Maharashtra
Development Report

सत्यमेव जयते

Planning Commission
Government of India

Maharashtra Development Report

सत्यमेव जयते

PLANNING COMMISSION
GOVERNMENT OF INDIA
NEW DELHI

Published by

ACADEMIC FOUNDATION
NEW DELHI

First Published in 2007 by
Academic Foundation
4772-73 / 23 Bharat Ram Road, (23 Ansari Road), Darya Ganj, New Delhi - 110 002 (India).
Phones : 23245001 / 02 / 03 / 04. Fax : +91-11-23245005. E-mail : academic@vsnl.com
www.academicfoundation.com

Published under arrangement with :
Planning Commission,
Government of India,
New Delhi.

Maharashtra Development Report
ISBN 81-7188-540-3

Designed and typeset by Italics India, New Delhi
Printed and bound in India.

Contents

...CONTD. ...

...CONTD. ...

The Core Committee

Following Members of Planning Commission, Government of India, served as Chairman of the Core Committee for different periods during the preparation of the Report.

- **Shri Montek Singh Ahluwalia**
- **Shri N.K. Singh**
- **Shri B.N. Yugandhar**

Following Principal Advisers and Advisers of Planning Commission, Government of India, served as the Member-Secretaries of the Core Committee for different periods during the preparation of the Report.

- **Smt. Krishna Singh**
  Principal Adviser
- **Shri L.M. Mehta**
  Adviser
- **Smt. Krishna Bhatnagar**
  Principal Adviser
- **Shri P.S.S. Thomas**
  Adviser
- **Ms. Sushma Choudhary**
  Principal Adviser

Following Additional Chief Secretaries, Planning Department, Government of Maharashtra, served as the Members of the Core Committee for different periods during the preparation of the Report.

- **Shri Jagdish Joshi**
- **Shri Nandlal**
- **Dr. D.K. Shankaran**

Core Committee Member, Editor and Coordinator

Dr. Vinod Kumar Sharma
Dean and Professor
Indira Gandhi Institute of Development Research, Mumbai-400 065 (India)
Tel: (91-22) 2840-0919/5653
Fax: (91-22) 2840-2752/5653
Email: vks@igidr.ac.in

Contributors and their Affiliation

Institute Coordinators:

IGIDR Coordinator: Dr. Vinod Kumar Sharma, Dean and Professor, Indira Gandhi Institute of Development Research, Film City Road, Goregaon East, Mumbai-400 065.

GIPE Coordinators: Prof. V. S. Chitre, Former Director and Dr. A. Narayanamoorthy, Reader, Gokhale Institute of Politics and Economics, Pune-411 004.

JBIMS Coordinators: Dr. R.K. Jadhav, Director and Dr. (Mrs.) H. Santhanam, Former Director, Jamnalal Bajaj Institute of Management Studies, University of Mumbai, Mumbai-400 020.

TISS Coordinator: Dr. Vidya Rao, Professor, Tata Institute of Social Sciences, Deonar, Mumbai–400 088.

Acknowledgements

This report is the outcome of the rigorous efforts and generous contributions of many individuals and organisations. The Planning Commission, Government of India, entrusted the task of coordinating and preparing the Maharashtra State Development Report (MSDR) to Indira Gandhi Institute of Development Research (IGIDR), Mumbai. Other collaborating partners of this report are Gokhale Institute of Politics and Economics (GIPE), Pune, Jamnalal Bajaj Institute of Management Studies (JBIMS) and Tata Institute of Social Sciences (TISS), Mumbai. We are grateful to all authors, experts and peer reviewers for their timely contributions.

Shri Montek Singh Ahluwalia, Deputy Chairman, Planning Commission, Government of India; Shri N.K. Singh, former Member of the Planning Commission and Shri B.N. Yugandhar, Member of the Planning Commission served as the Chairman of the Core Committee for different periods during the preparation of the MSDR. They took personal interest, gave their valuable time and suggestions and provided overall support for the report. Ms. Sushma Choudhary, Principal Adviser; Shri P.S.S. Thomas, Adviser and Shri N.D. George, Director, Planning Commission; efficiently coordinated the review of various drafts of MSDR and useful input from them and their colleagues helped a lot in improving the report.

Shri Jagdish Joshi, former Additional Chief Secretary and Dr. D.K. Shankaran, Additional Chief Secretary, Planning Department, Government of Maharashtra (GoM), have been very kind in convening several meetings to initiate the work, reviewing the progress of the report, arranging for crucial information and data and provide useful suggestions at various stages. Their efforts to get the drafts of MSDR reviewed in time by the concerned Principal Secretaries and Secretaries of the GoM improved the quality of the report to a great extent. In this regard, contribution of Ms. Maitreyi Das, Joint Secretary; Shri A.K. Tiwari, Joint Secretary, Ms. Chitkala Zutshi, Principal Secretary; Ms. S.M. Aparajit, Joint Secretary and of all anonymous experts who reviewed the report deserve a very high appreciation.

Dr. R. Radhakrishna, Director of IGIDR cooperated wholeheartedly in coordinating the work on the report and provided useful guidance and encouragement right since the inception of the report. He also reviewed and provided valuable contributions to various chapters of MSDR. Many other colleagues at IGIDR also contributed during this work. We highly appreciate the comments and suggestions received from Dr. Kirit Parikh, Former Director of IGIDR, and presently, Member of Planning Commission, and Professors D. Nachane, Nirmal Sengupta, M.H. Suryanarayana, Ashima Goyal, Shikha Jha, Jayati Sarkar, Rajendra Vaidya, P.V. Srinivasan, Kausik Chaudhuri, R. Nagaraj, K.V. Ramaswamy, Aldas Janaiah and Srijit Mishra.

Several municipal corporations extensively shared with us their information and data, which helped in updating different chapters of the MSDR. We are particularly thankful to the Municipal Commissioners of Amravati, Aurangabad, Brihan Mumbai, Kolhapur, Nashik, Navi Mumbai, Pune, Sangli-Miraj-Kupwad, Solapur and Thane. Various reports obtained from Mumbai Metropolitan Region Development Authority, Maharashtra Jeevan Pradhikaran and Maharashtra Economic Development Council were very useful.

We sincerely thank Dr. M.G. Rao of NIPFP, Delhi; Mrs. Anita Garware, Chairperson of Indian Heritage Society, Mumbai; Dr. Burange, Director of Centre for Advanced Studies, University of Mumbai; Mr. Shailesh Haribhakti, President of IMC, Mumbai; Mr. A.

Ramakrishnan, State Excise Commissioner; Mr. Chaini, President of MEDC, Mumbai and Mr. Gerson Da Cunha of AGNI Foundation for their support in this work.

Assistance of Ms. Sangeeta Thakore of IIT Bombay in editing the manuscripts, of Mr. Sam Thomas of IIT Bombay in designing the covers, of Mr. G. Badri Narayanan, Ms. Mary Cherical and Mr. S. Ghatak (all from IGIDR) in providing research assistance is highly appreciated. Formatting of manuscript was done by Mr. Mahesh Mohan of IGIDR. Cooperation and support from IGIDR's administration, library and computer staff has been uninterrupted and timely.

Vinod Kumar Sharma
Editor and Coordinator

एम. एस. आहलुवालिया
MONTEK SINGH AHLUWALIA

सत्यमेव जयते

उपाध्यक्ष
योजना आयोग
भारत
DEPUTY CHAIRMAN
PLANNING COMMISSION
INDIA

FOREWORD

One of the important Tenth Plan initiatives of the Planning Commission was to sponsor the preparation of State Development Reports with much of the work being done by reputed national level institutes. This exercise was undertaken in recognition of the fact that economic circumstances and performance in individual States varied considerably and it was necessary to examine development challenges for individual States in the light of State specific constraints and circumstances. The basic idea is to produce quality reference documents on development profiles of individual States and the possible strategies for accelerating growth, and reducing poverty and inequality.

The Maharashtra State Development Report reviews Maharashtra's experience and highlights issues critical for the State's development in the years ahead. I hope its publication will stimulate debate on growth strategies appropriate for Maharashtra. I am sure the road map indicated in the Report will stimulate a broader awareness of the critical policy issues facing the State and will assist the State to move to a higher growth path and to achieve all round human and economic development.

(M.S. AHLUWALIA)

योजना भवन, संसद मार्ग, नई दिल्ली – 110001 दूरभाष : 23096677, 23096688 फैक्स : 23096699
Yojana Bhawan, Parliament Street, New Delhi : 110001 Phones: 23096677, 23096688 Fax : 23096699, E-mail : dch@yojana.nic.in

सत्यमेव जयते

CHIEF MINISTER

MAHARASHTRA STATE

MANTRALAYA, MUMBAI 400 032 Phone : 22025151, 22025222 Fax : 22029214

MESSAGE

Maharashtra enjoys a historical reputation of being among progressive and well-administered States in the country. The State Government is aware that although progress has been achieved in various sectors since the inception of Maharashtra, much remains to be done in many fields. The Government is, therefore, undertaking strenuous efforts to provide basic minimum services to the people in Maharashtra.

I compliment the Planning Commission for collabrating with the State Government in preparation of Maharashtra Development Report (MDR), which provides an in-depth analysis of the present status of the State in various developmental sectors. Preparation of Maharashtra Development Report(MDR), thus, becomes a very relevant exercise for reviewing the documented effort of the State. The report reflects the potential of the State in the medium term as compared to other regions in India and the world. The objective of MDR is not merely to state policies and achievements of the Government, but it is a document that points out various lacuna that exist and the road map for the substantiable development of the State.

The report covers economic growth and its components including agriculture, industry and services over the last few decades. Its highlights the performance of the State in terms of growth in employment, availability of infrastructure poverty in the State, fiscal situation, various investments scheme and social indicators.

I am sure, that this authoritative and comprehensive document, so meticulously prepared, providing a realistic assessment of the current status of development of Maharashtra, will serve as a guide for future planning both within and outside the Government, in order to achieve the socio-economic progress of our people and improve the status of Maharashtra State.

I appreciate this endeavour wholeheartedly.

(Vilasrao Deshmukh)

B.N. YUGANDHAR
Member
Planning Commission
Government of India

सत्यमेव जयते

Yojana Bhawan
Parliament Street
New Delhi-110 001
Tel. : 23096566 (O)
23096567 (Fax)
E-mail: yugandhar.bn@nic.in

MESSAGE

Maharashtra, one of the most industrialised and progressive states of India, is currently at crossroads. The state has been facing enormous fiscal strain in recent years resulting in inadequate public investment in physical and social infrastructure. It is high time the state's economic policies are reviewed and corrective steps taken wherever necessary so that the state could realise its growth potential. The State Development Report (SDR), Maharashtra attempts a comprehensive and scholarly analysis of the major issues faced by the state's economy and puts forward a number of relevant and implementable recommendations.

The report reflects the growth potential of the state in the medium term. It suggests the need for better cohesion among various policy objectives and underlines the need for urgent measures for improving the social infrastructure, ensuring equity and human development, further, it recommends the participation of the private sector in infrastructure development and calls for sincere efforts from the government to prevent the widening imbalances at various levels.

I would like to place on record Planning Commission's appreciation to all those who have worked hard in preparing the Report, especially Indira Gandhi Institute of Development Research (IGIDR). Mumbai, the lead agency which coordinated the preparation of the report and the partner agencies i.e. (Gokhale Institute of Politics and Economics, Pune; Jamnalal Bajaj Institute of Management Studies, Mumbai and Tata Institute of Social Sciences, Mumbai.

I appreciate the efforts of Dr. Vinod Kumar Sharma, Professor, IGIDR and Coordinator of the Report in bringing out this valuable document. I would also like to thank Ms. Sushma Choudhary, Pr. Adviser, Planning Commission; Shri N.D. George, Director, Planning Commission; other officers and staff of Planning Commission; and the officers of the Government of Maharashtra for their help in the preparation of this Report.

Yugandhar

(B.N. Yugandhar)

List of Tables, Figures and Boxes

Tables

Figures

Boxes

Abbreviations and Acronyms

1 Lakh (or Lac)	= 100,000
10 Lakhs (or Lacs)	= 1 Million
1 Crore (or 100 Lacs)	= 10 Millions
46 Rs. (Indian Rupees)	= US$ 1
AAI	Airport Authority of India
ACGR	Annual Compound Growth Rate
AGRIND	Agriculture Related Industries
AMC	Akola Municipal Corporation
APDRP	Accelerated Power Development Reform Programme
APEC	Asia Pacific Economic Cooperation Secretariat
APMC	Agricultural Produce Market Committee
ARM	Additional Revenue Measures
ARV	Annual Rental Value
ARWSP	Accelerated Rural Water Supply Programme
ASEAN	The Association of Southeast Asian Nations
ASI	Annual Survey of Industries
AVF	Availability Factor
AWR	Annual Water Resource Per Capita
BAIF	Bharatiya Agro Industries Foundation
BC	Benefit Cost
BCCI	Bombay Chamber of Commerce and Industry
BCM	Billion Cubic Metres
BEAG	Bombay Environment Action Group
BEST	Brihanmumbai Electric Supply and Transportation
BIFR	Board for Industrial & Financial Reconstruction
BMC	Brihanmumbai Municipal Corporation
BMRDA	Brihanmumbai Metropolitan Region Development Authority
BMW	Bio Medical Waste
BOD	Biological Oxygen Demand
BOO	Build, Own and Operate
BOOT	Build Own, Operate and Transfer
BOT	Build, Operate and Transfer
BSES	Bombay Suburban Electric Supply
BSNL	Bharat Sanchar Nigam Limited
CADA	Command Area Development Authority
CAG	Comptroller and Auditor General
CAGR	Compounded Annual Growth Rate
CD	Credit Deposit

CETPs	Common Effluent Treatment Plants
CGR	Compounded Growth Rate
CIDCO	City and Industrial Development Corporation Limited
CLR	Computerisation of Land Records
CMPS	Cotton Monopoly Procurement Schemes
CNG	Compressed Natural Gas
CNN	Cable News Network
COD	Chemical Oxygen Demand
COPD	Chronic Obstructive Pulmonary Disease
COWDEP	Comprehensive Watershed Development Programme
CPCB	Central Pollution Control Board
CPI	Consumer Price Index
CPIAL	Consumer Price Index for Agricultural Labourer
CRD	Centre for Research and Development
CRISIL	Credit Rating Information Services of India Limited
CSFs	Cooperative Sugar Factories
CSO	Central Statistical Organisation
CST	Central Sales Tax
CWC	Central Water Commission
CZM	Coastal Zone Management
DA	Direct Advances
DAP	Draught Animal Power
DC (Handicrafts)	Development Commissioner for Handicrafts
DC (Handlooms)	Development Commissioner for Handlooms
DCs	Developed Countries
DCCL	Development Corporation of Cithara Limited
DCVL	Development Corporation of Vidarbha Limited
DELs	Direct Exchange Lines
DFID	The Department for International Development
DMI	Drip Method of Irrigation
DMO	Destination Marketing Organisation
DoT	Department of Tourism
DPC	Dabhol Power Corporation
DPC	District Planning Committee
DPDC	District Planning and Development Council
DRDA	District Rural Development Agency
DSC & WM	Directorate of Soil Conservation and Watershed Management
DTML	Devagiri Textiles Mills Limited
DWCRA	Development of Women and Children in Rural Areas
EAS	Employment Assurance Scheme
EC	Economic Census
EFC	Eleventh Finance Commission
EGS	Employment Guarantee Scheme
EIUS	Environment Improvement of Urban Slums
EMI	Employment Market Information
EOUs	Export Oriented Units
EPZ	Export Processing Zone(s)
ERI	Effective Rates of Interest
ESCAP	Economic and Social Commission for Asia and the Pacific
FAI	Fertiliser Association of India
FCI	Food Corporation of India
FDCL	Forest Development Corporation of Maharashtra Limited

FDCM	Forest Development Corporation of Maharashtra
FDI	Foreign Direct Investment
FHRAI	Federation of Hotel and Restaurant Association of India
FICCI	Federation of Indian Chamber of Commerce and Industry
FIRE (D)	Financial Institutions Reform & Expansion Project Debt Market Component
FMDC	Facility Management Development Company
FMI	Flood Method of Irrigation
FSI	Forest Survey of India
FYP	Five Year Plan
GCA	Gross Cropped Area
GCF	Gross Capital Formation
GDI	Gender Disparity Index
GDP	Gross Domestic Product
GEMS	Global Environmental Monitoring System
GFCFA	Gross Fixed Capital Formation in Agriculture
GFD	Gross Fiscal Deficit
GHGs	Green House Gases
GIA	Grants-In-Aid
GIA	Gross Irrigated Area
GIC	General Insurance Corporation
GLOBE	Global Learning and Observation to Benefit the Environment
GoI	Government of India
GoM	Government of Maharashtra
GP	*Gram Panchayat*
GSDA	Groundwater Surveys and Development Agency
GST	General Sales Tax
HMESC	Handicraft Marketing and Extension Service Centre
Ha	Hectare
HBCL	Haffkine Bio Pharmaceutical Corporation Limited
HC	Hydrocarbons
HDI	Human Development Index
HP	Horse Power
HPI	Human Poverty Index
HT/LT	High Tension/Low Tension
HUDCO	Housing and Urban Development Corporation
HW	Hazardous Waste
HYV	High Yielding Varieties
IA	Irrigated Area
IATA	International Air Transport Association
IATO	Indian Association of Tour Operators
IAY	Indira Awas Yojana
ICRA	Indian Credit Rating Agency
ICTs	Information and Communication Technologies
IDC	Irrigation Development Corporation
IDF	Infrastructure Development Fund
IDSMT	Integrated Development for Small and Medium Towns
IFMR	Institute of Financial Management Research
IH&RA	International Hotel & Restaurant Association
IIPS	International Institute for Population Sciences
ILO	International Labour Organization
ILP	Industrial Location Policy
IMC	Indian Merchant Chamber
IMFL	Indian Made Foreign Liquor
IMR	Infant Mortality Rate
INCID	Indian National Committee on Irrigation and Drainage
INS	International Network Services

IOTO	Indian Ocean Tourism Organisation
IPM	Integrated Pest Management
IPPs	Independent Power Projects
IR	Irrigated
IRDP	Integrated Rural Development Programme
ISP	Integrated Strategic Planning
IT	Information Technology
ITC	Indian Tobacco Company
ITDP	Integrated Tribal Development Project
ITES	Information Technology Enabled Service
ITI	Information Technologies Industries
ITI	Industrial Training Institute
JACK	Joint Action Committee Kanpur
JFM	Joint Forest Management
JNPT	Jawaharlal Nehru Port Trust
JRY	Jawahar Rojgar Yojana
KMC	Kalyan Municipal Corporation
KTDC	Kerala Tourism Development Corporation
kWh	Kilo Watt Hours
LDBs	Land Development Banks
LDCs	Less Developed Countries
LIC	Life Insurance Corporation
LIDC	Leather Industries Development Corporation of Maharashtra
lpcd	litres per capita per day
MAIDC	Maharashtra Agro Industrial Development Corporation
MC	Municipal Corporation
MCED	Maharashtra Centre for Entrepreneurship Development
MCGM	Municipal Corporation of Greater Mumbai
MDCL	Maharashtra Development Corp. Limited
MDR	Major District Road
MECL	Maharashtra Electronics Corp. Limited
MEDA	Maharashtra Energy Development Agency
MEDC	Maharashtra Economic Development Council
MERC	Maharashtra Electricity Regulatory Commission
MFPs	Minor Forest Products
MFSCDCL	Maharashtra Film, Stage & Culture Development Corporation Limited
MGWA	Maharashtra Ground Water Authority
MHa	Million Hectares
MHADA	Maharashtra Housing and Area Development Authority
MHDR	Maharashtra Human Development Report
MICE	Meetings, Incentives, Conferences and Exhibitions
MIDAS	Maharashtra Infrastructure Development and Support Act
MIDC	Maharashtra Industrial Development Corporation
MIG	Minor Irrigation (Groundwater)
MINARS	Monitoring of Indian National Aquatic Resources
MIS	Maharashtra Infrastructure Summit
MJP	Maharashtra Jeevan Pradhikaran
MKVDC	Maharashtra Krishna Valley Development Corporation
MLD	Million Litres a Day
MLDCL	Maharashtra Land Development Corporation Limited
MMB	Maharashtra Maritime Board

MMI	Major and Medium Irrigation
MMRDA	Mumbai Metropolitan Region Development Authority
MMRDC	Mumbai Metro Region Development Corporation
MNCs	Multi National Corporations
MNP	Minimum Needs Programme
MoA	Ministry of Agriculture
MoEF	Ministry of Environment and Forests
MoU	Memorandum of Understanding
MoWR	Ministry of Water Resources (India)
MPBCDCL	Mahatma Phule Backward Class Development Corporation Limited
MPCB	Maharashtra Pollution Control Board
MPCE	Monthly Per Capita Expenditure Class
MRCP	Maharashtra Rural Credit Programme
MSEB	Maharashtra State Electricity Board
MSFC	Maharashtra State Finance Corporation
MSFC	Maharasthra State Farming Corporation
MSHC	Maharashtra State Handloom Development Corporation
MSMCL	Maharashtra State Mining Corporation Limited
MSPHWCL	Maharashtra State Police Housing & Welfare Corporation Limited
MSRDC	Maharashtra State Road Development Corporation
MSRTC	Maharashtra State Road Transport Corporation
MSSCL	Maharashtra State Seeds Corporation Limited
MSTCL	Maharashtra State Textile Corporation Limited
MSTDC	Maharashtra State Tourism Development Corp Limited
MSW	Municipal Solid Waste
MSWC	Maharashtra State Warehousing Corporation
MT	Million Tonnes
MTDC	Maharashtra Tourism Development Corporation
MTFF	Medium Term Fiscal Framework
MTNL	Mahanagar Telephone Nigam Limited
MU	Million Units
MVA	Mega Volt Ampere
MW	Mega Watt
MWRC	Maharashtra Water and Waste Water Regulatory Commission
MWRPRA	Maharashtra Water Resource Planning and Regulatory Authority
NAAQM	National Ambient Air Quality Monitoring Programme
NABARD	National Bank for Agriculture and Rural Development
NAGRIND	Non Agriculture Related Industries
NBFCs	Non Banking Financial Institutions
NC	Nature Club
NCD	Non-Convertible Debenture
NCPA	National Centre for Performing Arts
NCR	National Capital Region
NCU	National Commission on Urbanisation
NDDP	Net District Domestic Product
NDP	Net Domestic Product
NEAC	National Environment Awareness Campaign
NEC	Not Elsewhere Classified
NEP	New Economic Policies

NFHS	National Family Health Survey
NFS	Non Farm Sector
NGO	Non Government Organisation
NH	National Highways
NHAI	National Highways Authority of India
NHDP	National Highway Development Programme
NIA	Net Irrigated Area
NIEs	New Industrial Economies
NIPFP	National Institute of Public Finance and Policy
NIRD	National Institute of Rural Development
NIUA	National Institute of Urban Affairs
NMC	Nashik Municipal Corporation
NMMC	Navi Mumbai Municipal Corporation
NOC	No Objection Certificates
NOx	Oxides of Nitrogen
NPAs	Non Performing Assets
NPK	Nitrogen Phosphate Potassium
NPW	Net Present Worth
NREP	National Rural Employment Programme
NRF	Normal Rainfall
NRY	Nehru Rozgar Yojana
NSA	Net Sown Area
NSDP	Net State Domestic Product
NSS	National Sample Survey
NSSO	National Sample Survey Organisation
NTPC	National Thermal Power Corporation
NWDB	National Wasteland Development Board
NWDPRA	National Watershed Development Project for Rainfed Agriculture
NWP	National Water Policy
O&M	Operations and Management
OAEs	Own Account Enterprises
OBBs	Off Budget Borrowings
OBC	Other Backward Class
OCMS	Online Complaint Management System
ODR	Other District Roads
OECD	Organisation for Economic Co-operation and Development
OL	Outstanding Loan
OMB	Open Market Borrowing
OSA	Official Secrets Act, 1923
PA	Protected Areas
PA	Plant Availability
PACS	Primary Agricultural Credit Societies
PAP	Project Affected People
PASTA	Plan of Action for Sustainable Tourism Development
PATA	Pacific Asia Travel Association
PCM	Pulgaon Cotton Mills
PDS	Public Distribution System
PESA	Panchayat's Extension to Scheduled Areas Act
PFCFA	Private Fixed Capital Formation in Agriculture
PHD	Public Health Department
PHRD	Policy and Human Resource Development
PLCP	Potential Linked Credit Plan
PLF	Plant Load Factor
PMC	Pune Municipal Corporation
PMGSY	Pradhan Mantri Gram Sadak Yojana
PMIUPEP	Prime Minister's Integrated Urban Poverty Eradication Programme
PPA	Power Purchase Agreement
PPP	Public Private Participation

PRIs	*Panchayati Raj* Institutions
PS	*Panchayat Samiti*
PSEs	Public Sector Enterprises
PSP	Private Sector Participation
PSU	Public Sector Units
PUC	Pollution Under Control Certificate
PWA	Potential Watershed Area
PWD	Public Works Department
RBI	Reserve Bank of India
RCA	Rent Control Act
RF	Rural Female
RFA	Rainfed Area
RIDF	Rural Infrastructure Development Fund
RLEGP	Rural Landless Employment Guarantee Programme
RM	Rural Male
RoM	Rest of Maharashtra
RPC	Relative Production Competitiveness Index
RPCGI	Relative Production Competitiveness Growth Index
RPM	Respirable Particulate Matter
RRBs	Regional Rural Banks
RTI	Right to Information
SARS	Severe Acute Respiratory Syndrome
SARITA	Stamp and Registration with Information Technology Application
SC	Schedule Caste
SCARDBs	State Cooperative Agriculture and Rural Development Banks
SDP	State Domestic Product
SDRs	State Development Reports
SEBs	State Electricity Boards
SEEPZ	Santacruz Electronic Export Processing Zone
SERCs	State Electricity Regulatory Commissions
SETU	Society for Promotion of Excellence and Transparency in Public Administration for Better Understanding
SEZs	Special Economic Zones
SFCs	State Financial Corporations
SFI	State of Forest Report
SGSY	Swarnajayanti Gram Swarojagar Yojana
SH	State Highways
SHG	Self Help Group
SIA	Surface Irrigated Area
SICOM	State Industrial and Investment Corporation of Maharashtra Limited
SIDBI	Small Industries Development Bank of India
SJSRY	Swarna Jayanti Shahari Rozgar Yojana
SME	Small and Medium Scale Enterprises
SMKMC	Sangli Miraj Kupwad Municipal Corporation
SO_2	Sulphur Dioxide
SPARC	Society for Promotion of Area Resource Centre
SPI	Small Scale Private Initiative
SPM	Suspended Particulate Matter
SPVs	Special Purpose Vehicles
SR1	Sub Round 1 (July to September)
SR2	Sub Round 2 (October to December)
SR3	Sub Round 3 (January to March)
SR4	Sub Round 4 (April to June)
SRR	Seed Replacement Rate
SS	Suspended Solids
SSI	Small Scale Industries

SSIDO	Small Scale Industry Development Organisation
STP	Software Technology Park
STs	Scheduled Tribes
SWD	Storm Water Drain
SWM	Solid Waste Management
SWOT	Strengths Weaknesses Opportunities and Threats
T&D	Transmission and Distribution
TE	Triennium Ending
TEC	Tata Electric Companies
TFC	Tenth Finance Commission
TFP	Total Farm Power
TIDC	Tapi Irrigation Development Corporation
TIMS	Tourism Information Management Systems
TMC	Thane Municipal Corporation
TOF	Trees Outside Forests
ToI	Times of India
TPD	Tonnes Per Day
TPDS	Targeted Public Distribution System
TRTI	Tribal Research and Training Institute
TRYSEM	Training of Rural Youth for Self Employment
TSA	Tourism Satellite Accounting
TSP	Tribal Sub Plan
TWA	Treated Watershed Area
UBSP	Urban Basic Services Programme
UF	Urban Female
UFW	Unaccounted For Water
UGD	Under Ground Drainage
UI	Unirrigated
ULBs	Urban Local Bodies
UM	Urban Male
UNDP	United Nations Development Programme
UNIDO	United Nations Industrial Development Organisation
USAID	United States Agency for International Development
UT	Union Territory
VAMBAY	Valmiki Ambedkar Awas Yojana
VAT	Value Added Tax
VOP	Value of Output
VPTs	Village Public Telephones
VR	Village Roads
WDP	Watershed Development Programme
WDR	World Development Report
WFRK	West Flowing Rivers in Konkan
WHO	World Health Organization
WIA	Well Irrigated Area
WMDC	Western Maharashtra Development Corporation
WPRs	Work Participation Rates
WRA	Water Regulatory Authority
WSC	Weavers Service Centre
WSP	Water and Sanitation Programme
WSSD	Water Supply and Sanitation Department
WTO	World Trade Organization
WTOBC	World Tourism Organization Business Council
WTTC	World Travel and Tourism Council
WUA	Water Users Association
WWDR	World Water Development Report
ZPs	*Zilla Parishad*

Map of Maharashtra

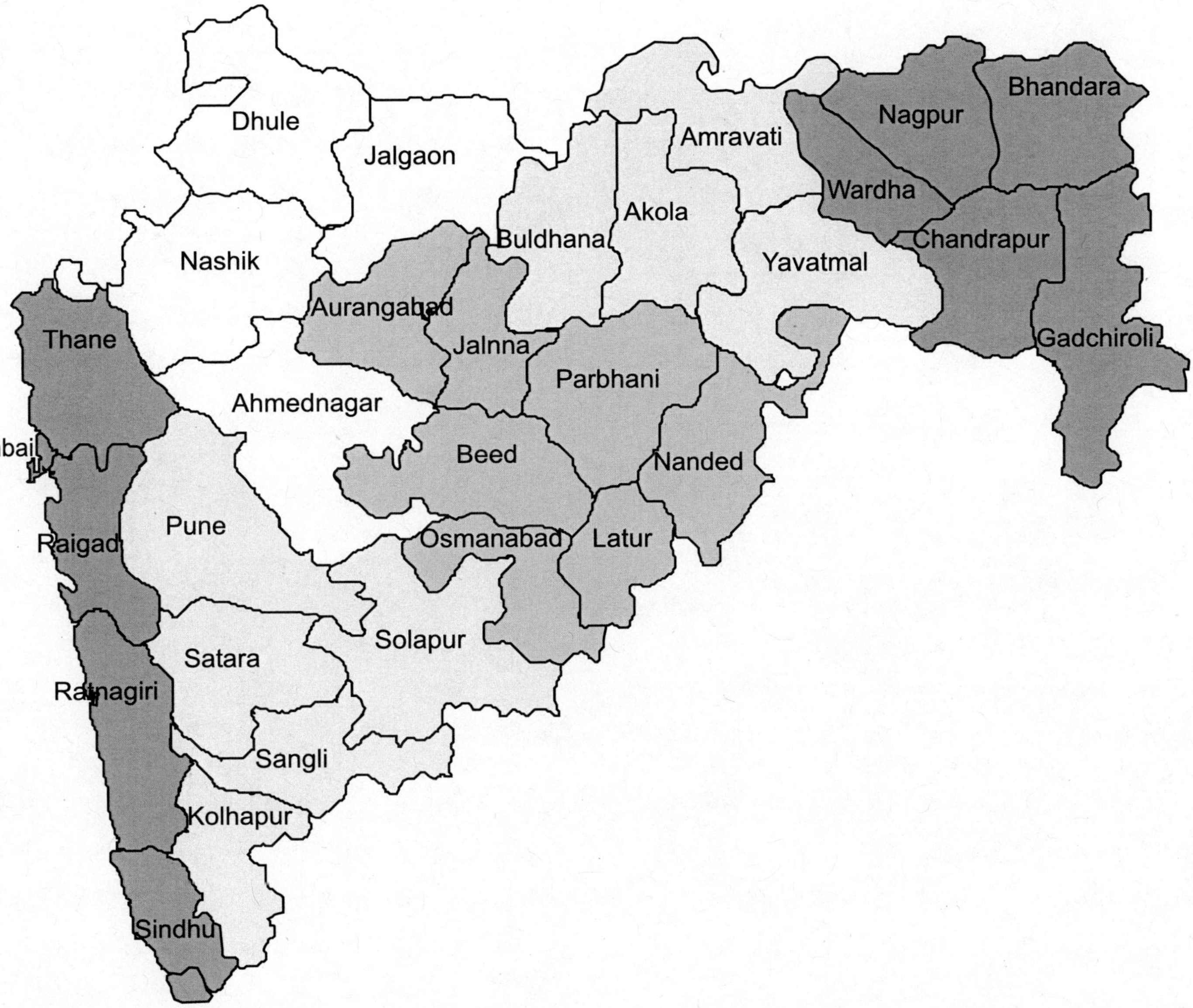

The Essence

India is a land of diversity, both in terms of natural and man-made systems. In order to alleviate poverty and improve the quality of life of its people, the country needs an accelerated process of development. However, it is imperative that this development process be economically feasible, socially equitable and environmentally sustainable. There are several interstate and intrastate disparities with regard to development and poverty. These regional imbalances call for the region specific development strategy and policies.

Preparation of the State Development Reports (SDRs) is a timely step, initiated by the Planning Commission, Government of India, which is aimed at producing a major policy document, in the form of the SDR, for each state. These reports could act as ready reference materials not only to review the reasons for success or failure on various fronts, but also as useful tools for the policy makers to decide the strategy for future development in each state.

Maharashtra enjoys the reputation of being one of the most industrialised and progressive states in the country. Over the years, the state has contributed to a large portion of the country's GDP, and has been exemplary to other states on many fronts. However, in the last few years, the overall rating of the state is fluctuating and showing a downward trend due to various reasons. Preparation of Maharashtra State Development Report (MSDR), thus, becomes a very relevant exercise for reviewing the major development sectors of the state. The report reflects the potential of the state in the medium term as compared to the other regions in India and the world. MSDR has been coordinated and prepared by the Indira Gandhi Institute of Development Research (IGIDR), Mumbai, India. Other collaborating partners are Gokhale Institute of Politics and Economics (GIPE), Pune, Jamnalal Bajaj Institute of Management Studies (JBIMS), Mumbai and Tata Institute of Social Sciences (TISS), Mumbai.

The objective of MSDR is not merely to state policies and achievements of the Government, but is rather a concerted effort to provide a document with guidelines for accelerated, improved and sustainable development in the state. It recognises that development is an all-encompassing process, which requires the State Government, the Civil Society, the *Panchyati Raj* Institutions and all other stakeholders to work in tandem. MSDR is organised in 16 chapters covering major sectors of development. The issues covered, the main findings and recommendations of each chapter are briefly described as follows.

Chapter 1 *Economic Profile and Development Strategy*, covers the economic growth and its components including agriculture, industry and services over the last few decades. It highlights the performance of the state in terms of growth in employment, availability of infrastructure, poverty in the state, fiscal situation, various investment schemes and social indicators. While identifying poor agro-climatic conditions as the weakness of the state, the chapter recognises abundant entrepreneurship as its strength.

The main finding of the chapter is that the state's success in achieving high rates of growth has been tarnished by its inability to reduce poverty, ignorance and disease. While the annual growth rate during 1985-1986 and 2000-01, has been 7.3 per cent, in the Ninth Plan, it reduced to 4.7 per cent. Foodgrain output has declined from 7.3 per cent in 1980-81 to less than 6 per cent in 2000-01. Though the state contributes about 19 per cent to the country's industrial output, the factory employment has decreased from 14.7 per cent in 1990 to 11.2 per cent in 1999. Maharashtra Industrial Policy 2001, focuses on high-tech industries, which may increase the industrial exports and employment. The service sector dominates the economy of Maharashtra, accounting for 69.3 per cent of the value of the output in the country. While the entertainment industry is doing fine due to various tax exemptions, the tourism sector is not harnessed well due to the lack of transport, hospitality and sanitation facilities in the spots of tourist attraction such as hill stations, beaches and national parks.

Amongst the major states, Gujarat, Haryana, Tamil Nadu, Kerala and Punjab had higher values than Maharashtra on the social and economic infrastructure index. The power sector is suffering due to pilferage, T&D losses, subsidies (mainly in agriculture sector) and obsolete equipments. The road length per sq km is better than the other states, however, their maintenance is poor. Of the total 5.5 million telephone connections, only 16 per cent are in rural areas. Maharashtra scores 0.523 on the HDI, as in 2001, and ranks fourth among the Indian states, by the value of the index, falling below Kerala, Punjab and Tamil Nadu.

There is an urgent need for Maharashtra to harness its resources of entrepreneurial, financial, managerial and administrative skills to achieve ever higher levels of human development and to grow at a sustainable rate of 8 to 10 per cent per annum over the decade 2002-2012. While the short-term strategy recommended is the generation of fiscal surpluses, the long-term strategy would require evolving institutions that would include the marginalised groups and give them voice and stake in the physical and social assets created in the process of growth. There is a need to improve the productivity of traditional crops and diversify the cropping pattern to water-saving commercial crops, horticulture, fruits and vegetables, etc. In order to make manufacturing globally competitive, upgrading the cities to the world-class status and substantial improvement in the infrastructure of power, transport and communication is required. With the use of information technology, biotechnology and knowledge-based industries, failures of the past can be corrected. A substantial improvement in the social infrastructure, equity and human development in the state is recommended. New institutions and new relationships have been put forward for enhancing the efficiency of the twin engines of the growth, namely, manufacturing and infrastructure.

Chapter 2 *Fiscal Situation and Policies* highlights fiscal position of the state government. The chapter dwells in detail, the reasons for persistent high fiscal imbalance in the state budget and its adverse impact on the long-term growth prospects on the economy. While easy fiscal policies in the short-run may have stimulating effect on the economy, in the long-run the same lead to lower growth. The state budget shows deteriorating revenue mobilisation and rising unproductive expenditure, resulting in growing fiscal and revenue deficits, leading to increase in debt and interest payment obligations. This has constrained the Government to undertake necessary productive expenditure in social and economic services.

The analysis of various components of revenue receipts shows that efforts towards revenue mobilisation have to concentrate on the own-tax revenues. Increase in tax buoyancy can come mainly from the sales taxes, electricity duty and motor vehicle taxes. This can be achieved by means of a simplified and efficient tax system, which may include introduction of VAT, removal of exemptions and revamping of tax administration through large-scale computerisation. The state would also have to bring the services sector in the tax-net in coordination with the Centre.

It is stressed that if the GoM does not undertake any significant fiscal reforms, and the underlying revenue and expenditure items exhibit the same trends as in the past, the current fiscal situation may become unsustainable. The state is already experiencing liquidity problems of unprecedented magnitude and is not able to cope up with the high levels of debt and deficits.

In order to identify the quantum of adjustment needed, alternative projections of future fiscal profile of the Government of Maharashtra has been drawn under two scenarios, *viz.*, base scenario (continuation of the present trend and policies) and reform scenario (to achieve sustainable debt and deficit regime). Reform scenario, in a way, is prescriptive and brings out the advantages of reforms and the quantum of adjustment needed in expenditure side and in the receipts side. The reform scenario shows that while fiscal deficit will be reduced in a targeted manner through greater revenue mobilisation and expenditure compression, there will be no reduction in expenditure particularly in the provision of merit goods such as primary education, water supply and sanitation, and basic healthcare facilities. In fact, the government will have more resources to spend for merit goods through refocusing and redesigning of government expenditure. In the context of decentralisation, it is suggested that fiscal autonomy of local bodies, such as *Panchayati Raj* Institutions and Urban Local Governments, needs to be raised so that they become financially less dependent on the higher tier of the government.

Chapter 3 covers *Agricultural Growth* and examines the status and the contribution of the agricultural sector in the state. It reviews the implementation of land reforms, changes in land use, cropping pattern and the input use in agriculture. It also discusses agricultural finance and investment in agriculture, horticulture and allied activities and marketing of agricultural products.

The findings reveal that, in Maharashtra, about 85 per cent of the districts have more than 60 per cent of workforce in the agricultural sector, thus, making it the key sector of the state economy. Technological changes in agriculture associated with the green revolution have brought about significant changes in the size, composition and productivity of livestock. The state ranks first in cotton production in the country and about 20 per cent of its farmers cultivate this crop. The consumption of pesticides in the state has come down to 173 g/ha from 320 g/ha during the Seventh Plan due to integrated pest management (IPM).

It is recommended that the constraints that jeopardise the growth of the agricultural sector should be removed and the strategies to accelerate agricultural growth, which in turn, would stimulate growth in other sectors of development, should be adopted. Top priority must be given to promotion of irrigation facilities and watershed development programmes. Further, promotion of rural non-farm employment will be beneficial so that burden on the agricultural sector is reduced. The GoM should withdraw its support to the cooperative sugar mills and the cotton sector and phase out the monopoly procurement scheme. Reforms pertaining to rural credit also assume importance in view of the poor repayment performance and high proportion of NPAs to total assets. Finally, the state government should capitalise on the export potential of its agricultural products.

Irrigation sector is discussed in **Chapter 4,** which focuses on nine major issues that are related to the irrigation potential, harnessed and utilised; investment in irrigation sector; growth of irrigation projects; trends and development of irrigated area; financial performance of irrigation sector; micro irrigation; water conservation measures (water users' association and watershed development programme); the demand and supply scenario of water; and irrigation and productivity nexus.

It is found that the state has the largest number of irrigation projects in the country, but its percentage of irrigated area is one of the lowest among the major states; area under surface irrigation is not equally distributed across the divisions and districts; crop-wise irrigated area too is not distributed in a desirable manner; area under micro irrigation (drip) has increased substantially; not only the productivity of major crops is lower in the state, but also the productivity of irrigated crops is found to be lower than the national average. Also, there seems to be an insignificant relationship between the level of irrigation and level of crop output across the districts.

It is recommended that irrigation policy should focus on completion of ongoing projects, even if it means foregoing new projects. Watershed Development Programmes (WDPs) must become central and not marginal to agricultural growth in Maharashtra. There is a need to establish Water Regulatory Authority (WRA) to manage and suggest strategies for improving the performance of the irrigation sector. Both supply and demand management strategies are to be introduced to avoid water shortage in the state.

Chapter 5 *Industrial Growth,* by analysing the process of industrialisation in Maharashtra *vis-à-vis* the other states, focuses on the future roadmap of industrial growth in the state. It gives an overview of employment in this sector and competition among various states. The chapter describes the state's industrial economy, infrastructure and policy incentives, competitive classification of the industries, and the status of sick and polluting industries and compares them with other states. It attempts to examine the structural changes in the state's industrialisation and its prospects for industrial growth. The chapter also analyses the status and prospects of small-scale enterprises using the cluster approach.

It is revealed that the sectoral composition of the SDP has been following the national trend of services-led growth. The state occupies a significant position in the manufacturing sector (mainly refined petroleum products, basic chemicals and other chemical products). Industries such as cotton textiles, wool, silk and synthetic fibre, textile products, wood and wood products recorded a decline. However, industries such as metal products, machinery, machine tools and parts, and other manufacturing industries recorded an increase in location quotient.

It is recommended that facilities such as power, port, and road network should be improved; better institutional support for developing industries in the backward regions of the state should be provided; development of Special Economic Zones and Single Window Clearance should be propagated in all the departments; the conditions of the state level financial institutions should be improved and sick small scale units and non-BIFR units should be revived. It is proposed to take steps for the development of the small scale industry in the state. As roughly 60 per cent of manufactured exports emanating from Small Scale Industries (SSI) sector originate in clusters, the development of such clusters is recommended.

Infrastructure Development has been discussed in **Chapter 6.** The problems of inadequacy and poor quality have infested almost all categories of infrastructure. Availability and problems of five basic physical infrastructure services (power; roads; ports and water transport; telecom and water supply to urban population) and the general issues pertaining to growth of infrastructure have been outlined in this chapter.

The state accounts for about 11 to 12 per cent of India's total installed capacity in power sector in the country and about 80 per cent of the population in the state has access to electricity. Construction of roads has been financed, to a large extent, by the non-plan expenditure. Maharashtra accounts for about 15.8 per cent of India's telephone subscribers. Financial losses of public utilities, distorted pricing, complex subsidy and cross-subsidy structures, regressive water pricing, peak demand deficits in power sector, lack of adequate modern facilities on ports, etc. are major concerns.

Recommendations include enlarging the scope of the private sector, which may improve both availability of infrastructure and efficiency through competition. This necessitates unbundling and rationalisation of tariff structure like removal of anomalies in tariff policies both across various infrastructures services (inter-services) and also within the same service (intra-services) and a careful scrutiny of infrastructure projects, which can enable the GoM to overcome some of these problems. Caution needs to be exercised so that the private sector participation leads to more competition rather than merely transfer of monopolistic power to the private operators. Integration of some of the infrastructure schemes, such as, construction of roads with the employment and income generation programmes will help in alleviation of poverty. Political willingness to implement the reforms can also enable the state to access more funds from the centrally sponsored schemes, as has been the case with some other state governments.

Chapter 7 *Public Sector Units: Restructuring and Reforms* examines the role and performance of public sector enterprises in shaping the economy of the state. It analyses the structure, pattern of investment and performance of public sector enterprises in Maharashtra, and discusses the need for, and the method adopted in, privatising the public sector enterprises in the state. The chapter also examines the measures adopted in public sector restructuring and provides an assessment of the progress of PSU reforms.

It is found that the single largest sector of public sector investment in the state turns out to be in construction activity (77 per cent). The public sector investments in Maharashtra are largely distributed in manufacturing, development organisations and in co-operatives. The highest average investment is in Maharashtra State Road Development Corporation Limited (MSRDC) that largely caters to the infrastructure requirements of the state. Most of the PSUs in Maharashtra are in financially vulnerable positions and continue to depend upon the grants and support from the government.

It is emphasised that there is an urgent need for restructuring and reforms, driven largely by the past performance and the present state of affairs in these enterprises. The analysis affirms that the restructuring and reform measures are too slow and far from being satisfactory, and require sincere efforts to formulate unit-specific policies. The method adopted for disinvestment needs to accept and highlight the distinction between public corporations and/or enterprises and cooperatives. The labour force should also be taken into confidence in coming to terms with the realities. Technical and conceptual capabilities are the needs of the hour in the programme of restructuring.

Chapter 8 suggests measures for *Human Resources Development of the Weaker Sections* and endeavours to present a different vision of development from the paradigm that inadvertently excludes majority of the people of Maharashtra. With strident liberalisation, it was expected that the demand for reservation would phase out. During the transition period, it was felt that measures to provide food and nutrition security for all by 2010, security of resources and sustainable livelihood, security of health, education for all and empowerment to ensure good governance should be taken up to prevent widening of rural-urban, regional, gender, tribe, caste and community disparities. Special measures to ensure access to education for children of migrant labour and other marginalised groups, to provide vocational and entrepreneurial skills from class VIII and extension of reservation in private aided/non-aided technical and professional training institutes are suggested.

Chapter 9 *Handlooms and Handicrafts* presents the current situation; post-independence policy and the problems faced by this sector due to liberalisation and government policies. It also focuses on product diversification, new developments and shift to the modern marketing era.

The handlooms sector is the largest generator of non-farm rural employment. It is a part of the textile sector, which comprises of the mill segment, the power loom segment, *khadi* & village industries segment and handlooms. Handlooms sector has many important features like it does not require power, its operations are manual, it has low capital investments, it has an extensive traditional skill base, etc. There is a decline in terms of quality of the goods produced, and in the number of devoted artisans in this profession, causing low sale of products.

The sector is still surviving and in some pockets it is successful, mainly because of its potential in providing gainful employment to the rural sector and contributing to the Indian economy. Its handicraft products have a deep cultural association with the masses, which is manifested in the traditional identity they provide to the users. Through market share of handlooms is dwindling, it still commands a huge loyal consumer base because of the emotional values it can provoke in its users. The sector thrives on raw material that is readily available and low-cost processing units, but in future, the sector will have to invest in quality measures that will improve the texture and design of its products. The products of the handlooms and handicrafts sector need to meet the expectations of the consumers and become competitive to qualify in the national and international markets. The products also require to meet the needs of efficient distribution, marketing and retailing. The adaptation to the modern marketing concept with consumer focus orientation will enable it to create consumer demand.

Governance issues are discussed in **Chapter 10,** highlighting some of the critical emerging concerns of governance in the state. The range of issues chosen for analysis includes the financial fiasco, the mismanagement and negligence of rural programmes, widespread inefficiency and lack of honesty in dealings. It also covers the significance and relevance of governance to the state; administration and bureaucracy; indicators of good governance; discrepancies in rural and urban areas; e-governance; law and order situation; right to information (RTI) and other Acts.

It is found that state debt is more than Rs. 80,000 crores. The GoM has been borrowing in the market primarily to repay its earlier loans, and to pay interest on its existing loans. The dynamics of corruption in the government starts with a systematic attempt at politicising the bureaucracy. The number of policemen per lakh of population is only 138. About 60 per cent of NGOs working on HIV/AIDS in the state is fraudulent. However, civil society and private sector participation are beginning to have a constructive impact on the political and administrative reforms of the state. All these issues have been critically examined, with fresh thinking and insights, providing constructive suggestions to resolve some of the inherent problems and their implications for the society.

It is recommended that the government should promote the ownership of the assets by local communities and local governments; improve the efficiency and transparency of government functioning and service delivery; plan resource flows to curb regional and class disparity; and work in close proximity with the private sector and NGOs. Quality in the Government services can be improved by integrating the citizen's charter and information technology initiatives under a holistic umbrella.

Chapter 11 *Integrated Village Development* deals with various aspects of rural regions including tribal areas and examines the major issues of village development in terms of socio-economic indicators such as rural population, poverty and literacy; status of rural infrastructure and regional imbalances. It also assesses various developmental programmes, employment generating schemes, and the impact and functioning of *Panchayati Raj* Institutions on village development.

It is found that the gap between rural and urban poverty and rural and urban literacy has reduced substantially. Fair progress has been made in provision of primary education, communication facilities and power to villages. About 45 to 50 per cent of the total income of the *gram panchayats* in the state comes from government grants.

It is suggested that participation of voluntary organisations could be encouraged in the areas like general education, welfare of women and children, and primary health services. Measures need to be taken to expand the medical facilities, transport facilities and *pucca* roads in rural areas. Devolution of more power to the *gram sabhas* with greater accountability and transparency is required.

Chapter 12 *Tourism* shows that the tourism industry has a great potential for generating income and employment in Maharashtra. Tourism is a major thrust area for economic growth in the state and the concept of sustainable tourism, future tourism development and the role of private sector is discussed. Tourism policies in the state are compared with those in other places.

Findings indicate that Maharashtra's share in total domestic tourist arrivals in India is 3.6 per cent. MTDC's budget outlay for tourism has increased ten-fold. The scenic 720 km long coastline of the Konkan has been included for development as the National Tourism Circuit.

A holistic planning approach involving sustainability, local participation and ecological conservation is required for giving fillip to the tourism industry. Also required is a marketing strategy to address the needs of domestic and international tourists and publicise the tourism potential of Maharashtra through appropriate media. In order to make the state a competitive destination, the government will have to bring in appropriate development control regulations, rationalise local and luxury taxes and make enabling provisions for speedier clearance of private sector investment proposals. Some other suggestions are- creation of legalised involvement of the local community in tourism planning at the destination level; need of Tourism Information Management System; urgent need to address the accessibility issue; need of larger role of private sector and single window clearance for private sector projects.

Chapter 13 *Urbanisation* discusses characteristics associated with urbanisation such as pattern of urbanisation, causes and consequences of growth of cities, approaches to urban development in national and state plans, urban policies and their results and future policies.

It is found that major towns of Maharashtra are experiencing an unprecedented population growth and exerting a tremendous pressure on urban infrastructure. About 44 per cent of the state's population is living in urban areas. Mumbai accounted for 37.4 per cent of the state's urban population in 1981, but it reduced to 29 per cent in 2001. Population growth is the root cause of city level problems of unemployment. Nearly 90 per cent of the housing shortage pertained to the weaker sections. There were 133 villages for every town in 1971, which reduced to 115 in 2001. The government has tried to improve the access of the poor to urban services. Levels of income increased over the 1990s though income disparities have widened. Although the state is highly urbanised, the levels of urbanisation are uneven across regions and districts within the state. Policies pursued to correct regional imbalance in urbanisation and development have met with limited success.

It is suggested that development of agriculture, non-farm service sector and basic infrastructure could go a long way to help correct the regional imbalance and help backward regions industrialise and urbanise. It is also suggested that the access of the social, economic and civic infrastructure to the poor should be improved, intra-city equity should be promoted and urban local bodies (ULBs) should be strengthened.

Chapter 14 *Employment* covers the issues related to the regional profile of employment in the state, employment by types of organisation (such as formal and informal), various policies and schemes and their achievements.

It is indicated that the relationship between the 'informal' and 'formal' sectors could be complementary as well as competitive. Several factors that influence the success of small and medium scale enterprises (SMEs) or informal segment entities are not amenable to easy monitoring, replication, assistance and/or regulation. Number of workers in manufacturing, mining and quarrying has increased but their share in production has fallen. Tertiary sector share has increased. The rate of growth of workers in urban areas is almost five times of the growth rate in rural areas. There is a fall in the share of formal sector and impressive rise in the case of informal sector.

Government agencies engaged in training, information services, and market intelligence or market building may be helpful and appropriate policy responses. Government can raise the demand for goods and services with the hope that the multiplier effect will enhance employment. However, the schemes involving subsidies may be infeasible and/or undesirable in the present precarious fiscal situation. Moreover, these are not likely to be very effective or capable of having any significant impact on employment. Other steps could be to strengthen and support specific sections or activities in anticipation of market trends and bolster the market trends and regulatory efforts to prohibit some of the practices like child labour, discriminatory wages and bonded labour. The government can increase demand for labour by undertaking works that are socially productive and useful.

Chapter 15 *Water and Environment* delineates the problems of major eco-systems in the state. Environmental subsectors covered in the chapter include water pollution (including fresh water, lakes, rivers and coastal areas); scenario of water supply and sanitation in rural and urban areas; air pollution (ambient and indoor); noise pollution; solid waste management including MSW, HW and BMW; Forests and biodiversity; and land degradation. International issues of climate change and trade and environment linkages and their possible impacts on state's economy are also discussed. Steps taken by the authorities and the reasons for state's under performance in the environment sector are given.

It is found that in view of the growing population, rapid industrialisation and large-scale urbanisation, the increased stress on environmental and natural resources is causing serious concerns in the state. Industries in Thane, Raigad, Kolhapur and Sangli districts discharge a very high BOD load. Satara district accounts for the largest share of industrial wastewater and solid waste released into the rivers, which is about 32.5 per cent and 22.9 per cent of total load generated in the state, respectively. Maharashtra tops all the coastal states in total wastewater generation and its disposal into the sea. The state accounts for about 21 lakh tonnes per year of HW, which is about 50 per cent of total HW generated in India. The actual forest cover, which accounted for 15.17 per cent of the total geographical area in 1999, has marginally increased to 15.43 per cent in 2001. Maharashtra soils show the greatest deficiency in nutrients in comparison to other states in the country.

Regarding the recommendations for this sector, it is worth mentioning that Maharashtra has been among the leading states both in recognising and solving the problems of environment. The state could maintain this lead by adopting an efficient environmental management system for sustaining the development process. Efforts are required to make all stakeholders well aware of the issues and to encourage private participation, increased involvement of NGOs and community participation in this sector. Environmental education requires significant capacity building in all sub-sectors of environment and at all levels such as schools, colleges, community, government, etc. In the water sector, there is a need to analyse the supply and demand, rationalise tariff structure and promote rainwater harvesting. Also, emphasis should be given to encourage the reuse and recycle of wastewater for irrigation and gardening.

Deteriorating air pollution scenario calls for improvement in transport infrastructure, particularly roads, improved vehicle design, alternate clean fuels and better traffic management. Promotion of renewable energy, installation of solar water heaters, and other photovoltaic systems is needed. Policies for SWM should be framed using the principle of the '4 Rs' i.e. reduce, recover, reuse and recycle. Source separations of waste would be of tremendous help in gainful recycling of waste.

Last, but not the least, conflicts between regulations of the central and state governments, which affect development plans of the state government, on environment grounds, should be avoided. It should be kept in mind that even the best planned development would have some cost to the environment. Therefore, a compromise has to be made in such a way that development process in the state causes the least possible damage to its natural resources and environment.

Based upon the findings of various chapters, overall *Conclusions and Policy Recommendations* are given in **Chapter 16.**

Chapter 1

Economic Profile and Development Strategy

Introduction

Maharashtra, with a population of 97 million in 2001, emerged as the second most populous state in India. With about 9 per cent of India's population, Maharashtra produces country's 19 per cent of industrial output, 15 per cent of service sector output, and about 13 per cent of GDP. Though the most industrialised of Indian states, it is not the most urbanised as it was till 2001 when Tamil Nadu pipped it to the second place. Its per capita income of Rs. 22,179 in 2000-01 makes it the third richest state in India after Punjab and Haryana (GoM, 2003). Despite that, the per capita income of the state has increased steadily at 3 per cent per annum over the last two decades. But its fiscal situation does not reflect its relative income position. As a per cent of GDP, its revenue deficit, fiscal deficit and debt stood at 3, 3.5 and 17.3 per cent, respectively in 2000-01. Over 87 per cent of its borrowings were financing consumption expenditure, adding to the unsustainablity of the debt being contracted.

Our objectives remain the same as before but the national and the international context in which we pursue them is no longer the same. Globalisation and the new technologies have changed it radically. Both create opportunities and pose new challenges. The strategy that we devise has not only to be in consonance with the changed context but it has to lead to sustainable growth. As Mr. Wolfensohn points out in the WDR 2003, we have to create new institutions and strengthen existing ones so that cooperative solutions emerge and are implemented. The growth of services sector, which largely comprise the new economy, contributed 8 per cent to the growth of Maharashtra's economy during 1997-98 and 2000-01. Seen in the context of the shrinking contribution of agriculture to the GDP (the agriculture sector showed a decline of 5 per cent in growth during the same period) and the near stagnant contribution of industries to the GDP during 1997-98 and 2000-01, we need growth strategies, for sustainable growth and development.

SECTION I

Economic Growth

In the Tenth Five Year Plan (2002-2007), Maharashtra has set for itself a GDP growth rate of 8 per cent with accelerated economic development through infra-structural development, with more private initiative in all possible sectors, ensuring high speed industrial development and creating large-scale employment.

Having experienced the growth rate of 8.9 per cent during the Eighth Plan (1992-1997), the target set for Tenth Plan seems quite achievable but deceleration of growth rate to 4.7 per cent per annum during the Ninth Plan (1997-2002) and the deterioration in the fiscal situation of the state makes the task daunting. The Tenth Five Year Plan document highlights the above scenario by pointing out to the "...disappointing progress in many social as well as infrastructural sector" (GoM, 2002a). It may also be relevant to see the interstate comparison of the growth rates during the last two Five Year Plans (Table 1.1).

Most states grew slower in the Ninth Plan than in the Eighth Plan, with the exception of West Bengal and Orissa. But for a fair comparison Maharashtra can be compared with other high income states like Andhra Pradesh, Tamil Nadu, Kerala, Karnataka, Gujarat, Punjab, and Haryana. If we examine the growth rates of these states, we find that during 1985-86 to 2000-01, Gujarat recorded a growth rate of 7.5 per cent, Tamil

TABLE 1.1

Growth Rates in State Domestic Product in the Eighth and Ninth Plans and those Targeted in the Tenth Plan

(Per Cent Per Annum)

Major States	*Eighth Plan 1992-97*	*Ninth Plan 1997-02*	*Tenth Plan (Targets) 2002-07*
Andhra Pradesh	5.4	4.6	6.8
Assam	2.8	2.1	6.2
Bihar	2.2	4.0	6.2
Gujarat	12.4	4.0	10.2
Haryana	5.2	4.1	7.9
Himachal Pradesh	6.5	5.9	8.9
Karnataka	6.2	7.2	10.1
Kerala	6.5	5.7	6.5
Madhya Pradesh	6.3	4.0	7.0
Maharashtra	**8.9**	**4.7**	**7.4**
Orissa	2.1	5.1	6.2
Punjab	4.7	4.4	6.4
Rajasthan	7.5	3.5	8.3
Tamil Nadu	7.0	6.3	8.0
Uttar Pradesh	4.9	4.0	7.6
West Bengal	6.3	6.9	8.8

Source: GoI, 2002a; GoM, 2002a.

Nadu 6.6 per cent, Karnataka 6.1 per cent, Andhra Pradesh 5.7 per cent, Punjab 4.5 per cent and Haryana 4.6 per cent. Maharashtra recorded a growth rate of 7.3 per cent. That being so, it would be appropriate to state that Maharashtra is poised to go on a higher path of growth provided it modifies its goals and priorities and devises new directions in the rapidly changing economy of not only the country but also the world. Such growth cannot be realised unless the human development indicators are in tandem with the growth in the industrial, social, and infrastructure sectors.

Since the aim of the planners is to make the economy world class, in comparison with some of the fast-growing Pacific-rim countries will be apposite. During the period from 1985-86 to 2000-01, while Maharashtra's economy grew at 7.3 per cent, Indonesia recorded growth rate of 7.1 per cent, Malaysia 7.3 per cent, Singapore 7.8 per cent, Taiwan 8.0 per cent, Thailand 8.7 per cent and South Korea 8.7 per cent. This comparison also fares well.

Sectoral Growth

Historically, economic development of the countries of the First World was accompanied by shifts in the shares of primary, secondary and tertiary sectors in their income and employment. The models incorporating the changes acquired prescriptive significance, though the historical experience was specific to the time and location. Development of East and Southeast Asia has been accompanied by the growth of tertiary sector ahead of the secondary. Globalisation and new technology have made predictions difficult; Maharashtra's experience in the last two decades suggests that the state may follow the East Asian rather than the Western path of sectoral change.

TABLE 1.2

Trends in Rates of Growth in Gross State Domestic Product at Constant Prices

(Per Cent Per Annum)

States	*Gross State Domestic Product (GSDP)*		*GSDP Per Capita*	
	1980-81 to 1990-91	*1993-94 to 1998-99*	*1980-81 to 1990-91*	*1993-94 to 1998-99*
Karnataka	5.4	8.2	3.3	6.4
Gujarat	5.1	8.0	3.0	6.2
Tamil Nadu	5.4	6.8	3.9	5.8
Maharashtra	**6.0**	**7.1**	**3.6**	**5.4**
Rajasthan	5.9	7.7	3.8	5.3
West Bengal	4.8	6.8	2.6	5.0
All-India	**5.6**	**6.8**	**3.3**	**4.8**
Kerala	3.2	5.5	1.7	4.2
Himachal Pradesh	5.0	6.7	3.1	3.9
Haryana	6.2	5.8	3.9	3.6
Andhra Pradesh	4.3	4.9	2.1	3.5
Punjab	5.4	5.0	3.5	3.0
Orissa	5.0	4.3	3.1	2.9
Bihar	4.7	4.2	2.5	2.6
Madhya Pradesh	4.0	4.4	2.1	2.3
Uttar Pradesh	4.9	4.5	2.5	2.3
Assam	3.6	2.7	1.4	1.0

Source: GoI, 2002a and 2002b.

The share of the primary sector in Maharastra's income decreased from about 28 per cent in 1980-81 to about 17 per cent in 2001-02. The share of the secondary sector reduced from around 32 per cent, to about 24 per cent and that of the tertiary sector increased from about 40 per cent to 58 per cent (GoM, 2004). We shall show later that the shares of employment changed in the same direction but slowly. The changes in output of the primary sector, the secondary and the tertiary sector in terms of per cent per annum during representative periods are shown in Table 1.3.

TABLE 1.3

Growth in SDP at Factor Cost by Sector: 1980-81 to 2001-2002

Year	*Sector*				
	Primary	*Secondary*	*Tertiary*	*NSDP*	*Per Capita SDP*
Share in SDP (%)					
1980-81	27.69	32.56	39.75	100	-
1990-91	22.88	32.90	44.21	100	-
1999-00	17.80	27.40	54.80	100	-
2000-01	17.40	24.80	57.80	100	-
2001-02	17.40	24.50	58.10	100	-
Growth % per annum					
1980-81	3.12	5.91	6.42	5.42	3.05
1990-91	3.83	6.30	7.56	6.40	4.64
1999-00	2.74	5.05	5.82	4.73	2.43
2000-01	-5.29	-12.25	1.95	-3.22	-4.99
2001-02	12.83	11.43	13.49	12.87	10.86

Source: GoM, 2004.

Sectoral Analysis

Agriculture

According to the 2001 Census, nearly 55 per cent of the workers of Maharashtra work in agriculture. They produced 10.1 mt of foodgrains in 2000-01. Maharashtra's share in India's foodgrain output has declined from 7.3 per cent in 1980-81 to less than 6 per cent in 2000-01. This has been due to decline in the share of area put to food crops. From a share of 79.1 per cent in 1982-83, the area declined to 71.5 per cent in 2000-01. This resulted in decline in food crops in the agricultural output from 22.3 per cent to 16.7 per cent during the period. Though the area under cereals declined, cereal production increased mainly due to improved methods to boost yield. Maharashtra ranked second in the production of coarse cereals. Yields also increased in cotton, oilseeds, vegetables and fruits. Maharashtra ranked first in India in the production of cotton and onions, and second in sugarcane. The state produced 18.65 per cent of the cotton in India, 35.56 per cent of the onions and 16.78 per cent of the sugarcane in 2000-01 (GoI, 2003a). The state ranked third in its share in production of pulses and oilseeds. Sugarcane production registered increase both in area and in yield. Sugarcane contributed significantly to the growth in the total value of agricultural output in the 1990s. It accounted for 80 per cent of the incremental gross value of agricultural output between 1993-94 and 1999-00.

There is no doubt that the cropping pattern is changing away from low-value cereals to high-value crops produced for the market. Commercial crops are immensely more profitable. A cotton farmer in Maharashtra harvests only 134 kgs per ha compared to 360 kgs in Haryana; a cane-grower produces 88 thousand kgs of cane per ha in Maharashtra whereas a farmer in Tamil Nadu produces 177 thousand kgs. The comparison can be there for all the crops but it is important to see that the output of foodgrains per ha in Maharashtra averages 103 kgs while that in Punjab is 1,032 kgs, almost 10 times. While this low yield may be due to scarcity of water, poor soil quality and small landholdings, there has also been a visible shift in the crop patterns. Farmers in Maharashtra are increasingly taking to commercial crops, which may be due to the pressures of globalisation, spurred by the WTO. A comparison of the returns to farmers in some of the commercial crops may provide the reason for such a shift. The yield per ha of grapes has been Rs. 2,36,000 sweet oranges Rs. 2,15,000, bananas Rs. 1,20,000 and mangoes Rs. 1,02,000. This is significantly higher than the return of Rs. 4,000 to Rs. 12,000 from conventional grains (GoM, 2002). This shift has put undue pressure on irrigation system, groundwater resources, etc. which needs to be addressed in a significant manner. The Tenth Plan envisages accelerated agricultural development programmes and search for new opportunities in other areas.

Irrigation

The gross irrigated area in Maharashtra was 3.65 million hectares in 2000-01, which was only 16.4 per cent of the total cropped area. This is three times more as compared to the area in 1960-61. Though this may sound impressive, it would not be possible to irrigate more than 30 per cent of the total cropped area, despite steep increase in expenditure on irrigation, from 14 per cent of the Third Plan's total expenditure to 33 per cent of the Ninth Plan's. Disproportionate accessing of the scarce resources by the cane-growers is also compounding the parsimony of the nature. Marginal holders stand little or no chance to improve their access to irrigation and, through it, to food and nutrition.

The scope for major and minor irrigation has also been exhausted. In the years of inadequate rainfall, the reservoirs do not get enough water and the need to provide drinking water reduces the availability of water for irrigation. Faulty pricing of water has not only created an excess demand for water but has also increased the wastage. The user prices are so low that they do not cover even the operation and maintenance expenses. But in September 2001, user charges were increased to cover full O&M costs and up to 20-25 per cent of the capital costs. This is an encouraging step.

Underground water is also being over-exploited, leading to some of the environmental issues, which will be discussed in Chapter 15. A user survey of groundwater reveals that the groundwater irrigation is mainly through electric pumps. Roughly 80 per cent of the groundwater exploitation is by farmers with average farm size of more than 4 ha.

Be that as it may, the irrigation potential created from all sources, major, medium and minor, till the end of June 2001 was 4.9 million hectares, barely 35 per cent of the potential. According to the National Sample Survey (NSS) data, over 75 per cent of the irrigation benefits accrue to farmers with average farm holdings of more than 2 ha and only less than 10 per cent of the irrigation benefits accrue to farmers whose average farm size is less than 1 ha.

The WUAs: Not Just Water but Water with Justice

The state government has encouraged formation of Cooperative Water Users' Associations (WUAs) so that irrigation management could be handed over to them to encourage community participation in common property rights. The policy also seeks to:

- reduce the gap between irrigation potential and actual utilisation,
- increase water use efficiency of irrigation management,
- restrict expenditure on maintenance and repairs of irrigation system, and
- recover government charges effectively.

The main responsibility for water resource development and management rests with the Irrigation Department. To overcome the hard budget constraint and claim its share of water under the Tribunal award, the Government created a number of Irrigation Development Corporations (IDCs). Most of the capital expenditures have shifted to the IDCs. Irrigation accounts for the largest share of off-budget borrowings of Maharashtra. Annual interest payment on the bonds issued by Maharashtra Krishna Valley Development Corporation (MKVDC), which have increased from Rs. 7 billion in 1996-97 to Rs. 13 billion in 2000-01, is made through GoM's budget. It is expected to increase to Rs. 50 billion in the next 6-7 years.

Industrial Structure

Growth with Diversification

Maharashtra contributes 18 per cent to the country's industrial output. The manufacturing sector in Maharashtra made net value addition of 21.5 per cent and deploys 17 per cent of the fixed capital in the organised industrial sector in 2000-01 (GoM, 2003). But the factory employment has decreased from 14.7 per cent in 1990-91 to 11.2 per cent in 1999-00.

The industrial activity in Maharashtra is concentrated in four districts, *viz.* Mumbai city, Mumbai suburban district, Thane and Pune.

The composition of the organised industrial sector in Maharashtra has undergone considerable change in the last two decades. In the early sixties, the consumer goods industry was more prominent than the capital goods and the intermediate goods industry. However, recently the capital goods and the intermediate goods industries have assumed greater importance than the consumer goods industry. The share of the capital goods and intermediate goods industries together in the value added has increased to 79 per cent in 1999-00 as against 48 per cent in 1960.

The industries in Maharashtra include chemicals and chemical products, food products, refined petroleum products, machinery and equipment, textiles, furniture, basic metals, motor vehicles, trailers, and other transport equipments. The shares of different industries are as follows:

- chemicals and chemical products–17.6 per cent
- food and food products–16.1 per cent
- refined petroleum products–12.9 per cent
- machinery and equipment–8 per cent
- textiles–6.9 per cent
- basic metals–5.8 per cent
- motor vehicles, trailers–4.7 per cent, and
- furniture–3.3 per cent.

The above industrial segments dominate the value addition in Maharashtra. These industrial segments together consumed 74 per cent of total inputs consumed by all industries in the state.

When the states are ranked by the value added in each of the 33 two-digit industries surveyed in the ASI, Maharashtra featured in the top three positions in 24 industries; and in 14 industries it ranked first. A more direct and decisive proof of Maharashtra's competitive edge in the industry segment would come from ranking of the states by the total factor productivity in each industry segment. In another way, we can also infer Maharashtra's superiority from Table 1.4. A factory in Maharashtra employs 16 per cent more fixed capital and 2 per cent more labour but produces 37 per cent more output and 51 per cent more value added than a factory in India. More elaborate discussion on the various issues of industrial development can be seen in Chapter 5.

TABLE 1.4

Fixed Capital, Value of Goods and Services, Net Value Added and Employment Per Factory, Maharashtra and India, 2001

Comparison Points	*Maharashtra*	*India*
Fixed Capital per Registered Factory (Rs.Lakh)	356	307
Production of Goods and Services per Factory (Rs.Lakh)	935	682
Net Value Added per Factory (Rs.Lakh)	178	118
Employment per Factory (Persons)	63	62

Source: GoM, 2002a.

Unregistered Manufacturing

The relatively less regulated sectors like unregistered manufacturing, trade, hotels and restaurants, communications, and transport other than railways experienced higher growth in the 1990s than in the 1980s. The growth rate of unregistered manufacturing was 9 per cent per annum, while it was 16 per cent per annum in communications in the 1990s compared to about 5 per cent and 6 per cent respectively in the 1980s (GoM, 2002b).

The advent of liberalisation has given impetus to the rapid industrial development in the state. Since August 1991 up to August 2001, 9,806 projects involving an investment of Rs. 2,222.64 billion in Maharashtra have been registered with the Government of India, and are in different stages of implementation. Of these, 4,298 projects have started their production. Major part of this proposed investment will be in Konkan (40 per cent), followed by Pune region (26 per cent) and Nashik region (13 per cent). The industrial development after liberalisation is also characterised by the participation of non-resident Indians (NRIs)/ foreign direct investors (FDIs). Under FDI scheme, 2,473 projects with an investment of about Rs. 464 billion were approved by the GoM up to October 2001. Of these approvals, 827 units have already been commissioned by January 2002. The liberalisation will affect the industry in the state in many ways. Liberalisation will force Maharashtra to specialise in the production of goods in which it has comparative and competitive advantage in the country.

Challenges of Globalisation

Globalisation will force the state to benchmark the total factor productivity in each industry with the best performer in the world. Progressive reduction in import duties will increase the competition in the domestic market and producers who cannot reduce their unit costs and prices to the level of their competitors would be forced to close down. Firms would try to become leaner and flatter. They would have to give up vertical integration and go for horizontal integration. They would like to hive off some of their activities and outsource. They would want to shift from their present high cost location to another where land and labour are cheaper.

Maharashtra Industrial Policy, 2001

The Maharashtra Industrial Policy, 2001 focuses on high-tech, knowledge-based industries. With the adoption of IT (information technology) and BT (biotechnology) based technologies the government hopes to increase industrial exports and employment. Maharashtra intends, as do other states, to discontinue incentives based on sales taxes but continue fiscal incentives. The Industrial Policy promises a new package of incentives such as exemption from payment of electricity duty, stamp duty and registration fees and refund octroi to all new industrial units in backward areas. It offers special capital incentives in the form of grant for setting up new small-scale industrial units in backward areas and interest subsidy to new units in textiles, hosiery and knitwear. It exempts all *khadi* and village industries from the payment of sales tax. It plans to establish self-governing industrial townships at 12 different places in the state.

Export Potential

The state's share of India's exports is estimated at 35 per cent. In 2000-01, Maharashtra exported goods worth Rs. 506.27 billion comprising largely engineering, chemicals, apparels, leather and leather products, electronics, and gems and jewellery. Between 1991 and 2001, 562 EOUs (export-oriented units) with investment worth Rs. 75 billion were set up in Maharashtra. The state has to attract much more investment in the infrastructure of ports, airports, warehousing and feeder roads to such facilities to exploit the export potential of the state. Studies by NCAER in 1994 revealed that India had substantial competitive advantage in the exports of bananas, grapes, lychees, onions, tomatoes, and mangoes. Maharashtra is one of the largest producers of mangoes, grapes, and onions. The export promotion drive would have to be synchronised with the state's changing crop pattern in agriculture towards horticulture, floriculture, animal husbandry, and food processing (MEDC, 2002).

Is Small Beautiful? Not Always if it is SSI

Of late, the policy related to giving incentive and subsidy, direct and indirect, to the small scale and *khadi* and village industries in the context of national development strategy is being debated. Rakesh Mohan (2002) has analysed different sources of data on SSI to show that the policy of reservation of products for SSI might have contributed to India's poor performance in comparison to China and some fast growing Southeast Asian economies in respect of growth of manufacturing output, employment and exports. It is stated that the fiscal incentives granted to the SSI dissuades the small entrepreneurs from exploiting the economies of scale and makes their existence conditional on the government subsidies. Whereas there was a decline in the share of household industry, the growth of non-household SSI benefiting from the fiscal incentives failed to compensate for the loss of household industry. The data produced by the SSIDO exaggerates the performance of the SSIs because it does not take into account the high mortality rate, endemic to SSI. Mohan argues that by and large, the policies of the government have helped sustain low productive employment without creating built-in incentives for the growth of high productive manufacturing employment.

Tertiary Sector

The tertiary sector consisting of transport, communications, banking insurance, real estate, public administration, and other services has grown at a compound annual growth rate of 7 per cent during 1993-94 to 2000-01. Highest growth was, however, seen in communications and banking and insurance. These are modern sectors and have experienced rapid growth. Mumbai, being the commercial and financial capital of the country, houses these largely. In contrast, the share of real estate in SDP declined.

The service sector dominates the economy of Maharashtra, accounting for 61.4 per cent of the value addition and 69.3 per cent of the value of the output in the country. Out of the above, the share of 'recreational services' was 63.2 per cent and 53.2 per cent, respectively.

India has a strong competitive advantage in knowledge-based industries and Maharashtra has qualitatively above an average infrastructure of knowledge industry in India. Approximately 25 per cent of the top 500 companies in the IT sector are in Maharashtra. The state accounts for 28 per cent of the software exports of India. Half of country's Internet users are in Maharashtra. The largest number of country's Internet providers are based in Mumbai. Specialised institutions in Maharashtra like C-DAC, Pune University, Mumbai University, IIT, VJTI and National Centre for Software Technology produce skilled technicians. The state government declared Maharashtra's Information Technology (IT) Policy in 1998. The Policy stresses the government's commitment to strengthen the state's leading position and to make its Information Technology industry globally competitive. It has initiated policies relating to human resource development, infrastructure, incentives to IT industry and computerisation of citizen-government interface. There are plans to set up Info-tech Parks through MIDC at Mumbai, Navi Mumbai, Pune, Aurangabad, Nagpur, Sangli, Solapur, Satara, Kolhapur, Ahmednagar and Nashik. The SETU Project initiated in seven districts is to be extended to other districts (MEDC, 2002).

Maharashtra has a good base of qualified personnel in biotechnology. Nature has bestowed upon the state immense biodiversity of flora and fauna. Biotech innovations come from small entrepreneurs and Maharashtra has no dearth of them. The Biotech panel has identified immense potential of the state in agri-biotech, drug development and manufacture, pharmacogenomics, environmental biotechnology and marine biotechnology. The market for biotech based products is yet to be explored. Besides, the industry lacks venture capital. While venture capital and angel fund investments in the info-tech sector grew from Rs. 0.7 billion in 1996 to Rs. 3.2 billion in 2000, the funding for biotech sector has so far been negligible. There is an urgent need for a proper 'intellectual property right regime' if biotechnology is to grow.

Entertainment Industry

The film industry in India has created a brand image for itself in the name of 'Bollywood'. The FICCI Anderson Entertainment Sector Report of March 2001 projects that by 2005 the total entertainment industry size would be Rs. 310 billion. Of late, from a highly unorganised sector based on individual ownership, the industry is moving towards corporatisation. There is an urgent need to promote the entertainment industry in Maharashtra in general and in Mumbai in particular. According to the Report of Price Waterhouse Coopers on film and entertainment industry, India ranked second in the number of screens in Asia Pacific. The number of screens is projected to grow from 13,400 to 21,000 in 2005. Despite the drop in admissions in recent years, India accounts for 78 per cent of the Asia pacific region's admissions. India ranks second behind Japan in box office spending in Asia Pacific region. The box office spending in India is expected to grow by 11 per cent per annum from $ 496 million in 2000 to $ 851 million in 2005. Total film exports from India are expected to increase from Rs. 6.65 billion in 1999 to Rs. 14.6 billion by 2005.

TV channels are reaching a wide audience—Zee reaches 27 million households, Sony 16.82 million and Star-Plus 14.82 million. Industry in Maharashtra should be able to capture a large chunk of this growth. Since the majority of films are made in 'Bollywood', the growth will be in Maharashtra. To give fillip to the industry, the government needs to reduce the entertainment tax rate from 60 per cent of the ticket price to around 20 to 25 per cent prevailing in most other states. To give a boost to the industry, the government has announced a three-year tax holiday for the multiplexes in the state and lowered the duty after three years (MEDC, 2002).

Tourism

Currently tourism contributes an estimated Rs.905 billion or 5.6 per cent to the GDP of India compared to the world average of 10 per cent. The travel and tourism sector created 9.3 million jobs directly and 17.4 million indirectly in 1999. This is expected to increase to 12.9 million jobs directly and 25 million indirectly by 2010. Maharashtra should try to get a sizeable share in the pie. The 720 km long coastal track of the Konkan characterised by abundant sunshine offers vast scope for developing beach resorts. The state could do well to learn from the development of tourism industry in Rajasthan, Kerala and Goa. Currently only 0.3 per cent of global tourists visit India annually. The infrastructure of transport, hospitality and sanitation is almost non-existent in the hill stations, beaches and national parks in the state. The state should lobby with the Central government to include tourism and hospitality in the infrastructure sector as recommended by Rakesh Mohan Committee on Infrastructure. This will help the industry to claim 100 per cent exemption from income tax payment for the first five years and give easy access to cheaper funds from the IDFC (MEDC, 2002).

TABLE 1.5

Index of Social and Economic Infrastructure, 1999

States	*Index*
Rajasthan	75.86
Madhya Pradesh	76.79
Assam	77.72
Orissa	81.00
Bihar	81.33
Himachal Pradesh	95.03
Uttar Pradesh	101.23
Andhra Pradesh	103.30
Karnataka	104.88
West Bengal	111.25
Maharashtra	**112.80**
Gujarat	124.31
Haryana	137.54
Tamil Nadu	149.10
Kerala	178.68
Punjab	187.57

Source: GoI, 2002b.

Infrastructure

Rapid agricultural and industrial growth depends on the availability of infrastructure facilities. Table 1.5

refers to an index, which is a composite comparative profile of the availability of physical, social and institutional infrastructure in the states. Amongst the major states Gujarat, Haryana, Tamil Nadu, Kerala, and Punjab had higher values on the infrastructure index than Maharashtra.

It is difficult to prioritise infrastructure because the economic criteria like cost-benefit analysis of the projects or their internal rates of return are not easily calculated for well-known reasons. WDR 1994 reports that one per cent increase in the stock of infrastructure increases GDP by one per cent too. The Maharashtra Vision 2005 (MEDC, 2002) refers to the need, estimated by the Rakesh Mohan Committee, to invest 6-7 per cent of the GDP in infrastructure to maintain a high rate of growth. This will be discussed in detail in the chapter on infrastructure (Chapter 6).

Power

Power is considered critical to economic development, as it is believed to have large backward and forward linkages relative to other infrastructure. Maharashtra, being more industrialised and more urbanised than India, per capita consumption of electricity in the state, 492.3 kWh in 2000-01 exceeded that in the country, being 356.4 kWh, by 38 per cent. Between 1961 and 2001, installed capacity in the state increased at the compound rate of 7.5 per cent per annum. The rate declined to 3.3 per cent in the 1990s (GoM, 2002). The per capita capacity in Korea, Malaysia and Argentina is 5-8 times higher than in India. In China, it is almost twice as high as in India (Kruegar, 2002). Lead over Maharashtra would be marginally less substantial.

Maharashtra has a relatively large market for industrial power. Nearly 40 per cent of its total sales are to industrial customers, compared to the national average of 30 per cent, and 23 per cent are agricultural customers which is well below the national average of 30 per cent (World Bank, 2001).

In Maharashtra, as in other states, loads-hedding is common in all districts of the state except two, *viz.*, Mumbai and Mumbai suburban. The extent of load-shedding when the demand peaks may be taken as a proxy for the shortfall in supply. The shortfall, though, has declined from 14 per cent of the peak to 9 per cent over the last two years but so has consumption of electricity by industry, agriculture, railways, and public water works. Total availability of electricity in Maharashtra was 75,000 million kWh in 2000-01, of which 62317 million kWh was generated in Maharashtra. Total consumption of electricity in the same year was 47300 million kWh. The production probably includes the power supplied by the Dabhol Power Company that is no longer available now.

There are well-known ways to manage the peak time demand and supply. The current excess of generation over peak demand may be just adequate if the technical problems associated with T&D and banking of power were tackled first. The real difficult problem is that of increasing installed capacity to meet the increased demand for power for the targeted growth of 8 per cent. The Maharashtra Vision 2005 estimates power consumption at 79062 million kWh in 2004-05. With three major power projects, the Dabhol, the Patalganga and the Bhadravati on hold, the chances of supply catching up with demand appear to be slim unless the state-owned Maharashtra State Electricity Board (MSEB) underwent a radical transformation. The MSEB incurred a loss in financial year 2000-01, which was met by a subsidy from the state government. The Board accounts for three-fourths of both the installed capacity and generation of electricity. The MSEB's T&D losses at 39.4 per cent in 2001-02 and 34.8 per cent a year earlier were intolerably high compared to the international standard of 10 per cent. The Central Electricity Authority of the Government of India has established a norm of transmission and distribution (T&D) losses at 16 per cent. Given that MSEB's average cost of purchases in 2000-01 was approximately Rs. 2 per kWh, had the losses been at the 16 per cent level, MSEB would have economised nearly Rs. 30 billion (World Bank, 2001).

Much of the supply in the state is not metered and monitored which encourages pilferage. Part of the losses in transmission and distribution is due to old equipments. Only half of the power supplied is billed and of the sales value, only 80 per cent is collected. Use of electricity in agriculture is highly subsidised. Agriculture consumes 27 per cent of the supply but contributes barely 7 per cent to the sales revenue. Industry bears the brunt of subsidies to agricultural and domestic users, not all of whom are poor.

Transport and Communication

Bad roads and communication infrastructure create uncertainties and delays in delivery. Producers who may be working on just-in-time inventory do not tolerate uncertainties of delivery schedules. In a competitive world, countries that lack efficient transport infrastructure loose their exports to others.

Total road length in Maharashtra in 2001 was 260,000 km. Maharashtra led India in road length standardised for area since 1981. In 1997, it was 117.62 km per 100 sq. km in Maharashtra compared to 74.93 km in India (GoI, 2002). Maharashtra has completed 90 per cent of the road development plan 1981-2001. The roads maintained by the Public Works Department (PWD) and *zilla parishads* measured 217,000 km. Of them about 82 per cent were surfaced.

The percentage interpreted as an indicator of quality does not compare too badly internationally. But the maintenance of the roads is poor. Nine out of every 10 inhabited villages in the state were connected by all-weather roads and 7 per cent, by fair-weather roads. Road connectivity plays an important role in building social, political and economic networks that reduce transaction costs all round. Roads, like other means of transport, extend the market for goods and labour. Equally importantly, village roads improve the access of the rural population to health and education.

The state spent 8 per cent of the expenditure on transport and communication in the Third, Fourth and Fifth Plan, 6 per cent in the next three Plans and the highest ever, 10.5 per cent, in the Ninth Plan. The State has allotted a little less than 7 per cent of the outlay to this sector in the Tenth Plan.

Ports: A Minor Berth

Along the 720 km long coastline of Maharashtra there are two major ports, Mumbai and Jawaharlal Nehru port, and 48 minor ports. The major ports are the responsibility of the Central government and the minor ports of the state government. Mumbai port handles both passenger traffic and cargo traffic whereas the JN port handles cargo only. The two ports are crucial to Mumbai's and consequently to Maharashtra's economy. Between 35-40 per cent of the exports of India pass through the Mumbai port.

The state government has decided to develop 7 of the 48 minor ports. The objective is to provide multi-user facility to handle all kinds of cargo, bulk, break-bulk, petroleum and chemical containers. It is expected that commercialisation of agriculture in Maharashtra and industrialisation of Konkan would increase export potential of the state considerably and proximity to ports would make the exports competitive. The development would relieve pressure on the Mumbai port. However the development requires large investments, well beyond the state in the present financial situation. The state has decided to tide over the difficulty by inviting private sector participation based on build-own-operate-transfer (BOOT) contracts. It established Maharashtra Maritime Board as a nodal agency in 1996 for acquisition of land, development of approach roads, supply of water and such other facilities. Techno-economic feasibility studies have been carried out in seven selected sites. Port Rewas-Aware is being developed as a multipurpose port and Port Dighi as chemical/liquid terminal (GoM, 2002).

Telecommunications

There were 5.5 million telephone connections in the state at end of March 2001. Of them, only 16 per cent were in rural and 84 per cent in urban Maharashtra. The density of telephone connections per 1000 population was 56.41. Mahanagar Telephone Nigam Limited (MTNL), which operates only in Mumbai, is having more than 2.4 million landline connections.

In the last couple of years, with the entry of private companies offering cell phones and landlines, the national and international connectivity in India and in Maharashtra has increased substantially. With the vision of making Mumbai a global financial centre, the telecom infrastructure in the state and the capital city would have to improve manifold.

SECTION II

Social Sector Attainments

Human beings are both the means and the end of development. The Human Development Index is an attempt to affix to a region an index, which is a constant weight aggregation of indicators of at least three aspects of human well being, *viz.*, income, health and education.

The Human Development Index constructed by the Government of India includes the following indicators: life expectancy at age one and infant mortality rate to represent longevity, proportion of literates to total population in age group of seven years and above, intensity of formal education to represent educational attainment, and per capita real consumption expenditure adjusted for inequality to represent economic attainment (GoI, 2002b). Maharashtra scores 0.523 on the HDI 2001 and ranks fourth among the Indian states arranged from top to bottom by the values of the index. It was below Kerala, Punjab and Tamil Nadu. Between 1981 and 2001, Maharashtra HDI improved from 0.363 to 0.523. In 1991, Tamil Nadu replaced Maharashtra in the third rank pushing it to the fourth (GoI, 2002b).

The HDI was much lower in rural than urban Maharashtra. In 1981, it was 0.306 for rural and 0.489 for urban Maharashtra. Rural-urban disparity was much greater in Maharashtra than in Kerala. The index improved faster in rural than urban Maharashtra in the 1980s and the rural-urban disparity was marginally lower in 1991 than in 1981.

The index is not of much use to the policy makers unless they find that the component of the index of the region they administer is poor relative to others. Hence, we need to look at the components of the index separately.

Attainment in Education

Literacy Levels

In 2001, 77 per cent of Maharashtra's population of seven years and over was literate. The state ran a poor second to Kerala with the literacy rate of 91 per cent, the highest among 16 major states of India. Maharashtra is ahead of India where only 65 per cent of its population of seven years and older could read and write a simple sentence. The adult literacy rate for population of 15 years and over was about 67 per cent in Maharashtra and 89 per cent in Kerala (GoI, 2002).

The Human Poverty Index

The UNDP's Human Development Index has spawned other indices based on various indicators of deprivation. Prominent among them are its own Human Poverty Index (HPI), and Gender Disparity Index (GDI) of the Planning Commission.

According to the more comprehensive of the two versions of the HPI of the Planning Commission, Maharashtra ranked 8th in 1991 and Kerala 7th, among all the states and union territories of India. According to UNDP's HPI for 1993-2001, Maharashtra stood 3rd and Kerala 4th among 15 large states of India (Table 1.6(a). The modified version of the UNDP index reported in Table 1.6(b) places Maharashtra in the 9th and Kerala in the 1st rank.

Disparities in Educational Attainment

Rural-Urban Differences

Literacy levels are lower in rural than in urban areas. Seventy-one per cent of Maharashtra's rural and 86 per cent of its urban population aged 7 years and over was literate in 2001. The corresponding literacy rates in Kerala were 90 per cent and 93 per cent respectively.

Gender differentials exist in both the states but are much wider in Maharashtra than in Kerala, much more

TABLE 1.6

Human Poverty Index : 1993-2001
(a) UNDP Method

State	*Health (Probability of Dying before 40) 1993-97*	*Education (Illiteracy Rate) (%) 2001*	*Provisioning (%) 1998-99*	*HPI Value 1993-2001*	*HPI Rank*
Andhra Pradesh	0.15776	38.89	28.85	30.22	9
Assam	0.23989	35.72	44.57	35.49	10
Bihar	0.22738	52.47	43.37	42.23	15
Gujarat	0.16999	30.03	30.25	26.33	5
Haryana	0.17783	31.41	30.12	26.89	6
Karnataka	0.15545	32.96	28.40	26.95	7
Kerala	0.0539	9.08	37.20	25.92	4
Madhya Pradesh	0.26038	35.89	46.17	36.40	13
Maharashtra	**0.13254**	**22.73**	**30.80**	**23.90**	**3**
Orissa	0.23906	36.39	44.17	35.51	11
Punjab	0.1498	30.05	21.80	23.21	2
Rajasthan	0.20358	38.97	43.77	36.26	12
Tamil Nadu	0.1364	26.53	20.73	20.95	1
Uttar Pradesh	0.32985	42.64	41.03	36.56	14
West Bengal	0.15504	30.78	32.05	27.45	8
India	**0.19634**	**34.62**	**36.50**	**31.09**	

Source: GoI, 2002b.

(b) Modified

States	*Health (Probability of Dying before 40) 1993-97*	*Education (Illiteracy Rate) Per Cent 2001*	*Children under Age 4 Undernourished (weight for age) Per Cent 1998-99*	*HPIM Value 1993-2001*	*HPIM Rank*
Andhra Pradesh	0.15776	38.89	37.7	33.46	6
Assam	0.23989	35.72	36.0	31.33	5
Bihar	0.22738	52.47	54.4	46.69	15
Gujarat	0.16999	30.03	45.1	34.09	7
Haryana	0.17783	31.41	34.6	28.90	4
Karnataka	0.15545	32.96	43.9	34.24	8
Kerala	0.0539	9.08	26.9	18.89	1
Madhya Pradesh	0.26038	35.89	55.1	41.44	13
Maharashtra	**0.13254**	**22.73**	**49.6**	**35.46**	**9**
Orissa	0.23906	36.39	54.4	41.16	12
Punjab	0.1498	30.05	28.7	25.67	2
Rajasthan	0.20358	38.97	50.6	39.77	11
Tamil Nadu	0.1364	26.53	36.7	28.32	3
Uttar Pradesh	0.32985	42.64	51.7	41.58	14
West Bengal	0.15504	30.78	48.7	36.40	10
India	**0.19634**	**34.62**	**47.0**	**36.45**	

Note: For HPI and HPIM, the state with the lowest value has been ranked 1.

Source: GoI, 2002b.

so in rural than urban areas. In 2001, 59 per cent of women and 82 per cent men in rural Maharashtra were literate. The corresponding rates for Kerala were 87 per cent and 90 per cent. In urban Maharashtra about 79 per cent of the women and 86 per cent of the men were literate compared with 91 per cent of the women and 93 per cent of the men in urban Kerala (GoI, 2002b).

Literacy by Income

Proportionately, more of the children in the age group of 6 to 14 years belonging to the richer households were currently in school than the children of same ages belonging to the poorer households. Children in Kerala belonging to the poor households were handicapped too. But the wealth gap in school enrolment was barely 9 percentage points compared with 29 in Maharashtra. Maharashtra could take some solace that the wealth gap in India was much wider at 44 percentage points (Table 1.7).

TABLE 1.7

Proportion of Children 6 to 14 Years Old 'Currently in School' by Economic Group

(Per Cent)

State	*Bottom 40 Per Cent*	*Middle 40 Per Cent*	*Top 20 Per Cent*	*Wealth Gap (Top-Bottom)*
Maharashtra	**67.1**	**83.9**	**96.2**	**29.0**
Kerala	88.7	96.1	97.5	8.8
All India	**50.0**	**76.7**	**94.2**	**44.2**

Source: World Bank, 1998 (Calculated from NFHS data 1992-93).

Simulated flow of 100 children through elementary schooling by economic group shows that in Maharashtra, 98 per cent of 15 to 19 year olds from rich households completed 1st Grade but only 59 per cent from poorer households did so. In other words, 4 out of 10 either never crossed the threshold of a classroom or left without completing the 1st Grade. In Kerala, almost all students who enrol are likely to finish Grade 1 irrespective of their income. In Maharashtra, 83 per cent of the children from rich households finished Grade 8, the end of the cycle of basic education compared to only 28 per cent of the poorer households (World Bank, 1998). Not only are the children of poorer household less likely to enrol but if they did, they are more likely to leave before completing either primary or basic education. To the extent students from poorer families do not enrol or drop out without completing basic education they lose the subsidies offered by the government.

Gender Differences in Educational Attainment

Literacy rate among women is higher in Maharashtra than in India. However, the state lags behind Kerala. In 2001, 68 per cent of the women and 86 per cent of the

TABLE 1.8

Gender Gaps in the Proportion of 15 to 19 Year Olds who have Completed Grade 8 by Economic Group

(Per Cent)

State	*All Quintiles*			*All Quintiles Lower 40 Per Cent*			*All Quintiles Top 20 Per Cent*		
	Male	*Female*	*Gender Gap*	*Male*	*Female*	*Gender Gap*	*Male*	*Female*	*Gender Gap*
Maharashtra	**67.2**	**49.0**	**18.3**	**42.1**	**13.8**	**28.3**	**87.0**	**79.9**	**7.1**
Kerala	72.8	76.8	-40.0	47.4	57.9	-10.5	90.9	93.7	-2.8
India	**53.7**	**35.5**	**18.2**	**31.3**	**9.5**	**21.8**	**85.2**	**79.6**	**5.6**

Source: World Bank, 1998 (Calculated from NFHS data 1992-93).

men in Maharashtra were literate. In Kerala, 88 per cent of the women and 94 per cent of the men were literate (GoI, 2002b).

The gender gap in schooling is wider for the poor than for the rich (Table 1.8). In the age group 15-19, 42 per cent of the boys and 13.8 per cent of the girls in the poorer 40 per cent of the households completed Grade 8. This difference reduces sharply in the richest 20 per cent with 87 per cent of boys and 79.9 per cent of girls completing Grade 8.

Among children in the age group 15-19 who complete Grade 8 the gender gap between the rich and the poor is 55 percentage points in Maharashtra. The gap between rich and poor girls is 66 and that between rich and poor boys 45 percentage points. In Kerala, there is reverse discrimination in favour of girls.

Attainment in Health

Life Expectancy

Attainment in health as indicated by life expectancy at age 1 increased from 64.5 years in 1981-1985 to 68.1 years in 1992-1996. Women could expect to live longer, 68.9 years in 1992-1996 compared to men who could expect to live for 66.8 years (GoI, 2002b).

Infant Mortality Rates

Infant mortality rate (IMR) is defined as number of deaths in the first year of a child's life per 1,000 live births in a given year. IMR reflects the probability of a child dying before reaching age one. Table 1.9 shows that the infant mortality rates have been falling for the past three decades in all the different categories, but remain high compared to the internationally accepted norms of 5 per 1000 live births. However, the disparity between rural and urban areas in terms of IMR remains the same, though the gender gap has fallen considerably. In 2001, Maharashtra ranked second amongst Indian states next to Kerala, but its IMR was three times as high as in Kerala. IMRs are higher in rural areas and for females (Table 1.9).

Nutrition

Maharashtra has not done well in improving nutrition. About 57 per cent of the rural and 55 per cent of the urban households consumed less than 2,700 calories per day. About a quarter of all rural and 28 per cent of the urban households reported an adequate calorie intake. Only 17 per cent of the households in the rural and urban areas reported more than adequate levels of calorie intake (GoM, 2002).

TABLE 1.9

Infant Mortality Rates (IMR)

Year	*IMR*	*Rural*	*Urban*	*Male*	*Female*
1981	119	131	67	131	106
1991	74	85	47	72	76
2001	45	55	28	43	48

Source: GoI (2002b), *SRS Bulletin* (2003).

Low level of food intake results in poor nutritional status of women and children. Nearly half the ever-married women 15-49 years old suffer from anaemia. The incidence is higher, 51 per cent in rural and 45 per cent in urban Maharashtra. Sixteen per cent of the children under 2 years of age were severely undernourished, with the weight for age index 3 standard deviation units (SD) below the mean, 41 per cent were moderately undernourished at 2 SD below the mean (IIPS, NFHS-2, 2000). The Bang Report reveals severe under- and malnutrition among the tribal population and backward areas of the state.

SECTION III

Distributive Aspects

While the state has done well in promoting growth, it has not done as well in securing its fair distribution across regions and sections of population. Equity in distribution is essential for sustainable growth. We preface our discussion of regional disparity with urbanisation, which reflects inequality in the distribution of population across space. A virtuous interaction between population and productive factors may at times transform a sleepy village into a city whose prosperity far surpasses that of the region in which it was situated creating a schism between rural and urban standards of living.

Urbanisation

Since independence, proportionately, far more persons lived in urban Maharashtra than in urban India. In 2001, 42.4 per cent of Maharashtra's population but 27.8 per cent of India's was enumerated as urban areas. As mentioned earlier, till 1991, Maharashtra was the most urbanised of the 16 large states of India. In 2001, it ranked second after Tamil Nadu though the latter's urban population was less than two-thirds of Maharashtra's. The state's urban population increased faster than its total population; which shows that cities of Maharashtra received migrants not only from rural Maharashtra but also from the villages and towns of the rest of India. They migrated overwhelmingly to the industrialised Mumbai-Pune region.

Distribution of Urban Settlements and Population by Size-Class

In 2001, Class I settlements or cities with population of 100,000 or over, formed nearly 11 per cent of the cities and towns in Maharashtra and they accounted for 80 per cent of the urban population of the state. Relative to India, a much greater share of Maharashtra's urban population lives in Class I cities. As in the country, so in Maharashtra, urbanisation slowed down in the 1990s relative to the 1980s but the number of Class I and II cities increased faster. In the past they absorbed at least 83 per cent of the increase in urban population in Maharashtra.

In 1991, there were 3 cities with population of a million or more. Their number increased to 7 in 2001. These 7 cities accounted for about 52 per cent of Maharashtra's urban population. Mumbai alone accounted for 29 per cent of the population of Maharashtra and 56 per cent of the population of 7 million-plus cities. Between 1991 and 2001, nearly 88.2 per cent of the growth of urban population was absorbed by 7 million-plus cities. The cities in Maharashtra, like those in most of the Third World, have failed to provide their citizen the basic amenities like housing, safe drinking water, sanitation and clean air. Globalisation is both a challenge and an opportunity to them. The cities are undergoing a painful structural adjustment. The strategy of industrialisation, import substitution and licensing had built up diversified but an inefficient large and small-scale industrial sector in the cities. It is now exposed to much fiercer competition from domestic and foreign producers. The transition from capital-intensive import-substituting industries to labour-intensive export-oriented industries based on flexible specialisation and information technology has just begun. Cities are likely to lose their relative advantage as producers of large-scale manufacturing. They are becoming junction-points for transfer of goods, finance, capital, people and switch-gears of information. To cope with the challenge the cities have to become attractive places to live, work and do business in. They would be required to provide high quality infrastructure of power, telecommunications, roads and all the civic amenities to attract foreign capital and reduce transaction costs all round. China in particular and East and Southeast Asian countries in general have succeeded in providing the necessary infrastructure and catapulted themselves into middle to high income countries as defined by the United Nations. The transformation requires a wide range of policies at all levels, national, state and local. They include population control, deregulation of laws, rules and regulations relating to land, labour and movement of goods and services. Daunting as the task may appear in the present context of financial crunch, Maharashtra can face the urban challenge by following strict financial discipline, efficient management of public sector and adopting innovative ways of eliciting cooperation from the domestic and foreign private sector. It would be difficult to meet the challenge if Maharashtra lapses into a state of financial instability and political and social turmoil. Chapter 13 gives a detailed exposition on the subject of urbanisation in Maharashtra.

Regional Disparities

The present state of Maharashtra with Mumbai as its capital was formed in 1960 by splitting the bilingual

Mumbai state and integrating the Marathi speaking regions, Vidarbha from Madhya Pradesh and Marathwada from Hyderabad with Konkan and Western Maharashtra. The four regions, Konkan, the Western plateau, Marathwada and Vidarbha, differed in their natural endowments and levels of economic and social development. To allay the fears of people of Vidarbha region, the Constitution of India was amended in November 1956 and the President was empowered to bestow on the Governor of the State, responsibility to appoint statutory development boards for Vidarbha, Marathwada, and rest of Maharashtra.

Dissatisfaction with regional inequality led to the appointment of the Fact Finding Committee chaired by Prof. V. M. Dandekar in 1984. The terms of reference required the Committee to decide indicators for assessing imbalance in development, to determine the district-wise imbalance and to suggest remedial action to remove the existing imbalance. The Committee chose 1984 as the latest year and compared the level of physical and social infrastructure built with public investment in each district in 1984. It calculated the public expenditure needed to raise the district's level in a specific sector to the state average.

The backlog in developmental expenditures was found to be higher in the districts of Marathwada and Vidarbha (GoM, 1984). Calculated per head of regional population, the backlog amounted to Rs. 327 for rest of Maharashtra, Rs. 772 for Marathwada and Rs. 859 for Vidarbha in 1984 (GoM, 1997).

The publication of the Report awoke the backward regions to the Constitutional provisions for the appointment of the statutory regional development boards. Dissatisfaction over the tardy implementation of the planned removal of the backlog simmered for a decade and led to the appointment of the Indicators and Backlog Committee in 1995 to find out if the backlog had increased between 1984 and 1994.

The Committee followed the same methodology as its predecessor, the Dandekar Committee, and concluded that it had. Intraregional disparity reduced in the rest of Maharashtra but widened in Vidarbha and Marathwada. The per capita backlog in 1994 in the rest of Maharashtra was estimated at Rs. 755 while it was five times higher, Rs. 3614, in Marathwada and Rs. 4001 in Vidarbha. The backlog in Marathwada and Vidarbha was made up largely of backlog in physical infrastructure while that of the rest of Maharashtra was largely contributed by a backlog of social infrastructure.

Seventeen districts were identified as backward in 1994, which accounted for 55 per cent of the area of the state, 37.5 per cent of the population and 76 per cent of the estimated backlog. Of these, three belonged to western Maharashtra, six to Marathwada and eight to Vidarbha. Needless to add, that these districts scored low on the HDI as well (GoM, 2002b).

The Central government had formulated a policy to reduce regional inequality by identifying the most backward districts. According to it the million plus cities were made out of bounds for new manufacturing industry and fiscal incentives were offered to attract it to the notified backward districts.

The Government of Maharashtra strengthened the industrial licensing policy of the Central government with its own location policy banning some sites for industry and providing infrastructure and incentives to it for situating them in backward districts. Consequently, the regional distribution of industry in the state has become more even than before.

Real per capita income net district domestic product (NDDP) in every district of the state increased between 1993 and 1998. It was marginally more dispersed in 1998 (CV=41.5 per cent) than in 1993 (CV=39.5 per cent). No district shows an increase in illiteracy. The neglect of public health infrastructure in the 1990s has contributed to an increase in both infant and child mortality in rural Maharashtra (World Bank, 2002). The widening rural-urban disparity would contribute to widening inter-district and regional disparity in infant and child mortality. There is a high correlation between per capita NDDP (1998-99) and HDI (2000). The Spearman's rank correlation coefficient (r) was 0.82. District-level poverty ratios are not available for recent years but, in 1993-94, per capita NDDP and district level poverty ratios were significantly but inversely correlated (r = -0.72) supporting both the trickle-down theory and the government intervention.

The HDI constructed for the districts of Maharashtra using the UNDP methodology for 2000 highlighted the backwardness of the districts of Marathwada and Vidarbha (Table 1.10). The state average value was 0.58. Only the districts of Mumbai—both city and suburban, Thane, Raigad, Sindhudurg, Pune, Satara, Sangli, Kolhapur, and Nagpur had values of HDI that were above the state average. Barring Nagpur, no other district of Vidarbha and none from Marathwada were above the state average attainment (GoM, 2002b).

TABLE 1.10

Human Development Index and Per Capita District Domestic Product in Maharashtra

District	*HDI 2000*	*Rank*	*PCDDP (Rs.) 1998-99*	*Rank*
Mumbai	1.00	2	45471	1
Mumbai (Subn.)	1.00	1	45471	2
Thane	0.82	3	33200	3
Raigad	0.70	6	30364	4
Ratnagiri	0.44	22	14354	25
Sindhudurg	0.60	9	20016	10
Nashik	0.51	13	20636	8
Dhule	0.36	30	11789	34
Nandurbar	0.28	32	11789	35
Jalgaon	0.50	14	16449	17
Ahmednagar	0.57	11	15251	22
Pune	0.76	4	28000	6
Satara	0.59	10	15563	20
Sangli	0.68	7	20411	9
Solapur	0.48	17	18097	13
Kolhapur	0.64	8	20925	7
Aurangabad	0.57	12	19365	11
Jalna	0.27	33	12047	33
Parbhani	0.43	24	13827	26
Hingoli	0.43	25	13827	27
Beed	0.47	18	15303	21
Nanded	0.37	29	13068	31
Osmanabad	0.38	28	12905	32
Latur	0.47	19	13677	29
Buldhana	0.41	27	13823	28
Akola	0.44	23	16069	18
Washim	0.36	31	16069	19
Amravati	0.50	15	17168	14
Yavatmal	0.22	34	13382	30
Wardha	0.49	16	16952	16
Nagpur	0.71	5	28878	5
Bhandara	0.46	20	14467	23
Gondiya	0.46	21	14467	24
Chandrapur	0.41	26	19325	12
Gadchiroli	0.21	35	17140	15
Maharashtra	**0.58**		**22763**	

Source: GoM, 2002a; GoM, 2002b.

Within western Maharashtra including Konkan, there are backward districts. The tribal district of Dhule and Nandurbar had low HDI. Nandurbar's HDI value was a mere 0.28. The districts of Marathwada are the most backward, with values lower than the state average. The HDI value for Jalna was 0.27. Except for Aurangabad, none of the other districts scored higher than 0.47. In Vidarbha, none of the districts were above or at par with the state average with the exception of Nagpur. Amravati and Wardha are relatively more developed of Vidarbha districts with HDI values of 0.50 and 0.49 and ranked 15th and 16th respectively. Gadchiroli, despite being in the second quartile in terms of per capita district domestic product, had the lowest HDI of 0.21 while Yavatmal had HDI of 0.22 (GoM, 2002b).

The districts of Mumbai and Mumbai suburban occupied the top slot. The difference in human development achievements in these two districts on the one hand and the others on the other hand is stark. The HDI reflects the regional disparities that persist in Maharashtra despite attempts made by the government to mitigate them through financial allocations for investment in physical infrastructure to ensure egalitarian economic growth. It also indicates that the high levels of income and the high social sector attainment of Mumbai has in fact pushed up the average income of the state and the average HDI value for the state.

Analysis of individual indicators of economic, structural and human development revealed that districts of Pune division were ahead of the districts from other regions of Maharashtra. However, they lagged behind on indicators of social and gender development such as percentage of girls married below 18 years of age compared to Konkan. Income levels are generally lower in the districts of Vidarbha compared to those in districts of Pune. The districts of Marathwada lag behind on economic, structural, social and human development indicators. Konkan emerged higher on economic, social and human development indicators. However, wide inter-district disparities exist in all regions (GoM, 2003).

Rural-Urban Disparity

Analysis of the National Sample Survey data on household consumption expenditure by Sawant and Mhatre (2000) shows that urban-rural disparity in consumption expenditure has widened. Two important conclusions emerge.

First, urban-rural consumption disparity increased for all as well as non-poor households. The former disparity increased from 1.64 in 1967-68 to 1.94 in 1993-94. The latter, increased from 1.95 in 1967-68 to 2.11 in 1993-94.

Second, amongst the 16 major states, Maharashtra had the highest urban-rural ratio for all households in all the survey years implying the highest urban-rural consumption expenditure disparity. Widening of urban-rural disparity in levels of living is inversely related to the rural per capita farm income and share of rural male workers engaged in non-farm employment. The rise in disparity is negatively related to growth in the state's agricultural income but positively to growth in non-agricultural income.

Poverty

The higher growth rate in per capita SDP in Maharashtra has not translated into a faster reduction in poverty. The state has been able to reduce the share of the poor in population from 43.44 per cent to 25.02 per cent and the number of poor persons from 29 million to 23 million between 1983 and 1999-00. In contrast, Kerala was able to reduce the share from 40.42 per cent to 12.72 per cent and persons living in poverty from 11 million to 4 million (GoI, 2002a and 2002b).

Haryana, Bihar, Himachal Pradesh, Karnataka, and Rajasthan experienced steep declines in poverty levels of more than 12 percentage points between 1993-94 and 1999-00. Uttar Pradesh, West Bengal and Tamil Nadu also registered significant reduction in poverty (Table 1.11).

TABLE 1.11

Percentage of Population Below Poverty Line, 1973-2000

(Arranged in Increasing Order of 1999-2000)

States	1973 -74	1977 -78	1983 -84	1987 -88	1993 -94	1999 -2000
Punjab	28.15	19.27	16.18	13.20	11.77	6.16
Himachal Pradesh	26.39	32.45	16.40	15.45	28.44	7.63
Haryana	35.36	29.55	21.37	16.64	25.05	8.74
Kerala	59.79	52.22	40.42	31.79	25.43	12.72
Gujarat	48.15	41.23	32.79	31.54	24.21	14.07
Rajasthan	46.14	37.42	34.46	35.15	27.41	15.28
Andhra Pradesh	48.86	39.31	28.91	25.86	22.19	15.77
Karnataka	54.47	48.78	38.24	37.53	33.16	20.04
Tamil Nadu	54.94	54.79	51.66	43.39	35.03	21.12
Maharashtra	**53.24**	**55.88**	**43.44**	**40.41**	**36.86**	**25.02**
All-India	**54.88**	**51.32**	**44.48**	**38.86**	**35.97**	**26.10**
West Bengal	63.43	60.52	54.85	44.72	35.66	27.02
Uttar Pradesh	57.07	49.05	47.07	41.46	40.85	31.15
Assam	51.21	57.15	40.47	36.21	40.86	36.09
Madhya Pradesh	61.78	61.78	49.78	43.07	42.52	37.43
Bihar	61.91	61.55	62.22	52.13	54.96	42.60
Orissa	66.18	70.07	65.29	55.58	48.56	47.15

Source: GoI, 2002a and 2002b.

Rural poverty in Maharashtra declined from 45.23 per cent in 1983 to 23.72 per cent in 1999-00. The number of rural poor reduced from 19.4 million to 12.5 million. In urban areas, poverty reduced from 40.26 per cent to 26.81 per cent but the poor increased marginally from 9.7 million to 10.3 million (GoI, 2002a and 2002b).

In the 1990s, rural poverty in Maharashtra declined faster than urban poverty. It declined at 7.8 per cent a year compound compared with 4.5 per cent in 1993-94 and 1999-00.

Projections for 2006-07 indicate that poverty ratio is likely to decline in Maharashtra to 16.18 per cent and the number of poor to 1.7 million. Many states would do better than Maharashtra. Unfortunately, in terms of poverty, the performance of Maharashtra comes closer to several of the less developed states in the country (Table 1.12).

TABLE 1.12

Poverty Projections for 2006-2007

States	Rural		Urban		Combined	
	Per Cent	No. (Lakh)	Per Cent	No. (Lakh)	Per Cent	No. (Lakh)
Andhra Pradesh	4.58	26.97	18.99	41.75	8.49	68.72
Assam	37.89	95.36	4.48	1.78	33.33	97.14
Bihar	44.81	482.16	32.69	54.74	43.18	536.91
Gujarat	2.00	6.88	2.00	4.38	2.00	11.25
Haryana	2.00	3.30	2.00	1.51	2.00	4.81
Himachal Pradesh	2.00	1.18	2.00	0.14	2.00	1.32
Karnataka	7.77	28.66	8.00	16.34	7.85	45.00
Kerala	1.63	4.03	9.34	8.01	3.61	12.04
Madhya Pradesh	28.73	192.07	31.77	74.46	29.52	266.54
Maharashtra	**16.96**	**101.61**	**15.20**	**72.68**	**16.18**	**174.30**
Orissa	41.72	139.12	37.46	23.57	41.04	162.69
Punjab	2.00	3.40	2.00	1.95	2.00	5.35
Rajasthan	11.09	54.41	15.42	23.44	12.11	77.86
Tamil Nadu	3.68	12.46	9.64	31.61	6.61	44.07
Uttar Pradesh	24.25	373.16	26.17	111.25	24.67	484.41
West Bengal	21.98	137.53	8.98	22.21	18.30	159.73
All-India	**21.07**	**1705.26**	**15.06**	**495.67**	**19.34**	**2200.94**

Source: GoI, 2002a and 2002b.

Employment Market

Maharashtra's population increased at 2.0 per cent per year, compounded from 78.9 million in 1991 to 96.8 million in 2001. The workers, main plus marginal, enumerated in the Census of 2001 increased a little faster at 2.2 per cent per annum from 33.9 million to 42.1 million. They increased faster than population irrespective of sex and rural-urban residence (Table 1.13). Contrary to the general impression, employment increased faster than population in cities than in villages.

TABLE 1.13

Main, Marginal and Total Workers by Sex and Rural-Urban Residence, Maharashtra : 1991-2001 and Rates of Growth : 1991-2001

	Main		Marginal		Total		Population	
Usual Status	*1991*	*2001*	*1991*	*2001*	*1991*	*2001*	*1991*	*2001*
				Rural+Urban				
Persons	31.01	35.67	2.90	6.38	33.91	42.05	78.94	96.75
Males	20.92	24.49	0.38	2.44	21.29	26.92	40.83	50.33
Females	10.09	11.19	2.53	3.94	12.62	15.13	38.11	45.42
				Rural				
Persons	21.38	22.75	2.65	5.35	24.03	28.11	48.40	55.73
Males	12.77	13.59	0.27	1.82	13.05	15.41	24.54	28.44
Females	8.61	9.16	2.38	3.53	10.99	12.70	23.86	27.29
				Urban				
Persons	9.63	12.92	0.25	1.03	9.88	13.95	30.54	41.02
Males	8.15	10.90	0.10	0.62	8.25	11.51	16.29	21.89
Females	1.48	2.02	0.15	0.41	1.63	2.43	14.25	19.13

Rates of Growth Per Annum

Usual Status	*Main*	*Marginal*	*M+Marg.*	*Pop.*
		Rural+Urban		
Persons	1.4	7.9	2.2	2.0
Males	1.6	18.7	2.3	2.1
Females	1.0	4.4	1.8	1.8
		Rural		
Persons	0.6	7.0	1.6	1.4
Males	0.6	18.9	1.7	1.5
Females	0.6	4.0	1.4	1.3
		Urban		
Persons	2.9	14.1	3.	2.9
Males	2.9	18.3	3.3	3.0
Females	3.1	9.9	4.0	2.9

Note: Rates of growth are compound rates of growth.

Source: For this table and tables that follow: NSSO, 1997 and 2001. Results of the Employment- Unemployment Survey for the 50th Round (1993/94) and 55th Round (1999/2000). Results for Maharashtra pulled out of the Central Sample Data.

Regrettably, secure organised employment stagnated at 3.7 million in the decade but its complement, the insecure unorganised employment, increased from 30.2 million in 1991 to 38.4 million in 2001 improving its share in total employment from 89 per cent to 91 per cent. Estimate of the share of the informal sector differs with the source of data and definition used.

If one used the NSSO and equated the formal sector with regular wage and salaried employment, informal sector would consist of self-employed and casual labour. In 1999-00, 88.2 per cent of the men and 98.5 per cent of the women were employed in the informal sector in rural Maharashtra. Their respective shares in urban Maharashtra were 46.0 per cent and 59.0 per cent. Work participation rates (WPRs) of men and women, rural as well as urban, increased between 1991 and 2001. This increase was the result of increased participation of marginal rather than main workers (Table 1.14). This corroborates the faster growth of the informal sectors.

TABLE 1.14

Work Participation Rates by Sex and Rural-Urban Residence, Maharashtra, 1991 and 2001

Usual Status	*Main*		*Marginal*		*Total*	
	1991	*2001*	*1991*	*2001*	*1991*	*2001*
			Rural+Urban			
Persons	39.28	36.87	3.68	6.60	42.96	43.46
Males	51.24	48.65	0.92	4.85	52.16	53.49
Females	26.47	24.10	6.64	8.49	33.11	32.59
			Rural			
Persons	44.18	40.82	5.48	9.61	49.66	50.43
Males	52.05	47.78	1.12	6.40	53.17	54.18
Females	36.08	33.57	9.96	12.95	46.05	46.52
			Urban			
Persons	31.52	31.49	0.82	2.51	32.34	34.00
Males	50.02	49.77	0.61	2.83	50.62	52.60
Females	10.37	10.58	1.07	2.14	11.44	12.72

Source: NSSO, 2001.

The net effect of the operation of the demand and supply in the labour market is seen in the changes in the rate of unemployment. Since the Census is yet to publish the data of 2001 relating to unemployment, one has to turn to the NSSO.

According to the NSSO, unemployment in Maharashtra increased among men and women living in villages or towns, irrespective of whether it was measured with the reference period of a year, a week or every day of the week (Table 1.15). Unemployment measured by the most comprehensive measure the CDS rate, increased from 4.3 per cent of the labour force in 1993-94 to 6.5 per cent in 1999-00 in rural Maharashtra and from 6.3 per cent to 8.1 per cent in urban Maharashtra. Urban women experienced higher rates of unemployment than urban men, both in 1993-1994 and 1999-00.

TABLE 1.15

Unemployment Rates by Usual, Current Weekly and Current Daily Status by Sex and Rural-Urban Residence, Maharashtra, 1993-94 and 1999-2000

Usual Status	*Usual Principal Status*		*Usual Principal+ Subsidiary Status*	
	1993-94	*1999-00*	*1993-94*	*1999-00*
		Rural		
Persons	1.2	1.8	0.8	1.4
Males	1.7	2.4	1.2	1.9
Females	0.7	1.1	0.3	0.7
		Urban		
Persons	4.9	6.4	4.4	5.8
Males	4.6	6.1	4.3	5.6
Females	5.8	7.8	4.7	6.6
	Current Weekly		*Current Daily*	
Usual Status	*1993-94*	*1999-00*	*1993-94*	*1999-00*
		Rural		
Persons	2.6	3.5	4.3	6.5
Males	3.0	2.7	4.6	6.3
Females	2.0	3.3	4.0	6.9
		Urban		
Persons	5.6	6.8	6.3	8.1
Males	5.3	6.5	6.0	7.7
Females	6.6	8.1	7.8	10.0

Source: NSSO, 2001.

TABLE 1.16

Unemployment Rates by Current Daily Status in Labour Force Entry Ages by Sex and Rural-Urban Residence, Maharashtra, 1993-94 and 1999-2000

(Per Cent)

Age Group	*Rural*				*Urban*			
	Males		*Females*		*Males*		*Females*	
	1993-94	*1999-00*	*1993-94*	*1999-00*	*1993-94*	*1999-00*	*1993-94*	*1999-00*
15-19	9.3	13.8	7.1	11.3	17.5	24.8	18.5	14.8
20-24	11.2	13.9	6.9	10.0	16.0	18.2	22.3	18.8
25-29	5.9	7.3	5.6	6.7	7.0	11.8	9.6	6.1
15-29	8.7	11.3	6.4	8.9	12.3	14.9	16.7	12.3

Source: NSSO, 2001.

Unemployment was essentially the problem of the young entrants to the labour force, much more in urban than in rural Maharashtra (Table 1.16). The current weekly status unemployment rates for the educated 15 years of age and over declined for rural men and women and urban women in the 1990s. Urban educated men 15 years and over faced higher rates of unemployment in 1999-00 than in 1993-94 (Table 1.17).

TABLE 1.17

Unemployment Rates by Usual Status and Current Weekly Status Among Educated 15 Years and over by Sex and Rural-Urban Residence, Maharashtra, 1993-94 and 1999-2000

Usual Status	*Usual Principal Status*		*Usual Principal+ Subsidiary Status*	
	1993-94	*1999-00*	*1993-94*	*1999-00*
		Rural		
Persons	7.1	7.0	4.7	6.1
Males	7.0	7.0	5.4	6.2
Females	7.7	7.2	7.2	6.0
		Urban		
Persons	6.9	7.5	6.3	6.9
Males	5.3	6.8	5.1	6.2
Females	14.5	11.7	12.7	10.5

	Current Weekly	
	1993-94	*1999-00*
		Rural
Persons	7.5	7.1
Males	7.3	6.9
Females	8.8	8.7
		Urban
Persons	7.1	7.5
Males	5.6	6.9
Females	14.8	10.6

Source: NSSO, 2001.

The state faces two major problems in respect of its labour force. First, its workers are overwhelmingly engaged in informal activities where incomes are low. Secondly, most of the unemployed are young belonging to the ages of 15-24, more so if they were educated as well. The employment policy of the state needs to address itself to the problem urgently.

SECTION IV

Strategy and Policies

We have delineated above the economic profile of Maharashtra highlighting its performance relative to other states in India. To devise a strategy for the future one has to set the objectives and assess our strengths and weaknesses and our achievements and failures.

Objective

To grow at a sustainable rate of 8 to 10 per cent per annum over the decade 2002-2012 is the objective. Sustainable growth implies not only a high growth rate and human development but also intra-and inter-generation equity. It requires building institutions to resolve conflicts over distribution of benefits from social assets. These conflicts prevent the creation of the assets in the first place.

Weaknesses

Agro-climatic conditions in the state are not favourable to growing cereals such as rice and wheat. Most of the state falls in the rain shadow and is dry and arid. Irrigation potential is low and its utilisation is much lower. Poor quality of land, its fragmentation and lack of water have resulted in low yields. Rural-urban and regional inequality of income and human development is high and so is poverty.

Strengths

Maharashtra has a relative abundance of entrepreneurship, thanks to the cosmopolitan character of its capital city Mumbai. The city's riches provide an insatiable market for the produce and labour of the hinterland. The state has a good physical, social and financial infrastructure. It is the most industrialised and second most urbanised and, judged by the per capita income, the third richest of the large states in India.

Performance

Maharashtra has maintained its eminence over the long haul since its formation in the 1960. Along with most other states of India, Maharashtra too suffered a deceleration in the second half of the 1990s largely due to successive droughts, implementation of the Fifth Pay Commission, the Asian meltdown and the world recession.

Failures

The biggest failure has been that to make growth sustainable and convert the high growth performance into equally high performance in human development. Neither did poverty decline fast enough nor did some of the aspects of human development improve as fast particularly in relation to the best performer, Kerala. In recent years, unemployment has increased. Available data show that rural-urban, regional and gender-based inequality has widened.

Basic Choices of the Strategy

The states in India base their strategy of development taking the cue from the strategy/perspective plan documents prepared by the Planning Commission. The long process of formal and informal consultations between the states and the Planning Commission results in the Draft Five Year Plan first at the national and then at the state level.

There are tensions between the philosophy of planning and that of the market. Assuming that the reforms agenda would be pursued regardless of the party voted in office, one could safely infer that the role of the market would increase and that of the plan would shrink. The state would be entrusted with the responsibility of increasing the supply of public goods, which are usually under-provided if left to the market. The government may encourage (discourage) the production of goods involving positive externalities (negative externalities). It could build, own and operate departmentally or it could enter into a BOT contract or even a BOOT contract with private producers.

These choices affect the size of the budget, resource mobilisation required and the macroeconomic policy. It is quite unlikely that the GoM would be able to mobilise through taxation and borrowing the resources to build the physical infrastructure of irrigation, power, telecommunication and transport on the one hand and social infrastructure of health and education needed for achieving growth with equity.

Strategy for Short Term

The state government, forced to borrow to consume, is under severe fiscal strain. In the short run, the government has to generate surpluses on the revenue account by prudent fiscal management. Surpluses are needed for better maintenance of public assets and investment in agriculture, irrigation and rural infrastructure where it is not likely to crowd out private investment.

Medium-to Long-term Strategy

The most crucial strategic question Maharashtra faces relates to the role to be assigned to agriculture. It provides food for the population and raw materials and labour to industry. Besides, it provides market for the products of industry. Because of the reasons referred to earlier, productivity of agriculture is low and has stagnated over time. Green Revolution did not spread to coarse cereals and though the price terms of trade increased, income terms of trade did not, at least for the small and marginal farmers. Prosperity is limited to water rich big farmers growing sugarcane and grapes and other commercial crops. Organised employment did not increase as fast as rural population and organised industrial employment declined in the 1990s.

The gloomy scenario has a silver lining in diversification of agriculture to horticulture, dairying, poultry and animal husbandry. The change is already underway. Its pace can be increased by establishing cold chains of cold storage and refrigerated transport and also by promoting food processing and canning industry. Since agriculture is carrying substantial labour slack, the benefits of diversification may not show up an increase in the numbers employed but it will in person-days employed. The pace of diversification will also depend on availability of power and road and rail transport.

Farmers particularly the poor among them take time to adopt new things. That is why agriculture would not respond immediately to diversification. Fortunately, globalisation frees the industry from the dependence on domestic agriculture for market. If industry in Maharashtra is competitive, it can readily sell its products in the international markets.

Twin Engines of Growth

Maharashtra would do well to concentrate on the two engines of growth, manufacturing and infrastructure. Factories in Maharashtra are bigger in scale and more productive than the all-India average. Maharashtra occupies top ranks in value added by most industries in India. The industrial structure of the state has diversified and matured over time. Capital and intermediate goods industries have improved their share in the value added quite substantially. With higher labour productivity industry in Maharashtra remains competitive despite higher wages. That the state is a better place to do business in, is certified by the fact that it leads other states in the inflow of foreign direct investment.

Maharashtra's Industrial Policy, 2001 emphasises development of high technology based industries in the state. This is a step in the right direction. Exports of high-tech industry will put the state on the industrial map of the world in the same way as exports of software industry catapulted Bangalore and Hyderabad. Globalisation, according to Ghose (2003), is really export of LDC manufactures to compete with the manufactures of the DCs. He shows how the LDCs that exported manufactures prospered in the current phase of globalisation whereas exporters of primary products, most of African countries for instance, suffered.

Infrastructure

Infrastructure is basic to material and social development. Researchers have tried to quantify the elasticity of response of GDP to variation in expenditure on infrastructure. We have referred to two estimates, one by Kruegar and the other by Rakesh Mohan in the text. The first relates to LDCs and the second to India. Their relevance to Maharashtra is not known. In development economics, average shares of expenditure on infrastructure in GDP of countries at different levels of per capita income are often accepted as norms for poor countries wanting to graduate to higher levels of income. Statement such as that India should spend say six per cent of its GDP on infrastructure or education or health is often rooted in norms derived from international experience. More relevant to Maharashtra is the index of infrastructure by states. It shows that Maharashtra lags behind Punjab, Kerala, Tamil Nadu, Haryana and Gujarat in social and economic infrastructure.

Infrastructure plays a crucial role in a highly competitive global context. Increasing production of perishable goods serves no use if they cannot be delivered cheaply and speedily to where they are demanded. Competition has forced producers to reduce costs of holding inventories of raw materials, spares and finished products. Just-in-time system requires very efficient infrastructure.

Infrastructure is difficult to prioritise but power is considered the most critical element of it because of its very high forward and backward linkages relative to other infrastructure. Per capita consumption of power is high in Maharashtra relative to the average in India but it is much less than in East and Southeast Asian economies including China. High cost of power caused by frequent load-shedding, inefficient captive power plants, high T&D losses, lack of maintenance, monitoring of consumption and proper pricing of electricity supplied to agriculture puts industry in Maharashtra at a disadvantage in relation to the manufactures from these countries in national and international markets. Addition to capacity has almost come to a standstill because of the Enron imbroglio but the Gordian knot has to be cut.

Next to power in importance is the infrastructure of transport and communication. Excepting some kinds of roads and minor ports, much of it lies in the central sphere. There is urgent need to develop Centre-state and private sector cooperation in the development of infrastructure. The rise of information industry and growth of the financial sector has increased the importance of communication infrastructure. Maharashtra has developed substantial advantage in knowledge-based industry which will reduce transaction costs all round, help exports of software and hardware and increase inflow of portfolio and foreign direct investment to the state.

BOX 1.1

Benchmarking with the Best

As a state aspiring for a place in the sun, Maharashtra should look at East and Southeast Asia for inspiration. Maharashtra has miles to go in improving literacy and life expectancy to levels that could compare well with those prevailing in the East Asian and Southeast Asian countries.

- Adult literacy rate was 84 per cent in China in 2000 while it was 67 per cent in Maharashtra in 1995-96.
- Life expectancy at birth was 70.5 years in China in 2000 and 65 years in Maharashtra in 1992-1996.
- Population below poverty line was 4.6 per cent in China in 1987-2000 and 25 per cent in Maharashtra in 1999-00.
- Total fertility rate was 1.8 in China in 1995-2000 and 2.8 in Maharashtra in 1995-1997.
- China spends 2.3 per cent of the GNP on education while Maharashtra spends 2.21 per cent of SDP on education. Singapore spends 3 per cent, Republic of Korea 3.7 per cent and Malaysia 4.9 per cent. Malaysia spends 1.4 per cent of its GDP on public health while China spends 2.1 per cent, Singapore 1.1 per cent, Republic of Korea 2.4 per cent. Maharashtra spends only 0.61 per cent of its SDP on public health.
- It is not only higher public spending but the quality ot service that is essential.

Social Infrastructure and Equity

We saw earlier that Maharashtra lags behind Kerala in human development. This could be attributed to two factors. First, Maharashtra spends a smaller share of its GDP on health and education than Kerala. Secondly, social, economic, cultural and political factors in Kerala have combined to empower women much more than in Maharashtra. Consequently, Maharashtra runs a poor second to Kerala in many respects such as reducing fertility, infant mortality and poverty on the one hand, and improving education and health on the other. Kerala has improved the access of the marginalised groups, women and poorer households for instance, to the social infrastructure of education and health much more than has Maharashtra.

Without the slightest intention of detracting from the achievements of Kerala, one should note the specific factors that favoured the laudatory outcomes in Kerala. Social anthropologist refers to prevalence of matrilineal family in the past. The long years of Communist rule may have helped women to fight discrimination.

Demographers point to the male out-migration that forced women to shoulder the responsibility of managing the household's land and other business, looking after the education of children, freedom from repeated childbearing caused by long absence of the husband and much else. Kerala is regionally not as diverse and as water-starved as Maharashtra. Even the human habitation pattern is a whole continuum of villages without much rural-urban differentiation.

Despite the collapse of time and space brought about by new technology, economic development takes time particularly when we try to achieve sustainable growth assuring intra-generation and inter-generation equity and justice. Conflicts over distribution are inevitable and need to be resolved by creating institutions to address them. In Kerala, ideology, political parties and trade unions helped by other NGOs led to such resolution and empowerment of women. Maharashtra has to await such a coalition to emerge.

Chapter 2

Fiscal Situation and Policies

Introduction

Maharashtra contributes 19 per cent of the country's industrial output, 15 per cent of the services output, and 13 per cent of the country's GDP. It is the state with third highest per capita income in the country. But, its performance is showing deterioration since the mid-1990s. The state's economy has slowed down in recent years after experiencing rapid and sustained growth till the mid 1990s. Trend GSDP growth rate of Maharashtra from a high of 7.3 per cent during the last 15 years has fallen to an average growth rate of 4.2 per cent during 1995-2002. Though, during fiscal years 2002-03 and 2003-04 the state had an average growth rate of 6.1 per cent, but the same is lower than the target growth rate of 8 per cent for Tenth Five Year Plan (2002-2007).

The current growth slowdown does not appear to be a cyclical downturn, but a result of many structural constraints afflicting the state's economy. Ranks of different states for growth rates in GSDP during the two periods, 1980-81 to 1990-91 and 1993-94 to 2000-2001, are given in Figures 2.1 and 2.2.

It can be seen from Figure 2.1 that Maharashtra ranked third in terms of growth rate in GSDP, behind Rajasthan and Haryana and followed by Andhra Pradesh, Tamil Nadu and Punjab. But the ranking for the period 1993-94 to 2000-01 shows that Maharashtra slipped to sixth place in terms of growth rate in GSDP and states—Karnataka, West Bengal, Rajasthan, Tamil Nadu, and Gujarat were ahead of it (Figure 2.2).

While the reasons for such a systematic decline in Maharashtra's growth rate are not well understood, it can be said with some degree of assurance that other states which forged ahead witnessed an acceleration in new growth sectors such as information technology and

FIGURE 2.1

Rank of Growth Rate in GSDP of Different States during 1980-81 to 1990-91

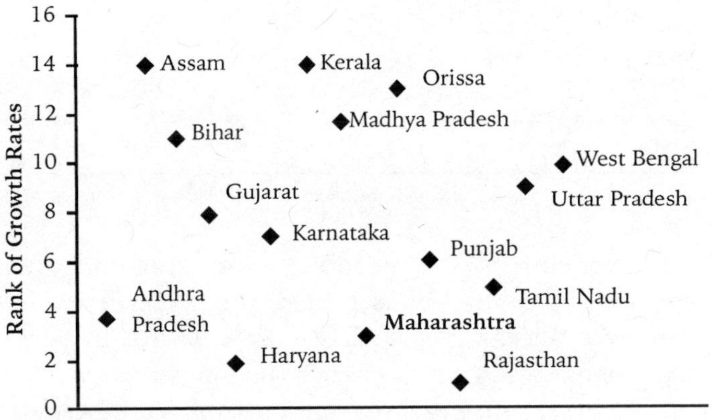

Source: Various GoI documents.

FIGURE 2.2

Rank of Growth Rate in GSDP of Different States during 1993-94 to 2000-01

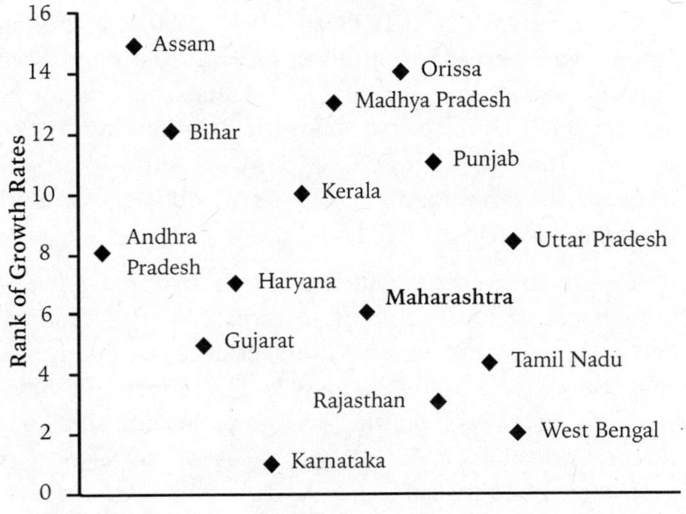

Source: Various GoI documents.

pharmaceuticals (World Bank, 2002, p.3). Table 2.1 gives the average long-term growth rate of various sectors during 1985-86 to 2000-01 and growth during 2002-03 in Maharashtra.

TABLE 2.1

Average Long-term Growth Rate of Various Sectors during 1985-86 to 2000-01 and in 2002-03 in Maharashtra (at 1993-94 Prices)

Sub-sector of the State Economy	*Growth Rate (%)*	
	1985-2001	*2002-03*
Banking and Insurance	12.8	6.4
Unregistered Manufacturing	9.0	5.8
Transport, Storage & Communication	8.7	8.3
Utilities	7.6	6.9
Trade and Hospitality	7.6	10.7
Registered Manufacturing	6.9	5.0
Public Administration	6.1	7.4
Agriculture	5.3	-2.4
Mining & Quarrying	5.2	4.1
Construction	4.1	11.5
Real Estate Services	3.7	4.5
GSDP	7.1	6.1

Source: World Bank, 2002 and *Economic Survey, 2003-04.*

Slowdown in the economy and stagnant own revenue effort has constrained the government to undertake necessary productive expenditure in social and economic services, especially in infrastructure. This had adverse consequences on the long-term growth prospects of Maharashtra's economy. Deteriorating revenue mobilisation and rising unproductive expenditure resulted in growing fiscal and revenue deficits with corresponding increase in debt and interest payment obligations. The gross fiscal deficit of major states as percentage of GSDP during the two five-year periods, 1990-1995 and 1995-2000, and during three year period of 2000-2003 and their relative rankings are given in Table 2.2. Maharashtra ranks at third, sixth and fourth, respectively during these periods. Though, during 2000-03 Maharashtra improved its relative ranking, its gross fiscal deficit was still nowhere near 1990-1995 level.

Theory as well as evidence shows that persistently high fiscal deficits could pose threats to the stability and growth of the economy. Experience also suggests that easy fiscal policies may in the short-run have stimulating effects on the economy, but in the long run, they lead to lower growth. Negative correlation is even stronger between deficit and growth, if the deficit is used for expenditure on current consumption purpose. The case of Maharashtra is one such example. Maharashtra borrowed primarily to finance its current consumption—to pay for salaries and pensions, losses in its PSUs and electricity boards. The low and declining buoyancies in both tax and non-tax receipts and decelerating resource transfers from the Centre worsened the situation. The government has taken some steps to correct the imbalance, but whether it is enough, remains to be seen.

TABLE 2.2

Gross Fiscal Deficit of States as a Percentage of GSDP and their Relative Ranking

States	*Gross Fiscal Deficit as Percentage of GSDP*		
	1990-1995	*1995-2000*	*2000-2003*
Andhra Pradesh	3.2 (5)	5.5 (5)	4.6 (7)
Bihar	7.0 (12)	4.1 (1)	4.5 (6)
Gujarat	7.4 (13)	6.3 (8)	5.7 (10)
Haryana	2.6 (1)	5.9 (7)	3.7 (1)
Karnataka	2.7 (2)	4.1 (1)	4.4 (5)
Kerala	6.6 (11)	5.3 (4)	5.2 (9)
Madhya Pradesh	3.8 (6)	5.2 (3)	3.9 (2)
Maharashtra	**2.8 (3)**	**5.8 (6)**	**4.1 (4)**
Orissa	6.4 (10)	9.8 (13)	7.8 (14)
Punjab	7.4 (13)	7.9 (11)	6.2 (12)
Rajasthan	3.0 (4)	8.9 (12)	6.1 (11)
Tamil Nadu	4.1 (7)	4.5 (2)	3.8 (3)
Uttar Pradesh	6.2 (9)	7.8 (10)	5.1 (8)
West Bengal	5.2 (8)	6.7 (9)	7.3 (13)
Average	4.9	6.3	4.97

Note: Figures in the parentheses are ranks.

Source: Various GoI documents.

SECTION I

Revenue Receipts

Powers of the states to raise resources are enumerated in the Seventh Schedule of the Constitution of India. Revenues of the states can broadly be divided into two heads—tax revenue and non-tax revenue. Major sources of tax revenue at state level are sales tax, state excise on alcohol, stamp duties and registration fees, motor vehicles tax and taxes on goods and passengers. Non-tax revenue includes mineral and forest royalties, fines and fees or user charges for publicly provided goods and services. The states also get transfer and grants from the Centre. Besides the above, the states also have access to capital receipts. These include internal loans of the state government and loans and advances from the Central government, recovery of loans and advances by the state government, receipts from public accounts such as small savings, provident funds, etc. Composition of revenue for Maharashtra from 1996-97 to 2003-04 is given in Table 2.3.

TABLE 2.3

Maharashtra's Revenue Composition

(in Per Cent)

Item	*1996-97*	*1997-98*	*1998-99*	*1999-00*	*2000-01*	*2001-02*	*2002-03*	*2003-04*
Own Tax	60.8	67.5	65.3	68.3	66.7	70.7	69.7	70.2
Own Non-Tax	19.5	17.9	16.4	15.6	18.9	15.5	13.9	10.1
Central Tax Shares	11.8	8.5	13.4	10.3	9.4	8.2	7.6	8.2
Grants	7.8	6.0	4.8	5.8	4.9	5.6	8.8	11.5
Total Revenues	**100**	**100**	**100**	**100**	**100**	**100**	**100**	**100**

Source: Finance Accounts, and *State Finances,* RBI, April 2004.

Profile of revenue receipts as percentage of GSDP for fiscal years 1996-97 to 2002-03 is given in Table 2.4.

TABLE 2.4

Revenue Profile of Maharashtra as Percentage of GSDP

Item	*1996-97*	*1997-98*	*1998-99*	*1999-00*	*2000-01*	*2001-02*	*2002-03*
Own Tax Revenue	6.61	7.05	6.66	7.15	7.09	8.02	7.73
Own Non-Tax Revenue	2.12	1.87	1.68	1.63	2.01	1.75	1.53
Central Rev. Transfers	2.13	1.52	1.86	1.68	1.52	2.39	0.33
Tax Share	1.28	0.89	1.37	1.08	1.00	0.92	0.77
Total Grants	0.85	0.63	0.49	0.60	0.53	0.63	0.51
Total Revenues	**10.86**	**10.44**	**10.20**	**10.47**	**10.62**	**11.33**	**10.54**

Source (Basic Data): *Finance Accounts, Economic Survey of Maharashtra,* 2003-04.

The own tax revenues as a percentage of GSDP though varied between 6.6 per cent and 7.7 per cent during 1996-97 and 2002-03 (going up in 2001-02 to 8 per cent) has been on rise. But non-tax revenues to GSDP ratio showed a secular decline from 2.12 to 1.53 per cent from 1996-97 to 2002-03. Central tax shares and grants have also been on decline, going down from 1.3 per cent to 0.8 per cent and 0.85 per cent to 0.5 per cent, respectively, during this period. But the overall revenue as a percentage of GSDP has been static around 10.5 per cent along a fluctuating trend. If we compare this to earlier years, we find that the ratio had increased from 12.2 per cent in 1980-81 to 15.6 per cent in 1986-87, and then started declining. It is often stated that reasons for such decline in the revenue receipts to GSDP ratio is due to a steady decline in the Central transfers. But it can be seen that shared taxes and grants as a proportion of GSDP had been declining even prior to 1986-87. But since own revenue—both tax and non-tax—was buoyant, it had more than made up for the decline and in fact, it resulted in an increase in the revenue to GSDP ratio.

FIGURE 2.3

Total Revenue of Maharashtra as Percentage of GSDP during 1990-91 to 2002-03

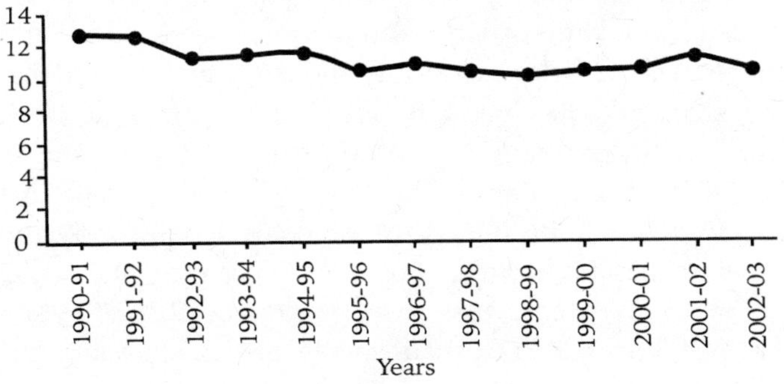

Source: (Basic Data): *Finance Accounts.*

Major heads of revenue receipts for the past three years, 2001-02 to 2003-04, are given in Table 2.5. As can be seen from the table, sales tax is the major source of revenue receipts of the Maharashtra

TABLE 2.5

Revenue Receipts during 2001-02 to 2003-04

(Rs. Billion)

Item	*2001-02*	*2002-03*	*2003-04 RE*
Sales Tax	121.31	134.88	154.85
Stamp and Registration Fees	24.43	28.23	31.0
State Excise Duty	17.87	19.39	23.0
Electricity Duties	10.34	11.49	12.8
Taxes on Income and Expenditure	9.86	10.32	10.2
Taxes on Vehicles	9.48	9.41	10.25
Taxes on Commodities & Services	6.87	8.11	8.61
Taxes on Goods & Passengers	10.27	2.45	6.65
Land Revenue	2.60	3.87	3.38
Taxes on Agriculture Income Tax	0.0016	0.00	0.00
Non-Tax Revenue	46.55	60.23	80.48
Share in Central Taxes	24.68	30.37	30.37
Grants-in-Aid from the Central Government	16.81	15.06	42.74
Total Revenue Receipts	**300.93**	**311.03**	**371.59**
Per Capita Revenue Receipts (in Rs.)	3077.46	3426.44	3762.56

Source: GoM Budget Document.

Government. Other tax sources, having relative significance during 2003-04 were stamp and registration fees (3.22 per cent), state excise duty (6.2 per cent), taxes on income and expenditure (2.74 per cent), taxes on vehicles and goods and passengers (4.54 per cent), and electricity duties (3.45 per cent).

Own Tax Revenues

Relative importance of various taxes can be analysed from the structure of own tax revenue of the Maharashtra Government. It can be seen from Table 2.6 that the major sources of own tax revenue are from the sales tax, followed by state excise and other taxes, *viz.*, stamp and registration duty, taxes on goods and passengers and electricity duty. It can also be seen that the share of sales taxes in total tax revenues declined from 61.60 per cent in 1996-97 to 56.94 per cent in 2001-02. This decline in the share of sales tax was due to the decline in the share of central sales tax and general sales tax from 10.80 to 9.56 per cent and 41.42 to 31.55 per cent, respectively. During 2002-03 and 2003-04, the sales tax share in the own-tax revenue has shown some rise, 59.1 and 59.4 per cent. Share of tax on motor sprit, etc. had also shown consistent rise during the period. But share of state excise duty had not been very encouraging, remaining below 10 per cent, except for two years 1996-97 and 2000-01 when it went up to 12 per cent. But thereafter during past three years 2001-02 to 2003-04, it has been around 8.5 per cent.

Stamp duty and registration fees and taxes on vehicles have also not been significantly rising. Share of stamp duty and registration fee in the own tax has been fluctuating around 11.5 per cent. Similarly the shares of other minor taxes have also remained more or less stagnant during the period. Land revenue also did not show any perceptive rise. Agricultural income tax remained a non-starter.

Sales Tax

As already seen, close to 60 per cent of the own revenue of Maharashtra comes from the sales and purchases tax, including the central sales tax. During the last two financial years, 2002-03 and 2003-04 (revised estimates), annual sales tax revenue of Rs. 134.88 billion and Rs. 154.85 billion were collected. If we take the ratio of the sales tax revenue to the

TABLE 2.6

Structure of Own Tax Revenue

(in Per Cent)

Item	*1996-97*	*1997-98*	*1998-99*	*1999-00*	*2000-01*	*2001-02*	*2002-03*	*2003-04*
Taxes on Agricultural Income	0.00	0.00	0.00	0.00	0.00	0.00	0.00	0.00
Other Taxes on Income & Exp.	3.29	3.16	3.02	3.26	2.89	4.63	4.52	3.91
Land Revenue	1.00	1.20	1.10	0.94	0.67	1.23	1.7	1.3
Stamps & Registration	7.96	11.81	11.30	10.88	12.32	11.47	12.37	11.89
Imm. Property Not Ag. Land	0.00	0.00	0.00	0.00	0.00	0.00	0.00	0.00
State Excise	11.74	9.99	9.79	9.12	12.03	8.39	8.5	8.82
Sales Tax	61.60	60.91	62.	62.23	57.04	56.94	59.1	59.39
Central Sales Tax	10.80	10.29	10.55	10.63	9.32	9.56	9.11	8.16
General Sales Tax	41.42	41.32	42.40	40.63	36.05	31.55	34.73	35.45
Tax on Motor Spirits, etc.	7.25	8.84	9.14	10.14	10.92	15.41	14.9	15.72
Sugarcane Cess/Purchase Tax	2.11	0.43	0.49	0.73	0.63	0.38	0.34	0.00
Turnover Tax	0.00	0.00	0.00	0.00	0.00	0.00	0.00	0.00
Others	0.02	0.02	0.01	0.10	0.12	0.04	0.04	0.06
Taxes on Vehicles	3.51	3.64	3.87	5.24	5.48	4.45	4.13	3.93
Taxes on Goods & Passengers	3.27	2.95	2.27	1.71	2.49	4.82	1.07	2.55
Taxes & Duties on Electricity	4.37	3.56	3.27	3.44	3.90	4.85	5.04	4.91
Other Taxes	3.26	2.77	2.78	3.17	3.18	3.23	3.56	3.30
Total	**100**	**100**	**100**	**100**	**100**	**100**	**100**	**100**
Own Tax Revenue (Rs. Billion)	**117.15**	**137.19**	**142.02**	**172.65**	**197.27**	**213.04**	**228.15**	**260.74**

Source: (Basic Data): *Finance Accounts.*

GSDP, we find that the ratio has been somewhat stagnant, hovering between 0.04 and 0.05 over the last 12 years (Figure 2.4).

FIGURE 2.4

Ratio of Sales Tax Revenue to GSDP during 1990-91 to 2002-03

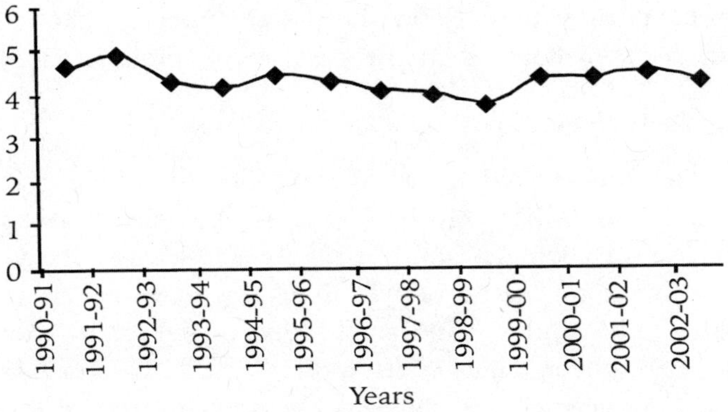

Source: (Basic Data): *Finance Accounts.*

In fact, the percentage of sales tax revenue in own-tax revenue has been showing a declining trend, from 63.59 per cent in 1990-91 to 56.9 per cent in 2001-02 (Figure 2.5). During the years 2002-03 and 2003-04 (RE), the share of sales tax in the own-tax revenue has however shown some rise, being 59.1 per cent and 59.4 per cent, respectively.

FIGURE 2.5

Percentage of Sales Tax Revenue to Own Tax Revenue of Maharashtra during 1990-91 and 2003 04

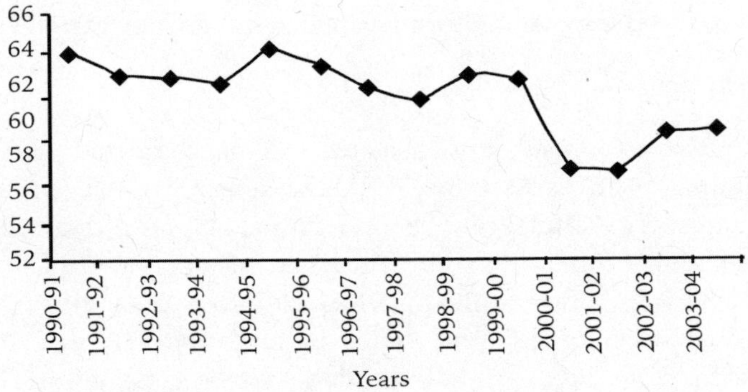

Source: (Basic Data): Finance Accounts.

This decline in the share of sales tax can be mainly due to decline in the share of general sales tax from 44.35 to 36.05 per cent and that of central sales tax from 12.40 to 9.32 per cent (Figure 2.6).

FIGURE 2.6

Percentage of Central Sales Tax (CST) and General Sales Tax (GST) in Own Tax Revenue

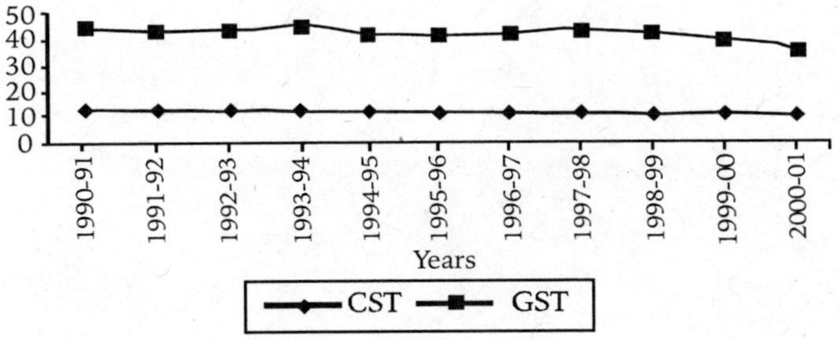

Source: (Basic Data): *Finance Accounts.*

Sales tax includes taxes on sales or purchases, central sales tax on interstate sales, etc. Most of the commodities are taxed at 13 per cent and 10 per cent, and there are 8 *ad valorem* sales tax rates from 0 per cent to 20 per cent. The average tax rate on non-exempt commodities was 8.17 per cent in 1998-99.

Major factors contributing to decline in sales tax collection appear to be widespread use of tax exemptions and deferrals and vertical integration of units to optimise tax liability under a first point regime. An estimate of revenue sacrifice from the exemptions and the package schemes puts it at Rs. 83.57 billion and Rs. 21.66 billion, respectively, which constitute about 25 per cent of the sales tax collections. Though the package schemes of incentives were discontinued some time back following an all-state agreement, their effect would continue to deprive the state of revenues for some time. With introduction of state-level value added tax (VAT) from 1 April 2005, some of these tax collection woes may be mitigated because a first point tax regime, unlike VAT, attaches a premium on vertical integration of activities by tax payers. With vertical integration, under a first point tax regime, hitherto taxable turnovers become endogenous to the firm and so cannot be taxed and the tax base narrows. With sales tax applicable on output and not on value added, a change in the composition of output towards higher value added products reduces sales tax revenue as a proportion of GSDP.

State Excise Duties

State excise duties are levied on the production of alcohol and other narcotic substances, besides licence fees for liquor wholesale and retail permits. During the last three years, the state excise duties have constituted around 8.5 per cent of the state's own tax revenue. Figure 2.7 shows the trend over last 13 years.

FIGURE 2.7

State Excise Duty as a Percentage of Own Tax Revenue

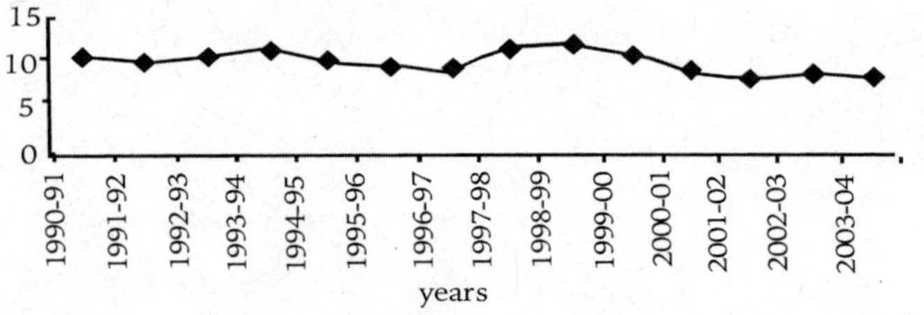

Source: (Basic Data): *Finance Accounts.*

Maharashtra is the largest producer of alcohol in the country. The chemical industry also has use of alcohol. Around 32 per cent of excise duty is collected from the country liquor and the balance from Indian made foreign liquor (IMFL), wine and beer. Over the last 10 years the percentage of excise duty in the tax collection of the state has remained at a long-term average of 11 per cent. But over the last three years there has been a declining trend in the excise duty despite *ad valorem* taxation. Fines and fees contribute about 10 per cent of the duties. Studies by the Excise Department show that unit realisation from beer has fallen by 18 per cent and that for country liquor by 33 per cent since 1997-98.

Professions Tax

Professions tax contributes about 4 per cent of Maharashtra's own revenue collections. This is one of the direct taxes levied by Maharashtra. This stream of tax has a wide scope to expand.

Stamp Duties and Registration Fees

The share of revenue from stamp duties and registration fees as a percentage of the state's own tax revenue is 11.46 (2001-02), 12.37 (2002-03) and 11.89 (2003-04 RE). Share in the total receipts during these three financial years was about 8 per cent. This share can be increased given that Maharashtra has high real estate values. But this is also a constraint as there is a persistent attempt to understate the value of property. Stamp duty on the property sales is 10 per cent of the property value and there are another 8 rates prevalent. As 10 per cent rate is high, large numbers of transactions (almost 70 per cent) are undervalued (World Bank, 2002, p. 9.30).

Due to high stamp duty, transfers are often shown as gifts, through General Power of Attorney, sale within the same cooperative society, etc. In fact concessional stamp duties and registration fees for housing cooperatives result in major loss of revenue to the state. Given the above situation, growth in revenues can only be secured through better implementation of market value scheme and procedural improvements. Besides, there are some inherent deficiencies in the legal provisions, which also require a closer look. For example, the current Registration Act only covers registration of documents and not property titles *per se*. Rate structures of the registration have not been updated for long. In the present scenario, they do not seem to cover even the cost of its administration.

Motor Vehicles Tax

The motor vehicle taxes are collected in the state under the Indian Motor Vehicles Act, State Motor Vehicle Taxation Act and as services and service fees and other receipts. In the year 2000-01, Rs. 0.86 billion was collected under Indian Motor Vehicles Act, Rs. 6.96 billion under State Motor Vehicle Taxation Act and a meagre Rs. 7.9 million as services and service fees.

Motor vehicle taxes contribute less than 4.5 per cent of the state's own tax revenue. In terms of GSDP, this is about 0.3 per cent. This is far less in Maharashtra as a proportion of GSDP than in other states. Besides the rate problem, lack of adequate collection from the state transport undertakings is a cause for poor collection of the motor vehicles tax. Another cause for the poor collection of taxes is illegal and clandestine operations and lack of enforcement mechanism. Some of the reasons for poor collection are difficulty in enforcement of permits for specified routes, non-rationalisation of rate structure and tax basis for interstate vehicles. Life tax system can be considered for small commercial vehicles apart from the non-transport private vehicles. The turnover basis can be converted to seating capacity basis and can be uniformly applied to private carriages.

Tax Effort of Maharashtra

Tax efforts of various states can be compared so as to make an assessment of Maharashtra *vis-à-vis* other states. Tax effort can be understood as a ratio of the tax collection and some measure of taxable capacity (Chelliah and Sinha, 1982). Figure 2.8 gives a comparison of different states in tax efforts. It may be seen from Figure 2.8 that Maharashtra's tax effort is lower than that of some major states like Kerala, Tamil Nadu, Karnataka, Haryana and Gujarat. One of the reasons for the lower tax-GSDP ratio of Maharashtra is that the octroi revenue in Maharashtra is not accounted in the state revenues, but it is considered as municipal revenue.

Even if we make allowance for that (octroi would account for not more than one percentage point of GSDP), Maharashtra would still not compare favourably with better performing states in terms of tax revenues (GoM Documents, 1999). Interstate comparison of tax-GSDP ratio also brings out the fact that there is considerable scope for improving the tax effort of Maharashtra. The state being the second highest per capita income state, the tax base and the fiscal capacity is much higher than other states including those states which are better performing in terms of tax-GSDP ratio.

FIGURE 2.8

Tax-GSDP Ratio of Major States (2000-01) Additional Revenue Measures in Own Tax Revenues

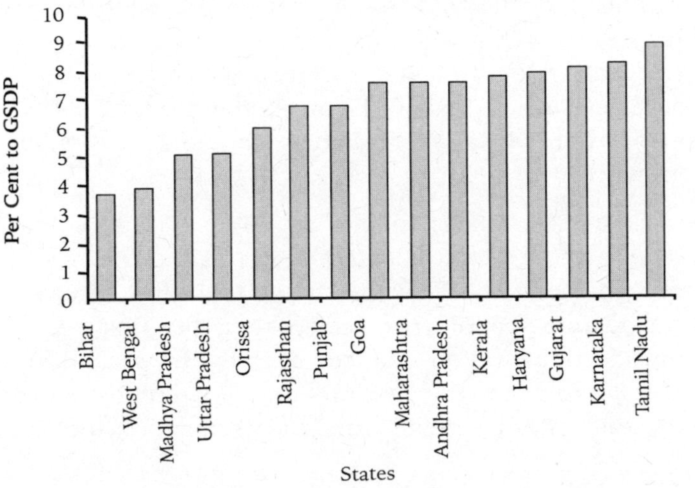

During 2002-03, Maharashtra Government raised Rs. 11.3 billion of tax revenue through additional revenue measures (ARM). Distribution of the above additional revenue in terms of value (Rs. billion) and percentage is given in Table 2.7.

TABLE 2.7

Additional Revenue Mobilisation (ARM) Measures of Maharashtra during 2002-03

Item	*Amount of Revenue Rs. billion*	*Percentage to Total Revenue Mobilisation*
Stamp Duty	0.05	0.4
Sales Tax	9.75	86.3
Electricity Duties	0.80	7.1
Entertainment Tax	0.65	5.8
Other Taxes	0.05	0.4
Total ARM	**11.3**	**100**

Source: RBI's Study of State Finances, 2003.

In comparison, Tamil Nadu raised Rs. 6.90 billion, Punjab Rs. 4.77 billion and Uttar Pradesh Rs. 2.46 billion through additional revenue mobilisation measures. It may be noted that as in the case of Maharashtra, so also in the case of other states, the percentage of revenue through ARM in sales tax is the largest.

Long Range Buoyancies of Revenues

Estimated buoyancies of major taxes of Maharashtra with respect to both non-agricultural GSDP and total GSDP are shown in Table 2.8.

Buoyancy gives an indicator for response of state taxes to the rise in output. Among the major taxes the highest buoyancy at more than 1.7 was shown by stamp duty and registration with respect to both non-agricultural GSDP and total GSDP (Table 2.8). Apart from stamp duty and registration fees other major taxes having buoyancies above one are state excise duties and tax on motor spirit, etc. The sales tax, which has the highest share in total taxes, showed buoyancy below one with respect to both the bases. Some of the taxes, which have shown buoyancy above unity, their combined share in total taxes is much lower than that of sales tax. Thus, the overall buoyancy of own tax revenues suffers and remains below one with respect to non-agricultural GSDP and marginally above one with respect to GSDP.

TABLE 2.8

Buoyancy of Major Taxes in Maharashtra: 1990-91 to 2000-01

Item	*With Respect to Non-agricultural GSDP*	*With Respect to Aggregate GSDP*
Own Tax Revenues	0.998 (24.01)	1.027 (23.70)
Land Revenues	0.609 (3.94)	0.624 (3.896)
Stamp Duty and Registration Fee	1.736 (16.84)	1.784 (16.03)
State Excise Duty	1.040 (16.83)	1.075 (19.44)
Sales Tax	0.962 (24.80)	0.989 (23.20)
Central Sales Tax	0.821 (23.03)	0.844 (21.76)
General Sales Tax	0.896 (19.53)	0.920 (18.42)
Tax on Motor	1.602 (6.1)	1.644 (6.21)
Spirit/etc.		
Sugarcane Cess/ Purchase Tax	0.864 (3.12)	0.902 (3.22)
Taxes on Vehicles	0.969 (6.55)	0.996 (6.53)

Note: Figures in parentheses are t-values.

Source: (Basic Data): *Finance Accounts*, World Bank, 2002.

Increase in the buoyancy (aggregate) is an important prerequisite for additional non-debt resource mobilisation. This needs to be done through an increase in the sales tax buoyancy above one and also through other relatively less buoyant taxes. The buoyancy estimates show that some of the worst performing taxes are land revenues, taxes on goods and passengers, and electricity duty.

An estimation of the long-run buoyancies of own revenue for nine major states has been reported in Table 2.9. From this (Table 2.9), it can be seen that stamp duty and the state excise duty are the two most buoyant sources of taxes. The sales tax follows the two. But as we discussed earlier, sales tax constitutes the major portion of the revenue receipts. Given the above scenario, it would be appropriate to shore up sales tax revenue collection in case the state has to improve the revenue collection. It should be noted that sales tax system suffers from various deficiencies and no comparable reforms have taken place in the area of sales taxes. Major problems of sales tax system, as already stated, are multiplicity of rates with large spread, plethora of exemptions and rate war between states. All these have contributed to a very complex structure of sales tax, which in turn contributes to large-scale evasion of tax, problems of enforcement and administration and compliance. Also, the sales tax being levied on gross value at the successive stages of production lead to considerable cascading, leading further to increase in the cost of production and the consumer price.

Direction of sales tax reform as suggested by various studies and expert groups include the following: eliminating cascading through full rebate on tax on inputs, zero rating of interstate sales tax, reduction in the number of rates and adoption of at least uniform floor rates for specified groups and commodities, reducing the number of exemptions, phasing out of sales tax incentives, and extending the tax to resellers on a value added basis.

VAT across the states, as a replacement of sales tax, has been introduced from 1 April 2005. The essence of VAT is in providing set-off for the tax paid earlier. This is given effect through the concept of input tax credit or rebate. Under this system, there will be only two basic rates—of 4 per cent and 12.5 per cent, plus a specific category of tax-exempted goods and a special VAT rate of 1 per cent only for gold and silver ornaments. The VAT system would cover about 550 goods, and so multiplicity of rates, which exist in the present system of sales tax, will be done away with.

Effects of the VAT system will be to rationalise the tax burden. This will stop unhealthy tax-rate war and trade diversion among the states, which had hitherto adversely affected interests of all the states. This will also improve tax compliance and ensure revenue growth.

Despite tax gains in the long run, it is feared that there may be revenue loss to states in the initial years of transition. The Government of India has agreed to compensate for 100 per cent loss in the first year of introduction of VAT, 75 per cent in the second year and 50 per cent in the third year of introduction, on the basis of an agreed formula for computing the loss.

Own Non-tax Revenue

Share of own non-tax revenue in total revenue over a period of 12 years, 1990-91 to 2002-03, has been declining from 23 per cent as shown in Figure 2.9. Non-tax revenue comprises mainly interest earning,

TABLE 2.9

Long-Run Buoyancies of Own Revenue and Components : 1999-2000

States	*Per Capita GSDP in Rs. (1999-00)*	*Own Revenue*	*Own Tax Revenue*	*Sales Tax*	*State Excise Duty*	*Motor Vehicles*	*Stamp Duty*
West Bengal	16054	0.92	0.98	1.02	0.91	0.41	1.13
Andhra Pradesh	16205	0.90	0.91	10.5	0.65	0.96	1.04
Karnataka	20269	0.94	1.00	1.06	0.89	0.98	1.24
Tamil Nadu	22179	0.94	0.97	0.98	0.98	0.91	1.04
Kerala	23089	0.93	0.99	1.04	0.85	1.04	1.05
Gujarat	24961	0.99	1.00	1.03	0.78	0.84	1.11
Haryana	25436	1.07	0.97	1.06	0.76	0.84	1.09
Maharashtra	**26486**	**0.91**	**0.95**	**0.96**	**1.07**	**0.89**	**1.48**
Punjab	26840	1.07	0.94	0.97	1.06	0.78	0.88
Average	**18027**	**0.97**	**0.99**	**1.02**	**0.99**	**0.90**	**1.14**

Source: World Bank, 2002.

dividends and profits from the state public sector enterprises (PSEs), earnings from general services, social services and economic services.

FIGURE 2.9

Share of Own Non-tax Revenue in the Total Revenue of Maharashtra

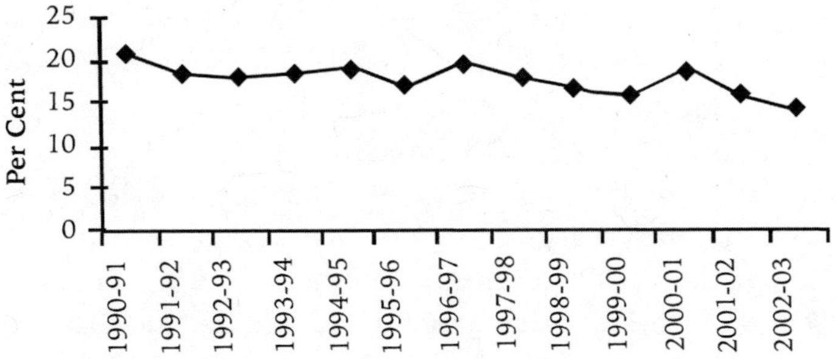

Source: (Basic Data): *Finance Accounts.*

Amongst all the sources of own non-tax revenue, interest earnings constitute the largest share in total non-tax revenues. In fact, its share in total own non-tax revenue had increased from 36.70 per cent in 1990-91 to 56.50 per cent in 2000-01 (Table 2.10). But during the last three fiscal years it has sharply declined to 39.65 per cent in 2001-02, 24 per cent in 2002-03 and only 8.54 per cent in 2003-04. Such sharp decline in the interest receipts may be due to reasons of declining interest rate, default in interest payment, and waiver of loans given to SEs. If we see the above along with sharply declining dividends and profits which in 1990-91 had a share of 0.49 per cent and was only 0.07 per cent in 2000-01, along with dismal recovery rates on the investments made in various corporations and public sector enterprises, we find that while government investment in Maharashtra increased in absolute terms from Rs. 8.48 billion in 1990-91 to Rs. 96.81 billion in 2000-01 (an increase of 11.4 times), dividend receipts and the corresponding rates of return on the equity invested are extremely low. The highest recovery rate was 1.03 per cent in the year 1990-91 which declined to 0.04 per cent in 2000-01 (Table 2.11). The situation demands that the state government should take up suitable steps to make these enterprises either profitable or else wind up the defunct and the perennially loss-making units, as it otherwise becomes a sink for the costly resources.

TABLE 2.10

Structure of Non-Tax Revenues during 1996-97 to 2000-01

(in Per Cent)

Item	*1996-97*	*1997-98*	*1998-99*	*1999-00*	*2000-01*
Interest Receipts	54.18	46.53	46.29	43.80	56.50
Dividends and Profits	0.25	0.26	0.17	0.10	0.07
General Services	7.67	8.74	7.90	11.02	9.77
Social Services	4.64	6.34	7.39	7.99	5.43
Economic Services	33.25	38.13	38.25	37.09	28.23
Total	**100**	**100**	**100**	**100**	**100**
Non-Tax Rev. (Rs. Billion)	**37.55**	**36.41**	**35.73**	**39.37**	**55.96**

Source: (Basic Data): Finance Accounts.

TABLE 2.11

Outstanding Investment and Recovery Rate

Item	*Investment at the End of the Year (Rs. Billion)*	*Dividend/Interest Received (Rs. Million)*	*Rate of Recovery (%)*
1990-91	8.48	87.5	1.03
1991-92	9.69	91.1	0.94
1992-93	10.47	56.0	0.53
1993-94	11.79	27.3	0.23
1994-95	14.17	37.9	0.27
1995-96	17.40	41.6	0.24
1996-97	18.74	92.7	0.49
1997-98	20.03	93.3	0.47
1998-99	54.40	60.1	0.11
1999-00	67.84	39.6	0.06
2000-01	96.81	39.5	0.04

Source: (Basic Data): *Finance Accounts.*

Also, the share of earnings from economic services declined from 41.79 per cent in 1990-91 to 28.23 per cent in 2000-01, and that from the general services declined from 16.12 to 9.77 per cent during the period. The share of earnings from social services, however, increased marginally from 4.90 per cent in 1990-91 to 5.43 per cent in 2000-01; though during the year 1999-00 the same share had gone up to 8.00 per cent. Studies have shown that the rates of recovery under social and economic services are very low across the states. Major reason for the low rates of recovery is the abysmally low user charges as most of the state PSEs are in utility services. Non-revision of user charges for years put the current prices of these services out of alignment with cost, resulting in huge subsidies. The recovery rates in social services and economic services, as estimated by Srivastava and Sen (1997) for Maharashtra, were as low as 4.53 and 18.24 per cent, respectively. Since goods and services provided by the public sector are classified as 'merit' and 'non–merit' categories. Merit goods and services are those goods and services that have strong externalities associated with their provision. Non-merit ones are the others. While low recoveries may have some justification in case of merit goods and services, it is hard to defend very low recovery rates for non-merit categories.

Central Transfers

Central transfers supplement the states' resources through tax devolution and grants, to eliminate both vertical and horizontal fiscal imbalances. It can be seen from the Figure 2.10 that the revenue transfers (tax share and grants) from the Centre showed a declining trend during 1990-91 to 2000-01. In 1990-91, it formed 20.52 per cent of total revenue of the state but was only 14.35 per cent during 2000-01. It further declined after that, and is now around 8 per cent.

FIGURE 2.10

Share of Revenue Transfers from Centre in the Total Revenue of Maharashtra

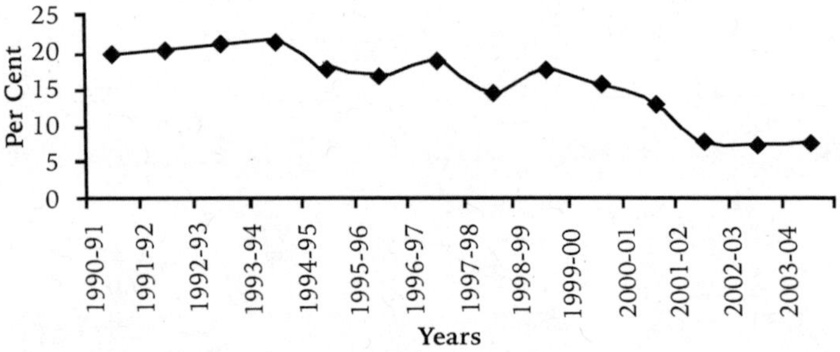

Source: (Basic Data): Finance Accounts.

Total central transfers to the state during this period, 1990-91 to 2000-01, also showed a declining trend in terms of its share in GSDP. The share of total transfers in the GSDP of the state declined from 3.20 per cent to 2.0 per cent during this period (Figure 2.11).

FIGURE 2.11

Total Central Transfers as a Percentage of GSDP

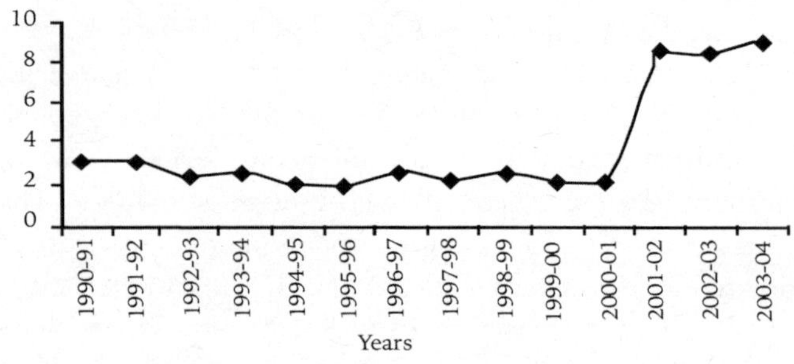

Source: (Basic Data): *Finance Accounts.*

The decline in transfers has been witnessed both in the case of shares in central taxes and the grants. Sharing of central taxes with the states is mandated by the Constitution and the principles involved in the sharing are determined by the Finance Commission for the vertical division of tax revenue between the Centre and the states and the horizontal division among the states. The tax shares as a percentage of GSDP has gone down from 1.44 per cent during 1990-91 to 1.08 per cent in 2000-01. The inclusion of all central taxes in the devolution of resources to the states as per the Eleventh Finance Commission recommendations resulted in sharing of taxes like corporation tax, customs duty, service taxes, etc. with the states. Though the rise in central tax shares during 2000-01 over the previous year was Rs.1.72 billion, its share in GSDP remained the same as that of the previous year (Figure 2.12).

FIGURE 2.12

Tax Share of Maharashtra as a Percentage of GSDP

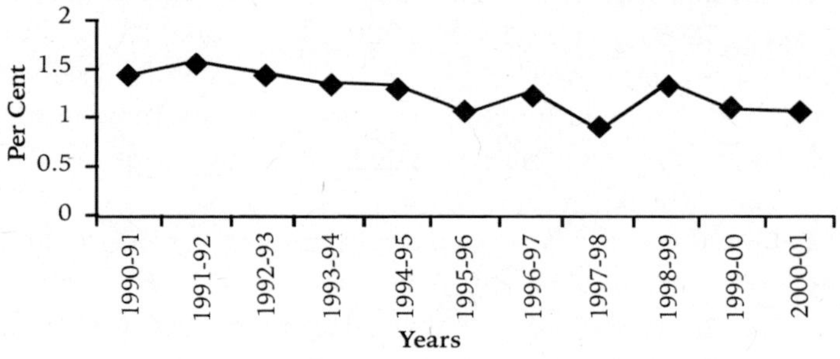

Source: (Basic Data): Finance Accounts.

The decline in quantum of devolution of share in central taxes, to a great extent, has been influenced by the deceleration in the growth of central taxes. The recessionary condition of the economy and low rate of industrial growth during later part of the nineties accentuated this problem. Continuance of the trend of decelerating growth in central taxes may actually defeat the goal set by the new devolution scheme involving all central taxes for sharing with the states.

A substantial part of Central devolution is received by the states from the Planning Commission in the form of Plan Grants for the state plans. This is distributed on the basis of Gadgil formula. The assistance given to the non-special category states (which is the case with Maharashtra) under the Gadgil formula is distributed on a 70 per cent loan and 30 per cent grant basis. Total grants to the state as a percentage of GSDP showed steep decline during this period. It went down from 1.16 per cent to 0.57 per cent of GSDP. Grants for State Plan Schemes, which were showing a higher trend as compared to the initial years, also declined after 1997-98 (Figure 2.13).

FIGURE 2.13

Total Grants (TG) and Grants for State Plan Schemes (GSP) as Percentage of GSDP

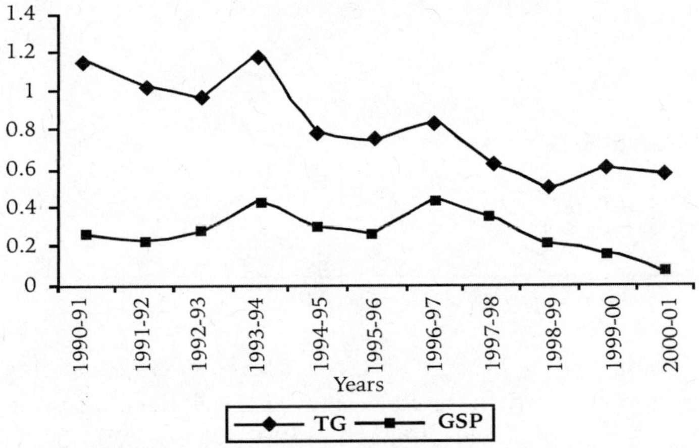

Source: (Basic Data): Finance Accounts.

Need for Revenue Mobilisation

Own tax revenue constitutes substantial part of the total revenue and so efforts towards revenue mobilisation have also to concentrate on the own tax revenues. Increase in tax buoyancy can come mainly from the sales taxes. Reform, therefore, should concentrate on sales tax under two broad categories of tax policy and tax administration.

As already stated, exemptions and concessions complicate tax administration and involve loss of revenue. Tax incentives should be looked upon as tax expenditure, as tax incentives are not only ineffective and it affects industrial investment in an adverse way. Since Maharashtra has traditionally been considered to have better infrastructure than most other states, the role of incentives in encouraging investment can at best be limited. So effort, while designing a tax system, should be on to have a tax system that is transparent, simple and promoting better tax compliance. Adoption of state level VAT with a wide base, multi-point taxation and a moderate rate would ensure that value added at all stages of production and trade are taxed, preventing artificial manipulation with the tax base.

Objective of good tax administration is to ensure that there is minimum leakage of taxes and compliance cost for the taxpayers is low. A good tax administration would promote tax compliance. It would frame a suitable audit strategy whereby high-risk categories of taxpayers are identified and taken up for detailed audit (possibly at the place of business). For this a good database would be required to be collated with supplementary information from the related sources. The tax department should maintain information about collection of taxes by commodity. Production figures can be obtained from other sources. These two sets of data should be used to infer about the level of compliance by a particular segment of dealers. A step in the direction would be to embark on a large-scale computerisation with an efficient and quick way of retrieving the data.

For all non-merit services, it would be imperative to increase the recovery rates. In fact in this respect it was seen that Maharashtra does not compare well even with some other states. Some of the best practices in India can be adopted by Maharashtra; e.g. Haryana has significantly higher recovery rate for transport and urban development, Goa for housing, etc.

SECTION II

Fiscal Deficit

The finances of Maharashtra have been under severe strain. Figure 2.14 captures the deteriorating trend of gross fiscal deficit (GFD) and revenue deficit of Maharashtra as a ratio of GSDP over the 10-year period, from 1990-91 to 2000-01. It can be seen that the GFD was 2.35 per cent in 1990-91, and increased only slightly to 2.79 per cent in 1996-97. But major deterioration in this came in 1997-98, and worsened

FIGURE 2.14

Gross Fiscal and Revenue Deficit of Maharashtra (Per Cent to GSDP)

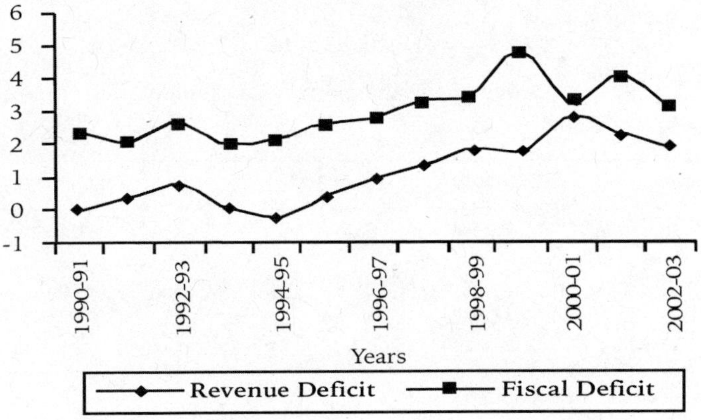

sharply from 1998-99 onwards, with a slight improvement in 2000-01. In 2001-02, 2002-03 and 2003-2004 RE, it was 4.1, 4.8 and 5.9 per cent, respectively.

Key financial indicators of Maharashtra over two five-year periods from 1990-91 to 2000-01 are given in Table 2.12. It can be seen that the ratio of primary deficit to GSDP increased nearly two and a half times during the five-year period 1995-2000 over the earlier period of 1990-1995. The interest burden of the state, calculated as a ratio of interest payment to revenue receipts, also increased from 11.50 per cent to 15.10 per cent i.e. a change by 31.3 per cent. The own-revenue resources declined to 60.6 per cent during 1995-2000 to finance the aggregate expenditures from an earlier position of 62.6 per cent during 1990-1995 i.e. deterioration by 3 per cent.

Primary deficit (fiscal deficit, net of interest payment) has further increased from 1.5 per cent of GSDP in 1995-96 to 3 per cent of GSDP in 2003-04.

TABLE 2.12

Key Fiscal Indicators of Maharashtra

Item	*1990-1995*	*1995-2000*
Primary Deficit/GSDP	0.90	1.83
Debt/GSDP	13.54	13.57
Interest Burden = Interest Payment/Revenue Receipts	11.50	15.10
Own Revenue Resources/ Aggregate Expenditure	62.60	60.60

Source: RBI, 2002.

In 1993-94, Maharashtra recorded revenue deficit and fiscal deficit of 0.1 per cent and 2.0 per cent of GSDP, respectively. In the year 2001-02, the same were recorded at 3.1 per cent and 4.1 per cent of GSDP, respectively. Table 2.13 gives the deficit figures from 2000-01 to 2003-04 RE.

TABLE 2.13

Deficits of Maharashtra Government

(Rs. Billion)

Item	*2000-01*	*2001-02*	*2002-03*	*2003-04 RE*
Revenue Deficit	78.34	81.88	93.71	90.37
Fiscal Deficit	85.76	105.92	148.81	184.60
Primary Deficit	33.51	41.62	75.95	97.58

Source: Economic Survey, 2003-04.

TABLE 2.14

Gross Fiscal Deficit

(Rs. Billion)

Item	*2000-01*	*2001-02*	*2002-03*	*2003-04 RE*
Revenue Deficit	78.34	81.88	93.71	90.37
Capital Expenditure Outside the Revenue Account	44.63	29.48	36.84	96.87
Net Loans and Advances Given by the State Government	-33.21	-2.39	12.35	7.53
Total Gross Fiscal Deficit	**89.76**	**108.98**	**142.9**	**194.77**
Total Gross Fiscal Deficit as Percentage of GSDP	**3.8**	**4.1**	**4.8**	**5.9**

Source: Economic Survey of Maharashtra, 2003-04.

The disaggregation of gross fiscal deficit consisting of revenue deficit, capital outlay and net lending given by the state government for 2001-02 to 2003-04 is given in Table 2.14. The gross fiscal deficit of the state has shown continuous increase over the years mainly due to high levels of revenue deficit. In fact, the share of revenue deficit in the gross fiscal deficit for the year 2002-03 was 65.6 per cent, and that for the year 2003-2004 (RE) was 46.4 per cent.

Revenue expenditure of Maharashtra grew at an average rate of 15 per cent between 1994-95 and 2001-2002 and the capital outlay grew at the average rate of 4 per cent during the same period. When seen with the increase in the government's deficit financing, this change in the composition of spending indicates that the state had borrowed primarily to finance current consumption, i.e., to pay for the growing salaries, pensions and the increasing interest payments. These items together accounted for close to 80 per cent of total revenues. This is also reflected in the ratio of revenue deficit to fiscal deficit, which reached 55 per cent in 2001-02. In the Budget for 2003-04, the development expenditure accounts for 41.6 per cent of the total expenditure at Rs. 624.62 billion, while the non-development expenditure constituted 58.4 per cent. If we look at the revenue and capital expenditures of Maharashtra during two periods, *viz.* 1993-1996 and 2000-2003, we find that while revenue expenditure increased from 10.68 per cent of GSDP to 14.10 per cent (an increase of 3.42 basis points), capital expenditure declined from 2.56 per cent of GSDP to 1.47 per cent (a decrease of 1.09 basis points). This puts across the budgetary deterioration of Maharashtra sharply if we compare the above to all state figures of revenue and capital expenditure during the same period. All state figures of revenue expenditure are 13.94 per cent in 1993-1996 to 16.67 per cent (an increase of 2.72 basis points)—a trend similar to Maharashtra but not as much; the difference is in capital expenditure, which was 2.66 per cent in 1993-1996 and 2.26 per cent in 2000-2003—a decrease of 0.40 basis points but not as sharp decline as in Maharashtra. The above comparison suggests that no doubt other states experienced similar expenditure shifts, but with a difference. Maharashtra was one of the top rankers in increasing revenue expenditure, only to be outranked by Orissa, Gujarat and Madhya Pradesh; the difference being that in all these three states there was an increase in capital expenditure rather than a decline—as in the case of Maharashtra.

Budgetary Deterioration

Composition of government spending in Maharashtra changed significantly between 1994-95 and 2001-02—with decline in capital and development outlays, non-wage O&M expenditure, reduction in certain social sector spending, but increase in salary, pension, interest payments and subsidy (Table 2.15).

TABLE 2.15

Changes in Composition of Expenditure

(As a Percentage of Total Expenditure)

Item	*1994-95*	*2001-02*
Salary and Pension and Interest Payments	51	60
Non-Wage O&M	15	13
Capital Expenditure	19	10
Subsidies	2	5
Others	13	12

Source: World Bank Report, 2002.

Increase in the committed liabilities—wages and salaries, interest payments and pensions, from 54.99 per cent of revenue receipts in 1990-91 to 82.70 per cent in 1999-00 led to the budgetary deterioration. This also reduced the share of revenues available for discretionary expenditure from 46.01 per cent in 1990-1991 to 17.30 per cent in 1999-00, which was alarming (Table 2.16).

TABLE 2.16

Incidence of Committed Liability on Revenue Receipts and Revenue Expenditure

Item	*1990-91*	*1994-95*	*1999-2000*
As a Percentage of Revenue Receipts			
Wages and Salaries	41.63	40.95	57.08
Interest Payments	10.12	11.66	19.33
Pensions	3.24	3.24	6.29
Total Share of Committed Expenditure	54.99	55.85	82.70
Share of Discretionary Expenditure	46.01	44.15	17.30
As a Percentage of Revenue Expenditure			
Wages and Salaries	41.37	41.73	48.83
Interest Payments	10.06	11.88	16.53
Pensions	3.73	3.55	5.50
Total Share of Committed Expenditure	55.16	56.96	70.86
Share of Discretionary Expenditure	44.84	43.04	29.14

Source: GoM Budget Documents.

Such limited resource availability both for Plan expenditure and non-wage operation and maintenance implied a thin distribution of resources across various projects and programmes which then were incapable of meeting the actual resource requirement for the upkeep of public services or completion of Plan projects.

Salary and Pension

Salary payments account for a major share of the committed expenditure. Maharashtra, like all other states, experienced a sharp increase in its salary and pension bill due to implementation of the Fifth Pay Commission's recommendations. While salary bill of GoM increased by 66 per cent in one year from Rs. 100.31 billion in 1998-99 to Rs. 166.35 billion in 1999-00, pension bill increased by 63 per cent from Rs. 12.49 billion to Rs. 20.34 billion in the same period. The pension bill continued to rise even in 2000-01, increasing by 51 per cent between 1999-00 and 2000-2001, before falling marginally in 2001-02 RE (World Bank: 2002, pp.10-11). The salary and pension bill fell modestly in 2000-01 to 24.4 per cent of the revenue receipts from 29.2 per cent in 1999-00, it was high in absolute terms for 2001-02 and 2002-03 at Rs. 72.35 billion and Rs. 74.63 billion, respectively.

If we calculate the above increases in terms of salary expenditure per employee to see the effect of Pay Commission recommendations, we find that during 1997-98 and 1998-99 average salary of an employee per annum was Rs. 58000 and Rs. 65000, respectively. This jumped to Rs. 100000 per annum in 1999-00. Though the same declined to Rs. 88000 in 2000-01 and Rs. 90000 in 2001-02; important to note here is the higher level of salary payment after implementation of Pay Commission recommendations.

Another reason for increase in salary and pension bill was increased recruitment in grants-in-aid (GIA) institutions. The revenue grants given to local bodies, educational institutions and other aided institutions, which was Rs. 34.73 billion in 1993-94 increased to Rs. 122.62 billion in 2002-03. Major parts of these grants were incurred on salaries and wages. Apart from the regular wage increases on the basis of the Central Government regulations, the growth in wage bill was also due to growth in employment. The number of employees in the state and local governments more or less remained the same over the last 6-7 years at between 0.6 and 0.7 million. While the average rate of growth in salaries of state and local government employees was 13 per cent during 1995-96 to 2000-01, the GIA salaries grew by 20 per cent during the period. During this period the employment in GIA institutions increased from 0.58 million to 0.68 million, an increase of 17 per cent. Besides the above, there were also separate SPVs (Special Purpose Vehicles) to manage large irrigation and road works with employment load and pay burden on the exchequer (World Bank, 2002).

Profile of annual growth rate of pension for Maharashtra is given in Figure 2.15, which shows decline from 1996-97 onwards. Pension also registered very rapid growth in the government budgets in nineties. Though the rate of growth of pension in Maharashtra was relatively lower than other major states in the country. During the period, 1991-92 to 1994-95, the rate of growth of pension was 14.74 per cent. This increased to 18.60 per cent during 1995-96 to 1998-99 (Table 2.17). Pension expenditure as a percentage of GSDP during 1993-96 was 0.36, this went up to 0.88 in 2000-03. The increase, though significant, was not as high as that for all-states average, where the average went up from 0.73 per cent during 1993-1996 to 1.56 per cent during 2000-2003.

If we see the pension payments as percentage of revenue receipts, we find that in 1999-00 there was sharp rise in pension payment, which continued rising up to 2001-02. Thereafter, it declined. Even if it is on decline, the expenditure in absolute terms was still very high. It was Rs. 27.81 billion in 2003-04. Given that the state has enormous financial burden, reforms of the existing pension scheme assumes importance. For the new employees, the state has introduced a new contributory pension scheme on the same line as the Central government.

TABLE 2.17

Growth Rate of Pension for Major States during the Two Periods 1991-1995 and 1995-1999

States	*1991-1995*	*1995-1999*
Andhra Pradesh	23.43	16.54
Bihar	24.58	21.94
Goa	16.16	47.29
Gujarat	15.92	35.15
Haryana	18.47	44.72
Karnataka	15.95	20.01
Kerala	18.00	19.87
Madhya Pradesh	23.10	32.10
Maharashtra	**14.74**	**18.60**
Orissa	22.32	30.86
Punjab	14.73	35.73
Rajasthan	17.68	31.23
Tamil Nadu	18.60	27.86
Uttar Pradesh	23.84	38.84
West Bengal	21.64	26.18
Total	**19.16**	**26.63**

Source: Report of the Eleventh Finance Commission, GoI.

FIGURE 2.15

Annual Growth Rate of Pension for Maharashtra during 1991-92 to 1998-99

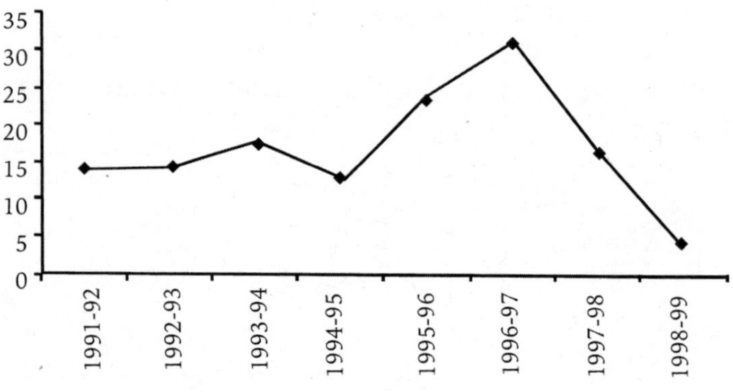

Source: Report of the Eleventh Finance Commission, GoI.

Procurement Schemes

Another source of increase in the committed liabilities was the functioning of cotton monopoly procurement schemes (CMPS) and the government support to the sugar cooperatives. Since 1994-95, CMPS incurred huge financial losses. In the year 1999-00, the amount of loss was Rs. 7.73 billion (World Bank,

2002, p. 58), which was to be financed through budgetary support. This increase in the loss was primarily due to an increase in the procurement price of cotton over the years. In the case of sugar cooperatives, mainly, the liabilities of the state government arose by way of default of guarantees given by the state on loans taken by these cooperatives from various financial institutions. The outstanding government guarantees to the sugar cooperatives was Rs. 33 billion. Unless these market interventions of the government in cotton and sugar are curbed, it would further add to the committed expenditures of the government.

Borrowings

The large stock of debt, much of which was borrowed during the period of high interest rates, had led to steady increase in GoM's interest payments. In 2001-02, interest payments amounted to Rs. 64.14 billion, nearly 21 per cent of revenue receipts. For subsequent years also the interest payments continue to be at 21 per cent. According to a recent report on Maharashtra's finances, the average effective rate of interest on state government borrowings is estimated at nearly 12 per cent per annum.

Given the state government's limited ability to undertake any significant debt restructuring exercise (like retiring high cost debt owed to the Central government by raising new debt from the market at a lower interest rate), and with many expensive off budget borrowings in its portfolio (more than Rs.10 billion was raised by one of the irrigation corporation through seven different bond offerings at an average interest rate of 17.5 per cent), the share of interest payments in total revenue expenditure is not likely to go down in coming years.

Many public sector undertakings (PSUs) in Maharashtra have also raised money in the domestic capital market with 'unconditional and irrevocable' guarantee from the GoM. These borrowings have been kept outside the purview of the budget, as they do not need the approval of the state legislature. The deficit of the GoM does not include the losses incurred by these state undertakings, including the losses of the cotton federations and the sugar cooperatives, which have grown over time.

The GoM did not engage in any off-budget borrowings (OBBs) prior to 1995-96, though it had been issuing guarantees on extra-budgetary borrowing since the 1980s. But now, OBBs have been growing at an average annual rate of 34 per cent between 1997-98 and 2001-02 RE, and they now account for nearly one-fifth of GoM's total liabilities.

Government Guarantees

The guarantees have grown at a breakneck pace of 44 per cent a year. These guaranteed borrowings have generally been used to finance commercial enterprises in cooperative and infrastructure sectors, cover up operating losses of PSUs, and finance their capital investment. Maharashtra had guarantees worth Rs. 549.04 billion outstanding on 31 March 2002. This is 12.77 per cent of GSDP. The structure of guarantee is shown in Table 2.18. The guarantees of various state corporations including statutory boards constitute more than 60 per cent of the total guarantee given by the state government. Though the share of guarantees given to them declined to 55.14 per cent in 1998-99, it started to increase from 1999-00 onwards.

Compared to 34 and 44 per cent growth rate of off-budget borrowings and guarantees, respectively, the corresponding average annual growth rate of budgetary borrowings and nominal GSDP are 19 and 10 per cent, respectively, indicating that the state's borrowing programme is clearly on an unsustainable path. Recognising the above problem, White Paper on the State's Finances noted that, "With the proportion of productive expenditure showing a declining trend, the capacity of the government to service the mounting debt without resorting to even larger borrowing is undermined. The situation has been further compounded in recent years with growing resort to off-budget borrowings through bonds floated by state sponsored corporations but with debt servicing (including interest and repayment of principal) being assumed by the state government" (GoM, 1999a).

Special Purpose Vehicles

Several states including Maharashtra have resorted to significant borrowing through the creation of new public corporations, generically called special purpose vehicles (SPVs). Reasons like falling revenues and an increasing wage bill of the GoM prompted creation of these SPVs. Primary objectives of SPVs was to carry out essential capital and infrastructure expenditure.

Some of these were newly created and some were the existing public bodies, like the Maharashtra State Road Development Corporation (MSRDC), the Maharashtra Jeevan Pradhikaran (MJP), the Maharashtra Water Conservation Corporation, and the Maharashtra Cooperative Development Corporation. Debt charges—interest and principal—of these SPV borrowing are paid directly from the state budget; therefore, these were part of the government's own borrowings. The state also extended guarantees liberally to these SPVs.

TABLE 2.18

Structure of Government Guarantees during 1996-97 to 2000-01

(in Per Cent)

Item	*1996-97*	*1997-98*	*1998-99*	*1999-00*	*2000-01*
Corporation including Statutory Boards	62.66	60.86	55.14	59.24	61.35
Government Companies	7.79	9.38	7.22	3.71	3.04
Banks	0.00	0.00	0.00	0.00	0.00
MCs/*Zilla Parishad*/ Other Local Bodies	4.04	3.75	3.35	4.23	3.56
Cooperative Banks	13.22	12.92	22.35	17.75	19.57
Cooperative Societies/ Sugar Factories	7.05	6.71	5.98	6.41	5.27
Other Cooperative Societies	5.20	6.34	5.92	4.90	3.99
Other Institutions	0.05	0.04	0.04	3.77	3.22
Total	**100**	**100**	**100**	**100**	**100**

Note: Others include government companies, MC and other local bodies and cooperative banks and societies.

Source (Basic Data): Finance Accounts.

In most cases, the financial returns on the investments fell far short of the interest and amortisation payments due on their borrowings. The current economic slowdown exacerbated the problem. So, there is a possibility that many of the guarantees given to these corporations are invoked in the coming years.

From the public expenditure management point of view, the borrowings by SPVs are not economical. Also the capacity of these SPVs to service debt is virtually nil. In fact, credit-rating agencies have recently downgraded the bonds issued by SPVs in the irrigation sector to categorise them for default of slipping up on interest payments. It is also reported that NABARD had alerted the Maharashtra Government about dues of Rs.7.50 billion lent to Land Development Banks (LDBs); 15 of these LDBs have been under liquidation on account of huge losses.

Subsidies

Reliable estimates of budget based and off-budget subsidies are not available for Maharashtra. However, information from several sources including various sectoral departments indicates that subsidies for public services are growing. According to GoM's own calculation, the subsidies that are administered through the state's budget have increased from Rs. 28. 63 billion in 1994-95 to Rs. 48.53 billion in 1998-99. A study by NIPFP finds that the total value of explicit and implicit subsidies taken together is around Rs. 188.27 billion or 7.5 per cent of the GSDP in 1998-99. The study also estimates the share of merit to non-merit subsidy as 50 per cent in social sectors and 33 per cent in economic sectors. The sectors that are major recipients of the subsidy include power, agriculture (cotton, sugar and onion), irrigation, grants-in-aid institutions (particularly education), transport, industry and food (milk). An estimate of power subsidies show that average retail tariff represents only 87 per cent of the average cost of generation, transmission and distribution. The agricultural customers pay only 26 per cent of the average cost of power supply. An estimate of power subsidy to farmers with pump sets puts the figure at Rs. 9,250 per beneficiary as the subsidy. Given that the average cost of power supply in 2000-01 was Rs. 3.4 per kWh and the recovery from the agricultural sector was Rs. 0.9 per kWh, the subsidy in 2000-01 was Rs. 7.20 billion.

SECTION III

Outstanding Liabilities

Composition of outstanding liabilities of Maharashtra over the past three years is given in the

BOX 2.1

Off-Budget Borrowings as a Means to Finance Investment

In Maharashtra, the government has authorised various PSUs in irrigation (Maharashtra Krishna Valley Development Corporation, Tapi Irrigation Development Corporation, Vidarbha Irrigation Development Corporation, Godavari Marathwada Irrigation Development Corporation, Konkan Irrigation Development Corporation), water supply (Maharashtra Jeevan Pradhikaran), roads (Maharashtra State Road Development Corporation) and power (Maharashtra State Electricity Board) to mobilise resources through bonds, which are guaranteed, and in many cases, also serviced by the government from the budget. The resources thus mobilised are partly used to finance capital outlays in the sectors.

Gross off-budget borrowings (bonds guaranteed and serviced by the state government) in Maharashtra have averaged Rs. 21 billion or 0.9 per cent of GSDP per annum over 1996-97 to 2001-02. Gross guarantees given for bonds (excluding bonds which are serviced by the government) have averaged Rs. 8 billion or 0.4 per cent of GSDP per annum over the same period.

Table 2.19. It may be seen that the share of internal debt of the Maharashtra Government has gone up from 12.88 per cent of the total debt at the end of March 2001 to 22.99 per cent at the end of next year. The same had further gone up to 29.17 per cent at the end of March 2003. On the other hand the corresponding share of loans and advances from the Central Government declined from 62.97 to 47.53 per cent during this period. The other two components of total debt though had gone up in absolute terms, but did not change substantially as a ratio of the total debt.

There are some variations in the figures reported in the *Economic Survey of the Maharashtra Government 2002-03* and the Budget for 2003-04. Figures reported in the budget document have been underlined in Table 2.19.

Perusal of the above figures suggest that the internal debt of the Maharashtra Government for the year 2001-02 actually declined from the revised estimates by Rs. 54.67 billion and the loans and advances from the Central Government increased by Rs. 46.71 billion, indicating more reliance on the Central loans and advances. The trend continued in the revised estimates for 2002-03 also. For the year 2003-2004, the Maharashtra Government had total debt of Rs. 801.49 billion in the budget (Table 2.20).

TABLE 2.19

Composition of Outstanding Liabilities at the End of March for Maharashtra

(Rs. Billion)

Items	*2001*	*2002*	*2003*
Internal Debt	64.82 (12.88)	140.54 (22.99) 85.87	203.65 (29.17) 181.45
Loans and Advances from the Central Government	316.89 (62.97)	323.93 (52.99) 370.64	331.75 (47.53) 375.59
Special Securities Issued to NSSF	56.39 (11.2)	75.45 (12.34) 70.74	84.77 (12.14) 75.65
Provident Funds, etc.	65.09 (12.93)	71.31 (11.67) 71.43	77.83 (11.15) 78.36
Total Debt	**503.19**	**611.23** **598.69**	**698.00** **711.07**
Percentage of GSDP	21.1	22.5 22.04	24.1 24.55

Note: Figures in parentheses represent ratio of the debt component to the total debt.

Source: Economic Survey of Maharashtra 2002-03 and the Budget for *2003-04.*

TABLE 2.20

Debt Position in 2003-04 (Budget Estimates)

(Rs. Billion)

Items	*Receipts*	*Repayment*	*Net*	*Closing Balance*
Internal Debt	207.21	136.12	71.09	252.55
Loans and Advances from the Central Govt.	16.87	13.12	3.75	379.35
Special Securities Issued to NSSF	22.04	13.79	8.25	83.90
Provident Funds, etc.	20.99	13.66	7.33	85.69
Total Debt	**267.11**	**176.70**	**90.41**	**801.49**

Source: Maharashtra Budget, 2003-04.

Interest Burden

The expenditure on interest payments, which was Rs. 1.1 billion in 1980-81 increased to Rs. 8.81 billion in 1990-91 and reached to Rs. 52.25 billion in 2000-01. It further increased to Rs. 71.30 billion in 2002-03. The expenditure on interest payments as percentage of revenue receipts was 5.4 in 1980-81. This increased to 10.1 in 1990-91 and reached 17.7 in 2000-01 and 20.2 in 2001-02. In 2002-03 it was 22.9 per cent (Table 2.21 and 2.22).

TABLE 2.21

Interest Payments as Percentage of Total Revenue Receipts in Maharashtra

Year	*Percentage of Revenue Receipts*
2000-01	17.7
2001-02	20.2
2002-03	22.9

Source: RBI's study of State Finances.

TABLE 2.22

Gross and Net Interest Payments of Maharashtra

(Rs. Billion)

Year	*1999-00*	*2000-01*	*2001-02*
Gross	48.83 (33.0)	55.84 (14.4)	64.14 (14.9)
Net	31.59 (56.5)	34.51 (9.20)	54.32 (57.4)

Note: Figures in parentheses represent percentage variation over the previous year.

Source: Economic Survey of Maharashtra, 2002-03.

Market Borrowings

Article 293 of the Constitution enjoins the states to obtain the Centre's approval for borrowing if they are indebted to the Centre. The reason for such stipulation is to ensure that the states do not borrow indiscriminately and a hard budget constraint is imposed. But as in the case of other states, and also in the case of Maharashtra, the gross market borrowings have gone up by 40 per cent over the last three years; the net market borrowing went up by 45.7 per cent during the same period (Table 2.23).

TABLE 2.23

Year-wise Market Borrowings of Maharashtra

(Rs. Billion)

Year	*Gross*	*Net*
1999-00	7.72	7.01
2000-01	8.09	7.70
2001-02	10.81	10.20

Source: *Annual Report of RBI*, 2001-02.

The maturity profile of these loans for March 2001 and March 2002 is given in Table 2.24.

TABLE 2.24

Maturity Profile of Maharashtra Government Loans at the End of March

(Rs. Billion)

Year	*0-5 Years*	*6-10 Years*	*Over 10 Years*	*Total*
2001	11.73	38.41	1.89	52.03
2002	15.80	48.51	-	64.32

Source: *Annual Report of RBI*, 2001-02.

In fact, the repayment of debt by the Maharashtra Government—internal loans, loans and advances from the Central Government, provident fund and other interest-bearing obligations is going to be in the manner given in Table 2.25.

As out of a debt of Rs. 698 billion at the end of March 2003, Rs. 331.76 billion was owed to the Central Government carrying an average interest rate of 11.5 per cent; retiring some of the loans was resorted to as the rate of interest then was not so high. During 2002-03, the Maharashtra Government retired Rs. 11.1 billion of the debt owed to Centre, Rs. 2.68 billion to the FIs and banks and Rs. 5.52 billion of the debt owed to investors in the off-budget instruments. Thus, a substantial part of the receipts went towards retiring old and expensive debts. This was done in spite of the fact that Maharashtra remained in the large open market for borrowing, which the Centre arranged through the RBI to retire old and high cost debts.

TABLE 2.25

Repayment of Total Debt by the Maharashtra Government at the End of March

(Rs. Billion)

Items	*2002 Actual*	*2003 Revised Estimates*	*2004 Budget Estimates*
Internal Debt	126.61	132.95	136.12
Loans and Advances from the Central Government	9.61	11.10	13.12
Reserve Funds	0.33	0.43	0.41
Deposit Bearing Interest	8.13	14.78	13.38
Provident Funds, etc.	11.78	12.89	13.67
Total Repayment	**156.47**	**172.15**	**176.71**

Source: *Budget of Maharashtra Government*, 2003-04.

Debt Relief Recommended by Tenth and Eleventh Finance Commissions

As an incentive for better fiscal management, the Tenth Finance Commission (TFC) designed a scheme linking debt relief to the fiscal performance of a state. The TFC measured improvement of fiscal performance by comparing the ratio of revenue receipts (including devolution and grants from the Centre) to total revenue expenditure in a given year with the average of corresponding ratios in the three immediately preceding years. Thus, each state was to be considered against its performance in the past. The TFC recommended that generalised debt relief could take the form of certain percentage of repayment falling due in each of the period of its recommendations being written off. The magnitude of relief with respect to two illustrative figures of percentage relief, namely, 5 per cent and 10 per cent indicated by the TFC can be seen from Table 2.26.

Under its terms of reference, the Eleventh Finance Commission (EFC) was required to make an assessment of the debt position of the states as on March 31, 1999 and suggest corrective measures as were deemed necessary, keeping in view, the long term sustainability for both the Centre and the states.

TABLE 2.26

Debt Relief (Incentive Scheme) to States on Repayment of Central Loans during 1995-2000

(Rs. Million)

States	*Repayments during 1995-00*	*Stipulated Relief under General Incentive Scheme at*	
		5%	*10%*
Maharashtra	**11247**	**562.35**	**1124.7**
Andhra Pradesh	8588.8	429.44	858.88
Tamil Nadu	6234.2	311.71	623.42
Kerala	4631.3	231.57	463.13
Karnataka	5676.8	283.84	567.68
Gujarat	10401.4	520.07	1040.14

Source: Study on Management of Public Expenditure by the State Governments in India, Planning Commission, 2001.

It was for the first time that the phrase long-term sustainability of debt was included in the terms of reference to a Finance Commission. The EFC looked at the relative position of the states in terms of interest payments to revenue receipts, which included the states' share of Central taxes and grants. Most of the states had ratio of interest payments to revenue receipts ranging from 25 per cent to below 10 per cent. The EFC felt that the scheme of general debt relief linked to the fiscal performance needed to be strengthened. Reasons for that were: a) states should get higher quantum of relief by improving their fiscal performance and b) higher relief would act as incentive for encouraging better performance for determining the quantum of relief. Based on the above, the EFC enhanced the factor of two to five and recommended that the extent of relief should be 25 per cent as against 10 per cent given by TFC.

Sustainability of Public Debt

The build-up of fiscal deficits results in the formation of public debt. Servicing or amortising public debt requires increased taxation and revenue generation or giving up productive expenditure. High and growing debt/GDP ratio is anticipated to make the public debt eventually unsustainable in the sense that they tend to increase interest rates, thereby increasing the debt service component of the budget. This, in turn reduces the flexibility of fiscal policy.

Though, there is no unique level of public debt, which can be considered unsustainable/sustainable, the judgment on sustainability of debt is to be based on an assessment of the rate of borrowing by the government, the rate of growth of GDP and the rates of interest on government borrowing. The familiar debt-dynamics equation shown below reveals that debt is sustainable as long as real rates of growth of the economy is more than the real rates of interest with a declining primary revenue deficit. When the economy's rate of GDP growth exceeds its interest rate, government could continue borrowing to repay interest, since the relatively high economic growth would reduce the relative size of the debt stock. Thus, the fiscal policy can be considered sustainable so long as the rate of growth of GDP remains above the interest rate. The growth-interest relationship depicted in the debt dynamic equation may not hold good in the long run. Consider the situation where an economy has a rate of GDP growth equal to or less than its interest rate. If the primary deficit persists over a long run, rising interest payments will increase the need for new debt more rapidly than the relative size of the decline in the outstanding stock of debt in relation to GDP. If this situation continues, the debt-GDP ratio would eventually explode and the fiscal situation would become unsustainable. If the debt level is too high, there is an urgent need to generate primary revenue surplus to arrest the growth of debt-GDP ratio (Shome, 2002).

The debt dynamics equation discussed above is presented below where the interlinkage between government borrowing, rate of growth and interest rate is examined.

$$X_t = X_{t-1} + X_{t-1} * r - P_{st}$$

$$X_t = (1+r) * X_{t-1} - P_{st}$$

$$\frac{X_t}{Y_t} = \frac{(1+r)^* X_{t-1}}{Y_t} - \frac{P_{st}}{Y_t}$$

$$\frac{X_t}{Y_t} = \frac{(1+r)^* X_{t-1}}{(1+g)^* Y_{t-1}} - \frac{P_{st}}{Y_t}$$

In a steady state condition

$$\frac{(1+r)}{(1+g)} = 1$$

$$r - g = \alpha = 0$$

$$X_t = \alpha_t X_{t-1} - P_{st}$$

Where α is the real interest rate (r) less the growth of output (g) (adjustment factor); P_{st} is the non-interest surplus net of seigniorage (seigniorage is the revenue from money creation by the Central Bank of any country); and X_t is the stock of debt.

It is to be noted that in India, the state government does not have access to monetisation of deficit and, thus, there is no provision of seigniorage. Thus, P_{st} represents the non-interest surplus. In order to find out the movement of the adjustment factor we plot the real rates of growth and real rates of interest. It is evident from the Figure 2.16 that the real rate of growth of the economy was more than real rates of interest in 1996-97. However, the sustainability condition got violated from 1997-98 onwards and that trend is continued till 2000-01. Violation of debt sustainability condition poses serious threat to the long run fiscal sustainability of the government of Maharashtra, unless corrective fiscal restructuring programme is undertaken.

We can also look at the sustainability criteria in terms of the ability to freeze the debt/GDP ratio. More stringent criteria could be to reduce the debt to zero at a particular future point in time. This would, however, need a highly restrictive fiscal stance, which may not be feasible.

In the literature, the condition that real rate of interest less than or equal to the real rate of economic growth is considered necessary for sustainability, but whether it is also sufficient is a debatable question as it is felt that it does not ensure that the initial stock of debt would be equal to the present discounted value of primary surpluses in the future.

For public debt to be amortised in n years it is necessary that the present discounted value of primary surpluses until period n be equalised to today's debt. The longer the horizon for the government to stabilise or repay the debt, the smaller is the primary surplus requirement. But the time period n cannot be indefinite (Figure 2.16).

FIGURE 2.16

Debt Sustainability Condition: Movement of Real Rate of Growth and Real Rate of Interest

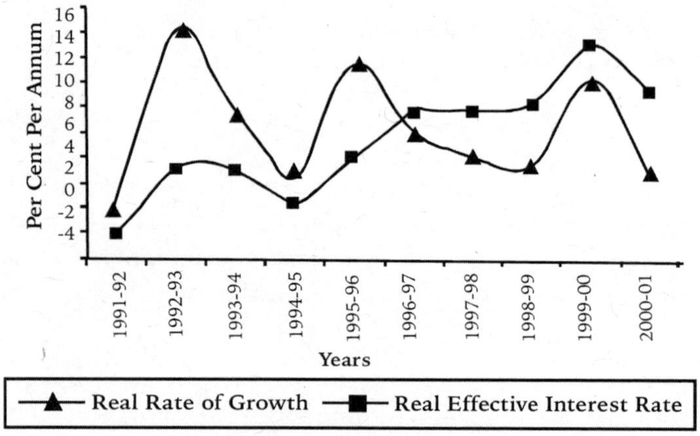

Source: GoM documents.

The Eleventh Finance Commission (EFC) observed that in order to ensure sustainability of debt over a medium term, the proportion of interest payments to revenue receipts of states including devolution should be about 18 per cent. The EFC, therefore, recommended that the states should keep this as their medium-term objective. Currently, as per the RBI report the proportion of interest payments to revenue receipts is more than 18 per cent in the combined position of all states and individually in many states. Since the public debt to GDP ratio of the states and the Centre combined stands at 63 per cent, the issue of its sustainability becomes relevant. The rationale of debt to GDP ratio can be construed to indicate that, were a country or state to retire its public debt in one step, how much of its GDP would it have to sacrifice. Since that would necessitate extraction of that portion of GDP so required, it should ideally exclude GDP required for subsistence.

The sustainability of public debt is usually discussed in terms of size of the primary deficit, fiscal deficit net of interest payment. Three criteria are tested for the sustainability of Maharashtra's public debt:

a) Debt should be zero at specified future period n.

b) Debt to GDP ratio at a future period n should be reduced to a specified fraction of today's ratio.

c) Debt to GDP ratio for the future is fixed at today's ratio.

The average interest rate of Maharashtra's public debt during 2002-03 was 10.15 per cent (total interest payment as per the RE of 2002-03 being Rs.72.22 billion on total debt of Rs. 711.07 billion). The nominal growth rate of Maharashtra's economy at current prices on the basis of figures available up to 2001-02 was 8.79 per cent, averaged over a period of six years from 1996-1997 to 2001-02. The situation worsens for the year 2003-04, if we assume the same growth rate for the economy, and compare that with the estimated interest rate of 10.36 per cent for the year 2003-04. As the nominal growth rate is lower than the nominal interest rate, it may not be possible to accommodate a primary deficit within a sustainable debt. In fact, a primary surplus is essential for a sustainable debt.

A simulation, based on the formula given below, can be attempted reflecting prevailing macroeconomic indicators (Shome, 1997). Nominal growth rate of the state economy 'g' can be assumed at 9 per cent. Average nominal rate of interest on public debt of the state (defined as interest payment of the state by the public debt) '*i*' can be assumed at 10 per cent.

The tests as stated above could be put in formula for testing as:

a) Debt should be zero at period n at specified interest rates (solvency).

$$PB = \frac{D_t * (1+i)^n}{\sum_{j=1}^{n} (1+i)^{n-j}}$$

PB = primary balance

D_t = public debt

i = interest rate

On the basis of an interest rate of 10 per cent for a time horizon of 15 years, a primary balance of 3.5 per cent of the GSDP (at the latest available estimates for the year 2001-02) would be needed for the present debt size of the state. For the time horizon of 10 years, however, the size of primary surplus would have to increase to 4.3 per cent.

In case the interest rate goes down to 9 per cent, the required size of primary balance for 15 years' time period would be 3.25 per cent of the GSDP at its estimates of 2001-02 and the same for 10 years period would be 4.09 per cent of the GSDP at 2001-02 estimates.

b) Debt/GSDP at period n is a given fraction α of current period (t) debt/GSDP (stabilising or reducing the debt to income ratio)

$$\frac{PB}{Y_t} = \frac{D_t}{Y_t} * \frac{[(1+i)^n - (1+g)^n * \alpha]}{\sum_{j=1}^{n} (1+i)^{n-j}}$$

Y = GSDP

g = rate of growth of nominal GSDP (Gross State Domestic Product)

In this case, the public debt to GSDP ratio is targeted to be reduced over a specified period of time. Let that the ratio is targeted to be reduced to 40 per cent, i.e. α is 0.40. In this case for a time horizon of 15 years, the state would need 2.24 per cent of the GSDP at interest rate of 10 per cent. At interest rate of 9 per cent and α of 0.60, the primary balance required for time period of 15 years would be 1.3 per cent of the GSDP. Thus, we see that the sustainability criterion is sensitive towards interest rates.

c) Debt/GSDP in future is fixed at today's (t) debt/GSDP (freeze change in debt to income ratio).

$$\frac{PB}{Y_t} \leq \geq \frac{\beta * (i-g)}{(1+g)}$$

Where β is the share of debt in GSDP (D/Y) at time (t-1).

To evaluate if the debt as on March 2004 (on the basis of budget 2003-04) is greater or less than the debt as on March 2003, we may take the effective interest rate at 10.15 per cent and the GSDP growth rate as averaged over the last 6 years at 8.79 per cent, we find that the debt to GSDP ratio on March 2004 would be less than the debt to GSDP ratio of March 2003. Thus, the debts are going down. In this calculation the GSDP has been taken at the 2001-02 value as reported in the budget 2003-04.

SECTION IV

Finances of Local Bodies

73rd and 74th Constitutional Amendment related to some fundamental changes in the functioning of local self-governments *panchayat raj* and urban local bodies. It also sought to empower the local self-governments through taxation powers and financial transfers. Constitution of State Finance Commissions to periodically review the financial positions and to make recommendations for resource devolution was mandated. As mandated by the Constitutional Amendment, Eleventh Finance Commission recommended measures to augment the resources of *panchayats* and municipalities. Certain criteria have been made which would form the basis of distribution of grants to the states to meet the requirements of the local bodies.

In Maharashtra, there are 27,832 villages *panchayats,* 33 *zilla parishads,* 224 municipal councils, 19 municipal corporations and 7 cantonment boards. The total income of all the local bodies together during 2001-02 was Rs. 177.82 billion and expenditure was Rs. 157.62 billion. Income during 2002-03 went up by 9.96 per cent to 195.54 billion. Correspondingly, expenditure also went up by 9.21 per cent to 172.14 billion in 2002-03. Table 2.27 gives local body-wise details of such income and expenditure. It can be seen that except for the municipal councils, the other local bodies have shown healthy increase in revenue and commensurate growth in expenditure.

Revenue Mobilisation by the PRIs

Receipts of the PRIs can be classified into four broad categories:

- Tax and fee receipts
- Non-tax receipts
- Borrowings
- Grants-in-aid and assigned revenues from the Central/state governments.

Amongst the above sources 'Borrowings' is almost non-existent by all three layers of the PRIs. Tax/fee receipts of the PRIs are major sources of revenue among the own revenue sources of the PRIs. In fact, in future, all the layers of PRIs are expected to rely on these sources. Taxes assigned to each tier of the PRIs can be classified into following four categories:

- Taxes imposed, assessed and collected by the PRIs (e.g. tax on land and buildings by the GPs).
- Fees imposed, assessed and collected by the PRIs (e.g. special water rate imposed by the GPs).
- Taxes imposed by the PRIs but assessed and collected by the state government (e.g. cess on land revenue apportioned to the ZPs and the PSs).
- Taxes imposed, assessed and recovered by the state government (e.g. stamp duty charges, which are partially apportioned to the ZPs and GPs).

TABLE 2.27

Income and Expenditure of Local Bodies in 2001-02 and 2002-03

(Rs. Billion)

Type of Local Body	*Number*	*Income*		*Expenditure*	
		2001-02	*2002-03*	*2001-02*	*2002-03*
Village *Panchayat*	27832	7.33 (29.9)	7.75 (5.7)	5.29 (32.58)	5.44 (2.83)
Zilla Parishad	33	66.39 (7.6)	66.19 (-0.3)	60.56 (6.94)	60.28 (-0.46)
Municipal Council	224	15.17 (-8.3)	15.60 (2.8)	13.28 (-9.35)	12.79 (-3.83)
Municipal Corporation	19	87.96 (21.9)	104.56 (18.87)	77.64 (17.37)	92.34 (18.93)
Cantonment Board	7	0.98 (13.9)	1.34 (36.73)	0.84 (13.51)	1.22 (45.23)
Total		**177.82 (13.3)**	**195.54 (9.96)**	**157.62 (10.85)**	**172.15 (9.21)**

Note: Figures in the parentheses indicate the percentage rise or fall over the last year.

Source: Economic Surveys of Maharashtra, 2001-02, 2002-03, and 2003-04.

Income of the village *panchayats* for the years 2001-2002 and 2002-03 are given in Table 2.28. The single major item of own receipts is the receipts by way of taxes/fees. This accounts for about 50 per cent of the total own receipts of the GPs. These tax/fee receipts have been growing at the rate of 17 per cent per annum over the last two years. Major tax/fee items in this group are tax on land and building, water rate, lighting tax and market fees. But there is considerable scope to enhance the receipts of all these taxes/fees by adopting measures such as better valuation of tax bases, improving the recovery performance, enhancement of rates and imposition of at least a minimal set of taxes and fees by every GP. Income of the *zilla parishads* for the years 2001-02 and 2002-03 are given in Table 2.29.

TABLE 2.28

Income of the Village *Panchayats* 2001-02 and 2002-03

(Rs. Billion)

Item	*2001-02*		*2002-03*	
	Actual	*% of Total Receipt*	*Actual*	*% of Total Receipt*
Opening Balance	1.727	-	1.931	-
Taxes on Houses	1.443	25.8	1.729	29.7
Other Taxes	11.104	19.7	1.129	19.4
Total Taxes	**2.547**	**45.5**	**2.856**	**49.1**
Government Grants	1.469	26.2	1.503	25.8
Contributions and Donations	1.089	19.4	0.911	15.6
Other Receipts	0.497	8.9	0.546	9.4
Total Receipts	**5.603**	**100.0**	**5.819**	**100.0**
Total Income	**7.331**	-	**7.750**	-

Source: Economic Survey of Maharashtra, 2002-03, 2003-04

TABLE 2.29

Income of the *Zilla Parishads*

(Rs. Billion)

Items	*2001-02*		*2002-03*	
	Actual	*% of Total Receipt*	*Revised Estimates*	*% of Total Receipt*
Opening Balance	3.934	-	4.571	-
Self-raised Resources	0.924	1.3	1.53	2.5
Purposive Government Grants	24.621	35.3	16.129	26.2
Establishment Grants	17.112	24.5	19.597	31.8
Plan	3.882	5.6	4.408	7.1
Other	8.104	11.6	7.371	12.0
For Agency Schemes	4.024	5.8	3.415	5.5
Total Revenue Receipts	58.667	84.1	52.449	85.1
Capital Receipts	11.090	15.9	9.173	14.9
Total Receipts	**69.757**	**100.0**	**61.623**	**100.0**
Total Income	**73.691**	-	**66.193**	-

Source: Economic Surveys of Maharashtra, 2002-03, 2003-04

It can be observed that as regards tax efforts by the PRIs, lowest strata of the PRI is better off than the two upper tiers. It has been further seen that the rates of taxation are low. Therefore, it would be imperative that measures like overall improvement in tax efforts, proper valuation of tax base, increasing the rates of taxation etc. are resorted to. In fact it has been seen that majority of GPs are imposing tax on land and buildings on a flat rate basis. This is not in accordance with the Act. This is primarily due to lack of knowledge on the part of members as well as the *gram sevaks*. Some of the ways and means to enhance receipts could be as follows:

- Impart training and orientation to the GP members and officials.
- Improvement in tax recovery status, particularly in rich GPs.
- Systematising the revaluation of tax base.
- Introduction of slab rates instead of flat rate basis.
- Complete restructuring of the prevailing structure of tax rates as prescribed by the Act.

Studies have suggested that if the measures suggested for the improvement of tax efforts are implemented, the tax receipts can go up by almost two-folds. It can also be seen that the share of own receipts of the ZPs and PSs in their total receipts is almost negligible, generally within 2 per cent to 3 per cent. Even its growth trend is moderate at around 11 per cent. Major contributing factor to these receipts is additional cess on land revenue. A significant growth trend has been observed for this source. Even measures like enhancement of the rates and so on will significantly help to increase the level of receipts from this source. The amount of self-raised resources for *zilla parishads* during 2000-01 was Rs. 1.42 billion, which is less by 30 per cent from Rs. 2.03 billion during 1999-2000. This is a matter of concern. In fact, the revenue of ZPs for the year 2000-01 was less by 8 per cent over the previous year 1999-00 and the same has grown only by 1 per cent in 2001-02.

Grants-in-Aid

Various grants to the (ZPs) are Purposive Grant, Establishment Grant, Plan Scheme Grants, Grant for agency schemes and Grant for assigned project work. In the total receipts of the ZPs, government grants account for major share. In 1996-97, the share of government grants in total receipts was 90 per cent. The same in subsequent years has gone down (Table 2.30).

TABLE 2.30

Share of Government Grants in Total Receipts of *Zilla Parishads*

(As Percentage)

Year	*Share*
1996-97	90
1997-98	83
1998-99	83
1999-00	86
2000-01	84
2001-02	77
2002-03	77

Source: Economic Surveys of Maharashtra.

Composition and Trend of the Local Expenditure

As far as the upper two layers of the PRIs are concerned, the total expenditure (revenue as well as capital) incurred by these two bodies are of three different categories—expenditure incurred out of its own resources, expenditure incurred from the various government grants received by them and expenditure incurred on the works assigned to them.

Of the three categories, the expenditures incurred on the assigned works are in a way pre-determined and hence, are not dependent on resource generation capacity and efforts of the PRIs. Corresponding funds are transferred for the work. Work on grants also have the same nature, except that for expenditure out of incentive grants the PRIs can choose their priorities. For the expenses out of the own resources of the PRIs, the choice and priority is set by the PRI itself.

An analysis of the expenditure pattern suggests that 80 per cent of the expenditure is in the nature of revenue and the balance, capital. But such distinctions are not always very sharp.

In the case of *gram panchayats*, major expenditures are on public works (roads, buildings), health and sanitation (including water supply) and general administration (Table 2.31). Last few years have shown a clear trend towards growth in the expenditure by the PRIs as compared to their receipts. These expenditures are more in the nature of revenue. In fact capital expenditure has shown a consistent decline for ZPs and PSs. This is a cause of concern (Table 2.32).

TABLE 2.31

Expenditure of the Village *Panchayats*

(Rs. Billion)

Items	*2000-01*	*2001-02*	*2002-03*
Administration	0.678	1.027	1.027
Health and Sanitation	1.073	1.461	1.482
Public Works	1.343	1.778	1.852
Public Lighting	0.235	0.324	0.298
Education	0.060	0.087	0.142
Welfare of People	0.318	0.395	0.455
Other Expenditure	0.287	0.223	0.188
Total Expenditure	**3.993**	**5.294**	**5.444**

Source: Economic Surveys of Maharashtra.

TABLE 2.32

Expenditure of the *Zilla Parishads*

(Rs. Billion)

Items	*2000-01 Actual*	*2001-02 Actual*	*2002-03 RE*
General Administration	4.657	4.699	3.831
Agriculture	0.673	0.695	0.615
Animal Husbandry	0.618	0.666	0.619
Forests	0.072	0.050	0.045
Irrigation	1.290	1.428	1.331
Public Works	4.116	3.416	3.213
Community Development	1.146	1.159	1.375
Education	26.300	31.407	23.539
Medical and Health Services	3.720	3.870	3.582
Public Health Engineering	2.048	1.720	1.547
Social Welfare	1.023	1.940	2.601
Other Expenditure	7.703	7.355	9.215
Total Revenue Expenditure	53.370	58.410	51.513
Capital Expenditure	7.4750	10.347	8.772
Total Expenditure	**60.850**	**68.757**	**60.285**

Source: Economic Surveys of Maharashtra, 2002-03.

Urban Local Bodies

There is much heterogeneity among the urban local bodies (ULBs) in Maharashtra. Unlike other states, where all the ULBs are governed by a uniform Act, ULBs in Maharashtra are governed by four Acts. The official categorisation of ULBs is as under:

Municipal corporations have population above 300000 while A class municipal councils, B class municipal councils and C class municipal councils have population ranging between 100000–300000, 40001–100000 and 25001–40000, respectively.

The number of municipal corporations in the state was 19 till 2001-02; 224 municipal councils and 7 cantonment boards. Of the 224 municipal councils, 21 were in A class (population of more than one hundred thousand) and 62 in B class (population of less than one hundred thousand but more than 40000) and the balance 141 in C class (population of less than 40000).

Income of Municipal Corporations

Revenues of ULBs can be broadly classified as revenue from own sources and those from external sources, such as grants and loans from the state. Own sources of revenue can be further categorised under tax revenues and non-tax revenues.

Following salient points emerge from Table 2.33:

a) Grants from the state government as a ratio of total income have hovered around 5 per cent between 1995-96 and 1999-00.

b) Share of loans in total income was 4.75 per cent in 1995-96. This has steadily risen to 11.73 per cent in 1999-00.

c) Share of octroi in the own income has been the highest among all income items. But it has registered a decline from 50.98 per cent in 1995-1996 to 47.72 per cent in 1999-00.

d) Share of property tax has gone up in the own income during the period, from 17.91 per cent in 1995-96 to 21.15 per cent in 1999-00.

The percentage of own income in the total income has shown a declining trend, which is disturbing. Growth rates of the income items is given in the Table 2.34. From this table, we can see that:

a) The loans and grants from state government have been inconsistent.

b) Income from own sources is declining steadily.

c) Water rates, property taxes have grown above the inflation, but since significant contribution may have come from expanding supply, it may not be possible to estimate whether recovery proportions improved.

TABLE 2.33

Share of 'Income Items' to all 'Income' of all 15 Municipal Corporations

(Per Cent of Total)

Items	*1995-96*	*1996-97*	*1997-98*	*1998-99*	*1999-00*
Grants from State Govt./Total Income	5.09	5.21	4.76	4.80	4.92
Loans/Total Income	4.75	5.91	6.99	9.83	11.73
Octroi/Own income	50.98	49.37	47.79	46.96	47.72
Property Tax/ Own Income	17.91	19.17	20.81	21.29	21.15
Water charges/ Own Income	10.86	13.20	14.55	13.67	13.43
Conservancy and Sanitation/Own Income	0.59	0.65	0.66	0.62	0.67
Licence fees and Entertainment/ Own Income	0.77	0.65	0.63	0.62	0.74
Building Rents/ Own Income	0.59	0.49	0.51	0.51	0.49
Own Income/ Total Income	**90.16**	**88.87**	**88.25**	**85.37**	**83.35**

Source: India Infrastructure Report, 2003.

TABLE 2.34

Growth Rate of 'Income Items' to 'Income' of all 15 Municipal Corporations

(Per Cent Per Annum)

Items	*1996-97*	*1997-98*	*1998-99*	*1999-00*
Grants from the State Government	20.83	3.48	18.45	17.48
Loans	46.61	33.89	65.50	37.01
Octroi	12.51	8.93	11.74	14.00
Property Tax	24.35	22.19	16.34	11.41
Water Charges	41.19	24.04	6.87	10.17
Conservancy and Sanitation	26.88	15.32	5.78	22.22
Street Lights	-	-	-	-
Licence Fees				
and Entertainment	-1.62	9.81	10.72	34.59
Building Rents	-3.13	17.48	13.38	8.48
Other Income	4.60	2.78	23.45	8.50
Total Income from Own Sources	**16.18**	**12.54**	**13.71**	**12.18**
Grand Total Income from all Sources	**17.86**	**13.33**	**17.56**	**14.89**

Source: India Infrastructure Report, 2003.

Further analysis reveals that smaller MCs rely for their revenue generation on octroi. The water charges do not show a healthy trend towards recovery. The smaller MCs need to take steps for widening the source base, and also for improving the recoveries.

Taxation and Levy Powers

Article 243X of the Constitution, inserted after the 74th Constitutional Amendment, envisages that the states would devolve additional taxation powers to the ULBs so as to make them financially competent for discharging the added functional responsibilities, mandated under the Article 243W. But in Maharashtra, no such devolution of taxation powers has taken place. Instead, taxation powers of small ULBs on octroi were withdrawn in March 1999. The taxation powers of the ULBs are limited to its traditional sphere and have not gone beyond various existing provisions.

Municipal Corporations in Maharashtra levy property tax as a percentage of 'annual rateable value' of the property, and ceilings for such percentages are laid down in different Acts of the state. These are summarised in Table 2.35.

TABLE 2.35

Rates of Property Tax (as Percentage of Value) in Municipal Corporations of Maharashtra

Components of Property Tax	*BMC Act*	*NMC Act*	*BPMC Act*
General Tax	26	12-13	Max. 12
Fire Brigade Tax	4	1	Max. 12
Water Tax	65	10-15	Autonomy to ULB
Water Benefit Tax	12.5	-	Autonomy to ULB
Sewerage Tax	39	12	Autonomy to ULB
Sewerage Benefit Tax	7.5	-	Autonomy to ULB
Education Tax	12	2-12	Up to 5
Street Tax	15	-	Max 10

It can be seen that BMC has no autonomy regarding the components and rate for each component of the tax, while Nagpur has limited autonomy. All other MCs have autonomy regarding the rate of tax in case of components related to water supply and sewerage only. However, there is no freedom to any MC regarding inclusion of any new component or changing the tax base to some other, say, area.

The external sources of revenues for the ULBs are grants from the state. There are about 30 types of grants. All these grants are purposive in nature and not untied. Many of these grants (octroi, profession tax, pilgrim, road, etc.) are also compensatory in nature. These grants are given subsequent to withdrawal of respective taxation powers of the ULBs, indicating centralising tendencies of the state. The distributive principles are not uniform. Generally, smaller classes of ULBs get grants higher than the ratio of their collections or expenditure.

Expenditure of Municipal Corporations

The EFC defined core services as being inclusive of water, streetlights, roads and sanitation. Expenditure of all corporations on these core services as ratio of total expenditure was 35.87 per cent in 1995-96. A very gradual increasing trend is noticed with the exception of 0.1 percentage point reduction in 1998-99. In 1999-00 the ratio stood at 39.18 per cent.

But the EFC defined core services do not have economic connotation. A more appropriate concept will be of local public goods. The local public goods share the characteristic of non-excludability with public goods. In this definition, water, as it can be metered and charged, is excluded but fire brigade is included. In 1995-96, the proportion of expenditure on these services was 24.14 per cent and in 1999–00, the ratio stood at 25.7 per cent. But if the local public goods were to be extended to include education, sanitation, fire brigade, water, roads and street lighting, the ratio of expenditure on these items was 46.02 per cent in 1995-96, and increased to 48.65 per cent in 1999-00. Table 2.36 gives a comparative picture of the growth rates of certain expenditure heads.

TABLE 2.36

Growth Rate of Certain Expenditure Heads in the Municipal Corporations of Maharashtra

(Per Cent Per Annum)

Items	*1996-97*	*1997-98*	*1998-99*	*1999-00*
General Administration, Salaries, Pension, etc.	14.05	19.04	11.92	14.69
Education, Libraries	15.53	12.64	2.40	24.52
Sanitation, Solid Waste Management	46.04	12.01	8.19	18.20
Fire Brigade	3.50	27.89	-3.97	38.50
Water Supply	28.34	20.46	22.60	10.88
Epidemics and Public Health	15.33	18.66	11.15	16.28
Roads	23.86	14.66	22.51	8.51
Street Lighting	27.27	2.66	19.37	8.59
Total Expenditure	**23.40**	**14.28**	**17.46**	**11.37**

Source: India Infrastructure Report, 2003

Municipal Bonds

Decentralisation initiative, following the 74th Constitutional Amendment, has increased the responsibilities of the municipal bodies, but commensurate measures to improve the finances are yet to be put in place. One such measure for mobilisation of resources, though nascent in India so far, is the municipal bonds. Two municipal bodies in Maharashtra, Nashik and Nagpur, have issued municipal bonds. The instruments issued by these municipal bodies were through private placements. Commercial banks, regional rural banks, provident funds, public enterprises, cooperative banks, and domestic financial institutions mainly subscribed to the issues. The revenue sources escrowed were octroi, property tax and water charges.

The Nashik Municipal Corporation issued Rs. one billion secured, redeemable, non-convertible bonds with AA-(SO) rating from CRISIL in 1999. The bonds had a coupon of 14.75 per cent per annum payable semi-annually. Nagpur Municipal Corporation received LAA-(SO) rating from the Indian Credit Rating Agency (ICRA). It went in for private placement of secured, redeemable, non-convertible bonds, worth Rs. 500 million, with coupon rate of 13 per cent per annum payable semi-annually.

Normally municipal bonds (so far only 9 of them in the country) are traded in the primary market, but municipal bonds of Nashik Municipal Corporation were traded in the secondary market also. As on March 2001, about 8.81 per cent of the total bonds were traded on the secondary market among 60 investors.

Though resource mobilisation by municipal bodies is needed for development of urban infrastructure, it is predicated on improvement in revenue collection. But as the property tax, one of the major tax instruments is calculated on annual rental value (ARV), which is the rent that would be paid by a hypothetical tenant to a hypothetical landlord for property use, efforts are made by the tax payers to keep the rental values artificially low, taking cover of the Rent Control Act (RCA). Thus, though the true market value of the property can be increasing, the yield from the property tax does not rise. Besides, the assessment of the properties which are not covered by the RCA are highly subjective, leading to contests in the courts and so, long delays in collection of taxes.

Revenue-generating capacity of municipal bodies is low. Average of the grants received from the state out of its revenue receipts during 1995-96 to 1998-99 was

1.27 per cent. Besides the growth rates for octroi, in overall, income indicates diminishing trend; this is more prominent for the smaller MCs, as they are more dependent on octroi. In the above background, significant steps need to be taken in case the ULBs see an opportunity in placing the municipal bonds for developing urban infrastructure. But factors such as lack of active secondary market for municipal bonds, lack of investor appetite for long-term paper, stiff competition from other financial securities, difficulties in rating municipal bodies and high cost of issuing bonds are some constraints in developing a municipal bond market.

In addition to the above constraints, the municipal bodies also need to remove an important constraint of replacing an outdated budgeting and accounting system. The municipal bodies in India use cash accounting system. This system of accounting does not capture information about the asset-liability profile of the municipality and the efficiency of a municipal body. These are critical considerations for investors and credit rating agencies so as to take an informed decision about the risk-return profile of the municipal body. The municipal bodies also lack a capital budgeting system.

SECTION V

Fiscal Situation of Maharashtra: Towards MTFF

Maharashtra's fiscal situation as analysed indicates that if the GoM does not undertake any significant fiscal reforms, and the underlying revenue and expenditure items exhibit the same trends as in the past, the current fiscal situation may become unsustainable. The state is already experiencing liquidity problems of unprecedented magnitude and is not able to cope with high level of debt and deficits. It is not that the GoM has been slow in understanding the nature of the problem or in recognising the corrective course of action. In fact it can be recalled that the GoM had brought out a White Paper on the state's finances in October 1999, which was presented and discussed in the State Legislature. The paper noted, "...Maharashtra's finances have been showing widening imbalances, with rising revenue and fiscal deficits. This has led to mounting debt and consequently galloping interest burdens, thus feeding a vicious circle of even larger revenue and fiscal deficits because expenditures have shown no sign of containment." Despite the above realisation, coalition politics and the coalition government in Maharashtra in recent years relied on populist agenda. This style of polity gave an unfocussed approach to key elements of institutional and policy reform such as restructuring of power sector, reduction in subsidy, reform in the grant-in-aid (GIA) institutions, restructuring of the PSUs, controlling guarantees and cooperative institutions, reduction in off-budget borrowings, reform in the civil service, etc.

Realising the above constraints, a vision document of fiscal reform programme was prepared some time ago. This document known as MTFF intended to provide a coherent quantitative statement of the government's three to five-year fiscal strategy. It defined a path towards fiscal sustainability and set targets for broad fiscal indicators in the medium term. It was expected to provide stability and predictability to fiscal policy setting, and greater transparency and accountability in the budget making process. It was a vehicle through which a particular fiscal trajectory could be charted to enunciate a medium-term development priorities, the role the government could take in shaping the economy and improving the institutional capacity.

The MTFF recommended: (i) improving efficiency in the revenue collection mechanism and processes; (ii) containing expenditure to generate budgetary surpluses; (iii) restructuring the role of the government by reducing involvement in a variety of activities; and (iv) building institutions with stakeholder participation to make the reform process durable.

Given the above scenario, a projection of the future fiscal profile of the Government of Maharashtra has been drawn. In order to arrive at the alternative fiscal projections we construct two fiscal scenarios, *viz.*, base scenario and reform scenario based on various assumptions on the key fiscal parameters.

Base Scenario

The base scenario is arrived by assigning alternative parameter values to the key fiscal aggregates. Objective of the base scenario is to arrive at a medium-term fiscal projection based on the assumptions that satisfy the past fiscal profile. In other words, the objective is to understand if the current fiscal situation is allowed to continue, what will be the likely fiscal situation in the medium term. In this scenario, key fiscal variables are allowed to grow on the basis of their trend rates of growth during the 1990s. The key assumptions of the base scenario are given in Box 2.2.

Based on these assumptions, we arrive at a fiscal profile of the state for the period between 2003-04 and 2009-10. It is to be noted that the base year considered for the projection is 2002-03, revised estimates. The study consciously avoided 2003-04, budget estimates for the base year of projection because there is always a problem of fiscal marksmanship (fiscal marksmanship is a tool to analyse the deviation of estimated budgetary aggregates from the actuals). It is generally noted that 'revised budgetary estimates' are closer to the actual. Thus, a reliable and meaningful projection can be undertaken if the 2002-03 revised estimates are considered as base year instead of 2003-04 budget estimates as the base year of projection. In both base and reform scenario, the state GSDP is assumed to grow at the rate of 15.28 per cent. This is the nominal rate of growth of GSDP observed for the period between 1990-91 and 1999-00.

BOX 2.2

Assumptions of Base Scenario

Receipts Side

Own tax revenues: Each tax at the state level are allowed to grow at buoyancy-based growth rates respective to each taxes on the basis of their historical buoyancies.

Non-tax revenues: Total non-tax revenue is decomposed into two components, *viz.*, interest earnings and the rest. The future stream of interest earning on loans and advances is estimated by estimating the profile of loans and advances and assigning a rate of interest estimated for the year 1999-00, which is 12.98 per cent.

Share in central taxes and grants: The central tax devolution and grants are assumed to grow at the rate of their historical trend growth rates of 9.2 per cent and 5.82 per cent respectively for the period between 1990-91 and 2001-02.

Expenditure Side

Interest payment is allowed to grow at its effective rates of interest assigning to the stock of previous year's stock of outstanding debt.

Pension, administrative service and other general services are allowed to grow at their respective trend growth rates.

Social services and economic services are allowed to grow at their respective trend growth rates.

Capital outlay and loans and advances are also assumed to grow at their respective trend rates of growth.

Based on the above assumptions, we arrive at the movement of key fiscal parameters which will enable us to give assess whether the current fiscal policy stance, if allowed to continue, will generate a sustainable debt and deficit regime. The key fiscal parameters projected are given in Table 2.37. It is evident from this Table that without any fiscal correction, the revenue deficit will increase from 2.06 per cent of GSDP in 2002-03 to 4.44 per cent in 2009-10.

The fiscal deficit will also increase from 3.64 per cent to 5.80 per cent during the same period and consequently the outstanding debt from 19.23 per cent to 30.11 per cent of GSDP. In other words, the result also indicates that if the fiscal situation is allowed to persist without any fiscal correction, there will be a sharp rise in the fiscal and revenue deficit and outstanding debt which in turn will increase the interest payment of the government from 2.05 per cent of GSDP in 2002-03 to 3.57 per cent of GSDP in 2009-10. Movements of all the key fiscal indicators projected reflect that current fiscal situation is unsustainable.

Reform Scenario

As the current fiscal policy stance is unsustainable reflected in the base scenario, a fiscal correction is a must to achieve a sustainable fiscal policy regime. The reform scenario built in this chapter accommodates these corrections and arrives at a sustainable fiscal regime. The fiscal corrections incorporated in the reform scenario are presented in Box 2.3. The fiscal correction as suggested in this Box, once incorporated

TABLE 2.37

Emerging Fiscal Profile (Base Scenario)

(Per Cent to GSD)

Items	*2001-02*	*2002-03 RE*	*2003-04*	*2004-05*	*2005-06*	*2006-07*	*2007-08*	*2008-09*	*2009-10*
Revenue Deficit	2.55	2.06	2.62	2.67	2.99	3.33	3.68	4.05	4.44
Fiscal Deficit	3.38	3.64	4.17	4.19	4.48	4.79	5.11	5.45	5.80
Primary Deficit	1.34	1.64	1.72	1.79	1.87	1.96	2.04	2.14	2.23
Interest Payment	2.05	1.99	2.45	2.39	2.61	2.84	3.07	3.32	3.57
Outstanding Debt	18.66	19.23	18.80	20.49	22.26	24.10	26.02	28.02	30.11

Source: Finance and Accounts and *Budget Document*, GoM, 2003-04.

in the base scenario, the fiscal situation improves significantly. In the reform scenario, revenue deficit as a percentage of GSDP declines from 1.77 per cent in 2003-04 and gets eliminated by the end of 2009-10 (Table 2.38).

BOX 2.3

Assumptions of Reform Scenario

Receipt Side

Own tax revenues: Own tax revenues are assumed to show improved aggregate buoyancy of 1.268 by assigning prescriptive to sales tax and other taxes.

Non-tax revenues: The targeted increase in the non-tax revenues is assumed to be from 1.28 per cent of GSDP to 2 per cent of GSDP between 2002-03 and 2009-10.

Share in central taxes and grants: In the case of reform scenario also, the Central tax devolution and grants are assumed to grow at the rate of their historical trend growth rates of 9.2 per cent and 5.82 per cent respectively for the period between 1990-91 and 2001-02.

Expenditure Side

A lower interest rate structure is assumed with an effective rate of interest of 9 per cent per annum. This is possible as the interest rates are falling and the states have been given to swap the high cost debts for low cost debts.

The reduction in interest payment and a decline in the expenditure under 'other general services' make a compression of expenditure under general services.

Release of resources, thus reallocated to two basic sectors, *viz.*, health and family welfare, and water supply, sanitation, housing and urban development.

Already declining share of 'economic services' in total revenue expenditure is allowed to continue.

Capital expenditure is assumed to increase from 1.72 per cent of GSDP in 2002-03 to 2.52 per cent.

Revenue deficit is expected to become zero and fiscal deficit is targeted to reduce to 2.25 per cent of GSDP by the end of the projection period.

The fiscal deficit also declines from 3.44 per cent of GSDP to 2.25 per cent during the same period. The burden of interest payment unlike base scenario increases marginally from 1.50 per cent of GSDP in 2003-04 to 1.56 per cent in 2009-10. Movement of outstanding debt behaves in a cyclical fashion with an initial increase up to 2006-07 and then shows a trend of decline. A comparison of the key fiscal profile, *viz.*, fiscal deficit, revenue deficit, primary deficit and outstanding debt in the base and reform scenarios is given in the Figures 2.17, 2.18, 2.19 and 2.20.

FIGURE 2.17

Revenue Deficit—Base Scenario and Reform Scenario

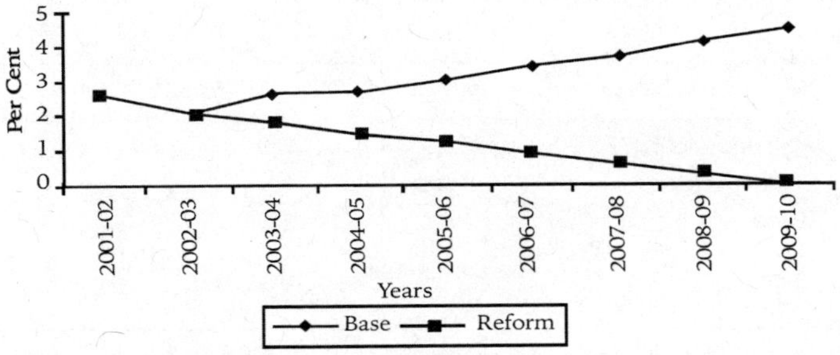

FIGURE 2.18

Fiscal Deficit—Base Scenario and Reform Scenario

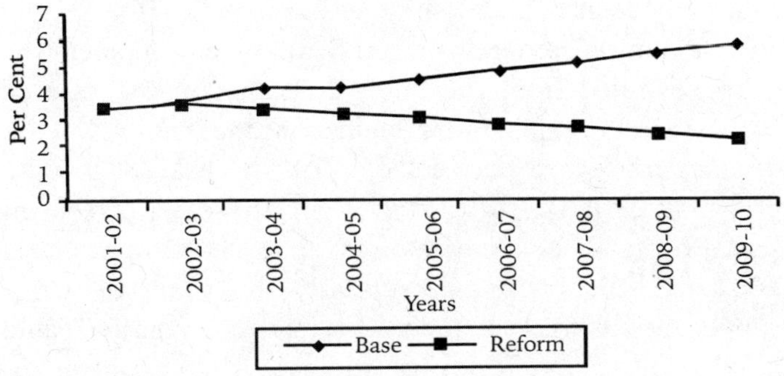

FIGURE 2.19

Primary Deficit—Base Scenario and Reform Scenario

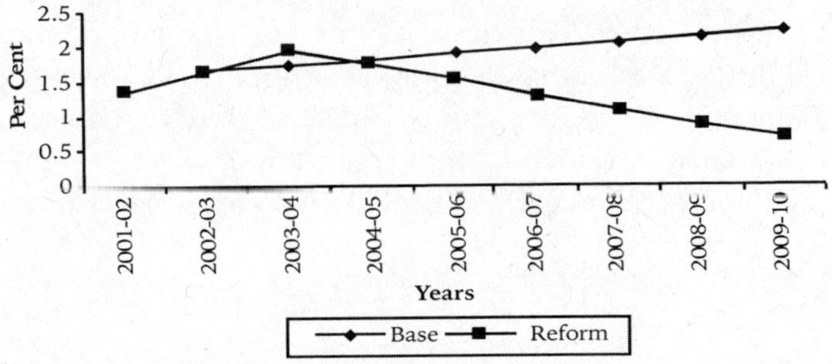

FIGURE 2.20

Outstanding Debt—Base Scenario and Reform Scenario

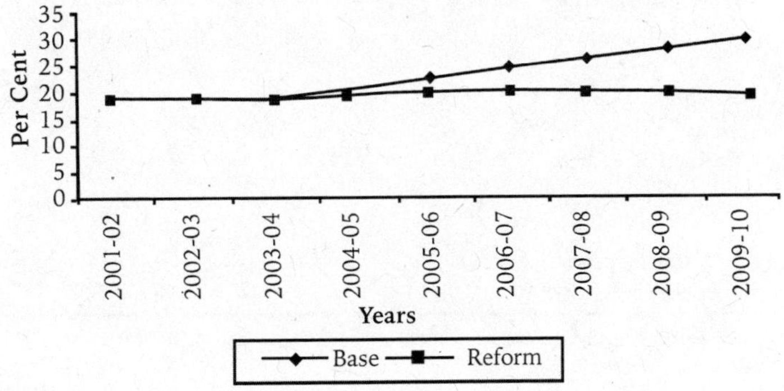

TABLE 2.38

Emerging Fiscal Profile (Reform Scenario)

(Per Cent to GSDP)

Item	*2001-02*	*2002-03 RE*	*2003-04*	*2004-05*	*2005-06*	*2006-07*	*2007-08*	*2008-09*	*2009-10*
Revenue Deficit	2.55	2.06	1.77	1.47	1.18	0.88	0.59	0.29	0.00
Fiscal Deficit	3.38	3.64	3.44	3.24	3.04	2.84	2.65	2.45	2.25
Primary Deficit	1.34	1.64	1.94	1.77	1.52	1.28	1.07	0.87	0.69
Interest Payment	2.05	1.99	1.50	1.47	1.53	1.56	1.58	1.57	1.56
Outstanding Debt	18.66	19.23	18.80	19.55	20.00	20.19	20.16	19.94	19.55

Source: Finance and Accounts and *Budget Documents*, GoM, 2003-04

The reform scenario, apart from targeting debt and deficit also ensures a restructuring of government expenditure away from general services to social services especially health and family welfare and water supply and sanitation and housing and urban development. It is to be noted from the Table 2.39 that in the case of base scenario, expenditure on health and family welfare declines from 0.56 per cent of GSDP in 2001-02 to 0.42 per cent in 2009-10. However, in the case of reform scenario, its share increases from 0.56 per cent in 2001-2002 to 1 per cent and similarly the share of water supply also increased under the reform scenario (Table 2.39). The above findings indicate that finances of Maharashtra broadly follow the nature of a fiscal crisis. Reasons for the problems are steady decline in the revenue mobilisation and rapid increase in the expenditure in the late 1990s. Reason for the increase in expenditure was upsurge in various committed liabilities. Decline in receipts, apart from poor own tax and non-tax revenue, was also due to steady decline in the Central transfers. Implementation of recent pay revisions accentuated the problems of fiscal imbalance.

On the basis of the above analysis, this study recommends three major areas of reforms:

- enhanced resource mobilisation effort,
- expenditure restructuring, and
- interest cost minimising debt management policy.

Enhanced Resource Mobilisation Effort

Resource mobilisation effort has to concentrate on both own tax and non-tax revenues. The own tax revenue, which had aggregate buoyancy (with respect to both agricultural and non-agricultural GSDP) of less than one during the 1990s, requires sufficient enhancement. The reform scenario constructed in this study puts an aggregate buoyancy of 1.268 for own tax revenues. The increase in buoyancy is expected to come mainly from the sales taxes (with a prescriptive buoyancy of 1.33), electricity duty and motor vehicle taxes. As already stated in Section I of this Chapter, tax reforms should be in the areas of tax policy and tax administration. Introduction of state-level VAT from

TABLE 2.39

Increase in the Share of Selected Services: A Comparison

(As a Per Cent of GSDP)

Items	*2001-02*	*2002-03 RE*	*2003-04*	*2004-05*	*2005-06*	*2006-07*	*2007-08*	*2008-09*	*2009-10*
Base Scenario									
Health and Family Welfare	0.56	0.50	0.49	0.48	0.46	0.45	0.44	0.43	0.42
Water Supply, Sanitation, Housing	0.31	0.58	0.58	0.58	0.58	0.58	0.57	0.57	0.57
Reform Scenario									
Health and Family Welfare	0.56	0.50	0.57	0.64	0.71	0.79	0.86	0.93	1.00
Water Supply, Sanitation, Housing	0.31	0.58	0.64	0.70	0.76	0.82	0.88	0.94	1.00

Source: Finance and Accounts and *Budget Documents*, GoM, 2003-04.

April 2005 would reduce the problems of double taxation of commodities and multiplicity of taxes, resulting in cascading tax burden. The present system of exemptions and concessions complicates tax administration and involves loss of revenue. VAT would have wider base with multi-point taxation and a moderate rate. Since tax in the VAT system would be collected at all stages of production and trade, artificial manipulation with the tax base would be prevented, ensuring better compliance. But this new system should also accompany a better tax administration. The present system should be revamped to have an improved computerisation, with facility to prepare a large database and its retrieval system, so that audit can be done on the basis of third party information system. Since the state contributes 15 per cent of services output of the country, it should try and bring the service sector within the tax net in coordination with the Centre. Chelliah *et al.,* (2001) had suggested that state can also tax on its own a few services, namely, entertainments, carriage of goods and passengers by roads and inland waterways, and some identified luxury services.

With regard to the non-tax revenues, the recoveries for all non-merit services assume critical importance. Corresponding user charges for these non-merit services provided by the government should be linked to the cost. For merit goods, such as primary education and basic health care facilities, this norm may not be applied. There is also sufficient scope for increasing the earnings in the form of interest, dividends and profits. The government must bring out a proper disinvestments policy for withdrawing from the sectors, which can be considered to be non-core areas. Proceeds of such disinvestments can be used to finance the high cost debts by introducing large-scale debt swap.

Expenditure Restructuring and Debt Management Policy

On the expenditure side, any reform is more difficult due to the steady increase in the share of committed liabilities like interest payment, pension and salaries and wages. But any reform would have to involve expenditure reduction also. One way of reducing the salary payments is to go for reduction of the number of state government employees. It can be suggested that the reduction in numbers can be 2 per cent per annum. This is so because average natural attrition rate is 2.8 per cent per annum. But such reduction should not be such as to affect critical service delivery. The state will have to device means of identifying slack and develop alternative means of ensuring service delivery. But this reduction should not be by way of transferring employees to GIAs.

Pension has also been a worrisome expenditure. Arresting the growth of pension would not be an easy task. New initiatives in this regard should be taken which can be in terms of introduction of 'Funded Pension Schemes' for the new employees. Though the government has already taken an initiative on this, a long-term pension policy can also be considered taking into account the hidden pension liability and take appropriate policy steps for its reduction.

Rapid reduction in the debt-servicing obligation both by reducing the fiscal deficit and also by a reduction in the cost of debt servicing is another area of focus. In the prevailing low interest rate regime, an active debt management policy should try to alter the high cost debt structure to low cost through large scale retiring of expensive debt introducing debt swapping. As mentioned, in the reform scenario, the fiscal deficit as a percentage of GSDP is expected to reduce from 3.64 per cent in 2002-03 (RE) to 2.25 per cent in 2009-2010. This would largely depend on the reduction in the effective rate of interest to 9 per cent during this period. It should also be noted that the effective rates of interest in Maharashtra government's outstanding debt is much higher than that of all state effective rates of interest. In other words, Maharashtra has relatively high cost debt structure compared to other states.

In order to achieve the targeted reduction of fiscal deficit during the medium term suggested by the reform scenario, expenditure compression is essential along with higher revenue mobilisation. But such expenditure reduction should not hamper the productive capital expenditure of the economy and that is only possible if the resources can be released through reduction in revenue deficit.

The debt management policy should examine the reasons for the high effective rates of interest of the Maharashtra Government and undertake steps to alter the debt structure towards low cost debt so that effective rates of interest comes down. As mentioned, this task is relatively less difficult in the context of current low interest rate regime if a debt swapping can be undertaken.

One of the major reasons for the very high effective rates of interest in Maharashtra is the transfer of debt servicing liabilities of very high cost government debt in the form of government guarantee given to various state level public sector units. It was seen that state public sector enterprises had an increasing interface with the budget of the government. It may be reiterated that these organisations are to provide functions on commercial lines, and so should provide adequate return on capital invested. But actual performances of these public sector enterprises have been far from being satisfactory. These public sector enterprises have been a drain on the government finances. Government has to undertake an assessment of their role. Key areas for such assessment or appraisal would be:

a) goods or services pricing rationalisation to ensure financial viability of the enterprises;

b) explicit and transparent subsides from the budget to the enterprises in case goods or service provisioning are at reduced rates;

c) assessment for closing down or liquidation of sick undertakings with adequate measures to enhance skills and capacities of employees; and

d) procedures to ensure that decisions for additional government investment are based on sound economic criteria.

On this issue of contingent liabilities management, as we have seen large number of guarantees being given by the Maharashtra Government, it is suggested that rationale for extending guarantees should be carefully examined and underlying risks documented. Some states have introduced legislation to curb the growth of guarantees. Such limits will also be an appropriate step for Maharashtra.

In the above context we can also recall that the Eleventh Finance Commission had set up an incentive fund, called Fiscal Reform Facility. Under this Facility the states were to achieve a minimum improvement of 5 per cent in the revenue deficit as a proportion of its revenue receipts each year till 2004-05 measured with reference to the base year 1999-00. Maharashtra's performance in this respect can be stated to be improving now, though there was deterioration in its performance when the Facility started. But it still has a long way to go. In a nutshell we can suggest the following to be the medium-term framework of its reforms programme:

- Adoption of VAT.
- Computerisation of the tax department, setting up a database for collation and quick retrieval of tax data.
- Improving tax administration and introducing tax audit on the basis of third party information.
- Increasing the recovery rates for non-merit services provided by the state government.
- Full computerisation of treasuries for better expenditure management and debt management.
- Better cash management and eliminating access to overdrafts from RBI.
- Mandatory financial viability analysis of every project—ongoing and new.
- Formulating expenditure ceilings for each agency.
- Identifying high risk programmes including contingent liabilities.
- Identifying programmes and projects that can be considered for scaling down or closing down.
- Streamlining pensions and considering reduction in employees numbers without compromising on the service delivery which are critical to the functions of the state.

Maharashtra has been a key state with high infrastructure and human development indices. It has potential for higher growth rate, provided urgent measures are taken to correct the fiscal imbalance. This would need a medium—term framework, strict compliance and discipline towards this framework, economies in expenditure through rationalisation measures, and improved delivery of services through decentralised decision making. These measures would put in place a growth oriented fiscal policy that would help it to achieve a sustainable fiscal regime in the medium term.

Chapter 3

Agricultural Growth

Introduction

Maharashtra, as compared to the other states of India, is one of the top economic performers with respect to per capita income. While the all-India per capita income was Rs. 10,254 (2000-01) at 1993-94 prices, the corresponding figure for Maharashtra was Rs. 15,172, i.e., about 1.5 times that of all–India. In 1999-00, Punjab had the highest per capita income, which was slightly higher (2 per cent) than that of Maharashtra.

The relatively high per capita income in the state, however, conceals the enormous urban-rural contrast and the regional disparities in per capita income. This gets reflected from the fact that in 2000-01, the per capita district domestic product for Mumbai was Rs. 31,779 (1993-94 prices) i.e. exactly double the state average. Only six districts, three in the Konkan region (Mumbai, Thane and Raigad), in addition to Pune, Kolhapur and Nagpur, have per capita income above the state average. The remaining districts have per capita income below the state average. Thus, about 82 per cent of the districts in the state have per capita income not only below the state average but also below the national average and it is in these districts, that agriculture is the main economic activity. Agriculture, thus, emerges as a key sector in the state, especially with respect to workforce.

While the same is true for the country, there do exist differences in the performance of Maharashtra's agricultural sector in comparison to that of India. Therefore, in this chapter, an attempt has been made to study the progress of the agricultural sector in Maharashtra, the constraints that jeopardise its growth and the strategies to accelerate its growth. Rapid growth in the agricultural sector, undoubtedly assumes importance, as growth in this sector will in turn, stimulate growth in other sectors.

Status of Agricultural Sector in Maharashtra

In this section, we have observed the status of the agricultural sector in the state and compared it with all India status.

Sectoral Contribution to SDP

The shares of the different sectors in SDP/NDP are undergoing major changes over the years (Table 3.1) and the contribution of the primary sector (agriculture and allied services) continued to decline over the decades at the all-India level as well as in Maharashtra. Taking into consideration the three decades (Table 3.1), the contribution of this sector was highest for all-India in 1980-81, but declined to 26 per cent in 2000-01. In Maharashtra, the contribution of the primary sector to SDP was much lower and declined to 14 per cent in 2000-01, while that of the tertiary sector rapidly increased to 52 per cent. At the all-India level also, the tertiary sector played the major role in terms of contribution to NDP.

TABLE 3.1

Sector-wise Share of Income in SDP/NDP in Per Cent

Sector	*Maharashtra*			*India*		
	1980-81	*1990-91*	*2000-01*	*1980-81*	*1990-91*	*2000-01*
Primary	28.0	21.4	14.2	41.2	35.0	26.0
Secondary	35.0	36.6	33.5	22.9	25.0	26.0
Tertiary	36.8	42.0	52.3	35.6	40.0	48.0

Source: Computed from *Economic Survey of Maharashtra* (Various issues).

Share of Agriculture in Workforce

While agriculture's contribution to income rapidly declined, the workforce continued to perpetuate in this sector, indicating limited employment opportunities in other sectors (Table 3.2).

TABLE 3.2

Share of Workforce in Agriculture

(Per Cent)

Year	Maharashtra			India		
	Culti-vators	Agri. Lab.	Total	Culti-vators	Agri. Lab.	Total
1981	35.0	26.6	61.6	41.0	25.0	66.0
1991	32.8	26.8	59.6	38.0	26.0	64.0
2001	28.5	26.8	55.3	32.0	27.0	59.0

Source: Census of India.

A comparison of the state with the national figures show that at the all-India level, 59 per cent of workforce (2000-01) is employed in agriculture, while the corresponding figure for Maharashtra is 55 per cent. Although, the share of workers in agriculture is lower in Maharashtra as compared to India, a district-wise analysis presents a different picture. First of all, if we exclude workforce only in Mumbai, which is the commercial capital of India, from total workforce in the state, the share of workers in the agricultural sector increases by 7 to 8 per cent for the years the data is presented. Further, in 2000-01, almost 20 out of 34 districts had more than 70 per cent of their workforce in the agricultural sector while 29 districts had more than 60 per cent workforce in agriculture. These percentages are more than those of the national average. This indicates that Maharashtra's economy is predominantly agrarian and barring a few districts, (Mumbai, Thane, Nagpur and Pune), a major portion of Maharashtra's workforce is still dependent on agriculture as its primary source of livelihood.

Further, regarding composition of workforce, it can be observed that both at the state as well as national level, the share of cultivators in the total workforce is declining, while that of agricultural labourers is more or less the same. Bhalla (2000), using the National Sample Survey data for 1993-94, observed that among different groups of rural workers, the incidence of poverty (headcount ratio) is highest among agricultural labourers (57 per cent).

Growth in SDP/NDP by Sectors

Since agriculture is the mainstay of Maharashtra's economy, it is necessary to observe how this sector is growing and how it compares with other sectors in terms of growth rates. It can be observed from Table 3.3 that for both periods as well as entire period the growth rate of SDP of Maharashtra grew faster than the all-India NDP average.

TABLE 3.3

Sector-wise Growth Rates in SDP/NDP (Constant Prices)

(Per Cent Per Annum)

Sector	1980-81 to 1989-90		1990-91 to 2000-01		1980-81 to 2000-01	
	Maha.	All-India	Maha.	All-India	Maha.	All-India
Agriculture	2.23	3.25*	3.33*	2.96*	3.98*	3.27*
Allied	1.93	0.97*	0.73*	3.44*	2.05	2.60*
Primary	2.19	3.00*	3.08*	3.03*	3.77*	3.18*
Secondary	6.20*	6.40*	6.01*	6.19*	6.72*	6.25*
Tertiary	6.60*	6.70*	8.50*	8.03*	8.43*	7.15*
SDP/NDP	5.33*	5.03*	6.67*	6.04*	6.80*	5.60*

Note: * Significant at one per cent; Maha—Maharashtra.

Source: Computed from data in *Economic Survey.*

An analysis of the sector-wise comparison, however, indicated that Maharashtra's performance was not always better than that of the national level. During 1980-81 to 1989-90, the growth rate in the primary sector in Maharashtra was only 2.19 per cent per annum and it was not statistically significant while all-India registered a statistically significant growth rate of 3 per cent per annum. Perhaps, this relatively lower growth rate could be partly explained by the state being affected by a severe drought in 1986-87. The growth rate during this period showed a better performance of 2.7 per cent per annum, and is also statistically significant if we exclude the drought year.

Agriculture in Maharashtra is heavily dependent on monsoons as barely 15 per cent of the gross-cropped area is irrigated. This is much below and even less than half the national average where 38.7 per cent of gross-cropped area is irrigated.

The secondary and tertiary sector for the state and also at the national level showed better performance compared to primary sector. Thus, the macroeconomic performance of the state as well as for the country as a whole, in different periods showed that growth rates were lowest in the primary sector. However, as noted earlier, a major portion of the workforce is still dependent upon this sector for their subsistence.

Land Reforms in Maharashtra

The theme of land reforms assumed importance in the post-independence period. Under the Indian Constitution, land reform is a state subject and all states began implementing their own land reform laws. The state of Maharashtra followed suit and the abolition of intermediary tenures began, soon after independence, with the abolition of *khoti* tenure in coastal districts, *malguzari* and *izardar* tenures in the Vidarbha districts, *jagirdari* tenure in the Marathwada districts; and came to an end with the abolition of the Revenue *patel watans* in western Maharashtra and *patwari watans* in the former Hyderabad, in 1965. The abolition of these tenures resulted in the intermediaries becoming revenue-paying occupants of only such lands as were under their personal cultivation while on the remaining land the tenants secured occupancy rights.

The Tenancy Acts amended in mid-fifties, required that in western Maharashtra and Vidarbha regions all recorded tenancy arrangements must be terminated. Landlords were permitted to retain land under certain circumstances and tenants were also free to voluntarily surrender land to their landlords. Finally, with effect from 1st April 1957, the 'tillers day', the tenants in possession of the leased land were declared as owners of land, subject to payment of price. In Marathwada, the law did not require the termination of all existing tenancies. Tenants were made owners of only a part of the land and the remaining was to continue under their tenancy as long as they did not surrender it. The latest information (*Economic Survey of Maharashtra*, 2001-02) reveals that right of ownership was conferred on about 1.4 million tenants with respect to 1.7 million hectares of land till March 2001.

The Tenancy Act in Maharashtra also provides that a new tenancy can be of only one year's duration and at the end of one year the tenant will be entitled to own (on payment of a prescribed price) so much of the leased land as the Act entitles him to, provided he applies to the Agricultural Lands Tribunal within one year of the commencement of tenancy. The Land Ceiling Act, addressing the third aspect of Land reforms namely ceiling on landholdings, came into force in all parts of the state in 1961. By the end of 1971, only about 4,600 landholders were found to hold land in excess of the ceiling. Barely 0.1 million hectares had been declared surplus with these landholders. The ceilings prescribed in the 1961 Act were revised and lowered from 2nd October, 1975. Under this Act, by December 2001, 0.3 million hectares of land was declared surplus and 0.2 million hectares of land had been allotted to 0.14 million landless persons and 75 cooperative farming societies (*Economic Survey of Maharashtra*, 2001-02).

Every landholder in the state has to keep proper documents about the record of his land and keep these updated. The state government also started the scheme, since May 1999, for distribution of up-to-date village form No. 7/12 to the landholders, which is now also available by post.

The trend in structure of operational holdings (Table 3.4) indicates that from 1970-71 to 1995-96, the

TABLE 3.4

Distribution of Number and Area of Operational Holdings in Maharashtra

(Number in Million and Area in Million Hectares)

Size Group	*Number of Operational Holdings*				*Area of Operational Holdings*			
	1970-71	*1980-81*	*1990-91*	*1995-96*	*1970-71*	*1980-81*	*1990-91*	*1995-96*
Marginal (Up to 1 Ha)	1.24 (25.05)	1.92 (28.07)	3.27 (34.58)	4.26 (40.00)	0.57 (2.72)	0.93 (4.55)	1.6 (7.73)	2.0 (10.5)
Small (1 to 2 Ha)	0.87 (17.60)	1.54 (22.44)	2.7 (28.80)	3.1 (29.80)	1.28 (6.06)	2.30 (10.93)	3.98 (19.03)	4.6 (23.2)
Semi-medium (2 to 4 Ha)	1.08 (21.82)	1.68 (24.57)	2.1 (22.45)	2.1 (20.20)	3.1 (14.78)	4.80 (22.55)	5.88 (28.10)	5.8 (29.5)
Medium (4 to 10 Ha)	1.22 (24.65)	1.39 (20.29)	1.17 (12.37)	0.94 (8.80)	7.7 (36.44).	8.40 (39.55)	6.85 (32.76)	5.43 (27.3)
Large (Above 10 Ha)	0.51 (10.38)	0.32 (4.63)	0.17 (1.80)	0.12 (1.20)	8.47 (39.99)	4.78 (22.41)	2.6 (12.37)	1.87 (9.45)
Total	**4.95 (100)**	**6.86 (100)**	**9.47 (100)**	**10.65 (100)**	**21.20 (100)**	**21.36 (100)**	**20.92 (100)**	**19.87 (100)**
Average Size of Holding (Ha)	-	-	-	-	4.28	3.11	2.2	1.87

Note: Figures for 1995-96 are provisional; figures in parentheses are percentage to total.

Source: Agriculture Census, GoM.

number of operational holdings increased by 2.2 times but the operated area over the years has not shown any remarkable change but rather disturbingly, shows a declining trend. The beneficiaries of the structural distribution were the marginal and small farmers. Their share in terms of number and area operated showed an increasing trend since 1970-71. In case of marginal farmers, their number as well as area operated increased by about 3.5 times from the period 1970-71 to 1995-1996. The same was observed in case of small farmers. This reveals the increasing marginalisation of farmers in Maharashtra as together 74.3 per cent of farmers belonged to marginal and small category. Obviously, the large farmers lost their share and area operated by them which was 40 per cent in 1970-71 steeply declined to 9 per cent in 1995-96. Another important feature relates to the average size of holding. The average size, which was 4.28 hectares in 1970-71, started reducing and the average size has come down to 1.87 hectares in 1995-1996.

Land Use and Cropping Pattern in Maharashtra

The state of Maharashtra located in the western coast of India has a geographical area of 30.7 million hectares, which is second largest in the country, next to the state of Rajasthan.

Land Utilisation Pattern

The land utilisation pattern displayed minimal changes since 1990-91 and its composition in 2000-01 is shown in Figure 3.1. While net sown area (NSA)

FIGURE 3.1

Land Utilisation Pattern

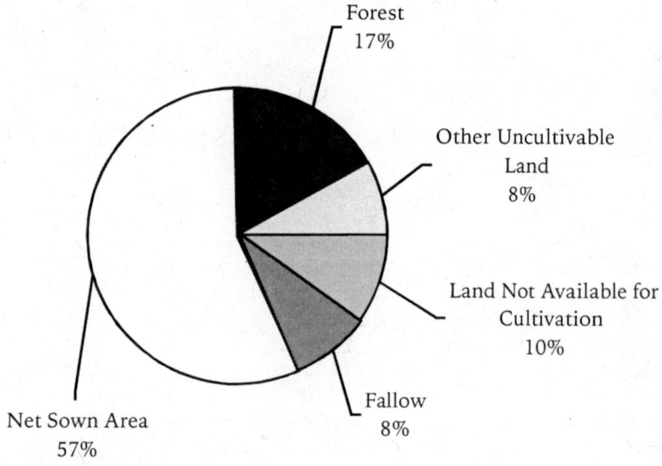

Source: Economic Survey, GoM, 2000-01.

was 60 per cent of the geographical area (18.56 million hectares) in 1990-91, it declined to 57 per cent (17.63 million hectares) in 2000-01. The share of fallow land increased from 6.4 per cent to 8 per cent during the same period.

Cropping Pattern in Maharashtra

Agriculture in Maharashtra continues to be dominated by foodgrains (Figure 3.2). While 70 per cent of the gross cropped area (GCA) was under foodgrains in 1980-81, this share declined to 60 per cent in 2000-01. Among foodgrains, the decline was with respect to cereals and the area under *jowar*, the main cereal in Maharashtra, declined by 23 per cent during this period. The area under pulses, however, showed a minor increase. The notable feature of Maharashtra's agriculture is that the cropping pattern is shifting towards commercial crops. The share of oilseeds increased from 9 per cent in 1980-81 to 12 per cent in the later decades. Cotton also showed an increase and its share went up from 12.4 per cent in 1990-91 to 14.3 per cent in 2000-01. Area under sugarcane also gradually moved up from 0.3 million hectares in TE 1980-81 to 0.6 million hectares in 2000-2001. The increase in area was more marked in case of fruits and vegetables and increased rapidly from 0.27 million hectares in 1980-81 to 1.26 million hectares in 2000-01. It may be mentioned here and will be elaborated later that government policies have been instrumental in inducing cropping pattern changes. The Technology Mission on Oilseeds launched in 1986 coupled with price support encouraged the shift in area towards oilseeds. Assured prices by cooperatives for sugarcane and guaranteed price for cotton through the government's Monopoly Procurement Scheme encouraged the production of these crops while the Horticulture Development Programme linked with the Maharashtra Employment Guarantee scheme accelerated the expansion of area under fruits and vegetables. After observing the share of various crops in the cropping pattern of Maharashtra, in Table 3.5 we present the growth rates of area under the important crops. The growth rates show that over the entire period (1980-81 to 2000-01), foodgrains registered negative growth rate whereas in the case of all commercial crops *viz.* sugarcane, cotton, oilseeds, fruits and vegetables, the growth rates were statistically significant. In the case of oilseeds, the growth rate was more marked in the first period whereas in the case of sugarcane and cotton the growth rates were higher in the second period.

FIGURE 3.2

Cropping Pattern in Maharashtra

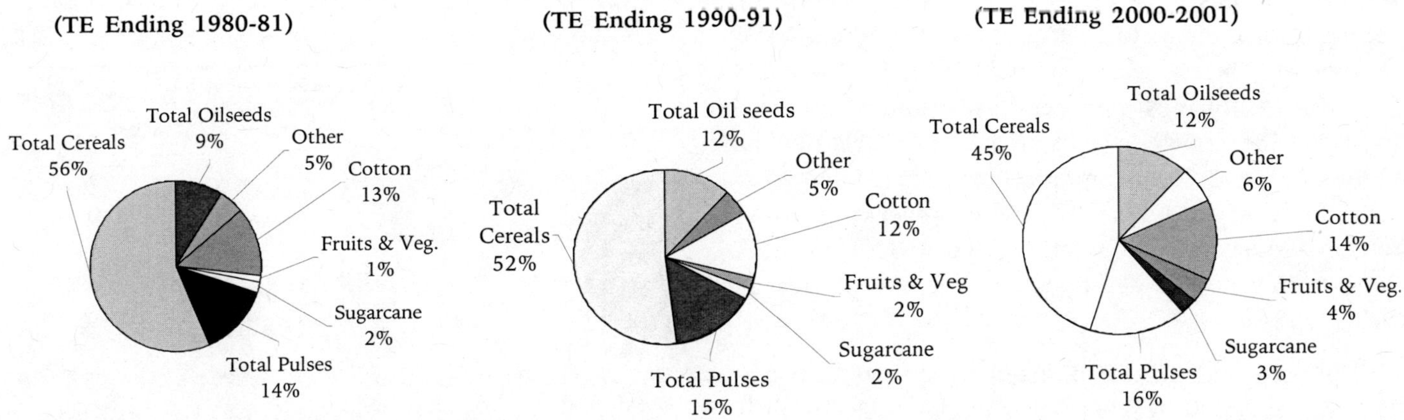

Source: Season and Crop Reports, various issues (GoM).

TABLE 3.5

Growth Rates by Area of Major Crops in Maharashtra

(Per Cent Per Annum)

Crop	*1980-81 to 1989-90*	*1990-91 to 2000-01*	*1980-81 to 2000-01*
Rice	0.58	-0.65*	0.17
Wheat	-2.30*	3.50**	-0.76
Bajra	2.40*	-0.80	0.50**
Jowar	-0.37	-1.69**	-1.40*
Total Cereals	**0.07**	**-0.67**	**-0.69***
Total Pulses	**2.70***	**0.91**	**1.69***
Total Foodgrains	**-0.27**	**0.61***	**-0.15**
Sugarcane	1.70**	2.40**	3.80*
Cotton	0.35	2.60*	1.14*
Oilseeds	6.70*	0.60	2.70*
Fruits & Vegetables	6.20*	8.00*	6.50*

Note: * Significant at one per cent; ** Significant at five per cent.

FIGURE 3.3

Commodity Composition (Per Cent) of Agricultural State Domestic Product : 2000-01 (1993-94 Prices)

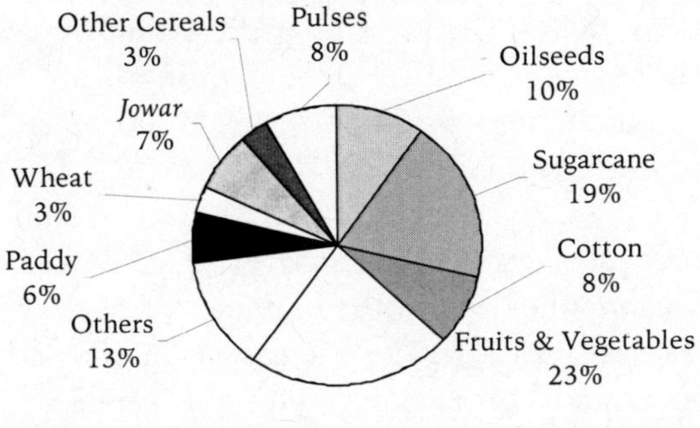

Source: Directorate of Economic and Statistics.

Finally, we look at the commodity composition of agricultural SDP (Figure 3.3). It has been observed that in 2000-2001, although the share of foodgrains in total area was 60 per cent, its contribution to state domestic product was only 25.5 per cent.

This can partly be explained by the fact that Maharashtra's foodgrain economy is dominated by low value coarse cereals such as *jowar*, which accounted for 52 per cent area under cereals and 23 per cent of GCA in 2000-01. Sugarcane, which barely constitutes 3 per cent of GCA, contributed to 19.3 per cent of state domestic product. Fruits and vegetables, which account for only 5.6 per cent of the GCA, accounted for as much as 24 per cent of agricultural state domestic product.

Production and Productivity of Crops

It was observed earlier that Maharashtra's cropping pattern is dominated by foodgrains, which constitute 60 per cent of the area under cultivation. However, Maharashtra contributes only 5.8 per cent to the foodgrain production of the country. This is mainly because *jowar* is the dominant cereal cultivated in the state and this crop is characterised by very low yield. The yield of *rabi jowar* is particularly very low and was 583 kg per hectare in TE 1996-97, while it constituted 62 per cent of the area under *jowar* during the same period. Rabi jowar is almost entirely unirrigated and this acts as a constraint on the use of high yielding varieties for *rabi jowar*. These factors also explain the fact that the yield of foodgrains in Maharashtra is about half that of the national level.

With respect to non-foodgrain crops also, with the sole exception of sugarcane, Maharashtra has lower yields than the national average. While 36 per cent of the country's area under cotton is in Maharashtra, the state contributes only 21.6 per cent to production (TE 1999-00), and the yield is 40 per cent less than the all-India level. This is again explained by lack of irrigation facilities as only 4 per cent area under cotton is irrigated. The growth rate of production (Table 3.6) and yield (Table 3.7), of major crops in Maharashtra indicates that foodgrains registered a negative growth rate in production, during the period 1990-91 to 2000-2001 mainly due to decline in growth rate of area and yield of *jowar*.

The area under *jowar* declined by 20 per cent from 1990-91 to 2000-01. This also explains the negative growth rate of production of cereals. Pulses, however, performed well, especially during 1980-81 to 1989-90 in terms of both production and yield. With respect to non-foodgrains, cotton and oilseeds showed an encouraging performance during the entire period as well as sub-periods. The Technology Mission on Oilseeds and the introduction of extra long staple high yielding varieties of cotton led to an increase in yield of oilseeds and cotton respectively. While production of sugarcane showed a statistically significant growth rate during the entire period (1980-81 to 2000-01), this was mainly achieved due to increase in area. The growth rate of yield of sugarcane, which is negative, is a disturbing feature especially because this crop is entirely irrigated. Pests often infest this crop, which lowers the yield.

TABLE 3.6

Growth Rate of Production of Major Crops in Maharashtra

(Per Cent Per Annum)

Crop	*1980-81 to 1989-90*	*1990-91 to 2000-01*	*1980-81 to 2000-01*
Rice	- 0.40	-0.13	0.70
Wheat	-0.40	3.70	2.03*
Jowar	1.40	-2.20	0.16
Bajra	4.40	0.55	4.60*
Total Cereals	**1.20**	**-0.50**	**1.10**
Total Pulses	**7.20***	**3.20**	**3.90**
Total Foodgrains	**1.90**	**-0.01**	**1.50***
Total Oilseeds	**9.20***	**4.30****	**6.08***
Cotton	3.30	3.80	4.20*
Sugarcane	0.64	4.20*	3.60*

Note: * Significant at one per cent; **Significant at five per cent.

TABLE 3.7

Growth Rate of Yield of Major Crops in Maharashtra

(Per Cent Per Annum)

Crop	*1980-81 to 1989-90*	*1990-91 to 2000-01*	*1980-81 to 2000-01*
Rice	1.50**	-1.40	0.00
Wheat	2.30	1.50	2.70*
Jowar	1.60	-0.40	1.60
Bajra	2.00	1.40	4.10*
Total Cereals	**1.10**	**0.39**	**-0.06**
Total Pulses	**4.60**	**2.30**	**2.30***
Total Foodgrains	**1.30**	**0.48**	**1.60***
Total Oilseeds	**1.60**	**4.20**	**3.10***
Cotton	3.10	1.50	3.00*
Sugarcane	-1.40*	0.70	-0.58

Note: * Significant at one per cent; ** Significant at five per cent.

Agricultural Inputs in Maharashtra

The major agricultural inputs besides water/irrigation are seeds, fertilisers, pesticides and machinery. The farmers can also treat agricultural extension service provided to the farmers as an important input as it includes various activities and mechanisms for ensuring efficient use of inputs. Use of better quality inputs and efficient input management and practices are extremely important for increasing the productivity of the given land.

Seed

Maharashtra is one of the major seed-producing states in India contributing to around 40 per cent of the total seed production in the country. Out of the total seed distribution, the public sector and the private sector, each, contribute 50 per cent. Entry of private sector in seeds market is expanding. It can also be noted that with reforms, seed production on *taluka* seed farms is on decline and many seed farms have been converted into agri-polyclinics, which is a welcome change. In Maharashtra, the production of certified seeds increased from 0.14 million quintals in 1980-81 to 0.41 million quintals in 1998-99, thus, registering a threefold increase in the last 20 years. As far as the research dimension is concerned, so far, 183 hybrid/HYV varieties of various crops have been released by the state. During mid-1980s, the number of such varieties developed was just 47. The increase is particularly high for oilseeds and cotton along with the cereals.

For understanding the progress on the seed front, data on two indicators can be observed. These are: area

TABLE 3.8

Achievement under Intensive Cultivation in Maharashtra

Category	*Wheat*	*Paddy*	*Jowar*	*Cotton*
Growth Rates of Area under HYVs 1980-2001 (%)	-0.52	2.35*	13.56*	35.87
Area under HYVs and Hybrids 2000-01 (%)	92.00	95.00	97.00	97.00

Note: 1. *= Significance at five per cent level. 2. For cotton, growth rate not calculated, as data is not available for adequate years, the figure indicates per cent change during 1992-93 to 2000-01. 3. For *jowar*, area under HYV for *kharif* season and the growth rate is for *rabi jowar* only. Growth Rate for *kharif jowar* is insignificant.

Source: District-wise *Agricultural Statistical Information of Maharashtra,* Office of Commissioner of Agriculture, GoM, Pune.

TABLE 3.9

Seed Replacement Rate Achieved in Maharashtra

Crops	*1985*	*1990*	*1995*	*2001*	*Target Fixed by GoM for 2003*	*Target Fixed by GoI, Ninth Plan*
R. Jowar	4	4	5	11	11	10
Paddy	2	4	14	18	20	14
Wheat	11	19	29	25	26	20
Groundnut	2	1	2	2	4	4
Sunflower (K)	17	14	23	28	28	20
Sunflower (R)	13	19	22	22	19	10
Soyabean	3	3	16	33	43	10

Source: Department of Inputs and Quality Control, Office of Commissioner of Agriculture, GoM, Pune.

under the HYVs and the seed replacement ratio (SRR) of the crop. Table 3.8 shows that the data on the per cent coverage under of HYV/hybrids relating to crops like *jowar* (*kharif* and *rabi*), wheat, cotton and paddy shows an increasing (though fluctuating) trend in the area under HYVs/hybrids. The latest figures show that the coverage is around 90 per cent for these crops. Over the period, area under HYVs and hybrids has been increasing at a very fast pace for *jowar*. There seems to be, thus, a scope for further increase. SRR which is the proportion of total (private + public) seed distribution to the total seed requirement and which indicates the rate at which the seeds get replaced *via* market is another important indicator. Thus, SRR is 100 per cent for the hybrids and lower for the traditional seeds, as the output cannot be used as seed in the next year in the case of the former as against the latter. Table 3.9 shows that at the state level, SRR of 100 per cent has been achieved only for the crops like hybrid *jowar* (*kharif*), hybrid *bajra* and hybrid cotton. SRR for the oilseed crops like sunflower and soyabean is seen to be comparatively higher. Pulses and cereals (other than hybrid *jowar* and *bajra*) have lower SRR indicating lesser extent of seed marketisation. For almost all the crops except groundnut it is seen that the targets set for the Ninth Plan have been achieved and SRRs for the year 2001 are seen to be closer to the target for year 2003.

Fertiliser and Pesticides

Like seeds, the fertiliser consumption in Maharashtra has been rising continuously. It is one of the major fertiliser consuming states in India with the share of around 10 per cent in the total fertiliser consumption in India. Annually around 3.8-4.0 million tonnes of fertilisers are consumed in terms of material and 1.8 to 2.0 million tonnes in terms of nutrients-nitrogen, phosphate and potassium (N, P, K). In 1995, per hectare consumption was highest in Punjab (167kg/ha.). Comparatively, in Maharashtra, it was around 65 kg (in 1995). However, it has increased from just 14 kg/ha in 1970-71 to currently around 75 kg/ha thus registering a five fold growth and a growth rate of 7.4 per cent per annum. As far as the level of NPK ratio is concerned, it was distorted from the normal level (4:2:1) to 8.1:2.3:1 due to the decontrol of phosphatic and potash fertilisers in 1992. It subsequently improved to 5.4:2.4:1, after the government introduced the Concessional Scheme of fertilisers to increase the consumption after 1992. With increasing area under horticultural and other high value export crops (which have significant nutrition requirement), fertiliser consumption might increase further.

However, it emerged out of the discussion with the government officials that there is still widespread ignorance among farmers about the appropriate application of fertilisers in terms of quantity and variety. Soil test-based application of fertilisers and application of micronutrients has still not become a rule. Application of fertilisers is governed by their prices. Thus, need-based application of fertilisers to avoid excess usage and wastage of fertilisers is the most important need today. At the regional level, in districts of western Maharashtra, per hectare usage of fertilisers is found to be very high (as compared to other districts) and this has affected fertility of soil adversely. Similarly, among various crops grown in the state, sugarcane is the crop, which consumes very high quantity of fertilisers. It was reported that the per hectare consumption of fertilisers for this crop moved up from 226 kg per hectare in 1972-73 to 501 kg per hectare in 1990-91 (Sawant *et al.*, 1999).

Biofertilisers are economical and pollution-free sources of plant nutrients. Under the integrated approach, implemented by the Government of India, balanced use of chemical fertilisers and biofertilisers/ organic manure is suggested to maintain the soil health. The state hardly uses 1,500 tonnes of these fertilisers as against the potential of 85,000 tonnes. On the other hand, the state consumes around 4 million tonnes of the chemical fertilisers. The state has about 41 production units of biofertilisers with capacity of 5,000-6,000 tonnes (*www.agri.mah.nic.in*). There is a large scope for further increase.

In the case of pesticides, the consumption in Maharashtra has come down to 173 g/ha from 320 g/ha during Seventh Plan due to integrated pest management (IPM). However, there is irrational distribution of pesticide use with maximum use on cotton (54 per cent) (GoI, 2003a). The use of eco-friendly IPM strategy has to be widespread.

Agricultural Machinery

Agricultural implements and machinery help farmers in speeding up agricultural operations and in utilising the land and labour resources more productively. In the post-Green Revolution period therefore, their importance has been increasing (Table 3.10). As against the availability of 1.16 tractors per ha of NSA, in 1982-1983, in 1996-97, 4.58 tractors were available. Importance of usage of electric pumpsets also can be noted. Usage of manually operated ploughs is clearly on decline.

TABLE 3.10

Agricultural Machinery in Maharashtra during 1982-83 to 1996-97

Implements/ Machinery	*Absolute Number* 1982-83	2002-03 (Provisional)	*% Change per Ha of NSA*
Plough	2586922	2206438	-14.06
Four Wheeled Tractors	20704	103964	402
Electric Pumpsets Used for Irrigation	448632	966713	116.46

Source: GoM 1997, 2003.

Agricultural Extension

Extension services provided to the farmers assume a great significance as various schemes for improving agricultural performance get actually implemented through this service. This basically includes dissemination of scientific information to and training of farmers as well as implementation of various schemes. Agricultural department of the state plays a major role in providing this service. A change in the approach towards provision of these services is being noted as far as the state is concerned. Earlier, these services were provided by the three separate sections of the department *viz.* crop husbandry, horticulture and soil conservation. With the recent reforms carried out in the department, 'single window system' was adopted since 1998, under which machinery of the three sections were integrated with an intention to provide extension services to the farmers with a holistic approach. Another welcome change observed is a gradual shift from individual–based government subsidies towards community and private-public partnership based subsidies. Also, recently, a more flexible approach has been adopted by the Central Government as far as implementation of schemes and delegation of powers to the state government are concerned. Lastly, it is observed that there has been entry and gradual expansion of the private sector for providing extension services.

Discussion with various government officials revealed that a major weakness of the system today is the poor quality of the manpower with department that actually interacts with the farmers and also weakening of the university scientist and agricultural assistant link. Better utilisation of other inputs definitely rests on these aspects.

Investment in Agriculture

Agricultural sector at the national level has been undergoing a disheartening trend of falling capital formation on government account. In contrast, the private investment's stepping up has been observed over a period of time. For Maharashtra, it was found that the gross fixed capital formation in agriculture (GFCFA) at 1980-81 prices was increasing at the trend growth rate of 2.39 per cent per annum during 1980-81 to 1993-94 (data for the later years could not be made available from the CSO). Though the share of public sector was 55.61 per cent (Gulati and Bathla, 2002), public sector investment was increasing only marginally and at a non-significant annual growth rate of 1.21 per cent while that of the private sector was 3.72 per cent. A similar picture emerges for per hectare investment in agriculture with per hectare public and private GFCFA growing at the rates of 1.3 per cent and 3.84 per cent respectively.

As far as the private sector investment is concerned, it was found that Maharashtra had achieved impressive growth in private fixed capital formation in agriculture (PFCFA). According to this study, PFCFA in Maharashtra was one of the highest in absolute terms in the country in 1981-82 (Rs. 1,669 million) and in 1991-92 (Rs. 6,592 million) thus, exhibiting a per cent change of 294 per cent. Maharashtra also recorded higher per cent change during this period in per hectare PFCFA (Chand, 2001).

Similarly, the composition of PFCFA has also been undergoing a change during the period from 1981-82 to 1991-92. A few important points can be noted from Table 3.11 in this regard. Firstly, though the share of 'orchards and plantation' increased only marginally, in absolute terms, the rise in expenditure has been considerable i.e. more than 400 per cent. This probably indicates the growing importance of horticulture in the state. Secondly, the share of 'wells' has reduced and that of 'other irrigation sources' (such as tanks and water channels) has increased over the period by more than 150 per cent. In absolute terms, the expenditure on latter item has increased by around 1000 per cent. This possibly can be attributed to increasing expenditure by the farmers on construction and maintenance of water channels and micro irrigation systems such as drip and sprinklers, which are relatively costlier. Together, wells and other irrigation sources contribute more than 50 per cent of the total PFCFA in Maharashtra, which is higher than the all-India level figure.

TABLE 3.11

Distribution of Fixed Capital Expenditure of Households in Different Categories of Farm Business in Maharashtra in 1981-82 and 1991-92

(Per Cent)

Categories	*1981-82*	*1991-92*
Improvement/Reclamation of Land/Buildings	20.52	14.13
Orchards and Plantation	1.96	2.61
Wells	37.39	34.16
Other Irrigation Resources	7.74	19.55
Agri Implements, Machinery, Transport Equipment, etc.	26.72	25.24
Farm Houses, Barns, Animal Sheds, etc.	2.09	0.96
Other	3.59	3.14
Farm Business—Total	**100.00**	**100.00**

Source: Calculated from data given in Gulati and Bathla (2002); Chand (2000); GoI (1988, 1998).

Agricultural Finance

Although there has been multi-agency setup for rural banking, the major institutional finance to farming community in Maharashtra comes from commercial banks and credit cooperatives. Further, the priority sectors such as agriculture and allied activities account for the major share in total annual credit plan outlay for the state of Maharashtra with activities relating to small scale industries (SSI) and non-farm sectors (NFS) accounting for the least share in the allocations in credit plan outlay. The estimates relating to Potential Linked Credit Plan (PLCP) outlays encompassing various sectors/activities show that among various regions, western Maharashtra alone accounts for around 50 per cent share in total PLCP outlay for the state of Maharashtra (Table 3.12).

TABLE 3.12

Potential Linked Credit Plan (PLCP) Estimates of Exploitable Potential for Different Regions of Maharashtra

(Amount in Multiples of 10 Million Rs.)

Regions	*1997-98*	*1999-00*	*2001-02*
Western Maharashtra	2552.87 (50.66)	3577.54 (50.17)	4945.71 (50.18)
Vidarbha	912.67 (18.11)	1361.47 (19.09)	1937.79 (19.66)
Marathwada	1159.36 (23.00)	1556.79 (21.83)	2048.29 (20.78)
Konkan	414.87 (8.23)	635.51 (8.91)	925.13 (9.38)
Maharashtra State	**5039.77**	**7131.31**	**9856.92**

Notes: Figures in parentheses are percentages to the total potential linked credit plan for the state.

Source: Compiled from official records, NABARD office, Pune.

The next important regions are Marathwada and Vidarbha, each accounting for about 20 per cent share in state's total PLCP outlay during the past five years. The allocation for Konkan region in state's total PLCP outlay is the least. As regards credit delivery from various rural financial institutions in Maharashtra, the trends over the past two decades as indicated in Tables 3.13 and 3.14 show a slower growth in institutional finance through both credit cooperatives and commercial banks during the decade of economic reforms (1991-2000) as against the decade preceding it (1980-1990). Not only this, the reform period is also seen to be marked with a slower growth in membership of credit cooperatives in Maharashtra (Table 3.13). On the other hand, the outstanding loans of these cooperatives have grown at much faster rate as compared to their loan advances during both pre- and post-economic reform periods. The commercial banks in Maharashtra have not only shown slower growth in their loan advances and deposits but also decline in their credit-deposit (C-D) ratios during the period of reforms as against the pre-economic reform period (Table 3.14).

TABLE 3.13

Cooperative Bank Finances in Maharashtra: 1980-2000

(Amount in Multiples of 10 Million Rs.)

Indicators	*Triennium Ending*			*CGR (%)*		
	1982-1983	*1990-1991*	*1999-2000*	*1980-1990*	*1991-2000*	*1980-2000*
I. No. of Cooperative Societies						
a. Apex	31	34	34	1.33	-	0.37
b. PACS	18565	19694	20378	-0.03NS	0.48	0.65
Total	**18596**	**19728**	**20412**	**-0.03NS**	**0.48**	**0.65**
II. No. of Members ('000)						
a. Apex	1109	1523	1340	1.01NS	-1.91	1.65
b. PACS	5595	7910	10432	4.90	3.48	3.35
Total	**6704**	**9433**	**11772**	**4.33**	**2.72**	**3.13**
III. Loan and Advances						
a. Apex	3318	9298	22195	14.47NS	7.12	8.64
b. PACS	288	929	2280	13.64	9.36	12.93
Total	**3606**	**10227**	**24475**	**14.08NS**	**9.74**	**10.76**
IV. Outstanding Loans						
a. Apex	1507	4811	15274	23.97NS	13.52	14.57
b. PACS	431	1521	3456	12.59	9.07	12.92
Total	**1938**	**6332**	**18730**	**18.50**	**12.98**	**14.64**

Notes: CGR-Compound Growth Rates.
All growth rates significant at one per cent level.
NS- Growth rates not significant at one per cent.
Apex institutions include SCBs and DCCBs.
Source: Computations are based on figures obtained from various issues of *Economic Survey of Maharashtra.*

TABLE 3.14

Rural Deposits and Credits of Commercial Banks in Maharashtra

(Amount in Multiples of 10 Million Rs.)

Period	*Rural Deposit*	*Rural Credit*	*CD Ratio (%)*
TE 1982-83	381	274	71.91
TE 1992-93	1964	1457	74.18
TE 1999-00	5145	3346	65.03
CGR (%)			
1980-90	19.05	17.08	-
1991-00	14.40NS	12.28NS	-
1980-00	16.28	14.91	-

Note: NS–Growth rate not significant at one per cent.
Source: Computations are based on figures obtained from various issues of *Economic Survey of Maharashtra.*

The C-D ratios of regional rural banks (RRBs) of this state have also fallen sharply over time (Table 3.15). So far as the rural finances are concerned, the most disquieting feature is the decline in loan advances of land development banks (LDBs) during the second half of the 1990s (Table 3.16). Not only the loan advances of LDBs of Maharashtra have declined sharply during the period of reform but the working capital of these banks also fell marginally during this period. The membership of LDBs of Maharashtra has also grown at slower rate during the period between 1991 and 2000 as against the period between 1981 and 2000 (Table 3.16).

TABLE 3.15

Progress of Deposit and Credit of Regional Rural Banks (RRBs) in Maharashtra *vis-à-vis* India

(Amount in One Hundred Thousand Rs.)

Period	*Deposit*	*Credit*	*CD Ratio (%)*
Maharashtra			
1981	557	824	147.94
TE 1985	1724	2034	117.40
TE 1990	8851	10709	120.99
TE 1995	22757	17373	76.34
TE 2000	75492	41562	55.05
All-India			
1981	33147	40682	122.73
TE 1985	97075	107492	110.73
TE 1990	353554	321839	91.03
TE 1995	861931	528835	61.35
TE 2000	2685412	1152160	42.90

Source: Computations are based on figures obtained from various issues of *Statistical Tables Relating to Banks in India,* Department of Banking Operations and Development for the RBI, Bombay.

TABLE 3.16

Progress of Maharashtra State Cooperative Land Development Banks (LDBs)

(Amount in One Hundred Thousand Rs.; Membership in '000)

Period	*Membership*	*Working Capital*	*Loan Advances*	*Loans Outstanding*
TE 1985	827	44405	5651	30627
TE 1990	926	66685	8932	49245
TE 1995	1111	107311	13668	82328
TE 2000	1189	144262	4875	99690
CGR (%)				
1981-00	2.79	6.07	0.54	9.21
1991-00	1.65	-0.27	-18.53	5.64

Source: Computations are based on figures obtained from various issues of *Cooperative Movement at a Glance in Maharashtra,* Office of the Commissioner for Co-operation & Registrar of Cooperative Societies, Maharashtra state, Pune.

The estimates relating to various rural financial institutions (RFIs) of Maharashtra also show a slower growth in their outstanding loans (OL), overdue from direct advances (DA) and bad debt in agriculture during the period between 1991 and 1997 as against the period between 1980 and 1990 (Table 3.17). However, the proportion of overdue to OL of RFIs of Maharashtra has grown at much faster rate during the reform period as against the pre-economic reform period. The reform period also shows increasingly high growth of Maharashtra's share in total overdue and bad debts in agriculture of RFIs in India.

TABLE 3.17

Some Broad Performance Indicators of Rural Financial Institutions (RFIs) of Maharashtra *vis-à-vis* All-India

(in Multiples of 10 Million Rs.)

Period	*Maharashtra*	*India*	*Share (%)*
Outstanding Loan (OL)			
TE 1982	842.12	7326.36	11.49
TE 1990	3084.77	25940.29	11.85
TE 1997	3521.57	34579.59	10.67
CGR (%)			
1980-90	16.12	15.21	0.91
1991-97	-1.02	2.01	-2.97
1980-97	10.51	10.75	-0.22
Overdue from DA			
TE 1982	294.99	2157.95	13.74
TE 1990	812.76	6712.71	12.03
TE 1997	1536.03	8912.23	17.10
CGR (%)			
1980-90	13.47	14.22	-2.97
1991-97	9.99	1.00	7.92
1980-97	11.75	10.13	1.45
Bad Debt in Agriculture			
TE 1982	46.97	244.44	19.30
TE 1990	112.01	771.98	14.50
TE 1997	185.84	1054.68	17.54
CGR (%)			
1980-90	11.78	15.65	-3.11
1991-97	4.91	-2.11	7.17
1980-97	10.12	10.83	-0.65

Notes: CGR-Compound annual growth rate; DA – Direct advances.

Source: Computations are based on figures obtained from Gulati, Ashok and Seema Bathla (2002).

The slower growth in institutional finances through commercial banks, credit cooperatives, RRBs and LDBs during the decade of 1991-2000 is due to adverse environment created by the financial sector reforms. One of the reasons for slowing down in institutional finance during the reform period could be the highly regressive and biased interest rate structure for priority sector during this era (Mujumdar, 1998). Another reason could be the emergence of new types of financial institutions like non-banking financial institutions (NBFCs) that provide loans for transactions on account of buying and selling of agricultural inputs and output. As pointed out by Mujumdar (1999), the new policy regime of financial sector reforms has grossly neglected the rural credit delivery system. Due to unfavourable policy framework, the entire rural credit delivery system encompassing rural branches of commercial banks, cooperative credit institutions and RRBs is reduced to a moribund state (Mujumdar, 2001). Mujumdar (2001) has also shown concern for the shrinking flow of financial resources to agriculture, both in terms of investment and working capital. In fact, the public investment in agriculture is reported to be declining (Thamarajakshi, 1999). However, the Ninth Plan not only recognises the role of priority sectors in the future growth of the country's economy but it also categorically emphasises upon the imperative of enlarging the flow of credit to these sectors.

It is to be noted that high transaction costs and poor repayment performance are the twin root causes of the moribund state of rural credit delivery system (Mujumdar, 2001). With a view to revive the agricultural credit delivery system, there is need to adopt innovative approaches like linking of self-help groups (SHGs) and (NGOs) with mainstream financial institutions. Such linkages are reported to have not only reduced transaction costs but also ensured better repayment performance. In Maharashtra, the strength of SHGs linked with bank credit grew from as low as 424 in March, 1997 to as high as 11,148 by June, 2001. One of the recent studies conducted in Maharashtra has shown cent per cent recovery of loans through SHGs despite having excessively high rates of interest (24-36 per cent per annum) on their loan advances (Kshirsagar and Shah, 2002).

As pointed out by Mujumdar (1998), one of the recent welcome developments in rural credit has been the establishment of the Rural Infrastructure Development Fund (RIDF) instituted by NABARD with the objective of advancing loans to state governments and state owned corporations for hastening ongoing projects, mainly those related to medium and minor irrigation, soil conservation, watershed management, etc. However, it is also being observed by Mujumdar (2001) that the utilisation of this fund is dismal at only 30 per cent. One of the further disquieting features of RFIs in Maharashtra has been the high proportion of NPAs to total assets, particularly of RRBs and state cooperative agriculture and rural development banks (SCARDBs), which are estimated to hover around 36-48 per cent during the mid-nineties. One of the reasons for such high incidence of NPAs of RFIs has been the familiar practice of debt forgiveness, which eroded repayment.

Marketing of Agricultural Produce

While technology and institutional factors play a pivotal role in agricultural growth, equally important is the role of agricultural marketing. In Maharashtra, most agricultural commodities are traded in regulated markets through auction method, but in the case of selected crops such as cotton and sugarcane, marketing is through state intervention.

Regulated Agricultural Markets and Rural Infrastructure

The Maharashtra Agricultural Produce Marketing (Regulation) Act, 1963, requires that all notified agricultural produce bought or sold within the market area must pass through the market yard or sub-yard managed by the Agricultural Produce Market Committee (APMC) constituted for each market. The APMC functions under the supervision of a state level Agricultural Marketing Board. No one is allowed to market any notified produce in the market area other than the principal yard or subyard. All functionaries like traders, commission agents, weigh-men and loading workers must hold licence of the APMC to carry out business. There are 857 regulated markets in Maharashtra consisting of 266 market yards and 591 sub-yards. The APMCs generate income by charging market fee, licence fee and rentals. The main objective of regulated markets is to protect farmers from exploitation by middlemen and to provide facilities for auctioning of produce so that farmers are assured of competitive prices. Rural infrastructure also plays an important role in enabling farmers to market their produce. In the year 2000 the total road length was 257,000 km. As per Census 2001, all-weather roads connected 79 per cent of villages, while fair-weather roads connected 8 per cent of the villages. The state had 676 warehouses with a storage capacity of 3.5 million metric tonnes.

Government Intervention in Marketing

The government of Maharashtra has been a strong proponent of cooperative marketing of agricultural produce. Cooperative marketing is especially predominant in sugar and cotton sectors and growers have an assured market as well as price for their produce.

Cooperative Sugar Factories (CSFs) in Maharashtra

Maharashtra has been the pioneering state with respect to setting up of CSFs and the first such factory (Pravara Cooperative Sugar factory) was set up in 1948. The successful establishment and operation of this factory initiated a trend in cooperative development with rapid multiplication of cooperative sugar factories in the state. There are at present 160 sugar factories in the state, out of which 147 are in the cooperative sector while only 13 are in the private sector. Also 57 sugar cooperative factories are in the initial stage.

The CSFs are involved in scheduling of planting, harvesting, transport and financing of the sugarcane crop. They purchase sugarcane supplied by farmers and process it into sugar. A committee of Ministers sets a mill specific cane price. On delivery of the sugarcane, within 15 days, farmers are to be paid statutory minimum price; a second payment is made when the balance sheet of the mills permit and a small final payment is made some months later, following a state audit of the mill.

The contribution of the state government to the share capital of every factory has been 32.5 per cent of the originally appraised cost of the project. The loan amount borrowed by every factory from the banks and financial institutions, for which the state government has been giving default guarantee, amounts to 60 per cent of the appraised cost of the project. In this way, the financial involvement of the state government in every cooperative sugar factory has been 92.5 per cent of the originally appraised cost of the project. In addition, due to cost overruns, the state government has been giving direct loans to the cooperative sugar factories as 'Last Mile Assistance' to enable them to complete their projects. Further, through government resolutions, soft loans and other forms of financial support were also rendered to sugar factories (Wadhwa, 2000).

In the initial years of independence, the sugar factories that were set up functioned efficiently and met with success. These factories were located mostly in western Maharashtra where irrigation facilities and other complementary inputs were available. Since western Maharashtra had a large number of sugar factories, northern Maharashtra, Vidarbha and

Marathwada followed suit, despite the fact that they were not gifted with the necessary factor endowments. The Godbole Committee (1999) noted that the most critical issue in the examination of applications for new factories was the assessment regarding the availability of water and the area, which was likely to be brought under sugarcane. However, certificates regarding present and future availability of water given by officers of Irrigation Department and Ground Survey and Development Agency were vague and misleading. This resulted in the shortage of sugarcane for the factories and all sugar cooperatives located in these regions began incurring losses. The normative costs adopted by financial institutions for sanction of loans were often outdated as actual costs turned out much higher. Since term loans were not available to meet this increased cost, the sugar factories often resorted to high cost short-term funds. This in turn led to shortage of working capital margins along with time and cost overruns. The state government also delayed releasing its share of equity and giving its guarantee for loans sanctioned by other institutional lenders. These factors led to a financial crisis among sugar factories and they defaulted in timely repayment of loans given by the government and other financial institutions. They were unable to make payments to labour as salaries and wages and also failed to pay interest and arrears of past loans, which were due for payment. A number of sugar factories had been paying much higher prices for sugarcane than warranted by their financial status. Cane prices were also paid by borrowing from banks or from diverting working capital, thus adding to financial liabilities. During the year 1998-99, out of 138 factories, only 31 sugar cooperatives were making profits while 107 factories were incurring losses. Thus, three-fourths of the sugar mills in the state were incurring huge losses and accumulating heavy debts. Further, while accumulated losses of 107 factories amounted to Rs 10.31 billion, the accumulated profits of the 31 mills was only Rs 0.20 billion. In Kolhapur district, out of the 15 sugar cooperatives, 10 were in losses amounting to Rs 420 million, while profits of the 5 mills were only Rs 10.8 million. The situation was similar in Sangli district, where the accumulated losses of the sugar mills amounted to Rs 520 million.

The records from the office of Sugar Federation revealed that the sugar factories in the state at present have the burden of short margin (the difference between the production cost and market price of sugar) to the tune of Rs 15.78 billion. The RBI and NABARD have shown willingness to convert the short-margin into medium-term loans, provided the government gives a guarantee. The government has given a guarantee for Rs. 10 billion as in the absence of this guarantee, a number of sugar mills may have to close down, while district central cooperative banks will face a grave crisis. Currently, a number of sugar factories are unable to pay the Statutory Minimum Price and as per the Sugarcane Control Order, if factories do not pay SMP within 15 days, they will have to face legal actions.

Besides being a threat on the fiscal status of GoM, sugarcane cultivation poses another problem. Sugarcane is a high water consuming crop and the amount of water conventionally utilised for sugarcane is several times that of other crops. As more sugar cooperatives are given licences, the area under sugarcane is bound to increase with the result that there would be pressure on scarce water resources and declining water tables. Excessive water use has led to waterlogging and increased salinity of land. While there are other competitive crops, that can also be grown, sugarcane, which does not require much effort to grow and often termed as 'lazy man's crop' continues to be a popular cash crop in Maharashtra. While some of the successful sugar cooperatives had helped to transform the rural areas especially in western Maharashtra, the fiscal burden on the government is heavy.

Government Intervention in Cotton

Maharashtra has the highest area under cotton in the country and about 20 per cent of the cultivators and their families in the state cultivate this crop. The marketing of this crop is characterised by a unique feature i.e. there is complete state intervention. A scheme of Monopoly Procurement of Cotton was framed and given a statutory form under the Maharashtra Raw Cotton (Procurement, Processing and Marketing) Act, 1971. With the enforcement of this Act, all private trading in cotton had been prohibited since the 1972-73 cotton season and the farmer was compelled to sell his crop only to the GoM's designated procuring agency, namely, Maharashtra State Cooperative Cotton Growers Marketing Federation. The hallmark of this scheme was the payment of guaranteed price, which remained the same throughout the season, and the cultivator was assured of it, even if the Federation could not sell at that price. In case the scheme made profits on its operations, the cultivator received 75 per cent of this surplus as bonus. The remaining 25 per cent was credited to a fund, to cover losses when needed. The scheme is now in operation for the last three decades. During the first two decades, the scheme made losses in eight years and to make good these losses a sum of Rs. 3.31 billion had to be transferred from the state exchequer to the Federation for its survival. Since the 1993-94 season, the scheme has been incurring massive losses and total losses from 1994-95 to 2001-02 season amounted to Rs. 40 billion. The Federation was surviving on budgetary support from GoM, delayed payments to farmers and debt rescheduling. There were several causes for mounting losses. First, in several years, the guaranteed price set by GoM was higher than ruling market prices in adjoining markets of neighbouring states. In some years high prices attracted illegal inflow of cotton from border-states in contravention to the provision of the Act. Thus the Federation, not only subsidised Maharashtra farmers but also those in other states. Second, although exports are now under Open General Licence, world prices are often depressed due to increased world production and thus in this global scenario the federation was unable to capitalise on exports. Also, the cotton is often contaminated and often not acceptable on quality considerations. The marketing practices of the federation often suffered from corruption in grading and inferior quality cotton was upgraded thus reducing potential revenues. Holding of massive stocks of cotton (worth Rs. 22 billion till 2000) deteriorated the quality of the fibre, forcing the federation to offer huge discounts on its sales. This also led to a huge increase in interest cost due to unsold stocks, (besides storage and insurance), which amounted to Rs. 10 billion (1999-00) and would sooner or later have to be borne by the state government. The operation of the monopoly scheme has built up a huge financial liability and to ease the situation, from the 2003-04 cotton season, CCI and private traders were allowed to enter the market. As a result of liberalising the monopoly scheme of cotton, the purchases by the Federation in the 2003-04 season were negligible and most of the purchase centres were closed down. However, the federation had to ensure that prices do not fall below the guaranteed price fixed by it.

Horticulture Sector

As noted earlier, agriculture in Maharashtra is diversifying into high value crops and horticultural crops are a major component of high value crops. Maharashtra has the highest area and production in the country devoted to fruits and fifth largest area under vegetables. It has 20 per cent share in the country's fruit production and 5 per cent share in vegetable production (1999-00). The state is the home of the renowned Alphonso mangoes and ranks first in the country in grape, cashewnut, pomegranate and orange production while it is first in banana productivity. It also has the highest share in onion production. The horticulture sector in Maharashtra contributes to the foreign exchange earnings as a large share of horticultural exports are from Maharashtra. With respect to floriculture, the area under flowers was 6600 hectares with an annual production of 28000 metric tonnes (2000-01). Besides, infrastructure created for the floriculture sector includes, 16 tissue culture units, 800 poly/green houses, 43 pre-cooling units and 101 cold storage units. The records of the state's Department of Horticulture reveal that 85 per cent of onions, 60 per cent of vegetables, 65 per cent of mangoes, 90 per cent grapes and 15 per cent of total fruits are exported from Maharashtra.

The area under fruits and vegetables which was only 0.5 million hectares in 1990-91, more than doubled to 1.25 million hectares in 2000-01. This increase came about due to concerted efforts on the part of the GoM which in 1990-91, launched an ambitious Employment Guarantee Scheme Linked Horticulture Development Programme, mainly to secure better returns to farmers and encourage them to bring wasteland under horticulture. Further, since horticultural production is labour intensive, this programme was intended to generate employment opportunities in rural areas. This programme of GoM has a high potential because a variety of horticultural crops can be grown in different agroclimatic zones of Maharashtra. Marketing of these crops is also facilitated by easy accessibility of major ports and well-established domestic and international airports.

The scheme open to all farmers, covers 88.5 per cent of villages in Maharashtra and includes 25 fruit crops, spices intercropped in coconut plantations and medicinal and aromatic plants. The scheme provides 100 per cent subsidy on wages and 75 per cent subsidy on material inputs for a period of three years. In order to supply high quality planting material to farmers, the government established 140 nurseries, while 24 nurseries were established in the 4 agricultural universities of the state. Further, 1674 private nurseries were set up to ensure easy availability of planting materials. Supporting infrastructure to facilitate the functioning of this scheme, included 21 tissue culture laboratories, setting up of two pesticide residue testing laboratories (Pune and Nagpur), and plant health clinics to test genetic purity. The number of beneficiaries selected since inception was 1.28 million and employment generated was 214.1 million man-days. Finally, a website on agriculture-horticulture was launched by the agriculture department to disseminate information about this programme.

Other schemes of the government as well as private sector initiatives served as complementary inputs for this horticultural development programme. For example, through a centrally sponsored scheme, subsidy is given to farmers for micro-irrigation and by 1999-00, 0.19 million hectares of fruit crops were under drip irrigation. The National Horticulture Board provided soft loans to cooperatives, associations of growers, etc., in all states, to strengthen the post-harvest infrastructure for horticultural crops. Accordingly, Maharashtra received Rs. 110.56 million, during the period 1993-94 to 1996-97, under the soft loan schemes. The private sector also contributed post-harvest infrastructure facilities such as pre-cooling equipment, cold storage, refrigerated transport, agro-processing units and extension services. Some commodity-marketing organisations, e.g. Mahagrapes and Mahamangoes have been instrumental in promoting exports of domestic produce. The GoM is also in the process of setting up Agri-Export Zones for promoting exports of certain fruits with the objective of providing remunerative returns to farmers on a substantial basis through improved access to exports.

The implementation of this scheme thus shows all round efforts on the part of GoM to commercialise agriculture in Maharashtra and despite water constraints, the state has tried to capitalise on soil and climatic factors as well as other infrastructure conducive to horticulture.

Allied Activities

Allied activities, namely, livestock, poultry, fishery and forestry have great potential for catalysing Maharashtra's rural economy. Change in food consumption patterns, from cereals to high protein diet, which includes meat, fish, eggs and dairy products, can give a boost to the livestock and fishery sectors. Forestry, besides creating employment and generating revenue also helps to maintain ecological balance in the state. Given the importance of allied activities, development in these sectors in the state over time is delineated in the subsequent sections.

Livestock Development

Technological changes in agriculture associated with the Green Revolution have brought about significant changes in the size, composition and productivity of livestock in Maharashtra as well as in several other areas of the country. The dynamics of changes in size and composition of livestock population in Maharashtra *vis-à-vis* India since 1956 are shown in Table 3.18.

The size of bovine head in this state registered an increase from 16.9 million in 1956 to 24.1 million by 1997. On the other hand, the total livestock population in the state grew from 23.8 million in 1956 to 39.6 million in 1997. In fact, Maharashtra accounts for around 8 per cent of the total livestock wealth of India and this share has remained by and large constant over the past 3-4 decades (Table 3.18). Further, over the course of time, the sex composition of bovine in the state has shifted in favour of females and breed composition in favour of crossbreeds (Shah, 1997). The male buffalo population in the state is seen to be in the process of erosion over time and females are replacing it. The poultry population in the state has shown much faster growth as compared to the growth in total livestock population. The total poultry birds in the state have grown dramatically from 8.8 million in 1956 to as high as 35.4 million in 1997 showing a fourfold increase (Table 3.18).

The scenario obtained over the past decade and a half also reveals dramatic transformation in livestock production of the state, particularly in the case of milk (Table 3.19). During the period between 1985 and 2000, the total milk production in the state registered a much faster growth rate as compared to that for India. The higher milk production in this state is mainly due to increase in productivity levels of various species of animals during the given period of time. Further, the ready acceptability of modern technology by the milk producers and intensive efforts of dairy cooperatives in providing balanced cattle feed, veterinary and health care services, and the availability of other infrastructure facilities have also played a positive role towards this increase in milk production in the state (Patel, 1993). However, there are still considerable regional imbalances in milk production. Regional imbalances in milk production are due to changes in agro-climatic conditions, extent of economic development, availability of irrigation facilities, etc. in different regions of the state.

TABLE 3.18

Livestock (including Poultry) Population Dynamics of Maharashtra and India

Indicators	*Maharashtra*			*India*		
	1956	*1972*	*1997*	*1956*	*1972*	*1997@*
I. Population Indicators Livestock (in 10^6)						
A. Cattle - Male	5.83	6.21	6.99	64.87	74.46	74.49
Female	4.27	4.58	5.89	49.89	56.40	64.36
Young Stock	4.06	3.92	5.19	43.80	47.48	65.73
Total	**14.16**	**14.71**	**18.07**	**158.56**	**178.34**	**204.58**
B. Buffalo – Male	0.30	0.30	0.31	6.51	8.07	8.09
Female	1.47	1.88	3.61	22.34	29.24	43.81
Young Stock	0.95	1.12	2.15	16.07	20.12	32.31
Total	**2.72**	**3.30**	**6.07**	**44.92**	**57.43**	**84.21**
C. Total Bovine	16.88	18.01	24.14	203.48	235.77	288.79
D. Sheep	1.96	2.59	3.37	39.25	39.99	50.78
E. Goats	4.61	5.91	11.43	55.41	67.52	115.28
F. Pigs	0.15	0.20	0.57	4.93	6.90	12.79
G. Equine	0.20	0.11	0.12	2.58	2.01	1.98
H. Camels	Neg.	Neg.	Neg.	0.78	1.11	1.03
Total Livestock	**23.80 (7.77)**	**26.82 (7.59)**	**39.63 (8.42)**	**306.50**	**353.34**	**470.86**
Poultry (in 10^6)	8.77	12.22	35.40	94.68	138.54	307.25
II. Other Indicators						
A. Draught Animal Population (10^6)	5.92	6.40	7.06	68.43	80.17	70.59
B. Draught Animal Power (DAP) (10^4 HP)	236.54	256.00	282.40	2737.20	3206.80	2823.60
C. Electric Pumpsets & Oil Engines (10^4)	2.88	34.35	96.40	16.80	317.50	1097.90
D. No. of Tractors	2320	6200	81353	20980	183800	1221800
E. Mechanical Power (MP) (10^4 HP)						
Pumpsets	1.05	84.90	425.90	23.00	809.00	3201.75
Oil Engines	13.36	86.84	57.75	61.00	778.50	2288.70
Tractor	5.80	15.50	203.38	52.45	459.50	3054.50
Total	**20.21**	**187.24**	**687.03**	**136.45**	**2047.00**	**8544.95**
A. Total Farm Power (TFP) (10^4 HP)	256.75	443.22	969.43	2873.65	5253.80	11368.55
B. Share of MP in TFP (%)	7.87	42.24	70.87	4.75	38.96	75.16
C. Share of DAP in TFP (%)	92.13	57.76	29.13	95.25	61.04	24.84

Note: It is assumed that one animal is equivalent to 0.4 HP, oil engines/pumpsets to 5 HP and tractor to 25 HP; @ - 1997 Livestock Census figures for India are not yet published. Figures in parentheses are percentages to the total livestock population of India.

Source: Computations are based on figures obtained from various livestock census reports of Maharashtra and India.

TABLE 3.19

Changing Structure of Livestock Production in Maharashtra *vis-à-vis* India

Production	*Triennium Ending*			*1985-2000*
	1987-88	*1991-92*	*1999-00*	*CGR(%)*
Milk Production (Million Tonnes)				
Maharashtra	2.47	4.10	5.40	7.13*
India	45.60	58.10	74.53	4.23
Share in India (%)	5.42	7.06	7.25	2.71
Wool Production (Metric Tonnes)				
Maharashtra	-	1487.54	1595.76	1.18*
India	-	40100	45500	2.04*
Share in India (%)		3.71	3.51	-0.85
Egg Production (Billion)				
Maharashtra	-	2.26	2.91	4.34*
India	-	23.04	30.07	4.51*
Share in India (%)		9.80	9.69	-0.17
Meat Production@ (in '000 MT)				
Maharashtra	159.257	151.210	203.056	2.30*
India	993.334	3420.667	3895.000	11.41*
Share in India (%)	16.03	4.42	5.21	-8.11*
Meat Production Per Animal (in Kgs)				
Maharashtra	21.577	24.054	27.857	2.80*

Notes: * - Implies significance of growth rates at one per cent level of probability; CGR - Annual Compound Growth; @ - excluding poultry meat.

Source: The estimates are based on figures obtained from various issues of "Report on Milk, Egg, Wool, Meat Production and Livestock and Poultry Keeping Practices in Maharashtra State", Department of Animal Husbandry, Maharashtra State, Pune.

It is also clearly evident from Table 3.19 that except for milk, all the products from livestock species in this state have shown slower growth during the period between 1985 and 2000 as compared to their growth for the nation as a whole. The growth rates in egg and wool production in the state have been marginally lower than the national average. The lower growth rate in wool production may be due to predominantly migratory nature of sheep flocks in the state. In the case of meat, the growth rate in production is so low that the state has shown a sharp decline in its share in India's total production of meat during the period between 1992 and 2000. The share of Maharashtra in India's total meat production is seen to have declined at the rate of 11 per cent a year during the given period (Table 3.19). It deserves mention here that meat in the state is produced from both authorised and unauthorised slaughterhouses. As the estimates of meat production from unauthorised slaughterhouses are unavailable, it is difficult to arrive at realistic estimates of meat production in the state. And, this might have caused a decline in Maharashtra's share in India's total meat production. Nonetheless, insofar as the meat production is concerned, the productivity levels of various species of animals in the state showed an upward trend during this period. This is also corroborated from the fact that the number of animals slaughtered in the state has shown a decline over time. However, there still exists vast scope for increasing livestock productivity in the state by following improved animal husbandry practices.

Fisheries Development

Maharashtra accounts for a significant share (around 16 per cent) so far as marine fish production in the country is concerned. The estimates relating to fisheries development in Maharashtra encompassing the period from 1979 and 1999 are provided in Table 3.20. The state of Maharashtra has 720 km of coastline. There are as many as 32 varieties of fish harvested/produced in Maharashtra. Among these varieties, shrimps, prawns, harpodon neherias, ribbon fish, otalithes, pomfrets, anchoviella, mackeral and cattle fish put together account for over 70 per cent share in total fish production of Maharashtra. As for various regions, Brihan Mumbai and Thane alone account for about 60 per cent of the total fish catch of Maharashtra. However, over the course of time, the shares of these regions in total fish catch of Maharashtra have declined marginally.

It is to be further noted that the share of Maharashtra in total fish production of India has steadily declined over the past two decades mainly due to a sharp decline in her share in total marine fish production of India (Table 3.20). However, over time, the state has shown considerable increase in the quantum strength of marine-fishing villages/hamlets, boats engaged in fishing, fish brought for curing, salt issued, cured fish removed, besides in the number of fish cooperative societies and their membership, etc. (Table 3.20).

Another disquieting feature of fisheries sector of Maharashtra is the decline in the number of fish curing yards, which have come down by 45 per cent during the period under consideration. On the other hand, the number of fishery schools in the state has stagnated at nine over the last two decades. The declining trends in inland water spread area, numerical strength of fish curing yards and stagnant number of fishery schools are certainly disturbing features of the fisheries sector of Maharashtra. However, in order to develop fisheries sector, the department of fisheries in the state is conducting various training programmes relating to carp fish seed production, fresh water prawn culture, integrated fish farming and management of aquarium, etc.

TABLE 3.20

Fisheries Development in Maharashtra: 1979-80 to 1998-99

Particulars	*Triennium Ending*			*1979-1999*
	1981-82	*1991-92*	*1998-99*	*CGR*
TCS	720	720	720	-
MFV	375	386	391	Neg.
BEF	12503	15712	18345	2.24*
BAOT	6834	9061	13005	4.21*
MB – D	3058	3939	4544	2.07*
MB – E	4072	7047	8734	4.41*
QFBC	8384	3083	15093	8.38
QSI	1732	697	2885	8.12
QCFR	6420	2140	10820	8.22
FP - M	340	372	436	1.37*
I	25	61	112	7.40*
T	365	433	548	1.86**
ALL India				
FP - M	1498	2347	2662	3.89*
I	912	1549	2381	6.08*
T	2410	3896	5043	4.81*
SMI - M	22.70	15.89	16.38	-2.43*
I	2.74	3.94	4.70	1.25
T	15.15	11.11	10.87	-2.82*
FCS 535	1547	2202	8.92*	
MCOOP.	177	190	221	2.29*
IWSA	310	301	300	-
FCY	20	7	11	-1.95*
FS	9	9	9	-
DFC	-	473344	536303	3.87*

Notes: 1) CGR: Compound growth rate (annual) (in %)
2) * and ** indicate significance of growth rates one and five per cent level of probability
3) TCS: Total coastline of state (in Kms.)
MFV: No. of marine fishing villages
BEF: No. of boats engaged in fishing
BAOT: No. of boats above one tonne
MB – D: No. of mechanised boats – departmentally
MB – E: No. of mechanised boats –existing
QFBC: Quantity of fish brought for curing (in tonnes)
QSI: Quantity of salt issued (in tonnes)
QCFR: Quantity of cured fish removed (in tonnes)
FP – M, I, T: fish production – marine; inland, total (in '000 tonnes); SMI – M, I, T: Share of Maharashtra in india (%)- Marine, Inland, Total
FCS: No. of Fish Cooperative Societies; MCOOP : Membership of Cooperatives (in '000); IWSA: Total inland water
Spread Area (in '000 Ha); FCY: No. of fish curing yard, fs: no. of fishing schools; DFC: Disposition of fish catch (in tonnes)

Source: Handbook of Basic Statistics of Maharashtra.

Forestry

Maharashtra accounts for about 7.3 per cent of the total forest area of India and the share of Maharashtra in country's total wasteland stands at around 12.3 per cent (GoI, 1998a). The land utilisation figures for Maharashtra during the period between 1980-81 to 1982-83 and 1994-95 to 1996-97 reveal a marginal decline in barren and uncultivated land and an increase in land put to non-agricultural uses. Permanent pastures and other grazing lands have also declined sharply during the given period of time. On the other hand, the current and other fallow lands have increased over time. While decline in barren and uncultivable land may be considered as desirable for the state's forest economy, the increases in land put to non-agricultural uses, current and other fallow land and at the same time decline in permanent pastures and other grazing land are certainly disturbing phenomena.

Growth in various forest related indicators of Maharashtra encompassing the period between 1980-81 and 1995-96 are provided in Table 3.21. A critical evaluation of Table 3.21 shows a marginal decline in value of forest produce harvested during the period between TE 1989-90 and TE 1995-96 in face of sharp increase in the same between TE 1982-83 and 1989-90. The decline in forest produce harvested is mainly due to sharp decline in forest area harvested, especially after the late eighties period. It is to be noted that during the late eighties the government had banned felling of trees in many parts of the state. This had not only affected forest area harvested, but also value of forest produce harvested. This had in turn affected revenue receipts from state forestry. On the other hand, expenditure on various forest-related activities grew sharply, so much so that a deficit of the order of around Rs. 900 million was noticed in revenue receipts from state forestry during the period between TE 1989-1990 and TE 1995-96. Further, in due course of time, there has been a considerable increase in outstanding forest revenue because of increases in amount of outstanding forest revenue due from forest contractors, non-receipt of dues from forest labour cooperative societies and non-receipt of *challans* from treasury.

The ban on felling of trees has also led to sharp decline in total number of coupes worked in forest area and also labour employment in forestry operations. On the positive side there has been decline in forest offences. The area under various plantation activities has increased considerably over time. Afforested area has grown over 10 per cent a year during the period

TABLE 3.21

Changing Structure in Forestry Related Indicators of Maharashtra: 1982-1996

Particulars	*Triennium Ending*			*1980-1996*
	1982-83	*1989-90*	*1995-96*	*CGR(%)*
Total State Revenue (in Rs.10 Million)	2341.67	6307.00	14878.00	15.17
Revenue from Forest (in Rs. 10 Million)	67.47	129.41	129.17	4.66
Forest Revenue to State Revenue (per cent)	2.88	2.05	0.87	-9.15
Total Expenditure on Forest (in Rs. 10 Million)	39.60	105.71	218.28	24.06
Total Forest Area (Sq. Km.)	62254	62882	64424	0.21NS
Forest Area as % of Total Geographical Area of State	20.87	20.75	20.22	-0.18NS
Labour Employed in Forestry ('000 Man-days)	26877	40518	35238	3.06
Wages Paid to Labour (in Rs. One Hundred Thousand)	1866	5819	9802	17.05
Total No. of Coupes Worked	825	664	279	-17.16
Outstanding Forest Revenue (in Rs. One Hundred Thousand)	765.36	1760.61	2267.27	9.57
Total Value of Forest Produce Harvested (in Rs. One Hundred Thousand)	5040.60	11556.31	11098.48	7.42
Total Forest Area Harvested (Sq. Km)	786.43	293.74	218.10	-17.58
Number of Forest Offences	87109	84121	66475	-2.14
Number of Fires	1376	1343	1633	1.72NS
Size of Fire (Sq. Km.)	214.67	336.89	436.67	5.16
Plantation under Various Activities (Ha)	23393	23781	58821	5.37
Afforestation under Various Activities (Ha)	28221	71032	87760	10.01
Percentage of Forest Area worked by – Forest Dept.	57.67	42.33	68.75	31.25
-FLCS	71.33	28.67	1.49NS	-3.19NS

Note: CGR-Compared growth rates; All growth rates significant at one per cent level of probability. NS-Not Significant at one per cent level of probability.

between TE 1982-83 and 1995-96. Another interesting feature of the state forestry is the increasing trend in outturn of minor forest produce (Table 3.22). This could be due to increase in the exploitation of minor forest produce, especially in the face of the ban on harvesting of major forest produce. It is to be noted that, of late, forest conservation and biodiversity issues have acquired newer dimensions. Therefore, management of minor forest produce as a viable alternative to major forest produce has begun to attract attention (Shah, 2000). The measures initiated by the government to conserve its forest resources are certainly a welcome development. However, the exorbitant cost of protection and preservation of forest resources could be a matter of concern, especially when there is deficit in revenue receipts from state forestry in more recent times. A more appropriate strategy could be to adopt such policy measures that not only prevent felling of trees in certain parts of the state but also help in intensifying afforestation in some other identified parts of the state and, at the same time, allow harvesting of high yielding varieties of major and minor forest produce in certain specific pockets of the state. The balance in the same could not only have helped to increase its revenue receipts from state forestry, but also in respect of achieving its goal of maintaining ecological balance in the state.

TABLE 3.22

Out-turn of Forest Produce in Maharashtra
(Quantity in '000 Cum and Value in '00,000 Rs.)

Forest Produce	*Triennium Ending*			*1980-1996*
	1982-83	*1989-90*	*1995-96*	*CGR(%)*
TVMNFP	1028.26	3188.07	5720.32	18.97
TVMJFP	4012.35	8368.24	5378.16	1.81NS
TOFP	5040.61	11556.31	11098.48	7.42

Notes: 1-3) As in Table 3.21; 4) TVMNFP: Total value of minor forest produce; TVMJFP: Total value of major forest produce; TOFP: Total out turn of forest produce.

Constraints on Agricultural Growth

Agriculture plays a major role with respect to employment as 55.3 per cent of the workforce is engaged in this sector. This figure rapidly rises to 69 per cent, when we exclude Mumbai, the commercial capital of India, indicating that in almost all districts in Maharashtra, agriculture is the main source of livelihood. This indicates very limited non-farm development. The problem is further aggravated because agriculture in the state is mainly rainfed as barely 16 per cent of the GCA is irrigated. More than half the districts have irrigated area below the state average. Further, one-third area of the state falls under rain-shadow region, with scanty rainfall. In fact, rainfall is uncertain in all districts, with the exception of the Konkan region. The state has the distinction of having more than 24 per cent of drought-prone area of the country. Almost 73 per cent of the area of the state falls in the semi-arid region. The state therefore faces major problems and constraints associated with rainfed agriculture such as low yields, crop failures and uncertainties due to erratic rainfall pattern. Lack of access to water also inhibits the use of other inputs such as high yielding varieties of seeds and fertilisers, thus widening the gap between potential and actual yields. Low value crops such as coarse cereals, therefore dominate the cropping pattern, which reduces the income generating potential of farmers. Thus, poor resources decrease the capacity of farmers to take risks and invest in improved technologies as well as land improvement.

Land degradation is also emerging as a major problem in Maharashtra. The National Bureau of Soil Survey and Land Use Planning estimated that about 86 per cent of land area in the Western Ghats and 75 per cent in the Konkan coast suffer from severe to strong soil erosion. Land degradation reduces the productivity of land and total loss to the state economy from soil erosion is estimated at Rs. 30 billion (Rural Development and Water Conservation Department, GoM).

The main source of water for agriculture in the state is groundwater. The area irrigated by wells accounts for 67 per cent of net irrigated area. This water is primarily drawn from the ground, using electric pumpsets. Excessive withdrawals of groundwater have contributed to the drying up of wells in several districts. Declining water tables may lead to scarcity of water in the future. There are also threats to the sustainability of surface irrigation due to deterioration of canal systems and inability to collect water charges from farmers.

While productivity levels are low due to natural constraints, government interventions to diversify agriculture, from low value coarse cereals to high value commercial crops such as sugarcane, cotton and horticultural crops, have not been free from problems. The direct and indirect support of the GoM to 147 sugar cooperatives in the state, besides 57 being in the erection stage is adding to the fiscal burden of the state as large number of them are sick and incurring huge losses. Further, since sugarcane is a highly water intensive crop, cultivation of this crop is leading to declining water tables and environmental degradation. Also, area irrigated with groundwater is through electric pump sets and the subsidy on power to agriculture further adds to fiscal crisis. Besides, increasing support to the sugar sector, total state intervention with respect to cotton is also a burden to the state exchequer. Further, the yield of both these crops is a cause for concern. White woolly sugarcane aphid, which is a common pest, infests the sugarcane crop and farmers are unable to combat this pest, which lowers their yield. In the case of cotton, about 166 different species of insect pests are reported to attack cotton at various stages of growth. Farmers lack adequate extension services on use of pesticides, which leads to pest resurgence. Further, often the quality of pesticides is sub-standard and spurious and timely availability of these inputs act as a constraint.

While attempts to promote the horticulture and floriculture sector are a welcome step, there are likely to emerge certain challenges and constraints in the development of these sectors. Plants have a high mortality rate in areas where there are water constraints and there is non-availability of specifically prescribed pesticides and nutrients. Besides infrastructure bottlenecks also exist such as poor condition of rural roads, improper post harvest handling, storage, processing, etc. In case of exports also there exist bottlenecks such as inadequate cold storage facilities at Mumbai international airport and shortage of cargo space on international flights. Also, meeting stringent export quality standards is made difficult as farmers lack awareness on scientific cultural practices. Due to such constraints, the state may not be able to fully capitalise on its export potential.

Under the State APMC Act, the law requires that all notified agricultural produce bought or sold within the market area must pass through the market yard or sub-yard managed by the APMC. This precludes any private agency from setting up an alternative marketing system to operate outside the purview of the notified markets. Thus besides natural constraints, at times even government policies impede agricultural growth, besides adding to the fiscal burden.

Policy Implications

About 58 per cent of Maharashtra's population continues to reside in rural areas with agriculture as the dominant source of livelihood. However, growth rate of this sector (1980-81 to 2000-01) is far lower than that of the secondary and tertiary sectors. Therefore, attempts have to be made to overcome the constraints and increase the productivity and competitiveness of this sector. The government may also have to reformulate its policies and priorities to create an environment suitable to agricultural growth. Equally important is the need to promote rural non-farm employment so that the burden in the agricultural sector is reduced. Growth in both these sectors will generate more rural income, stimulate consumer demand and give a boost to other economic sectors.

Agricultural productivity and hence its growth potential depend to a large extent on availability of irrigation. Irrigation helps *kharif* crops when there is a failure of rainfall and has a substantial effect in increasing the productivity of crops grown in the *rabi* season such as wheat, *rabi jowar,* etc. Water constraints also inhibit the use of complementary inputs such as HYVs and fertilisers. Thus, top priority must be given to bridge the gap between irrigation potential created and actual area under irrigation. The number of wells in the state is also increasing but it is burdensome for marginal and small farmer to bear the cost of a well. Constructing community wells may ease this problem. This may also lead to better utilisation of available groundwater. Besides development of irrigation facilities, watershed development is also very necessary to stabilise the carrying capacity of land and water resources in rainfed areas. A successful implementation of such programmes involves wholehearted participation of beneficiaries. These strategies generate employment and the bulk of the costs of such programmes can be accounted for by wages, which can be paid in kind, through grains obtained from Food Corporation of India (Mujumdar, 2002). Thus the GoM instead of thinly spreading the available investible resources over wide areas, should concentrate on few strategically selected areas for intensive development, such as completion of irrigation projects already underway and massive watershed development programmes. The state must also make fuller utilisation of resources available from NABARD's RIDF facility. Public investment in agriculture is reported to be declining. Agriculture and allied sectors, being the priority sectors in the future growth of the state, should be given due emphasis and necessary measures need to be drawn up for streamlining the credit flow in this sector.

Besides the development of irrigation facilities and watersheds, the government policy of encouraging the cultivation of very water intensive crops, notably sugarcane must be reconsidered. Increase in area under sugarcane is due to high profitability in cane cultivation relative to other crops, as well as preferential treatment extended to cooperative sugar factories. There are, however, concerns about the sustainability of this water intensive crop in water scarce state of Maharashtra. Use of micro-irrigation systems such as drip can be viewed as a solution to the growing water scarcity as well as to safeguard the sugarcane area from potential threats of waterlogging and salinity.

The GoM should also withdraw its support to the cooperative sugar mills and in the cotton sector; it should phase out the monopoly procurement scheme. Perhaps, a move is being made in this direction with respect to cotton, as during the 2003-04 cotton season, private traders as well as Cotton Corporation of India (CCI) were allowed to enter the market. Since state intervention in sugar and cotton sector have had a huge fiscal impact, alternative strategies to manage the uncertainty and risks inherent in agricultural markets, such as futures trading must be encouraged. The hedging and price discovery functions of futures markets will help to achieve efficiency in agricultural marketing. However, the physical markets of commodities encounter a number of impediments, such as government control and regulations, monopoly procurement (in the case of cotton), minimum support price, etc. Thus, all major hurdles that come in the way of proper functioning of futures trading must be removed so that it can function smoothly.

Attempts to shift to high value horticultural crops through an employment guarantee scheme is a step in the right direction. The state, which catered earlier to domestic markets, is now making inroads into international markets. Maharashtra has great export potential for fruits such as grapes and pomegranates because although there is competition from other countries, the basic advantage is that these fruits are available in the months of March and April only in Maharashtra. The state can therefore try and achieve maximum exports during these months. In case of floriculture also, there exists great export potential as there is peak demand in European markets in colder months due to festival season and the climate in India during these months is conducive for floriculture.

In order to fully capitalise on exports, it is necessary to invest in post-harvest technology and ensure that there are no infrastructure bottlenecks. While the establishment of WTO has led to the expansion of international economic activity, technical measures such as food quality and sanitary and phyto-sanitary requirements can impede trade. It is, therefore, necessary to educate farmers on quality standards and phyto-sanitary codes. The GoM is also in the process of setting up Agri Export Zones for Kesar mangoes, oranges, pomegranates, onions, etc. Marathwada has a good production base for Kesar mangoes and this region being drought prone with limited opportunities for agriculture can take advantage of the Agri Export Zone and become an important player in the international market. Similarly, an Agri Export Zone in Vidarbha for oranges may help to stimulate the agricultural economy of the region.

Barely 3 per cent of all fruits and vegetables from the state are processed as against 50 to 80 per cent in developed countries such as the USA and Brazil. As production of fruits is likely to increase, government as well as private sector, to promote value addition, must further promote agro-processing units. Private sector investment in agro-processing may be encouraged through contract farming through which farmers can receive inputs, extension services and all logistical support, besides an assured market. Use of IT for dissemination of information to farmers and upgradation of knowledge, skills, and communication capacity of extension personnel will help to increase agricultural performance. Necessary facilities for skill upgradation of graduates in agricultural science for setting up agri-business centres through training programmes under the ongoing 'Agri Clinics and Agri Business Scheme' of the Ministry of Agriculture must be availed.

Reforms pertaining to rural credit also assume importance. There is a need to increase PLCP outlay for Marathwada, Vidarbha and Konkan regions. Further, there is a need for cooperative and commercial banks to study the mechanism of new generation lending institutions like SHGs in terms of their pattern of loan recovery and interest rate structure, particularly in the light of the fact that they show high rate of recovery despite higher rate of interest on loan advances. In fact, the studies conducted earlier have clearly shown lower transaction costs and higher recovery performance of SHGs (Gulati and Bathla, 2002). These groups are also reported to have favourably impacted the social and economic status of their members. Further, the RFIs of Maharashtra are also seen to be beset with high levels of NPAs or overdues. There is, therefore, a need to take more stringent and cohesive measures for recovery of loans from chronic and heavy defaulters. In brief, in order to rejuvenate rural credit delivery system, the twin problems facing the system, *viz.*, high transaction costs and poor repayment performance, need to be tackled (Mujumdar, 2001). In fact, insofar as the rural credit delivery system is concerned, the focus should be on strategies that are required for tackling issues such as sustainability and viability, operational efficiency, recovery performance, small farmer coverage and balanced sectoral development (Puhazhendhi and Jayaraman, 1999).

The GoM must also reform the APMC Act, 1963, to allow private parties to develop agricultural markets in the state as this would facilitate the construction of more markets and also improvement in market infrastructure.

Allied activities, which provide supplementary and complementary employment and also add to the income of the farmers, must be promoted. With respect to the livestock economy, it may be noted that, first, while draught animals are not displaced by other sources of farm power, there is a sharp increase in the stock of female bovine population. This trend is desirable in the light of the growing economic opportunities for increasing milk production and for undertaking dairying as a commercial enterprise. In fact, the slowing down in the growth of work animals has been concomitant with the expansion of milch animal population in Maharashtra, which showed over 53 per cent growth between 1956 and 1997. One of the observations of Vaidyanathan (1987) and Nair and Das (1990) is also in favour of this trend. Second, the increasing use of mechanical equipment for cultivation in lieu of additional animal power will progressively increase the rural demand for energy, i.e., for electricity, diesel, etc. Therefore, there must be adequate investment in power sector in the future to accommodate this increasing rural demand for power. Lastly, as for livestock production, there still exists a vast scope for increasing livestock productivity by following improved animal husbandry practices. The prospects for increasing livestock production in the state will also depend on the extent to which farmers undertake fodder cultivation as an integral part of livestock production.

In order to develop fisheries sector in Maharashtra, there is need to educate fishermen with respect to dissemination of information relating to modern/ mechanised fishing techniques and efficient marketing of fish catch. Education of fishermen about modern fishing techniques is reported to have a significant impact on adoption of recommended fish culture practices by the farmers (Sivasankar, *et al.*, 1995). It is also pointed out that extension and mass media participation have strong positive relationship with adoption of fish culture practices (Prabhakara and Murthy, 1994). Nonetheless, inadequate infrastructure and flow of information technology have been cited as the major barriers for better market integration in the existing marine fish markets of India (Behura and Pradhan, 1998). There, however, exists vast scope for exploitation of offshore fishery resources through introduction of newly designed fuel saving multi-day mechanised fishing vessels and deep sea fishing vessels. Measures must also be taken to increase production of both marine inland fisheries from reservoirs, etc. and culture fisheries to increase the overall fish production.

With respect to forestry, afforestation of the waste and unproductive lands has acquired new dimensions and importance (Yadav, 1980; Chaturvedi, 1985). Unfortunately, the waste and other fallow lands in the state are increasing over time. Earlier, afforestation in wastelands of village *panchayats* was stressed by Joshi and Agnihotri (1983). Efforts, therefore, should be made to bring these lands under forest cover of the state. Further, efforts should also be made to curtail expenditure on forest related activities, which have shown to grow at an alarming rate of 24 per cent a year during the period between TE 1982-83 and 1995-96. Equally, important is to recover outstanding forest revenue.

On the whole, it appears that the state of Maharashtra must use water judiciously, reduce its intervention in sensitive crops like cotton and sugar, capitalise on its horticultural and floriculture sector, further promote allied activities, strengthen rural infrastructure and encourage private sector participation and investment in agriculture. Such strategies along with promotion of rural non-farm employment will stimulate the agricultural sector.

Chapter 4

Irrigation

Introduction

The irrigation sector in Maharashtra is one of the largest in the country, both in terms of the number of large dams and the live storage capacity. Nevertheless, the irrigation sector of Maharashtra has been facing multifarious problems. While the water availability for the future use of irrigation has been reducing at a fast rate, the demand for water for irrigation purposes has been alarmingly increasing due to agricultural expansion and intensification.

According to the estimate of the Maharashtra Water and Irrigation Commission (GoM, 1999), water available from both surface and groundwater can irrigate at most about 60 per cent of the cultivated land. The actual utilisation of irrigation potential created through major and medium irrigation (MMI) sector was only 1.73 million hectares (60.05 per cent) as against the created potential of 2.88 million hectares up to the end of Ninth Plan period (GoI, 2003a). This is very low when compared to the average utilisation percentage of the country (CWC, 2000). Besides this, the financial recovery rate of state's irrigation sector is also very low. Despite revision of water rates at a regular interval, the revenue of irrigation sector is not even enough to maintain the operation and maintenance (O&M) cost of the sector.

Though the state has the second largest live storage capacity, the percentage of irrigated area to gross cropped area is one of the lowest among the major states, mainly due to the improper distribution of water among different crops. New water-saving technologies such as drip irrigation have been introduced in the state aiming to improve the water use efficiency through subsidy programmes. Though presently the state ranks first in the area under drip irrigation, not many studies have attempted to find out its potential and prospects, including its economic viability. Keeping in view the above-mentioned problems, we try to examine the important issues that are faced by the irrigation sector of the state over the last 40 years. This study uses secondary level information for all its analyses.

This chapter is organised into nine sections. The first section deals with irrigation potential available, harnessed and utilised, since the First Plan. Changes that have taken place in the available water potential, trends in water potential harnessed and utilised, the gap between potential created and utilised among different sources of water are also examined in this section. The second section focuses on investment made on the irrigation sector since the First Plan across different sources. The pattern of public and private investment on different sources of irrigation, the relationship between the potential created and the investment made on different sources of irrigation, investment required to create one hectare of irrigation (cost efficiency), etc., are also studied.

The growth of irrigation projects and its associated issues are discussed in section three. Section four brings out the trends and development of irrigated area by crops besides looking at the consumption of water by crops and their importance in the economy of the state. Financial performance of the irrigation sector which includes prevailing water rates for different crops, changes introduced in water rates over the years, relationship between O&M costs and water rates, profits and losses, reasons for poor recovery rate, etc., are studied in section five. Importance of micro (drip) irrigation, water saving and productivity gains, economic viability of drip irrigation, its prospects and potentials etc., are studied in section six.

Section seven focuses on the role of users' participation in conserving water and its current status, the impact of watershed development programme on water availability, total investment made on watershed programmes including its area coverage, etc. The eighth section on demand and supply scenario of irrigation water highlights the sector-wise demand and supply position of water in Maharashtra including the present and future scenarios.

The ninth section on irrigation and productivity nexus discusses the productivity differences of irrigated and non-irrigated crops as well as the relationship between growth of irrigation and production of crops. Policy suggestions that emerge from the analysis are presented in section 10.

Irrigation Potential Harnessed and Utilised

As per the data of Central Water Commission (CWC), the total irrigation potential of the country is estimated to be 139.86 million hectares (mha) from all sources namely major and medium irrigation (MMI), minor irrigation surface (MIS) and Minor irrigation groundwater (MIG). Maharashtra's total irrigation potential is estimated to be 8.96 mha comprising of 4.10 mha from MMI, 1.20 mha from MIS and 3.65 mha from MIG. This accounts for only 6.40 per cent of the country's total potential of irrigation. Though substantial water potential is available along west coast (Konkan) of the state, it may not be easily possible to utilise the same because of want of suitable sites for construction of dams and also due to prohibitive cost of lifting the water to the east of Sahyadri for its use in the drought-prone area. This has resulted in lesser irrigation potential despite higher total water availability in the state.

Irrigation potential of the state is on the lower side in relation to its size of rural population and gross cropped area. For instance, the state ranks second in gross cropped area (GCA) in India by occupying about 11.45 per cent of GCA in 2001-02. Similarly, the share of rural population of the state is about 7.53 per cent in India in 2000-01. Given the limited availability of water and increasing demand for irrigation and from different sectors, there is going to be a tremendous pressure in the near future for water available in the state.

As regards trends in potential created and utilised, the status of the state up to the end of Ninth Plan was not very encouraging especially in MMI when compared to other states and national level average. The state has created a total potential of 2.88 mha through MMI source up to Ninth Plan period, of which only about 60 per cent is actually utilised. This is very low when compared to the average national level percentage of utilisation, which is about 89 per cent (GoI, 2003). What is interesting is that the utilisation per cent of MMI has been consistently declining from 83.6 per cent in Third Plan (1961-1966) to 60 per cent in 2001-02, a decline of 23.60 per cent points. The rate of decline of utilisation percentage is found to be faster in the state as compared to the national level average, where it declined only by about 5 per cent points (from 90.29 per cent to 85.02 per cent) during the same period (Table 4.1). The administrators who worked with the state irrigation department argue that the less utilisation of irrigation water in MMI sector is mainly because of two reasons. First, intensive irrigation to water consuming crops like sugarcane has drastically reduced the total area actually irrigated (when compared with projected irrigated area) and reduced the utilisation percentage. Second, the appreciable increase in allocation of water for domestic and industrial purposes from the reservoirs when compared with the allocation as per project planning has also reduced the utilisation percentage. However, this argument is somewhat different from the results of earlier studies, which show that inadequate availability of funds for developing hardware aspects of irrigation such as construction of main canals and distribution systems which take water to the farmers' field are the main reasons for the less utilisation of irrigation potential created (World Bank, 2002; GoI, 1992; Vaidyanathan, 1999). Although the reasons for low utilisation per cent of MMI are different, one would hope that the establishment of five Irrigation Development Corporations (IDCs) during 1996-1998 would take measures to increase both the creation of irrigation potential and percentage of utilisation relatively faster in the state in the future.

Utilisation percentage of MIS has also declined sharply in the state, from 82.1 per cent in Sixth Plan (1980-1985) to 65 per cent in 1999-00, which is comparable to the national level average, where it declined from 92.9 to 63.5 per cent during the same period. MIS caters to the needs of marginal and small farmers and therefore, any further reduction in it will have serious implications on these farmer groups. In contrast to surface irrigation sources, utilisation percentage of MIG (groundwater), which is predominantly owned and managed by farmers themselves, is relatively higher in the state. In fact, though the level of utilisation is only about 75 per cent at the end of 1999-00, the utilisation percentage of groundwater has been in the range of 96 to 97 per cent since 1980-81 in the state. Relatively higher number of electric pump sets used for lifting water from wells, flat-rate electricity tariff policy (on horse power basis) followed for agriculture and less availability of surface sources of water must have prompted the farmers to exploit groundwater and fully utilise the created potential of groundwater. Though the percentage of utilisation of irrigation is higher in the state as per the data of Planning Commission (GoI, 2003), the actual utilisation of irrigation potential created in the state sector, as per the Economic Survey of Maharashtra: 2000-01, was only 34.7 per cent (1.654 mha) as against the created potential of 4.769 million hectares at the end of June 2000 (GoM, 2002).

TABLE 4.1

Development of Irrigation Potential and its Utilisation

(Cumulative Area in Mha)

Source	*Fourth Plan (1969-74)*		*Ninth Plan (1997-2002)*	
	India	*M.S.*	*India*	*M.S.*
MMI				
Potential	20.70	0.84	34.99	2.88
Utilisation	18.69	0.49	29.75	1.73
	(90.29)	(58.33)	(85.02)	(60.05)
MIS				
Potential	6.96[a]	0.40[a]	13.02[b]	1.59[b]
Utilisation	6.96	0.40	8.27[b]	1.04[b]
	(100)	(100)	(65.32)	(65.41)
MIG				
Potential	16.44	0.93	53.07[b]	3.41[b]
Utilisation	16.44	0.93	41.08[b]	2.37[b]
	(100)	(100)	(77.41)	(69.50)
Total				
Potential	43.83	2.17	95.40	5.71
Utilisation	42.09	1.82	85.40	4.30
	(96.03)	(83.87)	(89.52)	(75.31)

Notes: Figures in parentheses are percentage of utilisation.
a- Utilisation figures are not available separately.
b- provisional figures up to 1999-00 and therefore, total may not tally.

Source: CWC (2002); GoI (2002).

Investment in Irrigation Sector

Considering the vast area under rainfed cultivation and the importance of irrigation in agricultural development of the state, planners have given adequate thrust for irrigation development since the Third Plan period—planning in Maharashtra started with the third five year plan. In the total plan expenditure of the state, the share of irrigation and flood control expenditure increased from 14.87 per cent (Rs. 0.65 billion) in Third Plan to 33.36 per cent (Rs. 153.93 billion) in Ninth Plan period (GoM, 2002). The total investment made on irrigation in Maharashtra is the largest as compared to any other state in India. Up to the Ninth Plan period (2001-02) for which we have comparable data, altogether Rs. 236.22 billion (in current prices) has been spent only on irrigation development (Table 4.2). This accounts for over 17.30 per cent of the country's total investment on irrigation, which is about Rs. 1360.65 billion, excluding investment on Command Area Development Programme and flood control. The state not only accounts for higher share in the total investment made on MMI but also in MI state as well as in MI institutional investment. While MMI investment of the state accounts for 17.78 per cent in India's total investment, MI state and MI institutional investments account for 16.91 per cent and 15.44 per cent respectively up to Ninth Plan period (CWC, 2002 and GoI, 2003).

TABLE 4.2

Sector-wise Total Investment in Irrigation up to Ninth Plan

(Rs. in Billion)

States	*MMI*	*MI*		*Total*
		State	*Institutional*	
Andhra Pradesh	111.05 (11.55)	16.32 (6.57)	22.60 (15.01)	149.97 (11.02)
Bihar	53.91 (5.61)	17.19 (6.92)	4.46 (2.96)	75.56 (5.55)
Gujarat	135.80 (14.12)	18.42 (7.42)	6.71 (4.46)	160.93 (11.83)
Haryana	29.84 (3.10)	5.03 (2.03)	7.04 (4.67)	41.91 (3.08)
Karnataka	103.33 (10.75)	13.12 (5.28)	10.51 (6.98)	126.97 (9.33)
Madhya Pradesh	64.20 (6.68)	24.87 (10.01)	11.33 (7.52)	100.39 (7.38)
Maharashtra	**170.96 (17.78)**	**42.02 (16.91)**	**23.25 (15.44)**	**236.22 (17.36)**
Punjab	12.20 (1.27)	5.18 (2.08)	7.37 (4.89)	24.74 (1.82)
Tamil Nadu	19.42 (2.02)	8.97 (3.61)	7.73 (5.14)	36.13 (2.66)
Uttar Pradesh	79.38 (8.25)	23.59 (9.50)	27.94 (18.55)	130.91 (9.62)
West Bengal	18.29 (1.90)	9.35 (3.77)	2.63 (1.75)	30.27 (2.22)
India	**961.63**	**248.44**	**150.59**	**1360.66**

Notes: Figures in parentheses are percentage to total investment.

Source: CWC (2002); GoI (2003).

In contrast to the traditional practice, one important change has taken place in irrigation investment in the

TABLE 4.3

Details of Irrigation Development Corporations Established in Maharashtra

(Rs. Billion)

Name of IDC	*Number of Irrigation Projects Incorporated*	*Total Funds Required*	*Govt.'s Share Capital*		*Funds to be Raised*	*Funds Raised up to 2001-02*	*Funds to be Raised during 2002-03*	*Targeted Irrigation Potential (mha)*
			Total	*Paid up to 2001-02*				
MKVDC (January, 1996)	23[a]/50[b]/324[c]/12[d]	95.64	35.00	14.25	81.60	54.63	4.14	1.085
VIDC (March, 1997)	14[a]/27[b]/55[c]	76.07	22.45	2.65	59.01	14.72	8.12	1.100
TIDC (March, 1997)	8[a]/37[b]/115[c]/10[d]	51.97	14.00	1.02	32.75	10.54	1.53	0.523
KIDC (December, 1997)	1[a]/4[b]/33[c]	9.37	2.73	0.49	6.17	3.98	1.54	0.109
GMIDC (August, 1998)	13[a]/24[b]/237[c]	32.66	13.00	2.41	26.00	13.90	5.81	0.561

Notes: a - Major; b - Medium; c - Minor; d - Lift Irrigation Scheme; Year of establishment of IDC is given in parentheses; MKVDC-Maharashtra Krishna Valley Development Corporation; VIDC-Vidarbha Irrigation Development Corporation; TIDC-Tapi Irrigation Development Corporation; KIDC-Konkan Irrigation Development Corporation; GMIDC-Godavari-Marathwada Irrigation Development Corporation.

Source: GoM, 2003.

state during the nineties. So far, almost the whole investment on irrigation especially on surface irrigation (MMI and MI) was directly made by the public sector. But, due to severe financial constraints, public sector was no longer in a position to allocate required investment for irrigation development. In order to avoid such constraints, a few states including Maharashtra established IDCs. Between 1996 and 1998, state government has established five IDCs, which mobilised Rs. 97.77 billion from public by selling state-guaranteed bonds up to 2001-02 (Table 4.3). Besides harnessing and utilising the water resources in different river basins, IDCs are responsible for surveying, planning, designing, executing, constructing and managing all projects in their respective river basins (World Bank, 2002). Though responsibilities of IDCs are many, these IDCs have been facing lot of difficulties in raising resources from the market by issue of bonds and debentures. For instance, it was planned to raise Rs. 32 billion from the market during 2003-04, but the actual realisation was only Rs. 2 billion till October 2003. Given the financial constraints, these IDCs will have to face severe challenges in accomplishing their objectives in the coming years.

While the investment on irrigation has been increasing in successive Plan periods, there is hardly any relationship between the investment on irrigation and area created from each Plan period. For instance, during Sixth Plan period, the state has spent Rs. 11.87 billion on MMI and created about 0.458 million hectares of irrigated area, by spending only about Rs. 25,921/ha. But, this has totally changed during Seventh and Eighth Plan periods (Table 4.4). With an investment of Rs. 37.07 billion during Eighth Plan period, the states could create only about 0.351 million hectares from MMI source. That is, the average investment required to create one hectare of irrigation increased to Rs. 10,5613 during Eighth Plan period.

TABLE 4.4

Plan-wise Per Hectare Cost of Creation of Irrigation Potential: Maharashtra and India

(Rs. in Current Prices)

Plan	*Maharashtra*		*India*	
	MMI	*MI*	*MMI*	*MI*
Third	4894	NA	2582	1953
Annual	4874	5249	2809	2777
Fourth	6252	15640	4763	2679
Fifth	12643	8761	6269	3614
Annual	26143	18660	10969	3637
Sixth	25921	10545	21667	4543
Seventh	59163	23476	49920	6801
Eighth	105613	10717	95219	15559
Ninth*	166712	47108	237729	15857

Notes: MMI – Major and medium irrigation; MIS – Minor irrigation surface; MIG – Minor irrigation groundwater; * - anticipated; NA- data not available separately.

Sources: Computed using CWC (2000 and 2002); GoI (2003).

Investment required to create one hectare of irrigation has also been increasing at a faster rate in Maharashtra when compared to many states. Since Maharashtra state falls in the hard rock area, the per hectare investment required for MI is relatively higher as compared to all-India average. As regards MMI, though uneven terrain condition and rolling topography of the state is partly responsible for huge increase of per hectare investment, incompletion of projects in time especially after Fifth Five Year Plan mainly due to paucity of funds is often cited as the main reason for poor cost efficiency of irrigation (Gulati, *et al.*, 1994; Abbie, *et al.*, 1982). Whatever may be the reasons, the existing poor cost-efficiency cannot be allowed to continue further. Therefore, unless all the ongoing projects are completed, new projects should not be taken up, as it will take away the limited funds available for irrigation development in the state.

Growth of Irrigation Projects

Altogether, a total of 3,596 large dams were completed in the country as per the latest information available from CWC (2002). Besides this, 695 projects are also under construction in the country, of which 300 (43 per cent) projects are in Maharashtra. Of the total projects completed in the country so far, 1,229 dams are in Maharashtra state alone, which is about 34 per cent of the total number of large dams in the country (Table 4.5). Thus, Maharashtra has the distinction of having the largest number of irrigation projects in the country. On an average, about 25 projects per year have been completed during the period 1951 to 1994. Number of projects that are constructed for irrigation purposes was very high during the seventies in the state and the same is true at the national level as well. While the projects completed between 1951 and 1970 were only 171 (about 8 projects per year), the same increased to 923 between 1971 and 1994 (about 40 projects completed per year). However, there are discrepancies in the number of projects given in CWC (2002) and the same reported in GoM (2000). For instance, as per GoM (2000), 33 major, 177 medium and 2032 minor projects have been completed in Maharashtra at the end of June 1999. Currently, 55 major, 126 medium and 908 minor irrigation projects are under construction in the state.

TABLE 4.5

Distribution of Large Dams in India and Maharashtra

Period	*India*	*Maharashtra*
Up to 1950	293	51
1951-1960	234	25
1961-1970	461	146
1971-1980	1190	589
1981-1989	1066	324
1990 & Above	116	10
Year Not Known	236	84
Under Construction	695	300
Total	**4291**	**1529**

Source: CWC, 1998.

As a result of a large number of projects, the state has a live storage capacity of 35.01 BCM from the completed projects, which is the second highest capacity created among the states in the country (CWC, 2002). Thus, Maharashtra does not seem to have fallen short in creating water storage or at least the state is comfortably placed at the top rank as far as creation of the storage capacity is concerned. But in terms of achievements the proportion of cultivated area under irrigation is only around 17 per cent of GCA as of today, which is one of the lowest among the states in the country. Thus, despite having the largest number of projects and high storage capacity, the state claims only the bottom rank in terms of percentage of irrigated area in relation to GCA.

A section of researchers feel that this imbroglio can be sorted out by allowing privatisation of construction and management of irrigation projects. But the real question is: can privatising construction and management of irrigation sector solve this problem? This needs careful consideration, as given the present situation, neither do we have sufficient experience of privatised activities in irrigation management nor can we rely on the private sector knowing the existing inequity in land distribution. It is essential to underscore here that the problem is not about the quality of construction but about the delay in completing the projects, which can be sorted out only by judicious planning of irrigation sector. The important issues to be understood here are: Why the projects sanctioned could not be completed in time? What are the time overruns and cost overruns of each project under construction? Is the non-availability of required fund the main reason for this or is there any other reason? It was not possible to study these issues in detail due to non-availability of required data on the extent of the time overruns and cost overruns.

TABLE 4.6

Time and Cost Overruns of Selected Irrigation Projects in Maharashtra

(Rs. in Million)

Project Name	*Started in Plan*	*Estimated Cost*		*Likely Exp. up to End of Ninth Plan*	*Spillover Cost*	*Likely Achievement of Potential up to End of Ninth Plan ('000 Ha)*	*Likely Year of Completion*
		Original	*Latest*				
Bhasta	V	1641.10	3224.90	2464.20	760.70	8.93	2007
Bhima	III	425.80	9190.00	8586.00	604.00	214.53	2007
Chaskaman	V	224.80	3471.40	2892.50	578.90	21.21	2005
Jayakwadi St.I & II	V	1273.60	7968.70	7793.20	175.50	236.93	2004
Khadakwasla	II	116.20	3450.40	3222.10	228.30	62.15	2005
Koyna Krishna L.I.S.	VI	2591.00	10830.00	9214.90	1615.10	4.52	2009
Krishna	III	276.60	3700.00	3889.70	-189.70	89.95	2007
Kuadi	66-69	179.00	9190.00	10524.50	-1334.50	94.88	2007
Surya	78-80	193.20	1751.40	2282.00	-530.60	22.55	2007
Tillari (IS)	78-80	2172.20	4240.60	4841.60	-601.00	1.33	2008
Upper Godavari	66-69	142.00	1332.30	1169.40	162.90	66.17	2007
Upper Penganga	V	844.80	8619.90	5484.40	3135.50	73.97	2007
Upper Pravara	V	158.70	2871.40	1200.30	1671.10	4.83	2007
Upper Wardha	V	398.80	6618.60	6180.30	438.30	73.33	2007
Vishnupuri	78-80	789.30	1932.20	1841.00	91.20	18.54	2007
Warna	IV	310.80	8920.00	4295.50	4624.50	18.81	2010

Source: GoI (2003), *Tenth Five Year Plan*: 2002-07, Volume II, Planning Commission, New Delhi.

However, we have presented the details of time and cost overruns of selected irrigation projects in Table 4.6.

Trends and Development of Irrigated Area

Though it is not fair to compare the growth of irrigated area of the state with the national level average because of its different terrain condition and topography, area under irrigation has been increasing in Maharashtra since 1960-61, at an equal pace with the national level growth. While the net irrigated area (NIA) of the state increased from 1.09 mha in TE 1962-1963 to 2.97 mha in TE 2000-01, the gross irrigated area (GIA) increased from 1.24 mha to 3.66 mha during the same period. The pace of growth of both NIA and GIA of the state is found to be almost similar to the growth achieved at the national level, where NIA increased 2.22 times (from 25.07 to 55.73 mha) and GIA increased 2.51 times (from 28.63 to 73.93) between

TABLE 4.7

Trends in Irrigated Area—Maharashtra and India

(Area in Mha)

Period	*SIA*		*WIA*		*NIA*		*GIA*	
	Maharashtra	*India*	*Maharashtra*	*India*	*Maharashtra*	*India*	*Maharashtra*	*India*
TE 1962-63	0.48 (44.04)	17.64 (69.29)	0.61 (55.96)	7.43 (29.64)	1.09 (100)	25.07 (100)	1.24	28.63
TE 1972-73	0.58 (43.61)	19.12 (60.70)	0.75 (56.39)	12.38 (39.28)	1.33 (100)	31.49 (100)	1.55	38.56
TE 1982-83	0.79 (41.36)	21.38 (53.49)	1.12 (58.64)	18.59 (46.51)	1.91 (100)	39.97 (100)	2.44	51.01
TE 1992-93	0.97 (36.06)	23.18 (46.93)	1.71 (63.94)	25.88 (53.08)	2.69 (100)	49.39 (100)	3.28	65.22
TE 2000-01	1.05 (35.35)	23.89* (42.87)	1.92 (64.65)	31.84* (57.13)	2.97 (100)	55.73* (100)	3.66	73.93*

Notes: * - relates to TE 1998-99; SIA – surface irrigated area; WIA – well irrigated area.:
Figures in parentheses are percentages to net irrigated area (NIA). GIA – Gross Irrigated Area.
Sources: GoI (various issues); GoM (various issues); FAI (2002).

TABLE 4.8

Growth Rate of Irrigated Area by Source in Maharashtra and India

(Per Cent Per Annum)

Period	Maharashtra				India			
	Surface	*Well*	*Net*	*Gross*	*Surface+*	*Well*	*Net*	*Gross*
1960-61 to 1970-71	2.49[a]	3.12[a]	2.85[a]	2.97[a]	1.93[a]	5.09[a]	2.19	3.13[a]
1970-71 to 1980-81	4.20[a]	4.76[a]	4.52[a]	5.59[a]	1.87[a]	4.16[c]	2.46	2.97
1980-81 to 1990-91	2.52[a]	4.04[a]	3.44[a]	3.18[a]	0.91[c]	3.13[a]	1.90[a]	2.30[a]
1990-91 to 2000-01	0.84[a]	1.92[b]	1.53[a]	1.55[a]	-0.08	3.51[a]	2.16[a]	2.38[a]
1965-66 to 1980-81	3.47[a]	3.61[a]	3.55[a]	4.36[a]	2.17[a]	4.81[a]	2.65	3.09[a]
1980-81 to 2000-01	1.77[a]	3.67[a]	2.93[a]	2.71[a]	0.63	3.47	2.19[a]	2.49[a]
1965-66 to 2000-01*	2.12[a]	3.25[a]	2.81[a]	2.99[a]	1.49[a]	3.89[a]	2.30[a]	2.66[a]
1960-61 to 2000-01*	2.20[a]	3.22[a]	2.82[a]	3.05[a]	1.72[a]	3.83[a]	2.19[a]	2.65[a]

Notes: a, b, c are significant at 1, 5 and 10 per cent level respectively;

\+ - Refers to only canal irrigation; * - India's growth rate is up to 1996-97.

Sources: GoI (various issues); GoM (various issues); FAI (2002).

TE 1962-63 and TE 2000-01 (Table 4.7). The trend growth rate computed for different time points shows that the growth of surface irrigated area is much higher during the first part of Green Revolution (1965 to 1981) as compared to the second part of Green Revolution (1981 to 2001) (Table 4.8). The important point observed from the growth analysis is that growth rate of irrigated area was very low during the period 1990-91 to 2000-01, despite spending substantial amount of money on surface irrigation development during this period. It is essential to examine as to why the growth of irrigated area has significantly slowed down during the nineties.

Though there are differences in the growth rate of different sources of irrigated area between Maharashtra and the national level average, the trends in the share of major sources of irrigated area is almost similar to the national level trend. The share of surface irrigation in the total net irrigated area has been coming down and the share of groundwater irrigation has been increasing both at the state and country level, though the decline rate of share of surface irrigation is relatively higher at the national level (Narayanamoorthy, 2002).

One of the important points that have been under discussion at different fora is whether the development of irrigation is equally distributed across regions or not. Available data shows that area under irrigation is not equally distributed across the divisions and districts in

TABLE 4.9

Division-wise Trends in Area under Irrigation in Maharashtra

(in '000 Ha)

Division	Surface Irrigation		Well Irrigation		Net Irrigation		Gross Irrigation	
	TE 1962-63	*TE 2001-02*	*TE 1962-63*	*TE 2001-02*	*TE 1962-63*	*TE 2001-02*	*TE 1962-63*	*TE 2001-02*
Konkan	10.97 (2.28)	25.43 (2.42)	9.77 (1.59)	27.40 (1.43)	20.77 (1.90)	52.83 (1.78)	21.37 (1.72)	63.73 (1.74)
Nashik	29.30 (6.10)	108.13 (10.30)	84.33 (13.77)	302.43 (15.76)	113.77 (10.41)	410.57 (13.83)	147.33 (11.84)	511.20 (13.97)
Pune	121.47 (25.28)	246.23 (23.45)	233.30 (38.09)	479.60 (25.00)	354.90 (32.47)	725.83 (24.45)	413.27 (33.22)	886.00 (24.22)
Kolhapur	75.80 (15.78)	158.33 (15.08)	87.17 (14.23)	249.50 (13.00)	162.97 (14.91)	407.83 (13.74)	194.37 (15.63)	495.90 (13.55)
Aurangabad	5.93 (1.23)	139.77 (13.31)	85.67 (13.98)	310.17 (16.17)	91.63 (8.38)	449.93 (15.16)	107.47 (8.64)	554.03 (15.14)
Latur	12.53 (2.61)	89.30 (8.50)	63.13 (10.31)	184.47 (9.62)	67.47 (6.17)	273.77 (9.22)	75.57 (6.08)	348.33 (9.52)
Amravati	0.53 (0.11)	47.73 (4.55)	25.97 (4.24)	129.00 (6.72)	26.57 (2.43)	176.73 (5.95)	26.63 (2.14)	225.03 (6.15)
Nagpur	231.87 (48.26)	235.17 (22.39)	23.27 (3.80)	235.93 (12.30)	255.23 (23.35)	471.10 (15.87)	257.50 (20.70)	574.60 (15.70)
Maharashtra State	480.50 (100.00)	1050.10 (100.00)	612.57 (100.00)	1918.50 (100.00)	1093.10 (100.00)	2968.60 (100.00)	1243.87 (100.00)	3658.83 (100.00)

Note: Divisions are as per the prevailing divisions in the state during the year 1994-95.

Sources: GoI (various issues), GoM (various issues); figures in parentheses are percentage share.

Maharashtra (Table 4.9). Four divisions namely Pune, Kolhapur, Aurangabad, and Nagpur together accounted for about 74.23 per cent (0.780 million hectares) of total surface irrigated area (1.050 million hectares) of the state during TE 2001-02. Though the same trend has been continuing since 1970s, the share of Nagpur division in the total surface irrigated area has sharply declined from 48.26 per cent in TE 1962-63 to 22.39 per cent in TE 2001-02. Since Nagpur division has relatively more area under tank irrigation, could this be due to reduction in area under tank irrigation in this region? If so, the worst affected farmers due to this must be poor resource owning farmers namely marginal and small categories, for whom alternative source of irrigation is not affordable (Vaidyanathan, 1999; 2001).

The distribution of area under well irrigation across divisions is relatively better than the surface source of irrigation. Except Konkan, Amravati and Latur division, the share of well-irrigated area in the net (total) irrigated area varies from about 12 per cent to 25 per cent in other divisions. Nashik and Pune divisions together accounted for over 40 per cent of well-irrigated area during TE 2001-02. What is interesting is that those divisions, which have higher share of surface irrigated area also have higher share of well-irrigated area, except Nashik and Nagpur divisions. The same trend is observed in both NIA and GIA. As irrigation is one of the important factors which determine the income generating capacity of the rural population and it also involves a large amount of public investment, the allocation of resources for irrigation development needs to be linked with the percentage of utilisation of irrigation potential across regions/administrative zones in the future.

Unlike the other states, crop-wise irrigated area too is not distributed in a desirable manner among different crops in the state. Out of the total irrigated area of 3.55 million hectares available during TE 2000-01, important foodgrain crops such as paddy, wheat, *jowar* and *bajra* together accounted for only 45.89 per cent (1.50 million hectares), while sugarcane alone accounted for over 18 per cent (Table 4.10).

Pulses and oilseeds are the important crops in Maharashtra accounting for about 28.33 per cent of GCA in TE 2001, but these two crop groups together accounted for only about 14.50 per cent of irrigated area during the same period (Table 4.10). Though net returns per unit of water generated by sugarcane is estimated to be very low when compared to most of the foodgrain crops (Rath and Mitra, 1989), available estimates show that major portion of irrigation water available in the state is still used only for sugarcane, which accounts for less than 3 per cent of gross cropped area in the state (World Bank, 2002). Irrigated sugarcane area accounted for over 18 per cent of GIA in the state, which is very high when compared to the national average figure of 5.36 per cent during TE 1992-1993. Inspite of severe water scarcity in the state, area under sugarcane has increased at a rate of 3.77 per cent per annum between TE 1972-73 and TE 2001-02.

TABLE 4.10

Crop-wise Share in GCA and GIA in Maharashtra

(Data are Triennium Ending Averages)

Crops	*Gross Cropped Area*					*Gross Irrigated Area*				
	1962-63	*1972-73*	*1982-83*	*1992-93*	*2000-01*	*1962-63*	*1972-73*	*1982-83*	*1992-93*	*2000-01*
Paddy	6.96	7.47	7.49	7.50	6.82	22.12	21.00	16.35	12.50	9.73
Wheat	4.74	4.64	5.16	3.47	4.26	11.29	17.65	21.25	15.96	19.58
Jowar	32.64	31.98	33.16	27.99	22.73	2.65	16.51	18.41	14.37	11.67
Bajara	8.80	8.88	8.08	9.13	7.99	0.14	2.88	2.14	2.20	3.32
Total Cereals	55.60	55.21	56.14	50.20	44.48	59.58	59.27	59.32	46.24	45.89*
Total Pulses	12.53	12.95	13.58	15.39	16.11	3.44	3.41	4.19	6.95	7.38*
Cotton	13.80	14.53	13.16	12.75	14.39	3.86	4.46	4.35	2.78	2.06
Sugarcane	0.78	1.12	1.83	2.63	2.59	11.91	12.94	14.62	16.91	18.12
Total Oilseeds	**10.11**	**9.60**	**8.50**	**12.18**	**12.22**	**1.61**	**2.07**	**3.64**	**9.57**	**7.18***
Others	7.18	6.59	6.79	6.85	10.22	19.60	17.85	13.88	17.55	19.90*
Total	**100**	**100**	**100**	**100**	**100**	**100**	**100**	**100**	**100**	**100**

Note: * relates to TE 1997-98.

Sources: GoI (various issues); GoM (various issues).

Considering the increasing demand for irrigation water and drastic decline in available water for future use, strict rules should be enacted wherein a farmer should not be allowed to cultivate sugarcane for more than a fixed area under surface method of irrigation.

Financial Performance of Irrigation Sector

Fully knowing the fact that gross receipts from irrigation water is only one of the direct benefits of irrigation, the performance of irrigation sector is often judged on the basis of the extent of recovery of working expenses through gross receipts. The policy towards water rates has been the major points of discussion right from the time of the First Irrigation Commission of Maharashtra (GoM, 1962). Among the suggestions on water rates given by the Second Irrigation Commission (GoI, 1972), the important ones are: (i) water rate should relate to the benefits rather than the cost, (ii) it should relate to the crop and the season, (iii) it should consider the cropping needs of the states, (iv) it should be fixed between 6 and 12 per cent of the gross income, and (v) it should be revised after every five years. Though the productivity of most of the crops is relatively lower in Maharashtra, the recommendations of the Second Irrigation Commission are broadly followed and the water rates are revised with the required frequency. In fact, in order to cover full operation and maintenance (O&M) cost of irrigation, water rates have been increased since September 2001. These charges will increase by 15 per cent every year and have been announced and also published for a five year period, 2001-05 (World Bank, 2002). It is worth mentioning here that no other state in India has taken this kind of bold decision in recent times. At present, the state has the highest range of water rates prevailing in the country (Table 4.11).

TABLE 4.11

Water Rates for Selected Crops and States as of September 2001

(Rs./Ha)

Crop	*AP*	*Kar.*	*Raj.*	*UP*	*Maharashtra*
Sugarcane	875	1000	574	474	3180-4673
Paddy	370-494	250	198	287	180-360
Wheat	250	150	148	287	360
Cotton	250	150	178	114	548-1088
Maize	250	88	67	---	270
Pulses	---	88	79	212	---
Vegetable	---	---	109	287	548-2040

Source: World Bank, 2002.

Though the water rates are very high in the state, the percentage of cost-recovery is not appreciably higher when compared to other comparable states. As per the data of CWC (2002), the percentage of recovery of irrigation and multipurpose river valley projects has declined from 166.02 in 1974-75 to 2.26 per cent in 1998-99 in Maharashtra, while the same has declined from 64.2 per cent to 6.30 per cent at the national level during the same period (Figure 4.1). However, as per the data of irrigation department, Government of Maharashtra, the cost recovery has increased recently from 19 per cent in 1997-98 to 56 per cent in 2001-02 (World Bank, 2002). One of the important reasons for the poor recovery rate is that the per hectare working expenses in Maharashtra are about five times of the average per hectare working expenses at the country level (CWC, 2002; Deshpande and Narayanamoorthy, 2001). Besides this, a relatively less amount of actual collection of water rates in relation to demand raised is also one of the reasons for poor recovery (Table 4.12). While efforts are needed to increase the collection of

FIGURE 4.1

Percentage of Cost Recovery in Irrigation Projects

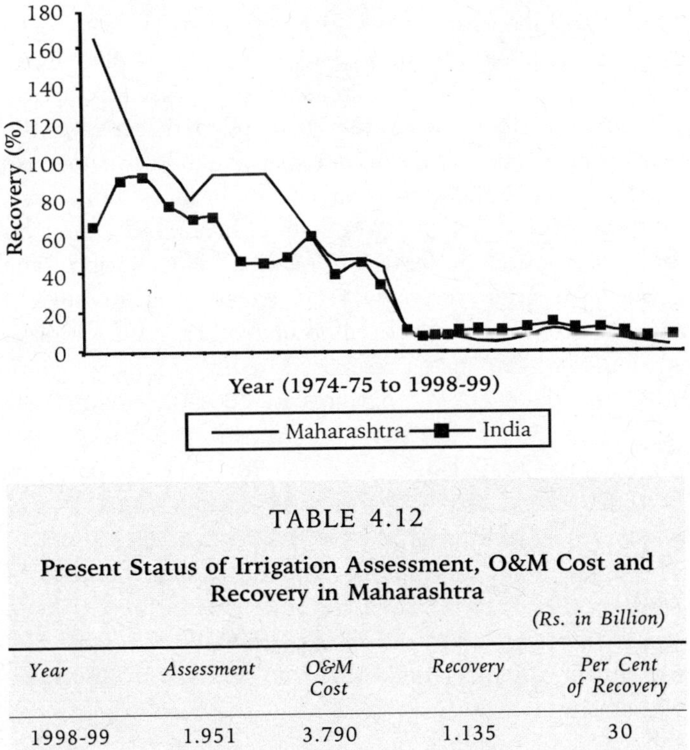

TABLE 4.12

Present Status of Irrigation Assessment, O&M Cost and Recovery in Maharashtra

(Rs. in Billion)

Year	*Assessment*	*O&M Cost*	*Recovery*	*Per Cent of Recovery*
1998-99	1.951	3.790	1.135	30
1999-00	2.762	4.326	1.729	40
2000-01	4.375	4.900	1.953	40
2001-02	4.535	4.500	2.516	56

Note: O&M cost includes establishment plus maintenance and repairs.

Source: GoM, Dept. of Irrigation.

charges by increasing the quality of service, working expenses being spent for managing per hectare of irrigation need to be drastically reduced in order to increase the recovery rate. Therefore, instead of working only on the revenue side (water rates) vigorously, it is obligatory to consider with equal vigour the expenditure side also so as to understand the increasing trends in expenditure and ways and means to cut down unwarranted expenditure. One of the options available for reducing working expenses and improving recovery rate is transferring the water distribution below the main canal systems to the Water Users Associations (WUAs) (Rath, 1997). In order to increase the participation of farmers in water management, Government of Maharashtra has taken a policy decision in July 2001 to hand over the irrigation management to WUAs within a span of three years in all irrigation projects. Though it seems to be a feasible solution, the working details of this have to be analysed keeping in view the ground realities about the irrigation department.

Micro-irrigation

One of the new methods introduced recently in India for increasing water use efficiency and yield of crop is drip method of irrigation (DMI). Unlike flood method of irrigation, which is followed predominantly in Indian agriculture, water is supplied directly to the root zone of the crops under drip method. Water use efficiency under DMI is very high as it saves substantial amount of water losses occurring through evaporation and distribution under flood method of irrigation. The growth of area under DMI is exceptionally high in Maharashtra when compared to any other state in India. Area under DMI increased from a mere 236 ha in 1986-1987 to about 217447 hectares in 2001-02, an increase of about 57 per cent per annum (Figure 4.2). Maharashtra state alone accounts for over 50 per cent of India's total drip irrigated area during 2000- 01, for which we have state-wise comparable data (Table 4.13). There are many reasons for the rapid development of DMI in the state. First, state government is very keen in promoting drip irrigation on a large scale by providing subsidy, technical and extension services. Maharashtra is the only state that has been operating a separate state scheme since 1986-87 for promoting drip method of irrigation by providing subsidy. All other states have been operating only central scheme, which started functioning from 1990-91. Second, irrigation availability from both surface and groundwater is quite low and hence, farmers have willingly adopted DMI in order to avoid water scarcity largely in divisions like Nashik, Pune, etc. Third, farmers were not able to cultivate more lucrative crops like grapes, banana, pomegranate, orange, mango, etc. by surface method of irrigation due to depletion of groundwater, which also forced the farmers to adopt DMI extensively in certain regions in the state. It is also adopted for growing high value crops such as floriculture, vegetables, horticulture, etc., under greenhouses.

FIGURE 4.2

Area under Drip Irrigation in Maharashtra

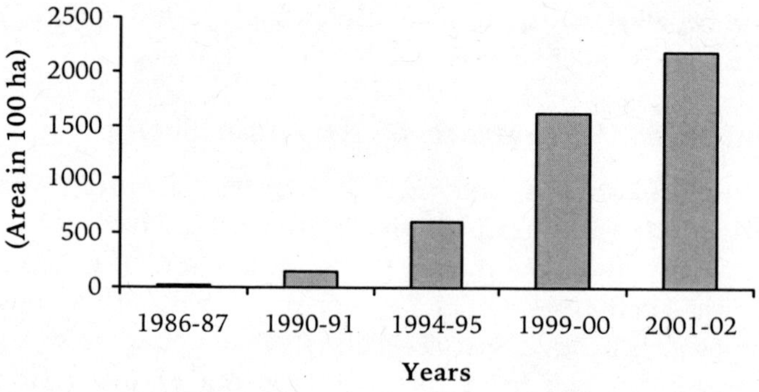

TABLE 4.13

State-wise Area under Drip Method of Irrigation

States	*Area ('000 Ha) Total Area*		*Per Cent to (Area)*		*ACGR*
	1991-92	*2000-01*	*1991-92*	*2000-01*	
Maha.	**32.92**	**160.28**	**44.64**	**53.16**	**19.23**
Kar.	11.41	66.30	16.17	18.03	19.55
T.N.	53.57	55.90	7.59	15.20	29.76
A.P.	11.59	36.30	16.41	9.88	13.52
Guj.	35.60	7.60	5.05	2.07	8.79
Kerl.	30.35	5.50	4.30	1.50	6.81
Orissa	0.04	1.90	0.06	0.52	53.56
Har.	0.12	2.02	0.17	0.55	76.74
Raj.	0.30	6.00	0.43	1.63	39.49
U.P.	0.011	2.50	0.16	0.68	82.74
Punjab	0.02	1.80	0.03	0.49	64.87
Others	2.12	5.40	0.00	1.47	10.11
Total	**70.59**	**367.70**	**100**	**100**	**20.13**

Notes: a- includes state subsidy scheme area of 58498 ha;

b- includes area under central and state schemes for development of oil palm and sugarcane; ACGR - Annual compound growth rate per cent per annum between 1991-92 and 2000-01.

Source: AFC, 1998; GoI (2004).

Though area under DMI increased significantly in the state since 1986-87, its development is not the same across the divisions and districts. While Pune, Nashik and Kolhapur divisions together accounted for nearly 67 per cent of the total area at the end of 1999-2000, districts like Nashik (14.53 per cent), Jalgaon (18.14 per cent), Solapur (9.82 per cent), Ahmednagar (6.67 per cent), Pune (5.53 per cent) and Sangli (5.37 per cent) together accounted for over 60 per cent of state's total area. Besides favourable cropping pattern, water scarcity prevailing in these districts forced the farmers to adopt DMI. As of March 2000, more than 26 crops are being cultivated using DMI in the state. However, the area is concentrated with only a few crops. Crops such as banana, grapes, sugarcane, citrus group of crops and pomegranate together accounted for 75 per cent of Maharashtra's total drip irrigated area (1,60,281 ha) at the end of March 2000.

Drip method of irrigation has many advantages over flood method of irrigation (FMI), which is followed predominantly in Indian agriculture. Besides saving substantial amount of water, it increases productivity of crops and reduces the cost of cultivation as well as consumption of electricity required for lifting water from wells. Studies carried out using experimental data show that while water saving under DMI ranges from 40 to 80 per cent in different crops when compared to FMI, productivity gains can be achieved up to 98 per cent as compared to FMI (INCID, 1994). Field level studies carried out in Maharashtra too established that DMI reduces water consumption and cost of cultivation besides increasing yield of crops to the extent of 19 to 29 per cent in crops like banana, grapes and sugarcane (Table 4.14).

DMI is considered to be a capital-intensive technology requiring an investment of Rs. 20,000 – 50,000 per hectare depending upon the crop (INCID, 1994). While the investment required for DMI is generally higher for narrow spaced crops as compared to wide spaced crops, it varies with type of drip materials to be used, distance between water source (well) and the field to be irrigated. One of the important questions often asked with regard to DMI is whether the investment on DMI is economically viable or not? Studies carried out using field level data collected from Maharashtra on three crops clearly show that the investment on drip irrigation is economically viable even without government subsidy, under 15 per cent discount rate. The benefit-cost (BC) ratio varies from 1.77 to 2.23 among the three crops under without subsidy condition. Even though subsidy is not needed to enhance the economic viability of the drip system, it is still needed to enhance the incentive for the widespread adoption of DMI particularly among the resource poor farmers. From the policy point of view, this result suggests that subsidy can be phased out eventually once the new irrigation technology covered an adequate enough to expand subsequently through the demonstration effect.

TABLE 4.14

Advantages from Drip Method of Irrigation over Flood Method of Irrigation: Results of Field Study

Particulars	*Banana*[a]	*Grapes*[a]	*Sugarcane*[b]	
	(Jalgaon)	*(Nashik)*	*(Pune)*	*(Ahmednagar)*
Cost Saving (Rs./ha)	1300 (2.47)	13400 (9.07)	5843 (11.78)	7250 (15.26)
Water Saving (HP hours/Ha)	3246 (29.15)	1968 (37.28)	1194 (40.69)	1632 (47.63)
Electricity Saving (Kwh/Ha)	2430 (29.15)	1470 (37.28)	896 (40.69)	1224 (47.64)
Productivity Gains (Quintal/Ha)	153.19 (29.00)	38.96 (19.00)	24.52 (20.99)	27.32 (25.27)
Net Present Worth (NPW) (Rs./ha)*				
With Subsidy	257635	551220	206692	166619
Without Subsidy	247753	540241	190025	149766
B-C Ratio*				
With Subsidy	2.36	1.80	2.16	2.02
Without Subsidy	2.23	1.77	1.98	1.83

Notes: a – data relate to the year 1993-94; b – data relate to the year 1998-99. Figures in parentheses are saving in per cent over FMI.

* - BC ratio and NPW are computed using discounted (at 15 per cent) cash flow technique.

Sources: Narayanamoorthy (1996, 1997 and 2001b).

Despite having many advantages, the area under DMI accounts for only 4.97 per cent in the net irrigated area of the state in 1999-00. The total potential area suitable for DMI roughly comes to about 1.95 million hectares, which accounts for nearly 52.69 per cent in GIA in 1997-98. Studies showed that slow growth of DMI is not mainly due to economic reasons but due to less awareness among the farmers about the real economic and revenue-related benefits of drip technology (Narayanamoorthy, 1997). This means that apart from the provision of capital subsidy, there is also an urgent need for an awareness campaign through an effective extension network including aggressive field demonstration. Moreover, since sugarcane consumes major quantum of surface water, it would be worthwhile to introduce drip on canal irrigation where sugarcane has been cultivated extensively in the state.

Water Conservation Measures

The fast decline of irrigation water availability and the increasing demand for water from different sectors has forced the policy makers to introduce strategies to conserve water. Among various water conservation measures, Water Users' Association (WUAs) and Watershed Development Programmes (WDPs) have proved to be important in conserving water resources. While WUAs help to improve the overall performance of the irrigation sector besides increasing the water use efficiency, WDPs improve the water and moisture availability in the rainfed areas, where poverty is widespread because of the slow growth of agriculture (Narayanamoorthy, 2001a).

Water Users' Association

In India, more emphasis was given to users' participation in water management only after the announcement of the National Water Policy (1987), wherein gradual involvement of farmers in system management was advocated. The policy states, "Efforts should be made to involve farmers progressively in various aspects of management of irrigation system, particularly in water distribution and collection of water rates" (GoI, 1987, p. 11). This has also been re-emphasised in the new National Water Policy of 2002 (GoI, 2002h).

Though WUAs are expected to improve the recovery rate and reduce part of the responsibility of the irrigation department, it is considered to be beneficial in many ways to users (farmers) as well. It has been clearly established that users-managed systems outperformed the systems that are managed by the irrigation agencies all over the world including India (Easter, 2000, Vermillion, 1997; GoI, 1992). The most commonly realised positive impact of users-managed systems are reduction in the cost of irrigation to farmers and government; enhanced financial self-reliance of irrigation schemes; expansion of irrigation; flexibility in cropping pattern; reduction in the amount of water delivered per hectare and significant increase in cropping intensity and yield of crops.

While the irrigated area managed by the WUAs is very limited as of today in India, a significant improvement has been made, at the policy level, in bringing more irrigation systems under WUAs in the recent years. Though, Vaidyanathan Committee on Pricing of Irrigation Water observes that, "The area covered by these initiatives is very small, less than one per cent of area irrigated at present" (GoI, 1992), the tenth five year plan document cites that currently about 15.25 per cent of the net irrigated area is partially covered under the participatory irrigation management scheme in India (GoI, 2003).

TABLE 4.15

Status of Water Users' Association in Maharashtra

Particulars	*As of September 1996*		*As of December 2003*	
	No.	*Area (Ha)*	*No.*	*Area (Ha)*
WUAs Functioning	100	43684	533	158923
Agreement Executed	34	9894	129	46367
WUAs Registered	180	60372	963	347399
WUAs Proposed	143	55211	847	244898
Total	**457**	**169105**	**2472**	**797587**

Sources: Naik, *et al.*, (2002); GoM (2002), DIRD (2004).

In Maharashtra, significant progress has taken place since 1992 as the irrigation department has been encouraging the farmers to form WUAs by explaining its advantages (Naik, *et al.*, 2002). As a result of the continuous effort by the irrigation department and non-governmental organisations, about 2472 WUAs have been functioning at different levels, which cover an area of 7,97,587 ha as of December 2003 (Table 4.15). Besides this, the NGOs promoted *Pani Panchayats* have been working reasonably well in many drought-prone and water scarce areas in Pune district (Deshpande and Reddy, 1990; Thakur and Patnaik, 2002). Though, the area brought under WUAs is only about 27 per cent of the net irrigated area so far, it has increased to as much as 372 per cent between 1996 (0.169 million hectares) and 2003 (0.798 million hectares). While the increasing role of WUAs is essential to increase the performance of irrigation system, there is no clear information about the performance of WUAs at the field level. Vaidyanathan Committee on Pricing of Irrigation Water observes that, "The general consensus among the knowledgeable people is that they have been fitful and have not made much of impact. For the most part the outlet and canal committees are there only in name; they are not consulted on substantive issues; nor are department officers required to follow their advice. There is also considerable reluctance, if not opposition, from the operational staff of irrigation departments to involving users in management; and even users themselves tend to be apathetic to the idea" (GoI, 1992, pp.126-127).

A number of strategies need to be introduced in order to increase the participation of farmers in water management activities. For this purpose, one needs to understand the factors responsible for the tardy progress of WUAs. The Ninth Five Year Plan (1997-2002) listed, among others, seven important reasons, which can be reconsidered while making strategies to improve the users' participation in irrigation management (Box 4.1). Similarly, while emphasising the importance of WUAs in irrigation management activities, the Maharashtra Water and Irrigation Commission (GoM, 1999c) also suggested various strategies to improve the users' participation in irrigation management (Box 4.2).

Water users associations are functioning mostly at the tertiary level, which cannot accomplish their duties in improving supply, and management of irrigation as the supply of water is controlled by the irrigation agency. Users' organisations that exist in small irrigation systems namely tank were able to perform their duty relatively better than the WUAs that exist in the large irrigation network namely canal. There are two reasons for this. First, the control of government agency is minimal under small irrigation systems like tanks. Second, users group can clearly understand the demand and supply position of water and make decisions accordingly. Therefore, priority should be given to create users group in all minor irrigation systems so as to improve the water use efficiency.

As regards WUAs in larger irrigation systems, the results are not encouraging so far. The turnover of irrigation systems has been slow in most of the large irrigation projects. There are reports that the staffs who are managing irrigation systems see WUAs as a potential threat to their jobs (Easter, 2000). Therefore, the wholehearted involvement in establishing and supporting WUAs by the agency staff may not be very high. Moreover, unlike other South Asian countries where WUAs have been working reasonably well, irrigation systems are very large in India and therefore, practically impossible to manage efficiently by WUAs without adequate support from the irrigation agency. In order to encourage the farmers' attachment with the WUAs, it is essential to demonstrate the benefits of WUAs in delivering water supply in the required quantity and time. Importantly, the WUAs should be able to reduce the cost of water over time in order to show the advantages of WUAs to the farmers (users).

BOX 4.1

Reasons for Tardy Progress of WUAs

- The prolonged prevalence of government managed systems has snapped the initiative of the farmers and made them dependent on the government.
- Non-availability of funds for PIM.
- Farmers are reluctant to adopt participatory approach unless deliveries of water can be made flexible and responsive to the need.
- Farmers fear that under new system, they might have to incur expenditure on O&M besides increased water rates.
- Farmers are reluctant to come together, because of differences of castes and classes, to form an association.
- Properly oriented, trained and motivated officials to implement this programme are lacking and there is no dedicated wing for this purpose.
- Lack of enabling law for the establishment of WUAs.

Source: GoI, 1997.

BOX 4.2

Some of the Recommendations of Maharashtra Water and Irrigation Commission

- In order to have proper utilisation of created irrigation potential, WUAs will have to be formed in large numbers.
- In order to legally enforce the participatory irrigation management, the existing Irrigation Act of 1976 should be amended forthwith.
- To speed up the setting up of water users' societies, there be an exclusive division in each CADA under the control of officers from cooperative department.
- Water from public canal system should be given to water users' societies on volumetric basis and water rates be charged accordingly.
- Tanks having irrigation potential up to 100 ha be entrusted to *gram panchayats* for their management while those having irrigation potential up to 1000 ha be entrusted to *taluka panchayat* samitie. The repair works on the tanks should be undertaken only after formation of water users' societies.
- Training needs to be given to the members of the office bearers of the WUAs in respect of working modalities of societies and their rights and responsibilities.

Source: GoM, 1999.

WUAs have to be legally established in order to increase their responsibility and decisions related to water management. It is always difficult for WUAs to provide better water supply and other services to their members without legal standing (Easter, 2000). With the improved service, WUAs can convince the farmers to pay the charges for water that they use. As rightly observed by the Committee on Pricing of Irrigation Water (GoI, 1992), "An essential pre–condition is to convince users that they will benefit from such group activity by getting more water, more assured supplies according to a pre-specified schedule (or according to the needs of the crops), greater flexibility in the use of water, or some combinations of these. Improvement in any of these dimension will almost certainly increase productivity and, therefore, induce farmers to take the idea of users' groups more seriously." Continued support from the government agencies is essential even after transforming the systems management to users group in order to sustain the participation of farmers. Importantly farmers at any level should not be allowed to think that the transfer of irrigation management is introduced in order to reduce the financial burden of the government. Before transferring the system to WUAs, it is also essential to restore the infrastructure created (main and sub-canals, etc.) to efficiently deliver water to each farmer's field, as farmers may not be in a position to do the same due to resource constraints.

Watershed Development Programme

One of the massive programmes introduced to improve the rainfed agriculture during the Seventh Plan in India is Watershed Development Programmes (WDPs). As water is important for improving the performance of agriculture and thereby the socio-economic conditions of the people living in rainfed areas, major thrust is given to improve the availability of water by constructing rainwater harvesting structures like *nalla bunds*, contour trenches, contour *bunds*, farm ponds, dugout ponds, masonry *bandharas* and other run-off management structures under WDPs. Though WDPs were introduced in a large scale in India during the Seventh Plan period (1985-86), it was introduced by the Government of Maharashtra under Employment Guarantee Scheme (EGS) in 1982 itself. The programme was entitled as 'Comprehensive Watershed Development Programme' (COWDEP). The centrally sponsored National Watershed Development Project for Rainfed Areas (NWDPRA) was implemented for the first time in 1986 in Maharashtra.

Considering the vast majority of cultivated area under rainfed cultivation (nearly 83 per cent as of today), the Government of Maharashtra has been giving high priority to the WDPs since early 1980s. Over the last 20 years, significant progress has been made in treating areas under the WDPs. Currently, WDPs are being operated under 16 different budget heads supported by the Central and state schemes (Table 4.16). While 10 budget heads are operated under state schemes, the remaining six heads are operated with the support of Central schemes. Between 1992-93 and 2002-03, a total amount of Rs. 26,005.48 million has been spent on WDPs.

TABLE 4.16

Budget Head-wise Expenditure Incurred for WDPs in Maharashtra

(Rs. Million)

Budget Head	*1992-93*	*2002-03*	*Total**
1. E.G.S.	1045.05	1839.81	9122.78
2. 100 Days Prog.	0.00	0.00	151.12
3. D.P.D.C (Plan)	137.74	52.02	1533.97
4. Backlog (Plan)	77.62	318.79	1832.15
5. C.D.B.	0.00	98.58	185.47
6. D.P.D.C (TSP)	24.95	18.34	1138.49
7. Backlog (TSP)	15.91	10.89	59.65
8. Jalsandharan	195.08	3.11	1728.96
9. World Bank	20.41	0.00	33.39
10. Other	21.38	366.19	1321.78
Total State schemes	**1538.13**	**2707.75**	**17107.76**
1. J.R.Y	35.41	0.04	1511.63
2. E.A.S	0.00	214.66	1834.93
3. NWDPRA	209.92	68.70	2543.47
4. Western Ghat	41.65	100.47	788.21
5. R.V.P	2.54	160.69	831.02
6. D.P.A.P	56.24	176.29	1388.46
Total Central Schemes	**345.76**	**720.85**	**8897.71**
Total State & Central	**1883.89**	**3428.59**	**26005.48**

Note: * - From 1992-93 to 2002-03.

Source: DSC & WD, 2003.

As of March 2002, about 8,322 micro watershed projects have been completed and 18,391 projects are under different stages of completion (Table 4.17).

TABLE 4.17

Division-wise Coverage of Micro-Watersheds in Maharashtra (March 2002)

Division	*PWA (mha)*	*Number of Watersheds*			*TWA (mha)*
		Started	*COM*	*ONG*	
Konkan	1.69	2041	421	1620	0.214
Nashik	2.63	3590	1611	1979	0.510
Pune	3.42	6865	770	6095	0.231
Kolhapur	1.73	1900	487	1413	0.237
Aurangabad	2.36	2563	1186	1377	0.344
Latur	2.85	3473	1954	1519	0.853
Amravati	3.36	3917	1236	2681	0.377
Nagpur	2.32	2364	657	1707	0.387
Maharashtra	**20.36**	**26713**	**8322**	**18391**	**3.154**

Notes: PWA- Potential Watershed Area, COM- Completed; ONG- Ongoing; TWA- Treated Watershed Area.

Source: DSC & WD, 2003.

Though, the number of completed projects seems to be on the higher side, the total area treated through WDPs is very limited in relation to the total potential area available for watershed development programmes. As per the estimate of Directorate of Soil Conservation and Watershed Management (DSC&WM), the total area available for WDPs is about 20.36 million hectares, of which, only about 3.15 mha have been treated up to March 2002. That is, only about 15.47 per cent of potential areas have been treated through WDPs so far. The achievement of the state seems to be reasonably good while comparing it to the total coverage of treated area at the national level, which is expected to reach about 27.5 mha at the end of Ninth Plan (GoI, 2001). Of this, Maharashtra state's share comes to about 11.45 per cent.

Though considerable amount of cultivated area has been brought under WDPs, the share of area treated through WDPs across divisions and districts is not equally distributed in relation to their drought prone and rainfed area. One might expect that division/ districts, which have higher share of rainfed and drought prone area, would have a higher share of treated area as well.

But this has not happened in the state as of today (Table 4.18). For instance, about 94 per cent of area in Amravati division is rainfed, but only 12 per cent of the area has been treated upto 2001-02. On the other hand, both Nashik and Latur division have relatively less rainfed area but their share in the total treated watershed area (TWA) is relatively higher when compared to Amravati division. While the exact reason for this imbalance is not known, high priority needs to be given to those areas/regions which have more drought prone as well as degraded area, as suggested by the Tenth Plan Working Group on Watershed Development, Rainfed Farming and Natural Resource Management (GoI, 2001).

Various evaluation studies carried out in different parts of the state clearly show that WDPs have increased the water and moisture availability (Deshpande and Reddy, 1991; Deshpande and Rajasekaran, 1995; Deshpande and Narayanamoorthy, 1999; Narayanamoorthy and Kshirsagar, 2000). A recent study carried out by Directorate of Soil Conservation and Watershed Management covering 2361 watersheds across different regions in the state clearly shows that there is a significant increase in water availability (irrigated area) including drinking water. Changes in irrigated area observed in some of the watershed projects are presented in Table 4.19.

TABLE 4.18

Division-wise Inequality Index of Watershed Development: 2001-02

Division	*PWA (%)*	*RFA (%)*	*TARFA (%)*	*NRF (mm)*
Konkan	8.30	93.66	27.91	2923
Nashik	12.94	83.11	24.94	838
Pune	16.78	77.09	9.53	785
Kolhapur	8.49	74.76	19.87	1101
Aurangabad	11.58	78.02	21.52	747
Latur	13.98	88.90	37.58	909
Amaravati	16.52	94.11	12.91	882
Nagpur	11.41	75.29	27.23	1301
Maharashtra	**100.00**	**83.11**	**21.54**	**1290**

Notes: PWA – Potential Watershed Area; RFA - Per Cent of Rainfed Area to Total Net Sown Area; TARFA - Treated Watershed Area to Rainfed Area; NRF- Normal Rainfall.

Sources: GoM (various years); DSC&WM, 2003.

TABLE 4.19

Impact of WDPs on Irrigation: Selected Watersheds

(in Ha)

Village	*Geographical Area*	*Irrigated Area*		
		Before WDP	*After WDP*	*Increase (%)*
Adgaon	1049	83	500	40
Ralegoan Siddhi	971	26	340	32
Naigaon	1528	60	400	22
C. Sastabad	1325	76	284	16
Kan. Mcoai	2281	68	315	11
Dhumalwadi	1221	32	235	17
H. Bazar	977	190	375	19
Kachpal	4241	281	979	16
Khawasapur	1375	162	817	48
Pachegaon	2356	221	364	6
Tipehalli	1457	220	430	14
Alegaon	2411	167	416	10
Gheradi	5383	289	372	2
Narale	1760	224	464	14
Ajnale	3872	625	705	2
Shivane	2892	576	810	8
Medshingi	2966	101	136	1
Bhandgaon	604	22	197	29
Wadner (H)	1157	110	536	37
Umrad	2316	1533	1988	20
Total	**42142**	**5066**	**10663**	**13**

Source: GoM, 1999.

While there are no two opinions about the fact that WDPs increase irrigated area, many scholars question the sustainability of WDPs. The report of the Working Group on Watershed Development, Rainfed Farming and Natural Resources Management for the Tenth Five Year Plan mention by citing a survey of 70 villages in Maharashtra and Andhra Pradesh covering several watersheds, that the increase in agricultural production and water availability did not last for more than two years, mainly because of lack of maintenance and poor mechanism for looking after common lands. The report adds further, that, "For watershed projects to be sustainable community managed system are needed and they can succeed only with farmers contribution and their commitment of time and resources. This has been amply demonstrated in watershed programmes implemented by some voluntary organisations, in 25 villages of Pune" (GoI, 2001i, p.17). Similarly, another study carried out in 86 villages of Maharashtra and Andhra Pradesh found that participatory projects performed better than their technocratic, top-down counterparts. However, participation combined with sound technical input performed much better than all other projects (Kerr, *et al.*, 2002). The message that emerges out from various studies is that users' participation is necessary for the sustained growth of watershed development programme. Therefore, instead of focusing only on technocratic and top-down approach (mostly followed in government managed projects), bottom-up approach that is mostly followed by NGOs is required to realise the full benefits of WDPs. Similarly, it is also essential to give greater focus on non-engineering and vegetative prescriptions and intervention for improving the productivity of land and also to obviate runoff.

Demand and Supply Scenario of Water

While demand for water from different sectors has been increasing due to intensification of agriculture and growth in industry as well as population across different states in India, the available water for future use has been declining. This is expected to create wide supply-demand gap in water use in the future (Saleth, 1996). In Maharashtra, as in the case of many other states, the present condition of supply and demand scenario of water is not very comfortable (MoWR, 1999; Iyer, 2003). As per the estimate provided by the Maharashtra Water and Irrigation Commission (GoM, 1999c), the annual average availability of water is 1,48,208 mm^3, of which, an amount of 1,39,227 mm^3 of water is available for planned use. Presently (in 1996) about 39,484 mm^3 of water is used for different purposes, which accounts for just about 26 per cent of the total water available for planned use (detailed estimate on demand-supply of water for different sectors across basins is available only for two time points namely 1996 and 2030. For the purpose of comparison, the year 1996 is referred as current period). In the total current use of water, agriculture, which includes irrigation and livestock, accounts for about 81 per cent and industry and domestic use accounts for about 3 and 7 per cent respectively at the state level (Table 4.20). However, the proportion of water used by

TABLE 4.20

Basin-wise Water Supply and Demand in Maharashtra: 1996 and 2030

(in Million m^3)

Basin	*Available Water for Planned Use*	*Demand for*									
		Domestic		*Agriculture (Irrigation+Livestock)*		*Industry*		*Others(Hydro+ Thermal Power)*		*Total Use*	
		1996	*2030*	*1996*	*2030*	*1996*	*2030*	*1996*	*2030*	*1996*	*2030*
Godavari	38882	874	2066	16653	40384	192	678	250	318	17969	43446
Tapi	9324	350	731	4126	10562	35	766	20.20	175	4531	12234
Narmada	343	3.50	6.46	29.40	245.20	0.00	0.00	0.00	0.00	32.90	251
Krishna	18356	603	1428	9471	27438	138	415	3112	3112	13324	32393
WFRK	72322	938	1952	1811	12030	877	1395	0.90	2.90	3626	15380
Maharashtra	**139227**	**2768**	**6184**	**32091**	**90660**	**1241**	**3254**	**3394**	**3617**	**39484**	**103705**

Notes: Figures rounded off to the nearest integer; WFRK—West flowing rivers in Konkan.

Source: GoM, 1999.

different sectors is not the same across different basins and sub-basins because of the varying nature of growth of agriculture and other sectors.

The demand scenario for water is expected to change drastically in the future because of the increasing demand for water from different sectors. The projections indicate that the total demand for water is likely to grow by about 162 per cent between 1996 and 2030 at the state level (GoM, 2003). That is, the total demand for water is expected to increase from 39,484 mm^3 in 1996 to 1,03,705 mm^3 in 2030. This means that about 70 per cent of the total available water for planned use will be utilised by different sectors in the year 2030. Water requirement for agriculture is expected to grow by about 182 per cent, from 32,091 mm^3 in 1996 to 90,660 mm^3 in 2030. This is very high when compared to the growth of water requirement for domestic and industry use, where the water requirement is expected to increase by about 123 and 162 per cent respectively. Water requirement for different sectors is also expected to increase substantially between 1996 and 2030 across all basins with varying rate of increase. Though, the projection indicates that there will not be any supply-demand gap for water up to the year 2030 at least at the state level, there is going to be a severe water shortage particularly in three major basins namely Godavari, Tapi and Krishna. This is because of the fact that the demand for water from all the three major sectors is expected to increase substantially between 1996 and 2030 in all these basins. The availability of water by sub-basins indicates that most of the sub-basins coming under Tapi and Krishna basin are going to have severe water deficit in the future. It is clear that there is going to be a gap in the demand-supply of water by 2030 particularly in two main basins namely Tapi and Krishna, both supply about 26 per cent of water to Maharashtra. Besides these, some sub-basins falling under Godavari basin are also facing water scarcity. It may be possible to a very limited extent to meet these demands, making good the shortfall by transfer of water from water surplus river basin. Transfer of surplus water from WFRK to Godavari and Krishna would not be an economically viable proposal because of the very high lift involved. In view of this, there is going to be extreme shortage of water in Krishna and Godavari basin. Therefore, there is an urgent need to prepare a master plan focusing on each basin with specific strategies that can be implemented to avoid supply-demand gap in water use. The plan to be prepared should include both demand and supply management strategies. Under supply side management strategies, volumetric pricing, periodic revision of water rates, etc are expected to save/conserve water. Establishing a large number of WUAs, shifting the cropping pattern from low-value-high water consuming crops to high-value-low water consuming crops and a large scale adoption of micro-irrigation (drip, sprinkler), etc. are some of the important options that need to be followed under demand side management strategies.

Irrigation and Productivity Nexus

By increasing the adoption of yield increasing inputs in crop cultivation, irrigation significantly helps to increase the productivity of crops. Productivity of crops is also found to be significantly higher in those lands that are cultivated using groundwater irrigation because of its better quality (in terms of reliability and controllability) as compared to other sources of irrigation. Since groundwater irrigation accounts for nearly 65 per cent of net irrigated area in Maharashtra, one might expect that the productivity of crops in the state would be higher than the national level average. However, against expectation, not only the total productivity of major crops is lower in Maharashtra but the irrigated productivity is also found to be relatively lower in the state as compared to the national level average (Table 4.21). Though the coverage of irrigation is relatively higher in crops like gram and groundnut in Maharashtra as compared to the national average, the irrigated productivity of these two crops is also lower when compared to many states (GoI, 2002). Does this imply that the marginal productivity of water is lower in Maharashtra? Or is water not used efficiently in Maharashtra? Only a disaggregated level analysis can throw some light on this.

TABLE 4.21

Irrigated (IR) and Unirrigated (UI) Yield of Principal Crops

(Kg/Ha)

Crops	*Maharashtra*				*India*			
	1980-81		*1994-95*		*1980-81*		*1994-95*	
	IR	*UI*	*IR*	*UI*	*IR*	*UI*	*IR*	*UI*
Rice	1684	1518	1634	1587	1695	1050	2053	1345
Jowar	1010	675	859	443	1096	613	1250	606
Wheat	1249	419	1696	717	1803	1057	2683	1100
Gram	505	312	794	543	791	604	990	761
Groundnut	1400	619	967*	741*	1028	678	1305	795
Sugarcane$	92.33	—	85.50	—	63.59	32.62	81.01	50.50
Cotton	197	68	759	402	308	97	923	455

Note: * Relates to year 1988-89; $ - Sugarcane yield is in tonnes.

Source: GoI (various years).

Irrigation growth is expected to boost the growth of production and productivity of crops. Therefore, to find out whether or not such relationship exists in Maharashtra, we have compared the growth of irrigated area with production and productivity of some selected crops for different time periods. Unfortunately, there seems to be no direct relationship between growth of irrigated area and growth of productivity of major crops in all time periods selected for the analysis (Table 4.22). For instance, area under irrigated sugarcane increased at a rate of 3.79 per cent per annum during 1980-81 to 2000-01, but its productivity growth was negative (-0.58 per cent) during this period. This indirectly reinforces the issue raised earlier about the possibility of declining marginal productivity of water among various crops in the state.

TABLE 4.22

Crop-wise Growth of Irrigated Area, Production and Productivity

Crops	*1960-61 to 1980-81*			*1980-81 to 2000-01*		
	IA	*Prod.*	*Yield*	*IA*	*Prod.*	*Yield*
Rice	2.29[a]	2.88[a]	2.16[b]	-0.12	0.66	0.56
Wheat	8.31[a]	5.92[a]	4.31[a]	2.00[a]	1.97[b]	2.86[a]
Jowar	2.80[a]	1.51	1.29	0.44	0.62	2.23[a]
Gram	4.23[a]	1.09	0.30	6.64[a]	8.29[a]	3.97[a]
Groundnut	6.59[a]	-2.21[b]	-0.01	3.89[b]	0.59	2.05[a]
Cotton	3.54[a]	-0.49	0.25	-0.08	6.25[a]	5.03[a]
Sugarcane	4.57[a]	4.90[a]	1.95[a]	3.79[a]	3.72[a]	-0.58[a]

Notes: a & b are significant at one and five per cent level respectively; growth rates are computed using log-linear function; IA – irrigated area.

Sources: GoM (various years); GoI (various years).

It is well known that the productivity of crops cultivated under irrigated condition is relatively higher than that of unirrigated crops. However, to what extent irrigation helps to increase the total value of crop output has not been studied using data from Maharashtra. To understand this, we have compared the value of crop output per hectare with the level of irrigation across 25 districts of Maharashtra for three time points: 1970-1973, 1980-1983 and 1990-1993. The value of crop output (in 1990-1993 prices) per hectare has been calculated by taking the production of 35 important crops, which cover over 87 per cent of the gross cropped area in the state (Bhalla and Singh, 2001). The results presented in Table 4.23 clearly show that there is no significant difference in the value of output between the less irrigated (< 10 per cent) and high-irrigated (>10 per cent) districts in Maharashtra (Figure 4.3). Could this be due to predominant cultivation of low value crops in most parts of Maharashtra? In-depth analysis using more disaggregated level data is needed to make any firm conclusion on this aspect.

TABLE 4.23

District-wise Irrigation and Value of Crop Output Nexus in Maharashtra

Year	*GIA/ GCA*	*No. of Districts*	*VOP (Rs/Ha)*	*NPK (Kg/Ha)*	*CI (%)*
1970-73	<10%	14	2176	11.94	104
	>10%	11	2476	15.33	109
	All	25	2308	13.43	106
1980-83	<10%	10	3588	20.23	109
	>10%	15	3614	32.35	113
	All	25	3603	27.50	111
1990-93	<10%	13	3888	51.06	117
	>10%	12	4478	137.39	116
	All	25	4261	67.15	115

Source: Computed from Bhalla and Singh, 2001.

FIGURE 4.3

District-wise Irrigation and Value of Output in Maharashtra: 1990-1993

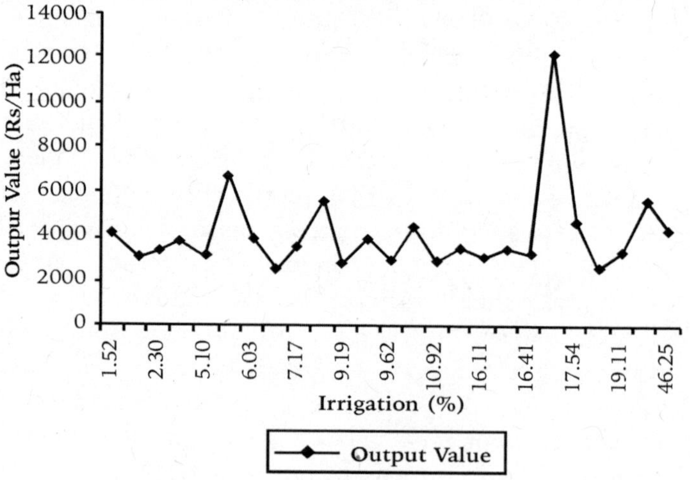

Source: Computed from Bhalla and Singh, 2001.

Further, to find out the contribution of irrigation to the value of output, regression (OLS method) analysis is performed by treating the value of output/ha as a dependent variable and percentage of irrigated area (GIA/GCA) as an independent variable for the above mentioned three time points covering 25 districts. As shown earlier through descriptive analysis, the regression results also suggest that there is hardly any relationship between the level of irrigation and per hectare value of crop output across districts (Table 4.24). All this seems to suggest that irrigation is not used efficiently in the state.

TABLE 4.24

Relationship between Irrigation and Value of Output: Regression Results

Year	*Constant*	*Slope*	R^2
1970-73	2617.58 (5.74)[a]	-17.73 (-0.39)[ns]	.006
1980-83	3459.83 (6.24)[a]	11.23 (0.30)[ns]	.004
1990-93	3835.60 (5.99)[a]	28.15 (0.66)[ns]	.018

Notes: a – significant at one per cent level; ns – not significant.
Figures in parentheses are 't' values.

Source: Computed using data from Bhalla and Singh, 2001.

Policy Suggestions

Among the important policy recommendations which emerge from this analysis the following may be underlined: (i) Irrigation policy should be focused on completion of ongoing projects, even if it means foregoing new projects; (ii) Watershed Development Programmes (WDPs) must become central, and not marginal, to agricultural growth in Maharashtra. Despite the rhetoric, only 15 per cent of the total area, which potentially lends itself to this programme has been so far covered. There is, therefore, an imperative need to launch a massive WDP designed to cover the bulk of the area within a short period of time. In fact, the year 2004-05 may be declared as a year of WDPs; (iii) Since users' participation is necessary for sustained development of WDPs, Government of Maharashtra should seek to involve *Panchayat Raj* institutions in both implementation and maintenance of projects under WDP; (iv) Government of Maharashtra should also seek foodgrains grant from Government of India for supporting massive WDPs envisaged under (ii) above; and (v) Since drip irrigation is an efficient water saving and yield enhancing technology, all potential area should be brought under this method. These recommendations are spelt out in the following paragraphs:

- Many of the projects started in different plan periods have not been completed in time, which have resulted in cost overruns besides delaying water supply to farmers. The investment required to create one hectare of irrigation under MMI sector has increased by about 17 times between Third And Eighth Five Year plan in Maharashtra. This has happened partly due to inadequate allotment of money required for completing the projects. Therefore, priority needs to be given to those projects, which are in near completion stage (over 75 per cent construction completed) by allocating the required money. If needed, no new project should be taken up for the next five years or till the completion of all the ongoing projects.
- It is essential to classify different irrigation schemes/projects in the state according to their level of sickness. Ideally, sickness of the projects should be judged by the performance in achieving its objectives. However, here sickness is defined in terms of time overrun, cost overrun, planning bottlenecks, financial performance and the level of completion of different development parameters for the purpose of making strategies. The projects can be grouped into three audit categories namely A, B and C, where audit grades refer to the performance of the scheme/project. Identification of problems and remedial measures can be planned after such categorisation.
- The entire irrigation sector of Maharashtra is currently managed by five IDCs established by the state government. However, the IDCs have been facing a lot of difficulties in making resources from the market by issue of bonds and debentures due to certain reasons. This is going to severely affect the progress of irrigation development in the state. Therefore, the state government should appoint a high level committee to find out ways and means to get out of this serious problem.
- The percentage of utilisation of irrigation to the total potential created especially in MMI sector is abysmally low in Maharashtra as compared to the national average. Inadequate allocation of funds required for constructing main and sub-canals are the important reasons for this. Therefore, efforts need to be taken to increase the utilisation per cent of irrigation potential by increasing investment on the hardware aspects of irrigation development.
- Surface irrigation, which is created and owned by the government, is not equally distributed across different regions in the state. Though the

unequal distribution of surface irrigation cannot be avoided because of variation in the available irrigation potential across the regions, this can be reduced to some extent by transferring water from the abundant basin to the scarcity areas. It is also possible to reduce the inequality in irrigation by investing more on minor irrigation and watershed development programmes in those regions/ districts, which have less area under surface irrigation.

- Despite periodically revising as well as charging highest water rates in India, the financial performance (recovery rate) of irrigation sector is not much different from other states. One of the main reasons that emerge out from the analysis is the very high working expense is required for managing the sector. Therefore, cost cutting measures need to be strictly followed by rationalising the staff strength for each one-lakh hectares of command area. There is also a wide gap between demand raised and actual collection of irrigation charges mainly because of differences in extent of service (water supply). In order to increase the collection of water revenue, a two-part tariff can be introduced, wherein all lands included in the command area should pay a flat annual fee on a per hectare basis for 'membership' of the system which entitles them to claim water and a variable fee linked to the actual extent of service (volume or area) used by each member, as suggested by Vaidyanathan Committee Report on Pricing of Irrigation Water (GoI, 1992b).
- Area under micro-irrigation (drip) has increased phenomenally (about 57 per cent/annum) since 1986 in Maharashtra, which is a leading state in India. Despite this, drip irrigated area accounted for just 4.97 per cent in the net irrigated area as of 1999-2000. Since drip irrigation has proved to be an efficient water saving and yield enhancing technology, all the potential area needs to be brought under drip method of irrigation through properly designed developmental programmes. Presently, the rate of subsidy is fixed uniformally for both more water-intensive as well as less water-intensive crops. This needs to be restructured and the rate of subsidy should be fixed based on the crop's water consumption. Sugarcane, which consumes major share of water in the state, is highly suitable for drip method of irrigation (Narayanamoorthy, 2001b). Drip irrigation can also be promoted in all those areas/ regions where there is over exploitation of groundwater.
- Since sugarcane consumes major quantum of stored water, it would be worthwhile to introduce drip on canal irrigation necessarily where sugarcane is grown. By constructing farm ponds or making use of existing wells in the command area, canal water can be stored and the same can be used for drip system. Availability of water from storage dams is going to reduce progressively due to siltation of reservoirs as well as increase in upstream watershed development works, etc. Introducing drip system in canal command areas would be handy in restoring the projected irrigation despite the reduction in water availability. Pilot projects should be introduced on major projects (where water availability is poor) under WUAs so that with the experience of its functioning, it could be replicated on a large scale on all major projects for sugarcane and other crops. Adoption of drip method in canal command area would also reduce damage of land due to waterlogging.
- Water User's Associations, which are expected to reduce the responsibility of the government besides increasing the water use efficiency, have made slow progress in the state so far: only about 27 per cent of net irrigated area has been brought under the control of WUAs as of December 2003. While there is no evidence to suggest that WUAs are working well at the large scale irrigation systems, a large number of studies have shown that WUAs can perform well at small scale irrigation systems. Therefore, all those irrigation systems that have less than 1000 ha of command areas should be brought under the control of WUAs. Experience from different countries indicate that it is difficult for WUAs to provide better water supply and perform all necessary duties without proper legal standing. Therefore, in order to promote the users' participation in irrigation management in an effective manner, there is a need to bring an Act, which empowers WUAs. One can only hope that "Maharashtra Farmers Management of Irrigation System Act-2003", approved by the cabinet and to be placed before the State Legislature, will stimulate the users' participation by giving required legal standing.

- Though the state has made tremendous progress in WDPs since 1982, it has treated only about 15 per cent of its potential area as of March 2002. Between 1994-95 and 2001-02, about 197 thousand hectares of area, on an average per year, has been treated through various intervention programmes under the WDPs. With the current rate of growth, it may take more than 100 years to treat the entire potential watershed area, which is estimated to be 20.36 mha. Therefore, since WDPs have proved to be effective intervention programme in increasing the water availability, thereby reducing rural poverty in the rainfed areas, new strategies need to be framed to cover at least one million hectares of area through WDPs every year. While selecting areas for WDPs, priority need to be given to those regions which have (a) more drought-prone area, (b) lower irrigation development, and (c) lower utilisation of irrigation potential. Greater emphasis should also be given for non-engineering and vegetative prescriptions and interventions for improving the productivity of the land and to obviate runoff.
- Currently, WDPs have been operated by different departments/agencies in the state without any coordination by any single agency. As a result, the overall working conditions of WDPs including utilisation of allocated funds are not clearly known. Therefore, by developing a convergent approach between various departments not only the funds can be utilised meaningfully but the areas for WDPs can also be selected appropriately for treatments.
- Demand-supply scenario of water is not very comfortable in many main and sub-basins, although the state level position is expected to be satisfactory up to 2030. Projections indicate that demand for irrigation water is expected to increase by 182 per cent between 1996 and 2030 at the state level. While no single strategy is going to solve the water scarcity problem, there is an urgent need to formulate appropriate strategies to reduce the demand for water. While watershed development programmes and reuse of municipal waste water may enhance the supply of water, volumetric pricing, turnover system of irrigation management, appropriate cropping pattern, large scale adoption of micro-irrigation, etc., can reduce the demand for water. Measures such as demand management and supply reassessment are necessary in water scarce Krishna basin. Policies on water resource development and management should be different for water surplus and water scarce basins. The state also should study the feasibility of transfer of water from water surplus basin to water scarce basin keeping in view the future demand for water.
- There is no doubt that bold reforms are needed in order to sustain the huge irrigation sector. But, at the same time, the performance of irrigation sector should not be judged only on the basis of financial recovery rate (direct revenue) as the gross benefits of irrigation are substantial Though they cannot be easily quantified (Gadgil, 1948). As suggested by a recent World Bank (2002) study on Maharashtra, "Meaningful and sustainable reform in the water sector require a well thought through strategy for change, and a commitment to participation of and communication with all interested parties. Since most of the changes involved are difficult to implement, strong political leadership and commitment are required to make things happen" (World Bank, 2002, p.56).
- Finally, since irrigation sector of Maharashtra is the largest in India, it is essential to establish Water Regulatory Authority (WRA), similar to State Electricity Regulatory Commission (SERC), to manage and suggest strategies for improving the performance of irrigation sector as well as to solve all water related disputes take place within the state. Water rates for different purposes and working expenses needed to maintain the sector should be approved by WRA.

Chapter 5

Industrial Growth

Introduction

This chapter presents an analysis of the structural changes of Maharashtra's industrialisation. The sectoral composition of the state domestic product of Maharashtra has been following the national trend of services led growth. With a limited potential in agriculture, the state needs to explore opportunities in the secondary sector. The share of the secondary sector in the state domestic product continuously increased up to 1986-87, but since then it has been gradually declining (Figure 5.1).

FIGURE 5.1

Changing Sectoral Composition of Maharashtra SDP

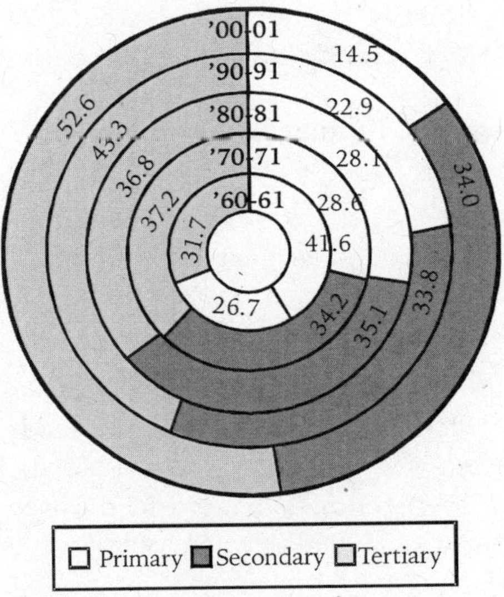

Maharashtra, the leading industrial state in India occupies a significant position as far as the manufacturing sector in the country is concerned. As per the Annual Survey of Industries (ASI) 1999-00 results, the value of output in the state originating from manufacturing sector (industry groups 151-369) was estimated to be Rs. 1,783.8 billion, which was 21.40 per cent of the country's output and in which 8 industries accounted for 51.71 per cent of the total output originating in the state. It is found that 44 industry groups of Maharashtra state had more than 10 per cent share in 1999-00.

The major manufacturing industries located in Maharashtra include refined petroleum products, other chemical products, basic chemicals, manufacturing n.e.c.—jewellery, musical instruments, sports goods, games and toys etc., spinning, weaving and finishing of textiles, other food products, sugar, cocoa, chocolates, noodles etc., basic iron and steel and motor vehicles. The principal industrial zone in Maharashtra is the Mumbai-Thane-Pune belt, accounting for almost 60 per cent of the State's output. Efforts are being made to promote other industrial areas like Nagpur, Nashik, Aurangabad, Solapur, Jalgaon, Raigad, Amravati and Ratnagiri, by building the necessary infrastructure and creating an environment conducive to industrial development.

In this study, we have used ASI data with old classification up to 1997-98 (Box 5.1) and with the new classification in three digits for the years 1998-99 and 1999-00. The ASI covers only registered manufacturing activities (broadly factory sector) and hence, this study has been confined to the registered manufacturing sector.

The analysis reveals that during the sixties, the value added by consumer-goods industry contributed 52 per cent of the total, while the remaining 48 per cent came from capital and intermediate industries. But by 1997-98, the consumer-goods industry accounted for a mere 16 per cent of the value added and capital and intermediate industries together contributed about 84 per cent.

BOX 5.1

NIC Classification—Two-digit Level

Industrial Code	*Description of Industry Group*	*Industrial Code*	*Description of Industry Group*
20	Manufacture of Food Products (includes Industry Group 21 Manufacture of Other Food Products).	30	Manufacture of Basic Chemicals and Chemical Products (except Products of Petroleum and Coal).
21	Manufacture of Other Food Products (includes Industry Group 20 Manufacture of Food Products).	31	Manufacture of Rubber, Plastic, Petroleum and Coal Products; Processing of Nuclear Fuels.
22	Manufacture of Beverages, Tobacco and Related Products.	32	Manufacture of Non-Metallic Mineral Products.
23	Manufacture of Cotton Textiles.	33	Basic Metal and Alloys Industries.
24	Manufacture of Wool, Silk and Man-made Fibre Textiles.	34	Manufacture of Metal Products and Parts, except Machinery and Equipment.
25	Manufacture of Jute and Other Vegetable Fibre Textiles (except Cotton).	35	Manufacture of Machinery and Equipment other than Transport Equipment (and excluding Manufacture of Scientific Equipment, Photographic/ Cinematographic Equipment and Watches and Clocks).
26	Manufacture of Textile Products (including Wearing Apparel).	36	Manufacture of Machinery and Equipment other than Transport Equipment (and excl. Manufacture of Scientific Equipment, Photographic/ Cinematographic Equipment and Watches and Clocks)
27	Manufacture of Wood and Wood Products: Furniture and Fixtures.	37	Manufacture of Transport Equipment and Parts.
28	Manufacture of Paper and Paper Products and Printing, Publishing and Allied Industries.	38	Other Manufacturing Industries (incl. Manufacture of Scientific Equipment, Photographic/ Cinematographic Equipment and Watches and Clocks).
29	Manufacture of Leather and Leather Products, Fur and Leather Substitutes.	39	Repair of Capital Goods.

Source: *Annual Survey of Industries*, CSO.

In Table 5.1, we find that Maharashtra, which was in a commanding position during the seventies as far as the share in manufacturing was concerned, faced a decline during the late eighties. But with the introduction of New Economic Policy in the nineties, the state has been able to regain and improve its position. At this juncture, it is felt that it would be useful to critically study the turn-around of the sector with a view to provide guidelines for future growth.

TABLE 5.1

Maharashtra's Share in Indian Manufacturing Sector

(Figures in Per Cent)

Year	*Number of Factories*	*Fixed Capital*	*Working Capital*	*Number of Workers*	*Value of Gross Output*	*Net Value Added*
1979-80	15.57	14.90	19.85	16.71	23.70	24.87
1985-86	14.82	15.63	27.73	15.14	22.54	25.88
1991-92	12.21	15.41	14.81	12.69	17.67	17.22
1997-98	13.74	17.18	18.26	12.70	19.05	19.42
1999-00(P)	14.45	17.52	18.61	13.60	20.19	22.32

Note: Estimated from various issues of *Annual Survey of Industries*, CSO.

Maharashtra's Industrial Economy

Value of Output

The analysis at three digit classification level for the state industries, i) based on inputs and ii) based on uses, reveals the following:

An input-based classification analysis (Table 5.2) indicates that Maharashtra's major industries are chemical, engineering and agro/food-based. The shares of output of chemical and agro/food based industries have declined in 1999-00 when compared to shares in 1998-99.

Further, an analysis of the use-based classification (Table 5.3) indicates that the major share is from the basic goods sector. This is followed by industries manufacturing consumer non-durable goods, capital goods and consumer durable goods. It is also observed that the share of output from industries manufacturing basic goods has gone down from 38.36 per cent in 1998-99 to 33.23 per cent in 1999-00.

TABLE 5.2

Growth of Value of Output: Input-based Classification

(Figures in Per Cent)

Classification	*Value of Output*	
	1998-99	*1999-2000*
Agro-based	15.54	14.50
Textile-based	7.45	8.13
Livestock-based	0.20	0.14
Forest-based	0.10	0.12
Metal/Mineral-based	11.41	10.22
Chemical-based	31.48	27.52
Engineering-based	23.25	25.46
Misc.-based	10.57	13.91

Source: Estimated from various issues of *Annual Survey of Industries*, CSO.

TABLE 5.3

Growth of Value of Output: Use-based Classification

(Figures in Per Cent)

Classification	*Value of output*	
	1998-99	*1999-2000*
Basic Goods	38.36	33.23
Capital Goods	21.34	22.27
Intermediate Goods	1.33	1.44
Consumer Durable Goods	12.23	16.25
Consumer Non-durable Goods	26.71	26.78

Source: Estimated from various issues of *Annual Survey of Industries*, CSO.

Employment

The estimated annual compound growth rate of employment for the period from 1980-81 to 1997-98 for all industries shows that the number employed in the state increased by 0.75 per cent per annum. This occurred mainly in the non-agriculture related industries (NAGRIND) while agriculture related industries (AGRIND) experienced a fall in employment during this period (Table 5.4). A large number of industries experienced a fall in the employment during this period *viz,* manufacturing of cotton textiles (23), wool, silk and synthetic fibre textiles (24), wood and wood products (27) and transport equipment and parts (37). However, industries such as food and food products (20-21), beverages, tobacco and tobacco products (22), textile products (26), leather and leather products (29), chemical and chemical products (30), rubber, plastic, petroleum and coal products (31), metal products and parts (34) and other manufacturing industries (38) are the major industries, which recorded an increase in the number of employees during this period.

TABLE 5.4

CAGR of Employment in Organised Manufacturing Sector of Maharashtra

(Figures in Per Cent)

NIC Code	*Number of Employees*	*Production Workers*	*Non-Production Workers*
20-21	1.03	1.18	0.79
22	2.23	2.42	0.12
23	-2.15	-2.23	-1.69
24	-1.70	-1.86	-1.06
25	-	-	-
26	3.32	2.79	5.09
27	-2.51	-2.86	-1.3
28	-0.29	-0.79	1.08
29	4.98	4.31	7.26
30	1.47	1.34	1.67
31	2.84	2.46	3.83
32	-0.05	-0.61	1.96
33	-0.34	-0.67	0.55
34	1.67	1.20	3.02
35-36	0.93	0.45	1.85
37	-0.97	-1.47	0.33
38	5.14	4.82	6.05
39*	4.38	3.82	7.09
Mfg.(2 3)	0.75	0.48	1.46
AGRIND	-0.30	-0.45	0.20
NAGRIND	1.59	1.31	2.21

Note: * Data are available from 1989-90.

Source: Various issues of *Annual Survey of Industries*, CSO.

In the case of employment in the manufacturing sector of Maharashtra, non-production workers such as persons holding supervisory or managerial positions or those engaged in administrative office, store-keeping section etc., recorded a higher growth rate than the production workers during the period. The industries such as cotton textiles (23), wool, silk and synthetic fibre textile (24), wood and wood products (27), non-metallic mineral products (32) and transport equipment and parts (37) recorded a substantial fall in the employment of production workers during 1980-81 to 1997-98 in the manufacturing sector of Maharashtra.

However, industries such as beverages, tobacco and tobacco products (22), textile products (26), leather and leather products (29), rubber, plastic, petroleum and coal products (31) and other manufacturing industries (38) recorded a substantial rise in the employment of production workers during the period. In the case of non-production workers only cotton textiles (23), wool, silk and synthetic fibre textiles (24), wood and food products (27) experienced a fall in employment during the period in manufacturing sector of Maharashtra. This peculiar pattern of growth of employment means that service-sector oriented employment is increasing, whereas in production, the rising capital intensity especially in large-scale industries is adversely affecting employment of production workers. This trend of employment in the state can be expected to adversely affect the income distribution pattern in Maharashtra.

Those employed in the manufacturing sector of Maharashtra realised an increase of 2.76 per cent per annum in real wages during 1980-81 to 1997-98. This rise was relatively more in the case of NAGRIND than that in AGRIND. In the case of production workers, increase in real wages is higher than that of non-production workers in the manufacturing sector. This trend in rising real wages may be one of the reasons for slow increase in the employment opportunities for production workers.

Capital and Output

The output (in real terms) of the manufacturing sector in Maharashtra increased by 8.07 per cent per annum during 1980-81 to 1997-98. The growth rate of output of NAGRIND is relatively higher than that of AGRIND during the same period (Table 5.5). The industries such as other manufacturing industries (38), leather and leather products (29), textile products (26), chemical and chemical products (30), transport equipment and parts (37) and machinery, machine tools and parts (35-36) recorded relatively high growth rate of output during the period in the state manufacturing sector. However, industries such as cotton textiles (23) recorded very low growth in the output while wood and wood products recorded a fall in the output during this period in the manufacturing sector.

In the case of gross fixed capital the manufacturing sector registered a growth rate of 10.08 per cent per annum during 1980-81 to 1997-98. This growth is relatively higher in the NAGRIND than in the AGRIND. The industries such as non-metallic mineral products (32), basic metal and alloys industries (33), rubber, plastic, petroleum and coal products (31), textile products and leather and leather products (29) recorded relatively higher growth in capital during this period in the state manufacturing sector. These are the capital-intensive industries. The higher growth rate of capital than that of output implies the rising capital intensity in these industries during the period. However, the industries such as cotton textile, wood and wood products registered relatively lower growth in capital.

TABLE 5.5

CAGR of Output and Fixed Capital in Organised Manufacturing Sector of Maharashtra (Constant Price; 1982=100)

(Figures in Per Cent)

NIC Code	*Value of Output*	*Gross Fixed Capital*
20-21	7.53	7.17
22	4.76	11.57
23	1.93	5.35
24	4.70	10.17
25	-	-
26	11.61	11.49
27	-0.78	6.68
28	5.50	9.75
29	10.01	11.26
30	9.45	9.90
31	7.84	13.81
32	7.48	17.17
33	6.98	14.16
34	6.01	10.89
35-36	8.15	8.57
37	8.88	7.23
38	19.11	9.82
39*	14.74	12.45
Mfg.(2-3)	8.07	10.08
AGRIND	5.94	7.98
NAGRIND	8.84	10.87

Note: * Data are available from 1989-90.

Source: Various issues of *Annual Survey of Industries*, CSO.

Location of Industries

In order to identify the industry-wise location status and their potential for higher growth, we have tried to use the Location Quotient (Florence, 1948) which is used to measure the concentration of any particular industry in any defined geographical area. In short, Location Quotient can be defined as the ratio of the percentage share of a given industry in terms of total employees employed in the manufacturing sector of a given state to the percentage share of that industry in the national level to the total number of employees in the national manufacturing sector. The location quotient can be defined as follows:

$$\text{Location Quotient}: \frac{(ES_i / ES_m)*100}{(EN_i / EN_m)*100}$$

Where,

ES_i = Employment in the ith industry of the state

ES_m = Employment in the manufacturing sector of the State

EN_i = Employment in the ith industry in national manufacturing sector

EN_m = Employment in the national manufacturing sector

TABLE 5.6

Location Quotient: Maharashtra

(Figures in Per Cent)

NIC Code	*1980-81*	*1991-92*	*1997-98*
20-21	0.63	0.81	0.73
22	0.87	0.80	0.90
23	1.25	1.25	1.19
24	1.68	1.15	1.03
25	0	0	0
26	1.31	0.9	0.51
27	0.48	0.35	0.36
28	1.01	0.98	1.08
29	0.17	0.21	0.27
30	1.48	1.4	1.31
31	1.35	1.24	1.27
32	0.60	0.56	0.52
33	0.69	0.66	0.67
34	1.62	1.30	1.71
35-36	1.31	1.25	1.43
37	1.17	1.13	1.16
38	1.61	1.74	1.91
39*	*	1.63	1.11
AGRIND	0.88	0.88	0.82
NAGRIND	1.14	1.11	1.17

Note: * Data are available from 1989-90.

Source: Various issues of *Annual Survey of Industries*, CSO.

If the location quotient of a given state in respect of a particular industry is more than unity, it means that the state has a larger share in the distribution of that particular industry than warranted by its share in the distribution of employment in the manufacturing sector. On the other hand, if the location quotient of a given state in respect of a particular industry is less than unity, it means that the state has a smaller share in the distribution of that industry than its due share in the country. The variation in the value of the location quotient of a given state in respect of a particular industry over a period of time reflects the changes in the relative importance of the state with regard to that industry. Precisely, location quotient explains the localisation of a particular industry in a given state.

The location quotient has been estimated for the two digit industries of Maharashtra for the years 1980-1981, 1991-92 and 1997-98 (Table 5.6). The location quotient in general is declining over the period for AGRIND in the manufacturing sector of Maharashtra. Industries such as cotton textiles, wool, silk and synthetic fibre, textile products, wood and wood products recorded a decline in the location quotient. However, industries such as metal products, machinery, machine tools and parts, and other manufacturing industries recorded an increase in location quotient.

Competition Among the States

During the 1980s many states realised their industrial backwardness and have been attempting to correct their industrial policies. These states started providing fiscal incentives, better infrastructural facilities, less bureaucratic administration, to name a few. States like Gujarat, Tamil Nadu, Karnataka, Andhra Pradesh, etc. are competing with Maharashtra and are trying to provide a better climate for the industrial relations.

Competitiveness of a state can be broadly considered as the overall health of the economy in terms of various observable economic and social indicators, which adequately demonstrate the level of development attained by the states. In a market economy, the relative competitiveness of the states becomes the guiding factor for the private corporate sector while evolving their future investment strategies. Therefore, it is necessary to analyse the relative competitiveness of Maharashtra on various performance indicators.

Availability of Physical Infrastructure

In this section, we discuss the availability of power, road and rail transport across the states. These constitute, *inter alia*, the physical infrastructure and are crucial for the growth and productivity performance of the states.

Availability of Power

Although the availability of power has improved in all states, there is hardly any drastic change (during the period 1991-92 to 2000-01) in the ranking of the states in terms of per capita availability of power or reduction in disparities in the distribution of power across states. Both in 1991-92 and 2001-02, the states with higher per capita availability of power (in descending order) as compared to the all-India level were Punjab, Haryana, Gujarat, Maharashtra, Tamil Nadu, Karnataka and Andhra Pradesh.

Availability of Road

It is seen that in states like Bihar, Uttar Pradesh and West Bengal, the road network is much poorer as compared to the proportion of population of these states. As against this, Maharashtra and Tamil Nadu are relatively better placed. Maharashtra seems to have improved the availability of road transport over the years as compared to other states. For other selected states, the disproportion between the road transport and population shares is not very striking.

Infrastructure Index

To arrive at an infrastructure index, we have considered all possible variables representing various sectors of infrastructure (transportation, power, etc.) and have categorised them into physical, financial and social infrastructure. Figure 5.2 suggests that Punjab is the top ranking state in terms of overall infrastructure development, followed by Gujarat and Maharashtra in the second and third positions respectively. These are followed by Kerala and Tamil Nadu, respectively.

FIGURE 5.2

Infrastructure Index

(a) Physical-Financial Infrastructure Index

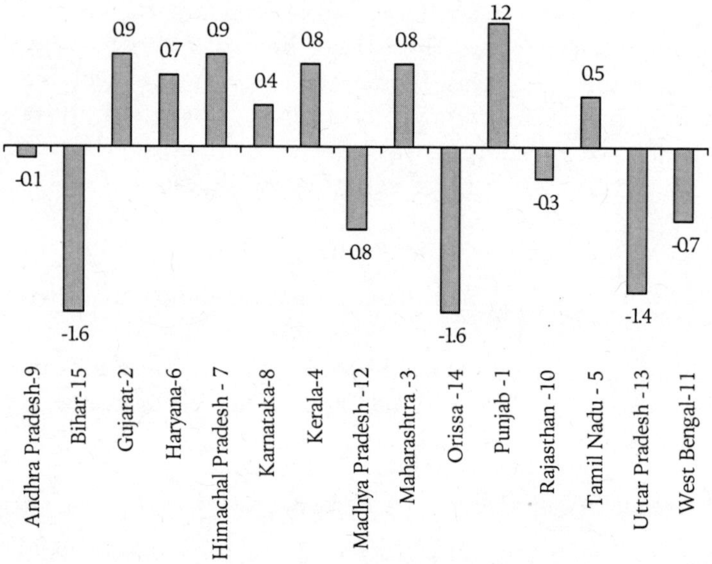

Note: The number against the name indicates the rank of each state.

(b) Social Infrastructure Index

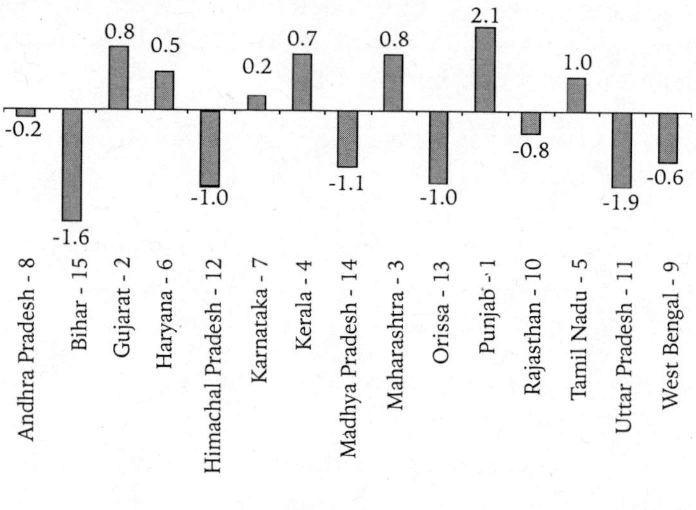

Note: The number against the name indicates the rank of each state.

In general, the trend observed is that the states of the southern and western region are relatively better off in comparison to other regions in terms of infrastructure availability.

Policy Incentives

Besides the availability of physical infrastructure, policy incentives can also activate productivity and growth process. Bajpai and Sachs (1999) have used various criteria such as incentives for investment, power sector reforms, industrial policy reform, infrastructure reforms and tax reforms implemented at the state-level to classify the states into three categories. These categories are: (i) reform-oriented states (Andhra Pradesh, Gujarat, Karnataka, Maharashtra and Tamil Nadu); (ii) intermediate reformers (Haryana, Orissa and West Bengal); and where the economic performance is measured in terms of growth rate, higher investment (both domestic and foreign), increase in software exports and improvement in primary health and education.

Competitive Classification of Industries

The relevance of labelling a state/national economy as competitive in the context of the changed global economic environment and the pursuit for competitiveness as an excuse for picking winners is a matter of continuous debate. Yet, this has become a pre-occupation of policy planners the world over. A country's industries can be classified into dynamic and non-dynamic product categories. There are several ways of measuring dynamism. For the purpose of this analysis, a three digit industry belongs to the dynamic product category if its share is seen as rising in the basket of output of the entire manufacturing industry. If the share is stagnant or declining over a period of time, then the three digit industry is in the non-dynamic category. Two key indicators were used to assess the competitive strength and weaknesses of manufacturing sector state-wise.

Relative Production Competitiveness Index (RPC)

This is defined as the production share of a particular industry or cluster (at the three digit) in total manufacturing of a state divided by the average share of the state in total national manufacturing of all products. A value greater than one indicates that a given state cluster or industry has a greater share of the country's production than average.

Relative Production Competitiveness Growth Index (RPCGI)

RPCGI is calculated by dividing the RPC for the current period 1999-00 by the RPC for the previous period (1998-99). A figure greater than one shows the competitiveness in production during the period under analysis. With regard to the economic status of a state, three digit industries can be classified into the following four categories using relationships between the above two ratios:

Rising Stars (RPC>1 and RPCGI>1)

Lost Opportunity (RPC>1 and RPCGI<1)

Falling Star/Possible Future Star (RPC<1 and RPCGI>1)

Retreat (RPC<1 and RPCGI<1)

On the basis of ASI 1998-99 and 1999-00 results, RPC and RPCGI have been calculated for Maharashtra state. The industries (at the three digit level) of Maharashtra state have been classified into these four groups (Table 5.7).

Rising Stars (RPC>1 and RPCGI>1): Dynamic industries in which the state's share in national industry product is increasing.

Lost Opportunity (RPC>1 and RPCGI<1): Dynamic industries in which the state's share in national industry product is declining.

TABLE 5.7

Relative Production Competitiveness Growth Index
(a) The Rising Stars

NIC Code	*Industry*
154	Manufacture of Other Food Products
155	Manufacture of Beverages
201	Saw Milling and Planking of Wood
210	Manufacture of Paper and Paper Products
222	Printing and Service Activities Related to Printing
223	Reproduction of Recorded Media
243	Manufacture of Man-made fibres
261	Manufacture of Glass and Glass Products
289	Manufacture of Other Fabricated Metal Products; Metal Working Service Activities
293	Manufacture of Domestic Appliances, n.e.c.
300	Manufacture of Office, Accounting and Computing Machinery
323	Manufacture of Television and Radio Receivers, Sound or Video Recording or Reproducing Apparatus, and Associated Goods
331	Manufacture of Medical Appliances and Instruments and Appliances for Measuring, Checking, Testing, Navigating and Other Purposes except Optical Instruments
353	Manufacture of Aircraft and Spacecraft
359	Manufacture of Transport Equipment n.e.c.
369	Manufacture n.e.c.

(b) Lost Opportunity

NIC Code	*Industry*
232	Manufacture of Refined Petroleum Products
242	Manufacture of Other Chemical Products
291	Manufacture of General Purpose Machinery
292	Manufacture of Special Purpose Machinery
341	Manufacture of Motor Vehicles
342	Manufacture of Bodies for Motor Vehicles; Manufacture of Trailers And Semi-trailers
361	Manufacture of Furniture

Falling Stars/Possible Future Stars (RPC<1 and RPCGI>1): Non-dynamic industries in which the state's share in national industry product is increasing; non-dynamic industries that have the potential to be dynamic.

Retreat (RPC<1 and RPCGI<1): Non-dynamic industries in which state's share in national industry is decreasing.

(c) The Falling Stars/Possible Future Stars

NIC Code	*Industry*
171	Spinning, Weaving and Finishing of Textiles
172	Manufacture of Other Textiles
173	Manufacture of Knitted and Crocheted Fabrics and Articles
181	Manufacture of Wearing Apparel, Except Fur Apparel
192	Manufacture of Footwear
221	Publishing
251	Manufacture of Rubber Products
252	Manufacture of Plastic Products
313	Manufacture of Insulated Wire and Cable
314	Manufacture of Accumulators, Primary Cells and Primary Batteries
322	Manufacture of Television and Radio Transmitters and Apparatus for Line Telephony and Line Telegraphy
332	Manufacture of Optical Instruments and Photographic Equipment
343	Manufacture of Parts and Accessories for Motor Vehicles and their Engines
351	Building and Repair of Ships and Boats
352	Manufacture of Railway and Tramway Locomotives and Rolling Stock

(d) Retreat

NIC Code	*Industry*
151	Production, Processing and Preservation of Meat, Fish, Fruits, Vegetables, Oils and Fats
152	Manufacture of Dairy Products
153	Manufacture of Grain Mill Products, Starches and Starch Products, and Prepared Animal Feeds
160	Manufacture of Tobacco Products
191	Tanning and Dressing of Leather, Manufacture of Luggage Hand-bags, Saddlers and Harness
202	Manufacture of Products of Wood, Cork, Straw, and Plating Materials
231	Manufacturing of Coke Oven Products
241	Manufacture of Basic Chemicals
269	Manufacture of Non-metallic Mineral Products n.e.c.
271	Manufacture of Basic Iron and Steel
272	Manufacture of Basic Precious and Non-ferrous Metals
273	Casting of Metals
281	Manufacture of Structural Metal Products, Tanks, Reservoirs and Steam Generators
311	Manufacture of Electric Motors, Generators and Transformers
312	Manufacture of Electricity Distribution and Control Apparatus
315	Manufacture of Electric Lamps and Lighting Equipment
319	Manufacture of Other Electrical Equipment n.e.c.
321	Manufacture of Electronic Valves and Tubes and Other Electronic Components
333	Manufacture of Watches and Clocks

Tables 5.7 to 5.10 indicate that though there is significant number of rising stars in Maharashtra's industries, the picture is marred by lost opportunities in some industries. Significant among these are refined petroleum products, other chemical products (pharmaceutical, medicinal chemicals and botanical products, soap and detergents, paints/varnishes, pesticides), special purpose machinery (agricultural and forestry machinery, machinery for food, beverages and tobacco processing), and motor vehicles industries.

Total Factor Productivity Growth Analysis

This section aims at assessing the efficiency of the industrial sector in Maharashtra at two digit level by Total Factor Productivity (TFP) analysis. The timespan covered in the study is 1979-80 to 1997-98. The summary of the results adopting the Translog index number approach to calculate TFP growth is provided in Table 5.8.

This attempts to bring out the relative performance of various two digit level manufacturing segments over the study period. This constitutes an analysis of the performance of the manufacturing sector in the light of 1991-92 liberalisation policy initiatives, mentioned as winners and losers in the Table 5.9. Changes that have come about in the comparative shares of the different inputs, their growth rates, and the resulting changes in the output and productivity have been looked into for this purpose. The study includes the analysis of data on 19 two digit level industries within the manufacturing sector of which, the data for 2 industries is not complete.

In line with the objectives of the New Economic Policy, manufacturing sector is expected to become more productive and efficient. Hence, we would expect higher growth rates in output and productivity. This, as expected, has been the general trend barring the non metallic products manufacturing sector (32), where the output registered an annual average growth rate of 1.6 per cent after liberalisation as against 4 per cent prior to liberalisation. Growth rates of output of a number of industries have shown notable increases, many of which (namely manufacture of wood and wood products, furniture and fixtures (27) and repair of capital goods (39) have turned from negative to significantly high positive figures.

In accordance with most common beliefs, liberalisation is known to displace labour from the production process due to the functioning of the free

TABLE 5.8

Comparison of the Pre- and Post-liberalisation Scenario in the Manufacturing Sector

Industry Code	*Capital Share in Output*	*Labour Share in Output*	*Intermediate Input Share in Output*	*Output Growth Rate*	*Capital Growth Rate*	*Labour Input Growth Rate*	*Growth Rate of Intermediate Inputs*	*TFPG*
20	0.027	0.052	0.767	0.026	0.015	0.023	0.031	0.000
20	0.021	0.042	0.891	0.037	0.049	0.009	0.042	-0.003
22	0.022	0.109	0.561	0.013	0.005	0.005	0.020	0.001
22	0.035	0.073	0.696	0.059	0.102	0.028	0.062	0.011
23	0.036	0.193	0.602	-0.005	-0.006	-0.021	0.000	-0.002
23	0.046	0.138	0.783	0.018	0.020	-0.006	0.027	-0.003
24	0.034	0.103	0.623	0.009	0.003	-0.004	0.013	0.001
24	0.064	0.066	0.708	0.052	0.153	0.005	0.059	0.001
25	0.008	0.044	1.042	0.164	0.689	0.123	0.261	0.152
25	0.042	0.044	0.666					
26	0.017	0.071	0.616	0.023	0.015	0.002	0.023	0.008
26	0.024	0.046	0.623	0.027	0.069	0.017	0.032	0.008
27	0.020	0.093	0.614	-0.012	-0.064	-0.018	-0.008	-0.002
27	0.026	0.067	0.691	0.067	0.109	0.004	0.084	0.002
28	0.051	0.128	0.589	0.022	0.025	0.002	0.026	0.005
28	0.056	0.078	0.675	0.036	0.081	0.030	0.043	0.001
29	0.020	0.105	0.596	0.013	0.037	0.000	0.012	0.006
29	0.022	0.081	0.660	0.068	-0.002	-0.005	0.032	0.065
30	0.039	0.083	0.634	0.015	0.036	0.005	0.021	0.000
30	0.051	0.054	0.668	0.052	0.025	0.012	0.047	0.018
31	0.022	0.028	0.793	0.033	0.042	0.014	0.035	0.004
31	0.046	0.023	0.895	0.042	0.070	0.026	0.051	-0.005
32	0.065	0.111	0.557	0.040	0.112	0.010	0.042	0.011
32	0.055	0.073	0.637	0.016	0.065	0.010	0.018	-0.001
33	0.035	0.066	0.733	0.027	0.041	-0.002	0.033	0.002
33	0.068	0.033	0.819	0.030	0.044	0.014	0.030	0.003
34	0.027	0.126	0.593	0.010	0.017	-0.011	0.016	0.002
34	0.052	0.084	0.705	0.069	0.091	0.044	0.076	0.007
35	0.033	0.125	0.547	0.030	0.016	0.015	0.039	0.006
35	NA	NA	NA	NA	NA	NA	NA	NA
36	0.032	0.115	0.585	0.035	0.032	0.016	0.043	0.006
36	NA	NA	NA	NA	NA	NA	NA	NA
37	0.046	0.126	0.611	0.028	0.010	0.011	0.031	0.008
37	0.029	0.075	0.719	0.052	0.080	0.019	0.068	0.000
38	0.024	0.110	0.571	0.032	-0.001	0.011	0.041	0.007
38	0.017	0.047	0.779	0.093	0.178	0.055	0.090	0.019
39	0.024	0.231	0.735	-0.006	-0.022	0.005	-0.026	0.007
39	0.026	0.312	0.460	0.093	-0.005	0.027	0.039	0.068

Note: Post liberalisation figures in lighter shade.

market mechanism. This has proved to be a misconception as the study reveals. Even though in 18 of the industries, labour share in total output declined after the reforms (only in industry 39—repair of capital goods, the labour share has increased from 23.1 per cent to 31.2 per cent during the same period), it is evident from the rate of growth of labour, that there has been a distinct tendency for it to increase. The fall in the share of labour in spite of a higher growth rate can be attributed to a relatively higher growth rate of inputs other than the labour. The only two industries showing a decline in the rate of labour growth are (20)—manufacture of food products and (29)—manufacture of leather and leather products, fur and leather substitutes. These fears of labour displacement thus seem to have been unfounded to a certain extent, at least in the case of the manufacturing sector in Maharashtra.

TABLE 5.9

Winners and Losers of Liberalisation (on the Basis of TFPG Averages)

Winners		Losers	
1.	Manufacture of Beverages, Tobacco and Related Products (22)	1.	Manufacture of Food Products (20) (includes Industry Group 21-Manufacture of Other Food Products),
2.	Manufacture of Wood and Wood Products: Furniture and Fixtures (27)	2.	Manufacture of Cotton Textiles (23)
3.	Manufacture of Leather and Leather Products, Fur and Leather Substitutes (29)	3.	Manufacture of Paper and Paper Products and Printing, Publishing and Allied Industries (28)
4.	Manufacture of Basic Chemicals and Chemical Products (Except Products of Petroleum and Coal) (30)	4.	Manufacture of Rubber, Plastic, Petroleum and Coal Products; Processing of Nuclear Fuels (31)
5.	Basic Metal and Alloys Industries (33)	5.	Manufacture of Non-Metallic Mineral Products (32)
6.	Manufacture of Metal Products and Parts, except machinery and Equipment (34)	6.	Manufacture of Transport Equipment and Parts (37)
7.	Other Manufacturing Industries (incl. Manufacture of Scientific Equipment, Photographic/Cinematographic Equipment and Watches & Clocks) (38)		
8.	Repair of Capital Goods (39)		

With respect to the share of capital in the total output, in majority of the industries, there has been a tendency for it to increase following the reforms. However, there have been cases where it either declined or remained unchanged. Corresponding to this, as expected, the rate of growth of capital has shown the same trend (barring the case of a few industries).

In most of the industries, the intermediate inputs have had the dominant share in the output and this share has increased in the post-liberalisation period. Corresponding to this, there has been a distinct rise in the rates of growth of intermediate inputs after the reforms in most of the industries except (34)—the manufacture of metal products and parts, except machinery and equipment. The study reveals that there are inter-industry variations in the growth performance within the manufacturing sector following the reforms. Certain sectors have fared better in the post-reform period as reflected in the total factor productivity growth rate while certain sectors have lost out in the process. Total factor productivity rate in nine industries were no less (in seven industries higher and in two unchanged) than the pre-reform average, in the remaining five industries on which data was available this rate came down from the pre-liberalisation level.

Small-scale Industries in Maharashtra

The small scale industry in Maharashtra contributes significantly to the SDP in terms of production, employment and exports, and therefore, this section tries to explore the potential of the same.

Of the 1,55,621 cumulative number of SSI units set up in Maharashtra till March end 2003, 268 are export-oriented. SSI happens to be a major source of employment as approximately 17 lakh workers are employed with an average of 7 workers employed per unit.

Though, the SSI sector is an important component of industrial development, it is plagued with sick industrial units. Maharashtra has done commendable progress in reducing the number of sick units from 8,056 in 2001 to 4,762 in 2003, but still lots need to be done. In this direction, the recommendations are as below:

Policy

Create a sound policy environment to help the sector cope up with the emerging challenges of globalisation. For this, state-level advisory boards need to be constituted and separate policy for tiny and micro enterprises is required. The investment limit for ancillary units should be upwardly revised while special thrust on modernisation and technology upgradation of existing units needs to be provided.

Industrial Legislation

Simplify the measures to include formation of high-powered committee for recommending single comprehensive legislation for SSI units and simplification of inspection procedures based on self-declaration and post-audit.

Credit

Strengthen credit delivery system through earmarking flow of bank credit to micro, tiny and small enterprises and introducing scheme for credit rating of small-scale units.

Rehabilitation of Sick Units

Put in place an appropriate policy framework for addressing the problem of industrial sickness through strengthening of State Level Inter-Institutional Committee (SLIC) for timely identification and rehabilitation of sick units and exploring the possibility of introducing statutory provision for the revival of viable sick units.

Technology Development

Modernise small-scale enterprises through a multipronged approach, *inter alia,* including formation of high powered committee to recommend linkages between R&D institutions, training institutions, technology banks and user groups and introduction of standards for testing.

Marketing

Extend comprehensive marketing support through Project Sub-contracting Promotion Policy and Vendor Development Programme for linkages between small, medium and large industries.

Fiscal Regime

Create an appropriate fiscal environment through rationalisation of taxes, tariffs and subsidies for small-scale industries.

Development of Small Enterprises: Cluster Approach

Clusters, from an international perspective, is a major strategic approach towards developing small and medium enterprises, because of its excellent linkages that are possible through key factors: service institutions, presence of units along various points in the value chain in fostering competitiveness, building relationships with big firms, developing niche markets, etc. Clusters of enterprises making the same, similar or complimentary products are fast becoming the norm world over. They have many advantages:

- **Recognition of heterogeneity:** Product characteristics, technology, type of markets served, production scale, etc.
- **Collective external efficiency:** A critical mass of firms producing a similar range of products attracts service providers. There is a free flow of useful information and market linkages are easily established. The cluster from which all the member firms derive benefits earns an image of collective efficiency.
- **Ease of customisation of support services:** Policy makers and development agencies in the cluster can ensure customisation of their policies and support systems. That helps the cluster to go on to a higher growth trajectory in comparison to generic support instruments applicable to all types of small enterprises.

Industrial clustering has become popular in India too. There are more than 350 modern SME clusters and over 2,000 artisan-based, rural clusters. Roughly 60 per cent of manufactured exports emanating from the small

TABLE 5.10

State-wise Concentration of Clusters

Types of Clusters	*UP*	*Rajasthan*	*Punjab*	*Karnataka*	*Haryana*	*Maharashtra*	*Gujarat*
Clusters	42	16	23	26	22	66	46
Natural	37	16	23	25	21	63	39
Induced	5	0	0	1	1	3	7
Modern SSI Cluster	18	14	20	13	18	53	37
Large Unit Centered	0	0	4	1	0	1	1
Horizontal	28	12	15	24	14	50	34
Vertical	6	1	1	0	1	8	4
Both	5	3	3	1	7	7	6

Source: UNIDO.

scale industries (SSI) sector originate in clusters. They are concentrated mainly in the northern and western regions of India as is evident from the Table 5.10.

Clusters in Maharashtra

Maharashtra has the highest number of clusters (66 including 55 modern ones). The important ones in Maharashtra are:

- Auto components in Pune and Aurangabad.
- Basic drugs in Mumbai, Thane-Belapur, Pune-Tarapur.
- Cashew processing in Sindhudurg, Vaugurla Ratnagiri.
- *Chappals* in Kolhapur.
- Cotton seed oil in Akola Amravati.
- Electronics in Pune and Mumbai.
- Raisins in Nashik and Solapur.
- Pharmaceuticals in Aurangabad.
- Power looms in Bewandi Malegaon, Bhivandi and Nagpur.
- Readymade garments in Pune, Nagpur, Mumbai.
- Rice milling in Bhandara, Chandrapur and Gadchiroli.
- Steel furniture in Nagpur and Nashik.

Table 5.11 provides a comparative statement of the clusters of Maharashtra *vis-à-vis* other states. It reflects the export orientation of the clusters of Maharashtra, which is comparatively much higher than the competing states. The number of market–based clusters too is high in Maharashtra.

Recommendations Regarding Clusters

Our policy recommendations regarding the implementation of the cluster approach are drawn from UNIDO's work on clusters as well as lessons learnt from successful clusters. These are listed below:

- The private sector should be providers of common services rather than state-level public sector agencies.
- FDI into clusters that have inherent export capabilities should be encouraged.
- The state should involve clusters in dialogues to evolve policies and plans on the industry.
- Flexible and unconventional support instruments should be introduced. A number of consortia could be formed for export promotion, mutual credit guarantee and purchases. The institutional capacities of local associations can be upgraded. These are some of the support instruments that can be exploited to the advantage of clusters and their local economies.
- Positive competition should be induced. Encouraging competition, both external and internal, for clusters based on quality rather than price would ensure motivation for upgradation, which is necessary for units in Maharashtra to retain their competitiveness.
- Cooperation mechanisms should be induced. Clusters could be encouraged to develop task forces so as to make them self-sufficient to the maximum extent possible.

TABLE 5.11

Comparative Statement on Clusters

Export Orientation	*UP*	*Rajasthan*	*Punjab*	*Karnataka*	*Haryana*	*Maharashtra*	*Gujarat*
High	28	8	15	17	7	26	1
Medium	6	0	5	5	8	23	12
Low	6	8	3	4	7	17	21
Infrastructure-oriented	0	0	0	0	1	1	5
Market-based	29	9	18	11	14	42	25
Resource-based	11	7	5	14	6	23	16
Competition with Large Units	28	7	15	11	9	29	30

Source: UNIDO.

- Stimulate induction of new firms: A continuous process of introducing new firms into the clusters and phasing out of ineffective ones could be performed. The process can be hastened by identifying the gaps in the value chain, which would necessitate the entry of a particular kind of firm. This is done not by the conventional system of providing financial incentives but through a positive approach of providing services and linkages with the local associations and research bodies.
- A database on clusters should be built. Clusters should be typecast into them according to their production and marketing at three levels: local, national and international.
- Policy support and developing assistance to protect the artisan clusters and promote the potential modern SSI clusters should be provided.

Spread of Industrialisation in Maharashtra

After taking a stock of industrialisation in Maharashtra, this section attempts to analyse the distributions of this progress, i.e., the geographical spread of industrialisation.

FIGURE 5.3

The Divisions of Maharashtra

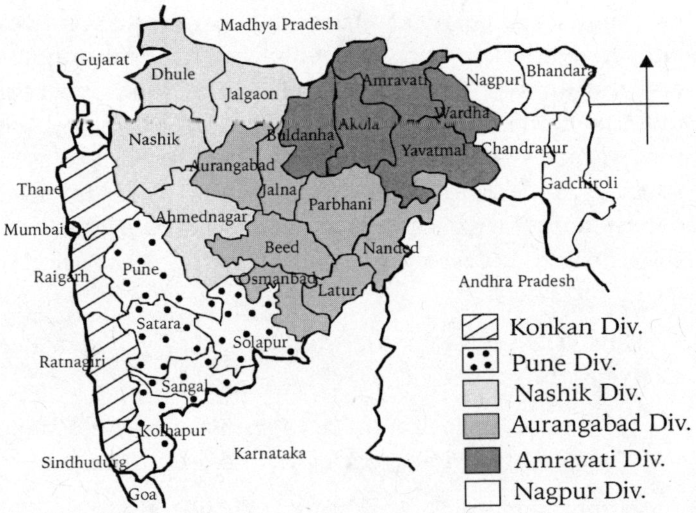

For this, the nature and extent of facility and incentives provided by the state government is used to measure the level of industrialisation. The assumption used is that a district with more number of blocks categorised as A grade is comparatively more industrialised than a district with blocks in D or D+ grade. The grading used in this analysis is the grading provided by SICOM.

Figure 5.3 shows the six divisions of Maharashtra and the districts in each of them.

Figure 5.4 shows the level of industrialisation categorised into four types *viz.*: backward, less developed, moderately developed and developed. It is noticed that industrialisation has happened in and around Mumbai. The districts of Pune, Thane and Raigarh are the developed districts with a few less developed pockets. Nashik and Ahmednagar are moderately developed while Satara, Sangli, Kolhapur, Aurangabad, Amravati and Nagpur are less developed. The rest of Maharashtra is backward.

FIGURE 5.4

Spread of Industrialisation

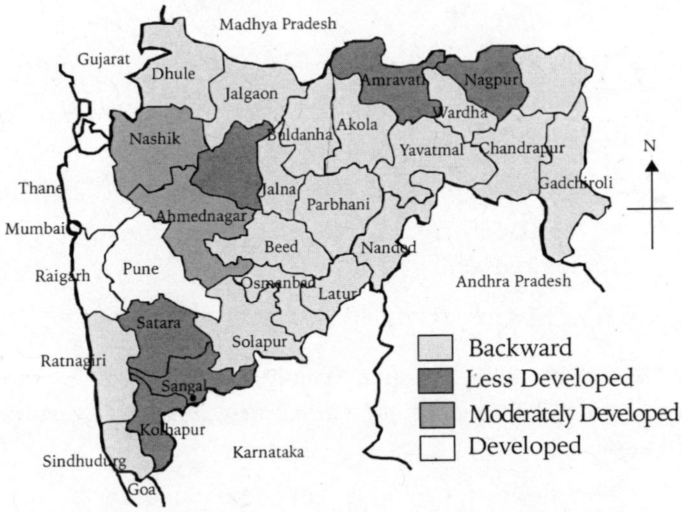

Attracting Foreign Direct Investment

This section focuses on the role of FDI and the measures taken by the state governments to boost the investment.

Factors Affecting Foreign Investments

In the studies related to foreign investment in India a number of factors influencing FDI inflow were identified. Market size is one such factor. Foreign investment is also attracted towards those host countries wherein probabilities or confidence of earning relatively higher profits happens to be more. Risk factors also play an important role in determining the FDI flows in a country. It is found that macro-economic policies are as important a factor in determining the inflow of foreign investment, as specific policies are themselves determinants in attracting foreign investment.

Since 1991, states in India have enjoyed more freedom in forming their respective industrial policy and are using this new opportunity most vigorously to attract private investment. States are now busy wooing private investors to invest and in this regard, provide investor companies with vast range of incentives. For each state, these incentives vary across industries, depending upon the scale of production, location of unit, export orientation and a host of other factors. These incentives may be classified as:

Financial Incentives

Defined as those where the government is directly involved in the financing of the projects and comprise:

- Provision of funds for financing investment operations.
- Government involvement in fixed capital investment for new industrial units.
- Financing and other assistance in setting up technologically pioneering and prestigious units.
- Expansion and diversification of external industrial units.

Fiscal Incentives

Fiscal incentives, which mainly aim at reducing the tax burden of (and/or providing subsidies to) investors include:

- Provisions for various sales tax exemptions.
- Deferment of tax schemes.
- Octroi exemptions.
- Reduction and exemptions of other taxes such as property taxes.
- Other incentives such as export-based incentives.

Other Incentives

- Help in formulating project analysis.
- Allowances for subsidised services like generating sets.
- Feasibility reports.

Incentives for modernisation schemes, special incentives and all other incentives that cannot be classified under a common head but basically which increase the economic viability of a foreign unit by non-financial means.

Do Incentives Matter to Investors?

It has been observed that the top-ranking factors influencing the decision to invest are related to infrastructure (namely transport, energy, telecommunication and water). Neither financial nor fiscal incentives are important, but rather good quality infrastructure that investors rank as the most important factor in investment decisions. It has been noticed that there is no strong relationship between investor friendliness and incentive provisions. However, it provides helpful hints about the attitude of the state governments.

Evidence suggests that the following factors influence FDI decisions more than incentives:

- market characteristics,
- production costs in the case of export-oriented offshore production,
- availability of resources,
- tariffs and other trade barriers,
- transport costs,
- exchange costs,
- political conditions and regulating environment, and
- administrative and institutional arrangements and, their effect on transaction costs, which help reduce uncertainty for potential investors.

However, it is found that there is a relatively weak but somewhat positive relationship between incentives and investment, and FDI shows a slightly higher correlation with the incentive index than internal investment decisions. It is therefore wrong to assume that incentives offered by states are irrelevant as a source for attracting FDI. When fundamental determinants across states are similar, incentives help the foreign investors towards making a particular locational decision.

Thus, we find that there are essentially two major strategies to attract FDI:

1) through creation of Export Processing Zones (EPZs) (providing exclusivity to FDI), and
2) through provision of 'tax holiday' (allowing FDI to move directly into the domestic zone and operate alongside local firms).

Industrial Sickness

Maharashtra Government has a policy of promoting industrial growth and dispersal of industries to the underdeveloped areas in the state through creation of necessary infrastructure. But along with the process of industrialisation, old industries have started becoming sick and a large number of industrial workers are being affected in the process. Table 5.12 provides an idea of the extent of the impact.

TABLE 5.12

Number of Small, Medium and Large Scale Industries Closed Down and Workers Affected in Maharashtra during the Period (1998-99 to 2002-03)

Year	*Small Scale Industries*		*Medium & Large Scale Industries*	
	Closed Down	*Workers Affected*	*Closed Down*	*Workers Affected*
1998-99	9274	47166	245	13602
1999-00	941	2891	95	1526
2000-01	4952	25209	333	52907
2001-02	5726	30769	203	27807
2002-03 (Up to the end of Dec.)	6249	28996	339	45509

Source: Directorate of Economics & Statistics, Planning Department and GoM, 2003.

Board for Industrial and Financial Reconstruction (BIFR) was set up in May 1987 to tackle this problem of industrial sickness. So far the board has received 620 references under the sick industrial companies (Special provision) Act, 1985 of which 119 cases were sanctioned for rehabilitation while 68 were recommended to be wound up. The state government created organisations like Maharashtra State Financial Corporation (MSFC), Maharashtra Industrial Development Corporation (MIDC), Maharashtra Small Scale Industries Development Corporation (MSSIDC), etc. In addition to the above organisations, central financing agencies such as Industrial Development Bank of India, Industrial Credit and Investment Corporation of India etc., also extended the financial assistance to the state.

Industrial Pollution

Industries are essential for the economic development of the state, but the industrial pollution by the way of waste disposal and emissions is causing health hazards and environmental degradation. According to ASI 1997-98 results, 60 per cent of total workforce of factory sector in India was engaged in such polluting industries. These industries contribute 68 per cent of industrial output, 69 per cent of net value added and 37 per cent of gross capital formation. In Maharashtra as per ASI 1997-98 results nearly 50 per cent of the factories in the state belonged to the polluting category. These industries contributed 58 per cent of the output, 50 per cent of value added in the manufacturing sector in the state. Around 50 per cent of factory workers are employed in such polluting industries. Table 5.13 classifies the industries of Maharashtra district-wise into varied levels of

TABLE 5.13

District-wise Classification of Industry by Red, Orange and Green in Maharashtra (as on 31.3.2001)

District	*Industry Type*												*Total*
	Large Scale				*Medium Scale*				*Small Scale*				
	Red	*Orange*	*Green*	*Total*	*Red*	*Orange*	*Green*	*Total*	*Red*	*Orange*	*Green*	*Total*	
Mumbai	99	22	1	122	75	44	34	153	875	539	3208	4622	4897
Navi Mumbai	92	12	8	112	39	24	22	85	820	260	1891	2971	3168
Raigad	32	4	-	36	35	4	4	43	271	261	411	943	1022
Kalyan	24	2	4	30	54	12	-	66	656	415	1337	2408	2504
Thane	32	2	3	37	101	43	73	217	1116	695	3577	5388	5642
Nashik	199	11	22	232	56	24	29	111	734	878	4759	6371	6714
Amravati	24	-	-	24	8	7	-	15	101	322	1364	1787	1826
Aurangabad	70	3	1	74	71	26	16	113	370	813	3416	4599	4786
Nagpur	112	2	2	116	83	19	3	105	494	1032	1872	3398	3691
Pune	135	20	26	181	121	57	29	207	801	812	3146	4759	5147
Kolhapur	60	31	-	91	92	66	-	158	536	729	5667	6932	7181
Total	**879**	**109**	**67**	**1055**	**737**	**326**	**210**	**11273**	**6774**	**6756**	**30648**	**44178**	**46506**

Source: MPCB.

environment friendliness. It shows the alarming proportion of industries of medium and large scale are polluting in nature. Due to this, environmentalists are threatening with complaints and PIL to shut down the polluting industries to protect the environment. From the said facts the economy cannot afford to shut down these industries on environmental reasons. Neither the present level of environment can tolerate further pollution due to these industries. The only choice, therefore left, is to rigorously pursue the pollution abatement measures in such polluting industries.

Information Technology in Maharashtra

When one thinks of IT in Maharashtra, the focus is narrowed down to Mumbai and Pune, the only two cities that can be considered as significant contributors to the IT revolution in the state. Of these, Mumbai attracts a majority of the investment flowing into Maharashtra for almost every industry and IT is no exception.

However, of late, there has been a growing perception that Maharashtra is fast losing out to other states, especially in the field of IT. This is no good news for a state that prides itself on an excellent track record. Consider the following figures put forward by Maharashtra Industrial Development Corporation.

- Maharashtra has the highest number of software export units (1,251).
- It contributes around 30 per cent of the country's software exports.
- The largest number of ISPs in India are based in Mumbai.
- Over 35 per cent of total PC penetration is in Maharashtra.

Moreover, specialised institutions like C-DAC, IIT, VJTI and NCST are churning out skilled technical manpower to spearhead the IT revolution. Mumbai was also the first choice of the early movers in the software space like TCS, Mastic, Datamatics and Patni. But, despite the impressive track record, recent reports indicate that Mumbai could be losing out to cities in more progressive southern states like Andhra Pradesh and Karnataka. Nasscom, which recently released a report titled, "Super Nine Indian ITES Destinations", to assess the competitiveness of nine Indian cities for IT enabled service (ITES) companies revealed some startling facts. According to Nasscom, the ITES industry in India is experiencing the third wave of growth in terms of geographical areas of operation and services offered.

In the first phase, the industry was dominated by captive centres of large multinationals such as GE, American Express and Swiss Air, who set up operations in metros such as Mumbai and Delhi. In its second phase, the growth of the industry attracted entrepreneurs who set up operations in and around Delhi (NCR) and Mumbai. The third phase of growth has been more geographically dispersed with new locations emerging such as Hyderabad, Pune, Bangalore, Chennai and more recently Kochi.

It is this shift that is hurting old-favourites like Mumbai, as every ITES company is looking to cut down operating costs. As factors like employee costs, transportation costs and cost of real estate in Mumbai is higher than those in emerging cities, ITES companies have naturally been attracted to cities like Kochi and Hyderabad, which offer lower operating costs. Hence, while other states are now going all out to attract IT or ITES companies, Maharashtra, which could earlier boast of its infrastructure facilities, is now grappling to build infrastructure in line with the new demands.

Maharashtra was the leading state in terms of infrastructure and in attracting IT companies, but this position has gradually been taken away by the southern states. Maharashtra lags behind because it did not aggressively take initiatives to stay in the number one slot. Compare this with southern states, where state governments are more proactive in interacting with foreign delegations. Also, one cannot be smug in the fact that our infrastructure was one of the best. In progressive sectors like IT, even in a short span of six months one can see infrastructure reach saturation levels. Hence, provisions need to be made on a continuous basis and infrastructure needs to be upgraded with the time. The southern states built infrastructure first and then invited IT companies to set up shop. Maharashtra is different from other states as it already has big companies operating and hence infrastructure needs to keep pace with the rising demand.

Despite these shortcomings, Mumbai still ranks among the very best in factors like telecom infrastructure and international connectivity. In fact, a recent study conducted by the research group Gartner ranked Maharashtra as the most preferred state in the country for the ITES industry. In terms of overall suitability, no other state can be compared to Maharashtra. When one looks at availability of trained and trainable manpower the state is way ahead of other states.

But, while Maharashtra touts impressive statistics, it has to realise that past laurels do not count in this competitive age and a state has to constantly adapt to changing times to attract businesses. For instance, the government has to take a serious look at the state of roads and try to reduce travel time.

There are certainly some areas that need immediate attention: road conditions, local transportation and hygiene. The problem of slums around these techno parks does not send positive signals. Solutions to problems like these are not easy but the state has to focus on these aspects. Broadening and quality improvement of roads must be taken up on a priority basis. Secondly, the government should undertake a serious view of slum management and provide basic amenities like toilets in sufficient numbers.

Another bottleneck that software companies in Mumbai face is with respect to getting imported equipment cleared through customs. This is despite the fact that Mumbai has more connecting flights than any other city in the country. Materials imported by air reach the city in a matter of hours, but on an average it takes 10-12 days between landing and permission for installation of the goods at the STP unit.

Another problem is with respect to the power supply outside of Mumbai. While Mumbai boasts of uninterrupted power supply, the same is not the case with cities like Navi Mumbai, where a large number of IT players have centres. Big companies can afford to install generators, but smaller players lose out in terms of revenues, as clients don't want to face the likelihood of data loss due to power failure.

While Maharashtra still has a considerably good infrastructure when it comes to factors like power, telecom infrastructure and international connectivity, it has to realise that being good in this competitive age is not sufficient—one has to be the best.

Conclusions

Maharashtra has made considerable progress in the field of industrial development over the past five decades. It was a front-runner among the developed states of the country in terms of overall economic progress till the mid-eighties. However, this situation has changed as seen from the analysis above.

It is time to have a fresh look at the policies, programmes and industrial setup for industrial promotion in the state. Past experience indicates that fiscal and financial incentives do help new ventures initially, but for their long-term viability, the state has to take aggressive measures to provide efficient and cost-effective infrastructure, skilled human resource, stable environment and good governance, which are the prerequisites for creating a proper investment climate for sustainable growth of industrial and commercial ventures. While it is important to attract new investments, it is equally important to address the problems and concerns of the existing industries, which are passing through a difficult time.

In the context of second generation economic reforms, Maharashtra Government came up with a Statement of Industrial Policy 2001, to accelerate the flow of investments in industry and infrastructure. To improve upon these efforts, the following can be recommended for the industrial development of the state:

- A growth rate of 8 to 10 per cent should be aimed at.
- The infrastructural facilities, especially, power, good port facilities and better road network should be improved.
- Better institutional support for developing industries in the backward regions of the state should be provided.
- Streamlining of the octroi assessment and collection procedures must be performed.
- Single window clearance should be propagated in all the departments.
- Development of special economic zones with world-class infrastructure to accelerate exports in the pattern of Schenzen in China could be planned and implemented.
- Development of social infrastructure should be enhanced.
- Export oriented units (EOUs) should be recognised as one of the thrust areas.
- Department of Industries should evolve suitable schemes and activate its district centres to adopt new management techniques for quality improvements, cost reduction, improved productivity and operational efficiency
- Sick small-scale units and non-BIFR units should be revived.
- The conditions of the state-level financial institutions should be improved.
- Film industry should be supported and promoted.
- Efforts should be made to emphasise the comparative advantage of host base.

Chapter 6

Infrastructure Development

Introduction

Growth of an economy can be constrained by the non-availability/inadequacy of infrastructure. Though the availability of infrastructure may be viewed as a necessary condition for growth, it need not be treated as a sufficient one. Traditionally, infrastructure services have been produced and provided through vertically integrated production units by the 'public sector'. This has been due to huge investment requirements, high upfront costs, uncertainty about returns and long payback periods. These characteristics of infrastructure service provision also lead to emergence of natural monopolies. Combined with these features is the generation of large positive and negative externalities, which make it difficult to translate the costs and benefits into the user levies for these services. Recent advancements in technology and management practices have made it possible to split the vertically integrated plants into various segments, i.e., by resorting to unbundling of these utilities into production, transmission or/and distribution units. The investment requirements and the risks associated with an unbundled sub-sector are fractions of those required for the vertically integrated plants. Thus, unbundling makes it possible to replace monopolies by more competitive market structures, wherein private sector can also participate.

Provision of infrastructure by the public sector in India has been due to two reasons. Huge investment requirement, as explained above, is the first reason. The second reason is that on the eve of planning process, India accepted a 'mixed economy' path or a 'socialistic pattern of society' and associated with such a system were the economic and social responsibilities of the state. Even as of today, rural electrification is deemed to be a basic minimum service to be provided by the state under the Prime Minister's Gramodaya Yojana (PMGY).

Attempts to run the infrastructure utilities on non-commercial principles have resulted in subsidisation, cross-subsidisation and distorted pricing. Naturally, the end result is financial non-viable operations of utilities providing infrastructure. The strain on fiscal sector and the fear of collapse of infrastructure utilities has compelled a paradigm shift in provision of infrastructure in India, i.e., a shift in favour of private sector participation. Many of these new experiments seem to be in the direction of replication of the successful examples witnessed in other countries.

In this chapter, we include the five basic physical infrastructure services, *viz.*, power, roads, ports and water transport, telecom and water supply to urban population. The scope of this chapter is confined to the description of the present status (availability and problems), reforms initiated and possible solutions for problems in efficient provisioning of the above-mentioned infrastructure. The contents of this chapter are organised as follows. First, we provide the context and discuss the general issues pertaining to growth of infrastructure. This is followed by the full-length discussions on each of the above-mentioned categories of infrastructure. Finally, the policy prescriptions and strategies for development of infrastructure sector as a whole constitute the concluding part of the chapter.

Backdrop: Context, Issues and Approaches

Kick-starting infrastructure projects at the national, state and sub-state levels is the priority of the policy makers. For this, coordination of policy decisions of centre, states and local bodies is essential. With the government funding becoming increasingly scarce and inadequate investment in crucial infrastructures, attempts are being made to 'commercialise' this hitherto heavily subsidised government dominated sector. The onset of rapid reforms since 1991 has led to considerable activity in terms of projects, policies, regulation and foreign collaborations. However, the state of physical infrastructure in the country is far from adequate both in terms of availability and quality. The state of infrastructure in India and its massive fund requirements have been clearly stated in Government of India (GoI, 1996). This report had estimated annual requirements of funds for infrastructure at US$ 26 billion during 1996-2001 and higher at US$ 43 billion during 2002-2006. The report had further added that about 15 per cent of the investment could be financed externally and 85 per cent should be domestically raised. An important reason given in favour of raising domestic finance was due to the fact that these projects will generate revenues in local currency and hence, in the long run it would be difficult to finance them out of foreign savings. Having briefly underlined the context, we now turn to the issues debated with respect to provision of infrastructure.

The first issue is whether the infrastructure should come first rather than later (Morris, 2001). This pertains to the lead and lag relationship between infrastructure provision and production. There are two views regarding whether infrastructure should be planned and created before the demand for it arises (infrastructure first) or whether demand for infrastructure should lead the production and provision of infrastructure (infrastructure later). If the infrastructure is created and the demand for it does not take off due to some reason, there is a danger of infrastructure being underutilised, leading to a heavy cost of infrastructure and financial losses.

The second issue is whether the infrastructure should be 'provided' by the public sector (with or without private sector participation, (PSP)) or by the private sector. Over the years, inefficiency in operations of public utilities has led to escalation of the cost of infrastructure services. The perceptions about the role of public sector in economic activity are changing in response to the performance of the public sector. Provision of infrastructure includes generation, transmission or/and distribution activities. As these services can be unbundled, it is possible to get hybrid systems, wherein, some services can be provided by public sector and others by private sector. As mentioned earlier, unbundling results in division of investment requirements and risks of provision of infrastructure. The various alternatives which involve PSP are: build-and-transfer (BT), build-lease-and-transfer (BLT), build-operate- and-transfer (BOT), build-own-and-operate (BOO), build-own-operate-and-transfer (BOOT), build-transfer-and-operate (BTO), contract-add-and–operate (CAO), develop-operate-and-transfer (DOT), rehabilitate-operate-and-transfer (ROT), etc. In most of these cases, the ultimate ownership of infrastructure projects is supposed to rest in the hands of the government.

The third issue is that of pricing of infrastructure services. The distinction between 'ownership' and 'commercial principle' is at the core of the pricing issue. The dilemma faced here is whether infrastructure services should be priced on the basis of commercial principles or according to social objectives. Linked to this issue is the dilemma as to whether commercial principles should be adhered to by the state or not. If the state also adheres to commercial principles in pricing, then the justification for state monopolies in these services is nearly lost. Again various hybrids can be experimented in this sphere as well. This is due to the fact that all infrastructure services need not be viewed as equally relevant from the point of view of social welfare, e.g., the case of water supply to poor cannot be equated with that of the provision of telecom services. The state cannot altogether absolve itself from the responsibility of provision of all kinds of infrastructure. A proper allocation of resources through budgets may have to be resorted to if the state allows private sector to provide these utilities. In this case, it will have to provide direct subsidies to the targeted consumers, if the state positions itself as a guarantor of social welfare of its people. Yet another alternative is to leave provision of these services to the private sector and provide an enabling policy environment to the private sector in the form of state guarantees, cheaper loans (*via* directives to financial institutions for infrastructure financing), tax incentives for infrastructure bonds, etc.).

The fourth issue is that of fairness to consumers. In order to combine commercial principles and efficiency, independent regulatory commissions both at central and state levels have been established/are mooted so as to protect consumers' interest and ensure that the services are provided to consumers at 'fair' prices. The regulatory commissions are also expected to ensure that the rules and regulations applicable to various service providers are not discriminatory and unfair.

Power Sector

The Constitution of India has placed power in the concurrent list, implying thereby, that the responsibility of taking and implementing decisions has to be shared both by the central and state governments. However, the primary responsibility at consumer end is that of the states. Thus, development of power sector in a state has to be within the framework of the national policy. In view of this, we first present a background of power sector in India covering its objectives, problems and reforms. This is followed by the discussion of power sector in Maharashtra and a comparison with the other major states.

Problems and Objectives of Power Sector Reforms

Power is a crucial input in the growth process. Per capita electricity consumption in India (355 kwh in 2000) is not only extremely low in comparison with developed countries, but also with those in comparable developing countries. In the year 2000, the global average per capita consumption of electricity was 2,176 kwh. The respective figures for some of the countries from the developing countries, *viz.*, Brazil, Mexico and China were 1,878, 827 and 1,655 kwh, respectively. As against this, the consumption levels in developed countries, *viz.*, France, Germany, Japan, UK and USA were 6539, 5,563, 7,628, 5601 and 12,332 kwh, respectively (World Bank, 2003). As stated in Electricity Bill, 2003, only 55 per cent households in India have access to electricity. Access is yet to be provided to about 80,000 villages (GoI, 2001a). Most of those who have access do not get uninterrupted reliable supply.

Cross-subsidisation in power sector is coupled with lack of assurance about the quality of supply. The timely and uninterrupted supply of power is necessary for industry to maintain growth momentum, as also to compete in the global markets. The crucial reasons why the growth of hardware segment of the IT sector has not complemented the growth of software industry in India are interruption and voltage fluctuations in power supply, besides the power shortages. In the absence of improved availability of power in the years to come, it will be difficult to sustain the growth of software segment of the IT sector and also to have it regionally dispersed.

The main problems facing the power sector in India are as follows.

- Huge investment requirement to meet the demand for power.
- Low coverage of population receiving power.
- Inadequate quantity (as reflected in energy and peak deficits) and poor quality of power.
- Large unmetered supply and high transmission and distribution (T&D) losses.
- Cross-subsidisation leading to financially unviable public utilities.

The basic objectives of the power sector reforms as laid down in the (GoI, 2001a) are as follows: (i) provide power on demand by 2012; (ii) make the power sector commercially viable and self-sustaining; (iii) provide reliable and quality power at an economic price; and, (iv) achieve environmentally sustainable power development. The policy makers have set the goal of electrifying all villages by 2007 and all households by 2012. This has also been advertised as reliable, affordable, quality 'Power to All: 2012'. The 16th Electric Power Survey (2000) has set the target of additional capacity installation to the tune of 107,000 MW (by 2012), so as to fulfil the objective of 'Power to All by 2012'. This means doubling the existing capacity in the next 10 years or replicating the achievements of more than 5 decades in the coming decade. The central, states and private sectors are expected to contribute about 61.0, 17.6 and 21.4 per cent of this additional capacity installation. Realism of this target has to be viewed against the additional capacity installation to the tune of about 36843 MW (52 per cent of the targeted additional capacity installation) during the Eight and Ninth Five Year Plans.

In conformity with the traditional view that infrastructure ought to be provided by the state, the public sector has been predominant in India's power sector. It is only recently that the continuing and unsustainable losses of the power utilities have made it mandatory to introduce reforms in the power sector.

Power Sector Reforms in India

Power sector reforms in India were initiated in the early nineties, as a part of stabilisation and structural reform package, power sector was opened to foreign investment. We also observe that since the year 2001, a number of committees and expert groups have been appointed by the Ministry of Power, Government of India (GoI) to identify the problems of power sector and to find solutions for the same. The major documents, which have been prepared by these committees and expert groups (along with the major policy documents/ announcements and legislative measures) have been listed in Box 6.1. These documents have shaped the course of the power sector reforms in India.

BOX 6.1

Major Documents on India's Power Sector

- The documents which have shaped/outlined the power sector reforms in India are as follows:
- Settlement of SEB dues, Report of the Expert Group (M.S. Ahluwalia, Chairman), Ministry of Power, (GoI, 2001a).
- Restructuring of SEBs, Report of the Expert Group (M.S. Ahluwalia, Chairman), Ministry of Power, (GoI, 2001b).
- Blueprint for Power Sector Development in India, Ministry of Power, (*GoI, 2001a*).
- Distribution Policy Committee Report (Ashok Basu, Chairman), Ministry of Power (GoI, 2002).
- Accelerated Power Development and Reform Programme (APDRP), (GoI, 2002b).
- Structure of APDRP, Reform Framework and Principles of Financial Restructuring of SEBs, Report of the Expert Committee on State-Specific Reforms (Deepak Parekh, Chairman), Ministry of Power (GoI, 2002).
- IT Task Force Report for Power Sector, submitted by IT Task Force (Nandan Nilekani, Chairman), Ministry of Power (GoI, 2002e).
- Report on Rating of State Power Sector, Submitted by ICRA/CRISIL, Ministry of Power (GoI, 2003c).
- Report on Distributed Generation, (A.V. Gokak, Chairman), Ministry of Power (GoI, 2003d).
- Electricity Act, 2003 (GoI, 2003e).
- National Electricity Policy (GoI, 2005).

The power sector reforms can be classified into three categories, *viz.*, legislative reforms, policy reforms and administrative reforms.

Legislative Reforms

The legal/institutional frame adhered to for the growth of power sector has been defined by the Indian Electricity Act, 1910 the Electricity Supply Act, (1948). The Electricity Regulatory Commission Act was passed in 1998, and it provides for setting up of a Commission at the Central level and also for regulatory commissions at state levels. The Central Electricity Regulatory Commission (CERC) was constituted in July 1998 and is in operation. In 22 states, the State Electricity Regulatory Commissions (SERCs) have been set (as on 16 Feb. 2005). As mentioned earlier, these regulatory commissions are meant to protect consumer interests in an environment of increasing privatisation. Lok Sabha has passed the Electricity Bill, 2003 on 9 April, 2003 and by Rajya Sabha on 5 May 2003. The Electricity Act, 2003 was notified on 2 June 2003 and became operational w.e.f. 10 June, 2003. The Act aims at creating a liberal framework for development of the power sector by distancing Government from regulation. It has replaced the earlier three existing legislations, *viz.*, Indian Electricity Act, 1910, the Electricity (Supply) Act, 1948 and the Electricity Regulatory Commissions Act, 1998. The salient features of the Electricity Bill, 2003 are provided in Box 6.2.

BOX 6.2

The Highlights of the Electricity Bill, 2003

- **Formulation of Policy/Legislations:**
  - Preparation of a National Policy Draft in consultation with state governments.
  - More stringent anti-theft legislation.
  - Constitution of an Appellate Tribunal to hear appeals against the decision of the CERC and SERCs.
  - The State Electricity Regulatory Commission to be mandatory.
  - Authorisation to Regulatory Commissions to fix ceilings on trading margins, if necessary.
- **Thrust on Generation and Management of Rural Electrification**
  - Licence free generation and distribution in the rural areas.
  - Local management (by *panchayats*, cooperative societies, non-government organisations, franchisees) of rural distribution.
- **Structural Reforms to Increase Competition and Efficiency**
  - Delicenced and captive generation of thermal power (though hydro projects would require clearance from the Central Electricity Authority).
  - Reorganisation or continuance of SEBs.
  - Mandatory metering of all electricity supply.
  - Open access in distribution to be introduced in phases.
  - Gradually phasing, out of cross subsidies.
  - Private licencees to be allowed in transmission open access in transmission from the outset, entry in distribution through an independent network.
  - Freedom to distribution licencees to undertake generation and generating companies to be permitted distribution.
  - Recognition of trading as a distinct activity.
- **Continued Role of the State**
  - A government company to act as transmission utility at the Central and state levels so as to plan and coordinate the transmission network,
  - Provision for payment of subsidy through budget.

Source: GoI documents released on 9 May 2003.

Besides this, emphasis is being laid on conservation of energy. Energy Conservation Act was passed in 2001 and it came into effect on 1 March 2002. A Bureau of Energy Efficiency (BEE) has been set up to reinforce the objectives of the Act. Central and state governments have been empowered to facilitate and enforce efficient use of energy and its conservation. Standards and Labelling (S&L) have been identified for improvement in energy efficiency. Standards and Codes (S&C) are to be applied for commonly used equipment in industries, such as, pumps, fans, blowers, compressors, boilers, etc., and efficiency gains of the order of 10 per cent are expected in use of these equipment. In the existing legislative framework, there is also a provision for imposing penalties in the case of wastage of energy.

Policy and Administrative Reforms

The resources required for additional capacity installation of about 1,07,000 MW during the Tenth and Eleventh Five Year Plans are estimated to be Rs. 8,00,000 crore (GoI, 2001). Of this amount, nearly one-fourth is required for the transmission system. In view of this huge sum required for installation of additional capacity, efforts have been made to facilitate private investment, including foreign capital as well. There is no ceiling on foreign equity participation in the power sector. Foreign direct investment (FDI) in transmission is being encouraged through two routes, *viz.*, joint venture (JV) and independent private transmission companies (IPTC). In view of the industry requirements and the time lag it may take to match the industry needs through additional capacity installation, development of captive power plants is being encouraged, especially in special economic zones.

A crucial component of the policy reforms pertain to the settlement of SEBs dues to central undertakings. Most of the SEBs are on the verge of financial collapse. As a result, these have not been able to pay for the power supplied to them by the central utilities. The total outstanding dues of SEBs to the central power utilities have risen to more than Rs. 4,10,000 crore and their losses have reached an alarming proportion of about 1.5 per cent of GDP (GoI, 2002). The recommendations of the Ahluwalia Group (GoI, 2001b) have been operationalised. The outstanding dues of SEBs towards CPSUs are being scrutinised by respective states with the clear understanding that the SEBs will pay their current dues.

Accelerated Power Development and Reform Programme has been one of the crucial policy measures. APDRP was introduced in February 2001 (as Accelerated Power Development Programme and later rechristened as APDRP in February 2002).

The objectives of the reforms as regards the distribution of power are to achieve 100 per cent metering, energy audit, better HT/LT (high tension to low tension) ratio, replacement of distribution transformers, use of IT solutions relating to power flow at critical points so as to ensure accountability at all levels, etc. These are expected to result in improvement in quality of power supply to the consumers, besides improving revenue realisation for the utilities. Sixty-three circles have been selected and are being developed as 'Centre of Excellence' for distribution reforms. The plan is to cover all the circles in the country in a phased manner. The funds to state governments are to be provided through the APDRP for: i) renovation and modernisation (R & M), life extension, uprating of old thermal and hydel plants; and ii) upgradation and strengthening of sub-transmission and distribution network (below 33kV or 66kV). This is to enable energy accounting and metering in the distribution circles. The upgradation, strengthening of transmission and distribution network is considered to be crucial. This can reduce the high aggregate technical and commercial losses (40-45 per cent of total losses arise at the distribution stage) and improve quality of power supply (low voltage)/availability/reliability. The funds are provided through a combination of grant and loan to the state governments as Advance Central Plan Assistance. The funding details are as follows:

- Hundred per cent project cost finance is provided to special category states (all Northeastern states, Sikkim, Uttaranchal and J&K) in the ratio of 90 per cent grant and 10 per cent soft loan.
- In respect of other states (non-special category), 50 per cent of the project cost is provided by the centre and the ratio of grants and loans is 50:50. The balance 50 per cent funds of the project requirement have to be raised by the state.
- The access of the states to the funds is based on agreed reform programmes, e.g. on the narrowing and ultimate elimination of the gap between unit cost of supply and revenue realisation within a specified time frame. Priority is accorded to projects from those states, which have committed themselves to a time bound programme of reforms. The financial aspects of these reforms have been discussed later whilst comparing the

TABLE 6.1

Mode and Ownership-wise Installed Capacity in Power Sector: Maharashtra and India

Sector/Utility/Region	*Mode and Ownership-wise Installed Capacity*							
	1997				*2002*			
	As a % of Grand Total for India				*As a % of Grand Total for India*			
	Hydel	*Thermal*	*Wind*	*Total*	*Hydel*	*Thermal*	*Wind*	*Total*
MSEB	1.58	7.48	0.01	9.07	2.29	6.99	0.01	9.29
Maharashtra (Private Sector)	0.50	1.55	0.00	2.05	0.43	2.45	0.30	3.17
Maharashtra (Total)	2.08	9.03	0.01	11.12	2.71	9.44	0.31	12.46
India	**25.24**	**73.70**	**1.05**	**100.00**	**25.03**	**73.53**	**1.44**	**100.00**
Grand Total for India (MW)				**85795**				**104918**
Sector/Utility/Region	*Mode and Ownership-wise Installed Capacity*							
	1997				*2002*			
	As a % of Total for Maharashtra				*As a % of Total for Maharashtra*			
	Hydel	*Thermal*	*Wind*	*Total (MW)*	*Hydel*	*Thermal*	*Wind*	*Total (MW)*
MSEB	17.47	82.46	0.07	7782	24.63	75.30	0.07	9744
Maharashtra (Private Sector)	24.26	75.74	0.00	1756	13.42	77.16	9.42	3331
Maharashtra (Total)	18.72	81.23	0.06	9538	21.78	75.77	2.45	13074
India	25.24	73.70	1.05	85795	25.03	73.53	1.44	104918

power sector in Maharashtra with the rest of Indian states.

The financial support available to states under APDRP is under two streams, *viz.*, investment and incentive streams. The former is aimed at developing 'demonstration projects' and the latter at reducing the gap between unit cost of supply and revenue realisation. In other words, the latter depends on the actual performance. The general financial losses of public utilities can be classified into two major types. These are: (i) deficits accumulated from the past, *viz.*, dues to suppliers of power and fuel such as NTPC and Coal India (or its subsidiaries); and, (ii) unfunded liabilities arising from future promises of payment, largely related to labour, such as, pensions, provident fund and gratuity.

Power Sector in Maharashtra vis-à-vis Other States: Present Status

Until early June 2003, three power utilities, *viz.*, Tata Electric Companies (TEC), Bombay Suburban Electric Supply (BSES) and Bombay Electric Supply & Transport (BEST) served the Mumbai area. BSES Ltd. was fully inducted into the Reliance conglomerate in early June 2003 and was renamed as Reliance Energy Ltd. (REL). TECs and REL are private companies, whereas, BEST is municipality owned. The remaining area of the state is served by the Maharashtra State Electricity Board (MSEB) which is a public utility created under the Electric Supply Act, 1948.

Maharashtra was ranked as one of the best states in terms of infrastructure availability. About 80 per cent of the population in the state has access to electricity. Though almost all households in cities and towns have access to electricity, this is not true for all the rural households. In Table 6.1, we provide a brief profile of Maharashtra's share (MSEB and private sector) in installed capacity in India.

Maharashtra accounts for about 11 to 12 per cent of India's total installed capacity in power sector. The contribution of MSEB in 1997 was more than four times that of the private sector. The provisional estimates for 2002 put the relative contribution of MSEB to about three times that of the private sector, thus indicating a greater role played by the private sector in the recent years as regards capacity installation in Maharashtra's power sector.

In 1997, the composition of installed capacity in Maharashtra was slightly more skewed in favour of thermal power as compared to that for India. Almost one-fourth of installed capacity at the all- India level was comprised of hydel power, whereas, for Maharashtra this figure was even less than one-fifth. Provisional estimates of composition of installed capacity for 2002 indicate a marginal shift in favour of both hydel and wind power and the mode-wise composition of installed capacity in Maharashtra has become similar to that for the country as a whole.

Though Maharashtra has ample power for the base load, it does face shortages of both energy and peaking capacity. The quality of supply is poor due to voltage drops, frequency fluctuations and load shedding. In Table 6.2, we provide data regarding the energy deficit and peak-deficit in Maharashtra (MSEB) and for India as a whole. Both energy and peak deficits for Maharashtra were lower than that for all-India in 1991-92 and 1996-1997. By 2001-02, Maharashtra recorded energy deficit that was higher than the corresponding figure for all India and the peak deficit became almost equal to the corresponding figure for all-India. Though the state suffers from energy and peak deficits, these deficits need to be interpreted with caution, as these are in relation to the requirements. A state that is stagnant (with recessionary conditions or economically backward) may not show deficits. Moreover, if peak deficits are to be avoided, then excess capacity installation becomes necessary. In fact, the Electricity Bill, 2003 does aim at creation of excess capacity in view of the need for uninterrupted availability of power. It may, however, be noted that underutilised capacity at non-peak hours implies higher costs of power and a choice has to be made between 'high cost of power with absence of deficit in peak hours' and 'a lower cost of power with peak deficits'. It may also be noted that the energy and peak deficits in Maharashtra have increased to 10.2 and 18.2 per cent, respectively, in 2003-04.

TABLE 6.2

Power Sector Deficit in Maharashtra and India

Year	*Energy Deficit (%)*		*Peak Deficit (%)*	
	Maharashtra	*India*	*Maharashtra*	*India*
1991-92	4.5	7.8	8.7	10.8
1996-97	5.6	11.5	8.7	18.0
2001-02	8.8	7.5	12.5	12.6

Source: "Annual Report 2001-02 on The Working of State Electricity Boards & Electricity Departments".

Despite the fact that Maharashtra is one of the most industrialised states of the country, the state has very low consumption of electricity per person in relation to the global standards. The per capita consumption of electricity in Maharashtra (411 kWh) was about 1.63 times that of all-India figure (253 kWh) in 1990-91. By the end of the decade, this multiple had decreased to about 1.47. In Figure 6.1, we provide a comparison of per capita consumption of electricity in Maharashtra with that for the country as a whole.

We can also see that in 1999-00 the per capita consumption of electricity registered marginal decline for both Maharashtra and for India. However, the fall in the former was more pronounced than for the latter. In 1994-95, Maharashtra served the highest number of consumers in the country (13 per cent of countrywide consumers). By 2000-01 (revised estimates), it served only 11.6 per cent of India consumers and also no longer remained a state serving the highest number of consumers. Tamil Nadu at present commands this enviable position.

FIGURE 6.1

Per Capita Consumption of Electricity (kWh)

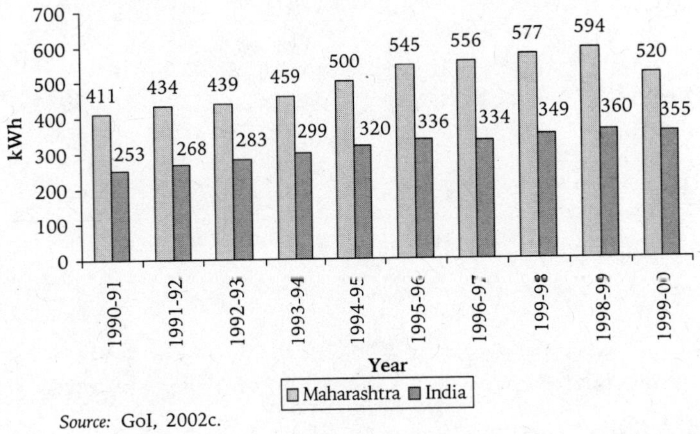

Source: GoI, 2002c.

Given the predominance of MSEB in provision of electricity in the state, its financial viability is one of the major concerns. The arrears of MSEB (as provided by the MSEB) have been rising in the recent years. These are as follows: Rs. 5,907 crore (2001), Rs. 7,114 crore (2002) and Rs. 8,765 crore (2003). Some of the major reasons for financial losses of MSEB are distorted pricing, technical and physical factors and hasty reforms.

Electricity Boards and Electricity Departments supply electricity to different categories of consumers at different rates. Hence, the financial sustainability of these utilities also depends on the composition of consumer categories, tariff structure across various consumer categories and the cost of supplying power. In Table 6.3 and Figure 6.2, we provide a synoptic view of the composition of the consumer categories in Maharashtra and compare the same with the national level figures.

Way back in 1960-61, about 10 per cent of electricity was supplied to the domestic and agricultural sector. In 2000-01, about 44 per cent of electricity by MSEB was supplied to the domestic sector (18 per cent) and agricultural sector (26 per cent). At the national level, these two categories account for about 50 per cent of electricity consumption. Electricity to these sectors is heavily subsidised and, therefore, it affects the financial viability of SEBs.

TABLE 6.3

Electricity Consumption by Different User Groups in Maharashtra

Year	*(% of Total)*				*Total (Mn. kWh)*
	Domestic	*Commercial*	*Industry*	*Agriculture*	
1960-61	9.6	7.3	68.1	0.6	2722
1970-71	9.6	7.2	69.4	4.7	7650
1980-81	12.7	6.8	57.9	12.3	14034
1990-91	16.9	6.9	49.1	22.0	29971
2000-01	18.1	15.0	40.6	26.3	41598
2001-02	25.7	9.5	37.6	18.8	46338
2002-03	24.6	9.3	36.4	21.3	49945

Source: GoI (2002c), MEDC (2000), GoM (2004); and author's calculations.

FIGURE 6.2

Consumer Categories: A Comparison of Maharashtra with India (2000-01)

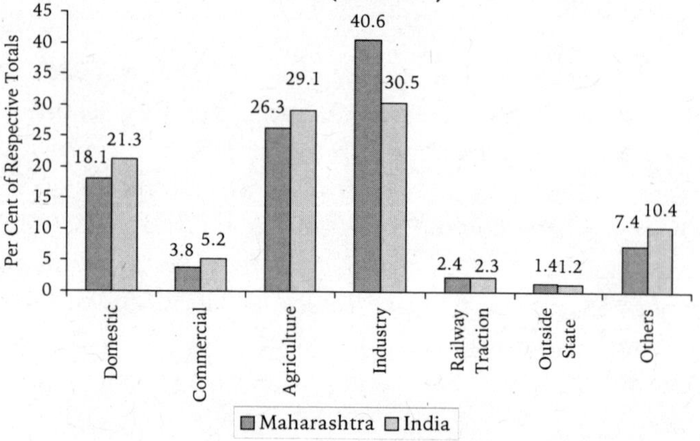

Source: Based on the data in "Annual Report 2001-02 on the Working of State Electricity Boards & Electricity Departments".

FIGURE 6.3

Cross-Subsidisation to Various Consumer Groups

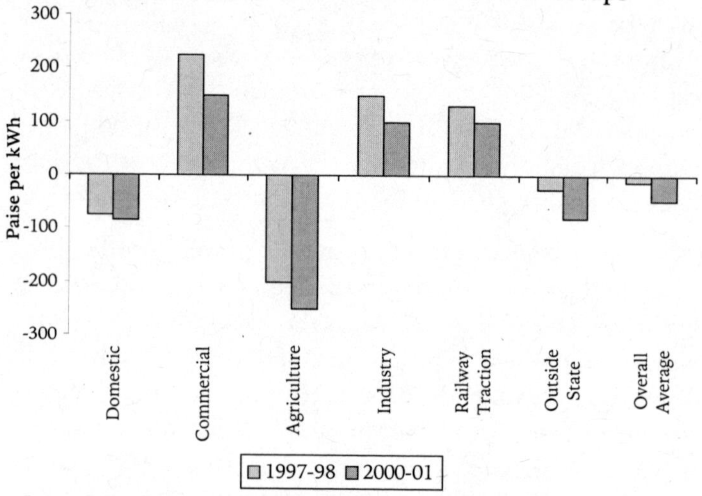

Source: Calculated from the "Annual Report 2001-02 on The Working of State Electricity Boards & Electricity Departments".

In Figure 6.3, we have plotted the margin of tariff over the cost of power supply for different categories of consumers. This difference provides us information about cross-subsidisation. From all these figures, we can conclude that, be it Maharashtra or the entire country, the domestic and agricultural sectors that account for more than 40 per cent of power supply have a recovery ratio (ratio of tariff to the cost of power supply) of less than unity. The opposite is true for industry, commercial and railway traction sectors. In other words, there is cross-subsidisation from these sectors to agricultural and domestic sector. It can be also seen from Table 6.3 that the proportion of electricity consumption by sectors other than household and agricultural sectors has been on a decline over the years and cross-subsidisation is one of the reasons of financial problems of the MSEB.

Cost of supply of power in Maharashtra has been lower as compared with the all-India average (revised estimate for India in 2000-01 was 327.1 paise per kWh). The cost of supplying electricity in Maharashtra in 1997-98 was 215.6 paise per kwh. The respective figure for 2000-01 (revised estimate) was 318.7. MSEB is not only one of the biggest SEBs in the country but has been historically known for its technical efficiency. It performed substantially better than the other electricity boards both in physical terms (plant availability and plant load factor) as also in financial terms. MSEB has been recipient of many awards for its technical efficiency. In the last two years, the losses of MSEB have been consistently falling and in fact, Maharashtra has also been able to get the incentive component of the ARPDP funding. Nevertheless, about 18 per cent of thermal generation plants in the state are more than 25 year, old and about 48 per cent are about 15 to 25 years old (GoM, 2002a). This results in high technical losses in the transmission process. Financing investment requirement for replacing these plants would be a daunting task and Maharashtra will have to face this challenge in the coming years.

The physical and financial performance of MSEB *vis-à-vis* the average of all electricity boards is provided in Table 6.4 and Table 6.5 respectively.

From Table 6.4, we see that both plant availability and plant load factors for MSEB have been higher than that for all Electricity Boards combined. The ceiling set by the Central Electricity Authority for T&D losses is 16 per cent. As regards, T&D losses, MSEB had substantially lower T&D losses as a percentage of its plant availability during 1996-97 to 1998-99.

TABLE 6.4

Physical Performance

Year	*Maharashtra*			*India*		
	PA (%)	*PLF (%)*	*T&D (%)*	*PA (%)*	*PLF (%)*	*T&D (%)*
1996-97	85.9	68.7	17.7	79.00	64.40	24.53
1997-98	85.0	68.3	17.1	79.40	64.70	24.79
1998-99	82.9	68.4	15.5	78.70	64.60	26.45
1999-00 (Provisional)	85.1	71.7	30.5 (31.8)	80.30	67.30	30.80
2000-01 (Revised)	86.4	72.6	30.0	80.50	69.00	29.90
2001-02 (Plan Estimate)	NA	74.5	28.0 (39.4)	NA	69.90	27.80

Note: (i) PA, PLF and T&D indicate plant availability, plant load factor of thermal stations and T&D Losses. (ii) Figures in parentheses indicate T&D losses reported in tariff filing with the MERC (World Bank, 2002).

Source: GoI, 2002c.

Thereafter, MSEB can hardly claim to be one of the better states with low T&D losses. High T&D losses of MSEB can also be partly attributed to a high ratio (approximately 2) of low tension to high tension transmission. Both high T&D losses and high cost of power from Dabhol Power Corporation (DPC) have led to deterioration of financial position of the MSEB in the recent years.

This is reflected in a yawning negative rate of return on capital of MSEB especially in the recent years, though it is below that of the average for all SEBs (Table 6.5). In view of this, several measures were undertaken to introduce the reform in power sector in Maharashtra. As mentioned above, some of these hastily implemented reforms themselves are responsible for financial deterioration of MSEB. We now proceed to outline the power sector reforms in Maharashtra and whilst doing so, we will also discuss the issue of hasty reforms with Enron saga as an example.

TABLE 6.5

Rate of Return on Capital without Subsidy

(Per Cent)

Year	*Rate of Return on Capital without Subsidy (%)*	
	Maharashtra	*Average of All SEBs*
1992-93	3.10	-12.7
1993-94	3.10	-12.3
1994-95	4.10	-13.1
1995-96	-5.30	-16.4
1996-97	-1.20	-19.6
1997-98	-0.14	-22.9
1998-99	1.92	-34.2
1999-2000	-16.52	-43.1
2000-01 (RE)	-13.85	-39.1
2001-02 (Annual Plan)	-31.72	-44.1

Source: GoI, 2002c.

Power Sector Reforms in Maharashtra

Maharashtra pioneered, in a temporal sense, as regards initiation of power sector reforms. This can be seen from the fact that though much of action on the part of Central Government has been seen since the year 2000, the Government of Maharashtra had taken several initiatives in the nineties itself. Moreover, the Government of Maharashtra has also undertaken reform initiatives so as to avail of benefits provided by the Central Government, which hinge on the reform milestones undertaken by the state governments. This is not to deny the fact that the implementation of reforms has been far from ideal. In Box 6.3, we present the initiatives taken by the GoM.

Maharashtra was one of the early states to rush in for foreign investment. Despite the fact that the entry of Dabhol Power Corporation (with its three-US based shareholders, *viz.*, Enron Corporation, Bechtel Enterprises Inc., and General Electric Company) was debated and criticised for several reasons and there were many a hiccups in clearing of the project, finally the approval was given on the build-operate-and-own (BOO) basis. DPC perhaps provides the best example of a hasty

BOX 6.3

Power Sector Reforms in Maharashtra

In order to initiate power sector reforms, the Government of Maharashtra appointed several committees and also brought out the White Paper. However, only a few of the suggested reforms have actually been implemented. In this box, we first summarise the suggested reforms by the various committees and later enumerate the reforms implemented/not implemented so far.

- Rajadhyaksha Committee was appointed in 1996. It suggested various measures so as to 'put MSEB on a viable footing'. One of its main recommendations was creation of a regulatory body. It also recommended the conversion of MSEB into a generation and transmission company with private sector owning shares of such a company. The other recommendations were 'privatisation of the distribution' of electricity supply. Of these recommendations, except for the creation and operationalisation of MERC, which was mandated by the power sector reforms undertaken by the Central Government, the other major recommendations have not been implemented.
- Upasani Committee was appointed in 2000 with the objective of formulating legislation so as to enhance powers of MERC's, and bringing its power on par with the other regulatory commissions in India. Maharashtra Electricity Reform Bill was drafted so as to widen the scope of powers of MERC and commence the unbundling process. The draft of the Bill has acquired the status of legislation now.
- Reforms undertaken as a part of APDRP: Under the APDRP, initiated by the Central Government, Maharashtra has signed the MoUs with the Ministry of Power, Government of India. Some of the reform milestones included in the APDRP are: setting up of regulatory commission; unbundling of SEBs; removal of cross-subsidies and tariff anomalies (issuing of tariff orders); providing budgetary support through subsidies to SEBs; introduction of privatisation; etc. In March 2001, GoM and GoI signed the MoU for undertaking measures for operating MSEB on commercial principles. The broad objective was to reduce systemic losses and eliminate all losses in distribution by 2003. GoM agreed to fully implement tariff orders of MERC. Two tariff orders have been issued, the last tariff order was issued in 2002. Under APDRP, the SEBs are required to sign a MoA with the Ministry of Power so as to carry out distribution reforms. The prime objectives of the MoA is to enforce accountability and commercial accounting, introduce online management information systems, reduce T&D losses, introduce benchmark for the prime indicators that reflect consumer satisfaction and stability of the system. MSEB signed the MoA with the Ministry of Power in June 2002. Another component of the APDRP is signing of a Tripartite Agreement (TPA) by the state governments with the Central Government and the Reserve Bank of India, as a part of one-time settlement of dues of the state utilities to central utilities. In March 2003, the Government of Maharashtra has signed the TPA. In order to reduce the technical and T&D losses, 85 per cent metering of 11 kv feeders and 86 per cent consumer metering has been completed. Though, The Anti-Theft Legislation has been passed, Maharashtra Electricity Reform Bill is yet to be passed.
- Energy Review Committee was appointed in February 2001. Dr. Madhav Godbole chaired the Committee. The main objectives of the Committee were to critically examine the contract with the Dabhol Power Corporation (DPC) and recommend a new framework for negotiation with the DPC and suggest measures to improve the financial performance of MSEB. The Committee recommended the following measures: (i) Restructuring of MSEB into various of generation and distribution utilities, though transmission was to remain a monopoly: (ii) Financial restructuring of the resulting generation and distribution utilities before their privatisation; (iii) privatisation of the urban distribution and implementation of credible solutions (such as, cooperatives-based solutions or privatisation based on the support of a subsidy programme which is transparent) for the rural areas; and, (iv) implementation of a multi-year tariff system so as to create incentives for private distributors to reduce losses. Except for opening up the private sector (both domestic and foreign) for generation of power and a more liberal policy for captive power plants, the other measures have not been implemented.
- In August 2002, Industries, Energy and Labour Department of Government of Maharashtra published a White Paper on Maharashtra Power Sector Reform. The reforms mooted in this paper are: internal reform, independent regulatory framework and structural reforms. The internal reforms consist of development of human resources, reduction of T&D losses, instituting anti-theft measures, energy auditing and metering, demand side management and instituting consumer grievance redressal system. The target for T&D loss reduction has been set at 1 per cent per year for technical losses and 3 per cent per year for commercial losses in urban areas. The respective figures for rural area are 0.5 per cent and 1 per cent per year. The regulatory commission is to address the issues of tariff rationalisation, phasing out of cross-subsidies in five years whilst protecting interests of poor consumers. Under structural reforms, unbundling and corporatising MSEB into separate generation, transmission and distribution companies is mooted.
- As regards implementation of the Electricity Act, 2003, there is no move to privatise MSEB by the GoM. However, restructuring of MSEB into separate state-owned companies for generation, transmission and distribution is under consideration. In order to ensure competition, a greater scope for private sector in generation and distribution is being envisaged by the state.

Source: World Bank (2002), GoI (2003), GoM (2001 and 2002) and MEDC (2003).

BOX 6.4

Dabhol Saga: An Example of Hasty Reforms

With the initiation of power sector reforms, in 1991, the Government of India decided to open up power sector for private sector through independent power projects (IPPs). The DPC—mainly a foreign entity domiciled in India agreed to establish a 2,184 MW power plant in two phases (740 MW first phase and 1444 MW in second phase) in Maharashtra. Along with MSEB, it had three US-based companies as its shareholders, *viz.*, Enron Corporation, Bechtel Enterprises Inc. and General Electric Company.

In May 1992, the MoU was signed. In September 1992, a World Bank team assessed the project and recommended against the project on two grounds. First, it was not the least costly option as the plant was liquid fuel-based, wherein, liquid fuel was to be imported from Oman. Coal or hydro plant would have enabled cheaper power generation *vis-à-vis* imported liquid fuel plant. Second, there was apprehension about the ability of MSEB to generate sufficient revenues to meet its payment obligations under the Power Purchase Agreement (PPA). Despite this, a draft PPA was initiated in November 1993, and concluded in December 1993. The financial closure was reached for Phase I in March 1995. DPC entered into a PPA with MSEB for sale of power on build-own-operate (BOO) basis for a period of 20 years. DPC agreed to a levelised tariff of Rs. 1.89 per unit at the exchange rate of Rs 32 per US dollar, at a fuel price of $13 per barrel and a plant load factor of 90 per cent. In anticipation of a high growth rate of the economy, the demand for electricity was also expected to increase rapidly. PPA implied that DPC sells power to the MSEB for which it is paid a sum that covers both fixed and variable costs. The payment of fixed cost was not tied to the level of generation, while the variable cost was linked to the amount of power being sold. This sum, divided by the amount of power sold, gave the per unit rate. MSEB and Government of Maharashtra gave guarantees about the payment to DPC. The GoI provided the counter guarantee.

In August 1995, MSEB was instructed by GoM to repudiate the transaction and to request DPC to stop construction as the doubts began to be expressed about the project. After lengthy negotiations involving GoI, GoM and MSEB, a revised PPA was reached and in December 1996, financial closure for the second phase was attained and the construction of plant was resumed. Phase I of the plant became operational in May 1999. During May 1999 to December 2000, DPC supplied 6,048 million units of electricity to MSEB at the rate of Rs. 4.67 per unit. This was much higher than the tariff of Rs. 1.89 negotiated with unrealistic assumptions. Due to the industrial deceleration, it was difficult for industry to absorb this escalated cost of electricity and this got reflected in the reduced growth rate of demand for electricity. The revisions in the estimates of demand for electricity made in the 16th Electric Power Survey of India (GoI, 2000) bear a testimony to this fact. Moreover, the cost of buying power from DPC was more than double the average purchase price from other suppliers. MSEB's finances deteriorated sharply due to the costly power purchase from DPC. It was able to pay for the power until December 1999. In May 2001, MSEB repealed the contract and halted the construction of Phase II.

The amounts at stake are considerable. The present exposure of the lenders is of the order of US$1.5 billion (Phases I and II), most of which has been arranged or guaranteed by the Indian financial institutions. five major foreign banks, *viz.*, Citibank, Bank of America, ANZ Bank, Credit Suisse First Boston and ABN-Amro, have communicated to the Finance Ministry that they be paid their $ 339 million exposure to the power project. However, the counterguarantees cover only $ 100 million in the first phase of which $ 10 million have already been repaid. The bankruptcy of Enron in November 2001 has also complicated the matter.

After the bankruptcy of Enron, the domestic financial institutions, led by the Industrial Development Bank of India (IDBI), have been making frantic attempts to sell the foreign equity stake in the Dabhol Power Company and get the company restarted. The interest of domestic lenders in restarting DPC can be understood as they expect to recover a part of their exposure to DPC through the sale of power to the Maharashtra State Electricity Board (MSEB). However, the foreign lenders are opposed to any such move as the guaranteed amounts are still pending. A few firms, such as, Reliance, BSES, Tata Power, Gail India, British Gas, Gaz de France and Shell had shown interest in having stakes in DPC and restarting it. Given the fact that foreign lenders have veto powers in this matter, the fate of DPC is still unpredictable.

The fiasco of DPC can be explained due to the following reasons. First, the mode of awarding the contract was through negotiations rather than through competitive bidding, despite the fact that the rationale for reforms is explained in terms of competition and efficiency. Second, the technical and economic aspects of the projects were not given adequate attention. Though the need was to augment the intermediate and peak capacity, the first phase of the project was to primarily create the base-load. Coal/hydro/gas-based plants would have enabled energy generation at a lower cost. Despite this, contract was awarded to the liquid fuel-based plant, which would import liquid fuel. Perhaps, optimistic perceptions about the growth scenario and foreign exchange reserves in future were behind the award of this contract, despite scarcity of foreign exchange at the time of the award of the contract. Sensitivity analysis regarding the cost of power to exchange rate, plant load factor, price of imported liquid fuel, etc., ought to have been conducted if the policy makers were serious about the reforms. Third, the structural aspects of reform process aim at introducing efficiency through market forces and how guarantees and counter-guarantees fit into the reform process is something which has to be convinced to people by the policy makers at both the state and the national levels. Naturally, the questions of governance are bound to arise. Finally, another faulty aspect of the structural aspect of this contract was opening up generation for private investment (with a single buyer model in which the entire risk is passed on to the government by private investor) without liberalising power distribution.

Source: World Bank (2002), GoM (2001), *and Business Standard* (January 7, 2003 and April 4, 2003).

reform in the power sector. In view of the relevance of this case for devising reforms, in Box 6.4, we highlight the problems with DPC. Phase I of DPC was started with guarantees and counter guarantees regarding the rate of return in foreign currency terms and commitment of MSEB to buy power from DPC.

As mentioned earlier, a high cost of obtaining power from DPC, *inter alia*, resulted in financial derailment of MSEB. The authorities themselves have admitted this. To quote the official position, "The optimistic expectations from the IPPs have not been fulfilled and in retrospect it appears that the approach of inviting investments on the basis of government guarantees was perhaps not the best way" (GoI, 2003c). The DPC saga, financial derailment of MSEB and introduction of power reforms by the Centre have made it necessary for Maharashtra to also go in for consolidation of the financial position of MSEB.

Basak (2002) claims that Maharashtra will become a power-surplus state in the next five years. He opined that MSEB can successfully compete with the private sector and that the Electricity Bill, 2003 (which has subsequently been enacted) is an opportunity rather than a threat to MSEB. This is due to MSEB's cost-efficiency and asset base. MSEB's cost of power production per unit ranges between 40 paise to Rs. 2.24, transmission cost per unit is 24 paise, distribution cost per unit is 65 paise, and asset value on replacement cost basis is Rs. 62,000 crore. Thus, MSEB's cost structure at present is much lower than the cost at which it bought power from DPC. However, there still remains a question as to whether MSEB will be able to meet the power needs of the state at this relatively lower cost even when the old plants will have to be replaced, given the fact that about half of the thermal generation plants in the state are about 15 to 25 year old.

Status of Power Sector Reforms in Maharashtra vis-à-vis Other States

One of the modes of assessing the progress of power sector reforms in Maharashtra *vis-à-vis* other states would be to examine the progress on the various reform milestones under APDRP.

As on 31 July 2003, SERCs have been constituted in 19 states, including that in Maharashtra. Maharashtra is also one of the 17 states in which SERCs are operational. Tariff orders have been issued by 15 states and Maharashtra has done it twice, the latest being in 2002. MoUs and MoAs have been signed by 27 states, including that in Maharashtra. Maharashtra is also one of the 25 states that have signed TPAs. As regards its progress towards metering, Maharashtra has made substantial efforts, though it has been outperformed by West Bengal. The core of power sector reforms lies in Enactment of Reform Bills at the state levels, unbundling/corporatising the electricity boards and privatisation of distribution. On all these fronts, the reform process has been rather slow, especially in Maharashtra. Only nine states have enacted both the reform bills and have unbundled/corporatised their electricity boards. West Bengal has done the latter but not the former. Maharashtra has done neither of these. Only Orissa and Delhi have taken initiatives in privatisation in distribution.

TABLE 6.6

Power Sector Reforms in Maharashtra *vis-à-vis* Other States (as on 31 July, 2003)

Reform Milestone	*Maharashtra*	*Total States & UTs*
Constitution of SERC	Yes	19
Operationalisation of SERC	Yes	17
Number of Tariff Orders	2	15
Signing of MoU	Yes	27
Signing of MoA	Yes	27
Signing of TPA	Yes	25
Reform Bill Enactment	No	10
Unbundling/Corporatisation	No	9
Privatisation of Distribution	No	2
11 KV for 100% Metering	85%	11
100% Consumer Metering	86%	5
Anti-theft Law	Yes	7

Source: GoI, 2003.

The states can avail finances from the Central Government under APDRP only if accompanied by their own initiatives. It can be seen from Table 6.7 that merely 8.9 per cent of the APDRP project costs have been utilised in India so far. Tamil Nadu and Delhi have utilised about 18 to 20 per cent of the APDRP costs. States like Karnataka, Andhra Pradesh and Rajasthan have utilised about slightly more than 10 to 15 per cent of the APDRP project costs. Maharashtra and Gujarat, despite being the most industrialised states have not been able to exploit this lucrative opportunity provided by the APDRP. As indicated earlier, the release of the financial assistance to states under the APDRP scheme is based on the performance of the states in terms of bridging the gap between the cost of supply of power and the tariff charged by them. This explains the low utilisation of APDRP funds in various states including that in Maharashtra.

TABLE 6.7

Progress of APDRP (as on 31 March, 2003)

State	*APDRP Cost (Rs. Crore)*	*APDRP Release (Rs. Crore)*			*Utilisation/ APDRP Cost (%)*
		Investment	*Incentive*	*Total*	
Andhra Pradesh	755.70	163.82		163.82	9.53
Bihar	368.99	66.11		66.11	1.69
Delhi	473.23	105.51		105.51	19.95
Gujarat	517.90	105.42	236.37	341.79	6.45
Haryana	226.71	56.33	5.01	61.34	11.04
Karnataka	580.60	145.15		145.15	10.73
Kerala	175.18	30.43		30.43	7.41
Madhya Pradesh	339.54	74.87		74.87	3.67
Maharashtra	**673.93**	**138.48**	**137.89**	**276.37**	5.65
Orissa	296.11	54.35		54.35	0.00
Punjab	353.19	53.98		53.98	6.89
Rajasthan	627.53	125.64		125.64	14.45
Tamil Nadu	484.09	111.57		111.57	17.80
Uttar Pradesh	406.43	80.12		80.12	0.00
West Bengal	102.13	19.02		19.02	4.57
Assam	408.54	96.97		96.97	0.01
India	**8737.60**	**1755.51**	**379.27**	**2134.78**	**8.90**

Note: It may be noted that the project costs are double of the APDRP costs.

Source: GoI, 2003.

An expert committee (GoI, 2002d) recommended restructuring models that include possibilities of competition and especially those that involve private sector participation in distribution segment. It also warned against using a single buyer model and opined that state governments should not engage in purchase and sale of electricity through any entity that is controlled or owned by it—either directly or through guarantees. In an unbundled electricity industry, it recommended that transmission utility should not trade in power in order to avoid potential misuse of its monopoly power. In this context, it is pertinent to note that in states, such as, Orissa, Andhra Pradesh, Haryana, Rajasthan and Uttar Pradesh have implemented power sector reforms and have gone in for a single buyer model. Effectively, the role of Electricity Regulatory Commissions (ERCs) has been confined to promotion of investment and growth of power sector. The presumption that regulatory bodies will protect interest of consumers' appears to be far-fetched in the case of power sector. Promotion of infrastructure and consumers' interest need not always coincide, is reinforced by the Dabhol experience in Maharashtra. Dabhol saga was caused by provision of guarantees and counter guarantees coupled with a single buyer model. These features of the contract went against the very principle of the market discipline.

Road Development in Maharashtra

Growth of a region depends, *inter alia*, on how well is it connected internally as well as with the rest of the world. Roads not only enable the masses to use the public road transport at economical prices but also help in smoothening interregional disparities in availability of goods (and hence, reduce dispersion of prices across regions).

Development of network of national highways is crucial to the development of a state. National highways provide connectivity to the states with other trading centres and ports of the country and constitute the first tier of road development plan (in a multimodal transport system).

Road development in India depends on efforts of both the central and the state governments. We first examine road development in Maharashtra through schemes initiated by the Central Government and later discuss the state initiatives. In December 1998, the Prime Minister's Task Force approved the National Highways Development Project (NHDP). The Golden Quadrilateral (GQ), one of the components of NHDP, aims at connecting Mumbai, Delhi, Kolkata and Chennai. It involves construction of road length of about 5,846 kms. In February 2002, except for Allahabad Bypass, civil contracts were awarded for various parts of the GQ. Earlier a substantial part of the project was to be completed by the end of year 2004, which has now been advanced to the end of 2003. Along with this, the north-south (NS) corridor, connecting Srinagar to Kanyakumari and east-west (EW) corridor, connecting Silchar to Porbandar, are also part of the NHDP. Four major sources of financing that have been identified for GQ and corridor projects are: (i) imposition of cess on petrol; (ii) external assistance; (iii) market borrowings; and, (iv) contribution of private sector. The total estimated cost of the project is about Rs. 58,000 crore. The contribution of the above four financing sources is expected to be approximately 34, 34, 21 and 10 per cent, respectively, of the total estimated project cost.

National highways passing through Maharashtra state account for just about 6.2 per cent of the total length of national highways in the country. A large 'interior' triangular area in Maharashtra, bound by Dhule, Nagpur and Osmanabad, still remains uncovered by the national highway network. Maharashtra and Gujarat account for around 8.3 to 8.4 per cent of proposed laning under GQ. This is lower in comparison to the share of Andhra Pradesh, Karnataka, Tamil Nadu, Rajasthan and Uttar Pradesh. Share of these states range between 10.7 and 17.4 per cent. Maharashtra accounts for just 6.0 per cent of the proposed laning of NS corridor. The main beneficiaries of NS corridor will be Andhra Pradesh, Jammu & Kashmir, Madhya Pradesh and Tamil Nadu. The EW corridor does not pass through Maharashtra and the direct benefits of this corridor will accrue mainly to Assam, Bihar, Gujarat, Rajasthan, Uttar Pradesh and West Bengal. The total share of Maharashtra in laning of both the corridors is just about 3.2 per cent, which is much lower than for many other major states of India. In order to exploit the full connectivity potential of this minor share in four/six laning of national highways, Maharashtra will have to complement this by construction of roads through its own initiatives, which would connect the GQ and the NS corridor. NHDP will also help the state in providing connectivity to about 44 of its ports (NHDA, 2003).

In view of the fact that there were about 1.60 lakh unconnected habitations (about 40 per cent of total habitations) in the country at the turn of the century, Pradhan Mantri Gram Sadak Yojana (PMGSY) was launched in December 2000. This scheme is dedicated solely to the construction of rural roads and aims at closing the gap between 'Urban India' and 'Rural *Bharat*'. The targets of PMGSY are to connect every unconnected habitation with a population of over 1,000 persons through good, all-weather roads by the year 2003. Habitations with a population of more than 500 persons are to be connected by the end of the Tenth Plan, i.e., by the year 2007. All habitations in the hill states, desert and tribal areas (with a population of more than 250) are also to be provided connectivity through PMGSY. The nodal agency for implementing the project in Maharashtra is the Ministry of Rural Development (Pradhan Mantri Gram Sadak Yojana, 2003).

In Table 6.8, we indicate the share of Maharashtra in the PMGSY. Maharashtra accounts for about 6.3 per cent of the total habitations of the country. The state accounts for about 9.1 per cent of connected and 2.5 per cent of unconnected habitations of the country. In other words, rural road network in Maharashtra seems to be better as compared to other states. Though Maharashtra is not going to be a major beneficiary both in terms of financial allocations and the coverage of habitations, yet there is a reasonable scope for improving the rural road conditions in the state and also meeting the other socio-economic objectives, if the scheme is implemented in an integrated manner with the other employment and income-generating poverty alleviation schemes. One of the major departures of this scheme from other developmental schemes is that the execution of the scheme is time-bound, without a possibility of cost escalations. Penalty clauses have been included in the cases of time overruns. However, the scheme assumes the ready availability of land, which opens up the crucial issue of governance, displacement and compensation.

TABLE 6.8

Maharashtra's Share in PMGSY

(% of All-India Total)

Maharashtra's Share in PMGSY	*Population*				
	1000+	*500-999*	*250-499*	*Below 250*	*Total*
Habitations	7.8	6.1	5.0	6.1	6.3
Connected Habitations	10.7	9.9	7.1	8.0	9.1
Unconnected Habitations	0.9	1.0	2.6	4.4	2.5
Habitations Covered under PMGSY Phase I (2000-2001)	4.5	1.8	2.5	0.3	2.3
Habitations Covered under PMGSY Phase II (2001-2002)	4.8	9.9	1.1	0.1	5.4
Habitations to be Covered under PMGSY Phase III (2003-2004)	2.3	1.5	0.7	2.5	2.1

Source: Author's calculations based on GoI (2003f).

Maharashtra is one of the major industrialised states of India. The city of Mumbai has acted as a magnet in attracting migrants from all over the country and has emerged as a hub of industrial, commercial, entertainment and financial activity. There has been a phenomenal increase in the number of mechanical vehicles in the state over the years. Inadequacy of roads due to disproportionate growth between the number of vehicles and the growth of road length also has resulted in poor quality of roads in the state. The road length at the eve of the formation of the state was just 39,242 kms. At the end of March 2003, the road length in the state increased to 2.25 lakh kms. Out of the above road length, 1.65 per cent (3,710 kms) was national highway, 14.98 per cent (33,705 kms) state highway, 21.4 per cent (48,192 kms) major district roads, 19.64 per cent (44,183 kms) other district roads, and the rest 42.30 per cent (9,150 kms) village roads. At the end of March 2003, the road length per 100 sq. kms of geographical area in the state was 87.40 kms (provisional). As per the 1991 Census, the road availability per lakh of population was 277 kms.

At the end of March 2003, out of 40,412 inhabited villages in Maharashtra, 93 per cent of villages were connected by all-weather roads and 4.77 per cent by fair-weather roads. Any type of roads did not connect remaining 2.23 villages. Of these unconnected villages 31 per cent were villages in tribal area and 69 per cent in non-tribal area.

Road Development Initiatives of Government of Maharashtra

To meet the ever increasing demand for better and wider road network in the state, two 20 year Road Development Plans, *viz.*, 1961-81 (Public Works Department, GoM, 2003b) Road Development Plan (Bombay Plan) and 1981-2001 Road Development Plan, have been implemented. The details of targets and achievements during the Road Development Plans 1961-1981 and 1981-2001 are given in Table 6.9. It can be seen from Table 6.9 that the original target of national highway was much higher in the Bombay Plan as compared to the revised target. These plans were preceded by the Nagpur Plan, the targets of which were almost met when the state of Maharashtra was formed in 1960. By the end of the seventies, the problem of deceleration in industrial growth had caught the attention of policy makers and the availability of infrastructure was considered to be one of the reasons for the same. In view of this, the efforts were made at the national level to prepare the Road Development Plan for the country as a whole for the period 1981-2001. Maharashtra finalised its own road development plan within the overall national road development plan framework The basic objective of the State Road Development Plan was to connect all the villages having population in excess of 500 in rural areas with at least one all weather road. This Plan also highlighted the problems of energy shortages, environmental degradation and road safety. The main components of the Maharashtra's Road Development Plan 1981-2001

TABLE 6.9

Targets and Achievements during the Road Development Plans in Maharashtra

Category of Roads	*1961-1981 Plan*				
	Length as on 1.4.61 (Kms)	*Target (Kms)*	*Revised Target (Kms)*	*Length as on 1.4.81 (Kms)*	*Achievement as a % of Revised Target*
NH	2312	5007	2956	2945	-0.4
SH	9804	13468	20374	18949	-7.0
MDR	11058	27426	29024	25233	-13.1
ODR	6954	32681	35714	25404	-28.9
VR	9114	35100	44230	28105	-36.5
Total	**39242**	**113682**	**132298**	**100636**	**-23.9**
Unclassified	-	-	-	40495	
Total	**39242**	**113682**	**132298**	**141131**	**6.7***

1981-2001 Plan

Category of Roads	*Targeted Length (Kms)*	*Revised Target (Kms)*	*Total Achievement (Kms)*	*As a % of Total Achievement*			*Shortfall as a % of Revised Target*
				BT or CC	*WBM*	*Unsurfaced*	
NH	3924	3112	2972	98	-	2	-4.5
SH	28282	35831	32380	95	4	1	-9.6
MDR	44047	48615	41166	57	280	6	-15.3
ODR	50794	51396	41701	26	58	16	-18.9
VR	76602	131304	72834	10	63	27	-44.5
Total	**207348**	**270010**	**191053**	**39**	**45**	**15**	**-29.2**

Note: (1) Abbreviations used in the above Table are as follow. NH: National highways, SH: State highways, MDR: Major district roads, ODR: Other district roads, VR: Village roads, BT:Black topped, CC: Cement concrete, and WBM: Water bound mecadam (2) Over achievement of target (*) is due to the fact that there was no target fixed for the unclassified roads in 1961-81 plan.

Source: Public Works Department, GoM, 2003a and author's calculations.

BOX 6.5

Progress of Projects Undertaken by MSRDC

Completed Projects	• Airoli Bridge Project
Ongoing Projects	• Fifty Flyovers (Mumbai Traffic Improvement Mega Project) • Amravati City Integrated Road Development Project • Aurangabad City Integrated Road Development Project • Bandra Worli Sea Link Project • Four Laning of Satara-Kolhapur-Kagal section of NH4 • Improvements to Satara-Chalkewadi-Patan Road • Mumbai-Aurangabad-Nagpur Highway Development to NH Standards • Mumbai Pune Expressway & Panvel-Bypass Project • Nagpur City Integrated Road Development Programme • Pune Integrated Road Development Project • Railway Over-bridges Project • Solapur City Integrated Road Development Project • Construction of Railway Over-bridges under Vidarbha Scheme • Widening of Thane Ghodbunder Road SH–42
Projects in the Project Development Phase	• Light Rail Transit (LRT) for Pune and Nagpur • Multi Modal International Hub Airport at Nagpur • Mumbai Trans Harbour Link (Nhava-Sewri sea link Project) • Mass Rapid Transit System for Thane City • Nanded City Integrated Road Development Project (Waghela MC) • Nandurbar Integrated Road Development Project • Development of New Mahabaleshwar as a Hill Station • Western Freeway Sea Link Project • Kolhapur City Integrated Road Development Project • Passenger Water Transport (PWT) Project of Mumbai
Projects under Mumbai Urban Transport Project	• Widening of Existing Jogeshwari Vikroli Link Road • Construction of Santacruz Chembur Link Road

Source: MSRDC, 2003 b.

were: (i) expansion of national highway (NH) network; (ii) construction of expressways on major traffic corridors; (iii) extension of state highways (SH) to connect district headquarters, industrial centres and tourist centres; (iv) construction of major district Roads (MDRs) to connect villages with population of 1000-1500; and, (v) construction of pedestrian footbridges (*Sakavs*) in hilly areas to serve the villagers living in remote areas by giving them access to their farms/other social amenities lying across rivers/creeks. Given the uphill task of raising resources for implementation of the plan, the finances were raised from different sources, *viz.*, assistance from the World Bank, National Bank for Agricultural and Rural Development (NABARD), private sector (on BOT basis) and Plan and Non-Plan allocations from annual state budgets.

In Maharashtra, construction of roads has been financed, to a large extent, by the Non-Plan expenditures. One of the major initiatives taken by the GoM towards development of road and road transport can be said to be the creation of MSRDC. MSRDC was established in July 1996 and is fully owned by the GoM. MSRDC was created mainly to deal with the properties and assets comprising movables and immovables including land, road projects, flyover projects, toll collection rights and works under construction which were vested with the State government and were under the control of the Public Works Department. These functions have been subsequently transferred to MSRDC. Some of the projects undertaken by the MSRDC have been listed in Box 6.5. Mumbai-Pune expressway is cited as one of the successful examples of the state initiative. The Government of Maharashtra entrusted the task of this expressway to MSRDC in March 1997 on build-operate-and-transfer (BOT) basis with the permission to collect toll for 30 years. The expressway opened for its full length from 1 March, 2002, though part of the route was opened a couple of years earlier than this. The project was completed in a record time and it is the first six-lane expressway in the country.

Financial Requirements

Roads are maintained by the various agencies, *viz.* public works department (PWD), *zilla parishads* (ZPs), municipal corporations/councils, etc. About 88 per cent of the total road length was maintained by the PWD and ZPs at the end of March, 2002. The classification of this road length according to the category of road is presented in the Table 6.10. As on end of March 2002, the financial requirements for maintaining the existing roads were estimated at Rs. 11,600 crores, whereas, to complete the remaining construction work under the Road Development Plan 1981-2001, the estimated cost was Rs. 15,800 crore. Besides this, Rs. 600 crores were required for acquisition of land for expressway. In other words, Rs. 28,000 crores of financial requirements was estimated to meet the set targets. Given the financial position of the state and a limited share of Maharashtra in the both NHDP and PMGSY, exploring other sources of funding seems to be inevitable.

TABLE 6.10

Road Length Maintained by the PWD and ZPs as on 31 March, 2002

Category of Roads	*Road Length (in Km.)*	*Percentage of Total*
National Highway	3710	1.7
State Highway	33405	15.0
Major District Road	47927	21.5
Other District Road	43906	19.7
Village Road	93618	42.1
Total	**222600**	**100.0**

Source: Economic Survey of Maharashtra, 2002-03.

Ports and Inland Water Transport

Maharashtra has a coastline of about 720 kms, which is about 10 per cent of the total coastline of the country. Out of 12 major ports in India, 2 belong to Maharashtra, *viz.*, Mumbai Port Trust and Nhawa-Shewa port. The state also has 48 minor ports. The minor ports of Maharashtra fall into 5 groups, *viz.*, Bandra group (9 ports), Mora group (11 ports), Rajpuri Group (9 ports), Ratnagiri group (11 ports) and Vengurla group (8 ports). In order to provide the multi-user port facilities, the state government has decided to develop 7 of these minor ports, *viz.*, Rewas-Aware, Dighi, Jaigad, Anjanwel (Dabhol), Alewadi, Ganeshgule, Vijaydurga, and Redi. Of these, development of the first three ports is in progress, whereas, the remaining ones are yet to be developed.

Development of major ports comes under the jurisdiction of Central Government, whereas, minor ports fall into the state list. As per the Port Policy of GoM (Nalinakshan, 2002), development of the minor ports is to take place through PSP on the BOOST basis. These ports are to be developed for multiple uses, such as, for handling all types of cargo like, bulk and break bulk, containers, petroleum and chemicals, etc. All the property of the GoM in the port (to be taken up for development) is to be transferred on lease to the developer company. The developer is to be exempted from payment of registration fee and stamp duty. The concession period is 50 years, including 5 years as the construction period. The state government can have equity participation of the order of about 11 per cent. In order to operationalise these projects, Maharashtra Maritime Board (MMB) was established in 1996 to act as a nodal agency. The Government will levy tariff of only Rs. 3.00 per tonne for the cargo handled by the port. This tariff can be increased up to 5 years, but at the end of 5 years it should not exceed twice the amount of the existing tariff. The developer is to be accorded full freedom to decide tariff rates for the various services provided at the port. The developer is also expected to develop facilities required for passenger water transport. However, the fixation of passenger tariffs is to be the prerogative of the GoM.

A coordination committee comprising of officers from the concerned Government Departments (under the Chairmanship of the Chief Executive Officer of MMB) is to provide a single window clearance to the investors. The investor will have to raise the required finance, develop the port, provide all services and manage the port as per the agreement entered with the GoM. The investor will be responsible for the construction of roads within the port boundary. However, the cost of construction of the approach roads and their maintenance are to be shared equally by the government and the investor. The investor will also be responsible for conservation of the port. Table 6.11 summarises the cargo handled at various groups of minor ports in Maharashtra. Bandra group basically handles coal and machinery. Mora group, which accounts for almost 70 per cent of cargo of minor ports of Maharashtra, primarily handles minerals and iron in various forms. Rajapuri ports handle iron in various forms. Ratnagiri port handles a diverse basket of commodities, whereas, Vengurla primarily caters to molasses cargo. With the development of Sindhudurg district as a tourism area, it is quite likely that minor ports could also be used for transporting consumption goods.

TABLE 6.11

Cargo Handled at Minor Ports in Maharashtra (2001-02)

Group of Minor Port	*Cargo Handled in (MT)*	*(% of Total)*
Bandra Group	350058	7.6
Mora Group	3235068	69.9
Rajpuri Group	787604	17.0
Ratnagiri Group	584067	12.6
Vengurla Group	20132	0.4
Total	**4627015**	**100.0**

Source: Data provided by The Maharashtra Maritime Board and author's calculations.

In Table 6.12, we provide the relative position of Maharashtra's minor ports. Gujarat accounts for almost 80 per cent of the cargo of minor ports of India. Maharashtra's share has been at best about 15 per cent in 1996-97 and in 2001-02 the provisional figure stood at about 5 per cent. Comparatively, Gujarat has an advantage over Maharashtra as regards geographic location. The former is closer to the north, central and even east bound cargo, while the latter's proximity is only to the south, which already has many ports. Besides, Gujarat being one of the most industrialised states also has the advantage of contributing to cargo handled at its own ports.

The GoM has also formulated a policy for captive jetties, which can facilitate both port development and the inland water transport. To encourage the development of captive jetties the GoM has announced that the land and site for a jetty will be leased out for a period of 30 years. The entire construction of the captive jetties and construction on the backup site will be on BOT basis. The construction, repair, maintenance and management of the jetties will also be the sole responsibility of the holder of these captive jetties.

TABLE 6.12

Relative Position of Cargo Handled by Minor Ports of Select States

Year	*Maharashtra*	*Gujarat*	*Goa*	*India Thousand Tonnes*
	As a Percentage of India			
1991-92	4.0	77.7	0.1	13258
1992-93	2.0	77.2	1.4	15403
1993-94	3.3	80.9	1.1	19470
1994-95	11.0	76.0	1.0	22282
1995-96	13.5	71.9	0.4	25710
1996-97	15.2	71.3	1.4	27832
1997-98	12.1	71.8	2.6	38607
1998-99	14.3	63.1	6.0	36306
1999-00	9.5	73.7	3.9	63383
2000-01 (P)	6.8	81.7	3.7	87249
2001-02 (P)	5.2	83.8	3.0	95126

Source: Data provided by The Maharashtra Maritime Board and author's calculations.

As per the port policy of the GoM, it will not recover any berthing dues from the vessels calling at the jetty. However, wharfage charges will have to be paid to the MMB as per the prescribed rate notified by the GoM through an official gazette. At the end of 30 years, the jetty and the super structure on the jetty will get transferred to the MMB.

Of late, the GoM has initiated development of inland water transport as the railway and road transport system in Mumbai has been extremely pressurised. Again, PSP is supposed to enable this. The inland water transport routes are to cover three routes, *viz.*, (i) Nariman Point to Borivali (western sea route) passing through Bandra, Juhu and Versova); (ii) The Eastern sea route (from South Mumbai/Gateway of India to Thane/Navi Mumbai; and (iii) the cross harbour route (from Gateway of India/ferry wharf/South Mumbai to Mandwa, Rewas, JNPT, Elephanta, etc.). The exact location at each of these sites has been finalised and the requirement of land has been worked out. A few remaining issues, such as, promulgation of the navigational channel and details of infrastructure required, are being addressed. The commuter ferry system has already been made operational on the Eastern Sea route and Cross harbour route. However,

TABLE 6.13

Major Telecom Sector Reforms in India

Year	*Nature of Reform*
1984	Manufacturing of the subscriber premises equipment opened up to the private sector.
1985	Department of Telecommunications established.
1986	Telecom services in Delhi and Mumbai corporatised under Mahanagar Telephone Nigam Ltd. (MTNL) and international telecom services were corporatised under Videsh Sanchar Nigam Ltd. (VSNL).
1989	Telecom Commission established.
1991	Telecom equipment manufacturing opened to private/foreign sector.
1992	Value added services opened up for private sector.
1994	Announcement of New Telecom Policy and broad guidelines for entry of private sector into provision of basic services, issuance of licences for cellular mobiles for four metros, tenders floated for bids in cellular mobile services in 19 circles (barring the four metros).
1997	Telecom Regulatory Authority of India (TRAI, formed by an Ordinance in 1996) starts functioning.
1998	Policy announcement for Internet Service Providers (ISPs).
1999	Announcement of Telecom Policy.
2000	Telecom Regulatory Authority of India (TRAI) Amendment Bill 2000 passed by the Indian Parliament; National Long Distance (NLD) services opened to private operators; Internet Service Providers (ISPs) permitted to set up International Internet Gateways for both Satellite and Landing Stations for submarine fibre-optic cables; Free right of way to lay fibre-optic cable networks along highways and roads. Ceiling on foreign equity in telecom services increased from 49 per cent to 74 per cent; the restriction on the number of players in cellular services removed; FDI up to 100 per cent permitted for ISPs that do not have satellite or submarine landing stations; reduction in customs duties on various telecom equipments; corporatisation of Department of Telecom Services (DTS); and formation of Bharat Sanchar Nigam Limited (BSNL).
2001	Announcement of policy for voice mail/audiotex incorporating a new service, i.e., unified messaging service, infrastructure providers of two categories (IP-1 and IP-2) allowed to provide end-to-end bandwidth and dark fibre, right of way, towers, duct space, etc.; Wireless in Local Loop (WLL) introduced.
2002	Private operators allowed in International Long Distance services, three licences issued.

Source: Adapted from Mani (2003).

better landing sites and infrastructure facilities are being planned so as to make the ferry system more attractive, convenient and safe.

Telecom Sector

Over the last decade, significant developments have taken place in the telecom sector. These changes have been in the arena of institutional reforms as well as technological advances. As regards institutional reforms are concerned, these have been in the nature of increased scope for private sector participation and globalisation leading to greater competition and efficiency. Technological progress has been in the form of reliance on radio waves rather than on fixed wired lines, which enables customers to use these services at a lower cost with greater mobility. The boom in information technology which has enabled the growth of telecom sector has, at least to some extent, relieved the constraints on growth imposed by inadequate and expensive transport facilities.

Telecom sector in India comes under the jurisdiction of the central government and hence, the progress of telecom sector of a state can only be viewed within the policy framework provided by the Central Government. However, the state governments can provide the enabling environment for the growth of this sector. In Table 6.14, we provide a synoptic view of the reforms pertaining to the telecom sector in India. It can be seen from Table 6.13 that the reforms in telecom sector in India allowed it to be opened to private operators, instituted regulatory authority and also were quick to move forward with the technological advances in this field.

TABLE 6.14

Relative Teledensity in Various Countries (US =100)

Country	*1991*	*2002*
China	1.1	6.9
France	90.9	87.7
Germany	80.8	83.7
India	1.1	2.4
Indonesia	1.1	3.3
Japan	80.9	76.1
Korea (Rep.)	56.8	67.0
Malaysia	16.4	27.7
Thailand	4.5	10.9
United Kingdom	80.8	81.3
United States	100.0	100.0

Source: Author's calculations based on data sourced from International Telecommunications Union (2003).

At present, India has a telephone network of 44.6 million lines and commands the sixth rank in the world and the second among emerging economies of Asia (next only to China). Though in absolute terms, the telecom network of India is large, teledensity in India is one of the lowest in the world. Barely about 2.6 per cent of the population owns telephones. Table 6.14 provides the relative teledensity in various countries.

In 1991, India, China and Indonesia had teledensity (telephones per 100 people) of about 1.1 per cent of that of the United States. China has improved its position significantly as compared to that of India. In fact, India has progressed slower than even Indonesia in this regard. However, one of the redeeming features of the growth of telecom industry in India is that it is growing at a phenomenal rate. Table 6.15 provides a synoptic view of the growth of telecom industry in India. Almost all growth rates are in double digits, except for the internet subscribers. In fact the growth of private Direct Exchange Lines (DELs) and cellular mobiles is closer to three digits than to two digits. Growth of private DELs was as high as 85 per cent in 2001-02. However, as the private DELs were barely one per cent of the public DELs, it will take almost a decade for the number of private DELs to surpass that of the public DELs (assuming constant growth rates witnessed by these segments in 2001-02). Another highest growing segment in India's telecom industry is the cellular mobile segment, which recorded a growth rate of 79 per cent in 2001-02. Even if the growth rates witnessed by DELs and cellular mobile phones in 2001-2002 are assumed to remain constant in the coming years, the number of cellular phones will exceed the number of DELs within a matter of six years. The pricing policy, apart from the convenience of mobile cellular phones, is also a key factor in propelling the growth of this segment of the telecom sector in India. In the recent past, there have been upward revisions in the tariff rates of fixed line phones, whereas, cellular mobile rates have been on a decline, i.e., the relative tariff rates of land lines have increased. Opening up of the cellular services to private sector have brought even the public sector companies into the ambit of competitive play.

Another feature of the India's telecom sector is the inequitable distribution of telecom services between rural and urban areas. The urban teledensity is around 13.71, whereas, the rural teledensity is just about 1.41. A silver lining is that in the recent years the growth of DELs in rural areas has been almost twice that of urban areas. Also new technologies, such as, Wireless in Local Loop (WLL) are expected to promote rural telephoney within a short span of time.

TABLE 6.15

Status of Telecom Sector in India

Description	*As on*		*Growth Rate in 2001-02 (%)*
	31-03-2001	*31-03-2002*	
Switching Capacity (BSNL and MTNL)	39.9	47.4*	18.8
No. of DELs	32.7*	38.5*	17.5
(i) Public	32.4*	38.0*	17.0
ii) Private	0.3*	0.5*	85.2
Cellular mobile phones	3.6*	6.4*	78.8
VPTs (Public and Private)	4.1#	4.7#	14.7
Rural DELs	6.7*	9.0*	34.8
PCOs	8.4#	10.7#	27.1
Internet Subscribers	3.0*	3.2*	7.7

Note: '*' and '#' denote measurement in millions and lakhs, respectively. VPTs are village public telephones and PCOs are public call offices.

Source: GoI (2003b), and author's calculation.

The advancements in technology and opening up of the telecom services to both domestic and foreign players have revolutionised the telecom industry in India by making it competitive, mobile and global. In fact, perhaps this is the only sector where advances in technology and knowledge have percolated in the form of lower prices to consumers and have made this infrastructure somewhat more affordable to the masses.

Telecom Sector in Maharashtra

As per the data provided by the Government of India (2003a), Maharashtra accounted for about 15.8 per cent of India's telephone subscribers, 9.5 per cent of total telephone connections, 9.1 per cent of connections in urban areas and 1.1 per cent in rural areas of the country (as on 31 Dec., 2002). About 8 per cent of cellular phones of the country are registered in Maharashtra. The Telecom Policy 1999, has set the targets of achieving an overall national teledensity of 7 by the year 2005 and 15 by the year 2010. It also targets the rural teledensity of 4 by the year 2010.

The overall, urban and rural teledensity recorded for Maharashtra (as on 31 Dec., 2002) were 5.77, 13.97 and

2.02, respectively. These figures are marginally above the national figure. The relative teledensity in India *vis-à-vis* other developing and developed countries (Table 6.15) indicates the distance that both India and Maharashtra have to travel in order to catch up with these countries. It is also noteworthy (Figure 6.4) that the overall teledensity in Punjab, Gujarat and Karnataka are higher than that for Maharashtra. Punjab leads the other states as regards the teledensity. It has teledensity almost twice as that of Maharashtra. It has already surpassed the overall national teledensity targets set for India for 2005 and rural teledensity target set for 2010. This is not true of Maharashtra. It is also pertinent to note that within Maharashtra, the teledensity is quite skewly distributed. Mumbai has teledensity (23.52), almost as high as urban teledensity in Punjab. The difference between teledensity in Maharashtra and Punjab may be a pointer to the fact that telecommunication industry growth is higher and more evenly dispersed if the urban-rural disparities in income are lower. In view of this, Maharashtra needs to pay attention to income and employment generation strategies so that its rural population is able to take the maximum advantage of the telecom revolution taking place currently.

FIGURE 6.4

Teledensity in Selected States of India (as on 31st Dec. 2002)

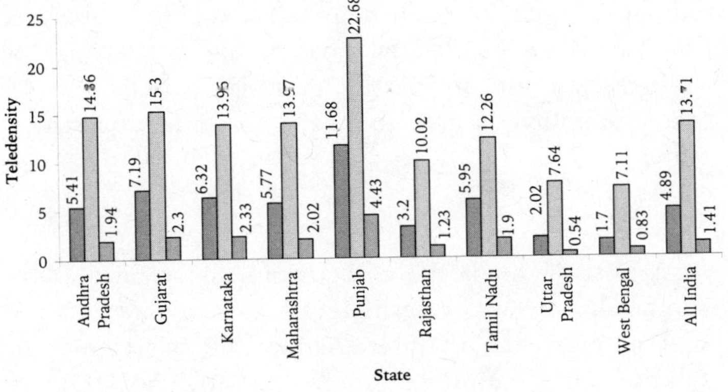

Source: GoI, 2003b.

Urbanisation and Water Supply

Year 2003 has been declared as the 'International Year of Freshwater'. The World Water Development Report (United Nations, 2003) has pointed out that water scarcity is one of the biggest challenges and the most vital developmental issues in the years to come. It has also reiterated the need for judicious use of water. Ensuring of basic needs such as right to health and food security (preconditions to poverty alleviation), protection of ecosystem, meeting competing needs due to urbanisation, supply of energy, etc., are crucially linked to availability of water. Some of the facts and figures provided by United Nations (2003) are as follows: (i) the Asian continent is the most stressed continent as regards the availability of water. It supports about 60 per cent of world population and accounts for just 36 per cent of the global water resources; (ii) about half of the population in developing countries is exposed to polluted water; (iii) climatic changes are supposed aggravate the problem of water scarcity; (iv) the bacteria levels from human wastes in Asian rivers are three times that of the global average. The lead content in these rivers are 20 times more of that of the industrialised countries; (v) India is among the third worst countries as regards provision of quality water, it ranks 120th among 122 countries rated for the water quality indicators; and, (vi) the extent of urbanisation of global population is about 48 per cent at present and is expected to increase to 60 per cent by 2030 and urbanisation not only increases the need for more water but also generates more waste water. One litre of wastewater pollutes about eight litres of freshwater.

Urbanisation and Water Supply in Maharashtra

Urbanisation in Maharashtra is higher than the all-India average. There is a wide disparity in the levels of urbanisation (as regards the numbers of cities and towns and populations contained therein) within the state of Maharashtra. For example, in Konkan division (comprising Mumbai, Mumbai Suburban, Thane, Raigad, Ratnagiri and Sindhudurg), about 72 per cent of the population resides in urban areas and almost all of it is in Mumbai, Mumbai Suburban and Thane. As against it, in Aurangabad division the corresponding figure is as low as only about 20 per cent. High levels of urbanisation and the regional variations in urbanisation lead to a high and lopsided pattern of demand for urban infrastructure. Naturally, the planning for provision of basic infrastructure to the urban population of the state is needed. Urban infrastructure includes urban transport, water supply, health care and other social services, and real estate and conservation of heritage structures. With increasing urbanisation in Maharashtra, the demand for all these above categories of urban infrastructure has been rising. However, in the years to come, water scarcity is anticipated to assume a proportion, which would be even more serious than that for oil. We have, therefore, addressed only this problem.

The 74th Constitution Amendment Act (1992) provided for constitution of State Finance Commissions (SFCs). SFCs recommend the basis for transfer of resources from state to local bodies and also specify the division of functional responsibilities between state and local bodies. Of course, this was made conditional to proper electoral procedures to be followed by the states.

The institutional and financial arrangements for supply of water in urban areas of Maharashtra are as follows. The entire range of activities related to water supply, *viz.*, augmenting water resources, treating the water, conveying the treated water, distributing it across consumers, operations and maintenance of billing and collection of user fees, etc., are currently being provided in the state either by the Urban Local Bodies (ULBs) or by the Maharashtra Jeevan Pradhikaran (MJP). Collection of the wastewater, conveying it to the pumping station and then to the treatment plant is also the responsibility of the ULBs. Thus, the entire chain involving water supply is vertically integrated. Similar to that in the case of power supply, there is scope for unbundling and privatisation in water supply service. The ULBs are responsible for providing safe drinking water supply and they find it difficult to fulfil this obligation due to huge financial requirements associated with this task. In order to circumvent this problem, the state government provides grants-in-aid (GIA) to ULBs. Besides this, the ULBs also receive soft loans from the institutions such as Life Insurance Corporation (LIC), Housing and Urban Development Corporation (HUDCO) and other multilateral agencies. It can be seen from Table 6.16 that larger is the size of ULB, lower is the GIA component in the financing pattern. Moreover, in the new financing pattern, the public contribution to the extent of 10 per cent has also been included. The restructuring of Capital Grants programme in July 2000, is aimed to provide incentives for improved performance of ULBs. Under this programme, 30 per cent of the state's grants are reserved for incentives. These incentives can be availed by plugging in leakages and reducing water thefts.

TABLE 6.16

Financing Pattern of ULBs in Maharashtra

Category of ULB	*Old Financing Pattern (%)*		*New Financing Pattern (since July 2000) (%)*		
	GIA	*Loans*	*Public Contribution*	*GIA*	*Loans*
Municipal Corporations	23.3	76.7	10	23.3	66.7
A-Class Municipal Councils	25	75	10	25	65
B-Class Municipal Councils	40	60	10	40	50
C-Class Municipal Councils	50	50	10	50	40
C1-Class Municipal Councils	100	-	10	90	

Source: GoM, 2000a.

Major Problems in Supply of Water in Urban Maharashtra

The problems in water supply are very similar to those in power supply.

Poor Service Coverage

About 171 towns in the state get water supply below the norms. The average percentage of water supply available in summer is below 60 per cent of the norms. Only 72 towns get water supply as per the norms (Pethe *et al.*, 2003). In Maharashtra, only 37 ULBs satisfy quantitative norms for water supply, whereas, 207 do not. The shortfalls are as high as 55 per cent. Besides, even though the quantitative norms may be fulfilled by some of the ULBs, there is a problem of supply of water only for a few hours during the day. More often than not, these hours are also not convenient to the public. Water availability in Western Europe is even lower than in India, but the supply is continuous unlike that in most of the urban areas of Maharashtra and also in the country. Unreliability of water supplied is also in terms of contamination of water.

Low Tariffs

Almost all municipal corporations and councils have uniformly low water tariff levels as compared to the cost of provision of water. As per the calculations of Sukthankar Committee Report (2000), the ULBs in Maharashtra have to hike the water tariffs at least 2 to 2.5 times, if they have to meet the cost of supplying water. Due to low tariffs and financial strain on ULBs, the paucity of funds for operation and maintenance functions can hardly be fulfilled satisfactorily. This also results in deterioration in the quality of assets of ULBs. Moreover, low tariffs act as disincentive for judicious use and recycling of water. With the increased power tariffs, upward revision of water tariffs has become all the more necessary, as increased electricity costs also lead to escalation in cost of supplying water. Needless to mention that, the rationalisation of water tariffs requires considerable political will. Maharashtra Industrial Development Corporation (MIDC) provides water to industrial estates at subsidised rates, if they are within the confines of the city. Industries can be asked to pay water charges based on commercial principles. Unlike many other infrastructure services, water is essential for survival and hence, poorest of the poor should not be denied of this source of life, even if state has to pay for it.

BOX 6.6

Direct and Indirect Initiatives to Improve Water Supply

- 73rd and 74th Constitution Amendment Acts (1992).
- Enactment of Groundwater Act (1993).
- Establishment of Maharashtra Jeevan Pradhikaran (1994).
- Publication of White Paper on Water and Sanitation (Brihat Arakhada) by Government of Maharashtra (1995).
- Establishment of Water Supply and Sanitation Department (WSSD) by Government of Maharashtra (1996).
- Established WSSD a core group in to prepare a roadmap for private sector participation in water and sanitation sectors in Maharashtra with support from Indo-US Financial Institutions Reform and Expansion (FIRE) Project (1999).
- Appointed of a Committee to prepare a road map for improved provision of water and sewerage services under the chairmanship of D.M., Sukthankar (2000).
- Restructuring of Capital Grants Programme to create incentives for water sector reform (2000). Submission of the report by D.M., Sukthankar Committee (2001).

Regressive Nature of Water Charges

Due to uneven distribution of water supply (for various economic and non-economic reasons), the poor are worst hit. For example, the residents of distant suburbs of Mumbai (primarily from lower income groups), have to depend on the water provided by tanker vendors who charge substantially higher prices as compared to the water tariffs paid by economically better-off residents to whose houses the piped water is supplied. This is also true of Delhi where the poor pay US$ 4.89 per cubic metre to vendors, whereas, households with piped connections pay just US$ 0.01 (United Nations, 2003). In view of this, it is necessary that water-pricing scheme should include mechanisms to protect the poor. A reasonable water tariff with assured supply to poor will serve them better as compared to pricing water extremely low and supplying it primarily to the better-off sections of society.

Contaminated Water Supply

As per the bacteriological analysis conducted by the State Public Health Laboratory, Pune (2000) for the samples (collected during Jan. 1999 and Dec. 1999) of water supplied by the various Municipal Corporations/ municipal councils in Maharashtra, about 10 were found to be contaminated by bacteria (Sukthankar Committee, 2000). A higher proportion of samples from Mumbai (14 per cent), Nagpur (12 per cent) and Kolhapur (11 per cent) were also found to be contaminated. Besides, the proportion contaminated samples; the extent of contamination also matters. Right to health is impaired by supply of such contaminated water and the adverse impacts on the poor are much severe. Though bacterial tests of water are conducted, but their official reporting to public is not a common practice. It may be also noted that there are hardly any tests of water for its physical and chemical contamination. The problem of contamination of water also arises from the fact that the supply systems are meant for continuous supply of water, whereas, water is actually supplied intermittently resulting in physical damages of the supply equipment and ultimately leading to water contamination.

Irrational Funding Policies

Funding for the new water projects by the Central government, financial institutions and international agencies has been much easier than for operations and maintenance of old projects. Due to this, many new projects have been initiated without budgeting for their proper operations and maintenance. This aggravates the financial stress on local bodies rather than solving the problem of water supply. One of the reasons for the poor asset quality has also been the irrational funding policies for water projects.

Deficient Institutional Arrangements

MJP is responsible for construction and commissioning of water system in most of the urban areas of Maharashtra. The responsibility of operations and management (O&M) is often transferred to ULBs, after commissioning of the projects. Due to the inadequacy of financial resources to finance O&M, ULBs refuse to accept their responsibility. About 43 ULBs have declined to take over the commissioned projects from MJP (FIRE (D), 2002a).

Lack of Accounting Norms

There is no accounting norm set up for ULBs and MJP. In the power sector, public utilities are expected to earn a minimum rate (three per cent) of return on capital. Similar norms need to be prescribed in the case of water supply providers.

Illegal Connections and Thefts

The difference between the quantity of water supplied by the ULBs and the metered quantity of water supplied is the unaccounted-for water (UFW). There can be two reasons for UFW: (a) physical losses due to leakage from pipes; and, (b) administrative losses due to illegal connections or thefts and unmetered water supply. In Maharashtra, the UFW ranges from 40 to 55 per cent of the total quantity of water supplied by the local bodies.

Augmenting Financial Resources of ULBs

Despite the fact that ULBs are responsible for providing and maintaining the urban water supply, in reality a significant proportion of population in almost every city has to depend on other sources, including the private sources, to meet its water requirements. In order to overcome the paucity of financial resources, three main approaches have been suggested in the literature. These are: (i) private sector participation (PSP) in financing and execution of the projects; (ii) floating of financial instruments by the ULBs in association with financial institutions; and (iii) internal generation of resources by the ULBs, such as, by rationalisation of tariffs.

We have already discussed PSP in the context of power and roads. The institutional change will require involvement of the financial institutions. Providing incentives to commercial banks for lending for water sector schemes could be one of the possible ways to boost investment in this sector. In order to access funds from the financial sectors, the ULBs will have to fulfil the obligations to maintain proper financial accounts and report them in a transparent and consistent manner. This will aid the process of rating the ULBs bonds. Commercial banks can also help in developing a vibrant secondary market for ULBs bonds.

The various ways of generating resources internally by the ULBs include, rational management practices, appropriate priorities for allocation of resources, cost cutting exercises, selection of appropriate low cost technologies, proper maintenance and timely replacement of outdated equipment, identification of socially essential subsidies and eliminating the inessential ones, etc.

It is also pertinent to take note of the recommendations of Sukthankar Committee, such as, revision and improved collection of water tariff, allocation of funds for O&M, training of manpower of ULBs, involvement of community (and in particular, of women) in water supply schemes in order to meet the spirit of the 73rd and 74th Amendments of the Indian Consititution, redefining the role of MJP, etc.

Strategies and Policies for Development of Infrastructure

As mentioned earlier, kick-starting of infrastructure projects has been a major concern of both Central and state governments. This is reflected in the fact that in the Budget 2003-04, the Finance Minister has listed 'infrastructure development' as one of the five priorities (labelled as 'Panch Priorities') of the government. He also stated that in order to exploit the full potential of technological progress and competition, it has become mandatory to provide quality infrastructure, such as, roads, ports, reliable power supply, safe drinking water, etc. Moreover, all these have to be provided at reasonable prices to the users. To achieve this, substantial improvement in efficiency in infrastructure sector generation and distribution cannot be postponed any further.

As regards the initiative at the state level, GoM has brought out a draft of the MIDAS Act (Maharashtra Infrastructure Development and Support Act). This is a comprehensive bill dealing with an entire gamut of issues, ranging from regulation to institutional aspects. It also deals with decision frame and policy implementation aspect, as well as, grievance redressal mechanism. Whilst this is an important state level initiative, the so-called Act completely bypasses the ULBs and hence, is open to possible criticism.

The strategies that are being tried to improve provision of infrastructure services include, introduction of competition (in order to improve efficiency) through private sector participation, unbundling so as to overcome the problem of bulky investment in vertically integrated plants, financial accountability and sustainability of infrastructure providers (through rational tariff setting and running the enterprises on commercial principles), checking thefts and leakages, setting up regulatory bodies to protect consumer interests, augmenting financial resources of ULBs through debt, etc. In line with the global trends, Indian infrastructure scenario too, is witnessing a changing role of government from its traditional role as a 'provider' of services to a 'facilitator' of services by ensuring that infrastructure services are actually delivered at reasonable prices. Establishment of various regulatory commissions is a testimony to this fact. In order to promote efficient provision of adequate and quality infrastructure, we suggest the following strategies.

First, as the provision of most of the infrastructure services involves Central Government, state governments and local bodies, a proper integration of roles, responsibilities and obligations of these layers of governments is required. Accelerated Power Development Reform Programme (APDRP) can be treated as a model, which provides efficiency-based incentives to states. Similar incentive schemes can be devised for other infrastructure services as well and states' efforts in promoting efficiency can be rewarded. It may also be important to note that the strategy for development of infrastructure will have to be a multi-pronged one. Mere announcement of incentives may not be adequate for the states to take advantage of these. This is confirmed by the fact that utilisation ratio of funds under the APDRP has been just about nine per cent.

Second, there seems to be hardly any option as regards more privatisation and unbundling, given the huge financial requirements for both creation of new capacity and also for the financial viability of existing public utilities. Tremendous possibilities exist to enlist private sector support in infrastructure. Private sector participation can take various hybrid forms including various parameters such as, responsibility of construction, transient ownership, operation, leasing and ultimate ownership. In the wave of privatisation and deregulation that has been sweeping across the globe, it is being increasingly recognised that ownership and operation of infrastructure facilities are separable. Sophisticated models exist to meet the desired characteristics for individual projects. The private operators can finance and build a project, operate and generate project income and eventually transfer ownership to government at the end of the concession period. Depending on the characteristics, an infrastructure project can be more or less suitable for a particular form of the private sector participation. As suggested by Pethe (2003), the projects that capture significant social benefits such as urban transport or water supply systems are more suited for traditional government ownership. This is because of the fact that non-exclusion characteristic comes into play, making pricing difficult. Indeed, in the first case even joint consumption comes into play making it close to the pure public good category. Of course, this may not be true if tolls are applicable (as in the case of flyovers or expressways) and if metered connections (which is generally not the case) exist, the above is not true for water. On the other hand, projects which offer commercial returns, such as, telecom, provide a greater scope for private participation. While private sector participation may accelerate development in infrastructure, the government would still remain a crucial player. Privatisation can also act as a substitute for the lack of political will to implement tariff rationalisation by the state utilities. Privatisation in distribution of power and water can help in reducing leakages and thefts and improve financial position of SEBs and ULBs.

Third, realisation of 8 per cent growth target specified in the Tenth Five Year Plan hinges on the speed with which we develop quality infrastructure. Financial institutions will have to play a vital role in financing these projects. The ratio of bank credit to infrastructure financing to the total bank credit was a meagre 2 per cent in 1998 and at present it is about 6.5 per cent. Financial institutions should rely more on credit appraisal of the infrastructure projects undertaken by public utilities and consistent monitoring of the projects financed by them rather than provide guarantees and counter-guarantees (MEDC, 2002).

Fourth, rational tariff setting is one of the most challenging tasks associated with provision of infrastructure services. As it has already been argued, a 'single uniform principle' of price setting for all types of infrastructure services may be inappropriate. This is because there are differences between the types of infrastructure. Some of them, such as water, may be required for human existence and invoking market principles for supply of water to poor would be an inappropriate developmental strategy. Some cross-subsidisation or direct subsidy will be needed for supply of water to poor. At present, we find that pricing of water is distortionary and that water charges are regressive rather than proportional or progressive in nature. Similarly, rural electrification programme may not be feasible without direct funding from the government. Nevertheless, it is possible to benchmark the minimum rate of return to be earned by public utilities in order to ensure their sustainability.

Fifth, removal of anomalies in tariff policies both across various infrastructures (inter-services) services and also within the same service (intra-service) needs to be carefully looked into. One of the examples of the former is that in power sector industrial sector subsidises domestic and agricultural sector. In the case of water, industrial sector is given subsidy by MIDC. This makes the subsidy structure irrational, complex and non-transparent. As regards intra-service anomalies, one can find them in the water sector in the form of regressive pricing. Those households from lower income groups who neither steal nor resort to obtaining water from unmetered connections, end up paying more for worse quality of water supplied by the tankers as compared to the water tariffs paid by the better off sections of urban population. Yet another example of such anomalies can be found in the form of tariff structure in power sector, wherein, cross-subsidisation is coupled with opening up this sector for captive power generation and for private sector. This has led to erosion of consumer base from commercial and industrial sectors, thereby, creating financial problems for electricity boards.

Sixth, proper sequencing and implementation of reforms in infrastructure sector are badly needed. Needless to mention that, the issue of governance cannot be ignored in this process. Dabhol case reconfirms that a supportive policies by the state does not mean that it should absorb all losses associated with ill-designed policies. In Maharashtra, there is no shortage of base generation capacity but there is the problem of peak deficit. Dabhol was to add to the base generation capacity rather than solve the problem of peak deficit. This is an indication that prioritisation of problems is needed before implementation of reforms. In order to address the problem of peak deficit, serious exploration of demand management approach by resorting to time zoning needs to be done. Guarantees and counter guarantees based on unrealistic assumptions seem more to be a problem of governance rather than opening it up for the private sector.

Seventh, the problem of high costs of infrastructure needs to be attended to. Regulatory bodies in various spheres, such as, Electricity Regulatory Commissions, Telecom Regulatory Authority of India, etc., have been established to protect consumers' interest. The concept of fairprice seems to be based on a reasonable mark-up for the infrastructure providers rather than based on efficient production and lowering of distribution costs. State initiative in promotion of appropriate and advanced technology and disseminating the same can also be experimented. In fact, in many countries, various state departments facilitate technology transfers to the private sector. A related issue, which needs to be addressed, is that the regulatory bodies should be able to function independently and objectively. Regulatory bodies cannot be watchdogs of public interest if their decision making is either influenced by the government or by business lobbies from the private sector.

Eighth, some of the infrastructure schemes, such as construction of roads can be integrated with the employment and income generation programmes. This will also help in alleviation of poverty.

Ninth, some awareness campaigns by the mass media may be required. Indian consumers have always been a victim of exaggerated claims of advertising campaigns for products. A multiplicity of private sector players in provision of infrastructure is something new, which is being witnessed by the Indian users of infrastructure. Only a few can grasp the implications of the deal, which they make with the service provider. This has been demonstrated in the telecom sector. Regulatory authorities can insist that users of infrastructure be provided complete and comparative details about the services offered to them.

Last but not the least, one of the most contentious issues in development of infrastructure pertains to the land acquisition and displacement of project-affected people (PAP). Philosophically, there is no ground for displacing people from their lands for welfare of others. Skirting this problem, if displacement does take place, the state should at least ensure proper compensation packages to the PAP to ensure development of infrastructure with a less inhuman face.

Chapter 7

Public Sector Units: Restructuring and Reforms

Introduction

Public sector, in the past, had been considered as one of the major instruments of state intervention in economic activity, in the development process of a developing country. It used to be an effective instrument to regulate the pace and composition of private economic activity in a mixed economy. The objective was to achieve efficiency along with the social objective of growth with equitable distribution by setting some of the 'core' economic activity in the public sector. Investment in the utility or infrastructure sector was not considered attractive to the private sector in a resource-scarce developing economy during the initial years of planned development and so, the public sector was to take the lead. Similar reasons also guided investment in the capital goods industries and other segments of the economy. The public sector was also intended to be a model employer whose employment and wage policies were to have a moderating influence on the corresponding policies in the private sector. These objectives guided the planners to import-substitution and other related policy formulations.

This chapter would largely focus on the need for, and the method adopted in privatising the public sector enterprises in the state of Maharashtra and the problems and prospects of the successful completion of the disinvestment process in these enterprises. Section I presents a brief description of the structure, pattern of investment and performance of the public enterprises in Maharashtra. In Section II, a discussion on the need for restructuring the public enterprises is presented. Section III deals with the measures adopted in public sector restructuring, while Section IV provides an assessment of the progress of PSU reforms in the state of Maharashtra. Section V gives the summary and conclusions of the present study.

SECTION I

Structure of PSUs

Public sector investments in Maharashtra were also guided by the principles mentioned in introduction. As on 31 March 2001, the state had 66 public sector undertakings (PSUs) comprising 61 government companies and five statutory corporations. Out of 61 government companies, 43 were working government companies while 18 were non-working government companies. All the five statutory corporations were working corporations. The number of non-working government companies increased from 17 to 18 during 2000-01.

Besides the state PSUs, a number of central public sector units are also located in the state of Maharashtra. Availability of infrastructure facilities, early industrialisation, and labour and resource advantages have been the major factors for the large inflow of central public sector investments. Some of these central PSUs, having headquarters in Mumbai, are in the financial sector—banking and insurance, as, from the pre-independence days, Mumbai developed as the financial capital of India. Similarly, the oil PSUs are also located in Mumbai, due to heavy dependence of India on the import of oil and petroleum products, the long coastline of Maharashtra and the pre-eminence of Mumbai port even before independence. Besides these, for historical reasons, textiles PSUs are also located in Maharashtra. Given the above background and other reasons, the share in assets in central PSUs increased from 8.63 per cent in 1980-81 to 20.34 in 1999-00. Table 7.1 gives the profile of increase in assets of central PSUs operating in Maharashtra.

Given the above structure of PSUs, Figure 7.1 presents the sectoral share of government investment in

Maharashtra, as on March 31, 2002. The single largest sector of public sector investment in this state turns out to be in construction activity (70 per cent). Among the industrial sector, textiles alone have a share of about 9 per cent in the total state public sector investment. Area development comes third with 5 per cent.

TABLE 7.1

Assets of Central Public Sector Undertakings Operating in Maharashtra

Year	*1980-81*	*1990-91*	*1994-95*	*1999-00*
Assets (per cent)	8.63	16.97	20.23	20.34

Source: Calculated from *Public Enterprises Survey*, 2000-01.

FIGURE 7.1

Sector-wise Investment in Working Government Companies in Maharashtra as on 31st March, 2002

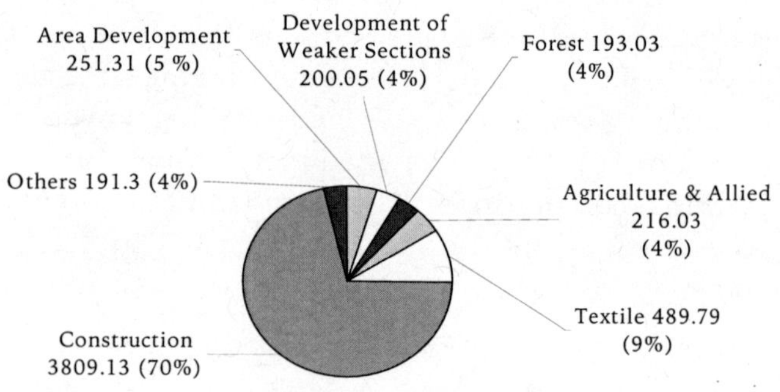

Source: CAG report on PSUs in Maharashtra, 2001-02.

Employment in PSUs

Directive Principles of State Policy contained in Part IV of the Constitution embody the concept of a welfare state. The Supreme Court of India has, in several of its judgments, held that the said principles supplement the fundamental rights in achieving a welfare state. As a welfare state, it has always been the endeavour of the Government of Maharashtra that the assets and resources of the state are so utilised as to bring maximum returns for the welfare and prosperity of the people of the entire state. It has also been the endeavour of the state government to ensure that there is an overall balanced social and economic development and progress of the whole state and the wealth and prosperity of the state are shared equitably by all the people of the state. Share of public and private sector in employment is presented in Table 7.2.

During the 25 year period from 1970-71 to 1994-95, the share of estimated employment in public sector increased, while that of private sector declined. Within the public sector, the share of central and state government enterprises show a declining trend, whereas the quasi-government and local bodies reveal an increasing trend. The share of small private enterprises has declined marginally from 2.37 to 2.08 per cent during this period. Table 7.3 provides the district-wise distribution of the factories and employment of public and private sector in Maharashtra in 1994-95.

TABLE 7.2

Percentage Share of Estimated Employment in Public and Private Sector

Years	*Public Sector*				*Private Sector*	
	C.G.	*S.G.*	*Quasi Govt.*	*Local Body*	*Large*	*Small*
1970-71	16.30	15.29	9.25	15.25	41.53	2.37
1980-81	15.11	13.35	15.04	15.05	39.37	2.08
1990-91	13.05	13.81	18.76	16.26	36.07	2.05
1991-92	12.75	14.47	18.45	16.38	35.95	2.00
1992-93	12.63	14.43	18.05	16.79	36.05	2.05
1993-94	12.62	14.03	17.96	17.23	36.13	2.03
1994-95	12.05	13.76	18.28	17.09	36.74	2.08

Note: C.G.–Central Government; S.G.-State Government.

Source: Calculated from *Statistical Handbook of Maharashtra*, 2000-01.

Table 7.3 shows that the dispersal of public enterprises was successfully achieved in this state. Excepting the developed places in the state like Thane, Nashik, Nagpur, Pune and Raigad and of course, Mumbai (which is a large metropolis), public sector factories and employment appear to be evenly distributed in many districts, although the share is very small. Moreover, the share of public and private enterprises in terms of the number of factories and employment seems to be following the same pattern in almost all the districts. This could largely be because of the fact that public sector investments in Maharashtra are largely distributed in manufacturing, development organisations and cooperatives. It could, therefore, be observed that in the case of Maharashtra, it was vital to distinguish between quasi-government and local bodies on the one hand and central and state-owned enterprises on the other.

It is quite likely that most of the cooperatives were included in the quasi-government and local bodies, and these cooperatives were growing in number. All the three categories of public enterprises have been getting sizeable government investment and policy attention.

TABLE 7.3

District-wise Share of Percentage of Working Factories and Employment in Public and Private Sector in Maharashtra: (1994-95)

Districts	*Public Sector*		*Private Sector*	
	No. of Factories	*EMP*	*No. of Factories*	*EMP*
B. Mumbai	22.77	38.76	37.44	32.96
Thane	4.95	14.64	15.96	13.66
Raigad	2.28	3.45	1.74	2.84
Ratnagiri	1.88	0.65	0.74	0.77
Sindhudurg	1.19	0.24	0.30	0.25
Nashik	5.25	8.04	4.64	4.42
Dhule	0.59	1.02	1.19	0.87
Jalgaon	4.36	3.19	2.51	2.04
Ahmednagar	3.37	0.79	1.74	2.45
Pune	10.59	6.03	11.61	14.96
Satara	3.66	0.88	0.86	1.44
Sangli	3.17	0.86	1.79	1.55
Solapur	2.87	2.22	1.20	1.89
Kolhapur	3.96	1.55	4.24	4.32
Aurangabad	3.07	1.35	2.05	3.71
Jalna	1.09	0.17	2.05	0.66
Parbhani	1.58	0.45	0.51	0.43
Beed	1.98	0.97	0.25	0.26
Nanded	1.98	0.91	0.47	0.93
Osmanabad	1.19	0.32	0.04	0.19
Latur	1.29	0.45	0.25	0.27
Buldhana	1.19	0.33	0.60	0.63
Akola	2.08	1.38	1.27	0.87
Amravati	3.17	1.02	0.93	0.67
Yavatmal	1.09	0.27	0.39	0.81
Wardha	1.39	1.51	0.50	0.69
Nagpur	5.64	6.73	4.41	3.70
Bhandara	0.99	0.18	0.95	0.57
Chandrapur	0.99	1.61	0.59	1.07
Gadchiroli	0.40	0.06	0.06	0.09

Source: Calculated from *Statistical Handbook of Maharashtra,* 2000-01.

Investment in PSUs

The total investment in working PSUs has increased from Rs. 191.4 billion as on 31st March 2000 to Rs. 196.7 billion as on 31 March 2001. The total investment in non-working PSUs also has increased from Rs. 0.47 billion to Rs. 1.31 billion during the same period. The budgetary support in the form of capital, loans and grants disbursed to the working PSUs decreased from Rs. 4.72 billion in 1999-00 to Rs. 2.82 billion in 2000-01. The state government also released loan of Rs. 96.5 million to one non-working company during 2000-01. The state government guaranteed loans aggregating to Rs. 29.89 billion (Rs. 29.84 billion to working PSUs and Rs. 47.5 million to non-working PSUs) during 2000-01. The total amount of outstanding loans guaranteed by the state government to all PSUs increased from Rs. 73.35 billion as on 31 March 2000 to Rs. 205.70 billion as on 31 March 2001. The total investments in five working statutory corporations for 1999-00, 2000-01 and 2001-2002 are given in Table 7.4.

TABLE 7.4

Investment in Statutory Corporations in Maharashtra

(Rs. in Billion)

Name of Corporation	*1999-2000*		*2000-01*		*2001-02*	
	Capital	*Loan*	*Capital*	*Loan*	*Capital*	*Loan*
Maharashtra State Electricity Board	14.79	110.99	34.65	96.91	34.65	104.40
Maharashtra State Road Transport Corporation	2.00	1.59	2.82	1.28	4.15	1.62
Maharashtra Industrial Development Corporation	-*	0.64	-*	0.84	-*	1.43
Maharashtra State Financial Corporation	0.63**	8.57	0.63**	8.02	0.63#	7.68
Maharashtra State Warehousing Corporation	0.08	-	0.09	-	0.09	-
Total	**17.5**	**121.79**	**38.19**	**107.04**	**39.51**	**115.13**

Note: * There is no investment of state government by way of share capital or loan in MIDC. However, the land is acquired by the state government and handed over to MIDC for development activities.

** Includes share application money of Rs. 1.45 crore.

Reduced due to refund of capital of Rs. 3.84 lakh to equity shareholders.

Source: CAG Report, 2001-02.

According to the latest report of the Comptroller and Auditor General (CAG), 17 working PSUs (15 government companies and two statutory corporations) earned aggregate profit of Rs. 0.62 billion. Against this, 28 working PSUs (25 government companies and three statutory corporations) incurred an aggregate loss of Rs. 30.38 billion as per the latest finalised accounts. Of the loss incurring working government companies, 13 companies had accumulated losses aggregating Rs. 5.08 billion, which exceeded their aggregate paid-up capital of Rs. 3.30 billion. Maharashtra State Road Transport Corporation, being a loss-incurring statutory corporation, had accumulated loss of Rs. 6.28 billion, which exceeded its paid-up capital of Rs. 2.82 billion by more than two times. Even after completion of five years of their existence, the individual turnover of 15 working and 11 non-working government companies has been less than Rs. 50 million in each of the preceding five years of latest finalised accounts. Further, four working government companies, which had turnover of more than Rs. 50 million, have been incurring losses for five consecutive years as per their latest finalised accounts, leading to negative net worth. As such, the government may either improve the performance of these 30 government companies or consider their closure.

Efficiency of PSUs

The Indian experience with the state owned sector is long enough to provide a backdrop for assessing comparative efficiency of public and private sectors. Needless to mention that it is very important to understand the comparative performance of state owned enterprises over the private enterprises, especially in circumstances where the state owned sector is a major player in the industrial arena, even after a decade of structural reforms and globalisation policy measures.

It is quite possible that private enterprises are earning, on an average, higher financial rate of profit but have a lower index of total factor productivity over the past decade, compared to the public sector. Improving the profitability alone does not strictly drive policy measures directed toward public sector disinvestments in India. As stated in the Eighth Five Year Plan, better utilisation of resources, improving efficiency and reduction in the dependence on the government transfer of funds is all of immediate concern.

From the beginning of the Eighth Five Year Plan, there has been concerted effort by the government, both at the Centre as well as at the state to privatise public enterprises. This is largely because of the fact that the plan document identified some of the principles governing public sector investments and stated that:

a) the public sector should make investment only in those areas where investment is mainly infrastructural in nature and where private sector participants are not likely to come forth to an adequate extent within a reasonable time period;

b) the public sector must withdraw from the areas where no public purpose is served by its presence; and,

c) the principle of market economy should be accepted as the main operative principle by all public sector enterprises unless the commodities and services produced and distributed are specifically for protecting the poorest in the society.

The performance of the public enterprises can be judged by several efficiency criteria. However, the financial performance assumes importance because one of the objectives of creating public sector enterprises was to generate resources for development by earning adequate returns. Most public enterprises in the state of Maharashtra have been incurring huge losses. Recent data for the year 2001-02 shows that in Maharashtra, 17 working PSUs earned an aggregate profit of Rs. 0.615 billion whereas, against this, 28 working PSUs incurred aggregate loss of Rs. 3.038 billion. The reform of the public sector in general and that of the loss making units in particular has, therefore, assumed importance in the context of the financial strain under which all governments, both at the Centre and the state, operate.

During the last two decades, many countries in the world have initiated measures of privatisation of state owned enterprises. The disinvestment or privatisation process has been initiated with the notion that the time has come to critically assess the sectors in which public enterprises must function. This is especially in the context that the resources available for the Centre and states are limited and are needed for extending the social infrastructure in a bigger way. Taking a leaf out of the Centre's book, several states have also decided to join the disinvestment bandwagon in order to raise critical fund for meeting the shortfall in fiscal deficit. The combined fiscal deficit of the Centre and states is expected to touch 10 per cent of the GDP this fiscal year. Already many international credit rating agencies and institutions like the World Bank and IMF have raised concerns about the dismal fiscal situation of both the Centre as well as the states. In the light of this, Punjab, Maharashtra and Gujarat have decided to offload their equity in the state-run companies to contain the ballooning fiscal deficit. For example, the Maharashtra Government has already announced its intention to sell strategic stakes in one of the automobile firms, which it has been holding, Maharashtra Scooters. Bajaj Auto is showing keen interest in buying the government's stake. Around 27 per cent of the equity in Maharashtra Scooters (3.1 million shares) is held by the Maharashtra Government arm WMDC, while Bajaj Auto holds 24 per cent.

Maharashtra Scooters' equity base is Rs. 114 million and at Rs. 50 per share, Bajaj Auto would have to pay Rs. 154 million for the purchase. Maharashtra Scooters shares have risen by over three times in recent months to around Rs. 90 per share on talk of a takeover by Bajaj Auto. However, the deal is yet to be finalised. There are many such instances that one comes across while analysing the restructuring of PSUs at the state level. Often, the experiences of different enterprises differ to a large extent and hence the lessons learnt could also be totally varied.

Financial Performance

The biggest problems in assessing the performance of these PSUs lie in the delays in finalisation of their accounts. The accounts of the companies for every financial year are required to be finalised within six months from the end of relevant financial year under Section 166, 210, 230, 619 and 619-B of the Companies Act, 1956 read with Section 19 of Comptroller and Auditor General's (Duties, Power and Conditions of Service) Act, 1971. They are also to be laid before the legislature within nine months from the end of financial year. Similarly, in the case of the statutory corporations, their accounts are finalised, audited and presented to the legislature as per the provisions of their respective Acts. However, as could be noticed from Annexure-2, in the latest CAG Report, out of 43 working government companies in the latest CAG Report, only 9 working companies and out of the 5 working statutory corporations only 4 working corporations have finalised their accounts for the year 2000-01 within stipulated period. During the period from October 2000 to September 2001, 22 working government companies finalised 23 accounts for previous years. Similarly, during this period two working statutory corporations finalised two accounts for previous years. Worse are the accounts of 34 working government companies and one statutory corporation, where the arrears for periods range from one year to 14 years, as on 30 September 2001. The cases of anomaly in some PSUs and statutory corporations are given in Table 7.5.

Moreover, statutory corporations, which account for a majority of the public sector investment and employment in Maharashtra, often end up being caught on the wrong foot by CAG. According to the latest report of the CAG, there are a number of cases in which losses amounting to crores of rupees could have been avoided by timely and efficient action.

TABLE 7.5

Anomalies in PSUs Reported by the CAG

Name of the Corporation	*Anomaly*
Maharashtra State Police Housing and Welfare Corporation Limited	Payment of processing charges for obtaining loan without ensuring government guarantee led to avoidable expenditure of Rs. 0.20 crore.
Maharashtra State Road Development Corporation Limited	Reimbursement of Works Contract Tax to the contractors in violation of contractual terms resulted in avoidable expenditure of Rs. 3.07 crore.
City and Industrial Development Corporation of Maharashtra Limited	Injudicious decision to construct a second banking complex without firm commitment from banks resulted in idle investment of Rs. 17.49 crore for four years with consequential loss of interest of Rs. 12.37 crore till August 2001.
Haffkine Bio-Pharmaceuticals Corporation Limited	Lacunae in terms of contract resulted in avoidable expenditure of Rs. 1.68 crore.
Maharashtra State Electricity Board (statutory)	Investment in equity of Dabhol Power Company in contravention of the recommendations of Negotiating Group resulted in payment of premium of Rs. 257.65 crore.
Maharashtra State Road Transport Corporation	Decision to construct bus station at a far away location despite permission received for constructing bus station within town resulted in idle investment of Rs. 1.25 crore.

Table 7.6 presents the financial profile of PSUs in Maharashtra. Government share in the total equity during the 1990-1999 ranges from 65.47 per cent to 81.03 per cent. However, the percentage share of state's debt in total debt of the PSUs has also remained very high from 1990-91 to 1997-98.

There is a sharp decline in the percentage share of state debt in total PSU debt in 1998-99, and the dividend paid is also substantially high during this year. This could be because of the improvement in the performance of PSUs during this year. However, the overall picture remains far from being satisfactory.

Moreover, public sector undertakings in Maharashtra can be classified into three categories: public corporations, enterprises and cooperatives. Group-wise structure and performance of the PSUs in Maharashtra is provided in the tables (Table 7.7 to 7.12).

TABLE 7.6

Financial Profile of PSUs in Maharashtra

Year	*Percentage Share of State Equity in Total Equity*	*Percentage Share of State Debt in Total Debt*	*Dividend*
1990-91	80.54	61.44	3.06
1991-92	81.03	62.43	3.44
1992-93	64.81	58.67	3.20
1993-94	76.89	47.55	4.13
1994-95	74.39	50.26	4.22
1995-96	65.47	58.09	4.41
1996-97	77.34	57.91	6.46
1997-98	74.17	57.03	5.83
1998-99	76.05	11.39	1070.14

Source: Estimation from the data provided by the Institute of Public Enterprises, Hyderabad.

Of the total 66 PSUs, data was largely available only for the 44 working PSUs. Out of 44 working PSUs, there are in all 25 public corporations in Maharashtra. It can be observed from Table 7.7 that the average state equity and investment are high in MKVDC, MIDCL, and MPBCDCL.

All the data presented here refer to the 1990s period, and they deal with average state equity, average total investment, average surplus investment, average accumulated losses, average net worth, average profit before tax, and average percentage share of state equity to total equity. The financial viability of these enterprises is being assessed by looking at their profitability before tax as a proportion of net worth and capital employed.

However, Maharashtra State Mining Corporation Ltd. (MSMCL) has the highest accumulated loss of Rs. 277 crore during the 1990s.

Three other corporations incurred an average accumulated loss of more than Rs. 10 crores, while two of them had less than Rs. 10 crores average loss. Eleven out of 25 public corporations have zero average

TABLE 7.7

Structure of PSUs (Public Corporations) during 1990-1999

(Rs. in Crore)

Name of PSU	*Avg. State Equity*	*Avg. Total Investment*	*Avg. Surplus Reserves*	*Avg. Accumulated Losses*	*Avg. Net Worth*	*Avg. PBIT*	*Avg. Percentage Share of State Equity to Total Equity*
MSTDCL	11.74	16.03	2.64	10.62	3.76	-0.28	100.00
CIDCL	3.95	1654.84	24.32	0.00	24.71	13.26	100.00
MSSIDCL	5.18	36.17	2.67	0.89	8.48	4.58	96.05
MSFC	28.98	838.82	33.17	10.82	78.85	1.40	51.00
MDCL	10.30	34.83	0.00	3.31	13.05	0.00	100.00
MMRDC	30.75	1547.95	0.00	0.00	435.46	0.00	7.61
FDC	21.34	73.50	85.43	0.00	106.75	10.35	100.00
MLDCL	3.00	50.07	0.00	13.50	0.00	0.00	75.00
MFDCL	0.97	1.54	0.00	2.19	-0.65	-0.12	100.00
MJP	0.00	548.03	99.98	0.00	311.83	6.56	0.00
MAIDC	1.86	58.11	12.55	0.06	15.52	4.42	56.35
MIDCL	1336.59	1373.19	16.72	0.00	16.72	2.72	100.00
MSPCL	7.77	9.66	0.00	8.94	-1.17	0.11	100.00
WMDCL	0.00	2.90	3.06	0.00	5.98	1.21	0.00
MSWC	3.42	13.35	26.96	0.00	33.63	7.33	51.07
MSSCL	1.89	20.87	13.31	0.17	17.26	6.84	47.91
DCVL	7.12	9.79	0.00	3.92	2.11	0.00	100.00
MPBCDCL	313.77	1438.75	0.00	0.00	0.00	-17.95	47.69
LIDCOM	4.23	4.62	0.48	0.81	4.72	0.67	100.00
MSMCL	206.69	385.56	0.00	277.32	-97.93	19.38	100.00
HBCL	4.73	8.36	4.03	0.55	7.85	3.13	100.00
MFSCDCL	3.93	7.38	0.00	2.44	1.49	0.39	100.00
TIDC	23.36	143.87	0.00	0.00	23.36	0.00	100.00
MSPHWCL	7.96	203.82	0.01	0.00	7.97	0.00	100.00
MKVDC	3878.67	5380.67	0.00	0.00	0.00	0.00	100.00

Source: Estimated from the data made available by the Institute of Public Enterprises, Hyderabad.

accumulated loss, which is surprising given the fact that these are all public corporations.

From Table 7.8, it can be noticed that except one public corporation, Western Maharashtra Development Corporation Ltd., no other public corporation had declared dividends during the period 1990-1999.

TABLE 7.8

Profitability and Dividends of PSUs (Public Corporations) during 1990-1999

(Rs. in Crore)

Name of PSU	*Avg. Per Cent PBIT/Net Worth*	*Avg. Per Cent PBIT/K-Employed*	*Avg. Dividends*
MSTDCL	-8.78	-4.11	0.00
CIDCL	64.01	2.02	0.00
MSSIDCL	54.60	12.22	0.00
MSFC	-1.38	0.61	3.22
MDCL	0.00	0.00	0.00
MMRDC	0.00	0.00	0.00
FDCL	11.14	7.23	0.00
MLDCL	0.00	0.00	0.00
MFDCL	20.35	0.00	0.00
MJP	1.60	3.42	0.00
MAIDC	7.80	6.89	0.03
MIDCL	36.85	7.20	0.00
MSPCL	19.03	3.39	0.07
WMDCL	20.03	15.09	118.84
MSWC	38.92	17.35	0.00
MSSCL	0.00	0.00	0.00
DCVL	-11.27	-2.46	0.00
MPBCDCL	0.00	0.00	0.00
LIDCOM	13.39	14.39	0.00
MSMCL	84.07	13.81	0.00
HBCL	37.35	26.70	0.21
MFSCDCL	17.06	6.11	0.00
TIDC	0.00	0.00	0.00
MSPHWCL	0.00	0.00	0.00
MKVDC	0.00	0.00	0.00

Source: Estimated by using the data made available by Institute of Public Enterprises, Hyderabad.

The picture shows a contrasting trend between profits estimated as a percentage of net worth and capital employed (higher in the case of former and lower for capital employed). Most enterprises appear to be earning less than one per cent return on capital employed during the period 1990-1999.

There are about 12 PSUs, which can be classified under 'enterprises' category. Table 7.9 provides data referring to the structure of these enterprises. In 8 out of 12, the state government has 100 per cent equity participation.

TABLE 7.9

Structure of PSUs (Enterprises)

(Rs. in Crore)

Name of PSU	*Avg. State Equity*	*Avg. Total Investment*	*Avg. Surplus Reserves*	*Avg. Accumulated Losses*
MSPCL	7.77	9.66	0.00	8.94
MPCL 8.39	8.39	0.40	0.00	
MECL.	9.53	45.49	7.72	15.84
DTML	0.00	13.85	0.16	9.43
Kalameshvar Textiles	0.00	16.65	0.00	7.87
Pratap Mill	0.00	16.37	0.04	15.26
PCM	0.50	12.65	0.00	9.46
MSTCL	86.32	183.28	2.92	96.73
MSFCL	2.75	34.41	0.00	15.05
MAFCO Ltd.	4.49	6.70	0.66	0.60
MSRTC	128.85	409.31	110.84	174.60
MSRDC7	5.00	1019.85	56.65	0.07

Source: Estimated by using the data made available by Institute of Public Enterprises, Hyderabad.

The highest average investment is in Maharashtra State Road Development Corporation Ltd. that largely caters to the infrastructure requirements of the state. The nearest corporation is the MSRTC, constituting 40 per cent of the investment that the state has made in MSRDC. However, MSRTC accounts for the highest average losses, to the tune of Rs. 1.75 billion during the 1990s.

It is closely followed by Maharashtra State Textile Corporation Ltd. Majority of the enterprises appear to be incurring heavy losses. The only exception is the MSRDC, which in spite of receiving the highest investment from the state is incurring a very low average loss during the reference decade. It is also the only undertaking to declare dividend during this period (Table 7.10). Many others show very poor performance in terms of profits by net worth and profits by capital employed.

There are seven cooperatives maintained by the state government. Average investment during the past decade has been the highest in the Tribal Development Corporation Ltd. The accumulated losses also appear to be the highest in this cooperative.

TABLE 7.10

Profitability and Dividends of PSUs (Enterprises)

(Rs. in Crore)

Name of PSU	*Avg. Per Cent PBIT/Net Worth*	*Avg. Per Cent PBIT/K-Employed*	*Avg. Dividend*
MSPCL	4.35	18.61	0.00
MPCL	5.37	5.90	0.00
MECL	-1.45	1.34	0.00
DTML	-92.05	-16.21	0.00
Kalameshvar Textiles	-0.41	0.27	0.00
Pratap Mills	31.32	-55.52	0.00
PCM	-142.16	-29.52	0.00
MSTCL	10.45	-10.96	0.00
MSFCL	29.46	-14.90	0.00
MAFCO Ltd.	15.19	10.30	0.00
MSRTC	-11.27	-2.46	0.00
MSRDC	0.00	0.00	0.41

Source: Estimated using the data made available by the Institute of Public Enterprises, Hyderabad.

It is very important to note that the state of Maharashtra, which has been giving a lot of importance to cooperatives, is not really suffering too much from the accumulated losses of all of them. The average accumulated loss of all other cooperatives is far much lower than the Public corporations or enterprises. Return on capital employed and nėt worth appear to be low for the cooperatives also. It is not really surprising given the fact that these cooperatives are more serviceoriented rather than profit maximising.

From the ongoing analysis, it can be observed that most PSUs in Maharashtra are not doing well in terms of return on capital employed or profit to net worth ratio. A few seem to be adding the burden on the exchequer with every year pass by. It is extremely important to tackle the problems of the loss-making ones on a priority basis. It is needless to mention that the focus of policy makers should also be to find out the problems and constraints of the individual corporations/enterprise/cooperatives and take adequate preventive actions.

TABLE 7.12

Profitability and Dividends of PSUs (Cooperatives)

(Rs. in Crore)

Name of PSU	*Avg. Per Cent PBIT/Net Worth*	*Avg. Per Cent PBIT/K-Employed*	*Avg. Dividends*
MHADA	12.35	15.90	0.00
MSHCFL	-24.19	-3.04	0.00
KCML	-8.34	-5.55	0.00
MSCMFL	12.40	6.52	0.25
MMSVM	0.00	0.00	0.00
MSCCGMF	5.61	3.88	0.00
MSCTDCL	14.53	25.74	0.00

Source: Estimated from the data made available by the Institute of Public Enterprises, Hyderabad.

SECTION II

Need for Restructuring and Reforms

To assist in the achievement of the objective of a welfare state, the Government of Maharashtra has established several state enterprises. However, it was noticed by the Government that in spite of several measures taken in the past for this purpose, the operational and financial viability of several state enterprises had deteriorated progressively, thereby not only straining the resources of the state but also

TABLE 7.11

Structure of PSUs (Cooperatives)

(Rs. in Crore)

Name of PSU	*Avg. State Equity*	*Avg. Total Investment*	*Avg. Surplus Reserves*	*Avg. Accumulated Losses*	*Avg. Net Worth*	*Avg. PBIT*	*Avg. Percentage Share of State Equity to Total Equity*
MHADA	0.00	423.64	218.45	0.00	205.19	15.75	0.00
MSHCFL	1.20	3.19	1.18	2.58	1.90	0.33	96.77
KCML	2.13	2.22	0.08	0.86	1.60	-0.13	88.89
MSCMFL	10.09	47.02	30.82	0.00	41.43	5.09	94.93
MMSVM	0.00	1.96	0.00	0.13	1.66	0.00	0.00
MSCCGMF	1.78	11.31	9.38	1.38	10.11	0.68	96.80
M.SCTDCL	1428.61	1560.74	29.57	81.45	3017.27	449.84	92.04

Source: Estimated using the data made available by the Institute of Public Enterprises, Hyderabad.

adversely affecting the objectives of these state enterprises. In addition, the rapid development of information technologies such as telecommunication, computers, microelectronics, robotics, fibre optics, and advanced and composite materials intensified the competition in both the global as well as the local markets. In this world of rapidly evolving technology, the public firms failed to keep pace, since their decisions were often taken by political considerations and also their response to changing markets and technologies were usually very sluggish. Moreover, these enterprises have also been largely overstaffed and depended heavily on subsidies and unilateral budget transfers for financial support.

Problem of Implicit Subsidy

Implicit subsidy implies excess of subsidy enjoyed by the PSUs out of the government investment either directly or indirectly. This causes cash losses, fiscal benefits and a notional 15 per cent return on the investment made by the state government in the form of equity, preference shares and accumulated reserves, if any. The summation of all—less the dividend (if any) paid back by the SPEs to the state government constitutes implicit subsidy. Thus, the concept of implicit subsidy means a burden on the state's exchequer. Comparing the implicit subsidy of Maharashtra between 1985-86 and 1997-98, it can be pointed out that Maharashtra's implied subsidy increased from Rs. 54 to Rs. 1,140 between 1984-85 and 1997-98.

Resource Generation and Wider Participation

Public sector disinvestments has also assumed considerable importance among the policy makers, as it is considered to be one of the major sources of resource generation and privatisation of these enterprises is expected to enable wider participation. Privatisation of public enterprises generate new sources of cash flow and finance for enterprises in both domestic and foreign markets, and also they in turn, reduce government's fiscal deficit by using privatisation revenues to retire external and domestic debt, reducing the fiscal transfers to state enterprises and increased tax revenues through higher profits generated by privatised enterprises.

Competitiveness and Improved Performance

Most public enterprises are important suppliers of goods and services to the private sector. Their poor performance, as a result, affects the performance of the private firms also, especially in a protected market. The state government being concerned to ensure that these state enterprises, which have been set up for the development of infrastructure in the state and for facilitating the availability of goods and services to promote social and economic development in the state, continue to play an effective role and remain financially viable. Therefore, necessity had arisen, of immediate intervention by the government by making available the services of an expert body to provide mandatory advice and assistance to the government as well as to such state enterprises with a view of enabling the latter to observe strict financial discipline and to revive or to reorganise and restructure themselves to become financially viable and operationally sound. For the aforesaid purposes, it was considered expedient to make and pass a special law and accordingly the Maharashtra State Enterprises (Restructuring and other special provisions) Act, 2000 (Maharashtra Act No. XXXIII of 2001) was passed. Under this Act, the state government has constituted Maharashtra Board for restructuring state enterprises.

The board would enjoy a whole gamut of powers for recommending measures for restructuring, amalgamation, merger, closure, and divestment of state public enterprises. Apart from the Chairman, the board would comprise of two other members. Under the provisions of the Act, the state government can make a reference to the Board in respect of a state enterprise where it wants to withdraw its ownership or management or divest its control especially when the financial condition of such enterprises is not satisfactory and requires remedial measures. The state government can also make such a reference when two or more state enterprises or subsidiaries can be merged for improving their financial position, operations and management.

SECTION III

Policy Measures for Restructuring

In accordance with the disinvestments measure adopted by the Central PSUs, a number of measures for restructuring the public sector units have also been attempted by the Government of Maharashtra. New Industry, Trade and Commerce Policy for Maharashtra for 1995, stated its policy on privatisation and the State Bureau of Public Enterprises of Maharashtra has explained the need for restructuring for the retained enterprises. The privatisation policy stresses the need for the privatisation of commercial and commercial-cum-promotional undertakings. It also seeks private sector participation in the construction of irrigation dams, roads, bridges, power projects as well as industrial estates and development of ports. The State Bureau of Public Enterprises suggests the formulation of specified minimum norms of returns, reduction/ control of administrative costs and closure of non-viable PSUs not serving any serious public purpose. It is generally felt that current profit, and/or current loss, need not necessarily be the appropriate criterion for disinvestments. Merely because a unit is profitable, it does not qualify to continue to be publicly owned, unless it meets a well-defined felt need. Loss making units need not be excluded from disinvestments, if there are buyers who can make it profitable.

As mentioned earlier, there are at least two major reasons adduced for the disinvestments. One is to provide fiscal support and the other is to improve the efficiency of the enterprise. The fiscal support argument has to be given adequate weightage. The demands on the state governments are increasing because of the compelling need to expand the activities of the state in the areas like education, public health, medicine and environment. It could be argued that a part of the additional resources needed for supporting these activities come out of the sale of shares built up earlier by the government out of its resources. Secondly, disinvestments in PSUs are expected to result in improving the efficiency of the enterprise. It is generally felt that the dilution of ownership results in the improvement in the efficiency of the enterprise, especially because of the increase in accountability of those in charge of the enterprise. The shareholders of the enterprise would require to be compensated and this in turn will compel the enterprise to operate more efficiently and perhaps earn more profit as well. Disinvestments can therefore be regarded as a tool for enhancing economic efficiency.

With regard to the extent of disinvestments, the level of disinvestments in an enterprise in any year should be derived from the target level of government ownership in that enterprise over the medium term. The target level could vary across enterprise and industry in which they operate. The target level of disinvestments should be derived from the desirable level of public ownership in an activity or unit consistent with the state's industrial policy. The approach paper of the Ninth Plan states that, "Disinvestments will be considered up to 51 per cent and beyond in the case of PSUs operating in non-strategic and non-core sectors." The most important aspect here is the identification of the enterprises in terms of core, non-core, strategic, etc. The consensus is that in the case of non-core and non-strategic sectors, the disinvestments can be beyond 51 per cent also. For the rest of the sectors, the criterion of disinvestments can be the extent of improvement and efficiency that can be brought about as well as the need to take care of the financial requirements of the government.

In addition, the government needs to identify the process to be adopted for disinvestments. This requires an appropriate valuation of the shares and the modalities to be adopted for sale. There are three methods of valuation of shares that are usually adopted: net asset value (NAV) method, profit earning capacity value method and discounted cash flow method. The NAV would indicate the value of the asset, but not the profitability or income to the investors. The discounted cash flow is a far more comprehensive method of reflecting the expected income flows to the investors. Valuation is a difficult exercise, especially because different methods can provide different results. The price at which a share can be sold is determined by the investor perception rather than a simple measure of its intrinsic worth. It is vital, therefore, to go in for full disclosure to generate credibility and investor interest. The Disinvestment Commission has identified two acceptable and transparent processes:

a) Offering shares of public sector enterprises at a fixed price through a general prospectus. The offer is made to the general public through the medium of recognised market intermediaries.

b) Sale of equity through auction of shares amongst predetermined clientele whose number can be as large as necessary or practicable. The reserve price for the public sector enterprises' equity can be determined with the assistance of merchant bankers.

Following these principles, the Government of Maharashtra constituted a Cabinet Sub-Committee to review the loss incurring non-viable PSUs. An Advisory Board, headed by Shri. V.G. Rajyadhyaksha was set up in 1986 to report on the working of PSUs and make recommendations on their restructuring and privatisation. The Board examined the working of 22 enterprises and suggested the following measures:

a) Reduction of equity to the Government of Maharashtra to 49 per cent and at a later date to 26 per cent by disinvestment and/or preferably by allowing the Haffkine Bio-Pharmaceuticals Corporation Ltd. to issue fresh shares to the public/financial institutions and at a minimum premium of Rs. 80 per share.

b) Setting up of joint ventures controlling seed production costs and producing only profit making seed varieties and go in for tax planning by the Maharashtra Seeds Corporation Ltd.

c) Closure of Overseas Employment and Export Promotion Corporation Ltd.

d) Reduction of overheads, formulation of new marketing strategies, development of new products, higher capacity utilisation by production plants and innovation in the spot decisions by Maharashtra State Oil Seeds.

e) Elimination of OBC schemes, weeding out of subsidy schemes and the concentration on training schemes by Mahatma Phule Backward Class Development Corporation Ltd.

f) Selling the company as a going concern or as a next step selling 51 per cent of the shareholding to a strong private sector partner or yet exploring the possibility of selling 51 per cent of its stock in the market/to the financial institutions/to State Industrial and Investment Corporation of Maharashtra Ltd. (SICOM) in the case of Maharashtra Electronics Corporation Ltd. The Board also suggested the strategy of separating three potentially viable divisions and forming joint ventures. The Board suggested that the funding of the restructuring and privatisation of Meltron could among other things be done by disposing off Meltron Semi Conductors Ltd.

g) Building up core competence in the area of training and withdrawing from agricultural activities in the case of Mahila Arthik Vikas Nigam.

h) Selling 51 per cent of shares to public, financial institutions, private sector in the case of MAFCO.

i) Restructuring of the sick Maharashtra State Financial Corporation, which has accumulated losses of Rs. 7 billion.

SECTION IV

Progress of PSU Reforms

Although, many state governments have been taking initiatives towards the disinvestments of public sector enterprises, the record of performance of disinvestments shows a varied picture. As can be observed from Table 7.13, the GoM has initiated disinvestments in only three enterprises out of six identified. This is a very poor record when compared to other states. However, Government of Maharashtra has simultaneously highlighted the need to have a relook at some of the regional corporations that it has created during the past few decades. The Government closed down four such corporations in 1992, which pruned the labour force of PSUs by a number of 8,000. Winding up decisions were taken in December 1993. It required the closure of three units including Gondwana Paints and Vidarbha Gems.

SICOM was privatised in 1996. Although, the process of privatisation started in 1994, a number of procedural formalities delayed its privatisation earlier. The privatisation of SICOM Ltd. was the trendsetter for privatisation of PSUs in Maharashtra and other states. Although the five irrigation development corporations have minimal investments from the government and have raised significant sums from capital markets/ private placements, there is a need to merge five irrigation development corporations. The State Electricity Board can also benefit from restructuring and privatisation, which may help it save some operational costs and mobilise funds for its maintenance and expansion. The most serious problem with the PSUs in Maharashtra, like in other states as well, is that although they continue to incur losses and their paid-up capital eroded, the state government has been providing funds to them in the form of equity capital, loans and grants/subsidy.

These funds are often taken for granted and, therefore, no serious effort is being made by the management of the PSUs to correct the imbalance and the dependence on the exchequer. This, in turn, imposes higher burden on the state government, which is struggling to make both the ends meet on its budgetary allocations. As pointed out earlier, there are 30 enterprises that have been identified to be ready for mergers, restructuring or disinvestments. No policy initiatives appear to have taken place in finding a solution for these enterprises.

In fact, according to the CAG report, the state government did not undertake the exercise of disinvestments, privatisation and restructuring of any of its public sector undertakings during the fiscal year 2000-01. At this rate, PSU reform and restructuring would continue to be a distant dream for the state of Maharashtra.

TABLE 7.13

Record of Disinvestments in States

State	*Approximate Number of State Level Public Enterprises (SLPEs)*	*Estimated Total Investment in SLPEs (Rs. in Crore)*	*SLPEs Identified for Disinvestment/ Winding Up/Restructuring*	*No. of SLPEs in which Process Initiated*
Andhra Pradesh	51	4444	21	10
Assam	42	3676	1	—
Goa	12	4869	1	—
Gujarat	49	23438	11	5
Haryana	27	4746	8	5
Himachal Pradesh	21	3143	15	—
Jammu & Kashmir	N/A	N/A	7	2
Karnataka	77	16641	17	9
Madhya Pradesh	34	8561	27	2
Maharashtra	**65**	**19186**	**6**	**3**
Manipur	14	N/A	10	—
Orissa	72	8544	N/A	N/A
Punjab	53	12425	9	2
Rajasthan	24	10838	11	—
Tamil Nadu	84	10158	13	3
Uttar Pradesh	50	17313	25	6
West Bengal	80	14081	2	2

Source: Public Enterprises Survey, 2000-01.

In all, there are four enterprises in which restructuring operations have been initiated during the recent times (before the year 2000) by the Government of Maharashtra. A brief description of the restructuring process in these enterprises is given below:

Maharashtra Small-scale Industries Development Corporation Ltd. (MSSIDC)

Incorporated in 1962, MSSIDC's activities include the procurement and distribution of raw materials required by small industries, assistance in marketing their products—both inside and outside the country and making available warehousing and storage facilities where required. MSSIDC's current employee strength is 458 of which 128 are officers/supervisors and 242 are clerical and 88 class IV employees. It is a profit earning company and its net worth stood at Rs. 98.72 million in 1996-97. The economic liberalisation has put the company in a tight corner as it does not enjoy the monopoly in raw materials procurement and faces price and incentive wars from its counterparts in the private sector.

It now operates in the buyers' market, where the buyer has the option to switch over from one to the other supplier on account of price, delivery schedule and quality. Further, the company cannot prolong its life only on trading. It is necessary for the company to have autonomy to make commercial decisions to face market driven business. It was in this backdrop that Government decided to privatise MSSIDC in 1995. An empowered Committee was set up to decide about the mode of privatisation. M/s Sriram Investments Ltd. was appointed to advise the Committee on the modalities of privatisation. This firm, in its report, suggested three routes for privatisation: outright sale; selling equity through public offer and; issuing non-convertible debentures (NCD) with warrants tradable at the end of 3 years with the guaranteed rate of return of 15 per cent p.a. The government is veering round the idea of preferring the NCD option as it will give adequate time to the management to restructure the operations of MSSIDC and continue to retain the state control to keep vigil on certain critical issues. Besides, the company will obtain immediate cash to overcome the financial crunch. The investors in NCDs pending privatisation will have the incentive to nominate one person on the Board of Directors per 10 per cent of the subscription to the NCDs. The MSSIDC is planning to commence many new businesses, which may include financial services, hiring of its godowns, involving in synergistic operations with SIDBI and SFCs to exploit the use of its existing network of the branches and funding of suppliers against deliveries. The company is proposing to issue bonus shares to the government.

Maharashtra State Road Transport Corporation

This Corporation was set up in 1964 to provide a coordinated, economic and efficient system of road transport services to the travelling public of the state. It had 1,12,146 employees on its role as on March 31, 1997. The Corporation incurred a net loss of Rs. 1.36 billion during this year. The Corporation on the directives of the state government is providing concessional travel, which alone made it incur a loss of Rs. 0.84 billion. The obligatory trips to rural areas resulted in a loss of Rs. 0.68 billion. The Corporation is facing a severe crunch impeding its fleet expansion and modernisation and also meeting POL expenses and wage costs. More than 51 per cent disinvestment seems to be the only way to make the Corporation work effectively in discharge of its objectives. The British Transport privatisation is being considered a good model, which may facilitate the setting up of a regulatory authority shouldered with the responsibility of promoting competition and regulation of tariffs. There is a need to reduce the bus-staff ratio and curbing the plying of private buses on nationalised routes. The disinvestment process in this premier transport corporation would take a long time to complete, and therefore the burden on the state government would continue for some more time.

Western Maharashtra Development Corporation (WMDC)

WMDC has a distillery unit at Chitali in Ahmednagar district. Since June 1993, molasses has been decontrolled and WMDC is finding it difficult to acquire molasses for its manufacturing processes and the distillery had to be closed for a number of days in a working season. As such, the government intends to privatise this distillery unit. Out of the various alternatives available, the conversion of the distillery unit into a subsidiary company and to offer on sale the equity to a private sector company/entrepreneur is finding favour with the government. This is a new approach that the government is taking. That is, instead of selling the shares of the company through the market, it wants to convert the distillery unit into a subsidiary company and sell the equities of that subsidiary to a private sector identified perhaps as a strategic buyer. Here again, the divestment process is still in the process of finalisation.

Development Corporation of Konkan Limited (DCKL)

DCKL has a rubber project in Sindhudurg district. DCKL has acquired 254 hectares of land from the farmers on a leasehold basis. Ownership rights are with the landholders and management rights are with the joint venture company i.e., DCKL and a private sector plantation company. DCKL has 24 per cent shares and the private company has 74 per cent shares in the equity. Private sector partner has paid 30 per cent of the cost of the project (estimated at Rs. 11.7 million) to DCKL at the time of signing the JV agreement. The balance amount has been treated as a loan of DCKL for which rate of interest is 16 per cent. The loan is repayable in 3 years in half yearly instalment and this will enable DCKL to recover the complete expenditure incurred in the project. DCKL was also involved in joint sector project involving oil palm plantation in which land of about 1,035 hectares was acquired from the farmers but they retain their ownership rights. DCKL has equity of 26 per cent in the joint venture and the private company has a 74 per cent share. The joint venture company (JVC) has management rights and will remain and take care of the plantation and yield for further processing. An oil factory has been erected by the JVC and it has started functioning since June 1999.

It is evident from these four cases that the Government of Maharashtra is adopting different methods in dealing with the PSU restructuring. Some of these methods are unit-specific, especially guided by the micro-level problems that the companies have been encountering, and are not strictly applicable in other cases. This approach, however, would be very time-consuming and hence there would be delays in finalisation of the process of restructuring. Such a unit-level approach to reform and restructuring, in spite of this time requirement is likely to be more effective and efficient method of reforming the aforesaid PSU. Efforts need to be directed to reduce the time taken in finalisation of the procedures of restructuring and effective and timely implementation of the same. The process of restructuring also requires the support of labour and other affected parties. Unit-level reform measures should also ensure that the labour unions are taken into confidence in the finalisation of the policies. Such process alone can ensure the successful completion of the reform measures and keep the cost of reform minimal. The analyses of the restructuring package introduced/used so far reveal that the State of Maharashtra is in the right direction, but moving with tremendous precaution.

Studies on the effect of different types of disinvestment in Central PSUs reveal that strategic sale using the first-priced sealed-bid method currently employed cannot always be counted upon to maximise efficiency and revenues (Ram Mohan, 2003). This is especially because under the strategic sale there is a danger of a large stake being sold cheaply. Further, there is also an element of irretrievability in strategic sale. On the contrary, empirical evidence in public sector disinvestment in India and other countries point towards the sale of government shares through an initial public offer (IPO) especially because the share issue privatisation (SIP) is consistent with post-privatisation improvement in the performance firms privatised through this route. Naib (2003) examined the impact of divestiture in Indian state owned enterprises and points out that in the case of partial divestiture, where divested equity is thinly spread with the majority shareholding still with the government, there has been no improvement in terms of profitability and operational efficiency. He suggests that strategic sale, where management control passes to the strategic partner will free the enterprises from political/ bureaucratic controls, enabling them to take decisions in line with the market demands. In profitable PSUs, however, equity should also be offered to the public and the employees (Naib, 2003). Learning from the results of these analyses, the Government of Maharashtra has tremendous scope for formulating an efficient method of restructuring the PSUs in the state. The method followed could differ across the nature and scope of the enterprises—especially on the basis of their strategic importance and performance.

SECTION V

Summary and Conclusions

This chapter provides an overview of the need for policy initiatives for restructuring and reforming of the public sector undertakings in Maharashtra. Most of the PSUs in Maharashtra are in financially vulnerable position and continue to depend on the grants and support from the government. There are at least 30 units where restructuring can take place immediately. Several of these 30 units operate at low efficiency and high cost. The government could easily merge some of them and form a single corporation. However, not many initiatives have been taken on these units so far. Moreover, there appear to be tremendous delays in the finalisation of the accounts of the PSUs in Maharashtra, which make most of the analysis extremely difficult to carry out. Added to this were the inefficient practices of some of the PSUs, which resulted in severe losses to the government. This has been pointed out by the CAG but appear to be over looked by the management of the enterprise and the government. An evaluation of the PSU restructuring in Maharashtra reveals that the restructuring process is far from being satisfactory. There are several problems, a number of which are unit-specific that need to be taken into account. Efforts have been made to formulate unit specific policies for restructuring. However, most of it has been very time-consuming and these delays have resulted in increasing the burden on the exchequer. The state seems to be traversing on a right path, however, very cautiously. Over-caution can create distrust among the potential buyers.

Further, outright sale of the equities of the public sector enterprises may not evoke much response; in the absence of a clear-cut portrayal of the role of the state as well as the enterprise in the industry and the economy in which the firm operates. Moreover, the acquisition (of assets of a public enterprise by the private sector firm) process often involves a bidder acquiring the shares of a majority shareholder in a target company at a negotiated price. Alternatively, the bidder could acquire shares *via* open market purchases. Following Anshuman (2003) it could be argued that all strategic sales of assets to the private parties result in a transfer of wealth from the majority shareholders to the minority shareholders. This is especially true when the government offers privatisation under 'dual-priced offers'. As a result, lower proceeds are raised in disinvestments involving strategic sale of PSUs with a public float. Also, empirical evidence in India points toward identifying a unit-specific disinvestment strategy. Such a strategy would go a long way to improve the efficiency and revenue generation capacity of the enterprise. The experience in the use of IPO method in the case of profit making Central PSUs in the petroleum industry could be an eye-opener for the state.

To sum up, Maharashtra's restructuring and privatisation agenda is only slowly gaining momentum. Privatisation and restructuring will provide a good deal of revenues to the state government and make the PSUs commercial entities in the true sense of the term. This drive has the tacit support of the Maharashtra Government. The state, however, needs to make a clear distinction between public corporations/enterprises and cooperatives in the manner in which it proceeds for disinvestment. The sooner it makes the distinction clear, the faster can the state proceed towards disinvestment. This is especially because the fiscal support for inefficient and loss-making public enterprises can no longer be sustained. Public sector cooperatives, on the other hand, have a welfare maximisation criterion, which would make formulation of disinvestment policy a bit difficult in these cases. Further, the labour force should also be taken into confidence in coming to terms with the realities. Technical and conceptual capabilities, which can provide impetus to this exercise, are the needs of the hour in the programme of restructuring and reformulation of the public sector undertakings in Maharashtra.

Chapter 8

Human Resources Development of the Weaker Sections

Introduction

The first seven goals of the UN Millennium Declaration adopted in 2000, namely, to eradicate extreme poverty and hunger, achieve universal education, promote gender equality and empower women, reduce child mortality and improve maternal health, combat AIDS, malaria and other diseases, ensure access to safe drinking water and ensure environmental sustainability, form the first axis of the frame of this chapter. Amartya Sen's proposition on development is the second. Sen argues that development must be seen as a process of expanding the real freedom that people enjoy and acuminate the major sources of lack of freedom, *viz.*, poverty, dominance, poor economic opportunities and systemic deprivation, neglect of public facilities as well as intolerance. What people can positively achieve is influenced by economic opportunities, political liberties, social powers and the enabling conditions of good health, basic education and the encouragement and cultivation of initiatives. The concept of human resources is the third. While the understanding is often limited to seeing human beings as a unit of economic production, human resources are involved not just in the production of goods and services, but more importantly contribute to the quality of individual and collective living, generate social capital, ensure freedom, liberty and foster civic engagement. Hence, while human resource development cannot be disassociated from the process of accelerating economic growth, it cannot be disengaged from equity either. The definition of weaker sections is the fourth axis, and brings within its ambit those who suffer from physical, economic and social deprivation, discrimination on the basis of caste, creed and patriarchy namely the STs, SCs, women and differently abled. With the four sides (axes) of the frame of this chapter clarified, the challenge of human resource development of the weaker sections is to combine acceleration of economic growth while strengthening equity, generate wealth ensuring distributive justice and enhance opportunity while engendering freedom.

Maharashtra—A Study in Contrasts

Maharashtra, with a per capita income of Rs. 24,736 in 2001-02, is the third richest state in India after Punjab and Haryana among 15 major states. In contrast to Punjab and Haryana's rich alluvial plains, Maharashtra has to be content with a narrow coastal plain and a vast parched plateau. Maharashtra's prosperity comes from Mumbai, the industrial and commercial capital of the nation. Maharashtra has also a long history of social reform.

Dnyaneshwar, Tukaram, Sahu Maharaj, Phule and Ambedkar are the more prominent among numerous reformers who advocated social equity. Movements of Dalits, Adivasis and peasants, movements for rehabilitation, water and land redistribution, against corruption are interwoven in Maharashtra's history. But behind the facade of prosperity and movements for equity, the lives of the majority of its people, particularly the SCs, STs and other disadvantaged groups, is less than enviable. Despite a glorious past and a prosperous present, the state has a quarter of its population below the poverty line.

Maharashtra—The Great Rural Urban Divide

It would not be an exaggeration to depict the state as islands of urban prosperity in a sea of rural poverty. Nowhere in the country is the divide so sharp as the comparison between the per capita product of Mumbai, which is consistently 2 to 2.5 times that of the rest of

Maharashtra as mentioned in Table 8.1. The ratio would be significantly higher if the per capita product of other highly industrialised cities of Thane, Pune, Nagpur, Nashik, Aurangabad and Rasayani-Nagothne, rated at 1 to 6 after Mumbai, were deducted from that of the rest of Maharashtra. This fact is reflected in the HDI constructed for 312 Indian districts for the year 1981. The ranks of districts ranged between 16 for Pune (No. 2 in Maharashtra) and 210 for Chandrapur (No. 10 in Maharashtra) (Prabhu, 1992).

TABLE 8.1

Net National Product Per Capita (in Rs.) Mumbai, Maharashtra Excluding Mumbai and India: 1970-71 to 1990-91

Year	*Mumbai*	*Rest of Maharashtra*	*India*
1970-71	1786	632	675
1980-81	4683	1858	1630
1990-91	8784	4105	3852

Note: NNP is at current prices.

Source: Mungekar, B., 2003.

Maharashtra's prosperity is concentrated in Mumbai and other industrial and commercial cities like Thane, Pune, Nagpur and Nashik, while her villages, where the overwhelming majority of her disadvantaged communities live, have no share in the prosperity but eke out a living on the fringes. While examining the relative position of agricultural, industrial, human resource and infrastructure development of the four regions of Konkan, Marathwada, Vidharbha and Western Maharashtra, Prabhu *et al.*, identify 11 districts as high, 3 districts in the middle and 15 districts as low on development. Significantly 7 of the 11 highly developed districts fall in the western Maharashtra region. The developed districts are built around a strong manufacturing centre, generally the district capital, while the hinterland and in most cases the adjoining districts are low on the development index. While on the whole the state stands 3rd among 17 states when the Human Development Index (HDI) was computed for the rural areas (Vyas and Vidyasagar, 1993) in 1981, the HDI value of 0.16 was near the bottom with only UP below it and 15 major states including poor states like Bihar and Orissa above. Table 8.2 gives a comprehensive picture of development status of districts using the parameters of agriculture, industry, human resources and infrastructure.

TABLE 8.2

Ranking of Districts according to Sectoral Development

District	*Agriculture Ranking*	*Industry Ranking*	*Human Resources Ranking*	*Infrastructure Total Ranking*
Ahmednagar	3	16	11	5
Akola	22	13	7	8
Amravati	12	13	2	15
Aurangabad	7	6	15	14
Beed	28	22	24	27
Bhandara	13	18	19	23
Buldhana	10	23	25	25
Chandrapur	23	9	23	18
Dhule	9	20	21	21
Gadchiroli	26	29	28	28
Jalgaon	5	7	22	10
Jalna	18	25	26	29
Kolhapur	1	7	8	9
Latur	23	28	17	22
Nagpur	11	3	3	7
Nanded	20	19	20	17
Nashik	2	5	12	12
Osmanabad	20	26	27	20
Parbhani	25	27	29	24
Pune	8	2	15	3
Raigad	18	10	9	2
Ratnagiri	29	17	9	11
Sangli	4	10	6	1
Satara	6	12	3	5
Sindhudurg	16	21	5	13
Solapur	15	4	18	4
Thane	17	1	14	16
Wardha	14	13	1	19
Yavatmal	27	24	13	26

Source: Mungekar, B. 2003.

Maharashtra attracted maximum foreign direct investment (FDI) between 1991 and 2001, but its share of Indian industry slipped down during the 1990s and its performance with respect to industrial employment is inferior *vis-à-vis* the national average. Burange (1999) suggests that rising capital intensity, fall in employment, substitution of capital for labour, low growth rate of value of output reflect unsatisfactory performance of the state in industrial activity. The FDI, ICT-led growth, however, resulted in an emphasis on urban areas development, uneven infrastructure, accentuated and worsened the regional and rural-urban disparities in the state. Push factors in the villages led to migration to high growth areas, resulting in decline in the quality of life in both rural and urban areas.

The Weaker Sections in Maharashtra—Facts Belie Presumptions

The relative prosperity levels of Maharashtra lead the undiscerning to presume that the weaker sections enjoy a measure of welfare security. But facts belie presumptions. The prosperity is ephemeral. Hard poverty is the fact for large sections of Maharashtra's rural population. This section explores ground realities by analysing six areas, namely, poverty, food security, health, employment, education and expenditure in the social sector.

Poverty

While poverty, indicated as percentage of people living below the poverty line, has steadily declined from 53.24 per cent in 1973-74 to 25.02 per cent in 2000, what is surprising is the decline in Maharashtra, even with its prosperity, is not better than the all-India percentage of 26.1 per cent. When compared with states with a similar per capita income like Punjab (6.16 per cent) and Haryana (8.74 per cent), the achievement of Maharashtra is poor. Karnataka and Kerala, with the same incidence of poverty in 1973-74, have done far better. The data of 1999-00 is harsher on Maharashtra; 10 of 16 states having a population of more than 10 million have lower levels of poverty than Maharashtra.

Food and Nutrition Security

Malnutrition of children is a fact of life in Maharashtra. Few districts can boast of being free of malnutrition deaths. It is disturbing that, going by the age-weight ratio, 58 per cent of all rural children under four suffer from malnutrition, and the number of malnourished children exceeds the national average.

Using quantity of cereal consumption and calorie intake values, MHDR (2002) shows that 57.4 per cent of rural and 54.8 per cent of urban households consume less than the standard 2,700 calories per day, a clear sign of undernourishment. This can be seen in Table 8.3. Only external inputs like ICDS have met with some success in addressing malnourishment among poverty groups. The problem for the weaker sections is compounded by the urban-bias in the PDS (Dev, 2003). The system is characterised by the fact that more than 50 per cent of the poor are not covered, bogus entries, and leakages particularly in rural areas and weak delivery systems in tribal tracts. PDS does not provide food security for the rural poor.

TABLE 8.3

Undernourished Children up to Four Years of Age: Maharashtra and All India: 1992-93

Item	*Rural*		*Urban*		*Total*	
	Maharashtra	*All India*	*Maharashtra*	*All India*	*Maharashtra*	*All India*
Weight for Age						
% below–3 S.D.	24.1	22.4	14.6	14.8	20.2	20.6
% below–2 S.D.	57.5	55.9	45.5	45.2	52.6	53.4
Height for Age						
% below–3 S.D.	26.2	30.9	15.7	22.0	21.9	28.9
% below–2 S.D.	50.8	54.1	39.1	44.8	46.0	52.0
Weight for Height						
% below–3 S.D.	4.3	3.2	3.8	2.9	4.1	3.2
% below–2 S.D.	21.5	18.0	18.3	15.8	20.2	17.5

Source: Family Health Survey for Maharashtra, IIPS, Mumbai, 1995.

Resources and Livelihoods

While examining access to land and land-based resources, data shows 57 per cent of SC households are landless and near landless. If marginal farmers were included, the share goes over 75 per cent. SC and ST households constitute nearly 40 per cent of the landless households and 37 per cent of the near landless households in the state. Table 8.4 indicates that only

TABLE 8.4

Distribution of Rural SC and ST Population—Economic Activity

Item	*1981*			*1991*			*2001*		
	SC	*ST*	*Others*	*SC*	*ST*	*Others*	*SC*	*ST*	*Others*
Cultivators	20.05	42.31	51.77	19.27	41.01	51.67	12.90	30.60	28.70
Agri. Labour	58.30	47.24	30.47	62.30	49.80	29.79	46.10	50.70	26.30
Others	21.65	10.45	17.76	18.43	9.19	18.54	41.00	18.80	45.00
Total	**100.00**	**100.00**	**100.00**	**100.00**	**100.00**	**100.00**	**100.00**	**100.00**	**100.00**

Source: Population Census 1981 & 1991 and *Economic Survey of Maharashtra,* 2003.

20 per cent of the SCs survive on their land, and most depend almost exclusively on their labour though the number of ST households depending on the land is marginally higher. What is observed is a slow but progressive decrease of dependence on land and growing dependence on wage labour due to falling land productivity and vagaries of the monsoon. Agriculture is losing ground as a livelihood, and, without stability of employment or social security, migration is the only alternative. Public works programmes such as EGS have been considered as solution to unemployment problem. But though government claims that 12.22 crore man-days were created in 2002 compared to 11.16 in 2001, employment created under EGS in the post-economic reform period has stagnated, adversely affecting the rural poor.

The Census 2001 notes that the work participation rate (WPR) in Maharashtra was at 43.5 per cent, a mere 0.5 per cent more than the 1991 level. The proportion of main workers to total workers declined to 84.8 per cent from 91.4, while their proportion to total population decreased from 39.3 per cent to 36.8 per cent in the decade ending 2001. The organised sector started outsourcing to remain competitive, using casual contractual labour and expertise from the nineties. Marginal workers, increased from 3.7 per cent to 6.7 in the same period with the incidence of female marginal workers being higher than males. Incidence of marginal workers was comparatively higher in rural areas. The growth rate of labour, with 93 per cent of workers in the unorganised sector, has been higher than the organised sector, which remained constant at around 7 per cent. Ninety per cent of total women workers are in the informal sector. In a milieu with no radical reforms and with benefits of growth flowing mainly to the rural and urban elite, the inadequate attention paid to basic education and health by state government blunted the only tools that were available to the disadvantaged sections to ensure their social mobility.

Health of the Poor

Maharashtra's achievements in the health sector are better compared to those in the education sector. Life expectancy increased from 53.3 years in 1970-75 to 63 in 1989-1993 for males, and from 54.4 years to 65.4 years for females, slightly better than all-India averages. Maharashtra's achievement is, however, overshadowed by Kerala's, a far poorer state as indicated in Table 8.5, IMR came down from 119 to 74 per 1,000 live births in 1991. However, gender bias is apparent— female IMR

TABLE 8.5

Trends in Education and Health Attainment: 1961-1991

Education	*Maharashtra*				*Kerala*				*All India**			
	1961	*1991*	*2001*	*% Change*	*1961*	*1991*	*2001*	*% Change*	*1961*	*1991*	*2001*	*% Change*
Literates Total (%)	14.67	53.77	77.27	266.53	31.90	77.96	90.92	144.39	15.13	42.84	65.20	183.15
Literates Female (%)	9.04	43.30	67.51	378.98	27.03	75.25	87.86	178.39	8.53	32.17	54.03	277.14
Literates Rural (%)	12.65	45.43	70.84	259.13	31.97	76.96	90.05	140.73	13.29	36.31	59.21	173.21
Literates Urban (%)	19.81	66.99	85.76	238.16	31.49	80.78	93.38	156.53	23.54	61.70	80.06	162.11
Health	*Maharashtra*				*Kerala*				*All India*			
	1951-61	*1989-93*	*1992-96*	*% Change*	*1951-61*	*1989-93*	*1992-96*	*% Change*	*1951-61*	*1989-93*	*1992-96*	*% Change*
Life Expectancy (Years)	45.2	64.2	65.2	44.24	48.3	72.0	73.1	51.34	41.2	59.4	60.7	47.33
Literates	*Maharashtra*				*Kerala*				*All India*			
	1981	*1991*	*1996*	*% Change*	*1981*	*1991*	*1996*	*% Change*	*1981*	*1991*	*1996*	*% Change*
Infant Mortality Rate	119	74	48	-59.66	54	42	14	-74.07	115	77	72	-37.39

Note: (a) Literacy rates have been calculated as literates to total population.

(b) Life expectancy has been calculated without adjustment due to decline in mortality.

(c) Infant mortality rate refers to number of deaths from birth to age one per thousand live births.

* Excludes Jammu & Kashmir.

Source: (1) Mungekar, 2003.

(2) *Primary Census Abstract, Census of India,* 2001.

(3) GoI, 2002b.

remained higher at 76 than the male IMR at 72. The decline in IMR is in proportion to rising education of women, standing at 72 for illiterate women and a low of 24 for women with high school education. (NFHS, 1994). The rural-urban divide was also apparent; the rural IMR at 58 was higher than the urban rate of 31 in 1996. Female IMR was particularly high in Yavatmal (126), Chandrapur (101) and Gadchiroli (117). The IMR was also higher in Ratnagiri, Nashik, Jalna, Buldhana, Amravati, Wardha, Nagpur, Bhandara and Chandrapur. Attention is drawn to the IMR in excess of 100 in Akola, Yavatmal and Gadchiroli. Importantly, these districts have a higher proportion of Scheduled Tribes (Prabhu and Kamdar, 1996, p. 345). While extensive data on maternal mortality is not available, available estimates indicate that the rate is higher than Kerala, and Tamil Nadu, relatively high proportion of non-institutional births being a contributing factor.

The prevalence rate of illness in Maharashtra, according to NCAER study in 1990, was 54.82 in urban and 70.46 per 1,000 in rural areas, lower than corresponding all-India figures. Incidence of diseases due to poor living conditions was 1,042 and immunisation for preventable diseases was 18.86 per lakh population in 1992 as compared to all-India level of 1,431 and 21.55 (Prabhu and Kamdar, 1996). Attention is drawn to the increasing proportion of deaths due to circulatory disorders, injuries, accidents, bronchitis, asthma, heart attacks, indicative of diet/ nutrition deficiencies, fast life, pollution, and environmental degradation. Reasons of restricted access to hospitals and chronic ailments due to lack of purchasing power are indicated in reportage of higher morbidity rates of disadvantaged sections. Availability of infrastructure facilities remains skewed as in the education sector with poor primary health facilities and better higher level tertiary facilities located in urban areas adding to the sharp rural-urban and interregional disparities. As against 0.62 PHCs per 100 sq. kms at all-India level, the number was only 0.53 in Maharashtra. Besides, only 53 per cent of the state's villages are approachable by all-weather roads affecting levels of access.

While leprosy eradication is a success story due to multi-drug therapy, TB resists eradication due to late detection and incapability of the health sector despite an elaborate control machinery. Malaria has staged a comeback due to delay and failure in treatment, sub-standard drugs and insecticides, lack of entomological surveys and staff shortage. While Maharashtra has highest HIV/AIDS incidence with a higher ratio of female victims, campaigns remain limited to surveillance of high-risk groups. The NFHS-I survey reports prevalence of partial blindness at 32 and complete blindness at 3 per 1,000 and higher incidence among rural women. Though safe drinking water and sanitation are important determinants of health, only 54 per cent rural and 91 per cent urban households had safe drinking water in 1991. None of the rural areas had underground drainage in 1993. Only 32 per cent in rural and 74 per cent in urban areas had garbage disposal facility in the state in 1993. To compound the situation, public expenditure on health and disease control is declining, while demand for health services has increased. Even then, a large proportion of health expenditure is on salaries with a negligible portion on medical supplies.

Education of the Weaker Sections

While Maharashtra ranks second in literacy rate among the major states in India, the picture is not heartening. Forty four per cent of all workers (NSSO, 55th Round) in the state are illiterate while 22.7 per cent received primary education level, the situation of the weaker sections is far worse. Only 33.3 per cent of the labour force can be termed as adequately qualified. While the state has well-developed infrastructure for education, rural-urban disparities are highest in Nandurbar, Gadchiroli, and Thane, which have high proportion of tribal population.

Free bus-pass, *vasti shala* for migrant workers children, Jyotiba Phule Shikshan Hami Yojana, school within a kilometre, free textbooks, uniforms, stationary, pre/post matric scholarships for special social groups, *ashram shalas,* hostels for backward class students, attendance allowance for disadvantaged girl children, mid-day meals, night schools for working children, special schemes such as DPEP and PEEP are some of the special attempts to increase school enrolment, retention, reduce dropout rates, improve access, and child participation. As a result, the state has achieved considerable progress in increasing literacy rate, enhancing enrolment and reducing dropout rate, but dropout rates remain high among the weaker sections, particularly among girl children. Dropout rates in 2000-2001 show that of 100 enrolments, only 80 complete primary education, 60 complete upper primary and only 40 complete secondary education. Overall passing percentages for the secondary school level examination are not impressive. Only 57 of every 100 students pass the SSC exam and only 32 appear for HSC exam. This shows that schooling opportunities do not get effectively translated into educational attainment in the state. In terms of technical education, the rate of increase of technical, vocational educational infrastructure neither has kept pace with the demand nor has it kept pace with the advancement of technology as shown in Table 8.6.

TABLE 8.6

Educational Infrastructure in Maharashtra : 2002-2003

Item	*Infrastructure (in No.)*	*Enrolment (Lakh)*
Primary School	68736	117.09
Secondary Schools	16647	83.97
Higher Secondary Schools/Junior Colleges	3904	16.97
Colleges	1195	10.35

Privatisation of technical, vocational, professional and higher education has put these beyond the reach of the weaker sections. The region-wise trends, provided in Table 8.7, throws some surprising results: primary schools are on the decline while secondary schools are on the rise across all the regions, exposing a serious flaw in the education sector which provides for higher education in urban areas rather than primary education. Primary schools per lakh population had declined in the state as a whole except Vidarbha in 1959-60 to 1990-91 period. The increase in schools, across regions except Mumbai, points out to increased privatisation of education in Mumbai. But when economic factors and lack of interest are given as the main reasons for non-enrolment and dropout rates, the disadvantaged sections of the population whose reliance on publicly provided infrastructure facilities is greater are punished with poor quality of schools and no schools.

Expenditure in the Social Sector

In the final analysis, commitment to the cause of the weaker sections is seen not in policies but in actual practice, which begins with resource allocation for the development of the weaker groups. Despite the reduction in public spending on social security, poverty alleviation and welfare programmes by Maharashtra in the 1990s, surprisingly poverty declined from 36.86 per cent in 1993–94 to 25.02 per cent in 1999–00, which was lower than the all-India level of 26.10 per cent as per the NSSO 55th Round conducted in 1999–00. But the incidence and severity of rural poverty in the state are higher than all-India levels. In absolute terms, more than 2.5 crore people in the state lived below poverty line, of which about 1.4 crore lived in rural areas. Further despite decline in incidence of poverty, a majority of rural and urban population is undernourished (MHDR, 2002).

Table 8.8 clearly indicates a withdrawal of the state from its responsibilities to the poor. Public sector spending was subjected to cuts, often ranging from 30-40 per cent during the last decade.

Due to inadequate provision made in the budget for matching funds in the social sectors, the state could not access its share of the funds provided by the Central Government for the centrally sponsored anti-poverty schemes. Provision for the programmes for the weaker sections declined. The share of elementary education in total education expenditure was 47.6 per cent in 1985-86, which declined to 41.3 per cent in 1990-91 (Prabhu and Chatterjee, 1993). This is in contrast to the situation in Kerala where, despite already high levels of primary education, the relevant figures were 51.9 per cent and 53.1 per cent. Expenditure on primary education per child aged 5-9 years in Maharashtra, Kerala and all-India when compared, Kerala is far ahead in this respect. The predominance of revenue expenditure on education and health, the negligible capital component, the inadequate allocation to lower level services, and a deceleration in the revenue expenditure on education and health since mid-1980s indicate low priority attached to human development concerns in the state (Prabhu and Sarkar, 1998). This can be seen in the Table 8.8.

A long history of social reform in Maharashtra is the bedrock of its widespread social capital, like two sides of a coin. The spirit of voluntarism, in the form of giving in cash/kind (PRIA) imbued an estimated 8.4 per cent of the rural and 19 per cent of the urban adult population to contribute Rs. 50.2 crore in 2000-01. Rural donors with an average contribution of Rs. 1384 outdid their urban counterparts at Rs. 625. What is significant is 91 per cent of the donors has an income below Rs. l lakh per year. About 80 per cent gave to varied organisations, 6.4 to religious causes, 5 to community associations, 2.7 for education and 4.5 per cent to government and related purposes. The spirit of voluntarism also motivated an estimated 8,47,350 persons. 1.7 per cent of the adult population to contribute 25.35 hours every month. About 94 per cent of the volunteers were males; 72 per cent in the 18-45 age group; 69 per cent were under-graduates and 95.1 per cent had incomes less than Rs.1 lakh. About 89 per

TABLE 8.7

Region-wise Trends in Education Infrastructure: 1960-1991

Region	*Institutions per Lakh Population*					
	Primary Institutions		*Secondary Institutions*		*% Change*	
	1959-60	*1990-91*	*1959-60*	*1990-91*	*Primary*	*Secondary*
Greater Bombay	26.32	21.95	9.63	8.92	-16.60	-7.37
Konkan	123.47	102.16	4.19	9.49	-17.26	126.49
Western Maharashtra	87.48	73.67	4.72	9.93	-15.79	110.38
Marathwada	83.67	77.96	3.64	11.08	-6.82	204.40
Vidarbha	81.83	82.19	6.06	11.97	0.44	97.52
Maharashtra	**83.26**	**73.15**	**5.33**	**10.39**	**-12.14**	**94.93**

Source: Mungekar, 2003.

TABLE 8.8

Per Capita Expenditure (in Rs.) in Social Sector in Maharashtra

Item	*Per Capita Expenditure in Rs. at 1993-94 Prices*		
	1980-81	*1990-91*	*1999-00*
Per Capita Expenditure Education			
Revenue	429.86	397.51	548.93
Capital	1.86	1.35	1.94
Total	**431.72**	**398.86**	**550.87**
Health			
Revenue	178.71	156.86	102.20
Capital	10.12	5.93	2.90
Total	**188.83**	**162.79**	**105.10**
Other Social Sectors			
Revenue	115.43	155.47	192.35
Capital	10.30	7.59	8.83
Total	**125.73**	**163.06**	**201.17**
Total Expenditure on Social Sectors			
Revenue	724.00	709.85	843.48
Capital	22.28	14.87	13.66
Total	**746.28**	**724.72**	**857.14**

Note: Based on data collected from the Directorate of Economics & Statistics, GoM, Mumbai.

Source: Mungekar, B., 2003.

cent were volunteers while 11 per cent (2.43 lakh) were paid employees. Around 95 per cent of rural non-profit organisation (NPO) workers were men. The urban NPOs had the opposite, with 93 per cent women associated with them.

Maharashtra, with an estimated 96002 NPOs, previously known as NGOs, has 52 per cent of the nation's estimated 1.2 million NPOs, engaged in welfare and development activities. NPOs accounted for 11.6 per cent of the nation's non-agricultural work force. About 51 per cent of Maharashtra's NPOs are rural based, the rest urban. Around 34 per cent are involved in religious activities, 25 in community service, 14 in sports and culture, 11 in education, 5 in health and 11 per cent in other activities. In 1999-00, the NPO sector generated an estimated Rs. 502.6 crores in the state. The social capital of the NPO sector, though less visible, is widespread. With the strength of social and human capital at its command, the involvement of the NPO movement in both planning, implementation and monitoring of the government campaigns and programmes for the welfare of the weaker sections is a challenge that Maharashtra can ignore at its own peril.

Scheduled Tribes

Introduction

With a population of 85.77 lakhs, the Scheduled Tribes account for 8.9 per cent of the population of Maharashtra (Census, 2001). A benchmark survey was conducted by the Tribal Research and Training Institute, (TRTI) Pune (1997) covering a population of 34.15 lakhs. The survey placed 91.11 per cent of the population below the poverty line (Rs. 11,000 per annum). Given the scenario of relative prosperity in the state, the issue of widespread tribal poverty cannot be dismissed.

While attempting to explain this situation, the first core issue to be examined is the intended and unintended effects of state policies and practices towards the tribal people. Though, Maharashtra followed the general principles of equality of culture and respect for diversity regarding tribal development, it operated on the premise that tribal cultures were backward and that tribals had to be modernised by bringing them into the mainstream. In chalking out a Vision for 2020, the role and relevance of the development thrust, the nature and impact of state intervention to develop tribals, and its impact on their access to resources for a life with dignity have to be kept in mind.

Welfare

Health

With the disintegration of the traditional system of health care and well-being on the one hand and an inappropriate 'modern' system superimposed on the other, the tribal health scenario is not encouraging. The IMR for tribal households is 73.6 per 1000, which is almost one and a half times higher than the state figure of 53.2. In the tribal areas of Yavatmal, the IMR is as high as 124. Child mortality rates are also much higher (e.g., 143 in Yavatmal, 144 in Gadchiroli and 137 in Chandrapur) than the state average of 58.1 per 1000.

Apart from the common water borne diseases (e.g. gastrointestinal dysentery), parasitic infections and malaria, genetic disorders like G6 PD deficiency, thalassaemia and sickle cell anaemia are highly prevalent among the tribals. Maternal mortality rates are high. According to the RCH Project Survey (1998-1999), 30 per cent of tribal women had at least one symptom of reproductive tract or sexually transmitted infection. As per NFHS–2 data, 64.2 per cent of tribal women have anaemia, 35.4 per cent of children are severely underweight for their age and 19 per cent are severely stunted. Weaning practices, nutritional deficiencies and excessive alcohol consumption lead to further health complications.

State-run health care infrastructure in tribal areas is inadequate. There are on an average 3 PHCs per one lakh population, while the actual requirement as per norms is 5 PHCs. Sub-centres are meant to serve a population of 3,000 but in reality serve 7-8,000 persons. In Thane district, as against population norms of 64 PHCs, only 48 are in existence. Similarly, instead of 431 sub-centres only 324 are existing. Further, 194 of these sub-centres have not been constructed. Many sub-centres are non-functional, with no resident medical functionary. More than 36 per cent of the multipurpose worker (MPW) posts are vacant in Thane district alone. Stock of drugs in all health centres is inadequate. Less than 50 per cent women receive complete antenatal care. Immunisation coverage is around 70 per cent.

The traditional healers and healing techniques based on a close understanding of nature and her healing powers have been de-legitimised by 'modern medicine'. However, the 'Bhagat' or 'Vaidu', who combines dispensing of herbal medicine along with the occult to effectively handle many ailments still continues to be the first choice for most tribal patients. Their involvement in the public health system would have given health praxis a strong foundation. Forest degradation and consequent unavailability of herbs is contributing to the ineffectiveness of the traditional tribal health practices. The situation is further confounded with the mushrooming of unqualified practitioners of allopathy, indulging in unethical medical practices. The three districts with the highest levels of Grade III and IV malnutrition are tribal dominated Gadchiroli (0.96), Nandurbar (0.84), and Amravati (0.78). (*Office Note:* Commissionerate of ICDS, 2002–03.) Within these districts there are certain pockets, where the malnourishment levels are alarming, e.g., Dharni in Amravati District (2.01), Taloda in Nandurbar District (1.76), Mokhada in Thane District (1.47).

Food Security

There has been a spate of malnutrition related deaths in Melghat, Nandurbar, Thane, Gadchiroli and other tribal districts. Four thousand Korku children died in Melghat between 1993 and 1996. In the 143 families surveyed in Nandurbar district, 158 children died, of which 42 per cent were in the age group of 1-6 years (TRTI, 2002). Table 8.9 shows malnutrition and mortality of tribal children.

TABLE 8.9

Indicators of Malnutrition in Maharashtra

Indicators	*Entire State*
Percentage Death 0 to 1 Year	3.08
Percentage Death 1 to 6 Years	1.18
Infant Mortality Rate	32.00
Still Birth Rate	19.00
Percentage of Children in Grade III Malnutrition	0.290
Percentage of Children in Grade IV Malnutrition	0.030

Source: Office of ICDS, Konkan Division, Konkan Bhavan.

The problem of food security is largely one of 'distribution' and 'the lack of purchasing power'. The Navsanjeevani Yojana launched in 1995, attempted to redress the problem of food security by clubbing EGS and SGRY, revamping PDS, establishing grain banks, improving nutrition levels through *anganwadis*, kitchen gardens, and focussed health interventions like rescue camps, pada swayamsevak scheme, etc. However, the functioning of many of these schemes has come in for serious criticism. While the need for intervention persists, the GoI has stopped the extension of the Anganwadi Scheme to 700 new centres across five tribal districts alone.

BOX 8.1

Various Welfare Schemes

Report by Dr. N.C Saxena, former Planning Secretary, GoI, Commissioner appointed by the Supreme Court in WP 196/2001, submitted on 27.1.2003 has these salient features:

"In many schemes, such as TPDS (Targeted Public Distribution System), SGRY, NMDS and *Annapurna*, the performance of the state is poor and the quota given to the state by GoI is not fully utilised...it is quite likely that these schemes are not functioning smoothly in village that has led to starvation or malnutrition deaths."

TPDS (Targeted Public Distribution System): Sixty three lakh BPL card holders identified, but a large number of the poor (including)...migrant population have been left out. About 30 per cent to 40 per cent of the state entitlement not being lifted from the FCI. Forest dwellers are not given ration cards.

Antyodaya Yojana: Identification (of *Antyodaya* beneficiaries) not completed in 50.5 per cent villages; in 27.5 per cent villages, grain not being distributed.

Annapurna Yojana: Only 8,000 beneficiaries identified in this category against a target of 60,000 set by GoI.

Sampoorna Gramin Rozgar Yojana: Distribution of foodgrains is much below the norm. Against the allocation of 3.74 lakh tonnes of foodgrains during the period 1.1.02 to 13.1.03, actual lifting was only 2.42 lakh tonnes.

Integrated Child Development Scheme: District data shows that only 0.74 per cent of tribal children suffered from grade III and IV malnutrition, while NFHS data for 1998-99 showed that 34.5 per cent of tribal children were malnourished. The state government must not allow such a degree of bogus reporting.

Mid-day Meal Scheme: Cooked meals are being given in less than one-third of the villages. Only 70 out of 1,324 schools in Nandurbar and 15 out of 564 schools in Yavatmal were supplying cooked food.

Resources and Livelihoods

Land

41.8 per cent of tribals in the state are landless, compared to 28 per cent of the general population. Landlessness is even higher among the Primitive Tribal Groups (PTG)—83 per cent (Katkaris) and 63 per cent (Kolam). Besides, tribal landholdings are small; 70.1 per cent are below 2 hectares compared to 58.9 per cent of non-tribals. The problem of non-recorded tenancies is widespread. Large-scale alienation of tribal lands without effective redress has pushed the tribals into the forest where they began to cultivate degraded forestlands. The cultivation has been treated as encroachment and attempts have been made from time to time to evict the encroachers. The government passed orders to regularise encroachments on fallow lands, grazing lands and forestlands in 1978, *Dalli* cultivations in 1971, and *eksali* lands in 1969. All these orders are yet to be implemented fully.

The Draft Tenth Five Year Plan observes that "Taking note of the most devastating impact of the growing incidence of tribal land alienation, high priority is accorded to prevent the same and restore the alienated lands to the tribals and if possible to put a total ban on the transfer of tribal land to non-tribals or even to the government in accordance with the SC order in the Samatha Case." However, Maharashtra's efforts to restore alienated tribal lands have met with limited success; 45,634 cases of alienation of tribal land and restoration were filed in the state till 2001. In more than 56 per cent of the cases, the land has not been restored to the tribals (Study to Determine Extent of Tribal Land Alienation in Maharashtra State, 1987-88, TRTI, Pune).

The Expert Committee on Tribal Land Alienation (GoI) in its report states that in the course of its visits in 2001–2002, it came across "sufficient evidence of official apathy and criminal neglect in respect to vital issues like the detection and filing of cases relating to the alienated tribal lands, their timely disposal, putting the tribal in possession of the alienated land and invoking the penal provisions of law against persons in illegal and forcible possession of the tribal lands." Action against defaulting revenue officers is recommended. There is a need for a Special Land Restoration Campaign through the active involvement of the *gram sabha*.

Forests

As forest dwellers, with an intimate understanding of and a symbiotic relationship with the forests, tribals were perhaps best suited to fulfil the role of effective stewards of the forests, managing and using the forest wealth sustainably. But interests of industry and commerce have prevailed and tribals have been reduced to being labourers, who are employed to clear, fell, and replant the forest with commercial varieties. While 7.3 per cent (46,143 sq. kms.) of the total forest area of the country is in Maharashtra, only 3.2 per cent of the total number of Joint Forestry Management (JFM) Committees is in the state. Further, in many JFM areas, the tribals feel that their actual involvement in decision making and forest protection is much less than what the policy promises. There is a need to reorient JFM to ensure greater stakes for the community, involvement of *gram sabha,* inclusion of agro forestry within its framework and greater flexibility in rules.

The National Forest Policy 1988, recognising their symbiotic relationship with the forest, specified that the forest dwellers' domestic requirements of fuel-wood, fodder, minor forest produce and construction timber should be the first charge on forest produce. The Draft Tenth Five-Year Plan (2002–2007) specifies that the protection of rights of the tribals in forests is key to the amelioration of their conditions. But today, viewing the tribals as an impediment to the scientific and economic exploitation of the forest resources, their rights and privileges have been converted into concessions and rigid restrictions have been imposed on them. The settlement of rights especially in former princely states is an issue that needs to be addressed.

The locus of the resolution of the forest encroachment issue lies in the concept of reciprocal rights. The 'right to cultivate' must be intimately linked with 'responsibility to care' for the forest. Hence, a policy, whereby the cultivator will be required to plant fruit and medicinal plants and care for adjoining forest area, needs to be put in place.

Suitable amendments are necessary to reclassify bamboo and tendu as minor forest produce, given the fact that they were removed from the classification in 1997 to bypass the requirements of the PESA Act, thereby denying tribals the access and benefits they would have otherwise received.

Displacement

Natural resources in tribal areas are being harnessed at the expense of the tribals. The colonial axiom that resources belonged exclusively to the state has continued. State policy has also encouraged migration of non-tribals into tribal areas. There is no credible data from both government and non-government sources giving the exact number of tribal households displaced due to construction of dams, power projects, highways, natural parks and sanctuaries, etc. Violation of traditional tribal rights over livelihood resources has subsidised the needs and luxuries of the urban dwellers. Rehabilitation of project displaced persons prior to displacement on land-for-land basis, has been possible only to a limited extent. Rehabilitation is further complicated because land records are yet to be updated, and land rights in forest areas are yet to be settled.

The Maharashtra Project Affected Persons Resettlement and Rehabilitation Act is being invoked mainly for irrigation projects, even though the Act suggests that the state government may apply the provisions of the Act for all projects that displace people. Neither are the guidelines for rehabilitation of the Ministry for Rural Development being followed.

Agriculture

Traditional tribal knowledge and agricultural practices lent themselves to organic agriculture, using biomass as a primary resource, multiplicity of seed types and crop varieties (of the coarser variety like highland paddy, *nachni, jowar* and *bajra*) to suit specific agro-climatic conditions and pest attacks. The traditional agricultural techniques were appropriate both in terms of the knowledge and skill base of the people and in terms of their independence.

The main thrust of the state has been on green revolution technology. Poor extension work, inadequate training and capacity building of tribal farmers to absorb technology, poor follow-up, and remedial action have also contributed to inappropriate use of this technology. Further, since most tribal lands are of poor quality, non-irrigated (95.66 per cent) and are located on slopes and hilltops, use of green revolution technology has been ineffective (BMS, 1997). This mainstream technology is routinely used, unmindful of the soil quality, drainage, climatic conditions, water availability and other social and economic infrastructure to absorb it.

About 94 per cent of the tribal population depends on agriculture either directly or as agricultural labourers accounting for 79 per cent of the total tribal income. Two hundred and seventy four Adivasi Cooperative Societies, affiliated to the Adivasi Vikas Mahamandal have been formed. Foodgrains (and MFP) are purchased through the Adivasi Vikas Mahamandal in the TSP Areas.

Animal husbandry is critical given the fact that tribals in Maharashtra possess 27 per cent of the cattle stock, 19 per cent of buffalo stock, 11 per cent of sheep, 22 per cent of goat population and 25 per cent of poultry stock. There is a need to strengthen animal husbandry technology based on resources, skills and competence already available.

Employment and Migrant Labour

The ranks of tribal educated unemployed are swelling. The following information from the Employment Exchange in Thane district tells the story (as in Table 8.10).

TABLE 8.10

Registration and Selection of Candidates in Employment Exchange in Thane District

Faculty	*Total No. of Registrations as on 30.11.03*	*Total No. of Candidates Selected*	*Candidates Selected as Percentage of Registrations*
Master's Degree	62	14	22
Graduate	1510	50	33
Medical	71	43	60
Engg. Graduate	12	0	0
Engg. Diploma	115	10	10
D. Ed./B. Ed./B.Ped/ M.Ped	856	662	78
ITI	1392	14	1
Total	**30017**	**1309**	**4**

TABLE 8.11

Indicators on Malnutrition and Mortality in Maharashtra

Indicators	*Entire State*	*Entire Tribal Area*	*Sensitive Tribal Area (Navsanjeevani Programme Area)*
Percentage Death 0 to 1 Year	3.08	4.07	4.07
Percentage Death 1 to 6 Years	1.18	2.08	2.53
Infant Mortality Rate	32.00	41.00	43.00
Still Birth Rate	19.00	21.00	22.00
Percentage of Children in Grade III Malnutrition	0.29	0.60	0.81
Percentage of Children in Grade IV Malnutrition	0.03	0.09	0.13

Source: Office of ICDS, Konkan Division, Konkan Bhavan.

In other words, only four per cent of all those registered in the employment exchanges obtain government jobs. Shockingly, only one per cent of ITI students are able to obtain government jobs.

Expenditure on EGS has declined despite the availability of funds (Planning Department (EGS), GoM, 2000–01). The Report of the Eighth state EGS Committee 2002-2003 has highlighted the delays in payment of wages and grain despite prevailing drought conditions. As a result, the Committee observed that the rural/tribal population could not depend on the EGS. Since the average wage per day on EGS works in 2001–02 was Rs. 45.28, while the average daily wage for unskilled labour in the market was between Rs. 70-80 for similar work, EGS is not acting as an effective mechanism to prevent seasonal out-migration. This has largely been responsible for the poor standard of living in the regions so the problem of malnutrition has aggravated. Various indicators of malnutrition and mortality are listed in the Table 8.11. It is, therefore imperative that the scheme is implemented as a supply driven programme rather than demand driven.

There has been an unprecedented growth in *adivasi* participation in the ranks of disaggregated casual labour. Entire families with small children abandon their villages simply to survive. Many are engaged by sub-contractors who double as commission agents for the contractors of large corporations and government undertakings for works as diverse as laying telephone cables, pipelines, working on the railways, on highways, construction work, etc. Others migrate under conditions of seasonal bondage to salt pans, brick kilns, on fishing boats, and for sugarcane cutting to repay consumption loans taken during the cultivation season.

These workers are often transported to far-off places, and are made to work under poor working conditions, with no provision of shelter or potable drinking water, and are subjected to physical assault and sexual harassment. According to a recent survey conducted by the Labour Department in 51 salt pans in Raigad district, as per orders of the Mumbai High Court in WP 343/2002, 88 per cent of employers did not issue appointment letters, identity cards, attendance cards or supply safety gear. In a large number of cases, when the work is completed, the sub-contractor simply disappears without paying the workers leaving them stranded. The law and the labour department have proved inadequate to protect the rights of *adivasi* migrant labour who are being reduced to a modern version of slave labour in the new economy subsidising the cost of globalisation and liberalisation.

Empowerment and Development

Education

The level of literacy among tribals was only 55.2 per cent as against the state average of 77.27 per cent (Census, 2001). In some districts, e.g., Dhule, Thane and Raigad, the tribal literacy is as low as 25 per cent, while in some ITDP areas of Gadchiroli, e.g., Bhamragad and Aheri, the rate was only 15 per cent and 20 per cent respectively.

From the standard V onwards there is a steady decrease in enrolment. (Deptt. of Education: GoM, 2002–03) While there are 975 *ashram shalas* in the state (422 government and 553 private) and 294 hostels (government), the lack of sufficient *ashram shalas* leads to a significant drop in enrolment at the 8th standard level (approx. 22 per cent). Even incentives (Rs. 500 for std. V to VII and Rs. 1,000 for std. VIII to X) have failed to stem the alarming dropout rate of girl students.

The 74 per cent dropout rate at standard X level is indicative of the quality of teaching in the *ashramshalas*. The level of teaching in the *zilla parishad* primary schools leaves much to be desired. The Mahatma Phule Shikshan Hami Yojana is no different, as the contracted teachers are unqualified and poorly paid. The generally poor conditions, poor quality meals, sexual abuse of girl students by teachers and employees contribute to the poor quality of education in *ashram shalas*.

The percentage of educated persons up to XII standard among males is 5.23, and among females it is only 2.40, while those holding professional degrees varies between 0.01 and 0.04 (TRTI Benchmark Survey, 1997). The enrolment of STs in technical institutes is not commensurate with their population and their quota remains unfilled or filled by non-ST candidates. Further, there is a high dependence on government institutions, implying that the privatisation of education with no quotas portends a disaster for ST students as the Table 8.12 indicates.

TABLE 8.12

Admission of STs for the Academic Year 2004-2005 in Degree Programmes

Type of Institute	*Percentage of Admission*			
	Govt.	*Govt. Aided*	*Unaided*	*Total*
Engineering. & Technology	4.25	4.46	0.32	0.74
Pharmacy	4.40	3.92	0.60	0.91
Hotel Management & Catering Technology	-	9.52	1.24	1.65
Architecture	-	4.96	0.69	1.15
Total	**4.3**	**4.50**	**0.36**	**0.77**

Source: Director of Technical Education, 2004-05.

The content, form, methods and techniques of schooling are identical to municipal schools with nothing to make them meaningful, relevant or contextual to tribal life and their needs. Further, with the quality of education being inferior, tribal children face a double jeopardy—they are implicitly forced to compete but inherently forced out of competition. The policy of mainstreaming in education has resulted in alienation of the tribal students from his/her culture, ethos and life. When the students return to their villages as school dropouts, they are neither equipped to work at home on their fields nor do they get any employment outside agriculture. The few, who have 'succeeded', have landed employment in government jobs, mostly at the lowest rung due to reservation policy.

Self-governance

The tribals were traditionally self-governing communities based on a consensus driven system of maintaining community harmony, a strength recognised by the Panchayats (Extension to the Scheduled Areas) Act of 1996 (PESA). The traditional councils were transparent, independent, self-defining and accessible bodies that managed the community's resources, adjudicated on social issues and disputes through the involvement and participation of the 'face to face' community. PESA "legitimises the involvement of tribals in their own empowerment process not only as active participants, but also as effective decision makers, implementers, monitors, supervisors and evaluators."

However, this traditional bedrock of self-governance has been replaced by a formalised, compartmentalised, non-transparent, state-sponsored *Panchayati Raj* system, based on a fractured polity and the rule of the majority. Maharashtra has passed a law as mandated by PESA. But there is wide discrepancy between the central and the state legislations, resulting in the dilution of the essence of the Central Act. The rules are yet to be formulated.

Today, the *gram sabha* is rarely being involved in decisionmaking. Knowledge of and participation in *gram sabhas* is low among the tribals. As a recent study by the National Institute of Rural Development notes, "The *gram sabha*, instead of being a sovereign, self-directing, all pervasive village institution, has been reduced to becoming a caricature of itself... that the *gram panchayat* endures to fulfil legal obligations."

The state government has published material and organised training programmes on *Panchayati Raj;* however, training programmes specifically on PESA are yet to be conducted.

Administration and Development Policy

While Reservation policy has offered opportunity where there was none, it has created pressures on the state government to grant scheduled tribe status to other sections, which do not strictly fall in the scheduled tribe category. The large number who have fraudulently obtained scheduled tribe certificates and jobs reserved for ST groups further complicate the problem. As a result of the inclusion of 'bogus' tribals, the tribal population has jumped from 23.97 lakhs (1961) to 29.54 lakhs (1971) to 57.72 lakhs (1981) to 73.18 lakhs (1991)—a more than 300 per cent increase in just 3 decades! (Census, 1991; Report of Working Group on Development of STs during Seventh Five Year Plan, GoI, 1984).

The Sukthankar Committee recommended that the Tribal Sub Plan (TSP) be formulated by the Tribal Welfare Department up to a ceiling indicated by the Planning Department. The Committee also recommended that the budgetary allocation for tribal welfare is to correspond to population share and therefore 9 per cent is to be allocated for Tribal Welfare. However, while the percentage share allocated to TSP peaked in 1997–98 at 8.51 per cent, it has been steadily declining in both percentage and actual terms since 1999–00 and has touched a low of 5 per cent in 2003–04. It is also necessary to assess the developmental backlog in tribal areas and provide additional funds to remove the backlog in a phased manner.

The TSP area, MADA pockets, mini MADA pockets and ATSP Areas collectively cover 8,487 villages in 123 *talukas* of 21 districts. These are covered by the 24 Integrated Tribal Development Project areas, including 11 sensitive ITDP areas, where special emphasis is laid. The Navsanjeevani Yojana began in 1995 for coordinated and effective implementation of all-important schemes. However, the programmes under TSP have neither been reducing poverty nor promoting growth as the schemes and plans are not related to the real needs of the tribals but instead are programmes meant for the general population, which are replicated under a separate Tribal Welfare budget head. Investment on infrastructure is as high as 78-80 per cent of TSP, to the detriment of development of scheduled tribes themselves.

Special Needs of Primitive Tribal Groups (PTGs)

As per the Annual Tribal Sub Plan 2002-2003, there are 3.66 lakh persons from the Primitive Tribal Group comprising the Katkaris (1.75 lakh); Kolams (1.18 lakh) and Madia Gond (0.67 lakh). However, the term PTG itself is a misnomer because it is a variant of the term 'backward' and does little to clarify the specificities of these communities and their special requirements. In fact, there is a need to change the nomenclature from PTG to Special Tribal Group (STG). The conditions of the Kolams and Madia Gonds have deteriorated through the suppression of their traditional means of livelihood *viz.* shifting cultivation, while the Katkaris are predominantly landless. Uprooted from their traditional livelihoods, the PTGs are forced to migrate for survival; hence, their numbers and actual living conditions are not accurately reflected in census and other records. Most of them become easy target for harassment and exploitation, and face continuous threats of eviction from their homes and lands. They live with high food insecurity and face continuous health threats. Any development plan must be based on a realistic appreciation of their special needs and not simplistic extension of plans and programmes made for other groups or tribes. There is a need to include groups like the Barda and Korku in the PTG category.

Special Needs of Nomadic Tribes

These tribes, for example, Dhangars, Pardhis, Lamans, Vasudevs, Gondhalis, Vanjaras have never been properly enumerated in the census. While the state government maintains a list of 42 Nomadic Tribes (NTs), they are not listed in any of the Constitutional Schedules. With changing times improvements in communications and markets, growth of the entertainment industry, emergence of new and sophisticated spiritual leaders, NTs have lost their occupations. Their education levels are very low. Being constantly on the move, both police and local people view them with suspicion and treat them as petty criminals. Many of them have begun to lead settled lives but face problems, as they have no land even to set up a house. It is, therefore, necessary to provide them with assistance and basic infrastructure if they desire to lead a settled life.

Special Needs of Denotified Tribes

Although, they are supposed to be free from stigma after denotification, in practice the former criminal tribes (e.g. Berad, Paradhi, Ramoshi, Waghari, etc.) are still harassed by the coercive arm of the state. There is a need to sensitise police, revenue and other officials so that both NT and DTs can lead their lives with dignity. Providing them protection by covering them under the Scheduled Castes and Scheduled Tribes (Prevention of Atrocities) Act 1989, would be useful. While the Social Justice Department has been entrusted with the implementation of schemes for their welfare, development and education, approximately 89 per cent of adults are still illiterate and are engaged in low earning economic activities. The absence of census data and exclusion from constitutional schedules is a severe handicap to developmental efforts.

Vision for 2020

The World Human Development Report, 2000, for the first time, introduced the enjoyment of human rights as an integral part and a necessary condition for human development. Three corollaries follow from this significant departure in defining human development *viz.*, the recognition that there is an organic relationship between the enjoyment of human rights and development. Further, the link between economic or material prosperity and human development is neither automatic nor obvious. And thirdly, human development has more to do with the quality of life than mere acquisition of material goods.

These corollaries are of particular significance to tribal communities who have been demanding recognition and access to land and land based survival resources. Conversely they challenge the development process being laid out before them as an essential part of their 'mainstreaming' without recognition of their traditional culture and rights. There is a serious flaw in categorising these communities as 'backward and primitive', while equating advancement with mainstreaming and development with 'modernity'. It is true that tribal 'tradition' is unable to negotiate an external modernity and is forced to be subsumed under the traditions of the mainstream and under the aegis of development. At the same time there is an inadvertent continuation of the colonial practices concerning their resources and an inadequacy of policy initiatives and practices that introduce external unsustainable inputs but fail to build on local strengths and resources. The strategies employed to date have at best created a miniscule elite in a morass of poverty. The incidence of poverty in the state under various sub sections is mentioned in Table 8.13.

TABLE 8.13

Incidence of Poverty by Social Groups

Category	*1983-1984*		*1987-1988*		*1993-1994*	
	Rural	*Urban*	*Rural*	*Urban*	*Rural*	*Urban*
			Persons			
S.C.	59.22	64.96	53.60	62.50	51.64	52.56
S.T.	61.18	N.A.	54.59	61.60	50.58	61.06
N.B.	N.A.	N.A.	61.50	67.70	N.A.	35.50
All	45.23	40.57	39.90 35.72 (OT)	38.20 34.00 (OT)	37.97 33.00 (OT)	35.50
			Households			
S.C.	51.95	58.54	45.00	53.30	N.A.	-
S.T.	55.38	N.A.	45.50	55.56	N.A.	-
N.B.	(N.A.)	N.A.	56.00	61.10	N.A.	-

Note: N.B.=Neo Buddhist; N.A.= not available.

Source: Mungekar, B., Mumbai, 2003.

Therefore, the thrust of tribal development should be to strengthen tribal communities to address the mainstream and negotiate modernity. PESA Act of 1996 has put in place a legal and Constitutional frame for tribal communities to reengage with their traditions, culture, common property resources, community management, development and exploitative processes through democratic processes which are founded on mechanisms of internal solidarity and equity, strengthen community and enhance participation. More specifically, strategies would include:

Eradication of Poverty, Ensuring Food Security and Good Health

Health

1. Formulation of a specific 'Tribal Health Policy' that seeks to integrate traditional healing, alternative herbal medicine systems and allopathy.
2. Strengthening of the public health delivery systems by increasing PHCs and sub-centres, filling up vacancies, upgrading existing health infrastructure, increased budgetary allocation for drugs.
3. Strengthening local involvement by replacing existing Pada Swayamsevak Scheme with a trained hamlet level woman health worker and strengthening community monitoring of health services and functionaries.

Food Security

1. Formulation of a nutritional policy with holistic cultural specific approach.
2. Formulation of a near-universal PDS policy allowing for regional variations.
3. Promotion of biodiverse cropping patterns.

Redistribution and Protection of Resources while Ensuring Sustainable Livelihoods

Land

1. Restoration of all alienated tribal lands.
2. Settlement of and implementation of all GRs regarding land and housing rights in forests.
3. Reduction of landlessness by granting of two hectares to all landless tribal families.

Forests

1. Reaffirmation of symbiosis of survival by involving tribals in forest stewardship through necessary reorientation of JFM.
2. Creation of legal framework for recognition of tribal customary rights and traditional privileges.
3. Creation of framework of reciprocal rights, linking regularisation of encroachments with forest protection.

Displacement

1. Ensuring no displacement without proper prior rehabilitation.
2. Ensuring completion of rehabilitation backlog prior to initiation of new projects.

Agriculture

1. Increasing productivity through popularisation of intensive biomass based sustainable agricultural practices.
2. Thrust on water harvesting and equity-based water management systems.
3. Strengthening of animal husbandry technology based on available skills and technology.
4. Capacity building of tribal farmers to adopt technology.

Employment and Migrant Labour

1. Provision of security to migrant labour through ITDP sponsored regulatory structure that ensures compulsory registration, payment of wages, and portable social security benefits.
2. Utilisation of surplus EGS funds to build community resources for sustained income generation.

Strengthening Tribal Communities to Address the Mainstream and Negotiate Modernity

Education

1. Strengthening the system of *ashramshalas* and reorientation of *ashramshala* syllabus to focus on natural resource development, sustainable agriculture, animal husbandry, agro-based industries, upgradation of traditional skills, introduction of modern technology and service sector skills.
2. Qualitative improvement of teaching methods with special focus on English and Mathematics.

Self-governance

1. Ensuring that *gram sabha* becomes a sovereign, self-directing, all pervasive village institution.
2. Imparting skills of accounting, development management, natural resource management, monitoring, prioritisation of scarce resources, conflict resolution and negotiation to *gram sabha* members and PRI representatives.

Development Planning

1. Focus on micro-watershed centered development planning with *gram sabha* participation.
2. Compilation of correct census and other database specifically on scheduled tribes to assist in development planning.
3. Strengthening the role of ITDP in development planning.

Administrative Reform

1. Continuation of reservation policy and extension of the same to private sector with proviso that reservation in jobs be limited to first generation beneficiaries.
2. Reorganisation of Scheduled Areas to include all MADA, mini-MADA and ATSP areas.
3. Reorganisation of all administrative boundaries in tribal areas (including Revenue, PWD, soil Conservation, Police, etc.) to correspond to TSP boundaries.
4. Creation of autonomous councils in accordance with Bhuria Committee recommendations.
5. Setting up mechanism to identify and revoke benefits allotted to bogus tribals.
6. Ensure allotment of nine per cent of state budget for tribal development.

Primitive Tribal Groups

1. Inclusion of groups like the Barda, Bhil, Korku and others in PTG category.
2. Special programmes to assist these communities

to render their traditional agricultural practices sustainable, upgrade skills and ensure food and health security.

Scheduled Castes

The scheduled castes (SCs) comprise an important section of the population of Maharashtra, not only demographically but also socially and politically. Facilitating development in general and of *Dalits* in particular in caste-based society having grave economic inequities is a complex task. Deeper transformation in social and economic spheres can ensure participation of the SCs in the development process. Besides recognising the specificity of the barriers to their development, it is necessary to focus on empowering Dalits economically and educationally. Development interventions in a caste-based society need not only to question caste-based discrimination vehemently, but also need to raise issues of redistribution.

At present, 59 castes are included in the list of SCs for Maharashtra. The Nav Baudhas were included in the list in the year 1991. Four main castes namely Mahar, Mang, Bhambi, and Bhangi formed the majority. The Table 8.14 gives the population distribution of scheduled caste *vis-à-vis* the total population.

TABLE 8.14

Total Population and Scheduled Castes Population in Maharashtra from 1961 to 1991

Year	*Total Population (in Lakh)*	*Scheduled Caste Population (in Lakh)*	*Percentage of Scheduled Caste Population to Total Population*
1961	395.53	22.26	5.63
1971	504.12	30.25	6.00
1981	627.84	44.79	7.13
1991	789.37	87.57	11.09
2001	968.79	98.81	10.20

Source: Census: 1961, 1971, 1981, 1991 and 2001.

Welfare

Stigma and Human Rights

The SCs' struggle against untouchable status/stigma have brought about considerable measure of freedom and dignity at the subjective level. Occupational change and economic independence has been possible in regions of commercial expansion. As the products such as leather goods, hand-made cleaning tools (such as broom), etc., have become redundant with the introduction of plastic items, they have taken to other menial jobs. The Chambhars (prefer to be known as 'Charmakars'), for instance, have shifted to agricultural labour in rural areas. The SCs, in general, have found acquisition of agricultural land difficult, but following the implementation of government orders regularising encroachments on village grazing and waste land, some have acquired land. This is reflected in the increase in ownership of land by SCs. Nevertheless, migration to towns has been most attractive option for securing newer choices and higher social status.

Irrespective of their economic standing, inhuman treatment in the form of untouchability meted out upon the SCs due to their low status in the caste hierarchy distinguishes them from other marginalised sections and makes them vulnerable. Despite the existing laws, *viz.* Protection of Civil Rights Act, 1955 and Prevention of Atrocities Act, 1989, the SCs continue to suffer from various forms of oppression ranging from the crudest forms of social ostracisation and denial of access practiced in the rural areas to the sophisticated forms of discrimination encountered even in the modern sectors in the urban areas. It is pertinent to remember that due to the economic dependency of the SCs on the perpetrators of atrocities, not every incident is registered. The number of registered cases of atrocities is on the rise, which is indicative of growing awareness and assertiveness on the part of the victims.

The Mahars, most assertive and politically organised community are often targets of discrimination. Even Matangs who have been targets of discrimination have organised themselves in recent times by iconising a revolutionary poet Shahir Annabhau Sathe. It is noteworthy that most of the atrocities occur around the issue of access to water and public hand pumps (Teltumbde, 2000), which could be easily curbed by stern state action. Persistence of caste-based prejudices and denial of access to land, education and political power has contributed to their increasing intolerance and militancy to claim their rights. These claims are increasingly met with coercive authority of the state, which further contributes to their economic marginalisation.

Poverty, Food Security and Nutrition

Average annual household income of the rural poor in Maharashtra was pegged at Rs. 5,754 in 1991. In comparison, the average SC family enjoyed an income of only Rs. 3,557 (NCAER/HDI Survey, 1991). But 71.6 per cent of the SC households earned less than an average income for the SCs and their per capita annual expenditure was less than Rs. 3,000. A staggering 91 per cent of the SC households in the state was below the state average for the rural poor.

Poverty for the SCs is not limited to their low incomes and calorie intakes, but it also impacts on their access to land, credit, health, longevity, education, safe drinking water, sanitation, and other infrastructural facilities. In essence, the SCs are not only poor but are also victims of structural deprivation and social oppression.

The state government has taken steps to extend various welfare measures for the economic upliftment of the SCs ranging from reservation in educational and employment opportunities to scholarships and different types of financial assistance.

Despite the efforts of the state government, less than 10 per cent of the rural SC poor were able to rise above poverty line in a decade. What is important to note is that the SC community's hope that migration to the urban areas was an important choice to improve their living conditions is not supported by data. While their move to the urban areas might have assisted them to break out from social oppression, it did not free them from grinding poverty. Hence, a larger percentage of SCs in the urban areas is below poverty line than their rural counterparts. In terms of households, the difference is significant at nearly 15 per cent. It is also important to note that in the 1987-88 to 1993-94 period, the rate of decline in poverty of the SCs was 3.65 per cent while it was 4.93 per cent for 'others' in the state. While the incidence of rural poverty among SCs is high compared to the general population, there is an in-built urban bias in the existing public distribution system.

More than 50 per cent of the SCs are not covered by the PDS with respect to most of the commodities (Dev, 2003). Delivery system in rural areas is poor. Extent of bogus entries by non-SCs and leakages is greater in rural areas. The overall functioning of the PDS is unsatisfactory in terms of food security for the poor in general and for the SCs in particular.

Health

Nutrition and health status attained are better indicators of overall well-being than merely income levels, although it cannot be denied that income levels do seriously impact on the nutrition and health status of the SCs. The limited evidence available for 1972-1983 period indicates that more than 80 per cent of the SCs both in rural and urban areas suffered from a shortfall in calorie intake, which has prompted analysts to call for appropriate (Suryanarayana, 2003) public action to ensure nutrition security.

Despite special efforts like the Child Survival and Safe Motherhood (NFHS, 1998–99), 81.4 per cent of SC children were suffering from anaemia; of them, 6.5 per cent suffered from severe anaemia. Neonatal mortality was at a high 40.2 per 1000 live births. Postnatal mortality was also high at 12.5 per 1000 live births, implying that one of 20 SC children born have a chance of survival. With a high 52.5 infant mortality, only one in twenty SC children will live up to the age of 5 years. With child mortality of 14.2, only one in 60 SC children will grow to adulthood. This is a matter of grave concern for policy makers. Table 8.15 gives a break-up of various ailments prevalent in the social groups.

TABLE 8.15

Prevalence of Ailments and Hospitalisation by Social Group, Maharashtra (Percentage): 1995-96

Item	*Social Group*		
	*ST**	*SC**	*Others*
Rural			
Acute Ailment	32	33	39
Chronic Ailment	7	16	16
Any Ailment	40	49	55
Hospitalisation	15	20	20
Urban			
Acute Ailment	26	40	35
Chronic Ailment	7	10	13
Any Ailment	33	49	48
Hospitalisation	29	28	26

Note: ST=scheduled tribes; SC= scheduled castes.

Source: GoK, 2002b.

The SCs in the urban areas, by virtue of access to health facilities enjoy a greater measure of health security in comparison to their rural counterparts. In the rural areas, the SCs have a larger degree of suppressed morbidity, which is not reflected in the statistics due to lack or denial of access to public health facilities. This remains a matter of concern.

In the case of preventive care, the public health services continue to play a lead role (MHDR, 2002). Inadequate and declining investment on public health and the regional disparity have accentuated the SCs' access to health services in Vidarbha, Marathwada, and north Maharashtra.

According to Human Development Profile of SC/ST in selected states (2000), only 50 per cent of the SC villages had a sub-centre and 50 per cent of the SC villages had a sub-centre/hospital beyond 5 kms in the state.

Resources and Livelihoods

Work Participation and Land Ownership

The most worrying issue now, besides untouchability, however, is the economic future of the SCs. Their low levels of literacy, lack of marketable skills to compete in the labour market ensures that economic liberalisation does not offer early advantages to marginalised groups. The existing structures of inequity are left intact and have become compounded with the disadvantages of marketisation.

Generally, given their highly deprived economic situation, the SCs are economically more active than the general population. Urbanisation, severe poverty, limited access to basic civic amenities, difficult living conditions, iniquitous structure of employment market, segmentation of labour market force them to work largely as casual workers in agriculture in rural areas and in the informal unorganised sectors in urban areas, as they have very little choice in terms of the sector of the economy where they could find work. The unorganised sector is plagued by job insecurity, low wages, and exploitative relations. Hence, notwithstanding their efforts, the SCs are forced into difficult and demeaning employments. More SC men in the rural areas and women in the urban areas work as casual labour. Lack of access to land, unavailability of jobs in non-farm sectors and low literacy levels prevent SCs access to better paid secure jobs outside agriculture in rural areas.

The implementation of the orders of the Government of Maharashtra in 1990 regularising encroachment by members of the SC on revenue waste and village grazing lands made a fair number of the SCs as land owners. The ownership, however, is ephemeral as the landholdings are marginal to sub marginal, soil quality is low and hence, productive use of these lands requires considerable investments. The new land owning SCs are not in a position to raise the financial resources personally, and hence the land remains effectively unproductive. There is apprehension that, the market forces, under liberalised economic conditions, may make land alienation inevitable, as there are no laws to check alienation of lands held by the SC farmers. Table 8.16 indicates the distribution of landholding among the SCs and others.

TABLE 8.16

Ownership of Agricultural Land Among SCs

(Figures in Per Cent)

Category (in Acres)	*Households Belonging to*			
	Scheduled Caste		*Others*	
	1982	*1992*	*1982*	*1992*
Landless	26.39	24.31	19.15	17.15
Sub-marginal(<0.49)	32.04	32.13	16.50	22.18
Marginal (up to 2.5)	17.00	17.49	15.20	18.06
Small (2.5—5.0)	11.38	12.9	16.06	14.82
Medium (5.0—10.0)	9.15	6.61	15.66	17.56
Large (above 10.0)	4.06	6.48	17.23	13.30

Source: Mungekar, B., 2003.

Rapid mechanisation in agriculture is displacing agricultural labour. Introduction of harvester combines and cane-cutting machines threaten to make more than half a million workers redundant creating massive unemployment. Labour displacing appliances in homes and offices have already reduced the need for domestic and conservancy labour in the informal sector. Restrictions on access to use of common lands, forest and water bodies have also had a deleterious effect on rural SC households to satisfy their need for fuel, food and fodder. The combined effect of the above change in their conditions has had an impact on the employment status of the SC women. Previously a considerable number of SC women, in urban areas, worked in 'other services', and in 'manufacturing other than household industry'. Household and construction industry together absorbed about 11 per cent. We now note an alarming change wherein of the SC women working in 'services', 50 per cent of them are employed as scavengers. Over 25 per cent of the SC women in the urban areas work as marginal workers.

A considerable number of SC women and men are also employed in the 'service' of operating dry latrines. Despite concerted efforts, only 14.3 per cent in rural areas and 85.7 per cent in urban areas have latrine facility (GoM, 2003b). Hence, dry latrines requiring manual disposal continues to be prevalent.

Introduction of pay-and-use public toilets are also operated by SCs only.

Scheduled castes continue to perform the 'service' of garbage collection and disposal in rural and urban areas. Solid waste management has not reduced the dependence on the SCs. In Mumbai city alone, more than one lakh contract labour who are SC men are engaged in solid waste collection and dumping.

Privatisation of garbage collection has reduced regular permanent employment in the municipalities and has created a new category of exploited, low paid, no-social security, contract labour, the majority of whom happen to be SCs. A gender division of labour among the SCs shows that waste disposal and menial task in hospitals is performed by SC women while garbage collection is performed by SC men. In the absence of data, it is difficult to estimate the magnitude of this phenomenon.

Notwithstanding the economic and technological advances that Maharashtra boasts of in its quest for modernity, traditional 'unclean' occupations such as disposal of the dead, handling bodies in the public morgues besides removal of dead animals, skinning them, and the like are performed by SC men as one of their traditional roles and are being carried over into the 21st century. Their wages are still determined by traditions that regarded these 'services' to be *gratis* or near *gratis*. This group, which performs critical function in society, is marginalised both economically and socially precisely because their caste predetermines their occupational status. Other than paying lip service to discrimination and indignity that is attached to such calling, no sustainable alternate livelihood opportunities are available to the 'safai kamgar', which could make a difference to their lives and quest for dignity.

Dalit Muslims have been excluded from all protection and assistance, which technically should have accrued to them under the Constitution. Though some are listed as OBCs and STs, they are victims of faith-based discrimination. Without any protective mechanism, assured access to employment or social security, under-privileged among the minorities, especially Dalit Muslim women continue to be victims thrice over—of poverty, gender-based oppression and faith-based discrimination. Their oppressive economic and social condition has pushed these workers into informal sector and the margins of Maharashtrian society today is not much different from if not worse than Dalits and Adivasis.

New employment opportunities in the IT sector remain out of reach of the Dalit poor. Their economic deprivation is a major deterrent to their social emancipation that this sector offers. Entry for the SC youth into this sector is highly unlikely without express supportive policies.

In a highly segmented urban labour market, 10.39 per cent unemployment among SCs has been reported. High levels of unemployment among the educated SC youth is indicated by the fact that thousands apply and appear for interview for the few posts of conservancy workers in railways, municipalities and other public sector organisations. Rural SC women reported highest levels of unemployment. Though a fourth of the SC non-workers actively sought work, social/economic disability, difficult living conditions were barriers to seek work (NSSO 55th Round, 2001).

Empowerment and Development

Education

The SCs have been particularly keen to acquire education seeing its emancipatory possibilities. Table 8.17 supports this argument. Education has also been seen as an important step for social advancement. The improvement in literacy rate between 1961 and 1991 among the SCs has been impressive. The growth in literacy among the SCs, though relatively high internally, and when compared to the national SC literacy level at 37.41 per cent, even at 56.5 per cent in

TABLE 8.17

Admission of SCs in Technical Institutes in Degree Programmes for Academic Year 2004-2005

Technical Institutes	*Government*		*Government-aided*		*Unaided*		*All*	
	SC	*Total*	*SC*	*Total*	*SC*	*Total*	*SC*	*Total*
Engineering and Technology	230 (13.57%)	1695 (100%)	212 (12.60%)	1683 (100%)	2208 (6.23%)	35440 (100%)	2650 (6.82%)	38818 (100%)
Pharmacy	14 (15.38%)	91 (100%)	15 (9.8%)	153 (100%)	202 (6.1%)	3308 (100%)	231 (6.5%)	3552 (100%)
Hotel Management and Catering Technology	-	-	5 (23.80%)	21 (100%)	60 (14.85%)	404 (100%)	65 (15.29%)	425 (100%)
Architecture	-	-	19 (15.70%)	121 (100%)	38 (3.75%)	1013 (100%)	57 (42.54%)	1134 (100%)

Note: Figures in parentheses are percentage to total.

Source: Director of Technical Education, 2004-05.

the state in 1991, is lower than that of the general population. The low literacy levels in Marathwada have affected the overall picture.

Three patterns in achievements in literacy are observable in Maharashtra (Velaskar, 2000). Table 8.18 shows the literacy rate among SCs in the state. In the first category are the districts (Mumbai, Pune, and Kolhapur), where the SCs have made impressive gains but their literacy levels are still lower than the general population of the region. The second category consists of districts (Jalna, Osmanabad, Latur, and Parbhani) where literacy levels of both SCs and general population are lower than the state average. In the third category are the districts (Thane, Wardha, and Nagpur), where literacy levels of both general and SCs population are above the state average.

TABLE 8.18

Literacy Rate Among SCs in Maharashtra: 1991

Year	*Total*			*Rural*			*Urban*		
	P	*M*	*F*	*P*	*M*	*F*	*P*	*M*	*F*
2001	71.9	83.3	60.0	67.9	80.6	54.7	78.3	87.6	68.4
1991	56.46	70.45	41.59	50.27	65.86	35.99	67.07	78.17	54.94
1981	35.55	48.85	21.53	30.21	44.00	16.01	47.13	59.02	33.96
1971	25.27	37.02	12.85	21.02	32.35	9.26	38.25	50.78	24.25
1961	15.78	25.46	5.70	12.15	20.62	3.51	28.77	42.17	13.93

Source: Census, 1991, 2001.

The rural-urban disparity in literacy was 6.5 per cent points higher for the SCs when compared to the general population; urban-based SCs have done better than their rural counterparts.

There are inter-caste variations as well among the SCs themselves. Middle castes among the SCs like Chambhar, Dhor, Bhangi, Khatik And Lingader enjoy high literacy levels. The same is the case for minor SCs, Mahayavanshi and Meghaval. The Chambars, for example, enjoy literacy rate of 57.33 per cent, the Mahars are a little lower at 54.5 per cent. The overall SC literacy rate is, however, pulled down by the literacy rate among Mangs, which stands at a low 32.99 per cent.

Higher enrolment of SC boys and girls in primary school is offset by a high dropout rate of SC girls. In most cases, the reasons for dropping out were economic compulsions. Scheduled caste boys and girls continue to drop-out interminantly with the inevitable fallout of only 12-14 SC children finally reaching the matriculate level. The dependence of the rural SC child on the government school for her/his social advancement and emancipation is a critical issue that should be kept in mind at all time. The Table 8.19 below gives the percentage of students completing matric education.

TABLE 8.19

Students Aged 17 and Above in Rural Areas Completing Matric Level Education (IX & X) 1994

(Per Cent)

SCs			*STs*			*All*		
Total	*Boys*	*Girls*	*Total*	*Boys*	*Girls*	*Total*	*Boys*	*Girls*
4.2	7.0	1.4	2.3	3.4	1.2	6.7	9.8	3.5

Source: NCAER/HDI Survey, 1994.

Percentage of SC enrolment to total enrolment in BE/BSc. (Tech.)/B. Arch during 1995–1997, for instance, increased from 4.2 per cent in 1995–96 to 4.46 per cent in 1996–97 (Chatterjee, 2000). The enrolment of the SC and Nav Baudha students in law colleges was 11.02 per cent in 1994-95 (Directorate of Education, 1994-1995). Not only are the gender disparities in the higher education of SCs an issue that requires serious consideration, the fact that even the 15 per cent reservation is not fully utilised remains worrisome. Inequality cannot be removed by enrolment alone (Wankhede, 2001) as continuing in institutions of higher education is impossible without scholarship. Though the number of SC beneficiaries of post-matric scholarship increased from 2,19,672 (boys 1,54,935 and girls 64,737) in 1995–96 to 2,66,084 (boys 1,88,528 and girls 77,556) in 1996–97 (Wankhede, 1999), it is difficult to accurately confirm what proportion of SC students who enrolled for higher education got post-matric scholarships. The Table 8.20 indicates their enrolment in ITIs.

In rapidly changing employment market, SC youth out of school, have to make quick decisions about educational courses to be pursued and move towards appropriate career options. But, state institutions and courses for which post-matric scholarships are available remain outdated. Private institutions where market oriented courses are available are not included in the list. Autonomous private colleges where such courses are offered are prohibitively expensive. Scheduled Caste youth are in a double mind; institutions that provide scholarship don't have market-oriented courses and *vice versa.* This complex situation effectively denies access to higher/technical/professional education to SC youth.

TABLE 8.20

Enrolment in ITIs in Maharashtra

Year	SC	Total
2000	7677 (17.62)	43580
2001	7455 (17.14)	43490
2002	7801 (18.42)	42340
2003	11631 (18.99)	61233
2004	12357 (18.75)	65887

Note: Figures in parentheses denote percentage of the total.

Source: Directorate of Vocational Training, GoM.

Those who manage to get enrolled discover that support services to help them cope up with the demands of higher education are not available. As a result, SC youth drop out or stagnate in professional courses. The lack of mechanisms that allow smooth transition from schools to appropriate career options had the inevitable result wherein SC students enrol late, enrol into less prestigious institutions, perform poorly, and take longer to complete (Chatterjee, 2000). The combination of poverty, lack of easy access to schooling, unattractiveness of education system, relative neglect of elementary/primary education, practice of untouchability, discrimination in schools, inequality of opportunities among the SCs themselves and patriarchy together result in educational backwardness of the SC (Aikara, 1996; Wankhede, 2001).

Self-governance

Currently, there is reservation for the SCs in the local self-government institutions. But in the discussion of issues related to participation of SCs, STs, women and minorities in local self-government, the crying need for their capacity building that would ensure effective participation have been sidelined. For instance, if a SC person gets elected as a *sarpanch*, issues about his/her livelihood are not discussed; so much so, even though he/she is the *sarpanch*, his/her family experiences extreme economic hardships. As a result, the SC *sarpanch* is forced to make decisions whether to pursue the political options or to give in to economic compulsions. The inevitable result is the ineffectiveness of the *sarpanch* and the imminent threat of being overthrown. The recent government directions that three-fourths majority is needed to pass a no confidence motion against a Dalit *sarpanch* is a good move. Despite having numerical strength at the *gram sabha* levels, the SCs generally have not been able to convert their numerical strength into concrete political/economic benefits (Jare and Kumar, 2001). As a result, the implementation of the 73rd and the 74th amendments have not benefited the SCs much in getting rid of the shackles of social stigma or facilitating their participation in local self-governance and empowering them.

Administration and Development Policy

There is no doubt that the reservation policy and development programmes specially meant for them have catalysed the little change in the quality of living of the SCs in the state and provided them some opportunity to enter the modern sectors of the economy in the 1980s.

Just when the SCs were beginning to carve out some space of their own in society, a crisis driven programme of economic reforms was introduced. Macro-policies introduced in the 1990s, especially new policies relating to population, health, women, education, industry, agriculture, information, communications, science and technology in particular, had differential impact because of prevailing gender and caste relations in the state. The relative distance between the SCs and others has remained the same or has worsened; out of the total population of 138 million Dalits, the number of reservations in services that the SCs have effectively accessed did not exceed 0.8 per cent (Teltumbde, 2000).

While the secular nature of the economic reforms challenged the traditional hierarchies to an extent, the 'creamy layer' among the SCs benefited to some extent leaving large sections of the SCs and the Dalit Muslims out of the reform process in the state. The 'development' has enabled those with political, economic and social power to reinforce their position at the expense of those without such power.

Recommendations Specific to Scheduled Castes

Effectively Implement Existing Laws Pertaining to Protection and Promotion of Civil Rights, Human Rights and Atrocities against the SCs by:

- Undertaking a massive public awareness campaign with the help of NGOs.
- Enlisting the NGOs in the community for the effective implementation of the existing laws.
- Sensitising the government functionaries to the Constitutional provisions to uphold human right and dignity.

Humanise Livelihoods, Provide Health Protection, Promote Dignity of Labour and Eliminate all Forms of Forced Undignified Occupations by:

- Intensifying campaigns to eradicate scavenging and to promote dignity of labour.
- Making water and sanitation available in rural and urban slum areas.
- Providing health safety net for all the 'safai kamgar' regardless of whether they are working independently or with a contractor or with private company.

Facilitate Equal Access to Technical, Professional and Higher Education in Private Aided and Non-aided Colleges by:

- Extending reservation policy to the private aided/unaided colleges with the help of suitable amendments to the existing statutory provisions so that access to technical/professional/higher education/vocational education can be assured.
- Including Dalit Muslims in the list of SCs so that access to education and vocational education can be assured.
- Updating the list of educational institutions in which SC students are enrolled to pursue technical, professional and higher education so that they can avail post-matric scholarships.
- Extending adequate post-matric scholarships covering all expenses connected with the educational programme.

Ensure Livelihood Security by:

- Enacting laws to prevent alienation of land held by the SCs.
- Extending reservation to the private sector employment.

Create More Political Space for SCs by:

- Recognising the SC habitat (Dalit *bastis*) as the smallest unit for self-governance in the respective legislations pertaining to PRI (currently they are clubbed with other revenue villages/habitats).

Women

In the light of women's multiple roles—their productive and reproductive labour and contribution towards the overall maintenance of the social fabric, changes in the economic policies have impacted women at two levels. Firstly, at the immediate experiential level, they continue to face lowered wages, less food and greater workload. Secondly, at a more structural or strategic level, informalisation of labour (Krishnaraj, 2003) has resulted in constricting the economic space available to the working class as a whole to negotiate from a position of strength. Further, while all sections of women were affected by the new development policies, the impact on Dalit, Adivasi and under-privileged minority women was greater.

Marginalised women such as the women working in the unorganised sector, women who are main bread-winners of their families, widowed, divorced, deserted women, women in institutions, victims of violence, mentally ill/challenged women, women ostracised as being 'possessed', sex workers, eunuchs and others are leading a precarious life. Female foeticide, female IMR, falling child sex ratio, unequal wages, violence perpetrated against them tell how precarious women's lives are in the state.

Welfare

Human Rights

Falling sharply from 934 in 1991 to 922 in 2001, sex ratio is as low as 908 in rural areas in the state. The declining sex ratio is the combined effect of increased migration of men, early marriage, teenage and repeated pregnancies. The child sex ratio was 917 in 1991 indicating worsening of the chances of survival for females in the state. Konkan, tribal eastern Maharashtra, most of the districts in Vidarbha have child sex ratio lower than the state average.

TABLE 8.21

IMR in the Three Indian States of High, Medium and Low Literacy Rates

State	*1991*			*2001*			*2002*		
	M	*F*	*T*	*M*	*F*	*T*	*M*	*F*	*T*
Kerala	45	41	42	14	9	11	9	12	10
Maharashtra	72	76	74	43	48	45	48	42	45
Bihar	62	89	75	57	68	62	56	66	61

Source: Datar, C., 2003.

Compared to Kerala, as seen in Table 8.21, Maharashtra has a long way to go as far as female IMR is concerned.

MHDR (2002) notes the regional variations in the female IMR, indicating the fact that, though the aggregate picture appears to be satisfactory, there are pockets where women's chances of survival is at risk.

Violence against women takes many forms ranging from the medical termination of the female foetus, a denial of nutrition, health and education to the girl child, domestic violence, sexual abuse, sexual harassment at work, and forcible sale of commercial sex workers. Witch hunting continues to be prevalent in the tribal areas (e.g. Nandurbar and Thane districts). Establishment of women's vigilance committees, establishment of women's police stations, special cells in police stations and other steps taken by the state government to prevent and protect women from violence has had some effect. At least some crimes against women get reported and there is some decline (MHDR, 2002) in the reported incidence. However, the fact is, most of the crimes go unreported due to various reasons. Alarmingly, 'accidents' is the second highest killer among women. With a view to curb domestic violence, a Domestic Violence Bill was drafted in 2002, but many have expressed reservations about the implementability of the proposed law.

Following the Supreme Court judgement in 1997, it has now become mandatory to have rules regarding action to be taken against perpetrators of sexual harassment at work. These steps may be of some assistance to the women employed in the organised sector. However, majority of the women employed in the unorganised sector suffer these indignities in silence.

Sexual harassment and abuse are the outcomes of poverty and harsh living conditions. Many women are pushed into prostitution as a result of poverty. There are no official estimates of the number of women trafficked for sex work or of the number of women engaged in sex work. Of those working as sex workers, around 30 per cent are minor girls (MHDR, 2002). Of these, 90 per cent were kidnapped and raped. Even though there is a law against trafficking in women, there has rarely been any conviction.

Growing urbanisation across the state and swelling urban population create pressures on housing, living and working conditions. Seasonal migrant women workers living in spontaneously sprung up shanties are the most vulnerable. Hardly 45.9 per cent of the households in the state have toilet or latrine facilities.

Victims of domestic violence, deserted women, divorced women, women who lose their mental balance temporarily due to various pressures, single women who work out of necessity, young women who have to acquire qualifications to be able to be economically independent, women with disability, elderly women without economic support require short/long-term safe affordable shelter. Currently, such facilities are few and far between.

Poverty and Food Security

Marginalised sections of women have to stretch themselves due to casualisation and informalisation of labour. They work for longer hours for less pay. More members from a household have to offer themselves in the labour market to be able to maintain their family's consumption levels. And, due to the insecurity of casual labour their incomes fluctuate. Women labourers in the unorganised sector often are not recorded or are merged in the *jodi* or gang. They do not get paid separately, and when they do, they have no control over their incomes.

In poverty conditions, food security becomes a special need for women who have less mobility. Women access such programmes as Food for Work Programme, the EGS and the SGRY. Due to lack of coordination between implementing departments and lengthy procedures, convergence of benefits under these programmes does not take place at the cutting edge (Dev, 2003).

Given the hegemonic patriarchal family dynamics, the brunt of poverty and difficult living conditions is borne by women in the households. They are malnourished and suffer ill health, which, in turn leads to low productivity and earnings, trapping women in the vicious cycle of poverty.

Health

Health status of women is determined by the interplay of a complex set of social, economic, cultural and political factors. This is indicated in Table 8.22. For instance, the main focus of women's health has always been their reproductive role. And as such, they are viewed as agents of human reproduction and as mothers rather than as individuals requiring health care. Health policy, within it, the population policy and family planning programmes have reduced women's bodies to targets for birth control at the cost of their health and well-being.

MHDR (2002) notes that, because female-based contraceptives are inserted without paying attention to reproductive tract infections, there are side effects. As it is difficult to negotiate safe sex, many women avoid contraceptives. Ninety-two per cent of women studied suffered from gynaecological diseases. Given the unequal status of women in society, women are more

TABLE 8.22

Health Status of Women: At a Glance

Pointers	*Maharashtra Percentage/ Figure*	*India Percentage/ Figure*
Life Expectancy at Birth	66.2 years (female), 63.8 (male)	61.8 (female), 60.4 (male)
Sex Ratio	922 women for 1000 men	933 for 1000 men
Child Sex Ratio (0-6 Years)	917 girls for 1000 boys	927 girls for 1000 boys
Anaemia	49 per cent women, 76 per cent children (6-36 months)	51.8 per cent women, 74.3 per cent children
Female Sterilisation	52 per cent (of currently married women)	34 per cent (of currently married women)
Male Sterilisation	5 per cent (of currently married men)	2 per cent (of currently married men)
Age at Marriage	30 per cent between 15 and 19 years	34 per cent between 15-19 years
Institutional Deliveries	57.1 per cent	33.6 per cent
Total Unmet Need for Contraception	13 per cent	16 per cent
Current users of Contraception	60.4 per cent	48.2 per cent
Using Spacing Methods (Pill, Condom, IUD)	7.7 per cent	6.8 per cent

Source: Datar, C., 2003.

prone to sexually transmitted diseases and HIV infection. With the rural-urban gap in availability of public health infrastructure, limited access to affordable private health care services adds to their woes. With rising costs of private health care services, often their own health needs are neglected (MHDR, 2002) in the household.

Apart from gender bias in child nutrition, nutritional status of children is an outcome of maternal health. Nutrition status of 42 per cent of women in the state is poor (NFHS, 2002).

Occupational health, mental health, unique health needs of disabled women, nutritional status, sexual abuse and violence and their impact on health of women remain unaddressed (Datar, 2003).

Resources and Livelihoods

Access to Resources

Women's participation was built into initiatives such as Joint Forest Management, Farmer Managed Irrigation Systems, Water Policy, 2002, Water Resources Planning and Regulatory Authority, 2002, Watershed Development and such other programmes only under the insistence of external funding agencies. However, water harvested through watershed development programmes and water users' associations promoted by government do not award water rights to women; and equitable sharing of the costs of water shortages has also been overlooked.

BOX 8.2

Urban Environment and Solid Waste Management with a Human Face

Municipal authorities have the daunting task of disposal of solid waste generated in cities. Till recently, two ways of solid waste disposal—dumping and incinerating have been practiced. Rag-pickers have shown us a more sustainable third way—recycling. Recycling was considered to be infeasible in our country because of the people's attitude, habits, difficulty in enforcing and enormity of the task.

'Parisar Vikas'—the project was launched by an NGO—Stree Mukti Sanghathna in 1998 on an experimental basis. The unique feature was that livelihood of poor, low skilled, low educated Dalit women engaged in rag picking would be protected while solid waste would be disposed off in environment-friendly and sustainable way. As it was a small-scale initiative, the Mumbai Municipal Corporation authorities responded positively on an experimental basis.

Today, more than 2,000 women are engaged in collecting garbage from houses, separating dry and wet garbage, selling the dry garbage (plastic, glass, metal), converting wet garbage into vermi-fertiliser and earn a living. Besides, they extend advisory services and training.

Considering the fact that employment opportunities in conservancy work are fully reserved for the SCs, the state government and the Municipal Corporation have facilitating role to play. A policy to segregate dry and wet garbage and rules for implementing it on a wide scale in all the big cities in the state have to be adopted. Besides saving the cost of transporting garbage to the dumping grounds, it will become possible to prevent pollution and generate resources by recycling the solid waste. Development of entrepreneurship in this area with a variety of policy support seems to be the direction for the future.

EGS implemented in drought-prone areas has not resulted in creation and regeneration of adequate water, forest and other common natural resources crucial to the survival of the weaker sections in rural areas, particularly the women, the SCs and the STs.

Women access land in three ways namely, through inheritance, purchase and as beneficiaries of land reforms. The state's women's policies have consistently promised amendment of appropriate personal and succession laws to confer land rights to women. So far, Hindu laws have been amended to confer equal share in the husband's/father's immovable assets. In the absence of data, it is not possible to say how much the marginalised women have benefited from these reforms. The state has implemented the rules pertaining to land transactions where women are now able to be joint owners of immovable property. Further, culturally, tenancy is not conferred to women cultivators.

Work Participation

The proportion of women's participation in work-force, comparatively, has always been high in the state. Table 8.23 indicates the same. However, entitlement to employment largely depends on endowments—of education, skills, assets such as land ownership and mobility, which resulted in a growing disparity among women themselves.

In rural areas, agriculture is the largest employer of women in the state (MHDR, 2002). While 48 per cent are agricultural labourers, 41 per cent are cultivators (MHDR, 2002: 117). The proportion of women cultivators is increasing; the Konkan region has a predominance of women cultivators.

TABLE 8.23

Labour Force Participation by Education

Labour Force	*Male*		*Female*	
	Urban	*Rural*	*Urban*	*Rural*
Illiterate	9.28	28.54	31.10	62.61
Primary	12.31	16.22	11.55	12.25
Middle	23.67	21.44	15.07	11.33
Graduate & above	15.13	4.37	18.08	0.63

Source: NSS 55th Round, Computation by Prof. Sarathi Acharya, TISS.

Horticulture, dairy, and poultry received a boost in 1970s and 1980s and has become the main source of income for some households. It is important to note that, though these are considered household activities, most of the work falls on women while the earnings are appropriated by men.

The 1990s saw an increase in the proportion of rural women engaged in subsidiary and marginal work as casual labourers. The MHDR (2002) observes that there is greater shift towards casual work of women in the state compared to the national trend.

The urban labour market for women is characterised by those with low skills, in dire need of employment on one end, and those with high levels of professional/technical education and skills at the other end. In the job market of production related activities, where some expansion took place, women lost out since their jobs were at the lower end in manufacturing and industrial activities (Datar, 2003). As per the NSS 55th Round, urban women are concentrated in manufacture, trade, hotel/hospitality, public administration, education, and commercial services. Of these, less than one per cent is in occupations with better pay scales requiring high levels of skill and education.

Weaker sections are self-employed as rag-pickers, hawkers, and domestic workers fisher women, washerwomen, childcare workers, personal care providers on a regular basis in urban areas. In garment manufacturing, construction industry, embroidery work, *beedi* rolling also a large number of women find employment. Though brick making is skilled, women are subsumed in the unskilled category. Women are completely left out of the purview of development planning because their work is invisible. Despite having Equal Remuneration Act, women continue to be paid less than men for same work.

Sub-contracting relationships allow expansion and contraction of production and shift costs of fluctuation to the vulnerable home-based units in which women and children are employed in large numbers. Employers have been taking advantage of legal loopholes and exploit women workers in rural and urban areas. No scientific or equitable procedure exists to determine payment in piece-rate system, widely prevalent in the home-based work. With the increasing informalisation and casualisation, the need to plug the gaps and to implement the labour laws diligently has assumed urgency. There is a scope for involving women's organisations, trade unions to inspect and file complaints against errant employers. There is a need to extend ESIS and other social security to these workers.

In urban areas, the proportion of women in professional occupations increased from 2.93 per cent in

1987-88 to 10.3 per cent 1999-00. Of the women in the organised sector, more than 16 per cent are in government employment. Of these, 49 per cent are in local government and the rest in state, central and quasi-government organisations. Generally, when women take to work either as contract workers or in government/organised sectors, they are found to crowd gender-stereotyped jobs implying little scope for upward mobility. Outsourcing, call centres require women to work at nights, which is proving to be detrimental to women's health and safety.

Efficiency of development functionaries working in rural areas such as the primary school teachers, ANMs and *anganwadi* workers, majority of whom are women, would be much more if the childcare, transport, convenient timings of water/electricity/bank, market, housing, school and physical safety support systems were available (Murdia, 1984).

With meagre support such as access to credit, extension services, input subsidies, marketing, and health coverage for the self-employed, the prospects of self-employment for women are not bright.

Empowerment and Development

Education

Maharashtra ranks 8th among India's states in terms of male literacy rate (86.27 per cent), but 11th in terms of female literacy rate (67.51 per cent). Despite enabling policies and programmes, about 13 million women remain illiterate. There has been a consistent effort by the state government to improve literacy among women in general, especially among women from marginalised sections. The literacy levels are shown in Table 8.24 (MHDR, 2002).

TABLE 8.24

Male and Female Literacy Levels : 1951-2001

(Per Cent)

Year	*Persons*	*Males*	*Females*
1951	27.91	40.49	15.56
1961	35.08	49.26	19.80
1971	45.77	49.40	31.00
1981	57.24	70.06	43.50
1991	64.87	76.56	52.32
2001	77.27	86.27	67.51

Source: Census, 2001.

Despite these efforts, in 22 districts of Maharashtra, women's literacy rates were below the state average in 1991. Osmanabad, Beed, Nanded, Parbhani, Hingoli, Gadchiroli, Jalna and Nandurbar have the lowest rates at 45.55 per cent (MHDR, 2002). In some districts, feudal history, social hierarchies, caste polarisation and isolation of tribal people have acted as inhibiting factors to literacy (Maharashtra State Commission for Women, 1997).

At the state level, the gap between SC men and women stands at 28.6 percentage points. The gap between total female literacy and SC female literacy is smaller (10.7 percentage points) indicating the general backwardness of all women but also the greater backwardness of SC women (Velaskar, 2000). Literacy among SC women is very low in Jalna, Parbhani and Nanded (around 20 per cent) and higher in Wardha, Nagpur and Konkan (above 50 per cent). Literacy among ST women was 1.75 per cent in 1961 and in 1991, it had increased to 24.03 per cent. The percentage of girls enrolled in primary, secondary and higher secondary schools in the state is given in Table 8.25.

TABLE 8.25

Girls' Enrolment

(Per Cent)

School	*2000-01*	*2001-02*
Primary	49	48
Secondary	45	45
Higher Secondary	42	41

Source: Datar, C., 2003.

A variety of indicators show that dropout rates at the upper primary grades are high for girls despite concerted government efforts. Girls fare better than boys—in 2000, 47.45 per cent of the boys who appeared passed; while the percentage of girls passed was 53.34 per cent. Though, girls fare better, only 64.5 per cent girls appeared for Std. X exam for every 100 boys in 1999. Girls' participation in higher education has considerably increased. Yet, more girls (77.33 per cent) go for under-graduate level vocational education (Directorate of Education, 1994-95). Table 8.26 gives an idea of the enrolment of girls at the degree level.

At degree level, girls go for gender-stereotypical degree programmes. The enrolment is very low for ST/SC women due to language, cost barriers, and lack of hostel facilities.

TABLE 8.26

Girls' Enrolment at the Degree Level

Institutions	*Girls Enrolled in 1994-95*	*Girls Enrolled in 1998-99*
Law	24.03	20.42
Agriculture	06.79	02.41
Veterinary Science	11.99	04.33
Engineering/Technical	-	07.47
Business Management	10.66	-
Library Science	44.44	-
Fisheries	08.06	-
Medicine	45.97	40.59
Social Work	33.22	-
Arts	37.69	-
Science	38.15	-
Commerce	40.81	-
Graduate	-	
Postgraduate	-	39.97
Research	-	
Diploma/Certificate	-	
Others	-	23.88

Source: General Statistical Organisation, 2000.

There are many special schemes to promote education of girl students as mentioned in the Table 8.27.

However, despite these schemes, many benefits do not reach the girl students as is apparent from the Table 8.28.

TABLE 8.28

Percentage of Girl Students Availing Benefit of Stipend Offered to Check the Rate of Dropouts

District	*Per Cent of Beneficiaries to Total SC/ST*
Thane	31.77
Dhule	18.40
Ahmadnagar	57.67
Pune	26.20
Satara	31.59
Kolhapur	21.34
Nanded	5.48
Buldhana	83.97
Bhandara	26.43
Gadchiroli	86.90
Chandrapur	46.45
Jalana	41.00
Beed	86.80
Parbhani	21.72

Source: Programme Budget, Overview on Education 1998.

TABLE 8.27

Schemes for Girls' Education in Maharashtra

Scheme	*Entitlement*
Ahalyabai Holkar Scheme (Started in 1996-97)	Girls in rural areas studying in Std. V to X are provided free travel in Maharashtra State Road Transport Corporation buses. Achievement: In 2001-02, about 4.5 lakh girls availed of this scheme.
Primary School Students of Educationally Backward Areas in 103 Blocks	Free textbooks, uniforms and writing material.
Ist and IInd Std. Students of 103 Backward Groups of *Zilla Parishad* Primary Schools	Free uniforms and stationery.
Government B.Ed colleges in nine districts having low literacy level namely Aurangabad, Jalna, Beed, Latur, Nanded, Osmanabad, Parbhani, Dhule and Gadchiroli	50% reservation for girls and education to be provided free of cost.
Education in Technical Institutions	25% reservation for girls.
Education in all Universities and Colleges	30% reservation for girls.
Daughters of *devdasis*	Free education.
Adarsha Stree Shikshan Puraskar	Encourage women teachers so as to check the dropout rates among girls.
Attendance Allowance (Implemented from 1992)	For girls (Std I-IV) BPL families in tribal sub-plan areas and SCs, one rupee per day. During 2001-02 4.75 lakh girl students were benefited. (GoM, 2002b).
Military School for Girls in Pune	
Free Education for Girls up to 12th Std. (and for Boys up to the 10th Std.)	

Source: Datar, 2003.

The government is running 42 hostels for SC girls to facilitate access to and retention in school in the state. There are 110 hostels for tribal girls. The Priyadarshini Vasathigrih Yojana was introduced in 1996-97 for girl students from rural areas for their college education. Currently, 13 hostels with a capacity of 650 girl college students are functioning. Though girls enrol in polytechnics, infotech educational institutes and engineering colleges, most being run by private managements, do not have hostel facilities. Income criterion for seeking accommodation in the working women's hostels is too restrictive that most women who work while learning and those who are in difficult family situation find it impossible to avail this facility.

Empowerment through SHGs

In urban areas, where literacy is high, supportive policies regarding finance/credit, marketing, etc. reportedly (MAVIM, 2002) have contributed to women's economic empowerment to some extent. Current strategy of entrepreneurship development adopted by Maharashtra Centre for Entrepreneurship Development consists mainly of sponsored programmes. With better coordination between the District Industrial Centres, *Mahila Arthik Vikas Mahamandal*, banks, backward classes finance and development corporations, state marketing federations, community polytechnics and state cooperative union, there is scope for increasing women's entrepreneurship. Special courses on micro-credit, micro-finance and micro-enterprise offered as a part of existing polytechnic, vocational courses and B.Com degree programmes would facilitate bringing out women's potential.

Mahila Arthik Vikas Mahamandal Ltd. (MAVIM) established in 1975 is currently working in 12 districts. A total of 10,438 SHGs organised by the MAVIM and the NGOs with a membership of 1,35,212 had distributed Rs. 28.88 crores and saved Rs. 14.72 crores till September 2003. The issue of how savings and credit can be linked to human development is critical. The decision to link sex ratio, teenage pregnancies, early marriage, low literacy levels with the activities of the SHGs on an experimental basis is a forward-looking step. The Annapurna Mahila Mandal, an NGO, has successfully linked training for self-employment, credit linked with savings, old-age security for women.

Such efforts to link SHGs to human development goals of the state would be a worthwhile avenue for the government to explore.

Local Self-governance

All round empowerment of women is a pre-requisite for women's participation in politics (Table 8.29). Women have had a presence in local self-government bodies in the state ever since the state formation. Initially, women with some exposure to public spaces, and belonging to political families contested elections as independent candidates. Now, their participation through political party membership is not insignificant. However, their integration into formal political structure has been slow. Surprisingly, their presence as voters and candidates has been declining in the state (Maharashtra State Commission for Women, 1997). Apart from lack of financial independence, low participation is attributed to fear of criminalisation of politics. Currently, the gender gap is 5.32 per cent though it is higher in some of the parliamentary constituencies.

Women's representation in the local self-governing bodies is lower than 33 per cent reserved by law.

However, it is a matter of concern that only 1.5 per cent of *zilla parishads*, 9.6 per cent of *panchayat samitis* and 29.4 per cent of *gram panchayats* were chaired by women. The three MCs of Thane, Nashik and Nagpur have had women mayors.

TABLE 8.29

Women in Politics—At a Glance

Elected Women Representatives	*In Per Cent*
Assembly	
1957	12.87
1972	10.33
1990	2.08
1995	3.81
Municipal Corporations (2000)	
All Municipal Corporations	33.1
Greater Mumbai and Pune (highest)	34.0
Sangli (lowest)	30.0
Municipal Councils	
All Municipal Councils	30.0
Nanded (Lowest)	5.2
Sholapur (Highest)	36.8
Zilla Parishad	33.0
Panchayat Samiti	32.7
Gram Panchayat	29.2

Source: Datar, C., 2003.

While substantial gains have been made by women in gaining representation in governance, both in rural and urban areas, Singh *et al.* (1992) found that dominant castes and classes ensure that their women gain entry into the local self-governments so that they can retain control. Effectiveness of women elected representatives has not been adequately researched. Women's representation in statutory committees, though ensured, remains mere tokenism.

Most women, especially first timers, and the SC/ST women are not aware of the list of development schemes being implemented at their level nor are they clear about their role and functions. By the time they familiarise themselves, their term comes to an end. Much capacity building work remains to be done.

There are three or four prominent NGOs engaged in the task of building capacities of elected women representatives, especially the *gram panchayat* and *panchayat samiti* members. Yet, capacity building of women-elected-representatives by both the government and NGOs remains episodic.

Women's participation in cooperatives has also increased over the years. The number of exclusively SC/ST women's cooperatives has also gone up. Except for the recent strategy to organise self-help groups of poor women, there are almost no specific schemes of financial assistance or other incentives to motivate women to form cooperatives. There is no reservation of seats for women in the managing committees, and boards of directors of cooperatives. Cooperatives in traditional occupations like dairy, animal husbandry, and fish vending could be explored. Mid-day Meal Scheme, supply of cooked food to ICDS also can be entrusted to women's cooperatives. In the formation and registration of urban cooperative banks, there is scope to provide 25 per cent of membership to women.

Women Belonging to Underprivileged Among Minorities

The underprivileged Muslim women are the most educationally backward. Literacy levels are particularly low, although only a smattering of empirical evidence is available. Some of them are included in the OBC and ST lists in the state. These women get left out from benefits due to covert faith-based discrimination. Having neither assured employment nor any kind of social security, the underprivileged among the minority women are simultaneously victims of poor material circumstances, patriarchy and faith-based discrimination. Those who work for wages and those who are own account workers in the informal sector find themselves pushed to the margins of Maharashtrian society today. With strident liberalism, patriarchy and communalism, they share the same fate as their counterparts—*Dalits* and *Adivasis*.

Persons with Disability

The right of a disabled beggar is a direct link between the chosen model of development and disability. With sex determination tests and legalised abortion, the differently abled do not even have right to life. Nearly half of all disabilities are preventable. People develop preventable disabilities because of i) malnutrition, ii) low birth weight, iii) low resistance to diseases, iv) lack of awareness about immunisation, v) lack of access to immunisation and primitive health services, vi) hazardous working conditions, vii) misuse of sex determination tests and abortion, viii) poverty, ix) negligence, and x) patriarchy and caste hierarchies. The road to new paradigm of development centring around life, dignity and livelihood security of the disabled includes opportunities and support for education, employment and access to public places.

Disabled, falling into five main categories namely locomotor disabled, vision impaired, hearing impaired, speech impaired and mentally challenged, are generally treated as a liability on society. Their ability and contribution is overlooked so much so that they were not enumerated in the census separately till a decade ago. It has been estimated that 1.1 per cent of the rural and 1.3 per cent of the urban population are reported having one or more disability, according to a special survey conducted in the state. In 2001, there were 2,61,276 persons with disability in the state. The estimated proportion of persons with different types of disability is given in Table 8.30.

TABLE 8.30

Per Cent of Disabled Persons in Total Population

Type of Disability	*Rural*	*Urban*
Mental	0.15	0.17
Vision Impaired	0.16	0.14
Hearing Impaired	0.15	0.15
Speech Impaired	0.12	0.11
Locomotor	0.67	0.80
Any	1.13	1.25

Source: GoM, 2003b.

Welfare

Human Rights

The persons with disability are not aware that their human rights are protected. Due to lack of awareness and lengthy procedure involved, the persons with disability have not sought redressal for the violation of their human rights in the state. For instance, they are not aware that simple right of mobility and access to public facilities is a human right.

Recently, Datrange (2003) conducted an audit on access of public places for the persons with disability in the state. A sample of public places like the state transport bus stands, collectors/*tehsildar's* office, police stations, and public hospitals in both rural and urban areas were covered in the audit. The state came out poorly. The government offices were not disabled-friendly. Following the findings of this audit, the state government has issued instructions to the Public Works Department to adopt suitable rules and standards to be observed while constructing the public facilities. But, there is no visible improvement in the situation. Without mobility and access, persons with disability are treated as liability rather than as a productive human resource.

Poverty

There is no data on the persons with disability who are below poverty line. The state government implements a pension scheme for destituted persons with disability. This social security is not only inadequate and intermittent, but it is availed by few, mainly due to procedural difficulty.

There is an entire official machinery and a set of laws for the welfare and development of the persons with disability in the state—the Commissionerate for the Welfare of the Persons with Disability, Finance and Development Corporation for the Persons with Disability, the Persons with Disabilities (Equal Opportunities, Protection of Rights and Full Participation) Act, 1995, and the National Trust For Welfare of persons with autism, cerebral palsy, mental retardation and multiple dsabilities. The state government's welfare schemes for the development of the disabled fall into three categories: i) education, ii) financial assistance, and iii) personalised welfare services. In addition, there is provision for grants-in-aid for NGOs.

The Disabled Person's Finance and Development Corporation has been extending financial assistance to the disabled in the state. In addition, if the persons with disability happened to be SCs, STs, women or persons belonging to minority communities, respective finance and development corporations extend financial assistance. There is no data about the number of persons with disability who have benefited from the financial assistance extended by these corporations. In 1999-00, the Disabled Person's Finance and Development Corporation extended financial assistance to about 351 persons in the entire state.

In addition, there are several concessions/relaxations in age, physical fitness, qualifications, travel by railways/roadways/air, income tax, custom duty, and in the cooperative sector.

There are three or four different grants-in-aid schemes to encourage voluntary organisations to establish special schools, sheltered training-cum-employment, counselling services, residential multipurpose institutions, vocational training, publication of reading material in Braille, production of mobility aids, etc.

Currently, more than 588 voluntary organisations are working for the rehabilitation of various categories of the disabled in the state. A good proportion of them work with children with disability, and are concentrated in urban areas. Comparatively, there are fewer NGOs working with adults, women and in rural areas. There are three or four national level voluntary organisations headquartered in the state.

The state government plans to encourage formation of cooperatives of disabled by providing financial assistance in the form of share-capital, grant, subsidy, loan, land, equipment in the coming years.

An enormous mass of uncared aged, orphaned, homeless, substance abusers, destitutes, beggars, delinquents, sex workers, families of undertrials, who are persons with disability subsist at the fringes of Maharashtrian society. With a little support, they will not only be able to lead a life in dignity but also will be able to contribute to human development. As they are voiceless and without political clout that would require the state to respond to their needs, their needs are largely not met. NGOs are currently meeting some of their needs, but the NGO response is patchy and scattered.

Reaching out to these groups would require joint intervention by government and NGOs, for, the chances are that exclusively state-centred action would in time render the interventions soulless and mechanical. And, NGOs may not be able to scale up.

On the whole, the approach has been in charity and welfare mode. This has to change. Ultimate aim is to ensure that interventions lead to their dignity and self-reliance. It is necessary to understand the distinct nature of their problems, vulnerabilities, needs and potential. A careful and innovative convergence of a range of existing poverty alleviation and welfare schemes, of the government, identification of do-able local community-based solutions with local resources and local leadership is required.

Employment and Livelihood

Work Participation

Despite three per cent reservation in educational institutions and government employment, due to social, economic, psychological, institutional and physical barriers, majority of the disabled are unable to avail this provision even though a Special Employment Exchange is in place. Table 8.31 indicates the percentage of disabled by age group.

TABLE 8.31

Per Cent of Disabled by Age Group

Age Group (Years)	*Rural*	*Urban*
0-4	2.8	3.1
5-14	16.4	15.6
15-59	57.4	58.9
60 and Above	23.4	22.4

Source: GoM, 2003b.

Of the total disabled persons in the rural areas in the working age group (Table 8.32), about 41 per cent were employed. 57.4 per cent in rural and 58.9 per cent of the disabled are in the productive age group of 15–59 years. This percentage was 35.04 per cent in urban areas.

TABLE 8.32

Per Cent of Disabled Persons in Total Population

Type of Disability	*Rural*	*Urban*
Employed	40.6	35.4
Unemployed	1.1	2.9
Neither Willing Nor Available for Work	58.3	61.7
Total	**100.0**	**100.0**

Source: GoM, 2003b.

Large proportion of the disabled persons (about 60 per cent) in both rural and urban areas was neither willing nor available for work due to difficulty in access —physical, psychological, institutional and attitudinal barriers.

Empowerment and Development

Education

There is no data about literacy levels among persons with disability. There is no data on the number of private schools and the number of children with disability completing matriculation in the state.

With a view to provide access to school education, the state government extended prematric scholarships to 36,900 disabled school-going children and to 15,955 students enrolled in vocational training institutions in 1999-00.

Every year, more than 2,000 persons are trained as special teachers. Table 8.33 provides data on educational institutions for the disabled. They are employed in special schools. The NGOs like the National Association of the Blind produce textbooks, reading material in Braille with the financial support of the government of Maharashtra and other national/international non-government funding agencies.

TABLE 8.33

Residential Institutions for the Adult Differently Abled (18-40 Years)

Type of Disability	*Government*	*Aided*
Blind	4	49
Hearing Impaired	3	152
Physically Handicapped	8	111
Mentally Challenged	-	125
Mixed	7	-
Total	**22**	**437**

Source: GoM, 2000-2001

Currently, residential facilities are available catering to nearly 20,707 persons. Often special schools cater to children up to VIIIth standard. Due to lack of special schools offering education beyond class eight, older children continue to attend the same school till they become old enough to attend vocational training institutions. Many a time, though teachers are trained in special education, due to lack of human, community and material support, the quality of education leaves much to be desired. There are several similar problems regarding access to education. As such, the full potential of persons with disability is not developed.

Local Self-governance

There is much talk of community-based rehabilitation of the persons with disability. Except for few NGOs in urban areas, this approach has not gained support. Dilasa, an NGO based in Kolhapur has been one of the few successful innovative initiatives. No effort has been made in the state to give effect to the National Trust Act in which the role of PRIs is significant. Despite progressive changes at the national levels, currently, the situation at the local levels continues to deny persons with disability their citizenship rights. The rules giving effect to the 73rd and 74th Amendments have not created public space for the participation of the persons with disability in local governance, especially pertaining to disabled-friendly infrastructure.

Recommendations Specific to the Persons with Disability

Eradicate Beggary, Destitution, Homelessness and all Forms of Forced Undignified Occupations by:

- Recognising them as citizen and by giving them voter ID cards.
- Meeting access and mobility needs *vis-à-vis* public places, public transport.
- Ensuring that children with disability will be able to complete primary education.
- Eliminating gender disparity in access to education.

Effectively Implement Existing Laws Pertaining to Violation of Civil Rights, Human Rights and Atrocities by:

- Undertaking a massive public awareness campaign with the help of NGOs.
- Enlisting NGOs in the community to facilitate community based rehabilitation and microplanning.
- Sensitising government functionaries to the special needs of the persons with disability.

Facilitate Equal Access to Technical, Professional and High Education where Job Opportunities are Opening up by:

- Extending adequate post-matric scholarships covering all expenses connected with the educational programme.
- Making suitable amendments to the existing reservation policy so that persons with disability can avail educational opportunities in private unaided schools/colleges.
- Extending special support services required by students with disability to complete respective educational/vocational training programmes.

Extend Livelihood Security to Persons with Disability by:

- Expanding opportunities for vocational training.
- Integrating entrepreneurship development with school education and vocational training.
- Achieving better coordination between NGOs, vocational training institutions, entrepreneurship development programmes, employers, financial institutions, and marketing agencies.
- Making credit available on soft terms.
- Giving industrial *galas* on concessional basis.

Empower Persons with Disabilities to Participate in the Local Self-governance by:

- Building capacities of the persons with disabilities to participate in the local self-government bodies.
- Making rules to facilitate their participation.
- Setting up a redressal mechanism to settle issues concerning their participation in the local self-governance.

Recommendations

The Way Ahead

In 2000 for the first time, the *World Human Development Report* affirmed that the enjoyment of human rights is an integral part and a necessary condition for human development. Three corollaries flow from this significant understanding of human development. First, there is an organic relationship between the enjoyment of human rights and development. Next, development is co-terminus with enjoyment of human rights and *vice versa* and the link between economic or material prosperity and human development is neither automatic nor obvious. Third, human development goes beyond mere acquisition of material goods to include enhancement of the quality of life. The development of the weaker sections, co-terminus with their emancipation, will pose major challenges in Maharashtra in the coming decades.

The approach for human resource development must be a judicious blend of several perspectives. First, among them stresses that security of life and livelihood is a condition precedent to development though development can on rare occasions result in security. The second perspective focuses on building on consolidating present strengths while stressing on special needs. In the rural areas, the approach will be strengthening capacities for sustainable increase in productivity of land and land-based resources to ensure food security and livelihood stability. The third concentrates on engaging in consolidation of literacy, functional and entrepreneurial skills to address present and future challenges effectively. The fourth concerns creating convergence in present policies and schemes to create productive skills and assets for cultivators, enable value addition in agriculture even while conserving the natural environment. The fifth relates to strengthening human and social capital to generate initiatives in governance that dovetail development with local conditions and emancipate people. The sixth stresses on building technical capacities that equip people to create employment opportunities in their local environment. The seventh calls for diversifying skills enhancement to ensure wider employment choices and opportunities in the region. The eighth calls for integrating the process in the present school curricula. The challenge of the exercise is to infuse choices and opportunities for development with dignity. With these perspectives in mind we recommend the following goals and tasks:

Goal 1—Security of Food and Nutrition for all by 2010

Formulation of a Statutorily Enforceable Time-Bound Universal Food and Nutrition Security Action Plan, Which Ensures:

a) Committed resource allocation for near universal PDS.

b) Revised BPL categories to include single mother, deserted and widowed women headed families, homeless, pavement dwellers.

c) Revised APL categories to allow the urban and rural poor, marginally above the poverty line, access to PDS at BPL rates.

d) Modified PDS providing for access to migrant workers at place of employment, regional specificities in cereal choice, seasonal demand variations.

e) Targeted Antyodaya for all BPL families for next decade.

f) Establish convergence of ICDS, Mid-day meal, Annapoorna Schemes into Integrated Nutrition Programme (Tamil Nadu pattern).

Goal 2—Security of Resources and Sustainable Livelihoods

Targeted Comprehensive Resources and Sustainable Livelihoods Action Plan with Specified Actionable Programmes to Ensure:

a) One guaranteed dignified year long livelihood for every family.

b) Vigorous promotion of micro-enterprises through comprehensive package of training in entrepreneurial skills, financial and technical inputs and development support.

c) Effective and time-bound implementation of land grant and restoration laws and schemes to provide inalienable land rights to STs and SCs.

d) Policy support and lab to land linkage for watershed development, sustainable agriculture, balanced cropping and appropriate agro-technology.

e) Reoriented EGS, using generated employment to create productive assets, while strengthening capacities to induct new agro-technology and alternative livelihoods for the rural poor.

f) Easily accessible Cluster Resource Centres focused on promoting appropriate technology, building necessary capacities, providing seed capital and resources and development assistance.

g) Strengthening tribal-forest interface by recognising tribal customary rights in forests and integrating livelihoods with forest conservation following guidelines of MoEF (GoI) of 20-12-1990.

h) Sheltered workshops for disabled in conjunction with industry and NGOs.

i) Introduction of 'livelihood stream' in school education with supervised apprenticeships with local professionals. Special incentives for girl students to develop entrepreneurial and microenterprise competencies.

Goal 3—Security of Health and Healing

Comprehensive Health Assurance Programme, which Includes:

a) Time bound implementation of recommendations of MHDR (2002) with special focus on SCs, STs, women and children.

b) Comprehensive and universal health insurance with state and employer contribution for all BPL and *antyodaya* families, migrant workers and workers in unorganised and informal sectors.

c) Strengthening and extension of primary health care with assured medical personnel and budget allocations for medicines and supplies.

d) Formulating a special 'tribal health policy' which integrates traditional healers and local knowledge and health traditions with current practices.

e) Strengthing of women volunteers as year round trained *pada swayamsevaks* to reach health to women and children, manage deliveries, combined with women-friendly policies and programmes for family planning.

f) Provision of safe drinking water and sanitation for all ST/SC villages or hamlets.

g) Comprehensive social security with state contribution for health insurance and old age pension for SCs, STs, aged, disabled, widow and deserted women headed families.

h) Social audit of public and private health clinics by ward/*gram sabhas*.

Goal 4—Education for All : A Literate State by 2010

Education Assurance and Action Programme Linked to Livelihoods with the Following Components:

a) Preferential admission for children of BPL, *antyodaya* and migrant labour families and disabled children in *ashram*/residential schools.

b) Inclusion of additional education stream from the VIII standard, which incorporates necessary local livelihood, vocational and entrepreneurial skills in collaboration with relevant institutions. Provision of vocational guidance from VII standard and preferential admissions to institutes of higher learning for livelihood skill competencies and frontier and sunrise technologies.

c) Open schools cum community polytechnics in co-operation with industries are combining academic, technical and entrepreneurial education at cluster level, with forward linkages.

d) Provision for multiple entry points in academic/technical institutions with bridge examinations.

e) Progressive incentive scholarships for PTGs/STs/SCs with selection examinations at IV, VII and X standards and special incentives for girl children.

f) Qualitative improvement of teaching methods in healthy and safe school environment by linking teacher incentives in state-run schools with 100 per cent of success at IV, VII and X standards.

g) Extension of reservation to private aided/non-aided technical and professional training institutes, particularly for the first generation learners.

h) Special coaching for CET/MCET/CAT and entrance tests for IITs, IIMs, IAS, medical, and management institutes.

Goal 5—Empowerment and Governance

Strengthening Community Participation and Leadership in Local Self-Governance:

a) Extension of the provisions of Panchayats (Extension to Scheduled Areas) Act, 1996 to SC hamlets.

b) Capacity building for effective participation in *gram*/ward *sabhas*, awareness training on rights, policies, programmes, procedures, benefits and skill development for management of natural resource and development.

c) Capacity building of PR functionaries and GS members to implement PESA effectively.

d) Empowerment of women's *panchayats* through statutory entitlements.

e) Transfer financial and functional powers concerning development programmes to *panchayat samitis* and *gram panchayats*

f) Gender audit of all development/welfare programmes.

Goal 6—Administrative Reforms

Ensuring Implementation through Supportive Rules, Regulations and Procedures:

a) Adoption of cluster approach with beneficiary/*gram sabha* monitoring of functionaries and implementation of all welfare schemes, assisted by a district committee constituted of representatives of beneficiaries, NGOs and implementing bodies.

b) Continuation of Reservation Policy and extension of the reservation policy to the private sector. Preference should be given to first generation beneficiaries. Extend reservation provisions also to underprivileged among minorities.

c) Continuation of subsidies (with provision for inflation) for the social sectors.

d) Extension of the provisions of PCR to other marginalised groups like NTs, DNTs, underprivileged among minorities.

e) Administrative reorganisation of tribal areas into compact areas with Autonomous District Councils combined with reorganisation of Schedule V areas to merge MADA, mini-MADA and OTSP areas.

f) Reorganisation of administrative boundaries of all departments with a view to provide a unified structure.

g) Statutory empowerment of POs (ITDP) to implement decisions of GS, administer all schemes and take legal steps to enforce protection of SCs/STs/NTs/ DNTs.

h) Empower State Womens' Commission, State Human Rights Commission, State Minorities Commission, and State Commission for Persons with Disability with statutory powers to protect rights and facilitate development.

i) Maintain budgetary provisions for tribal development as per Sukthankar Committee recommendations with district-wise allocations in proportion to population. Introduce similar budgetary provision system for SC/minorities development.

j) Establishment of fast track courts to expedite disposal of land alienation, restoration, atrocities cases.

k) Participatory planning and implementation with beneficiaries and representative NGOs for welfare schemes.

Chapter 9

Handlooms and Handicrafts

Introduction

Maharashtra is known for its rich and exquisite traditional handloom textiles and handicrafts. Handwoven textiles like Paithani brocades that have existed for more than 2000 years in original patterns, and woven with the same techniques even today, are prized heirlooms and possessions for many. New techniques and products were introduced by different dynasties, which ruled the state from time to time. These have left an indelible impression on the history of handwoven textiles and handcrafted arts of Maharashtra. Handlooms and handicrafts have played a crucial role in the state economy in providing employment and income.

However, since the early 20th century, with the introduction of mills and import of power loom fabrics by the British, the expanding mill and power loom sector in the country poses a threat to the handloom sector. Despite these constraints, the handlooms and handicrafts sector is an important segment of the rural economy. The immediate and essential requirements are careful nurturing and a development plan for facing market competition.

The production of these articles is achieved through labour-oriented methods by artisans/master craftsmen whose expertise and skills are handed down from one generation to the next, creating a distinctive regional identity and characteristics unique to the region. There have been improvements in designs, to a certain extent in technique, and in the use of contemporary fibres.

The use of modern technology is absent. This sector uses labour-intensive production technique, with less capital requirements; and it is best suited for India and underdeveloped countries, where labour is abundant and surplus, and capital is scarce. The technique has the potential to generate massive employment and raise the standard of living of people living below the poverty line. The handlooms and handicrafts, being cottage industries, production is carried out from household premises or in the open.

Under various schemes of the central and state government, efforts have been made to construct common worksheds and common facility centres. As a production unit, a combination of land, labour, capital and entrepreneurial skills are required in order to manage the economic activity.

As the handlooms and handicrafts sector is totally decentralised, individual weavers and craftsmen face difficulties in procuring finance, raw material and in marketing. The wages of weavers are also so meagre that they are not in a position to invest in any kind of change or improvement either in technology or in product diversification. Thus, as they are unable to sell their products at a price in order to earn the minimum wages to survive, they are shifting to other occupations, with the exception of the weavers who produce specialised products, which do not face any threat from the power loom sector or those fabrics, which cannot be economically produced on power looms.

High quality handloom fabrics and handicrafts were exported to England before the process of industrialisation in India acquiring recognition the world over. Mughal emperors, feudal lords and aristocrats were the main patrons of handlooms and handicrafts artisans and craftsmen.

The Industrial Revolution in England in the 19th century, British rule and the abolition of feudal lords led to the decline in the patronage of handloom weaving, and consequently, the handloom industry declined in India as it was unable to compete with technology-driven units of production with regard to price and consistency of fabric quality.

Post-Independence Policy on Handlooms and Handicrafts

In the post-Independence era, despite the thrust on heavy and medium industries for economic development of the country, due importance was also given to village and cottage industries because of the large employment potential. Handlooms and handicrafts sectors were the major sectors in terms of providing employment next only to agriculture.

Generation of massive employment is best-suited under Indian conditions, where capital is scarce and technology imports are not affordable by the nation; hence, the handlooms and handicrafts sectors are also best suited to achieve planned objectives of 'self-sufficiency' and 'self-reliance'. Owing to geographical specialisation, exports are possible, provided the production cost is minimal and the price is competitive in terms of the market.

Traditionally, these handcrafted products were patronised by royalty, the Indian aristocracy and foreigners. The quality of goods produced was not available elsewhere. Being labour-intensive, production takes its time and as there is an absence of modern technology, mass production is not possible. It is assumed that the use of modern technology leads to mass production, as it invariably brings down the cost of production and it is market competitive because of its cost advantage, i.e. produced at the least cost. While these characteristics may or may not be present in the production of handicrafts, with labour being in abundance and cheaply available compared to the cost of labour in western countries, this industry needs special skills handed down from one generation to the next, which are 'hereditary in nature.'

The Central Government, in coordination with the state government, proposed a number of schemes, which included conversion to power looms, supply of improved appliances such as take-up motions, etc. to improve the quality of handloom fabrics. To provide newer designs and training for using improved appliances to the weavers who were living in remote areas with no knowledge of changing trends in the cities, Weavers' Service Centres were started by the Government of India in various areas of the country, beginning with Mumbai in 1956.

The use of these appliances, which were developed for the production of better quality and uniform fabrics were not adopted by the weavers because of both physical and mental blocks. However, in certain areas, for production of plain medium-count fabrics, semi-automatic looms were adopted for ensuring a superior quality of fabric. This chapter is divided into four sections as follows.

SECTION I

Development in Handlooms Sector Apex Development Bodies

Ministry of Textiles, Government of India

The allocation of funds for the development of these sectors and for implementation of various schemes of the Government of India is done by the Ministry of Textiles through the Director, Weavers' Service Centre, Mumbai and Deputy Director, Weavers' Service Centre, Nagpur.

Development Commissioner for Handlooms, Government of India

The Office of the Development Commissioner for Handlooms, with its headquarter at New Delhi, directs the research, development and training for the handlooms sector in Maharashtra through its western region office headed by the Director with branch office in Mumbai and other sub-offices in Aurangabad, Kolhapur and Nagpur.

Department of Textiles, Government of Maharashtra

The State Textile Department is, headed by the Secretary (Textiles) who is in charge for the development of the handloom sector and assists in achieving targets through the Director of handlooms, power looms and textiles with headquarters located at Nagpur, and regional offices headed by Regional Deputy Directors at Mumbai, Solapur, Aurangabad and Nagpur.

Department of Industries, Government of Maharashtra

The state government, through Secretary (Industries) is in charge of the development of the handicrafts sector and provides assistance to the artisans.

Maharashtra Small-Scale Industries Development Corporation (MSSIDC)

MSSIDC was established in 1962, initially as an agency for the supply of raw materials to SSI units and to also extend marketing assistance to these units in selling their products. The basic objective was to help small-scale industries to develop and grow to the fullest extent, enabling them to play their role towards the realisation of the national objective of accelerating the industrial development, generation of employment and income.

In the handlooms and handicrafts sector, MSSIDC had undertaken the project of the training centre at Paithan in 1973 and still continues with it. MSSIDC has played a vital role in the revival of Paithani sarees of Paithan and Himroo weaving of Aurangabad. MSSIDC has also actively participated in the area of handicrafts by arranging training programmes, sales and marketing.

MSSIDC organises the marketing of handicraft items and also arranges to conduct training programmes in Paithani-weaving at Paithan and Yeola for the revival of this craft.

Maharashtra State Handloom Corporation (MSHC), Nagpur

The Corporation was set up in 1972 with the objective of providing gainful employment to handloom weavers not covered by the cooperative sector, by supplying raw materials and procuring the fabrics produced by the weavers after paying them conversion charges. The corporation, by these methods, has tried to generate employment for the weavers. This indicates that the corporation is a socio-economic organisation. The corporation has 13 production centres and 23 depots for selling fabrics produced by the weavers.

Private sector artisans and weavers are looked after by Maharashtra State Handloom Corporation (MSHC), Government of Maharashtra Undertaking. The coordination between the Director of Handlooms and MSHC is secured by appointment of the Director of Handlooms, Government of Maharashtra, as Vice-Chairman of the MSHC. The Chairman of Maharashtra State Handloom Corporation is a non-official political appointment. The Managing Director of MSHC is the chief executive of the corporation. Both the offices, viz. Directorate of Handloom and MSHC are located at Nagpur.

Maharashtra State Handloom Cooperative Federation Ltd. (MAHATEX), Mumbai

MAHATEX is a marketing organisation. Its main activity is to procure handloom products from member-weaver societies and arrange for its marketing through retail sales, wholesale, and exhibition sales.

Government of Maharashtra Schemes

Various schemes and subsidies are available and organisations such as Khadi and Village Industries Board, Small-Scale Industries Development Corporation, Mahila Arthik Vikas Corporation, Mahatma Phule Development Corporation and Annabhau Sathe Corporation are the facilitators to industrial artisans/units/cooperative ventures/NGO initiatives, providing marketing, training facilities, loan, subsidy and credit. However, the achievements fall far short of expectations and expected levels of performance.

Handlooms in Maharashtra

Handloom weavers in Maharashtra exist in pockets scattered throughout the state. The uniqueness of handloom is its regional specialisation of a particular kind of product that is known by the name of the place from where it is woven, e.g. Nagpur *sarees*, Paithani *sarees*, Mahendargi *choli khans*, etc. As this industry is totally decentralised, efforts have been made to assemble artisans under a cooperative fold so that they can avail themselves of the various schemes of the central and state governments in an organised manner.

Maharashtra is one of the most industrialised state in the country today with the basic infrastructure, which can promote development. The state is divided into four regions, *viz.*, Konkan, Western Maharashtra, Vidarbha, and Marathwada with a total population of above 96 six million (Census, 2001). The ratio of rural to urban population is approximately 5:3. The total strength of handlooms and power looms in Maharashtra is given in Table 9.2 and 9.3..

In view of the changes in the economic environment through technological acceleration in industrialisation and to maintain a balance of employment even in rural areas, it is essential to tap every possible resource of production, income and employment generation.

The handlooms sector, with an employment ratio per handloom of 1:3, has great untapped potential to increase income levels as well as to sustain employment levels and skills by appropriate design inputs, technology upgradation, creating value added fabrics and systematic marketing directed at the elite of society, apart from producing low and medium-cost fabrics for the masses. A SWOT analysis of the handloom sector given in Table 9.1, underlines the strength, weaknesses, opportunities, and threats to this sector. Keeping in view the intense competition from

TABLE 9.1

A SWOT Analysis of Handloom Sector of Maharashtra

Strengths	*Weaknesses*
• Skill availability	• Low yield
• Availability of raw material	• Not much change in technology and design
• Low capital cost/investment	• Lack of marketing linkages
• Presence of government support	• Products of average quality
• Work carried out from home	• Varied level of artisans
• Desire to upgrade	• Survival on government subsidies
• Supply of short length fabrics to valued clients	• Absence of professionalism
Opportunities	*Threats*
• Exclusive handwoven fabrics have good domestic and export market	• Competition from power loom and machine-made products
• Possibility of more value addition	• Moving to other occupations
• Dovetailing with available government schemes	• Competition of similar products from other states
• Versatility in changing designs and texture with minimum investment	
• Product innovation and diversification	
• Trust and capacity-building fashion fabrics for middle class and elite	

Source: Ramaswamy and Namakumari, 2002.

the power loom and mill sector, diversified production of fashion and high-value products should be stressed upon through channels of marketing. State Handloom Corporation were created to assist the weavers outside the cooperative fold and to function as a business organisation in order to sustain the industry by creating better products to suit contemporary market needs and organised marketing. There are various schemes for development, training, social welfare and marketing, offered by the Government of India (Table 9.3) through the Government of Maharashtra for the benefit of handloom weavers in the state under the aegis of the State Apex Handloom Cooperative Society, State Handloom Development Corporation, and Non-Government Organisations (NGOs).

Tables 9.2 and 9.3 indicate the total number of workers engaged in power looms and handlooms sector are 192,534 in the year 2003, of which 115,059 are in power looms and 77,475 in handlooms. In terms of percentage, power looms are 77.4 per cent and handlooms are 22.6 per cent.

Year 2004 scenario of power looms and handlooms is such that number of power looms are 29,853 and handlooms are 32,792, both together total number is 62,645, whereas in 2003 the total number of power looms were 153,012 and handlooms 44,724. The total of power looms and handlooms together is 197,736 in 2003. There has been a sharp fall in the number of

TABLE 9.2

Production and Employment in Power Loom Sector in Maharashtra

Year	*No. of Power Looms*	*No. of Workers*	*Total Consumption Year 2003 (in Kgs.)*	*Total Production in Metres*
2003	153012	115059 (59.76)*	24883251	272324413
2004	29853	-	-	-

Note: *Figure in parenthesis indicate percentage of total workers 192534 engaged in handloom and power loom sectors in the year 2003.

Source: Director of Handlooms, Nagpur.

TABLE 9.3

Production and Employment in Handloom Sector in Maharashtra

Year	*No. of Handlooms*	*No. of Workers*	*Total Consumption Year 2004 (in Kgs.)*	*Total Production in Metres*
2003	44724	77475 (40.24)*	699176	5897104
2004	32792	-	-	-

Note: *Figure in parenthesis indicate percentage of total workers 192534 engaged in handloom and power loom sectors in the year 2003.

Source: Director of Handlooms, Nagpur.

TABLE 9.4

Government of India Schemes for Handloom Weavers

Name of the Scheme	*Implementing Agency*
Input Related Scheme	
Scheme for supply of yarn at Mill Gate Price	NHDC
Development Scheme	
Deen Dayal Hathkargha Protsahan Yojana	State Govt. Agencies
Welfare Schemes	
Workshed-cum-Housing Scheme	"
Thrift Fund Scheme for Handloom Weavers	"
Group Insurance Scheme for Handloom Weavers	"
New Insurance Scheme for Handloom Weavers	"
Health Package Scheme for Handloom Weavers	"
Marketing Schemes	
Scheme for Marketing of Handloom Products through Exhibitions and Fairs	"
Scheme for Setting up of Urban *Haats*	"
Development of Exportable Products and Marketing Scheme (DEPM)	"
Training	
Decentralised Training Programme for Handloom Weavers (DTP)	WSC

Source: Compendium of Handloom, Development Commissioner (Handloom), New Delhi.

power looms and handlooms in Maharashtra. Hence, the Tables 9.2 and 9.3 indicate declining trends for the sectors in the state.

The Handloom Weavers are Covered under Three Basic Segments in Maharashtra

- Private operators/master weavers with captive looms and weavers who work for them,
- weavers under cooperative fold,
- handloom corporation covering the weavers outside cooperative fold.

The cooperative movement was started with the intention to free individual weavers from the clutches of master weavers and middlemen who consumed the higher proportion of the profit, thus reducing the weavers to poverty. The present status of handloom weavers, and the existing societies (as on March 2004) is given in Table 9.5.

Unfortunately, the cooperative system has suffered because of the intense competition from power loom and mill sector, except for specialised or value added products like the *Paithani*, top *padar, and tussar* sarees and dress materials, wall hangings and *dhurries,* which are uneconomical to produce by power looms. This is because the markets for the products in the handloom sector by private producers, power loom producers and foreign producers are distinctively different in terms of quality and customer preferences.

According to the Director Handloom, Power loom and Textiles, Government of Maharashtra, Nagpur, cloth produced by power looms is 25-40 per cent cheaper compared to handloom products. However, in spite of such competition, handlooms will survive because of the following advantages:

- Handloom cloth is eco-friendly.
- Handloom has great employment potential.
- It has immense foreign exchange potential.
- It has local demand.

Product Range

- Paithani *saree*
- Nagpur *saree*
- Solapur top *Padar saree*
- Pune *saree*
- Vidarbha *tussar saree* and dress material

TABLE 9.5

District-wise Weavers and Handloom Cooperative Societies in Maharashtra in 2000 and 2004

Districts	*Number of Handloom Weavers as on March 2000*	*Number of Handloom Weavers as on March 2004*	*Percentage of Handloom Weavers in Each District in the Year 2000*	*Percentage of Handloom Weavers in Each District in Year 2004*	*Number of Co-op Societies as on March 2000*	*Number of Co-op Societies as on March 2004*	*Percentage of Societies*	
							In 2000	*In 2004*
Mumbai	451	2303	0.58	1.81	5	8	0.64	1.16
Thane	0	-	0	-	-	-	-	-
Raigadh	0	-	0	-	-	-	-	-
Sindhudurg	65	-	.08	-	-	-	-	-
Ratnagiri	0	-	0	-	-	-	-	-
Nashik	1522	4199	1.96	3.30	7	6	0.90	0.87
Dhule	1010	277	1.30	0.22	5	3	0.64	0.43
Jalgaon	194	634	0.25	0.50	4	4	0.51	0.58
Ahmednagar	89	1490	0.11	1.15	10	13	1.28	1.89
Pune	733	86	0.94	0.60	6	1	0.76	0.15
Satara	474	340	0.61	0.27	1	2	0.12	0.29
Sangli	848	501	1.09	0.39	4	3	0.51	0.43
Solapur	15241	13443	19.67	10.55	175	173	22.40	25.10
Kolhapur	258	1986	0.33	1.56	70	14	8.96	2.03
Aurangabad	707	752	0.91	0.55	2	4	2.25	0.58
Jalna	20	1348	0.03	1.06	-	1	-	0.15
Parbhani	142	376	0.18	0.29	1	1	0.12	0.15
Beed	388	563	0.50	0.44	18	15	2.30	2.17
Nanded	1309	54725	1.69	43.06	24	23	3.07	3.33
Osmanabad	585	188	0.76	0.14	1	1	0.12	0.15
Latur	719	380	0.92	0.30	2	1	0.25	0.15
Buldhana	48	72	0.06	0.05	1	1	0.12	0.43
Akola	908	215	1.17	0.17	3	3	0.38	0.72
Amravati	2228	1054	2.88	0.82	6	5	0.76	-
Yavatmal	78	-	0.20	-	-	-	-	-
Wardha	332	544	0.43	0.43	7	4	0.90	-
Nagpur	40598	38935	52.40	30.63	392	386	50.90	56.02
Bhandara	5400	1813	7.0	1.42	29	12	3.81	1.74
Chandrapur	1124	870	1.45	0.65	5	5	0.64	0.75
Gadchiroli	2004	-	2.60	-	3	-	0.38	
Total	**77475**	**127094**	**100.00**	**100.00**	**781.00**	**689.00**	**100.00**	**100.00**

Source: Weavers' Service Centre, 2004.

- Solapur *Chadar*
- Bed covers and towels
- Furnishings
- *Dhurries* and carpets
- Wall hangings.

Table 9.5 indicates that the total number of Handloom Cooperative Societies in Maharashtra in 2000 was 781 which declined to 689 in 2004.

Nanded registered an increase in total number of weavers in 2004 to 54,725 against 1,309 total number of weavers in 2000. Nanded has 23 Cooperative Handloom Societies in 2004 as against 24 in the year 2000. The percentage was 3.07 and 3.33 in 2000 and 2004 respectively in Maharashtra.

Nagpur is the highest in terms of number of handloom weavers, which was 40,598 in the year 2000 and declined to 38,935 in the year 2004. The percentage of weavers was 52.40 in the year 2000 which declined to 30.63 in the year 2004. Nagpur is the first in Maharashtra state with highest number of cooperative handloom societies, 392 cooperative Societies in the year 2000 against 386 cooperative Societies in the year 2004. In terms of concentration of societies, Nagpur is the first in Maharashtra state registering 50.90 per cent cooperative handloom societies in the year 2000 and 56.02 per cent in the year 2004. Solapur is having second largest concentration of handloom weavers with 15,241 weavers in 2000 against 13,443 weavers in 2004 and percentage of handloom weavers was 19.67 in 2000 against 10.55 in 2004. Solapur also represents second highest number of cooperative societies in Maharashtra state which was 175 in 2000. It declined to 173 in 2004 and the percentage of societies was 22.40 in 2000 against 25.10 in 2004.

Following reasons are identified for concentration of handloom weavers and handloom cooperatives in Nagpur and Solapur:

- historical—since time immemorial,
- market is well developed at Nagpur and Solapur since time immemorial,
- availability of raw materials and prevalence of master weavers at Nagpur and Solapur is since time immemorial,
- Capacity of master weavers to hold on in profession at Nagpur and Solapur is extremely high,
- absence of above reasons at other districts in Maharashtra might explain the scanty distribution of handloom weavers in Maharashtra.

Problems Faced by Handloom Cooperative Sector

- Handloom cooperatives are primary cooperatives affiliated with the Assistant Registrar of Cooperative Societies and Deputy Registrar of Cooperative Societies, which function under several constraints and officials, find little time to devote to the development of the handloom sector.
- Members of handloom cooperatives are illiterate and unable to comprehend the schemes and the projects and its benefits; therefore, they are not able to implement them in letter and spirit in the cooperative sector. There is a need to train members of cooperative societies in managing them effectively.
- Power loom cloth is much more in demand in the market and is cheaper resulting in accumulated stocks leading to high inventories (Ref: Write up from MAHATEX, Mumbai and Handloom Development Corporation, Nagpur).
- Turnover in handloom is less compared to power loom fabric. Due to heavy inventories and no sales, cooperative handloom societies are economically crippled with no resources to buy raw materials and are consequently unable to offer work to weavers. Even Handloom Cooperatives are facing problems due to heavy losses. The losses are for the following reasons:
- Slump in the textile industry, leading to low demand for products of the corporation.
- Corporation has huge inventories.
- High rate of interest on the borrowed funds and quality of goods is poor.
- High cost of production and high establishment cost.
- Lack of professionalism in day-to-day functioning.

Current Issues and Concerns of Handloom Weavers

- Lack of consistent work and satisfactory wages. Children of handloom weavers do not opt for the weaving profession.
- Languishing traditional art, migration of weavers to non-craft activities.
- Lack of trust building, planned training with follow-up development, monitoring and support continuity.
- Poor infrastructure and support in design, technology and marketing.
- Low productivity and inconsistent quality.

SECTION II

Handicrafts in Maharashtra

Handicrafts are perhaps the oldest craft practised from the times of ancient civilisation since human beings started making utility tools. This sector is embedded in the socio-economic and cultural milieu of India. Handicrafts are 'skill-specific' and 'master craftsmen-specific'. Production of handicrafts is based on hereditary skills with its roots in caste-based occupations and is invariably economically and socially

TABLE 9.6

District-wise Distribution of Handicrafts in Maharashtra

Name of Craft	*Craft Pockets*
Kolhapuri *Chappals*	Kolhapur, Rashiwade, Sangrul, Jath, Malegaon, Bahireshwar, Miraj, Mandre, Maharashtra, Bazar, Bhogaon, Phanhala, Mumbai.
Hand Block Printed Textiles	Saoner, Sukhlibai, Pune, Aurangabad, Savergaon, Katol, Wardha, Mumbai, Kolhapur, Amalner.
Artistic Textiles/*Paithani/saree* weaving	Paithan, Yeola, Pune, Ahmednagar, Nagpur; Umerd, Bhivapur, Panani, Solapur, Sangli, Aurangabad, Maindargi.
Handmade *Chindi Dhurry*/Cotton *Dhurries/Punja Achalpur Akot*, Amravati, *Peth, Dhurry.*	Nagpur, Kamptee, Pratapgaon, Nandgaon, Chakur, Mumbai, Belapur, Khapa, Kandhar, Pilkhod, Kasoda, Parlhi, Dharangaon, Dhule, Nimgul, Mhasadi, Varesh, Mahergaon.
Silver Jewellery	Kolhapur, Hupari, Sangli, Nashik, Rendal, Pattankodoli, Pune, Mumbai, Thane.
Imitation Jewellery/Bead	Kolhapur, Hupari, Mumbai, Jewellery, Akola, Nagpur, Khamgaon, Amravati, Chandrapur, Buldhana, Chalisgaon, Kaij Aurangabad, Nanded, Thane, Saoner.
Silver Artware	Kolhapur, Nashik, Pune.
Terracotta/Pottery/Ceramics	Nagpur, Bhadravati, Kolhapur, Ajara, Sawantwadi, Pen, Khupire, Raigadh, Pune, Mumbai, Thane, Perth, Chikhali, Mehkar, Shegaon, Khamgaon, Darawah, Kalamb, Yavatmal, Anjangaon, Piroda, Mohadi, Jalna, Aurangabad, Hingoli.
Wood Carving and Lacqureware Toy	Kolhapur, Sawantwadi, Khed, Pune, Pen, Akhot, Ratnagiri, Gadchiroli, Umerd, Nagpur, Vanvas, Bhandara, Jalna, Solapur, Aurangabad, Hingoli, Daulatabad, Resigaon, Tanda, Ahmednagar, Badanpur, Paithani, Parbhani, Patoda, Pathari, Waithan.
Brass Sheet Work	Pune, Kolhapur, Tarapur, Nashik, Mumbai.
Copper Artware/Metalware	Pune, Thane, Murbad, Ambarnath, Mumbai, Buldhana Chitaroli, Warora, Chandrapur, Bhamragarh, Kurkheda, Jalgaon, Loni, Mardi, Parali, Tuljapur.
Oxidised Silver Artware	Kolhapur, Hupari.
Bidriware	Aurangabad.
Lace/Embroidery/Patch	Nagpur, Amravati, Kondhani, Hinganghat, Kolhapur, Pune, Satara, Ratnagiri, Sangli, Mumbai, Nashik, Jalgaon, Bead, Kamptee, Ichalkaranji, Aurangabad, Umred, Yerkheda, Andhalgaon, Chandrapur, Pusa-Gondi, Warora, Nandugra, Kerwadi, Chalisgaon, Rohini, Longe, Patna, Bhatpur, Parbhani, Paithan, Dharangaon.
Cane and Bamboo	Mul Ballarpur, Bhadrava, Nagpur, Karjat, Hinganghat, Wardha, Gadchiroli, Chandrapur, Sangli, Garghoti, Solapur, Ghoti, Jalna, Aurangabad, Hingoli, Nanded, Vaijapur, Kolhapur.
Dolls and Soft Toys	Nagpur, Akot, Chandrapur, Amravati, Akola, Kolhapur, Pune, Mumbai, Nashik, Ratnagiri, Aurangabad, Ahmednagar, Parbhani, Yavatmal.
Leather Artware	Nagpur, Miraj, Mumbai.
Paper Mâché and Plaster of Paris	Nagpur, Akot, Chandrapur, Yavatmal, Amravati, Kolhapur, Pen, Nashik, Ratnagiri, Koregaon, Mumbai, Sawantwadi, Kolegaon, Aurangabad, Kannad, Sillod, Nasirabad, Raver, Wasmat, Nagar, Jalna.
Warli Painting/*Chitrakathai*	Ganjad, Pinguli, Aurangabad Paintings/Ajantha Paintings.
Lac Bangles	Achalpur, Khamgaon, Akola, Aurangabad, Latur, Jalna, Dhule, Pachora.
Musical Instruments	Miraj, Mumbai, Nashik, Udgir, Sangamaeshwar, Pandharpur, Parbhani, Ahmednagar, Aurangabad, Ranisawargaon, Bhodne.
Carpet/*Dhurries*	Nagpur, Pratapgarh.
Cotton Wall Hangings	Maindagi, Solapur.
Sisal Fibre	Ahmednagar, Aurangabad.

Source: State Folder (Maharashtra) Office of the Development Commissioner, Handicrafts, Mumbai.

vulnerable. Irrespective of raw material used in the making of an article, these can be classified into two groups:

a) Utility articles like utensils, furniture, bags, etc. which are an essential part of our daily life.

b) Artifacts or decorative articles, which are used by practically every household for decoration.

Handicraft products are made by using the skill of the artisans varying with their ability of material handling capacity without much use of technology and is reflected in each piece they create. The quality and quantity of the product also depend on the craftsmen's ability and acumen. Artisans work mostly in their homes and at times in small workshops of master craftsmen. The distribution of handicrafts in Maharashtra is given in Table 9.6.

Production in this sector is unorganised, resulting in the absence of an institutional framework for marketing and support activities.

Handicrafts in Private or Cooperative Sectors

Handicrafts are 'skill-specific' and 'master craftsman-specific'; training is imparted only through master craftsmen and centres run by the state and Central Government agencies under various schemes. The key input is a 'master-trainer' who is identified as a 'master-craftsman', who is not required to be qualified in terms of school and college degrees but possesses hereditary skills in the production of handicraft goods. Master-craftsmen train artisans. These handicrafts have local and international markets and export potential.

Non-Government Organisations (NGOs)

In the absence of a corporation for the development of handicrafts, schemes and subsidies are offered by the Government, and NGOs are free to take initiatives in the sector. According to the Planning Commission, Government of India, there were 3,000 NGOs in India in 1999. These are charity organisations registered under the Charities Act, Trust Act and Societies Act. The wealthy contribute to charity *via* NGOs as tax concessions are available to those donating to NGOs. The Government of India and especially the finance department and some activists demand accountability and transparency in affairs of NGOs. NGOs have created a 'Credibility Alliance Rating Agency' since NGOs receive tax benefits along with donors to avoid collusion between NGOs and donors. Their assessment is expected to be on the basis of benefits offered to artisans/beneficiaries. There are several private agencies and IIM management professionals who have entered into NGO activities as foreign funds are also available for their initiatives. The lifestyle difference between NGO professionals and artisans is glaring and most of them are engaged in social work/welfare work/ charity work with organisational back up in the form of NGOs. The NGOs are supposed to create and set up self-help groups (SHG) of artisans but this objective has not been met by the NGOs adequately. Hence, the primary data collected for this project indicated that the formation of self-help groups must be left with the artisans themselves. The data revealed that NGOs were assigned funds to build facilitation centres, where artisans could interact with master craftsmen and provide training to new artisans but the NGOs have failed in this task.

Micro-credit Financing for Handicrafts Sector

National Bank for Agriculture and Rural Development (NABARD)

NABARD is a national level financial bank with its headquarters at Mumbai, designed to regulate credit/ financial facilities/subsidies, etc., for the promotion and development of agriculture, SSI, cottage and village industries, handicrafts and other allied activities in rural areas. It supervises national level cooperative structures in terms of credit and arranges for refinance to cooperative institutes, *khadi* and village industries and regional rural banks. The chief beneficiaries are the agriculture and non-agriculture sectors. Figure 9.1 presents micro-credit percentages for two sectors. NABARD also provides refinance to institutions for their lending activities in rural areas as well as loans to the state government for the creation of rural infrastructure.

FIGURE 9.1

Micro-credit Percentage for Agriculture and Non-agriculture Sectors

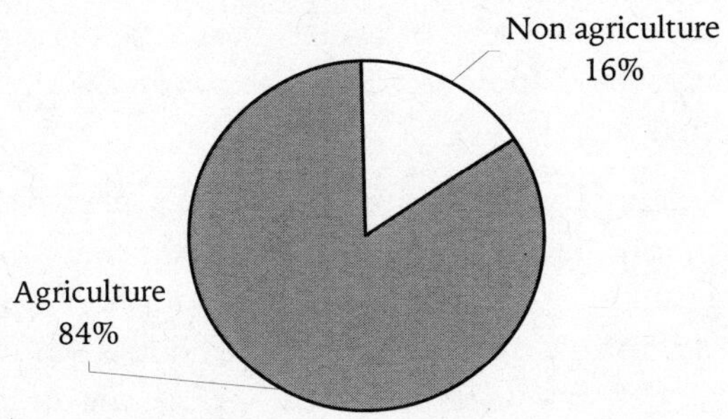

Source: Economic Research Publications 2001-2002, NABARD.

Handlooms and Handicrafts sectors come under the non-agriculture sector. Budget allocated to the handicrafts sector is 2 per cent, and *khadi* and village industries have an allocation of 10 per cent.

Handicrafts artisans are scattered all over the state and Government of India branch offices at Aurangabad, Kolhapur, Nagpur assist in the development of handicraft sector in Maharashtra. MSSIDC is not exclusively into handicraft sector.

SECTION III

Development Plan

With the changing times, the consumer's lifestyle and tastes are undergoing rapid changes. Need-base and secondary needs like buying an additional beautiful *saree* or dress, an extra bed cover, an additional set of linen or a few more pieces of handcrafted artefacts to be proudly displayed are emerging trends. Today, with extensive media exposure, the discerning customer is conscious about quality, value for the money spent and buys the best affordable product. Unfortunately, in the handlooms and handicrafts sector, this change has not kept pace with changing times. However, there are certain traditionally crafted articles, which still enjoy public demand having survived the vagaries of time because of the beauty and richness fashioned by exclusive craftsmanship. While working on these products, unique selling proposition is that the intrinsic aesthetic value is not diluted be it a handloom or a handicraft product. All this would require a carefully worked out development plan, promotional activities and a regulated marketing environment for buying.

Product Diversification and Development

This is a major thrust area because survival of handlooms is based on its inherent qualities, asthetics and it cannot be produced on power-operated machines. The specific requirement of a quality and fabric can only be delivered by handlooms. The areas of development are specified below:

- Developing value added products as per consumer demand based on continuous market surveys conducted periodically. Consumer demand for handloom and handicraft products must be separately assessed every year before the beginning of the year by government departments concerned and accordingly artisans plan production. It is necessary to involve professional management institutes in market survey and marketing exercises.
- Production of fashion fabrics by converting them into high-value garments. The government agencies have to seek coordination between artisans and fashion designers on continuous basis.
- Diversification of present production of household linens, furnishings into quality household linen and furnishings. The government agencies have to seek coordination between artisans and fashion designers on continuous basis.
- By bringing continuous change in design and colour. The government agencies have to seek coordination between artisans and fashion designers on continuous basis.
- Improved colour fastness is needed. The government agencies have to seek coordination between artisans and fashion designers on continuous basis.
- Revival of traditional *sarees,* maintaining its richness of workmanship and design. The government agencies have to seek coordination between artisans and fashion designers on a continuous basis.

Upgrading Entrepreneurial Skills of Artisans

- A massive training programme has to be undertaken to develop entrepreneurial skills of the artisans so that they are self-sufficient in the profession.
- This is one of the oldest industries in the country and has remained significant in the 21st century. Twenty-first century development plan is incomplete without the application of latest entrepreneurial and marketing skills. The handloom sector be given 'production priority' and assured market as in the past.
- Artisans, government agencies and private initiatives have to pay more attention to the changes to be brought about in the process of production and marketing. Research and Development input should be given top priority. Marketing is managed by managing quality of production and price is an important factor in consumers' decision to buy goods. The traditional philosophy that brand name, aesthetics and local specialisation would bring consumers to them is not valid in 21st century as the tastes and preferences of consumers have undergone radical changes due to global competition.
- Global competitive environment is based on the 'marketing concept', which not only begins and ends with the consumer but marketing thrust is totally 'consumer-oriented' based on four pillars *viz.*
    - Understanding the needs of the target market.
    - Translating needs into meaningful products and services that fulfil them.
    - Deliver the same to the consumer.
    - Making a profit for survival and future growth at the level of break-even point.

- Entrepreneurship training programmes for artisans are encouraged by the Development Commissioner for Handicrafts, Government of India, similar initiative by Maharashtra Government is necessary component of Maharashtra Development Plan.

Development of Showrooms

The showroom need not be like departmental stores but it should be a showcase where the beauty, value and aesthetics of each unique piece is available under one roof for consumer selection. Setting up few showrooms with the right assortment of products, ambience and environment at convenient location is appropriate for a city of Mumbai as it serves domestic and international clients. Purchasing power of consumer at a place like Mumbai is extremely good, this opportunity could be exploited by offering the best of handlooms and handicrafts of Maharashtra in the right ambience.

Revamping of Corporations into Business Organisations

Most corporations under the state government are running into losses, it is essential to strengthen and revamp them into business organisations manned by professionals with a clear vision of what to produce, where to produce and where to market the products. This requires a strategic planning and developmental thrust.

The government officials from the state cadres, who are in direct contact with artisans, must be well versed to develop awareness and utilisation of various schemes available for the artisans in the handlooms and handicrafts sector. They must have detailed knowledge about nitty-grittys of the scheme. Empowering the artisans is going to happen only when the officials are knowledge-based and well-informed.

One Window Clearance of the Projects Submitted by the Artisans

The problems faced by artisans relate to delays in sanction of assistance for their projects under the various schemes, and therefore, one window clearance should be set up to overcome such problems.

Coordination between Various Government Departments

The state departments involved in the development of artisans are listed below:

- Maharashtra State Handloom Corporation (MSHC), Nagpur,
- Maharashtra State Handloom Cooperative Federation Ltd. (MAHATEX),
- Development Commissioner for Handicrafts, Government of India, Regional Director, Handicrafts, Western Region,
- Maharashtra Small-Scale Industries Development Corporation (MSSIDC),
- District Project Officers/Project Officers for Tribal Development,
- Financial institutions like banks, National Bank for Agriculture and Rural Development (NABARD),
- The corporations designed for the development of the scheduled castes and scheduled tribes, other backward classes,
- Ministry of Textiles, Government of India,
- Department of Textiles, Government of Maharashtra, and
- Khadi and Village Industries Commissions.

All the above functionaries have same objective to develop handlooms and handicrafts sector, but there is a lack of coordination between them as they function as individual entities. They must draw a comprehensive plan together and implement it so that results in terms of developments are visible. It is essential that the officials of various departments meet together and work hand-in-hand at village-level, block-level, district-level, divisional-level, state-level and at the level of Government of India.

Tapping the Export Market

The private initiatives in the handlooms and handicrafts sector are highly successful in tapping the export potentials, but the government departments have not been successful in tapping the export market. It is evident that a beginning is made to showcase for the first time handloom and handicrafts products in Dubai Exhibition in 2004. Similar exercises are required to tap export market for the products and artisans. There are some foreign universities, such as Illinois Institute of Technology, Chicago and Massachusetts Institute of Technology, Boston, devoted to Research and Development of Technology in Handlooms and Handicrafts Sector. Coordination with such organisations is necessary. Government of Maharashtra may set up a corpus for undertaking the work of coordination with foreign universities and artisans as UNDP definition of handlooms and handicrafts accepts technological upgradation. A study should be conducted on the state-of-art on these sectors in foreign countries and to have buy back arrangement for goods produced by Maharashtra artisans. The benefits of export promotion council for handicrafts are confined to private sector agencies and steps should be taken to tap this export potential by the government functionaries. Maharashtra government should take steps in modifying the pattern of 'Kolhapuri Chappal' for export market. 'Kolhapuri Chappals' need to be more soft and fashionable for export market. A state-level export council should be set up for handicraft exports e.g. *Sawantwadi* and other artisans from Maharashtra.

Utilisation of the Services of Weavers' Service Centres, Handicrafts Marketing and Service Extension Centres

There are two Weavers' Service Centres under Development Commissioner for Handlooms, Ministry of Textiles, Government of India, in Maharashtra, one at Mumbai and the other at Nagpur, which are equipped to meet the requirements of training, product development and designs for developing handloom textiles in a more need-based manner. Similarly, the Office of the Development Commissioner for Handicrafts, Ministry of Textiles, Government of India with its regional office at Mumbai has its marketing and services extension centres at Aurangabad, Nagpur and Kolhapur. Their services can be utilised for the development of handicrafts sector in the state as it is exclusively for that activity.

The various schemes for development of handlooms and handicrafts sectors meant for improving the living conditions of the artisans, must be tapped in right earnest to make both these industries sustainable and subsidy-free.

Organising Exhibitions and Festivals and Promoting Advertising

The corporations, departments and commissions together must organise exhibitions, festivals etc., preferably at local, national and international levels so that the market is available to the products produced by the artisans of the handlooms and handicrafts in the state.

Organising Exhibitions in Foreign Countries

Frequent exhibitions for handlooms and handicrafts products by the state must be held in foreign countries to tap export market. A beginning is made in this direction by organising a festival in Dubai, similar initiatives go a long way to tap international market.

Awareness of brands like MAHATEX and Indrayani be enhanced and new brands be introduced for the state of Maharashtra by the government agencies.

Advertising Campaigns through Net

Since the professional channels are expensive, the cheapest is net advertising. Net advertising can reach global market, which must be utilised for the benefit of the sector. A comprehensive website development is necessary for this sector.

Apex Body and Self-help Groups

There is need for formation of an apex body and Self-help groups formed by artisans. Apex bodies like Co-optex in Andhra Pradesh, Karnataka, and Tamil Nadu are necessary for the state of Maharashtra.

Provision of common facility centres at district level or convenient places is required as they provide interaction and training between master craftsmen and new artisans.

Audit and accounts are not maintained by the artisans and for the same, training be provided by the government functionaries to them.

Design specialists are available with the Development Commissioner of Handicrafts. Specialists from Indian Institutes of Technology, foreign universities are also available. Government bodies must provide for collaboration between artisans and technologists to give boost to this sector.

Post-liberalisation Effects

Private operators in handicrafts are able to export through Export Promotion Council. Artisans from Maharashtra should be organised by government agencies for export purpose.

Organised Production

Handicrafts sector is totally unorganised in Maharashtra and government agencies should take care of this sector to convert it into well organised sector or assign this task to some interested management institutes.

Statistical data and economics related to handlooms and handicrafts are not available for the state, and therefore, policy and strategy forecast for the sector are not possible. Continuous, reliable and authentic data generation is required for development of this sector.

Handicraft Sector

- There is a need for setting up of a Board for handicrafts development for Maharashtra.
- Artisans cannot handle big orders due to their limitations like illiteracy and small size. Hence, management training programmes for artisans to equip them with basic skills need to be organised by the state.
- Cooperative societies, self-help groups in handicrafts should be set up with the help of government agencies.
- Enhancement of micro-credit facility and budget for the development of this sector is required.
- Inadequacy of training inputs and design specialists in handicrafts sector has restricted its growth, hence, it is to be rectified.
- Common facility centres are very few and not effective and they have to be geared up to meet the need of employment generation.
- Ambedkar Hastkala Vikas Scheme, 2003 is a comprehensive scheme and artisans can benefit from this, provided awareness and utilisation of schemes by artisans is ensured by government agencies.

Field Visits Observations

- The relationship between artisans and officials of government agencies is strained and inter-personal relations among officials are not smooth. This is leading to 'gaps' and 'barriers' in the implementation of the schemes and procedures.
- Training provided to artisans is restricted to few artisans and mass training for employment generation is necessary to justify need for development of this sector.

Brands

- MAHATEX, Indrayani, Paithani brands exist in handloom sector in Maharashtra state, similarly brands like 'Kolhapuri Chappals' are well received in export market besides existing brand enhancement and there is scope for creation of new brands in handicraft sector. Undertaking campaigns, exhibitions, festivals fairs, etc. have to be ensured for development of this sector.
- Formation of atleast 150 retail outlets in Mumbai to sell all products at one place *viz,* handlooms and handicrafts produced in Maharashtra state is needed.
- Handloom Textile Zones, at Nagpur, Solapur and Wardha, and Handicraft Zones at Districts/divisions, having concentration of handicrafts, should be given priority.
- Government agencies, cooperatives, NGOs and artisans operating in this sector lack professionalism and training in communication and managerial skills, etc. and the same be introduced to them with the help of interested prestigious management institutions.
- Entrepreneurial skills of the artisans should be developed through specially designed programmes, on priority basis, involving management institutions.
- Handlooms and handicrafts products should be moved from lower-end to upper-end market through niche marketing.
- Intellectual property rights should be protected for artisans *viz., Paithani* and other products and handicrafts artisans where skills are on the verge of extinction.
- Minority Commission's Report about minorities' earnings indicates that compared to general population in similar activities, Muslims earn less than Christians and Jains. The FAO report states that SC and ST face worst fate and their participation in common facility centres is not ensured. Therefore, efforts should be made to have common facility centres for SC/ST artisans and minority artisans.

SECTION IV

Conclusion

Maharashtra, a highly industrialised state in India, with its rich cultural heritage and natural beauty, boasts traditional age-old handwoven and handcrafted articles along with the availability of most advanced technology. Handlooms and handicrafts have the potential to provide gainful employment to thousands of weavers and craftsmen with a minimum financial investment. Developing and exploiting these inherent skills in producing consumer-oriented merchandise, with design and quality intervention, and marketing in the right environment, would better sustain this industry. The tradition and richness of the hand-made textiles and handicrafts must survive along with technological advancements in order to bring an economic balance and maintain job opportunities in rural areas. Mumbai, with about 12 million people, is itself a big market. It is, therefore, imperative to sustain this industry with careful nurturing and create an awareness for appreciation of the value of our traditions in future generations.

Chapter 10

Governance

Introduction

'Good Governance' has become the buzzword and magic recipe for development. Although the concept of good governance is not something new, it has, of late, come to signify some sort of panacea to root out the ills of authoritative or corrupt administration. It has entered into political and academic parlance as the World Bank and other aid providing agencies have made it a part of precondition for economic aid or for a process of reform qualifying for such aid. According to the World Bank, good governance is epitomised by predictable, open and enlightened policy making, a bureaucracy imbued with a professional ethos acting in the furtherance of the public good, the rule of law, transparent processes, and a strong civil society participating in public affairs (World Bank, 1994). Good governance is therefore, the basic building block for a cluster of government policies necessary for ensuring sustainable human development. Only when there is an environment of transparency in policy formulation, a culture of accountability among government officials, and stakeholder participation in decision making, can one expect an overall development and visible change. Governments can no longer afford to support rigid, bureaucratic, reactive, rules driven administrative organisations, rather today's administrative system ought to be flexible, consultative, result-oriented and proactive, at the same time encouraging and supporting creativity and innovation from the bottom to the top in order to govern and provide services to the citizens at large.

The Significance of Governance

Historically, Maharashtra has been India's most industrialised state. It is also perceived to be one of the country's best-administered states, with the state capital, Mumbai, being the financial and commercial capital of the country. But unfortunately, in spite of being India's fastest growing and the most industrialised state, Maharashtra has not been able to establish an overall development record. While dealing with the targets and achievements of its economic goals, somehow the underprivileged sections of the community got neglected as the trickle-down theory did not work up to the expectations. Access to opportunities in education, employment and health care did not reach the poorer sections of the society. The myopic vision and the reluctance to undertake long term planning led to the oversight of the fact that however, high the economic growth, it is not necessarily a sufficient condition for better human development. The pattern of growth, its employment generating capability, its human and social dimension, its ability to create competitive industries and skills are equally important.

There is more to translating growth into development and this has to do with the governance and institutional reforms. The United Nations Development Programme (UNDP) has been at the forefront of the growing international consensus that good governance and sustainable human development are indivisible. According to the UNDP's (2003) report, India is ranked 127 in a list of 175 countries, in the Human Development Index (HDI), which is a simple summary measure of three dimensions of the human development concept: living a long and healthy life, being educated and having a decent standard of living.

As per the National Human Development Report 2001, Maharashtra ranked fourth among the 15 major states in HDI. The Government of Maharashtra has since realised the challenges it faces on the human development front.

It brought out the Maharashtra Human Development Report (MHDR) in June 2002 and ensured that the human development agenda comes to the forefront of the state's vision for the future and its development priorities. This underscores an important reality that economic growth is a means to sustainable human development and not an end in itself. UNDP defines human development as expanding the choices for all people in society. This means that men and women—particularly the poor and vulnerable—are at the centre of the development process. This ensures the creation of an enabling environment in which all can enjoy long, healthy and creative lives. For example, countries that do well when ranked by per capita income often slip down the ladder when ranked by the human development index. A country's human development index speaks of its success in removing deprivation and creating conditions conducive to meeting its basic social needs. Brenda Gael McSweeney, at the launch of the MHDR quoted a fellow member "... effective governance is central to human development" (McSweeney, 2002). It follows that developing the capacity for good governance should be—the primary way to eliminate poverty. 'Good governance' puts people into the centre of development. 'Where people grow, profits grow', this well-tried business rule is applicable to development policy as well. Where there is long-term investment in people's health and education, where both men and women, regardless of their social status, have access to the necessary means of production, extension and credits, they can take their fate in their own hands and make use of opportunities to improve their quality of life. The role of what in economic parlance are called social sectors is considered crucial in this regard. Social sector activities are considered as those that emphasise the improvement of quality of life by offering education, employment and health facility to that part of the population, which is less privileged and suffers from malnutrition, with high mortality rates and diseases, low income and lack of education.

Relevance of Governance to Maharashtra

The inability of Maharashtra to translate an above average economic growth into visible development and poverty reduction on the scale achieved by the Southeast Asian economies with a similar growth record reveals that growth does not always lead to development if governance is poor. Maharashtra had a growth rate of 7.3 per cent during the period 1985-2001, marginally overtaking Malaysia's 7 per cent (1981-1996) and just below Singapore's average growth of 7.8 per cent for the same period of time. But at the end of the period, Malaysia had a per capita gross domestic product of over US$ 3,000, while Maharashtra had less than a third of that. In Malaysia, just about 15 per cent of the population was below the poverty line; in Maharashtra, the ratio was almost double to that. (Baru, 2002). The *raison d'être* being that the Malaysian government brought about changes in structure, procedures and processes, which brought about visible changes in its governance. In Malaysia, public sector agencies had obtained ISO 9000 certification for their services and the government was expected to serve as a regulator rather than service provider. A similar model has been suggested and worked out for Maharashtra. The International Consultancy firm McKinsey has in its 10 year development plan for Mumbai recommended that corporate management techniques be adopted with a designated CEO vested with authority for the city's overall development. When implemented, Mumbai can compete with Kaula Lampur as a global city (*Times of India*, (Mumbai) July16, 2003).

It is a paradox that, in spite of having the highest per capita income in the country, Maharashtra's economic growth has tumbled since the mid-nineties. While growth has declined for India as a whole, the sharpest decline, among 14 major states, has been in Maharashtra. The average annual growth rate fell from 7.8 per cent (the average over 1984-85 to 1994-95) to 5.3 per cent (over 1995-96 to 1999-00) and according to many estimates is now less than 3 per cent.

Although Maharashtra has the highest per capita income in the country, the human development indicators shown in Table 10.1 reveal that the state's performance in the social sector is pretty disappointing. Around 50 per cent of its rural population do not still have easy access to drinking water and the coverage of sanitation facility is also poor. Till 1997, only 6 lakh families (6.25 per cent of a total of 96 lakh rural families) had toilet facilities. Total coverage of rural sanitation in the state has now risen from 15 per cent to 20 per cent (Thakre, 2002). Improvements in hygiene and health are necessary for enhancing the quality of life, increasing productivity and providing a platform for sustainable higher levels of economic growth and for reducing poverty.

Another area of concern is that although poverty levels have fallen over the years, 25 per cent of the state's citizens still live below poverty lines. Poverty line is defined in terms of expenditure required for daily calorie intake of 2,400 per person in rural areas and

TABLE 10.1

Human Development Indicators

States	*Literacy % (2001)*	*Life Expectancy at Birth (Years) 2000*	*Infant Mortality Rate 1997-99 3-year Moving Average*	*Population Served by Doctors/ Population (1999)*	*% of Rural Population Having Access to Drinking Water (2000)*	*% of Rural Households Without Sanitation Facilities (2000)*	*Per Capita Income (Current Prices) 1999-00*
Andhra Pradesh	61.11	63.90	66	83.3	33.0	85.5	14,750
Bihar	47.53	65.20	63	N.A.	14.7	N.A.	5,540
Delhi	81.82	N.A.	31	48.5	N.A.	N.A.	N.A.
Gujarat	69.97	63.61	63	24.3	66.0	79.9	18,625
Karnataka	67.04	64.44	58	26.7	38.5	88.9	16,343
Kerala	90.92	73.34	14	22.8	14	23	18,262
Madhya Pradesh	64.11	58.60	90	N.A.	16.0	N.A.	11,244
Maharashtra	**77.27**	**68.26**	**48**	**N.A.**	**49.8**	**85.5**	**22,604**
Orissa	63.61	59.90	97	182.4	21.4	96.1	9.162
Punjab	69.95	70.90	53	24.5	16.6	67.9	23,040
Rajasthan	61.03	62.50	81	N.A.	36.1	87	12,533
Tamil Nadu	73.47	68.40	52	29.5	56.0	88.5	19,141
Uttar Pradesh	57.36	63.80	84	9.5	15.2	90.6	9,765
West Bengal	69.22	67.70	52	N.A.	N.A.	76.0	15,569

Note: N.A.- not available

2,100 in urban areas. The expenditure is officially estimated at Rs. 228.9 per capita per month in rural areas and Rs. 264.1 in urban areas at 1993-94 prices. As regards poverty levels Maharashtra lags behind the states of Andhra Pradesh, Gujarat, Karnataka, Kerala and Tamil Nadu (NHDR, 2001). This is despite the fact that poverty programmes constitute a substantial part of the state budget (Bardhan, 2003). The regional disparity is also a matter of concern: levels of poverty and social infrastructure development in different regions of the state differ greatly. While in some regions poverty was as high as 50 per cent in 1993-94, in some regions it was 14.8 per cent (*Indian Rural Development Report*, 1999).

Regional imbalances also exist in rural health infrastructure. Some districts have low literacy rates and in some other districts female literacy is particularly low. So one can visualise the urgency for the development of a system that will result in good governance, which does not neglect the social sectors especially with respect to the regional disparity. Table 10.2 shows the index for selected Indian states, which measures the interstate differentials in infrastructure. This index of the social and economic infrastructure takes into account the economic competitiveness and certain social parameters and brings out the differences in the levels of development of various states. This

TABLE 10.2

Index of Social and Economic Infrastructure

States	*Index*
Andhra Pradesh	103.30
Arunachal Pradesh	69.71
Assam	77.72
Bihar	81.33
Gujarat	124.31
Haryana	137.54
Himachal Pradesh	95.03
Karnataka	104.88
Kerala	178.68
Madhya Pradesh	76.79
Maharashtra	112.80
Orissa	81.00
Punjab	187.87
Rajasthan	75.86
Sikkim	108.99
Tamil Nadu	149.10
Uttar Pradesh	101.23
West Bengal	111.25

Note: Cited from Final Report, Administrative Reforms Committee, GoM, (December 2002). p.9.

Source: T.C.A. Anant, K.L. Krishna and Uma Dutta Roy Choudhry (1999). *Measuring Interstate Differentials in Infrastructure.*

FIGURE 10.1

Ingredients of Good Governance

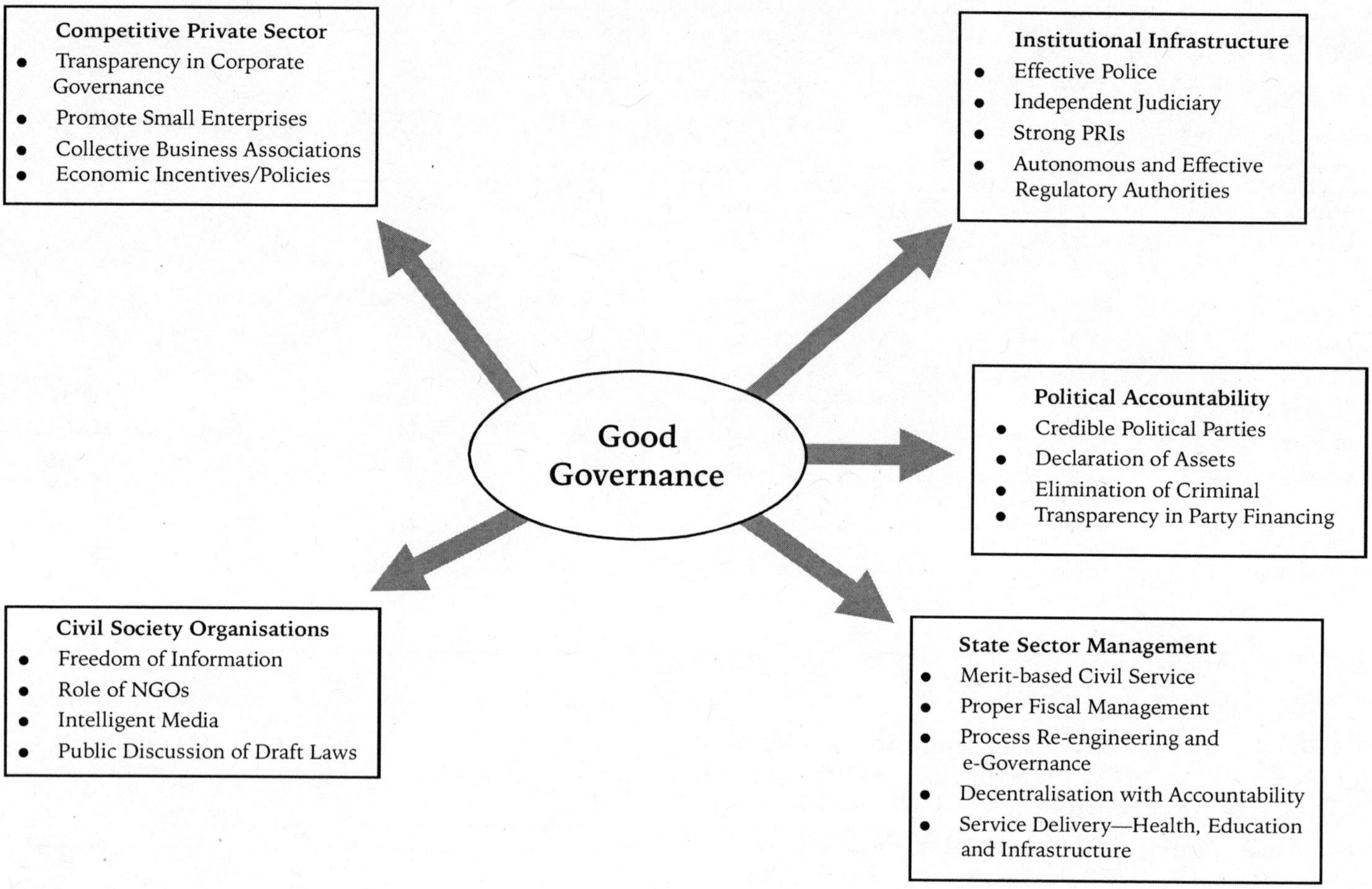

Source: The World Bank, May, 2002.

index reveals that Maharashtra ranks sixth while Punjab, Kerala, Tamil Nadu, Haryana and Gujarat are better positioned. There is a need to invest in social infrastructure as much as in economic infrastructure. It is a very difficult situation since, over the past five years, Maharashtra has been experiencing a deceleration in its rate of growth. If the social infrastructure does not improve, it will be difficult to attract investment as states like Karnataka and Tamil Nadu are showing better records in the economic and social indicators. In a well-governed state, it is easier to get all information and the permission required to quickly start and continue business, which increases their attractiveness for business. In order to maintain its commanding position, Maharashtra should retain its investment climate especially with regard to foreign direct investment (FDI). Foreign Direct Investment gives rise to development and, in the process, brings development of clusters, prosperity and jobs.

FDI also increases the attractiveness for setting up further businesses. So far, the investor perception in Maharashtra has been very positive. Nevertheless, there has been a significant decline in the approval of FDI to the state, with Maharashtra's share of FDI approval in all of India falling from 24 per cent during the first half of 1990s to 15 per cent during the latter half of 1990s. Notwithstanding this decline, Maharashtra remains the most preferred destination for FDI in India. If proper care and encouragement is not given, Maharashtra may slip further. With the abolition of licensing, FDI is not forced to go in the direction of the governments' preferences. The sales tax-based incentives have also been abolished and therefore, the FDI will find its way to the states that are perceived to be better governed, places where investors feel, are better suited for business. Maharashtra should not lose out on FDI due to malgovernance (Singh, 2003).

There is no quantifiable annual index available on good governance based on certain agreed indicators such as birth rate, death rate infant mortality rate, literacy rate, electrification of rural households, availability of safe drinking water, crime rate, custodial deaths, rural and urban unemployment, revenue surplus and deficits, loan repayment liability, capital expenditures, tax performance, disbursement of subsidies as a percentage of gross state domestic product (GSDP) etc., to show where the state stands (Godbole Report, 2001). However, the social and economic indicators are good signals that point out that governance has deteriorated over the decade.

They include the entire set of norms, practices and institutions that define the way that a society works in the areas of politics and public administration, law and the judiciary and business ethics and corporate governance. Governance, therefore, is not restricted to the state, it definitely encompasses the state, but it transcends the state by including the private sector and civil society organisations (CSO). The domain of governance consists of the state, the private sector and the civil society, encompassing all three, good governance defines the processes and structures that guide political and socio-economic relationships.

Public accountability and transparency are relevant to all sections of the society and good governance is possible only when all sections of the society conduct their affairs in a socially responsible manner. The Figure 10.1 gives a comprehensive picture of the various ingredients that are contained in the concept of good governance in the Indian context. From the figure, it is apparent that for good governance to take root certain fundamentals need to become a part of the system, such as:

- democracy particularly decentralised democracy;
- respect for human rights and the rule of law;
- efficiency, accountability and transparency in government and public administration;
- peoples participation;
- equity and poverty concerns; and
- commitment to good government at all costs.

A Critical Appraisal

Administration and Bureaucracy

The Maharashtra Government Administrative Reforms Committee Report (2002) brings to the fore the public perception of the government, which is characterised by the four 'D's—discourtesy, delay, dishonesty and deficiency. The 'Four Ds' have affected its capacity for effective governance. Reflecting on why this has come about, it can be pointed out that over the years, the State got involved in sectors far more than what it could handle. The state got involved in physical infrastructure, agricultural development, industrial promotion, and also in the production and distribution of various goods and services. Initially they were justified on the grounds of speeding up economic development but over time the increase became really overwhelming. The state at the time of inception had only 12 departments and the current number is 26. It is not only that the number of departments has increased, but also departments have witnessed internal expansion. Besides affecting the capacity for governance the stretching of the government has become very expensive.

Financial Management

Proper financial management is a very important and a key issue, as the objective of the fiscal policy is to ultimately improve the socio-economic fabric. Bad fiscal governance will lead to a financial crisis. Maharashtra was considered a well-administered state mainly because of its financial stability and financial prudence but unfortunately over the past six to seven years there has been a precipitous fall in this. This is a major reason for the poor performance of the government in various sectors.

After 1995, the state government's economic status deteriorated, both in terms of fiscal stability and economic growth. The proportion of debt to State Domestic Product (SDP) rose sharply from 11.6 per cent in 1995-96 to 18.93 per cent in 2000-01. Its liabilities were higher than the value of its assets by a margin of Rs. 3,263 crores in 1998-99, according to the White Paper on the state's finances published by the government in 1999. According to the latest reports, the state debt is more than Rs. 80,000 crores and this is the biggest problem confronting the government today (Balakrishnan, 2003). The fiscal slippage in Maharashtra, documented in a World Bank study, shows that the government debt is well in excess of levels that would be considered optimal or consistent with inter-temporal solvency (World Bank, 2002). This is a testimony to the collapse of governance in India's most developed state. The World Bank report has warned that Maharashtra is heading towards insolvency by 2005-06 unless its revenue and deficits besides debts (including off-budget borrowings) are reined in. The government of Maharashtra has been borrowing in the market primarily to repay its earlier loans, and to pay interest on its existing loans. The fiscal deficit caused by borrowing for expenditure on development, such as, building roads, dams, etc., which will improve the standard of living of the people, and hence, their productivity is in fact acceptable. The total development expenditure has been steadily decreasing from 69.3 per cent of total expenditure in 1996-97, to 66.7 per cent in 1997-98 and 50.2 per cent in 1998-99 (Padmanabhan, 1998). The taxes levied by the state go entirely for payment of salaries and pensions of government and quasi-government employees and the interest on its outstanding debt. "Governments in such situations may become merely employment agencies rather than agents of development or poverty reduction" (Stern, 2001).

Another major area of concern is the question of subsidy, which was Rs. 18,825 crores in 1997-98. There are genuine doubts whether subsidies are going to the deserving and right end. An example is the subsidy given for diesel purported to be used by mechanised fishing vessels. There are a number of debatable discrepancies. The state government provides subsidised electricity to agricultural consumers and households at the expense of commercial and industrial users, and cash-crop farmers who grow sugarcane benefit while other farmers do not. Irrigation water subsidies accrue mostly to farmers with average farm holdings of more than two hectares. The benefit of the high procurement price paid to cotton growers under the Monopoly Procurement Scheme are not going to the cotton farmers but to the rent-seeking intermediate traders and corrupt officials (*Hindu*, 25 Oct., 2002).

The financial bankruptcy of the state government also comes in the way of utilisation of development funds provided by the Central Government. To cite an example, according to the Prime Minister's Rozgar Scheme educated unemployed can avail of loan up to rupees one lakh from state owned banks for starting some small business. As they are not trained in the art of entrepreneurship, there is a central subsidy for such training and in the state of Maharashtra the Maharashtra Centre for Entrepreneurship Development (MCED) gives such entrepreneurial training. It is learnt from the MCED that the subsidy for such training for the year 2002-03 was already disbursed by the Central Government but the MCED never received the funds. Further they have been informed by the central authorities that the next tranche of the subsidy was ready to be disbursed after receiving the utilisation report. Such cases of diversion of funds have become common. When there is no certainty of funds, and no counterpart funds, plans will not be implemented. According to the MCED their programmes do continue with their own funds, but then in such situations the quality of expenditure naturally tends to get poor. There are numerous examples of diversion of funds but surprisingly there seems to be no shortage of development programmes.

Very often, the state makes an announcement of a development scheme for one region and soon has to follow up with similar schemes for other regions without making detailed provision for funds or making sure that the particular scheme is suitable for the region concerned. The announcement of a special development programme for Vidarbha in 1996 inevitably led to the announcement of similar schemes for Marathwada, Konkan and other regions. According to reports, the new schemes were announced despite the fact that the budget was not able to support even the existing schemes. Government had been taking up one ambitious project after another evidently without identifying the sources of funds. To name a few, the projects include a scheme to rehabilitate Mumbai's slum dwellers by providing them with free housing; various Maharashtra State Road Development Corporation projects, including the construction of about 50 flyovers in Mumbai and a programme to provide drinking water to all villages in the state. Many questioned the high priority being accorded to the construction of flyovers, pointing out that even if one accepted the contention that flyovers facilitated substantial savings in fuel consumption, the savings would not benefit the state exchequer to any great extent. On the other hand, the construction of roads and power plants in the areas of heightened industrial activity would lead to the creation of more jobs and the generation of more income, which in turn would benefit the exchequer.

The Slum Rehabilitation Scheme originally envisaged a purely supervisory role and zero financial liability for the government. The idea was to rope in real estate developers to build the houses in return for the government facilitating the construction of saleable premises by them. But this has ended with the state government getting involved with huge financial implications, the government owning a company, Shivshahi Punarvasan Prakalp Limited, and a debt of Rs. 600 crores towards its seed capital (Padmanabhan, 1998). In many instances, the state was compelled to go in for bond issues and other means to borrow not to mention the furnishing of guarantees. The gestation periods of quite a few of the projects taken up by the government were considerably longer than the maturity periods of the bonds floated. Sources wonder how, given the fact that the government is resorting to borrowing even to service the existing debt; the newly incurred debt will be serviced five to six years down the road. A classic example of a faulty revenue model is the case of the Maharashtra Krishna Valley Development Corporation (MKVDC). Having guaranteed the bonds, the cash-strapped state government today reportedly spends a major chunk of its irrigation budget on repayment of principal and payment of interest to bondholders.

Rural Governance

Good governance can work only when democracy is strengthened not only at the top but also functions effectively at the grassroot level. Democracy gives a voice to needy people and protects them from many different forms of economic and political abuse (Sen, 1999). Villages are compact; decision making and action is in close proximity; stakeholders are interested and the domain of local governments covers those subjects that vitally affect peoples' daily lives. But, in spite of the 73rd and 74th Amendments to the Constitution making *panchayats* and municipalities 'institutions of self-government,' there appears to be no forward movement visible to empower *Panchayati Raj* Institutions (PRI). Maharashtra is one of the states that have taken a very keen interest in this kind of governance. There are 27,000 village *panchayats* under whose ambit nearly six crore people or two-thirds of the state population falls (Narayana, 2003). But unfortunately although *de jure* the *panchayat raj* system opens for widespread participation in grass root democracy, *panchayats de facto* do not seem to have become democratic bodies. Like in most unequal societies, in Maharashtra too, the elite has easily captured local bodies. State governments have firm control over functioning of *panchayats* besides promoting parallel structures outside the PRIs. The *gram panchayats* cannot solve these problems because they neither have the funds nor the necessary powers to sanction the needed schemes.

Major problems in rural areas are drinking water and sanitation. Although, many villages are cash starved, there are many instances where funds are flowing but yet there have been no result, for example, the Mhaswad Water Scheme. The total cost of the scheme so far has been Rs. 12 crore, while the population of the village, according to 1991 Census, is 14,000. This means that around Rs. 8,600 has been spent per person for drinking water. Today, however, despite the vast expenditure per family, Mhaswad village is still only getting non-filtered water.

It is not that there are no success stories. The Darewadi Watershed Project and the Watershed development through community participation at Ralegan Siddi are examples of which Maharashtra can be truly proud. Many such programmes get World Bank and other foreign funding but suffer delays due to government apathy and administrative neglect. For instance, the Maharashtra Rural Water Supply and Sanitation Project with the Japan Policy and Human Resource Development (PHRD) funding of US$ 300,000 and credit/loan of US$ 150 million for a US$ 200 million project has been finalised. Japan PHRD has built a strong partnership between the World Bank, the Government of Japan and developing countries for more than 10 years. This partnership has culminated into stronger client institutions, better skilled development experts working in effective programmes designed to alleviate poverty in the developing world. There are certain advantages in involving external donors in such development programmes. Firstly, it creates additional resources and secondly international agencies insist upon proper documentation of project proposals followed by mid-term evaluation and final evaluation. Implementation of mid-term evaluations become easier and the wealth of data generated by donor promoted consultancies can be of great use. Such projects benefit a large section of the society, but as donor appointed consultants might not be aware of field conditions, proper implementation and sustainability of the project is left to the local authorities. It requires good governance on the part of the state administration to make a success of such projects by making a determined effort to ensure that the development objectives of the project, which in the above mentioned case is to: (i) increase rural communities' access to improved and sustainable drinking water and sanitation services; and (ii) institutionalise decentralisation of rural water supply and sanitation service delivery to rural local governments are achieved.

Figure 10.2 demonstrates that for all development programmes, there should be a real paradigm shift in governments' thinking (especially with reference to rural water supply), moving from a centralised, supply-driven approach to a people-centred, demand-driven approach that focuses on decentralised delivery through local governments.

The government should also promote the ownership of the assets by local communities and local governments. The primary objective of such programmes should be to achieve environmental, institutional and financial sustainability.

This sort of paradigm shift will not only make sure that the rural development takes place according to the requirements of the region but will also ensure accountability and transparency in all the projects and will minimise the political and bureaucratic influence which is largely responsible in the corruption and diversion of funds.

FIGURE 10.2

Paradigm Shift

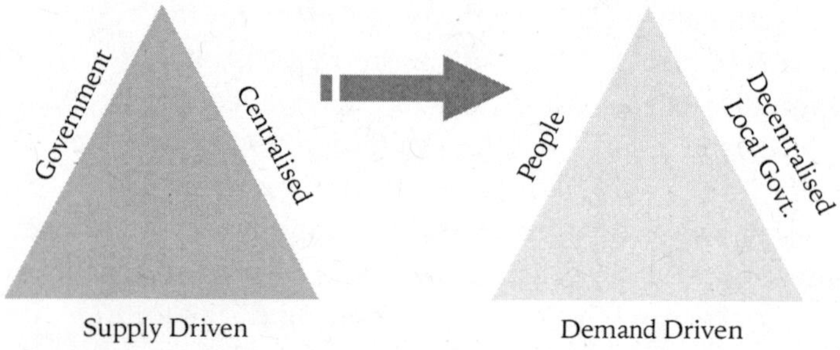

Diversion of funds affect the development of backward regions of the state namely Vidarbha and Marathwada. Way back in 1984 the V.N. Dandekar Committee on backlog determination put the backlog in development expenditure at Rs. 3,186.98 crores. Between 1985-86 and 1999-00 the backlog was around Rs. 8980 crores and the subsequent Bhujrangrao Kulkarni panel appointed to check the backwardness pointed to a backlog of Rs. 15,355 crores (Vijapurkar, 2001). In order to ensure equity in allocations for development of the backward regions and liquidating the backlog three statutory development boards were set up in 1994. The Governor under Article 371(2) is mandated to steer the efforts at neutralising the backlogs through the medium of these boards (Vijapurkar, 2001). In spite of concentrated efforts by the GoM to bridge the gap between the developed and developing regions of the state and despite massive infusion of funds, over nearly two decades to neutralise backlogs in the backward regions of Vidarbha and Marathwada, the backlogs have only grown, and the coastal Konkan regions—Raigarh, Ratnagiri and Sindhudurg continue to receive major share of the investment.

Another area of governance that needs focussed attention is integrating the socio–economic development of the most underprivileged sections of the Indian society, the Scheduled Tribes (STs) and Scheduled Castes (SCs) in a coordinated and planned manner. Scheduled Tribes account for about 9.4 per cent of the state population. The districts of Raigad, Yavatmal, Chandrapur, Gadchiroli, Thane, Nashik, Dhule and Nandurbar have a high tribal population with the percentage ranging from 10 per cent to 22 per cent. Lack of accountability of implementation agencies either to the government or to the people has been the single major cause for diversion of development funds away from backward regions and communities.

The problem of raising the living standards of scheduled tribes, scheduled castes and other weaker sections of the population is complex and calls for sustained endeavour over a long period.

Urban Management

Cities and towns are now recognised as 'engines of economic and social development.' With high concentration of human beings, cities give birth to ideas; they foster creativity and innovation; and they create jobs. However, they also generate and intensify social exclusion. And in the process they tend to deny the benefits of urban life to the poor, to women, to youth, and to religious or ethnic minorities and other marginalised groups. Urban poverty cannot be seen from the mere perspective of rural poverty. It is infinitely more complex and dynamic comprising deprivations of housing, employment, services and physical safety. In Maharashtra too, like the rest of the country there has been a significant migration of rural poverty to select urban locations in search of employment and livelihood. These migrants, however, have become vital contributors to the city economy without whom many of the support systems for city life would collapse. Strengthening urban management, through capacity building, is therefore a key area by which Maharashtra's cities can meet the challenges of urban development. This entails the creation of a conducive and enabling environment for urban institutions to effectively perform their functions, and for city managers to acquire the knowledge, skills, and expertise necessary to plan, manage, and govern their cities. In Maharashtra's cities, especially Mumbai, the problems of proliferating slums, contaminated water and collapsing infrastructure have raised questions. There is no lack of studies or reports, the McKinsey–Bombay First (July, 2003) being the latest addition. The recommendations of a few earlier studies that promise to make Mumbai into a world-class city have yet to be implemented. Some of the earlier studies include the 1993 McKinsey Report to make Maharashtra an economic leader; the 1994 Cooper and Lybrand strategies to improve waste management; the 1997 Tata Consultancy Services feasibility study for underground railway; the 2001 Crisil plan to make Mumbai a financial Centre (*The Times of India*, 7 July 2003). A recent study conducted by Bombay First, an NGO, revealed that young graduates prefer Hyderabad or Bangalore to Mumbai, as the social infrastructure is better in those cities. It is high time that the local authorities in charge started implementing not only the suggestions of the reports but also by looking at experiences and best practices that demonstrate practical ways of meeting the challenges of urbanisation. Since the process of urbanisation cannot be reversed it has to be regulated in a manner that would help absorption of surplus rural labour in urban areas and lead to a balanced development of small, medium and large towns. Perhaps emulating the Chinese model could be a good option. China's distribution of urban population has become much more balanced, with a higher proportion of population living in the small and medium cities. A lot can be achieved with the proper political leadership. Unless the political machinery is committed to eliminating the lethargic attitude to these problems good governance will remain a distant dream.

Corruption and Criminalisation of Politics

The general perception that India is a very corrupt country has been supported by the Transparency International Corruption Perception Index which has rated India 72nd in a list of 99 countries, and with a score of 2.9 in a scale of 1-10. There is little doubt that corruption in present-day India pervades all levels and all services. The administrative as well as the police and judicial services are often in the picture charged with colluding with the political leadership to indulge in systemic corruption, making a mockery of democratic governance. Indian laws, rules, regulations, procedures and methods of transaction of government business, however, sound and excellent cannot by themselves ensure effective and transparent administration if the political and administrative leadership entrusted with their enforcement fails to do so and abuses its powers for personal gain (Sondhi, 2000). Corruption shifts government expenditure priority from social sector spending to areas, where the opportunities for rent seeking are greater and the possibilities for detection are lower (Kumar, 2001). Allocating government funds to a few large defence contracts or mega-projects may be more attractive to the corrupt persons in power, than spending it to build numerous rural health clinics (Bardhan, 1997). Political incentives to respond to the needs of ordinary people are more often than not offset by incentives to respond to the demands of the rich and powerful.

The dynamics of corruption in government starts with a systematic attempt at politicising the bureaucracy. The simple instrument, by which the political executive has found that the bureaucracy can be made to dance to its tunes, is the instrument of transfers and postings. Not only is there a fear of transfer for non-compliance, but also of late there have been reports of officials getting the desired postings by way of payments. The postings, often termed as 'wet postings' and 'dry postings' have different magnitudes of bribe and the amount for the former can be staggering. According to a report quoted by Vittal, the former Chief Vigilance Commissioner (CVC) an official is supposed to have paid Rs. 4 crores to get a particular posting in Mumbai. He goes on to explain that if a person pays Rs. 4 crores to get a posting in Mumbai, he must be able to make at least Rs. 40 crores if not Rs. 20 crores from that investment (Vittal, 2001). This may be a stray case but the media has often reported about the bribe amounts for 'wet' postings in Mumbai and Delhi for jobs that have interface with the public especially in the revenue concerned departments to vary between Rs. 20 lakhs to Rs. 25 lakhs.

Moving on to crime and organised crime including mafia in the state sector, the state of affairs is truly alarming. The mafia and organised crime have given a new dimension to the concept of corruption. The organised crimes are large-scale rackets run by extensively organised crime syndicates carried on over long period of time and relying on public officials for protection from the law. G.V.G. Krishnamurthy, the former Election Commissioner, revealed the depth to which the country's politics has been criminalised. He also revealed that there are at least 110 organised criminal gangs in Maharashtra, of whom no less than 55 are in Mumbai. The concentration of criminal gangs in Mumbai is not a reflection solely of the city's wealth, but also of the close links that they have forged with the dominant political parties in the city (Jha, 2002).

The reasons for the criminalisation of politics are murky financing of political elections, the doubtful quality of many electoral candidates and the non-transparent ways in which many political parties function (Paul, 2002). Under Indian law, there exists no legal method for political parties to raise more than a small fraction of the amount they need. Various decisions and enactments over the last three decades have, on the one hand, made it progressively more difficult to raise political funds legally, and on the other hand, vastly increased the political parties' need for funds. This has thrown the politicians into the lap of criminal and corrupts elements. Honest and sincere officials (and there is no dearth of them) holding senior positions are hesitant in openly expressing their views on this matter, leave alone work towards their elimination from the system. The incapacity to legislate meaningful institutional checks against abuse of authority and corruption, despite recommendations of various committees like Santanam Committee in the sixties and the Vohra Committee in the nineties has disillusioned many an honest civil servant. The Vohra Committee report has brought out startling revelations of how the various crime syndicates/mafia organisations are able to operate with significant muscle and money power alongside established linkages with government functionaries and political leaders. The rationale for establishing such commissions is questionable as it costs time, money and huge effort to finally give results that can be simply rejected at will or accepted only if found convenient. Nothing gets done to introduce mechanisms that will disallow politicians so much liberty to dispense justice, when they are often the guilty party. The state and the country need a system, which ensures that commissions of inquiry are, firstly, based on evidence and not allegation, and secondly, that action is taken wherever called for. This does not mean a blanket acceptance of all commissions but for a system that is less political and fairer in dealing with the commission's reports.

Although the picture looks very grim there is a silver lining. According to N. Vittal, although corruption is so widespread, out of the 100 crore people of India may be 5 crores are corrupt and one crores in a position to be corrupt. This will include all the corrupt politicians, bureaucrats, criminals and businessman. This means 95 crores are not corrupt. But the main problem is that they are not organised, while the corrupt people are organised. What then is required is a good instrument to fight corruption in the country and to sensitise the people at large about the need for fighting corruption. It is expected that information technology (IT) will drastically reduce corruption and red tape. Bribery, which is a common practice in the official corridors across the country, will hopefully be significantly reduced with the introduction of e-governance.

Process Re-engineering and e-Governance

During the last decade, there has been a wide conviction that modern Information and communication technologies (ICTs) can be used to promote development and bring the benefits of modern ICTs to the citizen. Once unknown ideas, 'IT for the masses' and 'bridging the digital divide' have suddenly leapt to the forefront of consciousness in the world of development. Literally crores of rupees are committed to the belief that ICTs can enable the rural areas to 'leapfrog' traditional problems of development like poverty, illiteracy, disease, hunger, unemployment, corruption, and social inequalities so as to move rapidly into the modern information age.

Information technology is not an end in itself, but means to provide better quality of life to the citizens of the state. It does not aim at merely automating existing process but the target is to use IT to improve overall organisational efficiency and pass the benefits to the citizens of the state. E-governance (electronic governance or digital governance) is the effective use of IT to improve the system of governance that is in place, and thus provide better services to the citizens (Moni and Vijayaditya, 2003).

There is a widespread belief that information technology does, can, or could produce transparency, accountability, responsiveness, citizen empowerment, freedom from corruption, and a host of other benefits and that e-governance promises 'a new governance and a new politics', "redefining the vision and the scope of the entire gamut of relationships between citizens and government" (Bedi and Srivastava, 2001).

E-Governance, therefore, is the use of ICT to support good governance. In practice, e-governance involves two distinguishable activities. First is the computerisation of government functions themselves. This proposes connecting the central and state government to district officials, and computerising registrations, legal proceedings, land records, state offices, etc., for the benefit of the administrators of the state. Second, e-governance may mean government-to-people and people-to-government connections whereby citizens obtain direct access to records, rules, and information about entitlements that they need or want in their daily lives. (Keniston, 2001) This is a blessing especially where the public service is complex with red tape creating delays and corruption that result in slow and ineffective output. E-governance simplifies the government procedures so that accountability and transparency is total at all levels of management. Citizens need not hire middlemen to manoeuvre through the opaque bureaucracy and handle time-consuming procedures like the manual copying and indexing of documents and their storage in paper form.

Maharashtra has been acknowledged as one of the first few states in the country to have given e–governance an important status and it has been successfully spearheading the implementation of the state government's IT policy. The state initiated the computerisation of various departments and field offices of the government in a major way in early 1998 by setting up the Directorate of Information Technology, and is now taking IT right down to the grassroots level. There has been a continuous effort to make a significant improvement in the quality of service at the interface between the government and citizens.

Notable among the departments which have gone online is the public works department (PWD). The PWD, which was computerised in a phased manner, now boasts of a website. Notices of tenders above Rs. 5 lakhs are posted on the site. Contractors can register on the site and specify projects of their interest. Whenever a new tender is posted on the site, contractors get an automatic e-mail detailing the nature and needs of the project. Another unique experiment pertains to the Registration Department, which after being computerised has reduced the transaction time from a week to 25 minutes. The pilot project, which started in four offices of the department, has now been replicated among 386 offices state-wide. Apart from convenience for citizens, it also offers immense cost-reduction opportunities for the government (Khullar, 2003). It has also increased revenues by plugging leakages. There is also a proposal for sales tax department to jump onto the bandwagon, making it possible for businesses to file returns online.

To ensure time bound service delivery to citizens, the government has initiated citizen facilitation centres. These single window counters will perform various routine citizen services such as registrations of letters, application for various certificates and redressal of grievances. One such centre has already been set up by the Thane collectorate. Known as 'Setu', this centre gives out 23 odd certificates in less than 24 hours and also has an online query system by which citizens can track the status of their files. Such centres, which are operational from 8 a.m. to 8 p.m. irrespective of holidays, will be replicated in 400 locations encompassing district headquarters and *talukas*. The services provided in the facilitation centres will include NGOs at the front end and government administrative process at the back-end. Computerisation of land records (CLR) is a mission that aims at delivering excellent grassroots e-governance within the domain of land management. This can be successfully accomplished by bringing in land reforms and by utilising the far-reaching potential of IT. In a true sense, CLR could safely claim to be the first initiative of e-governance at the grassroots level.

One can cite a number of success stories from different parts of the state. Experiments like the Warna Wired Village are using Internet not as an elitist medium but as a social phenomenon that has the power to touch the day-to-day lives of every Indian. The project has resulted in a web-based information system on the agriculture produce market, agriculture schemes and crop technology, village information system, employment and self-employment schemes, educational and vocational guidance and many more. It allows wired management of sugar cane cultivation and marketing over the Intranet. Land record documents will also soon be made available through the system (Agarwal, 2003). A good deal of money is required to keep these kind of projects going. In this case, the sugar cooperative has the resources to sustain it. While Warna is a good model, it must not be overlooked that this region has the advantage of being one of the richest areas in southern Maharashtra as it has enough water, good soil and a high literacy level. It is not clear whether it will work in less favourable circumstances. Besides, Warna's literacy level is about 70 per cent and that made the project much easier to promote. More important than all is the importance of sugar industry to the socio-political life of Maharashtra. If IT has to empower people, it should cover every category of worker connected with the industry—right down to the sugarcane cutter, who is a landless labourer and who is often homeless (Katakam, 2002).

Maharashtra has entered into an agreement with World Tel, a private limited company in UK to work on developing state-wide Internet connectivity. World Tel has been asked to create the infrastructure and build an organisation that will operate community Internet centres on a commercial basis. The purpose is to use Internet in areas like: (a) admission to schools and colleges, (b) job search, (c) health care, (d) public distribution, (e) public grievance redressal, (f) distance education, (g) tourism, (h) agricultural and crop management (i) disaster warning (j) housing scheme (k) land record, (l) water management, etc. (Goswami, 2001).

The question is whether one can justify the expense of IT in a nation where so many basic needs are unmet. In a village where more than half of all the men, women and children are below the poverty line, there are other priorities, *viz.*, food, education, water, medical care, basic rights, social justice, freedom from corruption and meeting these priorities must be the core criteria for any use of modern information technologies rather than the infrastructure needed for modern IT (Bhatnagar and Schware, 2000). There is a general belief among hardliners that due to certain inherent weakness of our administrative system, e-governance cannot create social opportunities for the poorer section of the society. A critic observes: "The apprehension is that while e-governance might work wonders for the limited few among the elite, it might bypass the vast majority of commoners. As of now, all electronic impulses tend to get dissipated in the ace of the tangled maze of complex procedures and practices" (ICT, 2001). However, it is hoped that IT can play an important role in empowering the masses and enable them to reap the fruits of development. It is becoming increasingly clear that IT is not an urban phenomenon and that with the increasing cooperation from the village level stakeholders the concept of IT in rural areas can work. It is hoped that e-governance will ultimately help eliminate corruption, as even the institution of law and order seem to have been gripped in this spiral of corruption.

Law and Order, Police and Criminal Justice

An efficient and honest police force is the principal safeguard for the citizens against violations of basic rights and for the maintenance of law and order. In Maharashtra, the ratio of policemen per lakh of population is 138 (Borwankar, 2003). A basic drawback therefore, is the shortage of police force. In substantial part of rural areas, police have hardly any presence.

Although the traditional tasks of the police force has been to maintain law and order, to prevent and detect crime, of late, there has been diversification into various other spheres which have assumed significance. The police is most of the time asked to handle a variety of functions beyond law and order, or crime-control. Many a time, the VIP duties to which the police personnel are assigned have no valid place within the realm of their work, although they continue to be among the top purposes for which they are used. This huge wastage on non-essential service has resulted in hampering their normal duties.

The politicisation of the police force or exploitation of the police force or some of the officers for partisan political or personal ends undermines the reputation and public perception of the police. Political connections are most important to secure a degree of immunity from arrest, and more often than not, criminals use this link. If one does not bend to the wishes of the political bosses, there is the threat of transfer. Politicians often use police as a weapon, or as a facilitator for some illegal operation. A simple example is the carting of truckloads of people for a public meeting. Carrying people in a truck is against the Motor Vehicles Act, and the person doing so can be booked immediately. It is a hazard to life. But this is a regular feature and no policeman can prevent this from happening. There are many cases of police officers that resist unwarranted pressures from a wide range of sources, even as there are many cases where they succumb or enter into mutually enriching arrangements with compromised and partisan elements. The reality is far more complex than the simple stereotypes in the public mind and those who stand by their principles often have to pay a price that can hardly be imagined (Gill, 2001).

The number of lacunae in the legal systems also unwittingly hampers police functioning and facilitates the criminals. The success of good governance depends on the capacity to deliver especially when it comes to investigation and successful prosecution. As far as the dispensation of speedy justice is concerned, it is not only Maharashtra but the entire country is facing problems. The pendency of cases in courts is probably the single most important reason for this state of affairs. There are close to four crore cases pending in the Indian courts today while the average conviction rate is a mere five per cent. This is an index of the complexity of the situation. It points to the enormous strain on the criminal justice system. No single player is to blame. The Law commission in its report on manpower planning in 1987 placed the judge population in India at 10.05 judges per 10 lakh people as against 50.09 in UK, 57.07 in Australia, 72.02 in Canada and 107 in the USA. The credibility of the judicial system suffers when on an average disputes take 20 years to get sorted out. There are an estimated 2,80,000 undertrials who have been waiting in jails longer than the maximum mandatory sentences for which they are being tried (*Economic Times*, 15 May 2003). In Maharashtra in the year 2001 only 13.1 per cent cases tried by the courts resulted in conviction and only 26.3 per cent cases of murder ended with conviction during the same year (Borwankar, 2003). There are many reasons for acquittal e.g. witnesses turning hostile, poor quality of presentation in court, non-cooperation from witnesses etc. Wherever the fault may lie the citizens get disillusioned as they feel that they are getting a raw deal on this account and this is leading to a total loss of faith in the law and order system and in policing of the state. According to the police the rise in crime both in the urban and rural regions is a reflection of the collapse of the criminal justice system.

It has been the experience of governments the world over that suppressing data about crime is no longer profitable and is actually fraught with undesirable consequences to all players concerned—the executive, the police and society. The annual crime publication should be widely disseminated and debated. Access of such information will enable citizens to force the government to respond besides being an eye opener to policemen themselves (Raghavan, 2000).

Right to Information (RTI) and Repeal of Official Secrets Act

The greater the access of the citizen to information, the greater would be the responsiveness of government to community needs. Information is the currency that every citizen requires to participate in the life and governance of society. The citizens have a right to get information about all aspect of government functioning and in a democracy as all public servants exercise power only on behalf of the people, it would be an anathema if what they did were hidden from the people. Information promotes openness, transparency and accountability in governance and so there is a critical link between lack of transparency and corruption. If democracy is to be successful, then the right to information plays a very important tool. An important ingredient of good governance was enacting the RTI on a national level. The Freedom of Information Act (2002) is a landmark one as it puts India among only a handful of countries that have legislated a measure that can provide transparency, openness and accountability in government functioning. At the state level, the states of Maharashtra, Rajasthan, Karnataka, Assam, Delhi, Tamil Nadu and Goa have all passed legislation on RTI. The Maharashtra Right to Information Act was passed in 2000. It had many flaws and proved inadequate, as it was unable to empower citizens to demand transparency in the functioning of the government. After much protest about the inadequacy of the Act of 2000, the GoM eventually promulgated an ordinance the Maharashtra Right to Information Ordinance, on September 23, 2002. The Ordinance is very comprehensive and is one of the best models in terms of legislation on the issue in comparison with other states in India that have laws on RTI. The Government of Maharashtra forwarded a proposal to repromulgate the Right to Information Ordinance in February 2003 for the assent of the President of India. Meanwhile, the pending bill on Right to Information came to be passed by the State Legislature in Summer 2003. Consequently the proposal for assent to the Ordinance was withdrawn and proposal for assent of the President to Right to Information Bill, 2002 was forwarded. The assent of President was received on August 10, 2003. Accordingly, the Right to Information Act 2002 and the Rules framed thereunder came into force retrospectively with effect from September 23, 2002.

The RTI makes information sharing an obligation and duty of the state. But unfortunately, the archaic Official Secrets Act, 1923, (OSA) continues to survive and this ensures a cloak of secrecy and provides a cushion of safety for the corrupt. The OSA makes it an offence to disclose certain information without proper authorisation. Due to the OSA being in force, in spite of having the RTI, a common man, who does not have access to government files, cannot prove a charge against a public official.

Ignorance of the law is a major obstacle in the path of the rural poor for whom the right to know has the potential to be most effective. Many are simply unaware that such legislation exists. There has been no effort on the part of the government to educate these people and inform them of their legal rights. Political activists or NGOs have had to take responsibility for creating greater awareness of the legislation. By distributing pamphlets and public discourses, they have been educating the people about their rights and instilling in them social values and the benefits of a political climate characterised by openness, transparency and accountability (Wilson, 2002). In

USA, there are many NGOs who keep collecting classified information using the USA's Freedom of Information Act and keep publicising that classified information.

The RTI movement in these past few years has been a significant part of strengthening democracy and fighting corruption in India. The electoral reforms bill, which makes it mandatory for candidates to disclose their criminal background, is also based on people's right to know. But despite all this there is a long way to go if this right has to be properly implemented for giving good governance. In that sense, the current Bill merely gives teeth to our fundamental right, by setting up a mechanism by which information can now be obtained by the people.

An unbiased media is very essential for disseminating correct information. The media can use the RTI very effectively. Mass media can play a key role in enabling citizens to monitor the actions of incumbents and to use this information in their voting decisions. Amartya Sen has pointed out that the media increases the salience of government performance in famine situations by providing information on the actions of politicians, which citizens can use in their voting decisions (Sen, 1984). Though suggestive, the Sen analysis does not establish a robust link between development of mass media and government responsiveness. Analysis of the role of media in influencing government policy has recently been deepened by Besley and Burgess (2002). Using panel data for Indian states for the 1958-1992 period, they look at two policy response systems. First, public distribution of food as a response to fall in food production associated with droughts. Second, spending on calamity relief as a response to crop damage caused by floods. They then examine how newspapers and politics affect, how responsive state governments in India are to these shocks. They find that higher newspaper circulation is associated with government being more responsive to falls in food production and flood damage. The magnitudes of the effects that they find is large—a 10 per cent drop in food production is associated with a 1 per cent increase in public food distribution in states which are at the median in terms of newspaper circulation per capita whereas for states that are in the 75 per cent percentile a 10 per cent drop in food production is associated with a 2.28 per cent increase in public food distribution. According to this survey, Maharashtra ranks 2nd both as regards responsiveness as well as newspaper circulation. Interestingly Besley and Burgess (2002) find that it is newspapers published in the regional languages that are driving their results. The media is a strong instrument that can create a public opinion in favour of responsible actions by the government. Quick and correct information is now possible through the vast spread of ICT, which the media should judicially use to bring unbiased information before the public. Public pressure can also be exerted through CSOs and NGOs.

Civil Society Organisations

During the past decade, there has been a great upsurge in CSO namely NGOs. Many of them are voluntary agencies engaged in the delivery of services in the field of education, health, poverty alleviation, environment etc. catering to various sections of the population—women, children, the aged, the disabled etc. CSO/NGO have come to be widely viewed as an important agent for limiting authoritarian governments, strengthening popular empowerment, reducing the socially atomising and unsettling effects of market forces, enforcing political accountability, and improving the quality and inclusiveness of governance. Some of them are activist, vigilant groups who try to monitor the working of both public and private organisations. The CSO/NGO can have a constructive impact on the administration of the state by helping to foster fairer, more honest, transparent, democratic and accountable governance. In Maharashtra social activists like Anna Hazare have been appealing to the government (or even pressure them) to improve their performance in the desired areas. They also acquaint ordinary people both with the possibility of better governance (which puts pressure on government to improve) and can provide people with participatory experience that inculcates the skills needed to make such governance a reality. The contribution of civil society to good governance may be summarised under four headings: public policy and decision making; enhancing state performance; transparency and information; and social justice and the rule of law.

A vast section of civil society in India does not at all relate with the policy system. It is primarily engaged in direct service delivery or socio-cultural pursuits. A vast section of the civil society does not even understand how policy is formulated, implemented or not—the political economy of public policy making remains largely an unknown territory for much of civil society. In this connection, the law on RTI will go a long way in bringing to light many of the policy decisions that lead to discussions and public debate. The CSOs and NGOs who are at present engaged in such activities that will promote policy decisions will get the support and push required from the society at large if there is public awareness. Such engagement by civil society can result in inclusion of certain constituencies and perspectives in policy making. For example, a number of public policies for urban poor primarily focus on slum-dwellers who have an identified location of living—illegitimate, illegal—as it may be. However, pavement-dwellers and invisible street children get neglected in public policy on urban poor unless specific civil society engagements have been made to highlight their plight. Thus, policy inclusion as a mode of engagement by civil society can have long-term policy gains for the marginalised communities.

What has been happening so far is that civil society action begins when policy has actually been made and gets presented in the public domain. It is then that civil society organisations recognise that these policies may have negative impacts on their constituencies. Although late, such actions have led to reversal of policy decisions, after the commencement of projects. The Bombay Environment Action Group (BEAG) has helped to fashion and install legislation for Mumbai's heritage buildings and precincts. BEAG has saved large tracts of Panchgani and Mahabaleshwar, hill resorts near Mumbai, from looting builders. Citizens' Forum for Protection of Public Spaces (Citispace) was formed to deal with the takeover of Mumbai's streets and pavements by illegal hawking. They were successful in obtaining favourable court orders. Citispace now also looks at recreation grounds, playgrounds and other public space that is vanishing, as also the repeated 'regularisation' of illegal constructions to serve vote-bank politics. Society for Promotion of Area Resource Centre (SPARC) assists the Maharashtra government, in a scheme, supported by the World Bank, to rehabilitate project affected persons. Encroachment on railway property had to be cleared and the displaced communities rehabilitated. Government has trusted the capabilities and efficiency of SPARC and other such NGOs (Cunha, 2002).

The Brihanmumbai Municipal Corporation (BMC) has also been cooperating with civil society organisations for good governance. BMC is the local body that manages the governance of Mumbai, India's largest metropolis and the financial and business centre. Praja Foundation is one of India's leading non-government organisation committed to bettering the lives of citizens through better governance and cooperation between government agencies and citizens' bodies. Praja pioneered the citizen's charter a few years ago and has been working actively with the BMC to improve governance mechanisms, internal systems and communications with citizens. The Online Complaint Management System (OCMS) is a joint effort by the BMC, Praja Foundation (Praja) and Nixel Technology (Nixel). This initiative has been taken on by Praja to harness the web, make communications for citizens simpler and facilitate better delivery of services by the BMC to citizens.

Not all CSOs/NGOs are faultless. There are also cases where NGOs have vested interests. For example, there are foreign agencies ready to pump in money for certain causes like AIDS. It has been reported that starting an NGO for the AIDS cause is fast becoming an instant-returns industry. The Maharashtra assembly's estimates committee tabled a report stating that there were a large number of bogus NGOs working in the field of HIV/AIDS prevention. While some confined their work to putting up stickers in local trains, a large number merely existed on paper, "...the report is an eye-opener. It says over 60 per cent of NGOs in HIV/AIDS in the state are frauds. This is significant since the biggest share of funds from all sources is diverted to Maharashtra and many of the big-budget NGOs in the state are run by political parties" (Kumar, 2001).

Some of the NGOs represent some sort of a peoples movement in the country, contributing to the evolution of an alternative political process emanating new consciousness in many of the cities and villages of the country. With the help of NGOs many village organisations are able to interact with leaders, legislators and ideologues of various political parties, providing information and important documents and discussing issues with them.

The Private Sector

The private sector covers private enterprises (manufacturing, trade, banking, cooperatives and so on) and the informal sector in the marketplace. The private sector players influence social, economic and political policies in ways that create a more conducive environment for the marketplace and enterprises. Sustainable human development depends in part on creating jobs that provide enough income to improve living standards. Most states now recognise that the private sector is the primary source of opportunities for productive employment. The three G's, namely, growth, governance and globalisation are the core drivers of economy today (Haribakthi, 2003). Economic globalisation is fundamentally changing the ways in which industries and enterprises operate. Private enterprise must be encouraged and supported to be more transparent and competitive in the international marketplace. The business community's involvement in governance can go a long way in preparing the good infrastructure that will result in better telecom, roads, ports, a more friendly tax regime, competitive financial infrastructure and business-friendly negotiation of international accords. There are talks of the Federation of Indian Chamber of Commerce and Industry (FICCI) working with the Airport Authority of India (AAI) to pursue operational and constructional changes in the city airports. Recognising the fact that the Indian business forms a powerful constituency with the potential to influence and transform the culture of governance in the country the Indian Merchants' Chamber (IMC), Assocham and Bombay Chamber of Commerce and Industry (BCCI) have organised a forum on governance. The focus will be on what corporates can do to transform the standards and quality of governance.

Conclusions

Measures for Policy Consideration

Good governance is not a luxury. It is a *sine qua non* for sustainable development and improved economic performances. In a rapidly changing world, the state is under pressure to become more effective and to adapt to the increasing pace of change opportunities for improvement are also opening up as new technologies and change in management theory and practice usher in a wide range of possibilities for better governance. The increasing demands on the state are arising on account of various reasons, an important one being that the public is becoming more demanding with regard to the quality of service. A series of measures for policy considerations discussed below may be useful as a framework for building up mechanisms that improve governance and institutional constructs to involve stakeholders.

(1) ***Political accountability:*** Most of those in politics have become victims of circumstances to survive in power. Therefore, mere elections that will bring about a change in players are not enough and the rules of the game need to be changed. What is required is a systemic change starting with electoral reforms and system improvements. Electoral reforms will have to start with process improvements like prevention of polling irregularities, arresting and reversing criminalisation and checking abuse of unaccountable money power. Systems improvement should include political party reform (Narayan, 2003).

(2) ***Quick implementation of reports:*** The report on good governance submitted by Dr. M.D. Godbole, (2001) commonly referred to as the Godbole Report and the Report of the Administrative Reforms Committee (2002) under Mr. D.M. Sukthankar need to be implemented. Both have given a number of proposals that will bring about good governance. The practice has been that as soon as a committee submits its report on important issues it becomes a secret document until it is placed before the legislature or the cabinet. This takes time, the subject gets relegated to the background and the issue gradually fades from public memory. There is no reason why reports should not be made public as soon as it is presented. It makes sense that the government gets response from different sections of the community and the committee should consider the suggestions and should make sure that the suggestions are included. If the committee reports are priced then the amount of money spent on the preparation of the report can be recovered. A time frame should be set for the implementation of any report after it is submitted.

(3) ***Weeding the statute book of outdated laws:*** Repeal of old and obsolete legislation is necessary for good governance. There are age-old legislations that still hold well. A list prepared by a commission said that there were 400 obsolete laws in the country. These Acts that were formulated ages ago have ceased to have any relevance today and they come as a hurdle in the development of the state. As already dealt with earlier, the Right to Information Act will lose its significance with the existence of the Officials Secrets Act. There are a number of laws related to land in Maharashtra that are antiquated and irrelevant–Land Revenue Code, Tenancy Act, Land Ceilings Act, etc. The Doctrine of Sovereign Immunity is long abandoned by the British yet survives in India, although diluted where Human Rights have been violated. This law goes against the concept of the Rule of Law. There are some Acts that have

been repealed by the central government but the state government has not followed the lead, for example Urban Land Ceiling Regulation Act. The State Law Commission should tackle the task of identifying obsolete laws as quickly as possible.

(4) ***Financial management:*** Fiscal Responsibility Bill and fiscal and public expenditure reforms are important steps towards reversing the fiscal deterioration, expanding allocations for critical sectors such as education and health, and strengthening financial accountability. Budget should be easily understood and be transparent. Andhra Pradesh has started the process of consultation with the stakeholders, public, the NGOs, etc. in advance of the budget formulation exercise. Fiscal consolidation—incorporating expenditure restructuring, cuts in non-merit subsidies and increases in the user charges should become major planks of action. Non-merit subsidies should be slowly phased out. It is necessary that all subsidies are made transparent and shown explicitly in the budget so that it can be known that they are well targeted and they reach the target group. It is necessary to identify areas that need subsidy—those that will become financially viable over a period of time and those that have a tremendous social profit need to be subsidised. In other cases subsidies should be eliminated. Likewise unproductive schemes, overlapping schemes and schemes with miniscule outlay should be discontinued. The objective should be for the state government to provide only merit goods and services with positive externalities, where a non-payer cannot be excluded. Fiscal Responsibility Bill should be enacted as early as possible.

Therefore, fiscal reforms at the level of the state that would correct the deteriorating governance situation and improve the development potential would include efforts to:

- Improving the tax system for example, tax simplification, introduction of VAT, introduction of taxes on agricultural incomes and land.
- Plugging leakages in collection of taxes and improving the tax to GSDP ratio.
- Reforming public sector enterprises including private service provision, privatisation, retrenchment and redeployment.
- Reprioritising spending, increased social sector and infrastructure spending, consolidation of the numerous welfare programmes, better targeting of social subsidies, downsizing and upgrading the administrative service.
- Improving cost recovery particularly in power and irrigation, sectors that are key to the reform process.

(5) ***Administrative reforms:*** are necessary to improve the efficiency and transparency of government functioning and service delivery. Downsizing and rightsizing of government departments is an important step towards this. There is an urgent need to reduce the size of the government establishment and reduce established expenditure from the present 60.9 per cent to 50 per cent of revenue expenditure. Rules for the transfer of civil servants are another important task. From time to time the government has issued transfer policy guidelines that have been mostly sidelined. The Sukthankar Committee Report suggests the establishment of Transfer Boards. This will ensure more equitable and objective consideration of each transfer proposal and minimise the probability of corruption and other malpractices that are in existence today. This will also ensure a fixed tenure of reasonable span, thus improving the efficiency of the officials. The adoption of Transfer Policy on the lines proposed in the Sukthankar Committee Report would be a useful step.

(6) ***Decentralisation:*** Decentralisation can become a reality only by a paradigm shift from supply driven model of service delivery to demand driven approach—top-down to bottom-up. Empowerment and involvement of the community in the planning and implementation stage will bring about a sense of community ownership and responsibility.

The following principles drive such programmes:

- services should be delivered at the lowest appropriate level;
- adoption of a demand-driven and participatory approach;
- community to have a sense of ownership of asset;
- focus on village level capacity-building;

- integrated approach for instance water supply, sanitation and hygiene promotion;
- partial capital cost recovery and full operations and maintenance financing by users; and
- well-informed community with strong *panchayati raj* and urban self-governing institutions.

(7) ***Government role:*** Government should be more a facilitator for rather than a service provider. The government need to rethink its role and endeavour to withdraw from a number of areas so as to strengthen its role in selected sectors. It should drop the excess baggage and let it be handled by the private sector. In fields like higher education etc., it makes better sense to let the private sector take over.

(8) ***Simplification of procedures and jurisdiction:*** High degree of coordination and breaking down of the wall of official jurisdiction is required. To implement any scheme, various departments of the state government get involved. It is not easy with the present system to get things done when a scheme has to get sanctions and clearance from multiple departments as the jurisdiction demarcation often come in as stumbling blocks. Citing the example of the Mhaswad Water Scheme, initially, to acquire the land needed to carry out the project, permission of the revenue department was required; to lift the water, permission of the irrigation department was required; and for the electricity supply not only permission of the electricity department was mandatory but, according to their conditions, Rs. 36 lakhs had to be deposited with them. Mhaswad Municipal Council did not have the funds, so the government of Maharashtra deposited the money. It proved very difficult to deal with the various departments involved. It took nearly seven years for the initial hurdles to get pass. Presently, the different departments at the national level as well as the state level look after the natural resources like land, water, forests and biodiversity. There is need to adopt the integrated approach for the development of natural resources. Unless the integrated concept is adopted, development programmes in isolation for different resources and by different departments may not bring the desired result (Swaminathan, 2002).

Apart from simplification of rules and procedures, all unnecessary or marginally relevant requests and provisions for obtaining NOC, licences, permits, approvals, sanctions, registrations etc. should be done away with. Citizens Charters should be prepared for each department laying down time limits and procedures mentioning the grievance redressal mechanism in those tasks. Academics, trade and professional organisations and NGOs should work hand in hand with the government (Ranganathan, 2003).

(9) ***Planning resource flows to curb regional and class disparity:*** Once the Appropriation Bill gets passed by the Legislature expenditure should be totally in accordance with the appropriation. There is an urgent need for group specific public interventions especially in situations of historically disadvantaged groups and backward and remote geographical areas locked into poverty. These cases need to be addressed going beyond the usual policies and need to be carefully identified without being pressurised by strong lobbies. Preferential policies towards some groups or areas designed to cope with historical handicaps can carry the risk of being difficult to reverse.

Programmes for bringing scheduled tribes, scheduled castes and other backward classes to the level of the rest of the community are among the most significant tasks. For this the government should make sure that there is tremendous reduction in the proliferation of schemes. If there are too many schemes then administering them becomes a Herculean task. In Maharashtra, although there is a separate department of Tribal Development to be able to cater to the developmental needs that are special to tribal areas, the department has more than 250 schemes under which assistance is provided to tribals.

(10) ***The police should become instruments for upholding the Rule of Law:*** For this, they need to be insulated from political interference in operational matters. The police should also be made accountable to the law, for them to be accountable certain protections like Section 132 and 197 of the Criminal Procedure Code have to be removed. There is also the recommendation for the appointment of a Criminal Justice Commission, which has not been accepted by our politicians at large. It is necessary to raise the status of the police to make him trustworthy in the eyes of the citizens. Regulating police behaviour through internal controls and external supervisions can do this. Mandatory judicial

enquiry in custodial crime, death in custody, rape in custody etc., need to be formalised.

(11) ***Grievance mechanism:*** The institution of *Lok Ayukta* to be made more transparent to the public. It will facilitate the grievance mechanism if a state Vigilance Commission is appointed and also if it uses the services of the Anti-Corruption Bureau when desirable. All powers of prosecution should be vested in the Commission. There should be a time limit set for the decisions by the *Lok Auykta*. A levy of a small fee on applications should also be considered as this may curtail unnecessary applications (Iyer, 2003).

(12) ***Public procurement:*** Karnataka has Transparency in Public Procurement Act, 2000, and it will do well for Maharashtra to follow suit. The Maharashtra government is a significant purchaser of goods and services. It tenders for various civil engineering and other works through its PWD and irrigation departments. The Industries Department is the nodal agency, which issues formal orders and policy directives regarding procurement. The present process, which is very elaborate, needs to be simplified. There is no statute that governs purchase tendering and contract procedures. Such an Act will bring about transparency and procedural reforms.

(13) ***Public distribution system (PDS):*** While the Centre is responsible for procurement, storage and transportation of the PDS products up to the godowns and making them available to the states, the onus for distribution to the consumers through the fair price shops and administration of the PDS lies with the state governments. The private agencies can be used in the PDS. To give an example, 3,006 fair price shops service the needs of 36,33,904 families in Mumbai and Thane. The PDS is supposed to provide foodgrains at a subsidised rate. But these good intentions ran into a number of problems like difficulty in obtaining ration cards, black marketing, poor quality grains, adulteration, etc. Though NGOs were aware of it, a systematic partnership between Rationing Kruti Samitee (RKS) an NGO and the government (Controller of Rationing) came about only in 1992. Over the next two years a number of objectives were met i.e. simpler procedure to obtain ration cards, displaying samples of grains to counter adulteration, police raids to deal with black-marketing, etc. (YUVA *et al.;* 1996). This partnership succeeded to a large extent and did achieve what it was meant for. The actors in the model i.e. the NGOs, the department of rationing and the shopkeepers were able to sort out their differences in order to make the whole scheme viable at least for the initial period. However, on the last count i.e. sustainability, the whole project failed. The Controller of Rationing for Mumbai was supportive of it, but the enthusiasm of the government for the scheme waned after his transfer. The communities, on the other hand, were not equipped to continue with the scheme.

(14) ***Working in close proximity with the private sector and NGOs:*** Public private participation (PPP) can promote good governance. This system has been tried out for the registration of documents. A private party was appointed for operating a computerised system in all the registration offices in about 350 *talukas*. The private party invested the capital, appointed personnel, processed the documents, assessed fees and approvals obtained from the sub-registrar. By this the government revenue went up and the public too were happy with the efficiency and speed of service. The experience of SETU and SARITA has shown public–private partnership can bring the efficiency of private sector to bear upon the provision of public services. It not only reduces the pressure on the government funds but also makes the interface between the citizen and the government friendly and efficient.

(15) ***Widespread dissemination of good practices especially in e-governance:*** Maharashtra has had a number of good e-governance initiatives. For instance SETU is a good e-governance initiative for the issue of various types of certificates and SARITA for registration. Adopting the best practices of success stories and avoiding the mistakes of failed initiatives should become the general rule. Some of the good work in other states need to be studied for implementation in Maharashtra especially those that will reduce red tape and corruption. The Bhoomi project in Karnataka for instance is expected to eliminate corruption and red tape at the village level. The project is designed to help 6.7 million farmers

get copies of record of rights, tenancy and crops, a document essential in their dealings with the government and financial institutions. The Gujarat Road Transport Department's 'computerised checkpost project' has eliminated corruption at 10 octroi posts on the state's borders, and increased the revenue from Rs. 60 crore in 1998-99 to Rs. 250 crore in 1999-2000 (Aram, 2002). The moment a truck enters the state, its weight is recorded and the vehicle is video graphed, and the data is instantly accessible in Ahmedabad. This allows little room for local officials to take bribe. Compared to the additional revenue earned, the heavy capital investment of Rs. 18 crore is nothing. Other good projects to take note of are Haryana Registration Information System (HARIS) the web enabled electoral rolls in Haryana, Saukaryam the online civic services in Vishakhapatnam (Andhra Pradesh), computerisation of driving licences in Delhi, computerisation of district administration of Thanjavur in Tamil Nadu, etc. Some of them have been partially or fully implemented in Maharashtra, but the pace needs to be accelerated. Such initiatives will reduce the interface of public functionaries with the citizens and will reduce the chances of corruption besides ensuring quick service.

(16) ***Quality of services:*** The state government is providing a lot of services, but the problem lies in the quality of services. Quality in government services can be improved by integrating the Citizen's Charter and Information Technology initiatives under a holistic umbrella. Twenty-two departments have framed citizens charter indicating the level and type of services citizens are entitled to. These charters set concrete and measurable goals for all citizens to see and defaulting agencies are to be held accountable. However, there is no system to find out whether they are being enforced. There should be a proper monitoring of the citizens charters preferably by an NGO, they should be easily available without difficulty and should be given wide publicity.

Although there is an increasing demand for the public to have a greater say in the business of governance, the intelligentsia and the vast majority of the educated middleclass, those who can effect a change, tend to be silent spectators without any involvement—many of them do not even cast their votes. For institutionalising good governance the key stakeholders—the middle class—should take time to value and care for the process of change and should be willing to commit themselves towards this belief. The 'middle class' should rise to the occasion and get actively involved in bringing about good governance for if they remain indifferent the mountains of resources would constitute a scrap heap in the path of the destiny of the state.

Chapter 11

Intergrated Village Development

Introduction

The saying, "India lives in its villages" is relevant even today, in the new millennium. Like India, Maharashtra too, has a large number of villages and a substantial proportion of its population living in the rural areas. About 58 per cent of the total population of the state lives in 43,722 villages; thus the rural areas need provision of adequate infrastructure to ensure a decent quality of life. Village life in the state is governed by dependency on agriculture, which in turn is plagued by the problem of low yields and low irrigated acreage, which further compounds the developmental problem. To ensure the development of villages, it is necessary to address the problem of introducing modern methods in agriculture, provision for identification of alternative sources of employment, provision of quality health facilities, education facilities, communication facilities, power supply and finally building up village institutions to empower the people. To assess village development in Maharashtra, major socio-economic indicators of development for rural Maharashtra have been examined. In addition, the programmes undertaken in the rural areas of Maharashtra have been discussed. The functioning of *Panchayati Raj* Institutions (PRIs) is also assessed to see its impact on village development.

Villages in Maharashtra: Some Socio-Economic Indicators

Inhabited villages in Maharashtra have grown from 35,851 in 1961 to 35,776 in 1971, 39,352 in 1981, 40,412 in 1991 and 43,722 in 2001. Villages range from small, having a population of 200, to large, having a population of more than 10,000 persons. A larger number of villages are concentrated in the smaller size class (Table 11.1). The total inhabited villages of the state, distributed across districts for various years, show an almost equal proportion of inhabited villages in every district, the proportion being 3 to 4 per cent. Only Sindhudurg, Sangli and Osmanabad have a low proportion of the total inhabited villages of the state (below 2 per cent).

TABLE 11.1

Size-Distribution of Villages in Maharashtra: 1991

Population Size	*No. of Villages*
Less than 200	3461 (8.56)
200-499	8242 (20.39)
500-999	12408 (30.70)
1000-1999	10632 (26.31)
2000-4999	4715 (11.67)
5000-9999	762 (1.89)
10000 & above	192 (0.47)
Total	**40412 (100.00)**

Note: Values in parentheses are percentage to total.

Source: GoM (1996a).

Rural Population

The proportion of rural population of the state has fallen from 72 per cent of total population in 1961 to 58 per cent in 2001. Maharashtra has a much lower rural population, compared to many other Indian states, indicating the rapid urbanisation in the state. District-wise rural population shows that with the exception of Mumbai, Thane, Nagpur and Pune, all other districts are predominantly rural, having between 60 to 90 per cent of their population, in rural areas.

Rural Poverty

The proportion of population below the poverty line for India, and for rural and urban Maharashtra is shown in Table 11.2. Population below poverty line for rural

Maharashtra is lower than that for rural India. The incidence of rural poverty in the state increased between 1973-74 and 1977-78 and has declined thereafter. Reduction in rural poverty in Maharashtra has moved almost at the same pace as that of India. Rural poverty which was at a higher level than the urban poverty in the state till 1993-94 has come down to 23.82 per cent as against an urban poverty ratio of 26.91 per cent. Regional variation in rural poverty does not appear to be significant as seen from Table 11.3.

TABLE 11.2

Population Below Poverty Line

(Per Cent)

Year	*Maha. Rural*	*Maha. Urban*	*All India Rural*	*All India Urban*
1973-74	57.71	43.00	56.44	49.20
1977-78	63.97	40.60	53.07	47.40
1983	45.23	40.60	45.65	42.20
1987-88	40.78	39.00	39.00	40.10
1993-94	37.93	35.15	35.15	32.46
1999-00	23.82	26.91	27.11	23.65

Source: Planning Commission, New Delhi.

TABLE 11.3

Region-wise Rural Poverty Rates in Maharashtra, 1999-2000

Region	*Districts*	*HCR*
Coastal	Sindhudurg, Ratnagiri, Raigarh, Thane, Gr. Bombay	15.2
Inland Western	Kolhapur, Sholapur, Sangli, Satara, Pune, Ahmednagar	16.2
Inland Northern	Jalgaon, Dhule, Nashik	43.3
Inland Central	Latur, Osmanabad, Nanded, Beed, Parbhani, Jalna, Aurangabad	42.2
Inland Eastern	Akola, Buldhana, Amravati, Yavatmal, Wardha, Nagpur	46.6
Eastern	Bhandara, Chandrapur, Gadchiroli	45.2

Note: Based on the use of probability of being poor functions estimated at regional level.

Source: Deaton (2003).

The regional variation in rural poverty is along expected lines. The coastal and inland western regions are the least poor whereas inland northern, inland central, inland eastern and eastern regions are relatively poorer.

Rural Literacy

Literacy rate in Maharashtra is among one of the highest in the country. It ranks after Kerala and some smaller states and union territories. Maharashtra has seen a rapid increase in literacy in the last decade. Rural literacy too has increased rapidly in the previous decade; an increase of almost 15 per cent as against urban literacy which increased by 6.56 per cent. The noticeable point is the decrease in the gap between rural and urban literacy over the 20 year period from 1981 to 2001 (Table 11.4). Rural literacy in all divisions barring Aurangabad, ranged from 69.45 per cent in Nashik division to 75.03 per cent in Amravati division in 2001. Aurangabad division had the lowest rural literacy: 65.99 per cent in 2001 and 45.7 per cent in 1991.

TABLE 11.4

Literacy Rate in Rural/Urban Maharashtra

(in Per Cent)

Year	*Total Literacy*	*Rural Literacy*	*Urban Literacy*	*Gap Between Rural-Urban*
1981	57.24	46.70	76.31	30
1991	64.87	55.52	79.20	24
2001	77.27	70.84	85.76	15

Source: Census of India 2001. *Series 28*, Maharashtra.

There is no major imbalance in the rural literacy across divisions or regions of the state excepting that Aurangabad division lagged behind other divisions in 1991 and 2001. Amravati division has made rapid strides in rural literacy because of which it has the highest rural literacy rate among all divisions in 2001.

Provision of Village Infrastructure: Maharashtra *vis-à-vis* Other States

According to an index, developed by National Institute for Rural Development (NIRD) to assess the availability of social and physical infrastructure in rural areas, Maharashtra's performance *vis-à-vis* other states is average. Among the top 10 per cent states on the Social Development Index of rural areas, Maharashtra enjoys that position only with regard to the facility of primary school. With respect to other social indicators like *pucca* house, safe drinking water, toilet, medical facility and taps, Maharashtra does not figure in the top 10 per cent. In fact, in case of safe drinking water, it falls in the bottom 30 per cent of the states. For the remaining indicators of social development, the state's performance falls in the middle range. In case of some of the physical infrastructure like electricity and post and telegraph, Maharashtra falls in top 10 per cent of the states (NIRD, 1999). In short, the performance of the state *vis-à-vis* other states in terms of providing social and physical infrastructure to rural areas is average. In the following sub-section, an attempt is made to see how villages in Maharashtra are provided for with different amenities that comprise the social and physical infrastructure. This is done by examining the percentage of villages in the state and each district having a specific amenity. The amenities considered are those recorded in the census (Table 11.5).

TABLE 11.5

Villages Served by Various Amenities

(Per Cent of Total Inhabited Villages)

Amenity Provided	*1981*	*1991*
Education	90.44	93.27
Medical	17.40	31.01
Drinking Water	100.00	100.00
Post and Telegraph	28.57	29.63
Market/*Haat*	10.92	10.55
Communication	47.32	64.44
Pucca Road	37.44	42.23
Power Supply	67.08	95.76

Source: Compiled from Census, 1981, 1991.

Provision of Village Infrastructure: State and District Level Performance

The performance across types of amenities shows that the state has been most successful in providing primary education to its villages with most districts providing this facility to up to 99 per cent of its villages (Table 11.5). In the case of safe drinking water, data show that 100 per cent villages of all districts have been provided this facility. However, this figure seems to be doubtful since the NIRD report shows that in terms of safe drinking water Maharashtra falls in the bottom 30 per cent of the states. Since mid-1970s, there have been recurrent water shortages in the state. These have been dealt with using *ad-hoc* measures like provision of water with water tankers, etc. Since the problem persists even today, some long-term solution is called for. Provision of power supply shows progress over the decade. For most districts, up to 80 per cent of villages have this facility. In all districts, except Gadchiroli, 50 or more than 50 per cent of the villages have been electrified. The performance in this shows improvements in 1991, with up to cent per cent of villages of some districts and 90 and higher per cent of the remaining districts being electrified.

The above are the only two facilities, (education and power) among those considered, for which the provision is satisfactory. With respect to other amenities, the performance is far from satisfactory and a wide gap remains to be covered.

In case of medical facility, there is an improvement over the decade of the eighties. Only 17 per cent of villages had this facility in 1981, though in 1991 this improved to 31 per cent. However, in absolute terms it is still low. If we look at the district-wise performance, it ranges between 6 per cent (Gadchiroli) of villages with medical facility to 37 per cent (Kolhapur) in 1981. In 1991, this is between 11 per cent (Raigad) to the best of 54 per cent (Sindhudurg) Table 11.6.

With respect to communication facilities, the performance shows an improvement from 47 per cent in

TABLE 11.6

Region-wise Percentage of Villages Served by Various Amenities

Amenity	*Year*	*Konkan*	*Northern*	*Western*	*Marathwada*	*Vidarbha*	*Maharashtra*
Education	1981	92.64	93.07	98.13	97.64	78.78	90.44
	1991	93.17	95.66	98.02	97.69	85.11	93.27
Medical	1981	21.94	14.81	26.28	13.63	13.04	17.40
	1991	26.17	28.67	32.26	34.83	27.78	31.01
Drinking Water	1981	100.00	100.00	100.00	100.00	100.00	100.00
	1991	100.00	100.00	100.00	100.00	100.00	100.00
Post and Telegraph	1981	29.35	29.35	44.19	27.13	18.82	28.57
	1991	27.37	35.10	43.39	25.52	20.98	29.63
Market *Haat*	1981	4.92	8.75	12.50	9.92	14.23	10.55
	1991	4.76	8.07	10.90	7.30	12.12	10.55
Communication	1981	61.61	61.99	62.45	44.22	27.18	47.32
	1991	74.52	78.18	74.08	64.70	44.23	64.28
Approach by *Pucca* Road	1981	43.25	35.75	43.93	34.80	32.95	37.44
	1991	50.25	39.63	47.70	41.14	35.64	42.23
Power Supply	1981	65.67	72.03	75.89	69.20	58.76	67.08
	1991	98.89	95.04	98.97	99.56	88.94	95.76

Source: Compiled from *District Census Handbook.*

1981 to 64 per cent in 1991. The district-wise dispersion is not skewed. Most districts have around 30 to 60 per cent of their villages with communication facilities. In both years, Gadchiroli is the worst performer with only 12 per cent in 1981 and 23 per cent in 1991 of its villages having communication facilities.

Provisions of post and telegraph services also show a poor record. The coverage of villages, which was 29 per cent in 1981, increased to 30 per cent in 1991. District-wise performance is not skewed and the range is small in both years. Gadchiroli is the worst performer here too, in both years. In 1991, only 10 per cent of its villages were being served by this facility.

In 1981 only 11 per cent villages of the state had a market *haat* and there was very little change in this in 1991. Since this facility is not provided for, but is a feature of village life, its presence indicates the demand for this facility. Whether this needs to be improved on a priority basis or not, is not clear. Approach by *pucca* road is one of the major infrastructural requirements of village development and therefore, its inadequacy could prove to be the major bottleneck in village development. On this key indicator, Maharashtra did not show a promising picture in 1981, with only 37 per cent of its villages linked with *pucca* roads. The coverage improved to 42 per cent in 1991. District-wise performance shows that Ahmednagar was the best performer in 1981 (58 per cent coverage) and Aurangabad in 1991 (61 per cent coverage). The worst performer in both years was again Gadchiroli (19 per cent coverage in 1981 and 17 per cent in 1991).

Overall, Maharashtra has been able to address some of the requirements of village development in terms of provision of infrastructure but is lagging behind in some important ones. Primary education, communication and power seem to be the areas where the state has done a fair job so far. However, other areas such as medical facility, *pucca* road and most probably safe drinking water need attention. These are crucial to village development as they provide the necessary physical and human capital required for sustainable development. Among districts, Gadchiroli stands out for being a laggard in the provision of all the amenities discussed here. One has to bear in mind the way these amenities are defined, before concluding about what has been achieved so far and what needs to be done. For example, safe drinking water is assumed to be available if there is a tap in the village. The tap may or may not be working, water may or may not be available, but presence of a tap is taken to mean availability of safe drinking water. Moreover, it is not possible to comment on the quality or the maintenance of the amenity provided; one can only infer about the quantity.

Regional Imbalances in Provision of Village Amenities

Regional imbalance is one of the key features of Maharashtra and its development. It is mainly due to wide differences in the topography and agro-climatic variations among the five major regions of the state. Vidarbha, Marathwada and Konkan are relatively backward compared to the more developed regions of northern and western Maharashtra. Developmental efforts attempt to bridge these differences wherever possible.

In case of provision of primary education, wide disparities are not seen. Vidarbha is lagging behind other regions but the gap has narrowed in 1991. In case of medical facilities and posts and telegraphs too there are no wide disparities in either 1981 or 1991. Western Maharashtra is the best performer with respect to these amenities. In the case of communication, some regional disparity is seen in 1981 with Vidarbha and Marathwada lagging behind the other regions. This disparity declined to some extent for Marathwada in 1991. There appears to be little disparity across regions in provision of *pucca* road and power supply. However, once again Vidarbha lags behind in the provision of power supply. On the whole, there are no major disparities across regions in provision of village amenities except that Vidarbha as a region lags behind in the provision of amenities like power supply, communications and education. However, it is to be noted that in terms of market/*haat* Vidarbha has a better coverage than the other regions. This is due to the fact that Vidarbha has been a long-standing supplier of raw materials like cotton, oilseeds, etc.

Regional Development Boards were set up in 1991 for removing the developmental backlog and correcting the regional imbalance. However, their functioning has not been satisfactory. They have been viewed as aiding the divisive forces in the state rather than as pragmatic solutions to removal of the developmental backlog. There have also been criticisms of misuse or diversion of funds for other purposes. Their functioning needs to be improved to address the long pending problem of regional imbalance more effectively.

Village Development Programmes

To accelerate the pace of development of rural areas, a variety of special programmes sponsored by the Centre, state or partly by both are used. Different programmes are aimed at different aspects of rural development. These programmes can be categorised broadly as: a) employment generating, b) anti-poverty or poverty alleviating, and c) rural infrastructure creating programme. Any one programme may be addressing more than one of the objectives.

Budgetary allocation for rural development, as per cent of total plan outlay, has been 11 per cent in the Eighth Five Year Plan (1992-1997), 9 per cent in the Ninth Five Year Plan (1997-2002) and 10 per cent in the Tenth Five Year Plan (2002-2007). Within rural development, programmes for employment generation have been allotted 59 per cent of the total allocation for rural development in the Tenth Five Year Plan whereas IRDP, an anti-poverty programme, is allotted 3.3 per cent. This underlines the importance of the employment generation programmes for the rural areas of the state.

Employment guaranteeing programmes like the Employment Guarantee Scheme (EGS) or Employment Assurance Scheme (EAS) are meant to tackle immediate problems of widespread poverty due to calamities like droughts, floods, etc. These are meant to offer immediate relief and generate some work and income for the very poor in rural areas either during the non-farming season or during the farming season when there is a drought or flood and agriculture is badly affected. To tackle the problem of rural poverty on a sustainable basis, however, the above effort is not enough. Hence, some assistance in asset creation at a personal level is necessary to enable the rural poor to raise themselves above the poverty line. The Integrated Rural Development Programme (IRDP) was launched with this aim. The third category of programmes, i.e., those meant to develop rural infrastructure, are necessary because an effort has to be made to develop the rural area not only with respect to increasing incomes level but to develop infrastructure to help the poor. Hence, some programmes are aimed at giving incentives to people to build up their personal assets, e.g. smokeless *chulhas* or constructing better dwellings. Examples of these types of schemes are Indira Awaas Yojana, water supply schemes, and biogas plants, etc. All the three categories of programmes are addressing the problem of rural poverty and underdevelopment at different levels. One major programme in each of the categories mentioned above is discussed in the sub-sections to follow.

Employment Guarantee Scheme

The EGS was launched formally in 1972 to check the rural to urban migration as well as to provide employment to those willing to work for a minimum wage. The objective of EGS is to provide gainful and productive employment to the people in the rural areas and in the areas of 'C' class Municipal Councils who are in need of work and are prepared to do unskilled manual work on the principle of work on demand.

The budget provision on EGS has continuously increased from Rs. 22.3 million in 1972-73 to Rs. 6,670 million in 2000-01. Data show that the utilisation of funds has been satisfactory. This indicates that the demand for the scheme continues to be strong. One of the major requirements of the EGS is that more than 60 per cent of the expenditure is to be spent on wages to ensure generation of labour-intensive work. This has been achieved successfully in all the years with the wage component being at times 90 per cent of the total expenditure.

The average daily attendance is seen to be high, ranging between 0.5 million to 0.6 million during seventies and even early eighties. In the late eighties it started to decline to around 0.27 to 0.38 million. After 1995, it further declined to around 0.096 to 0.17 million. Hence, a continuous decline in the average labour attendance is seen over the years.

The break up of activities taken up under EGS, from 1990s, shows that while irrigation and forestry works have declined, works related to roads, horticulture, Jawahar wells, etc. have increased. Agriculture related works have remained more or less the same.

Because of its success and need, the EGS was modified to include horticulture programme (1990), Jawahar wells (1988) and Shram Shakti Dware Gram Vikas programmes. This was to bring in new area like horticulture and total village level planning and building infrastructure required by the village as a whole. The norm for expenditure on labour was also relaxed in 1997.

Several studies show that EGS funds are mainly generated from taxes paid by the urban population. Dev (1995) contends that the contribution of EGS to income of EGS households is substantial. Other indirect benefits are stabilisation of incomes of rural poor (even if there is no increase) and creation of durable rural assets. He finds evidence (Sathe, 1991) that assets created under EGS led to improvement in income of agriculture and rural non-agricultural households. Moreover, it was found that the EGS wage rate influenced the general agricultural wage rate in the state. The importance of EGS lies in its guarantee of work, which acts as an assurance. It also performs much better than other poverty alleviation schemes/ programmes like National Rural Employment Programme (NREP), Rural Landless Employment Guarantee Programme (RLEGP) and IRDP (Acharya, 1990; World Bank, 1989).

Problems in the working of EGS have also been studied and discussed. There have been problems of leakage of funds, corruption and also of the wage rate where the recipients have not always got the minimum wages (due to the complicated piece rate system). Moreover, starting an EGS site requires a lot of advance planning of work in groups of villages and then on execution of these plans by officials of the irrigation, agriculture and forestry departments. Regarding the assets created, there is a concern on the quality and development impact of these assets.

Despite these drawbacks, the EGS is a popular scheme in Maharashtra. It is successful in its target of providing relief to the poor and unemployed in rural areas during the lean season or the agriculture season (in the case of drought) as well as in creating rural assets. The demand for EGS is still high especially in districts like Solapur.

Some aspects of EGS may be reviewed, one being that of the assets created not being durable. This can be tackled by making provision for undertaking maintenance works of the assets created as part of new EGS works. The other question that is often raised is that of allowing some machinery to be used to make asset more durable. For this, the norm of 60 per cent expenditure on labour has already been relaxed. Often a question is also raised whether EGS should remain a temporary drought relief programme or be converted into an anti-poverty programme. It may be said that until Maharashtra does not address its problem of irrigation adequately, programmes like EGS will be needed.

Indira Awas Yojana

In June 1985, Government of India pronounced that some part of fund of Grameen Bhumiheen Rojgar Hami Karyakram be kept aside for the construction of houses for people of SC, ST and *mukta vetbhigari* (bonded labourers who are now freed). From this fund, the Indira Awas Yojana (IAY) was started as sub-scheme of Grameen Bhumiheen Rojgar Hami Karyakram in 1985-86. But soon after, when the Jawahar Rojgar Yojana (JRY) was started in 1989, IAY was continued as a sub-scheme of JRY. Out of total funds of JRY, 6 per cent was allocated for implementation of IAY. From the year 1993-94 the scope of IAY was increased to include the non- SC/ST families below poverty line. Taking this fact into consideration, funds allocation for implementing the scheme was increased from 6 to 10 per cent of the JRY budget at national level, provided that the distribution of funds to BPL non-SC/ST families should not exceed 4 per cent of total allocation of IAY. As of now, IAY is separated from JRY and from 1 January 1996 it is functioning as an independent scheme.

The purpose of IAY is to provide houses free of cost to the poor (BPL) families in the rural areas. Under this, from 1999 the government has fixed Rs. 30,000 per house of which Rs. 1,500 will come from the beneficiary. The scheme was modified to allow for construction of new houses (80 per cent of funds) and upgradation of unserviceable *kutcha* houses (20 per cent of funds). For the latter, Rs. 10,000 per unit are allowed. These can also be used for constructing sanitary latrines and smokeless *chulhas*.

Utilisation of funds of IAY is above 55 per cent in almost all the districts in Maharashtra in all the years (1997-98 to 2000-01). The percentage of ST population covered is decreasing in all the districts in Maharashtra. Highest number of ST beneficiaries has been covered in Thane in all the concerned years (from 1997-98 to 2002-03). The percentage of houses completed to the annual target is seen to be decreasing over a period of 1997-98 to 2002-03 from more than 60 per cent in the initial years to below 25 per cent in all other districts. However, work in progress on new houses and upgradation as percentage of target is substantial, i.e. more than 50 per cent. IAY is picking up rapidly and is addressing the question of providing shelter to the rural poor. There is a demand for this and such a scheme must be further strengthened.

Integrated Rural Development Programme (IRDP)

The Integrated Rural Development Programme (IRDP) was initiated in 1978. The objective of this programme was to integrate different activities locally in micro-level planning framework at the district and block levels. But in the Sixth Five Year Plan, when the programme was extended from selected districts to the whole country, it was simplified to being mainly a small loan-cum-subsidy programme (Loan of Rs. 7 to 8 thousand at 1991-92 prices). It was meant to generate self-employment among families identified as below the poverty line (families whose annual income did not exceed Rs. 3,500 at 1980-81 prices).

IRDP was criticised mainly for its administrative targeting approach, for the excessive centralisation in decision making and for the utilisation of loan by the beneficiaries (Rath, 1985; Dreze, 1990). However, according to studies based on large samples by RBI, NABARD, Planning Commission and IFMR, IRDP has not been an absolute failure. These studies found that half the sample households in each study had received IRDP funds and 21 to 50 per cent had crossed the poverty line. It was observed that majority of respondents are satisfied with IRDP (NIRD, 1999). Another study concluded that the more developed regions and families nearer to the poverty line showed a better performance when compared to others. Assistance went to deserving poor and the communities had adequately participated in beneficiary selection, the assets distributed were sectorally balanced and the record of repayment was no worse than that in other government programmes (Kurien, 1987).

Despite some of the encouraging assessment of IRDP as noted above, the government noted that IRDP has not been successful as expected since the number of people crossing poverty line were few and the over dues were very large (GoI, 1992). Considering the strengths and weaknesses of this scheme, various alterations were made to it through Seventh and Eighth Plan such as decentralisation through District Rural Development Agency (DRDA) and block authorities playing an important role to ensure people's participation as well as meeting location specific requirements. It was also decided to refinance some of those families who had not been able to cross the poverty line. Up to 30 per cent reservation was to be made for women although this was family targeted programme.

Swarnajayanti Gram Swayamrozgar Yojana (SGSY)

Currently, SGSY is the single self-employment programme for rural poor. It was initiated on 1 April 1999. It replaced the earlier self-employment and allied programmes like IRDP, DWCRA, TRYSEM, etc.; these programmes are no longer in operation. Table 11.7 shows the performance of SGSY.

TABLE 11.7

Performance of SGSY, up to December 2002

Beneficiaries		*SHGs*	
Swarojgaris (No.)	22663	Groups Members Assisted	10546
Subsidy to *Swarojgaris* (Rs. Millions)	225.6	Groups Assisted (No.)	928
Credit to *Swarojgaris* (Rs. Millions)	401.2	Subsidy to SHG *Swarojgaris* (Rs. Millions)	109.7
Assistance per Beneficiary (Rs.)	27658	Credit to SHG Swarojgaris (Rs. Millions)	155.5
		Assistance per SHG (Rs. App.)	276077

Source: Economic Survey of Maharashtra, 2002-03, p.215.

The objective of SGSY is to bring the assisted poor families (*swarojgaris*) above the poverty line by ensuring appreciable sustained level of income over a period of time. It is rooted in the belief that rural poor in India have competencies and given the right support, they can be successful producers of valuable goods/services. So persons assisted under this programme will be known as *swarojgaris*.

The programme targets mainly the rural poor and that too the most vulnerable among them. At least 50 per cent of *swarojgaris* will be SCs/STs, 40 per cent woman and 3 per cent disabled. One of the distinctive features of the programme is the group approach. This would involve organisation of poor into self-help groups. SGSY is a credit-cum-subsidy programme. Credit is a critical component while subsidy will be only an enabling element of this programme. Credit will be multiple-credit rather than one time credit injection. Subsidy will be uniform at 30 per cent of the project cost subject to ceiling of Rs. 7,500 and for SCs/STs it would be 50 per cent with the ceiling of Rs. 10,000. For self-help groups, subsidy would be 50 per cent of the project cost with the ceiling of Rs. 0.13 million. But for the irrigation projects there will be no limit. Institutions like banks, *panchayats*, *gram sabhas*, NGOs and technical institutions have an important role to play in the planning, capacity building, choice of activity of SHGs, selection of individual *swarojgaris*, pre-credit activities and post-credit monitoring including loan recovery. SGSY is a centrally sponsored scheme and funding is shared by the Central Government (75 per cent) and state government (25 per cent).

Appraisal of SGSY

Under SGSY, up to December 2002, 928 SHGs were assisted with Rs. 109.7 millions and Rs. 155.5 millions of credit. Utilisation of funds of SGSY in all the districts of Maharashtra is above 60 per cent. In case of Ahmednagar, Nanded, Bhandara, it is about 100 per cent. The percentage of SC beneficiaries to total has not increased remarkably over the years in the state. It has been relatively greater in Pune and Aurangabad divisions during 1990 to 2002. In the latest year, i.e. 2002, it is highest in Kolhapur (49.32 per cent) and lowest in Dhule (1.75 per cent). The percentage of ST beneficiaries is higher in districts of Thane, Nashik, Dhule, and Gadchiroli in the year 1990, 1995 and 2002. Since the coverage of the SC/ST beneficiaries under SGSY is less than the guidelines of 50 per cent, the field level machineries have been directed by the government to increase the percentage of SC/ST beneficiaries. Percentage of woman beneficiaries under SGSY has increased substantially. Among the SHGs, 90 per cent are women's groups. In fact, SHGs have become so popular that the problem now facing the government agencies is to make adequate credit available to the SHGs. This indicates that the rural poor, particularly women, have been motivated to empower themselves. On its part, the government is making several attempts to improve credit availability. For instance, joint workshops of NGOs, bank representatives, and field officers were arranged at state as well as division level to overcome the common problems arising in disbursement under the scheme. Also, this issue is always raised at the State Level Bankers Committee (SLBC) and State Level Co-ordination Committee (SLCC) under SGSY. Activities undertaken under SGSY are predominantly activities under the primary sector like irrigation, land development, animal husbandry and others. Out of total number of loans, almost 70 per cent are for dairy activity. However, the percentage coverage of primary sector is decreasing over time and the coverage of the secondary sector is increasing in all divisions of Maharashtra excluding Aurangabad and Amravati division. Under secondary sector, activities undertaken are those of *masala* making, vegetable vending, tailoring, etc. With greater participation of women in SGSY, the challenge now may be of identifying adequate and viable commercial activities for them to pursue. In this respect, the government machinery ensures that the commercial activities are selected based on the availability of inputs in the local areas and marketing facilities for the goods produced by the SHGs. To provide marketing facilities to the products produced by the SHGs under SGSY, government arranges an exhibition-cum-sale named 'SARAS' at the state and national level every year. However, lack of credit or viable commercial activities need not become the main stumbling block in a programme like this because empowerment of women or the poor need not be only through increased income generation. This should not be seen as a failure of the programme or the developmental effort. Raising awareness of the poor through these programmes is also a way to empower them.

Sampoorna Gramin Rojgar Yojana (SGRY)

The SGRY was proposed in the Tenth Five Year Plan as an important poverty alleviation scheme. It combined the earlier two schemes, namely, Employment Assurance Scheme (EAS) and the Jawahar Gram Samridhi Yojana (JGSY). Though the scheme was implemented from September 2001, in Maharashtra it came into effect in January 2002. The main objective of this scheme is to provide food and nutrition to the poor, and to create durable community assets in rural areas. SGRY has both cash and kind component. While 5 kgs of foodgrains (wheat and rice at the rate of Rs. 5 and Rs. 6 per kg respectively) is made available per manday to the workers, the rest of the wage is paid in cash. The SGRY is implemented in two streams: the first at the district and *panchayat samiti*, and the second at the village *panchayat* level. Under the first stream, 22.5 per cent of funds are provided to individual beneficiaries of SC/ST families living below the poverty line. In 2002-03, (up to December 2002) 11.8 million man-days of employment was generated. Under the second stream, 50 per cent of funds are spent for creations of need-based village infrastructure in SC/ST habitation/ward. During 2002-03 (up to December 2002) the second stream provided 11.6 million man-days of employment.

All the anti-poverty programmes, especially IRDP, have been criticised mainly because they could not achieve what they had meant to achieve. Changes were incorporated in their designs (e.g. DWCRA was launched as sub-scheme of IRDP, then SHGs in the form of the Maharashtra Rural Credit Project (MRCP)) to enable a better success rate. It is now seen that probably the modifications made in the IRDP over the years may be ensuring better success. The SHGs based programmes e.g., MRCP or now SGSY, are showing a much better performance in Maharashtra as they are in other states as well. Of course, these too are not problem free but they are perceived to be better than the earlier IRDP by all agencies concerned, namely the government, the banks/lending institutions and the beneficiaries.

In conclusion, intervention for village development has seen some success and it is necessary to build on this success to further catalyse, and speed the pace of development of the villages in Maharashtra.

Village Development in Tribal Areas

Maharashtra has 10.17 per cent of India's total tribal population according to the 2001 Census. The tribal population is 8.85 per cent of the total population of the state. There are in all 47 scheduled tribe communities (*Tribal Research Bulletin*, 2000). The total tribal area of Maharashtra is 307,713 sq. km, which is 19 per cent of the total geographical area of Maharashtra. These scheduled areas of Maharashtra spread over 11 districts of Thane, Nashik, Dhule, Jalgaon, Ahmednagar, Pune, Nanded, Amravati, Yavatmal, Gadchiroli and Chandrapur. The district-wise proportion of tribal population to total population of these tribal concentrated districts is shown in Table 11.8. The Bhils, the Varlis, the Katkaris, the Kolams and the Gonds are some of the major tribes found in the state.

To assess the development of the tribal areas, the following approach has been adopted. Firstly, the districts having a high concentration of tribal population have been identified (Table 11.8). Secondly, the schedule tribe population of the various *tehsils* of the above-mentioned districts have been looked into. From here, the *tehsils* having a high tribal population and those with low tribal population have been selected. High tribal population is defined as: schedule tribe population above district average (1991) and low is defined as scheduled tribe population below district average.

With this, the tribal and non-tribal *tehsils* in the districts have been demarcated. The tribal areas comprise of the *tehsils* with high tribal concentration. The development of tribal tahsils *vis-à-vis* the development of non-tribal *tehsils* has been assessed by examining some social indicators of development. The findings are given in the following paragraphs.

Literacy rate of tribals (STs) is much lower than the literacy rate of general population except in case of Thane. Difference in the literacy rate of tribals in tribal and non-tribal *tehsils* is substantial in the case of districts like Amravati, Thane and Gadchiroli, but the difference is not so marked for Dhule, Nashik and Yavatmal.

TABLE 11.8

Tribal Population: 1991 and 2001

District	*Tribal Population as a Percentage of Total Population*	
	1991	*2001*
Dhule	40.87	26.00
Gadchiroli	38.70	38.30
Nashik	24.18	23.90
Yavatmal	21.46	19.30
Chandrapur	19.70	18.10
Thane	18.12	14.70
Amravati	14.38	13.70
Maharashtra	**9.72**	**8.85**

Source: Census of India, 1991, 2001.

In the case of education, post and telegraph, market/*haat*, communication, *pucca* road and power supply, the non-tribal *tehsils* of all districts have a better coverage than tribal *tehsils*. Among districts, Thane shows minimal difference between the tribal and non-tribal *tehsils*. Across facilities, education shows a better coverage and along with the facility of market/*haat*, displays minimal discrepancy between coverage of tribal and non-tribal *tehsils*.

In the case of medical facility, the percentage of villages having medical facility (primary health centre) at district level is low in all the tribal districts (16 to 37 per cent). Dhule, Amravati and Thane have a lower percentage of villages having medical facility in tribal *tehsils* than in non-tribal *tehsils*. For Gadchiroli, Nashik and Yavatmal the picture is reversed; in these districts, tribal *tehsils* have a higher percentage of villages with medical facility as compared to the non-tribal *tehsils*. This could be due to special tribal health programmes initiated at the districts of Gadchiroli, Nashik and Yavatmal.

Programmes like IAY, aimed at the tribal populace are aiding development of the tribal areas. About 38 per cent of the state's ST population has been covered under the IAY. There are regional variations; Konkan and northern Maharashtra have a better coverage (above 55 per cent), Vidarbha region shows 38 per cent coverage and western Maharashtra and Marathwada are lagging behind with a low coverage of the ST population (Table 11.16).

Overall, within the tribal districts, the tribal *tehsils* are backward relative to non-tribal *tehsils* in terms of the social indicators and infrastructure considered here. The exception is medical facility. In Nashik, Yavatmal and Gadchiroli, provision of medical facility shows a better coverage in the tribal *tehsils* compared to the non-tribal *tehsils*. This may be attributed to the special health programmes operative in these districts.

Panchayati Raj and Village Development

After the formation of the unilingual state of Maharashtra on 1 May 1960, the then Chief Minister Y. B. Chavan advocated the creation of a democratic socialist state with the help of PRIs. In pursuance of the recommendations of Balawantrai Mehta Committee, the state government appointed the V.P. Naik Committee in 1960. The latter opted for a three-tier structure like that of the Mehta Committee. But unlike the Mehta Committee, it suggested that the *zilla parishads* (ZPs) be all powerful in the hierarchical structure of *panchayats*. It recommended the devolution of power of taxation and disbursement of development funds to the ZPs. Thereafter, the Maharashtra Zilla Parishad and Panchayat Samiti Act, 1961 was enacted. Village *panchayats* had already been in existence under the Bombay Village Panchayats Act, 1958. Thus, the three-tier *panchayati raj* system in the state comprising the *gram panchayat* (GP) at the lower, *panchayat samiti* (PS) at the middle, and ZP at the highest levels, was introduced. As recommended by the Naik Committee, the government also appointed Panchayati Raj Evaluation Committees periodically to review the functioning of *panchayats*. The notable among them are the Bongirwar Committee and Patil Committee. Maharashtra is considered one of the few states, which has satisfactorily implemented the *panchayati raj* system in the wake of Balwantrai Mehta Committee report of 1957 (Mathew, 1994).

In compliance with the 73rd Constitutional amendment, the Maharashtra Zilla Parishads and Panchayat Samitis' (Amendment) Act, 1993 was enacted. As most of the provisions of the 73rd Constitutional Amendment were already in operation, only minor changes have been made. Many provisions of the 73rd Constitutional Amendment were similar to the recommendations made by the Patil Committee earlier. In pursuance of the Provisions of Panchayats (Extension to Scheduled Areas) Act, passed by union government in 1996, the Maharashtra Zilla Parishads and Panchayat Samitis (Extension to the Scheduled Areas and Amendments) Act was passed in 1997.

The government, placing emphasis on the district as the basic unit of planning and development, in 1974 facilitated the formulation of the District Planning and Development Councils (DPDC), and its executive and sub-committees. In view of the 74th Amendment, the DPDCs have been dissolved since March 1999. However, the District Planning Committees (DPCs) as per the provision prescribed under Article 243 ZD (1) of the Constitution has not yet been constituted like that of Karnataka, West Bengal, Kerala, Madhya Pradesh and many other states. The main functions of the DPCs include preparation of the draft plan and the Five Year Plan for the district, monitoring and reviewing of development plan, recommending the sanctioned development plan of the district to the state government, etc.

The first elections for the ZPs and PSs were held in 1962, and then in 1967, 1972 and 1979. The elections were postponed on some political pretext or the other and in certain areas ZPs were superseded by the government (Sirsikar, 1995). After a lapse of 13 years, elections were then held in 1992, 1997 and 2002. These elections are party based. In fact, the PRIs and co-operatives were looked upon as the training grounds for the emerging political leadership.

Structure of PRIs

The ZP is an autonomous body with a corporate character. It is composed of directly elected councillors (numbering 50 to 75) and chairman of the PSs as per the amendments made to the Zilla Parishad Act in the light of the 73rd Constitutional Amendment Act, 1992. The amended Act abolished the earlier provision of inclusion of the chairpersons of cooperative societies and the director of Land Development Bank as the associate members. The president and vice-president of the ZP are elected from amongst the elected members. While the term of the members is five years, it is one year each for the president and vice-president.

The Zilla Parishad Act provides for a committee form of governance. According to the Maharashtra Zilla Parishads and Panchayat Samitis Act, 1961 (amended in 1966), each ZP has a standing committee. Besides, there were six subject committees each dealing with finance, works, agriculture and cooperation, health, education and social welfare. On the recommendation of Patil Committee, three more subject committees have been added to deal with animal husbandry and dairy, women and child welfare and water conservation. The standing committee consists of the president of ZP as its chairman, chairmen of the subject committees, seven elected members and two coopted persons having special knowledge and experience. It has the power to override decisions taken by the subject committees and provide the necessary checks and balances. The chairman of the ZP is the ex-officio member of all the subject committees, thereby coordinating all the works.

The PS consists of only the directly elected members. Every ZP has two PSs. The members of PSs are elected from the electoral colleges in the Block for which each ZP electoral division is divided into two electoral colleges. The chairman and deputy chairman of the PS are elected from amongst the directly elected members. The term of membership is five years, and for the chairman and deputy chairman one year each. Unlike ZPs, there is no committee system at the PS level. In the overall structure of *panchayati raj* in the state, PS is given a negligible role. It acts almost like an agency of the ZP for all practical purposes (Khanna, 1994; Sirsikar, 1995; World Bank, 2000).

The *panchayat* is composed of 7 to 17 directly elected members (depending upon the population). The GP members elect the sarpanch and the *up-sarpanch* for a five-year term. Of course, it is against the provision of direct election for the *sarpanch* and *up-sarpanch* as per the 73rd constitutional amendment.

Reservation of Seats for Hitherto Excluded Groups

As per the provisions of the Zilla Parishad and Panchayat Samiti Act, 1961 and the Bombay Village Panchayat Act, 1958 seats were reserved for the SCs and STs in ZPs, PSs and GPs. Following the Patil Committee recommendations, 30 per cent reservation for women was provided in all the PRIs since 1992. In fact, Maharashtra was the first state in the country to provide 30 per cent reservation for women in the *panchayati raj* bodies. The Zilla Parishad and Panchayat Samiti Act, 1961 and the Bombay Village Panchayat Act, 1958, which were amended in conformity with the 73rd constitutional amendment, enhanced the provisions of reservations for women (up to 33 per cent) and introduced reservation for the backward classes (27 per cent) on rotation basis. Offices of *sarpanch*, chairperson of the PS and president of the ZP are reserved for the scheduled castes and tribes as per the proportion of their population and 27 per cent for the OBCs on a rotation basis. One third of the number of these offices (including those reserved for SC, ST and OBC persons) are also reserved for women by rotation. Of the nine subject committees of the ZP, the chairperson of social welfare committee should be from SC/ST communities, and the chairperson of the women and child welfare committee from amongst the women councillors.

Financial Resources and Expenditure Pattern

The local bodies receive grants from the state and central governments for implementing the development programmes. The state government releases grants to the ZPs, which in turn, finance the PSs and GPs. The finances of the ZP comprise self-raised resources like taxes, fees, cess on land revenue, assigned revenues and government grants. The grants made to a ZP include purposive grants, establishment grants, incentive grants, plan grants, grants for agency schemes, local cess matching grants, etc. Consequent upon the recommendations of the successive evaluation committees, the state government has attempted to strengthen the resources of the ZPs. The recommendation of the Bongirwar Committee that cent per cent grants be given to the ZPs for meeting the expenditure on transferred schemes and establishment was accepted. The recommendation of Patil Committee for the enhancement of the financial resources of the ZPs has also been more or less accepted and a finance commission has been constituted at the state level for determining the quantum of resources to be transferred to the ZPs. The last three years average annual income from all sources (Table 11.9) shows that the ZP of Pune has the highest income in the state having over Rs. 4 billions. Some other districts like Nashik, Ahmednagar, Satara, Solapur and Amravati have income between Rs. 2 to 3 billions. Sindhudurg, Wardha,

TABLE 11.9

Classification of Districts based on the Average Income of ZPs

(in Rs.)

Particulars	*No.*	*Name of Districts*
4 to 5 Billion	1	Pune
3 to 4 Billion	Nil	-
2 to 3 Billion	5	Nashik, Ahmednagar, Satara, Solapur, Amravati
1 to 2 Billion	20	Thane, Raigad, Ratnagiri, Dhule, Jalgaon, Sangli, Kolhapur, Aurangabad, Jalna, Parbhani, Beed, Nanded, Osmanabad, Latur, Buldhana, Akola,Yavatmal, Nagpur, Bhandara, Chandrapur
0.50 to 1 Billion	3	Sindhudurg, Wardha, Gadchiroli
Up to 0.50 Billion	2	Washim, Nandurbar

Note: Based on average income of last three years (1998-99, 1999-00 and 2000-01).

Source: Bureau of Economics and Statistics, Maharashtra.

Gadchiroli and some of the newly created districts have income up to only Rs. 1 billion.

As regards the average income from their own resources (Table 11.10), a majority of the ZPs has income from Rs. 20 to 50 million only. The ZP of Pune has a maximum income (Rs. 50 to 90 million). The ZPs having income up to Rs. 10 million from own resources are from districts like Sindhudurg, Aurangabad and Latur.

TABLE 11.10

Classification of Districts according to Average Income of ZPs from Own Resources

(in Rs.)

Particulars	*No.*	*Name of Districts*
50 to 90 Million	1	Pune
20 to 50 million	19	Raigad, Thane, Nashik, Jalgaon, Ahmednagar, Satara, Sangli, Solapur, Kolhapur, Jalna, Parbhani, Beed, Nanded, Buldhana, Akola, Amravati, Yavatmal, Nagpur, Chandrapur, Bhandara
10 to 20 Million	4	Ratnagiri, Dhule, Osmanabad, Gadchiroli
Up to 10 Million	6	Sindhudurg, Nandurbar, Wardha Aurangabad, Latur, Washim

Note: Based on average income of last three years (1998-99, 1999-00 and 2000-01).

Source: Bureau of Economics and Statistics, Maharashtra.

It is reported that the share of government grants to the total income of the ZPs has increased noticeably since 1994-95 (as per the data provided by the Project Formulation and IRDP Cell, Department of Rural Development and Water Conservation, GoM). In the state as a whole, the government grant-in-aid constitutes nearly 75 per cent of total income of ZPs in 1999-00. The ZPs of the western region are relatively less dependent on government grants (63 per cent). The share of government grant to total income is less in Pune ZP (42 per cent). Over 87 per cent of the total income of the ZPs of the Konkan region is covered by government grants. In almost all the ZPs there is an increased dependence on government grants. To go by the Economic Survey of Maharashtra, the proportion of self-raised financial resources of the ZPs has declined over the years. It has come down to only 3 per cent in 2000-01 as against 9 per cent in 1970-71.

The PS does not have independent sources of revenue, as it is not a corporate body. It receives block grants from the state government through the ZP and prepares, executes, supervises and administers developmental schemes financed from these grants.

The main sources of finance of a GP are the land revenue and the cess thereon as also the grants from the state and central governments. In addition, it levies taxes (on buildings, fairs and festivals, pilgrimage, trade, general sanitary cess, etc.) under Section 124 of the Bombay Village Panchayat Act, 1958. The GPs in the districts of Raigad, Jalgaon, Pune and Kolhapur have incomes over Rs. 0.25 million each on an average (Table 11.11).

TABLE 11.11

Classification of Districts according to Average Income of GPs

(Rs.)

Particulars	*No.*	*Name of Districts*
Above 0.20 Million	9	Raigad, Jalgaon, Pune, Kolhapur, Thane, Ratnagiri, Sindhudurg, Satara, Nagpur
0.10 to 0.20 Million	10	Nashik, Dhule, Ahmednagar, Sangli, Solapur Latur, Nandurbar, Parbhani, Amravati, Yavatmal
Up to 0.10 Million	12	Aurangabad, Jalna, Buldhana, Osmanbad, Akola, Washim, Wardha, Bhandara, Chandrapur, Gadchiroli, Beed, Nanded

Note: Based on average income of last three years (1998-99, 1999-2000, 2000-01).

Source: Bureau of Economics and Statistics, Maharashtra.

The GPs of 12 districts in the state have less than a Rs. 0.10 million of income. The GPs depend to a large extent upon government grants. It is reported that the share of grants and donations to total income of GPs shows an increasing trend across the districts.

About 45 to 50 per cent of the total income of the GPs in the state comes from government grants. The GPs of the Konkan region particularly of Thane are to a large extent self-supportive. The government grants and their income from own sources is negligible. The *panchayats* of the majority of the districts in the state have an income of less than Rs. 50,000 from their own resources (Table 11.12). As a result, they are unable to undertake development work independently.

TABLE 11.12

Classification of Districts according to Average Income of GPs from Own Resources

(Rs.)

Particulars	*No.*	*Name of Districts*
Above 0.10 Million	1	Raigad
0.05 to 0.10 Million	7	Thane, Nashik, Jalgaon, Pune, Satara, Kolhapur, Nagpur
Up to 0.05 Million	23	Ratnagiri, Sindhudurg, Dhule, Nandurbar, Ahmednagar, Sangli, Solapur, Aurangabad, Osmanabad, Latur, Buldhana, Amravati, Wardha, Chandrapur, Gadchiroli, Jalna, Parbhani, Beed, Nanded, Akola, Washim, Yavatmal, Bhandara

Note: Based on average income of last three years.

Source: Bureau of Economics and Statistics, Maharashtra.

Paucity of financial resources as a major weakness of the *panchayati raj* bodies has been noted by the Evaluation Committees and other studies (1971, 1986; Sirsikar, 1995; World Bank, 2000). To go by the Report of the Eleventh Finance Commission of India (2000-2005), the income from own resources (tax and non-tax) of the PRIs in the state as a whole constitutes only 3.40 per cent of their total revenues, which is less than the all-India average (3.49 per cent). The share of own income of PRIs to total revenue is many times higher than Maharashtra in states like Punjab, Haryana and Kerala. There is an increasing trend of dependency on government grants. The government grants are mostly scheme bound. Of the 27 total recommendations made by the State Finance Commission on devolution of grants and taxes to PRIs, the state government has accepted only 12 recommendations fully. While 4 recommendations including the one on share in profession tax were rejected totally, 11 recommendations were accepted partially (Mathur, 2003).

The single largest item of expenditure of ZP in the state is education, which amounts to nearly half of the total expenditure (Table 11.13).

The expenditure on social welfare, community development, etc., is not substantial. Establishment charges also constitute an important item of expenditure of the ZP. The rising trend of establishment costs of ZP has been observed by other studies also (Vithal and Rao, 1997). Bulk of the expenditures of the GPs in the state is incurred on items like administration, health and sanitation, and public works. The expenditure on health and sanitation as well as public works has increased (Table 11.14).

TABLE 11.13

Average Expenditure of ZPs under Various Heads

(Per Cent)

Various Heads	*1987-88 to 1991-92*	*1992-93 to 1996-97*	*1997-98 to 2000-01*
General Administration	10.82	8.60	6.19
Education	54.71	48.63	49.28
Medical	8.51	7.62	7.50
Agriculture	0.47	1.81	1.91
Animal Husbandry	1.65	1.19	1.19
Building & Communication	8.59	9.63	8.43
Social Welfare	1.69	1.90	2.02
Community Devt.	0.27	2.58	3.01
Forestry	0.50	0.35	0.19
Public Health Engg.	2.95	3.62	4.37
Irrigation	3.91	5.61	3.54
Others	5.94	8.46	12.36
Total	**100.00**	**100.00**	**100.00**

Source: Economic Survey of Maharashtra, relevant issues.

TABLE 11.14

Average Expenditure of GPs under Various Heads

(in Per Cent)

Items	*1987-88 to 1991-92*	*1992-93 to 1996-97*	*1997-98 to 2000-01*
Administration	22.07	20.54	15.94
Health & Sanitation	20.83	26.36	31.83
Public Works	30.82	31.12	32.54
Public Lighting	10.13	7.89	5.46
Education	3.50	1.97	1.51
Welfare of People	6.06	8.57	6.90
Others	6.59	3.56	5.83
Total	**100.00**	**100.00**	**100.00**

Source: Economic Survey of Maharashtra, relevant issues.

Accountability Mechanism

Passing a no-confidence motion, by a vote of simple majority, can do the removal of heads of ZP, PS and GP. The standing committee of the ZP can also remove *sarpanch* or *up-sarpanch* on the grounds of misconduct.

Similarly, the state government can also remove the chairperson and vice-chairperson of the PS and the president and vice-president of ZP. The Gram Panchayat Act and Zilla Parishad and Panchayat Samiti Act have made provisions for holding the *gram sabhas* at the *panchayat* level and *gram sabhas* at the block levels to strengthen the peoples' participation. A *sarpanch* (or in his absence the *up-sarpanch*) has to call at least four meetings of the *gram sabha* during a financial year to approve the budgets, identify the beneficiaries of various programmes, etc. To build the linkage between the three tiers, Prabhag Committees are formed at the block level where the ZP councillors, PS members and *sarpanchs* participate. However, the *gram sabha* has very limited power. In September 2002, the state government decided to amend the Gram Panchayat Act to give more powers to *gram sabhas*. The GP will have to seek a prior permission of *gram sabha* before implementing any government scheme or programme. A *gram sabha* will also decide about the prospective beneficiaries of these schemes. It will have the power to seek information in cases of corruption or irregularities by the local government employees and submit a report to the authorities that are expected to take action within three months.

The major challenge that the PRIs in the state face is the corruption at various levels, which is the common practice in many states. Instances of misappropriation of funds by *sarpanchs, gram sevaks* often appear in the local newspapers. However, the recent initiatives of the government to empower the *gram sabha* by recalling *panchayat* representatives under certain circumstances, in response to social crusader Anna Hazare's demand, may check such incidents. Moreover, the wider anti-corruption movement initiated by Anna Hazare and his campaign for the people's right to information could generate effective and vigilant public opinion against the individuals and groups involved in such practices.

Schemes and Programmes

Based on the recommendations of the Bongirwar Committee and Patil Committee, most district level schemes have been transferred to the ZPs. Their activities as envisaged by the 73rd Constitutional Amendment are given in the Schedules I and II of the Zilla Parishad Act and the Schedule I of the Village Panchayat Act. As many as 234 schemes have been transferred fully to the ZPs which include those relating to education, public health, family welfare, water supply, sanitation, etc. The ZPs can also undertake the execution of government development works and schemes as an agency basis under the Zilla Parishad and Panchayat Samiti Act.

Forty-four schemes have been transferred to the ZPs on an agency basis for which three per cent (now raised to five per cent) agency charges are given to them for implementing these schemes which cover employment guarantee, natural calamities, arts and culture, rural development programme, medical and health, general education, family planning, crop development, MLA fund, social security and welfare. Most schemes dealing with development programmes at the district level such as agriculture, animal husbandry, primary and secondary education, drinking water supply, health and sanitation, primary health centres, women and child development, biogas and improved *chulhas* have also been transferred to the PRIs. A recent estimate is that schemes and programmes worth Rs. 20 billion per annum are with these bodies in 2001.

However, many schemes are only partially transferred to the PRIs. The Line Departments and District Rural Development Agencies continue to have major control over the planning and implementation of the schemes. The PRIs mostly act as the delivery units.

Impact of PRIs on Village Development

Despite the constraints and weaknesses, the state has been recognised as one of the progressive states in the field of *panchayati raj* in the country, which was considered worthy of emulation, by other states. Of course, comprehensive data are not available to assess the impact of the functioning of PRIs on quality of rural development particularly in post-73rd Amendment period. Given the historical background of rural local governance in the state, one would expect exemplary development in the rural areas in terms of literacy and education, reduction in the incidence of poverty, supply of drinking water, infrastructural facilities, etc. Though in terms of primary education, power supply and communication and few other items, the state has done a fair job so far, it lags far behind many other states as well as national average in several important indicators. It is believed that Maharashtra's better performance in the field of primary education is mainly due to the effective role of PRIs because the primary and secondary public education in the state is entrusted to them. Viewed from a different perspective, the PRIs have succeeded in bringing qualitative changes in the rural society in terms of stimulating popular participation and local leadership (Inamdar, 1970; Sirsikar, 1995; Mandlekar, 1991; World Bank, 2000).

The participation of women, which was unheard of in the rural local governance in the state, emerged after the introduction of the three-tier *panchayati raj* system. Way back in 1963 all-women *panchayat* was formed in Nimbut village of Pune district. In 1984 another village of the same district came up with an all-women *panchayat*. As many as 13 women attempted to challenge the male dominance in local governance by contesting *gram panchayat* elections in 1984 in 2 villages of Satara district. Further, in 1989 eight and in 1992 two *panchayats* came up with all women representatives in the districts of Pune, Ahmednagar, Amravati, Jalgaon, Yavatmal, Solapur and Wardha. The Shetkari Sanghatan and Shri Anna Hazare inspired most of them.

As a result of the provision of reservation, the participation of the members of the hitherto excluded groups in local decision making process has increased noticeably in the post-73rd Amendment period. According to the election results of 1997 and 2002 (Table 11.15), over 33 per cent of the elected representatives were women. In 2002 their representation at the PS level has gone up to 36 per cent. Similarly, the number of representatives belonging to the scheduled castes and tribes was also significant. The percentage of tribal representatives, which was relatively less in 1997 at the GP level, has increased to 14 per cent, i.e., more than the proportion of their population (9 per cent). It indicates that these groups were also elected from the unreserved seats.

According to the Maharashtra Human Development Report, 2002, over 22 per cent of the chairpersons of standing committees of ZPs, 40 per cent of chairpersons of PSs and 29 per cent of *sarpanchs* of GPs were women as on 1 April, 2001. It is found that the number of *sarpanchs* belonging to the scheduled castes and scheduled tribes has also increased noticeably across the districts as compared to the pre-73rd Amendment period (Directorate of Economics and Statistics, Mumbai). The proportion of tribal *sarpanchs* has gone up to 66 per cent in Nandurbar district followed by 46 per cent in Gadchiroli and 37 per cent in Thane in 1999-00.

Besides, in March 2000 over one thousand elected women representatives from different parts of the state assembled for two days at Saigata village in Chandrapur district to look back on the five years of women's participation in PRIs and take decisions to strengthen their role in the future. They announced *Mahila Rajasatta Andolan* and urged women to contest for unreserved seats also to increase their strength in local governance. *"Vote Hamara, Raj Hamara, Leke Rahenge, Leke Rahenge"* (Vote is ours, Governance is ours, we will get it) was the prime slogan of the Saigata Convention. As a result, 145 organisations are working together in as many as 129 *talukas* covering 30 districts. In fact, this movement in the state has given ample scope for women to share their experience, efforts and problems on local governance. Following a government directive and consistent efforts by several voluntary organisations, the national flag was hoisted by women *sarpanchs* on 26 January 2003 (54th Republic Day) and women *gram sabhas* were also held across the state. According to a survey the PRIs in Maharashtra has inspired more trust in women than men, unlike the national average as well as many other regions (Mitra, 2001).

In fact, the increasing participation of the hitherto excluded groups is not only due to the reservation provisions for them it may also be attributed to the impact of their strong movements against the privileged groups. The movements led by Phule and Ambedkar and the subsequent organised activities of the lower castes, and the Bhil and Koli tribals' movements in Dhule,

TABLE 11.15

PRIs and their Elected Representatives

Level	*1997*					*As on February 2002*				
	No.	*Total Elected Members*	*% of SCs*	*% of STs*	*% of Women*	*No.*	*Total Elected Members*	*% of SCs*	*% of STs*	*% of Women*
Gram Panchayats	27619	303545	13.43	5.58	33.33	28553	232644	11.53	13.68	33.33
Panchayat Samitis	319	3524	16.61	12.85	33.31	349	3902	11.46	13.53	36.06
Zilla Parishads	29	1762	11.69	13.17	33.31	33	1951	11.53	13.68	33.73

Source: Department of Rural Development and Water Conservation, GoM, Mumbai.

Gadchiroli and Thane districts encouraged the *Dalits* and tribals to ascertain their rights in all spheres. The same could be said about women also. Although the women have been elected and have formed *panchayats,* they have not been empowered except in a few cases (Bhandari, 1995; Mohanty, 1995). In many cases, the elected representatives of the hitherto excluded groups were also unable to challenge the dominance of the privileged groups. The assertive women members are harassed by the dominant male prejudice. This is more so in the case of Dalits women representatives. The all-women *panchayat* at Gokawadi of Pune district was reported to be under the control of the male members and women were the representatives only for namesake. The *purush mandali* managed the *panchayat* affairs (Indian Express, March 8, 2001). It is well known that the illiterate woman *sarpanch* of Panjawadi *panchayat* (Nashik district) unknowingly put her thumb impression on her resignation letter prepared by the *panchayat* officials. Recently it was reported that a Dalits woman *sarpanch* of Maratha-dominated Pethvadaz village of Nanded district was humiliated and opposed by the upper caste *up-sarpanch* and his associates.

Besides, the local level bureaucrats particularly the *gramsevaks* also find it easier to dominate a scheduled caste or tribe woman *sarpanch*. It was reported that the *sarpanch* of *Tirth Gram Panchayat* of Osmanbad district, who was a scheduled caste woman, was bypassed by the *gram sevak* in many of the *Panchayat* affairs (Mathew, 2001). In a number of cases the women contest elections to retain the seat for the male members of their family and these women representatives often act as proxy for men. Apart from this, in many cases the elected representatives of the privileged groups have succeeded in removing the *sarpanchs* and presidents of ZPs and PSs belonging to the reserved categories by using the provision of no confidence motion against them. A study lately undertaken in Tuljapur block of Osmanbad district shows that of the 22 *sarpanchs* removed by the no-confidence motion, 19 belong to the reserved category (Jare and Kumar, 2001). Some time back, the woman president of Wardha ZP was also removed through a no confidence motion. However, the recent amendment that the motion against a woman *sarpanch* can be passed by a majority of not less than 75 per cent of the members may strengthen the position of women *sarpanchs*.

Overall, the inclusion of hitherto excluded communities has generated a kind of awareness among them on many aspects of local governance. Participation in the election process, becoming representatives, attending meetings and expressing viewpoints at various levels shows signs of changes in lives of the members of hitherto excluded groups. There are some micro-level studies, which provide firm evidence in this regard (Baviskar, 2002; Patil, 2002). The widespread participation of women and members of the scheduled castes and tribes has helped them to be the beneficiaries of various rural development schemes. In fact, the beneficiaries of SGSY which is the single self-employment programme for the rural poor, is considerably higher among these groups compared to their demographic strength in most districts and regions.

The number of women beneficiaries has gone up to 68 per cent in the state as a whole and it is over 80 per cent in many districts. Similarly, in the case of IAY the numbers of scheduled caste and scheduled tribe beneficiaries are also higher in relation to the proportion of their population across the districts (Table 11.16). However, the greater beneficiaries from these disadvantaged groups are also due to guidelines of these schemes in favour of them.

The Success Stories

The experiment at Ralegaon Siddhi provides firm evidence as to how the socio-economic development at the local level can be achieved by activating the *panchayat* through the people's initiatives and participation. The village has witnessed remarkable development on many fronts during the last 25 years under the able leadership of Anna Hazare. It shows that the government can only provide financial and technical assistance up to a certain limit, but the people of a locality as also their leadership ultimately shape the quality of development. Projects like the watershed development, which is the key to the exemplary economic development of Ralegaon Siddhi, is successful because of the people's involvement in decision making in the *gram sabha*. Matters related to the ban on *nasbandi* (sterilisation), *nashabandi* (ban on alcohol), *kurhadbandi* (ban on tree felling), *kuranbandi* (ban on grazing) were decided in the *gram sabha*. The *gram sabha* meetings are held periodically to discuss the issues relating to the welfare of the village and a final decision is made. The GP is answerable to the *gram sabha* just as the cabinet is answerable to the assembly. In short, the *gram sabha* acts as the decision making wing and the *gram panchayat* as the executive wing. Members of backward classes and women take part in the decision making process in the *gram sabha*. The village had all-women members in the *panchayat* in 1990-1995 and the present *sarpanch* is a Dalit.

TABLE 11.16

Distribution of Beneficiaries of IAY and SGSY

(Per Cent to Total Number)

Districts/ Region	Population-1991		IAY Beneficiaries 2002-03		SGSY Beneficiaries 2002		
	SC	ST	SC	ST	SC	ST	Women
Thane	5.18	18.12	5.39	59.58	3.79	63.12	59.18
Raigad	2.79	12.82	15.63	35.94	4.28	56.62	60.29
Ratnagiri	1.77	0.96	64.91	12.28	14.09	0.00	29.82
Sindhudurg	5.10	0.47	81.48	0.00	14.64	0.00	46.79
Konkan Region	4.15	12.47	10.39	55.15	8.73	32.50	48.03
Nashik	8.48	24.18	13.18	52.72	14.90	45.17	54.19
Dhule	5.30	40.87	5.52	88.76	2.77	71.43	60.05
Jalgaon	9.25	9.84	26.71	27.36	26.96	21.57	64.51
Northern Region	7.90	23.82	11.19	69.33	16.09	43.45	59.14
Ahmednagar	12.41	7.12	41.13	18.30	6.40	8.18	53.10
Pune	11.41	3.91	39.29	21.43	23.69	15.29	76.01
Satara	9.50	0.75	62.82	0.00	23.61	0.00	53.11
Sangli	12.56	0.49	55.56	0.00	28.93	0.00	96.62
Solapur	15.41	1.50	59.69	0.00	47.41	1.29	77.41
Kolhapur	12.75	0.49	65.60	0.00	49.32	0.00	58.14
Western Region	12.33	2.77	52.28	8.22	30.58	3.64	68.36
Aurangabad	13.79	3.77	35.69	20.82	30.30	6.61	79.34
Jalna	12.93	2.07	N.A	N.A	27.82	2.45	72.50
Parbhani	11.02	5.26	48.22	1.52	41.63	9.01	62.66
Beed	13.41	1.13	60.00	0.00	13.33	0.00	30.00
Nanded	18.15	11.48	42.22	21.11	40.26	6.99	77.50
Osmanabad	16.34	1.76	56.52	4.35	23.96	2.08	69.79
Latur	19.06	2.24	N.A	N.A	39.50	1.25	73.35
Marathwada Region	14.92	4.53	47.06	9.84	33.51	4.60	72.07
Buldhana	11.49	5.06	50.44	9.97	26.29	4.76	47.42
Akola	11.95	7.03	N.A	N.A	41.21	12.36	58.00
Amaravati	17.48	14.38	27.62	34.76	35.08	33.11	89.28
Yavatmal	10.92	21.46	27.64	38.91	16.86	37.25	78.38
Wardha	14.05	15.59	29.92	29.55	30.08	23.25	80.81
Nagpur	18.84	13.92	29.32	30.96	27.93	20.88	44.28
Bhandara	16.87	14.70	N.A	N.A	42.18	20.75	71.05
Chandrapur	16.90	19.70	24.91	35.23	22.33	29.97	86.74
Gadchiroli	12.20	38.70	15.46	43.46	16.61	19.84	79.03
Vidarbha Region	15.02	14.95	26.60	34.50	29.56	24.25	72.26
State	**11.09**	**9.11**	**26.74**	**38.33**	**26.75**	**20.98**	**67.76**

Source: Department of Rural Development and Water Conservation, GoM, Mumbai.

The success story of Ralegaon Siddhi is gradually spreading across the state (Box 11.1). In 1992 the Government of Maharashtra started the Model Village Project to multiply the success in other villages. This project is in progress in 75 villages of 10 districts of the state with the help of 29 NGOs. Though such a project may generate development consciousness among the people, it alone may not be able to replicate leadership like that of Anna Hazare which was the driving force for village development in Ralegaon Siddhi. The pre-conditions for such leadership could be created by providing appropriate orientations at the institutional levels of family, school and community/ neighbourhood through inculcating values of honesty, social service and commitment for local development.

BOX 11.1

Ralegaon Siddhi, a Model Village

Ralegaon Siddhi, like many other Indian villages, was stricken by poverty, unemployment, illiteracy and social discrimination. There was hardly one acre of irrigated land per family and the agricultural production was inadequate to sustain the village population for the whole year. Men were migrating to cities in search of livelihood. The village *panchayat* was monopolised by the privileged groups. The socio-economic transformation in the village began in 1975, under the leadership of Anna Hazare, who mobilised people for village development through *gram sabha*. The *gram sabha* emerged as the important forum for collective decision making in the village and it nominated the *sarpanch* and other officials through general consensus. The women and the members of the scheduled castes came to the forefront of the *gram sabha*. The success of the watershed development programmes which changed the economic profile of the village by tremendously enhancing the irrigation facilities and thereby the agricultural output, is mainly due to the people's participation in the decision making process of the *gram sabha*. Now, the village has 2 percolation tanks, 30 *nulla bunds*, about 90 wells and 10 borewells that are viable all through the year. There are 17 self-help groups, a grain bank and several cooperative and registered societies to monitor the various developmental activities in the village.

Similarly, Hiwarebazar *panchayat* of Ahmednagar district has emerged as another success story of the *gram sabha*. It has been transformed from a drought-prone village to a green and prosperous model village under the leadership of Popatrao Pawar who replicated Anna Hazare's model of village development on the lines of Ralegaon Siddhi. The village has undertaken several development projects effectively with the active involvement of the people from all sections. The *gram sabha* prepares the development plan for the village, which serves as the guideline for the *panchayat*. The noticeable economic development of the village in the recent years has often been cited in the media reports. The same could be said about another small drought-prone village called Nimbavi in Ahmednagar district. The health project in Jamkhed *taluka* initiated by a doctor couple—Rajnikant Arole and Mabelle Arole—with the support of local resources and personnel also provides an example of participatory development.

Recently the Thane ZP has undertaken a programme called *Apla Hati Apla Vikas* which has charted out an action plan to organise *gram sabha* simultaneously in 924 villages of 6 scheduled area *talukas*. As a result of this campaign, over 83 per cent of *gram sabha* meetings were held which were attended by a remarkable number of women.

PRIs and NGOs

Maharashtra has been a torch-bearer in promoting voluntary organisations because of sustained services rendered by a large number of eminent social workers and their dedicated followers. The state has a long tradition of voluntarism. In each district of the state, one finds a number of voluntary organisations, which cater to the local developmental needs. Their activities include education, health care, welfare of weaker sections, etc. The existence of these organisations helps not only in improving the people's awareness and participation in rural development schemes, but also gives direction to the leadership of PRIs to attain development more effectively.

The Patil Committee specifically mentioned that general education, welfare of women and children, and primary health services are the areas where participation of voluntary organisations could be encouraged. Though the representatives of the PRIs can identify the felt needs at the local level, many technicalities are involved to convert them into plans for development. While at the district level, the people's representatives may get technical assistance from various governmental agencies, planning particularly at the *gram panchayat* level, will have no such facilities. Such technical assistance could be provided by the voluntary organisations working in the related areas of the concerned locality. Many voluntary agencies have expertise and competence in programmes relating to watershed development, water management and planning, resource mapping, implementation of land reforms, development of fishery resources, income generation projects for community members, etc. Recently the Pune ZP entrusted the entire responsibility of managing all the public health activities in a number of villages of the hilly areas to an NGO named Savadham Trust. It is working as a mother NGO for 10 districts of Maharashtra for the programme of reproductive and child health care. Similarly, another NGO—Aamcha Arogya Aamcha Hath—is undertaking the work of health services in the tribal district of Gadchiroli. It may be mentioned that an NGO—Resource Support Centre for Development (RSCD) along with its regional network partners—has addressed many of the women representatives in PRIs to take active part in the decision making process.

Conclusions and Policy Implications

Integrated village development implies improving all the aspects of village life. Maharashtra, like all other states, is predominantly rural and is characterised by poverty, illiteracy and inadequate physical and social infrastructure. Developmental intervention over the years has brought about a marked reduction in poverty and illiteracy. Specifically, the gap between rural and urban poverty and rural and urban illiteracy has declined. With respect to primary education and electricity too, the state has performed well. However, measures need to be taken to expand the medical and transport facilities, post and telegraph services, market and *pucca* roads to a larger number of villages. These measures should be addressed not only to the number of villages provided for with these facilities, but also their quality and maintenance. Special attention is required for Vidarbha region, which is lagging behind. In terms of developmental intervention through special programmes, EGS, despite the drawbacks, has helped in tackling problems of rural employment and poverty. Similarly, IAY is becoming a popular programme in improving the living conditions of the rural poor. SGSY too is showing a good response as against the earlier IRPD. The challenge lies in providing adequate credit to the SHGs formed and identifying commercially viable activities suitable for rural areas, which can be undertaken within these programmes. Schemes like SGRY are aiding the development initiatives by focusing on the provisions of employment and village infrastructure, particularly in the SC/ST habitations. Special programmes for tribal areas also supplement the developmental effort. In short, these interventions are catalysing socio-economic development in villages and should be further strengthened. However, from a long-term policy perspective, attention needs to be paid for the expansion of area under irrigation, allotment of land to the landless, improvement of infrastructure, particularly relating to the health sector.

The PRIs have imparted a new strength to the entire process of planning and implementation, particularly in the post-73rd Amendment period. It helped in the emergence of leadership and contributed for the improvement of quality of rural life. Given the strong foundations of the Maharastrian society based on Dalit, tribal and women's movements, as well as the long history of rural local governance, the PRIs have the potentiality to strengthen democracy at the grassroots level and improve the quality of village development in the state. However, Dalit movement has become ineffective due to factional politics and women's movement remains as a middle class bastion. The *panchayati raj* system in the state has to be geared up further to catch up with states like West Bengal and Karnataka, which are cited as the progressive states in terms of people's mobilisation and participation at the local level (Lieten, 1996; Manor, 1998; Vyasulu and Vyasulu, 1999). Devolution of more power to the *gram sabha* with greater accountability and transparency at all levels could enhance the people's participation and empowerment. As indicated by the State Planning Board in its approach papers to the Tenth Five year Plan, the *gram sabhas* have to be empowered to prioritise the projects for their villages and also to monitor their implementation. The *panchayats* should be endowed with adequate responsibilities and necessary powers in the area of financial administration so as to ensure greater autonomy in the decision making process at their levels. In addition to funds allotted for the state/centre sponsored schemes, financial assistance could be provided to the *panchayats* to undertake independent development programmes as per the local requirement. Efforts could be made to provide certain percentage of grants to the *gram panchayats* as untied grants, subject to the broad guidelines under which such untied funds could be utilised. Authorisation to *panchayats* to levy, collect and appropriate taxes, duties, tolls and fees and making such amendments which are in Consonance with the provisions of Article 243H of the Constitution and recommendations of the State Finance Commission could be considered for policy option. District and *panchayat*-wise allocation of plan and non-plan funds in the annual budgets of the government could enhance the financial strength of these bodies. The merger of DRDA with *zilla parishad* like that in Rajasthan could be considered to provide greater autonomy to the ZPs.

PRIs can invite the cooperation of NGOs with respect to watershed development and management, forest management, health related issues, etc., to make use of their experience and expertise for better results. The PRIs, now extended to the tribal areas, may also work in collaboration with the NGOs, which have done appreciable work relating to tribal development.

Chapter 12

Tourism

Introduction

Maharashtra, one of India's premier commercial and industrial states, has recognised tourism to be a major thrust area for economic growth in the state. The Budget 2002-03 for Tourism and Investment Incentive Package 1999 gives clear indications that the Government of Maharashtra realises the potential of tourism for wealth creation and employment generation. In 2001, Maharashtra emerged as one of the states, which received the highest numbers of international tourists and emerged as India's 2nd most used port of entry. At the same time in the domestic tourist arrivals, the state ranked fourth amongst Indian states. The travel and tourism industry including transport, storage and communication, trade, hotels and restaurants accounted for around 20-22 per cent of the gross state domestic product and 3.5 per cent of the state's employment. The government's promotion and development initiatives to harness Maharashtra's tourism potential reflect the state's commitment to this industry.

Paradoxically, however, along with the growing recognition of the importance of travel and tourism by the Government of Maharashtra, there seems to be a lack of appreciation of its scope, complexity and dynamism. This industry works beyond the local boundaries at a global level bringing together diverse industries and stakeholders. It encompasses development of other areas of economic activity, as well as growth in the social and environmental context. The government of Maharashtra, working on its bullish initiatives, should inculcate this appreciation of travel and tourism industry to obtain long-term gains for the state.

The urgent need is for the government of Maharashtra to view tourism in a holistic sense, beyond its national and global boundaries, bringing together the internal dynamic elements like its stakeholders—the community and the private sector to work towards a tourism concept that benefits all and retains tourism assets for future. The concept of sustainable tourism is one such approach that balances tourism with its stakeholder relationships, managing the effects of globalisation, to the advantage of its tourism strengths and opportunities. It offers a solution to the internal dynamics of diverse stakeholders and responds to the trends and happenings beyond geographical boundaries that generate a stable and growing tourism economy.

Sustainable tourism is an approach that has found much favour recently, both in the academic and the business world. The WTO, WTTC, IH&RA amongst others, have taken a keen interest in harnessing its use in tourism. Countries similar in culture and nature to India and characterised by dynamic growth like Turkey, Hong Kong, China, Thailand and Malaysia have taken the path of sustainable tourism and are a part of the Plan of Action for Sustainable Tourism Development in the Asian and Pacific Region.

India too, realising the capability of sustainable tourism has, in its National Tourism Policy of India (GoI, 2000), made its "Mission to promote sustainable tourism as a means of economic growth, social integration and creating larger foreign exchange earnings and conditions for more foreign direct investment."

This chapter takes this initiative forward and attempts to define policy implications of using the concept of sustainable tourism in Maharashtra in its broader stakeholder market-product form and not just in an ecotourism or environment aspect. It looks beyond the boundaries of Maharashtra, to the globalised and interdependent world, where tourism in

Maharashtra affects and is affected by the changes in the world, India and Maharashtra environment.

The chapter is divided into three sections. The first section is on sustainable tourism, as a concept is understood, followed by the section with an analysis of the present condition of internal and external environment of tourism in Maharashtra based on the strengths, weaknesses, threats and opportunities. The third section is on recommendations for a sustainable tourism framework in Maharashtra, that customise the sustainable tourism concept to cater to Maharashtra's strengths, opportunities and minimise its weaknesses and threats.

Sustainable Tourism: Definitions and Principles World Initiatives

The World Commission on Environment and Development for the United Nations has defined a sustainable development policy as one that "Meets the needs of the present without compromising the ability of future generations to meet their own needs."

The sustainable development approach was further elaborated and expressed in Travel and Tourism Agenda-21 in 1995 at the United Nations Conference on Environment and Development, popularly known as the Earth Summit, held in Rio de Janeiro in 1992, that was adopted by the conference. Since then, many national governments have adopted sustainability as their fundamental development policy. The World Tourism Organization (WTO) has adopted the sustainable approach to tourism, and applied sustainable development principles in all of its tourism planning and development studies. The WTO has defined sustainable tourism as one that, "Meets the needs of present tourists and host regions while protecting and enhancing opportunities for the future."

Sustainable tourism has also been recognised as a holistic model form of economic development that is designed to improve the quality of life of the host community; provide high quality of experience for the visitor and maintain quality of the environment/heritage/art and culture of which the host community and visitor depend. Tourism that is developed by using 'sustainability' as a guide can fulfil economic, social, and aesthetic needs while maintaining cultural integrity and ecological processes. It can provide for today's hosts and guests while protecting and enhancing the same opportunity for the future.

Sustainability considers tourism in its ecological, socio-cultural, economic and experiential dimensions. The guiding principle for sustainable tourism development is to minimise the negative impacts of tourism in order to maximise visitor enjoyment and local benefit. Sustainable tourism delves into the dimensions created by the relationship between the various stakeholders—the tourist, the government, the host community, the industry with each other and most importantly the tourism asset (environment, heritage, art and culture) and creates a dynamic development framework to ensure continuity, strength and growth of these relationships.

Environmental/Heritage/Culture Sustainability

Sustainable tourism ensures ecological and cultural sustainability, where development is compatible with the maintenance of essential ecological processes, biological diversity, biological resources and conservation of heritage and culture.

Economic Sustainability

Economic sustainability ensures that development is economically efficient and viable and that all the stakeholders—government, private sector and local community enjoy the financial benefits of tourism.

Experiential Sustainability

The experiential dimension relates to the relation between the tourist and all other stakeholders. A high level of tourist satisfaction is maintained in order to retain the marketability and popularity of the tourist destinations. If the tourists are not satisfied with the tourism area, the destination not only loses its tourist markets but also becomes an unviable investment.

Social Sustainability

Tourism emanates from society and hence people become a part of any tourism product. Sustainable tourism development is planned and managed so that the socio-economic benefits of the tourist destination are spread as widely as possible throughout the society.

World Initiatives in Sustainable Tourism

Worldwide, the concept of sustainability in tourism has been approached intensively. International government and private organisations have realised the benefits of developing tourism in a sustainable manner and are initiating plans for its development. The World Tourism Organization (WTO), World Travel and Tourism Council (WTTC), Economic and Social Commission for Asia and the Pacific (ESCAP), Pacific

Asia Travel Association (PATA), The International Hotel and Restaurant Association (IH&RA), Asia-Pacific Economic Cooperation Secretariat (APEC), Indian Ocean Tourism Organisation (IOTO), United Nations Educational, Scientific and Cultural Organization (UNESCO) and Principal Regional Office for Asia and the Pacific are undertaking initiatives for sustainable tourism development. Some of their initiatives by these organisations include:

- Agenda—21: Programme of Action for Sustainable Development (WTO, WTTC, Earth Council).
- Escap, Plan of Action for Sustainable Tourism Development in the Asian and Pacific Region (PASTA).
- WTO's Tourism Satellite Account for economic impact assessment.
- WTTC's Green Globe Environment Awareness programme.
- WTTC India Chapter Manifesto for India.
- PATA Code of Environmental Conduct.
- IH&RA 'Environmental Action Pack for Hotels' and 'Environmental Good Practice in Hotels' APEC Tourism Charter.
- IOTO's set of principles for coastal zone management (CZM).
- WTO's indicators for sustainable tourism management and carrying capacity assessment.
- WTO's quality standards.
- APEC/PATA Code for sustainable tourism.

In India too, there have been attempts at initiating sustainable tourism. The WTTC's India Imperative; WTO's TSA implementations in Kerala, Rajasthan and Goa; Khajuraho Conservation and Sustainable Tourism Strategy, 1998; the People's Charter and Draft Guidelines on Sustainable Tourism for Kumarakom are few examples. Also CII, PATA India Chapter and IATO etc. have made many supportive reports.

Recent Trends

Foreign tourist arrivals have increased from 0.88 million in 1995 to 1.07 million in 2000 indicating a compounded growth rate of 4.1 per cent in this five year period. Figure 12.1 indicates international tourists' arrivals in last six years in the state, where domestic tourist arrivals increased from 6.16 million in 1995 to 8.30 million in 2000, indicating a compounded annual growth rate of 6.14 per cent. However, both of these growth rates are less than those of major tourism states like Kerala, Rajasthan and Karnataka. The tourist arrivals in Maharashtra for the year 2001 are estimated by the Ministry of tourism, Government of India, to have a share of around 16.8 per cent in total international tourist arrivals in India. In the past year, tourist arrivals from abroad have shown a decrease in growth rate, mirrored at Maharashtra's most important tourist destination of Ajanta-Ellora. Mumbai International Airport is the second most used international airport in India catering to 26 per cent of the foreign tourists to India, after Delhi. The government of Maharashtra realises that out of the 1.08 million tourists visiting Maharashtra, only 5-6 per cent of foreign tourists move on to tourist destinations in Maharashtra. Out of the total tourists visiting tourist destinations in Maharashtra, only 10-12 per cent are of foreign origin and not many of the 26 per cent of all foreign tourists who enter the country through Mumbai, spend time or money in the state. Mumbai has had growth of around 2.5 per cent in international tourists' arrivals over a five year period till 2000 as per the report by the Jones LaSalle in 2000.

FIGURE 12.1

International Tourist Arrivals in Maharashtra

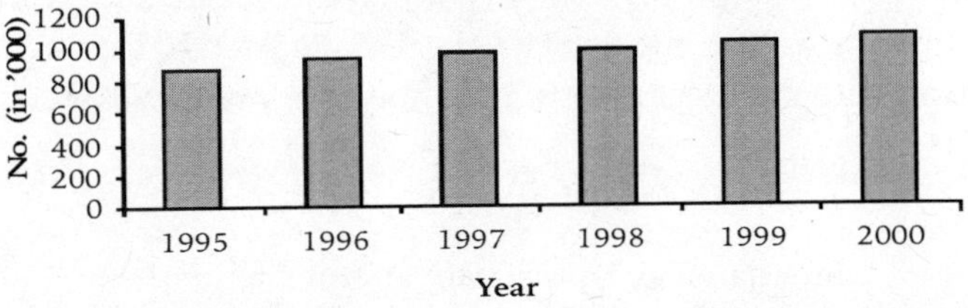

Source: GoM, 2000.

Maharashtra's share in total domestic tourist arrivals in India is 3.6 per cent. Out of the total tourist visiting tourist destination in Maharashtra, about 15-20 per cent tourists are from other Indian states. The majority in Maharashtra contains domestic tourists from within the state.

International Tourist Profile

There is no clear, real information on the profile of tourists visiting Maharashtra. Hence, with respect to the profile of an international tourist for Maharashtra, it is assumed that it can be represented by the tourist profile for India as also by the tourist profile for Maharashtra's premier international destinations of Ajanta-Ellora and Mumbai. Figures 12.2 and 12.3

indicate international tourists' composition at Aurangabad and Mumbai respectively. Most of the international tourists here were mostly one-night stay tourists and had a Japan-USA-Europe mix.

FIGURE 12.2

International Tourist Mix at Aurangabad in 1992

(in Per Cent)

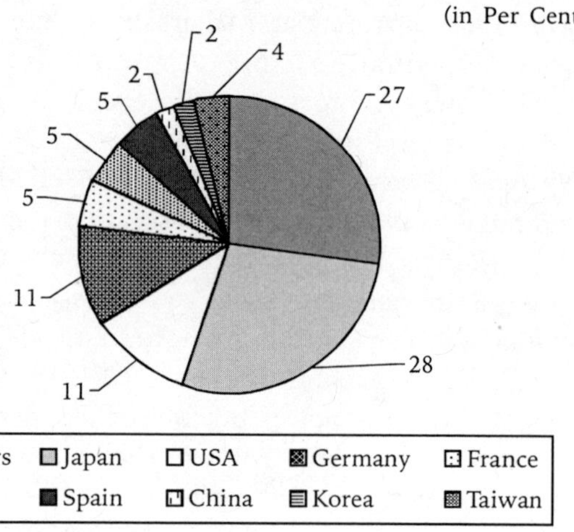

Source: GoM, 1992.

Mumbai, Maharashtra's most visited destination's largest source market traditionally has been Western Europe. The UK represents more than 80 per cent of the Western Europe demand and was the largest source market for Mumbai followed by West Asian and North America as per the Jones Lang LaSalle Hotels the "India Hotel Report 2000"—Mumbai tourism market overview.

FIGURE 12.3

International Tourist Mix at Mumbai in 1999

(in Per Cent)

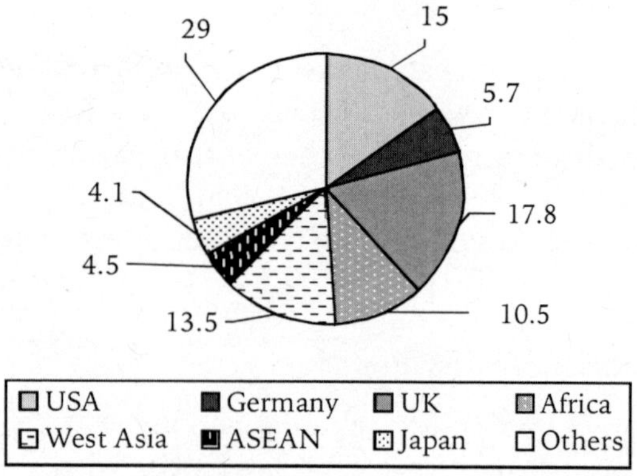

With respect to domestic tourists, the Maharashtra Economic Development Council, an NGO for defining domestic tourist profile, conducted a small survey that observed that most visitors from other states mostly holidayed and stayed with family and friends. Another study survey conducted for GoM tourism found that interstate tourism was restricted to popular destinations like Ajanta-Ellora, Matheran, Mahabaleshwer and Mumbai from neighbouring states like Tamil Nadu, Gujarat and Karnataka.

Future Tourism Development

In Maharashtra, the primary government agency responsible for tourism growth and development is Maharashtra Tourism Development Corporation (MTDC). MTDC has been from its year of incorporation is working to boost the tourism industry in the state. Some of the initiatives in tourism development in Maharashtra by MTDC are explained below.

With the main thrust, to market Maharashtra as a premier global tourism destination, thereby generating employment and enhancing productivity through tourism, the award-winning promotion campaign—'Maharashtra...Unlimited', has been created by MTDC. It aims to highlight the unlimited potential of the state.

MTDC has commissioned many master plans for various regions in Maharashtra, Sindhudurg, Vidarbha, Ajanta-Ellora, and forts being some of them.

MTDC's budget outlay for tourism has increased ten-fold as compared to its previous budget. Its present budget of Rs. 101 crores has been segregated as—Rs. 55 crores has been allocated for Ajanta Ellora, Rs. 12 crores for Ashta Vinayak, Rs. 5 crores for the Konkan Riviera, Rs. 5 crores for wildlife and ecotourism in the Vidarbha region and Rs. 10 crores for Shivneri. In addition, Rs. 7.95 crores has been sanctioned purely for publicity and promotion, a seven-fold increase over last year.

MTDC's strategy for development of Konkan region on the lines of the French Riviera, Bali and Gold Coast, comprises of the development of self contained resorts on under populated and under productive lands, strong public-private collaboration in the development of infrastructure, creation of training schools for absorption of local populace in the tourism industry, aggressive marketing. The GoM has allocated Rs. 5 crores in this budget for the Konkan Riviera.

For Maharashtra, luxury train—The Deccan Odyssey has been planned, with interiors that will showcase pristine beaches, forts, legends, gods carved in black monolithic rock, and opulent palaces dedicated to kings, from north to south. This luxury train offers to take its passengers on a journey through the kingdom of the Marathas, Maharashtra.

Shirdi, recognised as the second largest religious centre in terms of visits after Tirupati, is a religious destination slated for upgradation. The government in collaboration with the Shirdi Trust has charted plans to promote the desired objective. Shirdi falls under the 'Special Area Development Plan' of the Maharashtra government, where public policy management schemes have been planned to ameliorate the region. Measures have been adopted to amend the drainage and sanitation system and the Shirdi Trust, besides setting up a few five-star properties, has also built accommodation facilities in the form of dormitories.

Promotion of *vipassana* and ayurveda tours, especially at the Vipassana Kendra at Igatpuri near Nashik has been slotted for promotions.

Participation in tourism fairs, both national and international, has been on the agenda of the state's promotional drives. The state has participated in tourism fairs at Berlin and London, where the Government of India has identified Maharashtra along with Kerala, West Bengal and Rajasthan as partners. MTDC also has plans to work with CNN. Promotion of fort tourism and development of beach tourism by improving accessibility to the beach areas is underway. Promoting the concept of coastal cuisine, especially Malwani cuisine, is under consideration.

The Sindhudurg district, which was declared by the Maharashtra government as the "Tourism District", has, in fact, the best beaches in the region. Shiroda, Tarkarli, Mochemad, Mandwa, Kihim and Janjira have been identified for further beach promotion drives. MTDC has plans to implement the Sindhudurg Tourism Development Project here. The scenic 720 km long coastline of the Konkan has been included for development as the National Tourism Circuit and Tarkarli has been chosen as the new port of call for Hebridean Cruise Liners.

The state tourism department has identified promotion of adventure and wildlife tourism in the state, especially in the Nagpur belt. Joining hands with the neighbouring Madhya Pradesh government to further these plans, along with introducing the concept of historical tourism, to provide an insight into the Sanskrit culture in certain identified areas in the state, has been conceptualised.

MTDC has developed an incentives package with special concessions for Sindhudurg district to attract private sector investments in tourism industry. Also, state-level tax rates have been lowered, the entertainment tax is 6 per cent while sales tax stands at 15 per cent for food and 25 per cent for beverages.

MTDC plans to position Mumbai as a potential destination both for leisure and corporate travel. Apart from promoting Mumbai as a single destination, special activities and highlights that are area specific can also be promoted. There are a number of gateways from Mumbai that can prove to be excellent destinations for one-day trips. There are potential hill stations around the region that can be marketed to these tourists. Further, the caves around the city can be marketed and promoted as potential heritage sites and as cave circuits. The city's waterfront is also planned to be utilised, as a number of activities can be developed around the coastal region. Bollywood, is Mumbai's unique feature that MTDC plans to promote as a city of stars.

On the initiative of the MTDC, the Bombay Municipal Corporation has recently set up a special committee for the first time to look into matters concerning the promotion and welfare of tourism in the region, headed by the commissioner. Along with MTDC there are other stakeholders that are contributing to tourism development.

The National Action Plan for Tourism have identified 21 travel circuits, 12 destinations and 33 pilgrim centres which include destinations/places of tourism potential in remote/hilly areas for intensive development through the joint efforts of Central and state governments and the private sector in order to strengthen infrastructure facilities. From Maharashtra, the travel circuit of Raigad Fort-Janjira Fort-Kuda-Caves, Sirivardhan, Harihareshwar, Sindhudurg, the destination of Ajanta-Ellora (Aurangabad) and pilgrim centres of Shirdi, Nanded and Jyotiba have been identified.

MSRDC has undertaken the development of New Mahabaleshwar Hill station. It plans to develop the region from Mahabaleshwar to Koyna backwaters/Patan as New Mahabaleshwar Hill Station. Pre-feasibility study of this area has been carried out by MSRDC. The Government has approved the project in principle. In addition to the above projects, MSRDC has undertaken road development projects as well as the development of Nagpur multinodal international airport that could help in strengthening basic infrastructure at various tourist destinations.

CIDCO Golf Course and Country Club of Navi Mumbai are involved in the development of an 18-hole

Executive Golf Course and a country club at Nerul, Navi Mumbai.

MMRDA has undertaken to convert the warship INS Vikrant into a maritime museum at Mumbai.

The Forest Development Corporation of Maharashtra (FDCM) Ltd. has appointed the Indian Society for Environment, Art and Cultural Heritage (Indsearch) to conduct ecotours in the vicinity of the forests in Maharashtra. There is excellent potential for eco-tourism since Maharashtra has an estimated forest cover of more than 103 sq km. The FDCM along with the forest department of Maharashtra plans to utilise the existing available infrastructure for the development of eco-tourism along with Indsearch, who will conduct guided tours in various forests, sanctuaries.

Private Sector Role

The government has played a central role in tourism for Maharashtra, while the private sector role has been more supportive. Major national and international hotel chains—including Taj, Oberoi, Le Méridien, Best Western, Hyatt and ITC have already established hotels and resorts in the state. The latest year for which a detailed breakdown of hotel accommodation supply is available is 2000. As shown in the Table 12.1, most development has been in the one- to three-star categories.

TABLE 12.1

Maharashtra's Classified Hotel and Room Capacity, 2000

Category	*No. of Hotels*	*No. of Rooms*
5-star Deluxe	13	4064
5-star	14	1795
4-star	15	1097
3-star	50	2295
2-star	83	2564
1-star	47	1368
Heritage Resorts	1	22
Unclassified	19	667
Total	**242**	**13854**

Source: IHR, 2000.

Mumbai, Maharashtra's most prominent destination had 93 government-registered hotel establishments comprising 7,003 rooms, as of March 2000. Figure 12.4 connotes rooms' percentage in different categories of hotels in Mumbai.

In contrast to the 1990s, room supply in the 5-star deluxe and 5-star segments of the market is expected to increase in the near future for Mumbai as per the Jones Lang LaSalle Hotels India Hotel Report (IHR) 2000. In the absence of the large land parcels that can be developed, most of this additional supply is concentrated in North Mumbai with the opening of ITC Grand Maratha International, Airport Inter-Continental, Grand Hyatt International and Leela Suites International Airport in close proximity to the emerging business districts of Andheri-Kurla Road and Bandra-Kurla Complex. The domestic traveller continues to be of importance across all hotels in Mumbai accounting for 76.3 per cent of all guests. Domestic business travellers represented the largest percentage of hotel guests at 39 per cent. Foreign leisure travellers and groups, who prefer luxury and heritage hotels, comprised 25.7 per cent and 29.4 per cent of the heritage market respectively. UK provided the largest demand at 15.4 per cent, followed by the US at 14.2 per cent, and Germany at 8.9 per cent. Foreign business travellers primarily drive hotel rooms in Mumbai.

FIGURE 12.4

Percentage of Rooms in Mumbai

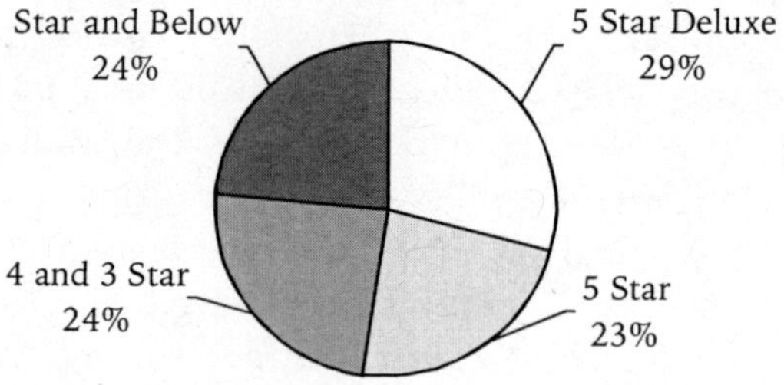

Source: IHR, 2000.

According to the FHRAI report on cities for 2002, despite the huge increase in the new room supply in the Mumbai market, occupancy levels have declined only by 3.5 per cent. This indicates a large surge in demand for hotel rooms. It is estimated that this increase in demand has consistently grown at 25–30 per cent over the past 2-3 years. New room supply has, however, had a detrimental effect on average rates, which declined by 40 per cent. In the other prominent city of Pune, overall occupancies in luxury and mid-market hotels have remained steady. Average rates, however, have decreased dramatically across the board at nearly 49 per cent. The city is witnessing a lot of hotel activity and at least 2-3 hotels are to change hands in the next year. FHRAI expects the overall market to improve in 2002-03.

The role of tour operators in Maharashtra has been limited. According to statistics available till 2000, there were 24 tourist transport operators, 78 travel agents and 24 tour operators approved by the Ministry of Tourism in Maharashtra. International tour operators like Cox and Kings, Thomas Cook and national leading operators like Sita Travels, Raj Travels, Raja Rani tours have offices in Mumbai, though they mostly cater to outbound market and national market. Niche tour operators for Maharashtra are very local and offer basic packages for travelling to religious and heritage destinations here.

Recently, with a view to increase the role of the private sector, a joint task force, focusing on private-public sector partnership, is being set up with major industry players and other stakeholders as members, to act as advisors to the state government with regard to tourism development activities.

SWOT Analysis

Strengths, weaknesses, opportunities and threats (SWOT) analysis has been used to create a quick map of the internal organisation and the fundamental external dynamics involved. Analysis of Maharashtra's tourism sector is based on national and global factors and environmental considerations.

Strengths

Most obviously, Maharashtra has immense tourism potential with its natural beaches, heritage and culture. Most of the other states in India too have similar offerings. So, the strengths for Maharashtra will lie with its unique perspectives. The strengths are answers to these questions: What is the value proposition offered in relation to the other states in India? Why should a tourist visit destinations in Maharashtra when he has so many options?

The primary strength of Maharashtra is Mumbai. It is a commercial and entertainment capital of India and now planning to be a top urban tourist destination. Its strengths are:

- **South Mumbai:** The South Mumbai area houses the Gateway of India, museums, shopping malls and designer showrooms. It offers Victorian buggy rides, walking down Kala Ghoda's art district in an aesthetically designed surrounding. With its proximity to the world heritage site of Elephanta, south Mumbai can become the primary activity oriented destination.
- **International airport:** Mumbai's international airport brings around 26 per cent of international tourists to India. It has the advantage of getting most of tourists to the state before any other state in India does.
- **Bollywood:** Mumbai is the entertainment capital of India. Major studios, actors, and designers, reside in Mumbai. Bollywood has received international attention and is of prime interest to population of Indian origin in the source markets of USA and the UK.
- **Commercial Capital:** Mumbai primarily caters to international and domestic business tourists. Mumbai's new prime hotels are close to the airport to convenience the business tourists visiting the North Mumbai business areas of Santacruz Electronic Export Processing Zone (SEEPZ) and Bandra-Kurla complex.
- **Amusement Parks:** The premier amusement parks of Essel-world and Water Kingdom are at close proximity to the international airport, and offer an excellent one-day outing of its kind.
- **Sea Forts:** Maharashtra has a huge cache of sea forts, most of which are in the Konkan belt and offer a distinct uniqueness. Also, the sea forts of Alibag and Murud-Janjira are close to Mumbai.
- **Maharashtra residents:** Maharashtra is the largest generator of domestic tourism with around 40 per cent of its population showing a high propensity to travel. Moreover, an India profile study by British Tourist Authority shows that the primary source-state for Indian outbound to Britain is Maharashtra.
- **Nationally known religious sites:** Maharashtra homes prominent religious places with nationwide following. Shirdi, Ashtavinayak and even the Mumbai famous Siddhivinayak temples are a must in the itinerary of domestic tourists visiting Maharashtra.
- **Tangible and intangible culture:** Maharashtra's richness of culture lies in the arts of Warli, Chitrakathi, Bidriware and music traditions at Elephanta, Balgandharva, Banganga, Kalaghoda and Kalidas. These handicrafts and tribal arts indeed add to the unique value of Maharashtra.
- **Rich Buddhist cave architecture heritage:** Not just Ajanta-Ellora, but also the caves of Bhaja and Bedsa, Karla, Pandavleni, Junnar and Pithalkhora are Buddhist heritage sites, each offering the view of ancient 'cave architecture'. According to the Convenor of the Indian National Trust for Art

and Cultural Heritage, this architecture is one of its kinds in the world thus offering a unique perspective of the Buddhist culture.

- **Specialty tourism:** The rise in rural and eco-tourism world-wide, finds ample opportunity in Maharashtra with its forests and national parks as well as special areas like Lonar.
- **Beaches:** A 720 km coastline dotted by beaches in the Sindhudurg and Ratnagiri region along with a potential to attach culture and nature is one of the main assets for Maharashtra.

Weaknesses

- **Long haul tourist dependence:** Maharashtra depends highly on the leisure tourist long-haul markets of UK, USA, France and Germany. One of the most prominent disadvantages of a strong long-haul market is their unpredictable nature. Any security and safety issues at the destination initiate cancellation of vacations. Effects of economic slowdown and 9/11 are most prominent for the long-haul markets. WTO-Tourism 2020, South Asian sub-region (of which India forms more that 50 per cent) states: "South Asia region relies on long-haul tourists, mostly ultra long-haul tourist (Europe and America). For these tourists, high budgets are necessary. It will be vital for South Asian countries to consolidate these sources through well-directed and appropriate marketing, and seek to avoid 'monoculture' by developing and penetrating other regional sources."
- **Mumbai's host ambience:** Mumbai represents the most visited destination site of Maharashtra. When tourists land at Mumbai they make their first impressions. Mumbai's poor condition of the western express highway, touts and beggars creates a very poor host ambience. Most of the tourism experts interviewed stressed on this aspect being the most important problem area for Mumbai.
- **Mumbai's transit destination status:** In spite of having around 50 per cent of tourists visiting India, through Mumbai airport, only a 5-8 per cent of international tourists travel to Maharashtra destinations. There are no clear indications whether the tourist spends any time visiting Mumbai attractions.

Lack of Competitive Advantage

- **High priced destination:** According to the World Travel and Tourism Council (WTTC) research (World Travel and Tourism Tax Policy centre 'Key Issues in taxation'), the tax paid by tourists in India is around 40 per cent, which is the highest in the world. Mumbai is among the least competitive destinations with the highest tax burdens (*Economic Times*, 2002). A recent study conducted by AF Ferguson & Co. for FICCI showed that lowering tax rates could increase tourist arrivals. The study reveals that cutting tax by 50 per cent could double the potential number of households who can afford tourism at that level and can actually increase the total revenue for government.
- **Connectivity to destinations:** Present leisure tourists looking for value for money and time want to reach their destinations without time gaps and inconveniences. If a domestic traveller wants to go to Tarkarli, he has to first come to Mumbai and then travel *via* pre-booked trains or buses. Destination connectivity is grossly lacking. Also majority of the source markets are long-haul making it necessary that travel time to get to end destinations should be minimal.
- **Mumbai's dependence on business tourism:** Most of the hotels in Mumbai cater to the high return business tourist and have not focused on leisure tourism. According to the Jones Lang LaSalle Hotel report on Mumbai, foreign business travellers primarily drive demand for high-end accommodation.
- **Lack of innovation:** Maharashtra's tourism products have not been built around catering to the 'new experience' requirements of today's highly aware tourists. The world tourism trends indicate growth of adventure tourism and rural/ethnic tourism [World Tourism Organization Business Council (WTOBC) 1999].
- **Unfocussed development and lack of co-operation:** Many contributors to Maharashtra tourism—MTDC, MSRDC, Ministry of Railways, FMDC, ASI, etc. have followed their own objectives and plans and are working on separate platforms. There is lack of an overall vision and strategy to guide tourism planning and development. Also, lack of cooperation between various governmental organisations involved in

tourism creates inconvenience for the tourist. A visit to Ajanta World Heritage Site requires a tourist to purchase as many as seven tickets due to a distinct jurisdiction issue.

- **Information availability:** Most obviously, Maharashtra does not have a proactive information strategy to attract a tourist at the decision making point, since most of the tourists worldwide, tap into websites for information and purchase of products. Hotel websites at 5.5 per cent had the highest growth rate over the previous year especially in the heritage sector, where it accounted for 12.4 per cent of all advance reservations. This reflected a dramatic 600 per cent increase over the previous year. Overall increase in web-based reservations reflected a growth of 400 per cent.
- **Lack of analytical data:** Every vision strategy and policy should be based on data. In the case of tourism, information, like destination-wise source, country-wise tourist arrivals, spending patterns, etc. would offer an opportunity to make intelligent analysis. Maharashtra does not maintain any such data.
- **Lack of quality human resource:** Tourism is a people-centric activity. A tourist meets 'people' throughout his/her travel and interacts with them for purchases, advice and guidance and services. Thus, the quality of experience a tourist has, is highly dependant on the 'human resource' element. In Maharashtra, there is the Institute for Hotel Management, Catering Technology and Applied Nutrition at Dadar, as well as university affiliated Garware Foundation that offers travel and tourism courses and small private institutes offer IATA certification courses, ticketing and airline services courses that are mainly operational. But, a clear human resource policy is required that singularly focuses on quality.

Opportunities

- **Domestic tourism:** Domestic tourism's predictability and controllability has been seen as virtue post 9/11 and is stated for high growth world-wide (Dave, 2002). World-wide many countries are undertaking initiatives to attract domestic tourism as a tourism growth strategy. Indian Government's work on the Golden Quadrilateral highway project and North-South and East-West corridors is expected to increase accessibility and promote domestic tourism (GoI, 2002). Also with Maharashtra's nationally known religious sites and the city of Mumbai, this growing market can be an opportunity.
- **Growing Buddhist populated source markets:** Growing tourism source countries of Japan, China and neighbouring Sri Lanka have Buddhist populations (Buddha Dharma Education Association). Their interest in Buddhist architecture and heritage can be an opportunity for Maharashtra to offer them its unique 'cave architecture'.
- **Proximity to economically growing ASEAN countries:** The economic situations of source markets affect their outbound tourist expenditure. The projected economic growth for emerging markets such as the members of ASEAN or those in Eastern Europe, have been maintained or even raised. The proximity to these growing economies is an opportunity to tap high spending tourists.
- **China outbound market:** Although China's outbound tourism market is rarely analysed, a 1999 survey ranked travelling as third, in all desired expense items among Chinese consumers. China has overtaken Netherlands and Canada in tourist spending and together with Hong Kong, China is becoming increasingly important in terms of expenditure, spending more than even France. It is the second-largest source of travellers in Asia Pacific after Japan—18 million in the same year.
- **India's tourism prospects:** The WTTC has identified India as one of the world's foremost tourist growth centres in the coming decade. After Turkey, India is expected to achieve the fastest rate of growth of the total amount of economic activity, likely to be generated by travel and tourism, at 9.7 per cent over the next 10 years (WTTC, 2002). The growth in 'visitor exports' or spending by international tourists is likely to be the fastest in India at 14.3 per cent per annum over the next decade.
- **Growth in cultural tourism:** World trends have shown that an increasing number of tourists want a unique cultural experience. Most of Maharashtra's present source markets of Europe and USA have interest in experiencing the art and culture (McIntyre, 1993).
- **Transit visitors:** Most of India's international

visitors use Mumbai as the transit port of entry or exit. This existing captive audience can be changed from transit visitors to tourists. In most gross terms, the benefit of this opportunity was explained by Mr. Pradip Madhavji as a $42 million increase in tourism earnings for every additional day spent in Maharashtra by every transit tourist. India's foreign exchange earnings of around $3 billion from 2.5 million tourists to India implies that approximately $1,280 per person was spent in 31 days, i.e. $42 per tourist, per day. For Maharashtra, if 94 per cent of 1.08 million tourists that transit through, spend an additional one day it means approximate tourist earnings of $42 million per day.

- **Nostalgia and roots tourism:** Many countries today have a large NRI population e.g. UK, USA, South Africa, Australia, etc. Also, WTO has declared the world-wide growing trend of nostalgia tourism.
- **Indian outbound market:** India's outbound tourism is approximately four million. Malaysia, Dubai, UK, Mauritius, Singapore, China and even Tunisia have tourism offices in India wanting to tap the value for money Indian tourist as well as the MICE market. Tourism boards of various countries are planning to step up their advertising expenditure by about 25 per cent to target Indian outbound travellers who have emerged as the highest spenders. India's foreign exchange earnings from 2.5 million tourists to India of around $3 billion means approximately per person spend of $1,280 spent in 31 days. A per day tourist spend of $42. For Maharashtra, 94 per cent of 1.08 million tourists that transit through spend one more day it means approximate tourist earnings of $42 million per day (*Business Standard*, 2003). If Maharashtra can offer this class of tourists an opportunity to see added values—experiences, this growing outbound market can be shifted to domestic tourism. Also according to the report of British Tourist Authority, Britain's primary Indian state source market is Maharashtra with 36 per cent of the Indian outbound market to UK residing in Maharashtra (British Tourist Authority, July 2002).
- **Business tourism and MICE market:** An FHRAI study observes that 57 per cent of all guests in Indian Hotel Industry comprise of business guests. Most travel agents interviewed during this study agreed that business travel had grown for the last couple of years by 10-15 per cent annually. The Meetings Incentives Convention Exhibition (MICE) market is growing worldwide, India being no exception. Most of the South East Asian countries are tapping the source markets for India namely—Mumbai, New Delhi, Chennai and Bangalore. According to Express Travel and Tourism "The MICE segment will be the important driver for corporate travel in India, enhancing traffic to key cities like Mumbai and Delhi, while increasing traffic to emerging nodal towns like Pune, Hyderabad and Bangalore" (WTTC, 2003). The Union Budget's announcement of the proposed establishment of two global standard international convention centres at an estimated cost of Rs. 1,000 crore, one being in Mumbai, will be a big boost for the MICE market (Express Travel and Tourism, March 25, 2003).
- **International airport at Goa:** Goa is planning an international airport in North Goa, just a few kilometres away from the high tourism potential district of Sindhudurg. Accessibility to this region will certainly assist in increasing tourist interest in this region as also encourage premier hotel groups to build facilities in Sindhudurg.

Threats

- *Perception:* An issue that is essential in stabilising tourism growth is the factor of 'perception'. How your present and potential tourist markets perceive the destinations in Maharashtra State is important in defining their travel options. The bomb blasts and scares have caused a setback to tourism in Maharashtra. The dispersed marketing initiatives do not clearly give an idea to a tourist as to which destination he can choose or visit.
- **Global and national effects:** The comments of Mr Frangialli, WTO president that, "There is an increasing awareness that risk is no longer associated exclusively with specific destinations; that risk can exist in one's own backyard", bring out the global nature of tourism. Recently, WTO news has mentioned the Asian destinations that have not recorded major cases of infection to date, (India, Indonesia, Malaysia, Cambodia, the Philippines, Thailand...) have suffered almost as much as the areas actually affected, China, Hong Kong and Singapore. Thus, in spite of India being a part of Asia and in close proximity to the affected regions in Southeast Asia, tourism has

been affected. Also, India being such a vast country, the rest of India does not essentially feel the effects of security and safety tensions in one part. Yet tourism to India, in general, has been affected by such incidences.

- **Safety and security issues in Mumbai:** In today's information-savvy and global world, safety and security issues in destinations have primary importance. How present and potential tourist markets perceive the destination, beyond its leisure, fun, shopping, etc., image, in terms of health and safety has found prominence after the 9/11, SARS and Gulf War.
- **International airports at other Indian metros:** Thiruvananthapuram, Hyderabad and Chennai already have international airports, while Goa is on the verge of building one. As these airports become popular with leisure and business tourists, offering convenient connecting time, Mumbai might lose out on its transit status.
- **Economic situations at source market:** The outbound tourism is inevitably linked with the general economic situation of the source market countries. The International Monetary Fund published its World Economic Outlook last September, in which it lowered its economic development projections for most countries. The figures show a generalised reduction in growth among the developed countries, which are the main generators of tourism.
- **Competition from other Indian states:** The small cache of foreign tourists visiting India predominantly travel to the five states: Kerala, Rajasthan, Tamil Nadu, Delhi, Maharashtra and Goa. According to DOT data, Maharashtra ranks second in India's tourist destinations. But that ranking can be attuned to the existence of the international airport at Mumbai. Goa, Rajasthan and Kerala have already initiated the Economic Impact Assessment workings with support from WTO and WTTC. Kerala has initiated the Vision 2025 for long-term sustained tourism development. These states depend highly on the tourism industry. With international airports within the state and large-scale charter flights, all have accessibility support. The governments in these states have supported tourism in a big way through large budgets and promotions. Maharashtra faces competition from these states in the areas of heritage tourism, special interest tourism—backwater, palaces and beach tourism.

Policy Recommendations—Sustainable Tourism for Maharashtra

From the SWOT analysis, it is evident that Maharashtra has a great potential and opportunities to develop tourism as a basis of economic development. The state can use its strengths to take advantage of its opportunities for sustained tourism growth by following an approach that inculcates the principles of sustainable tourism. Sustainability of tourism in Maharashtra during this short-term Five Year Plan period, primarily depends on its ability to increase tourist spend at the existing tourist destinations, like Mumbai and Ajanta-Ellora and to increase tourist arrivals to other attractions in the backdrop of strong leadership, planning systems and procedures.

The report recommends the following policy implications for tourism in Maharashtra that match the sustainability concept to the advantage of its strengths and opportunities, while reducing its threats and weaknesses. These recommendations take into consideration that a state's tourism policy should provide the most explicit statement of the government's approach to sustainable tourism development and the roles that all stakeholders in the tourism sector are expected to play. Some of the examples of sustainable tourism policies and actions are given below:

Sustainable Tourism Planning in Turkey

Recent growth of the tourism industry in Turkey has followed the global pattern of rapid expansion, in line with, rising standards of living, increased leisure time for travel and improved infrastructure. The tourism industry in Turkey contributes significantly to its foreign exchange earnings and employment. Government gives priority to training qualified personnel. Most activities to develop human resources are carried out by the private sector, although the government provides vocational training.

The Turkish Tourism Policy aims to extend the economic benefits from tourism to the people, while ensuring that tourism policies are environmentally sound and sustainable. Tourism is primarily a private sector industry, but tourism facilities must be licenced either by municipalities or the Ministry of Tourism. Such licensing by the Ministry is intended to guarantee that the quality of services conform to international standards.

The government is responsible for research and statistics to help evaluate the impact of tourism.

Turkish Tourism Policy ensures the continuity of natural and cultural assets, by prioritising environmental protection and the cultural heritage. Turkey has a number of environmental management projects, such as the Mediterranean and Aegean Coastline Tourism Infrastructure Management Project and the Blue Flag Campaign to ensure water quality. The Government of Turkey is responsible for infrastructure and public services, although incentives are granted under the Tourism Encouragement Law.

The Ministry of Tourism provides the overall orientation and coordination, though publicly owned tourism establishments will be gradually privatised. Foreign investment in the tourism sector is encouraged according to Foreign Investment Law number 6224, which is based on a country report prepared by Plan of Action for Sustainable Tourism Development (PASTA plan 1999-2005), "A Progress Report".

Sustainable Tourism Planning in China

China has a seven-point strategy as a basic framework for sustainable tourism development that seeks to balance rational use of resources for positive economic impact with environmental protection. It emphasises on giving full play to market mechanisms and promoting the government's role in establishing a cooperative institutional safeguard system. This would help at the macro-economic level by replacing some traditional industries that used resources inefficiently and caused pollution.

China has strengthened its legal and technical standards in order to protect tourism resources. Since the 1980s, it has included the Law on Environmental Protection, Rules and Regulations on National Scenic Spots and Regulations on Forests and Parks. The National Tourism Administration of China has proposed guidelines for promoting tourism.

China has also emphasised public awareness and education campaigns on sustainable tourism development, and there have been pilot projects on eco-tourism. One initiative under China's seven-point strategic policy for tourism development involves setting up model ecotourism projects. An important part of eco-tourism projects involves action to preserve and maintain the continuity of the cultural heritage, which is based on a country report prepared by the China National Tourism Administration, Beijing, China, (Translated) in Plan of Action for Sustainable Tourism Development in the Asian and Pacific Region (1999-2005), "A Progress Report".

Sustainable Tourism in Kumarakom, Kerala—A Case Study

Kumarakom, a backwater tourism hub is gaining a strategic place in the map of tourism due to its natural, scenic and aesthetic beauty. Tourism Development in Kumarakom started with the lease of KTDC land (bird sanctuary area) to Taj Kerala Resorts Limited in 1989. Tourism has developed rapidly in the area after that and Prime minister Vajpayee's visit and his popular Kumarakom musings has created much hype among tourists in this otherwise calm destination.

Kumarakom *Panchayat* at present has 5 big resorts contributing to 344 beds and creating direct employment opportunities of 515 and indirect employment opportunities of 164. There are 7 small resorts and more than 20 lodges and home stay facilities contributing to another 100 beds. *Panchayat* is earning 20 lakhs as tax from the industry and it claims that the tourism industry's revenue amounts to around 30 crores in this small destination.

Initially, the arrival of tourism industry was well-received by the local people with the land value increasing many folds in the potential areas for tourism ventures. They offered their agricultural lands and paddy fields for tourism construction at an exorbitant price. Although the conversion of land reduced the agricultural yield and employment, the temporary employment opportunities in the construction sector with relatively higher wages, made the local workers happy.

In the years to come, however, the negative impacts of tourism for the local community started showing:

- **Employment:** Eighty per cent of the regular employees in big hotels were appointed from outside Kumarakom. A study revealed that most of the labourers lost their traditional occupation. Women and agricultural labourers were displaced from the lands converted for tourism could not be compensated with alternative jobs.
- **Occupation/income loss:** The clustering of the resorts on the banks of Vembanad Kayal denied the local people involved in fishing and shell collection, access to the Kayal. The increased number of speedboats, motorboats and houseboats plying as a part of tourism development, resulted in the damage of their fishing nets. Tourist resorts have even gone to the extent of privatising and appropriating the Kayal to promote their business without due regard to the

regulations placed by the *panchayat*. The natural banks of the Kayal, once covered with thick mangrove forest, are replaced by granite walls by the resort owners in order to get uninterrupted view of it from their property. The cutting down of these mangrove forests has also completely destroyed the breeding grounds for several fishes, resulting in their diminishing numbers. For e.g the half beak (*Hemiramphus*) species, which were once abundant in the lake are now reduced, also resulting in the unemployment of many fishermen.

Environment Loss

- The two mangrove swamps on the northwest corner of the KTDC complex were the only breeding ground for Night Herons in Kerala in the eighties. The clearance of trees in the entrance area of the complex has ensured the vanishing of one third of the bird population in the last decade.
- The bird census conducted in the area periodically has clearly shown the impact of tourism development on bird population. The survey conducted in 10 selected areas of Kumarakom featured 36,498 birds in 1993, 22,195 birds in 2001 and a meagre 13,274 birds in 2002.
- The wastes from hotels and those from houseboats, including human excreta are dumped into the lake. The total coliform count in the lake is much higher than the maximum prescribed value. The number of coliform in 100 ml of lake water is 1,500 to the permissible limit of 500 maximum/100 ml for ecologically sensitive and contact water sports. In Kumarakom, improvement of the infrastructure development and the development of service and productive sectors has received no contribution from the tourism industry.

Equations conducted a Technical Session on 29th August, 2002 for the *panchayat* members, on the Powers and functions of the *panchayat*, devolved as per the Kerala *Panchayat Raj* under the broad mandate of the 73rd Amendment of the Constitution useful for the proper regulation of tourism. Motivated by this knowledge, the *panchayat* members came up with a People's Charter and Draft Guidelines on Sustainable Tourism for Kumarakom, which demanded the preparation of master plan for tourism development and put regulations on new constructions, tourism activities and utilisation of common resources. The Charter also insists that the tourism industry ensures direct and indirect employment opportunities for the local people and contributes to the projects of priority, for the well being of the community and conservation of the environment, in the backdrop of overall socio-economic development of the region. A thrust has been given to the concepts of social obligations of tourism industry and its corporate accountability. The Charter also demands the creation of an expert committee to look into the conceptualisation, planning, implementation and monitoring of tourism development within the Kumarakom *panchayat*. To realise these objectives, the *Panchayat* is now planning to create a Functional Committee on Tourism as per Section 163(1) of the Kerala Panchayat Raj Act, which allows the *panchayat* to form functional committees on different subjects.

On 23rd April 2003, the *Panchayat* convened a meeting of members of the tourism industry and others concerned with tourism, to initiate a democratic discussion on the People's Charter and Draft Guidelines. The representatives of the tourism industry consented to the contents of the Charter and the process of its ratification is underway.

The implementation of the Charter and community-based tourism initiatives will lead to sustainable tourism with the components of conservation, participatory processes and benefit sharing to all the stakeholders concerned in Kumarakom (Sustainable Tourism in Kumarakom, A Case Study).

The Sustainable Tourism policy approach brings together the stakeholders involved in the tourism product, consisting of the industry with top hotel groups like the Taj, Oberoi, ITC and tour operators like Thomas Cook, Cox and Kings and Raj Travels along with many local well-known players. Also, the dynamic government leadership of MTDC and the Government of Maharashtra, Ministry of tourism, the local community that has a variety of artisans and entrepreneurs, the people of Maharashtra and most importantly the tourist who still mostly transits through Maharashtra and may yet contribute to the economic development of Maharashtra by increasing in numbers and spending.

The report recommends a policy approach, where the government plays the role of initiating investment and involvement from private sector and local community, while investing in tourism asset conservation and capacity building. The private sector plays a larger role by offering more innovative options for tourists and investing in infrastructure and services. The local community becomes a part of this broader approach by increasing entrepreneurship and their involvement in all stages of planning and development of tourism. Thus each of the stakeholders needs to provide the following:

- Support through defining and following policies, systems and procedures.
- Investment in infrastructure and economic growth.
- Involvement in the social progress and growth.
- Responsibility towards environment, heritage and culture.
- Partnership in tourism planning development and management.

Plan for Long Term

- Create state leadership involvement in tourism, the travel and tourism industry's role, as Maharashtra's sustained economic driver requires the involvement of the highest authority like, the chief minister at the policy/planning, implementation and management stages of tourism initiatives. Tourism being a diverse industry, involves coordinated working of different areas like public works, power and water works, law and order, urban and rural planning, environment, conservation, which need holistic and decisive decision making. Thus, tourism, without the support and involvement of the chief minister, may just be relegated to being an elitist industry and tourism plans on sustainable principles will not be implemented. The need is for tourism to be politically acceptable without compromising on its sustainability.

This report recommends that a Cabinet Committee chaired by the chief minister be established with appropriate ministers as members. This committee would be coordinated by the MTDC, the Ministry of Tourism, and GoM and all its decisions would be binding on its members. The tourism initiatives in Maharashtra undertaken by diverse groups and agencies, like CIDCO, MSRDC, FDCM can be brought under this committee.

- **Establish destination-based development authorities:** Maharashtra has some of India's best nature and heritage sites like Sindhudurg, Matheran, Elephanta and Ajanta-Ellora. However, unplanned development, overcrowding, short-term initiatives can hamper their appeal as major tourism destinations, prime examples being the eco-sensitive zones, like Mahabaleshwar and Panchgani. Thus, the government must ensure that other destinations do not undergo the same fate. With regard to this, the report takes into consideration the recommendation of the 'Development Authority' for the Sindhudurg Development Plan and the government initiatives for Mahabaleshwar hill station development.

Destinations in Maharashtra demand focussed development with less duplication of efforts, an integrated approach and shared knowledge through regular interface with local partners and stakeholders. Since each destination has its own problems and issues a local perspective needs to be brought in.

The report recommends that development authorities based on the concept of 'Destination Management Organisations' (UNEP for Sustainable tourism) be created for major destinations, like Ajanta-Ellora, Sindhdurg Tourism Zone and Mumbai where, the local authorities provide leadership, with the involvement of local NGOs, community and indigenous representatives, academia, and local chambers of commerce. The DMO would be responsible for developing master plans for the destinations and its implementation.

Any development for tourism services would fall under the purview of the DMO. These authorities would be independent in their working, though they would be accountable to MTDC for any lapses. The DMO should define its own strategy and objectives and develop promotion and can be funded by the state in its preliminary years and later be created as a self-funded agency.

- **Create responsibility and accountability systems:** Maharashtra has nature reserves, heritage and cultural attractions that are vulnerable to the negative impacts of tourism over development, pollution and loss of cultural authenticity. In order to preserve these tourism attractions, accountability systems should be created as a part of monitoring plan of the DMOs. Each stakeholder should be made responsible and accountable for its actions. For example, any local entrepreneur mass-producing 'local handicrafts' should be fined. Or any company creating visual, noise or waste pollution should be stopped from any further production till corrective action is taken.

In addition, it should adopt the principles of ecological preservation as outlined in Agenda 21, developed for the travel and tourism industry after the 1992 Rio Earth Summit by WTTC, the World Tourism Organization and the Earth Council. The report recommends that a series of policies and guidelines be framed for development of ecotourism, culture and art tourism, heritage tourism and urban and religious tourism.

Also specific guidelines for tour operators, guides, hotels, restaurants, local communities, small and independent entrepreneurs should be prepared at the state level that can steer the workings of the DMOs at the destination level. The government can take the cue from already existing guidelines from Pacific Asia Travel Agents Code of Environmental Conduct, International Hotel and Restaurant Authority 'Environmental Action Pack for Hotels' and 'Environmental Good Practice in Hotels' APEC Tourism Charter, IOTO's set of principles for Coastal Zone Management (CZM), WTO's Indicators for Sustainable tourism management and Carrying Capacity Assessment, WTO's Quality Standards and APEC/PATA Code for Sustainable Tourism.

- Strategy, focused and planned development: Maharashtra has many high tourism potential attractions, each capable of being a major tourist destination by itself. But all of them cannot be developed and promoted simultaneously as the success of tourism also depends on their readiness for it. This report notes that readiness for tourism in Sindhudurg depends, to a certain extent, on issues of accessibility and local support.

Thus, the Government of Maharashtra should consider development of destinations based on their present readiness for tourism.

This report recommends that destinations can be developed based on classification of:

- **Primary products:** These are the products having tourism infrastructure and services and receiving majority of the tourists coming to Maharashtra. The destinations of Mumbai and Ajanta-Ellora-Aurangabad fall into this category. Mumbai has many options for international and domestic markets—heritage, museums, cuisine and culture, business, nearby beaches, nightlife, shopping and fashion. Ajanta caters mostly to the tourist interested in heritage, specifically Buddhist heritage. Ellora would interest most international and domestic tourists. Also major religious destinations like Shirdi and the Ashtavinayak circuit can be primary destinations.
- **Secondary destinations:** are those near the primary destinations, which can be attached as add-on products. Aurangabad, e.g, is the transit place for visiting Ajanta-Ellora, and having historical tourist attractions it can initiate an additional day stay. Another special tourism site is Lonar that is accessible from Aurangabad and can command high interest amongst international tourists. Pune and Matheran can be secondary destinations for Mumbai, the former being covered, as a destination is the Deccan Odyssey.

Also potential destinations, like the Sindhudurg region will become accessible with the implementation of the international airport in Goa thus, making Sawantwadi, Sindhudurg Fort and Tarkarli secondary destinations. Potential ecotourism destinations–national parks and forests can be tapped with neighbouring states for domestic tourism.

Manage Tourism Proactively

- **Create tourism management system:** Tourism is a demand-based economic model; the tourism product can be viable only if the demand for the product exists. Thus, the government of Maharashtra should encourage research and collection of data to aid the development decision making. The ESCAP region's Plan for Sustainable tourism in Asia Pacific region explains that the effectiveness of policy making by the government policy makers and stakeholders depends on reliable information and timely data of good quality to enable better understanding of tourism's complex and long-term interactions with the rest of the economy.

At the state level, the report recommends the Tourism Information Management Systems (TIMS) undertake:

- Profiling of domestic and international source markets.
- Feedback mechanism of tourists at the entry and exit points to mark their expectations and satisfaction levels.
- Economic impact assessments.
- Environmental impact assessments that can provide useful information for planning future strategies.

- At the destination level, the data on:
  - Tourist arrivals at the destination and at specific tourist attractions within the destination, with characteristics, like nationality, and for domestic tourist, the region they reside in, purpose of visit.
  - Spending patterns, age-sex groups, income levels, group/individual travel, length of stay, port of entry and seasonal patterns.
  - Satisfaction levels of tourists at the destination, with respect to the type and quality levels of infrastructure and services.
- **Accommodation:** room types, availability, rates and quality should be compiled. The data collection and analysis should form a part of a system procedure that is regularly updated. Tourist surveys can be periodically taken during the peak and off-peak seasons that can assist in future developing trends/developments.
- **Establish monitoring systems:** The government of Maharashtra is undertaking a dynamic plan for tourism promotion and development. The progress and effect of this plan has to be duly monitored to ensure that tourism is on the right track and to detect any problems and take proactive remedial action before they become serious. An overall evaluation of the tourism policies and plans can include management, through a set of indicators of sustainable tourism at given destinations or regions, which in turn can help the planners and managers of tourism to anticipate and prevent those tourism activities which may threaten key attributes. An example is the core indicators of sustainable tourism published by the WTO as shown in the Table 12.2. This set of indicators can be complied on a regular basis at the destination level.
- **Perception and public relations for stakeholders and tourists:** An issue that is essential in stabilising tourism growth is the factor of 'perception'. How your present and potential tourist markets perceive the destinations in Maharashtra state is important in defining their travel options. Tourism in Maharashtra, from the point of view of safety has suffered a setback due to the frequent bomb blasts and scares.

TABLE 12.2

Core Indicators of Sustainable Tourism

Indicator	*Specific Measures*
Stress	Tourism numbers visiting site per annum/peak month.
Use Intensity	Intensity of use in peak period.
Social Impact	Ratio of tourists to locals.
Development Control	Existence of environmental review procedure or formal control over development of site and use densities.
Planning Process	Existence of organised regional development plan for tourist destination (including the tourism component).
Critical Ecosystems	Number of rare endangered species.
Consumer Satisfaction	Level of satisfaction by visitors, tourist revisit levels, spending patterns.
Local Satisfaction	Level of satisfaction of locals, income levels, crimes against tourists.
Tourism Contribution to Local Economy	Proportion and growth pattern of total economic activity generated by tourism alone, multiplier effect; leakage percentage.

Source: WTO (1997). "A Practical Guide to Development and Use of Indicators."

The report recommends that a regularised, public relations and perception management exercise be undertaken by the government to portray Maharashtra as a safe destination.

The local communities in various destinations of Maharashtra also suffer for want of information on tourism plans and developments. Tourist awareness plans must be made at the destination and state levels, offering information on the government's plans for tourism while giving a platform to air views and queries and find appropriate answers.

Emphasise Tourism as an Economic Driver

- **Develop integration with other industries:** Maharashtra's gems and jewellery, horticulture, breweries, floriculture, sugarcane industries are well known. These industries can be tapped as an extension of the travel and tourism industry. The Sindhudurg district, along with being a potential tourist destination, also has horticulture as its prime industry that can be attached to tourism. Mumbai has the entertainment and fashion industry while Kolhapur has the textile industry. The report recommends that the destination plans are integrated and developed with other industries that are local to that area. The government of Maharashtra can offer incentives for entrepreneurs that create synergies between local industries and tourism.

- **Make local community a partner in tourism:** Local communities in Maharashtra are yet to be given prominence in tourism planning and development. The government of Maharashtra should appreciate that tourism as an economic driver can succeed only if the economic benefits, generated through the tourists, percolate to the local level. Moreover, their support for tourism is an essential aspect to actually sustain it at any destination. Such support will exist only if the rights and interests at regional and local levels, the property owners and relevant indigenous people who may exercise traditional rights or responsibilities over their own land and its significant sites, are protected.

This report recommends that the Government of Maharashtra can create legalised involvement of the local community in tourism planning at the destination level. The local community should be involved in establishing goals, strategies, policies and protocols for the identification, conservation, management, presentation and interpretation of their heritage resources, cultural practices and contemporary cultural expressions, in the tourism context. Support for local companies should also be provided so that they can develop access to technology advances and compete more effectively with suppliers in competing destinations. The government should incorporate local approval, employment and minimum leakage as an essential aspect for tourism plans.

Develop Tourism Asset Capital

- **Human resource development:** The government of Maharashtra needs to realise that sustained tourism growth demands the development of human asset. Tourism is a people centric activity. The quality of experience a tourist has is highly dependant on the 'human resource' element. The success of tourism industry depends as much on the availability of requisite infrastructure, as on the availability of trained manpower to work as guides, interpreter, and tour operators and above all to serve in hotels and restaurants, so as to ensure a comfortable and happy stay for the tourists. Hence, trained persons in tourism related subsectors are seen as a *sine qua non* for the tourism industry.

Also, one of the main considerations in tourism is to draw advantage in terms of employment multiplier effect resulting in creation of additional employment opportunities. It is estimated that an investment of Rs. 10 lakh in tourism, results in creation of 89 jobs in the hospitality industry as compared to 45 in agriculture and 13 in manufacturing.

In Maharashtra, the Institute for Hotel Management, Catering Technology and Applied Nutrition, at Dadar is one of the best institutes. There are many organisations, like the Garware Foundation, that offer travel and tourism courses with university affiliations. In fact, this Foundation is now planning to start distance learning tourism courses, for local community in Sindhudurg that will be extended to a full-fledged college in the years to come. Small private institutes offer IATA certification, ticketing and airline services courses that are mainly operational.

The Government of Maharashtra needs to prioritise education and training as a part of its tourism policies. Along with development of quality institutions that create a 'profession' label for tourism, continuous training programmes should be organised to train various categories of people engaged in the tourism industry, such as the staff at government tourist offices and information centres, the policy makers, local government representatives and community leaders. Emphasis must be on training of taxi drivers, cooks, waiters, guides, information office assistants, etc. that come in direct contact with tourists.

- **Encourage conservation and preservation as an intrinsic aspect of tourism development:** Maharashtra's most potential tourist attractions are heritage and cultural sites that are in semi-urban and rural areas. These sites are the backbone of Maharashtra's future tourism growth. Thus, the Government of Maharashtra should realise that growth in tourism along with benefits of foreign exchange earnings and employment, also introduces commercialisation of culture and history, arts and traditions, loss of natural environment and societal distortions. World-wide, there have been cases wherein crafts are mass manufactured in other sites and sold to tourists as homemade traditional stuff. There have been instances of staged weddings, dances, art and handicrafts being offered to tourists, which though, earlier encouraged by pride in their culture, become a professional show performed by paid actors. Also, cheap imitations of intricate handicrafts are being sold to the ready market, and areas, traditionally owned lands by the locals are used for constructing tourist facilities (findings at UNESCO workshop on sustainable tourism development in world heritage sites—planning for hue). The result, as exemplified at many tourist destinations, is the commercialisation, of culture and traditions, loss of authenticity of artisan products and traditional skills, modification of traditions to please the tourists, and an erosion of social values. Such an effect would end up degrading the tourism attraction, rather than reviving it.

The report recommends that the Government of Maharashtra gives serious consideration to the conservation and preservation aspect of tourism and develops broad policies to guide the service providers, tourists and local community.

- **Build education institutions to retain the art, crafts and cultures:** Maharashtra's arts and crafts that are potential attractions for the growing, 'experience oriented' tourist segments world-wide, needs to be sustained through inculcating a sense of pride amongst its artists and craftsmen. The report recommends that special educational institutions be set up at the local destination level, offering short courses/internships, to encourage the locals to learn their local arts and crafts. Further, the institutions can exhibit these arts, and also provide one-day workshops for tourists. This initiative would create a brand name for its destination and the state of Maharashtra, while offering a way of income earning for the artists and craftsmen.

Develop Competitive Advantage—Advantage Maharashtra

- **Tax intelligently:** Tourist tax comprises of a host of central taxes like service tax, expenditure tax along with Government of Maharashtra's sales and luxury taxes. In the Union Budget 2003-04 the expenditure tax was removed though the reimposed service tax on tour operators, was increased.

This report urges the GoM to appreciate the effect of taxation on the volume of tourist arrivals and the multiplier effect of tourist spend, and accordingly design a tax policy, that balances volume *versus* revenue issue. The report notes that the Government of Maharashtra state taxes for travel and tourism industry are lower than most other states, though the WTTC's tax barometer declared Mumbai, one of Maharashtra's premier tourism investment centre, as one of the highest taxed and the least competitive destinations. Tables 12.3 and 12.4 reflect a comparison among four metropolitan cities of the country in terms of sales and luxury taxes respectively.

TABLE 12.3

Sales Tax (Decided by the State)

City	*Food %*	*Beverage %*
Delhi	7.01	15.01
Mumbai	15.01	25.01
Calcutta	22.5	22.5
Chennai	6.01	6.01

TABLE 12.4

Luxury Tax (Decided by the State)

City	*Rates %*
Delhi	Nil
Mumbai	10 now reduced to 6
Calcutta	12.5
Chennai	20.01

Source: India Info-line Hotel Report (Dec' 2002).

In many cities throughout the world, tax policies have been adopted which not only slow the revenue generating capacity of travel and tourism, but also slow or completely stifle job creation. WTTC observes that in some cities, such as New York, the failure of policy makers to thoroughly consider the implications of increasing hotel room tax rates has actually resulted in a net loss of tax proceeds and jobs, for the city and state. It is estimated that New York state lost $962 million in taxes on visitor spending to collect $463.2 million from a 5 per cent room tax.

- **Encourage diversity and innovation in products:** Maharashtra has a plethora of intangible cultural tourism assets like its cuisine, music, Bollywood, theatre, arts like Warli, Ganjifa and Chitrakathi along with its tangible heritage structures and natural parks. It is necessary to build around these intangible assets, to tap the full potential of tourism growth and to cater to the 'new experience' requirements of today's highly aware tourists.

The report recommends that the government should offer incentives to open specialty of Maharashtra cuisine, music and craft workshops and experiences at major destinations while creating a 'brand' through promotions. Entrepreneurship in new tourism experiences, like adventure tourism, rural and ethnic tourism should be encouraged by offering micro-finance and promotion support.

- **Diverse strategies for different markets:** The international source markets for Maharashtra are primarily the USA, UK, Germany and Japan. These are also the world's largest travelling and spending tourism source markets. Also NRIs and growing source markets like China form important, yet specifically untapped markets.

On the domestic front, the present outbound market, regional leisure tourists are potential source markets.

Each of these markets has a distinct relationship with Maharashtra and hence each market should be treated as a different entity having differing needs and wants. Japan is one of the world's largest source markets that require specific facilities. For example, Japanese-speaking guides should service Japanese tourists visiting Ajanta-Ellora. Similarly, NRIs can be offered special religious or shopping tourism packages, while the domestic tourists can be offered entertainment shows.

Also, with the potential of domestic market playing a larger role, a specific strategy should be made to target this market. The strategies should aim at increasing the number of tourist arrivals and spending.

- **Prioritise on, 'information reach' 'branding' 'higher visibility' for Maharashtra's tourism products:** Sustainable tourism for Maharashtra needs to reach the increasingly competitive global marketplace, to create a strong branding of destinations. Information dissemination and branding mediums like the Internet, tour operators, travel shows, print media, expert views and road shows can be created to tap the potential tourism source markets.

One important medium is the Internet that can offer visibility to a large market. Maharashtra State Development Corporation has taken a step in developing a website that offers useful information and at the same time promotes its potential. But this website needs to be regularly updated to give visitors the latest information on new destinations and developments. Also the website can develop relationships with private operators to distribute their packages.

Apart from the Internet, which is an impersonal medium of information distribution, there are tour operators and travel agents that have direct contact with tourists. The government should create partnerships with them to offer Maharashtra's destinations.

Tourists have become very influenced by travel shows on television channels and travel magazines that portray a real and practical view of tourist destinations. The government must invite and create opportunities to cover its destinations on such shows that directly reach the tourists.

The system should cater to the needs of the diverse markets according to their use of the mediums.

Create a Viable Investment Environment

- **Increase government support and investment:** Though the present state budget for tourism has a 10-fold increase it forms a minor percentage of its overall budget. Taking a cue from WTTC's observation that India is one of the lowest spenders on tourism—153rd out of 160 countries —while its neighbouring competitors and China invest far more: Malaysia (5.1 per cent), Nepal (5 per cent), Indonesia (8.4 per cent), Maldives (15.7 per cent), China (3.8 per cent), the government of Maharashtra should increase its budget for tourism.
- **Increase accessibility at tourist destinations:** Maharashtra needs to strengthen its overall infrastructure significantly not only in the interest of tourism, but also for the general economic development of the state. Specifically, there is an urgent need to address the accessibility issue that affects the volume of tourist arrivals, their satisfaction and investment viability for the private sector. This report notes that one of the reasons for large international hotel groups that have been given landholdings in Maharashtra's prominent Sindhudurg tourism district, not starting development, might be accessibility.

In the paper titled Dimensions of Domestic Tourism by Mr. Uttam Dave, the development of inter-state highways has been observed as an essential thrust for domestic tourism. The interstate highways, as well as roads connecting tourism destinations, need to be upgraded to international standards. This network of world-class highways would allow Maharashtra's numerous tourist attractions to be fully enjoyed. Maharashtra also has apart from airports in Mumbai, a spate of local airports close to tourist destinations. The government must look into involving the private sector as a major player in reviving these airports through charter flights.

Most of the domestic tourists in India use trains as a mode of transport. The Ministry of Railways is presently taking an aggressive stance at offering tourist conveniences. The Maharashtra State Government should work with the Ministry to provide better tourist facilities.

- **Participation of private sector investment:** The private sector in Maharashtra needs to start paying a larger role in travel and tourism industry. Presently, the government of Maharashtra plays the role of support for initiating investment and involvement from the private sector and the local community. Infrastructure development that has been a government undertaking can be shifted over a period of time to the private sector. Kerala has already taken a stand to develop infrastructure through the private sector in its action plan for Tourism 2025. The Government of Turkey too, though presently responsible for infrastructure and public services, is moving towards private sector investment through incentives granted under the Tourism Encouragement Law.

The report suggests that along with infrastructure, tourist services, like different kinds of tourism transport-luxury coaches, air-conditioned cars, luxury boats, yachts and speedboats, innovative accommodation like tree houses, entertainment services can be offered as incentives, for private sector participations

- **Facilitation/convenience to stakeholders:** Maharashtra's numerous stakeholders would be working together to build sustainable tourism in the state. Thus, it is essential to facilitate each one of them to smoothen any problems and to convenience their workings.

The report recommends that the private sector be aided by offering a single window clearance, for projects. It is noted that MTDC has plans to work on this issue. Removing barriers to a satisfying tourist experience should facilitate the most important stakeholder for Maharashtra, the tourist. The entire tourist process should be studied to understand the issues—information availability, host-ambience, quality of services, etc., that can be dealt with through supportive actions. For example, a visit to Ajanta-Ellora requires the tourist to pay toll, purchase tickets, etc., around five times due to a jurisdiction difference between the central and state government. Mumbai suffers from a lack of host ambience with condition of roads, hygiene and beggars being the major issues. These should be resolved to offer a better experience to the tourist.

Recommendations for Future Studies in Maharashtra Tourism

The report also recommends that as an extension to this exercise undertaken by the Planning Commission, a set of more specific studies be undertaken in the future. As a result of the data collected and analysed during this study, it is recommended that the following projects be considered as an appropriate next step. The projects represented are not in the order of priority and can be undertaken simultaneously.

Project I: Market profiling and analysis: The main objective of this study is to remove barriers to an informed and intelligent decision making process. Information about Maharashtra's present key markets, their spending patterns, future interests, and economic conditions should form the basis for tourism product developments in Maharashtra. Growing tourism source markets like China should also be covered. Similarly, the domestic tourism source areas can be identified and their profiles can be analysed.

Project II: Tourism information system: This project involves working with Ministry of Tourism, Government of India and the Government of Maharashtra to develop a long-term standard system of tourism data collection and analysis. This information should provide latest trends in tourists visiting Maharashtra and other competitive states.

Project III: Sustainable tourism guidelines, policies and standards: This study is crucial for the development of sustainable tourism in Maharashtra. It aims at creating handbooks for various stakeholders and policies and standards that overall guide the development and management of destinations.

Project IV: Economic impact assessment: Tourism Satellite Account implementation in co-operation with WTO and WTTC India.

Project V: Tourism and hospitality education: The objective is to develop a high level of education for all levels of tourism professions to supply to the tourism industry of Maharashtra. The project considers the levels and targets for future demand.

Project VI: Tourism awareness programme for general public and for small-scale service providers: The first objective of the tourism awareness programme is to increase the knowledge of the people of Maharashtra and specifically Mumbai about its tourist attractions and encourage young people to engage in tourism courses and undertake tourism as a profession. Secondly, the programme can inform the small-scale service entrepreneurs or providers about the tourism business.

Along with general studies, specific sustainable tourism destination plans for Mumbai and Ajanta-Ellora–Aurangabad should be undertaken in the short-term followed by such studies being undertaken for other destinations over medium and long term.

Chapter 13

Urbanisation

Introduction

Urbanisation is an integral part of economic development. As the economy develops, there is an increase in the per capita income and also in the demand for non-farm goods in the economy. These goods are not heavily land-dependent and use more of other factors of production, especially labour and capital. They are cheaper if produced in the urban sector of the economy, since urban settlements enjoy economies of agglomeration in manufacturing, services and provision of infrastructure. Economic growth influences the rate of urbanisation, while urbanisation in turn, affects the rate at which the economy grows. As the country urbanises, the share of national income that originates in the urban sector also increases.

Urbanisation brings in its wake a number of challenges, such as rapid population growth in urban settlements, which is cited as the biggest challenge in most literature on this subject. This is a consequence of births exceeding deaths, migration of rural population to urban centres and also the classification of rural settlements as towns. Apart from growing population, there are other challenges too. The first set of challenges relates to the inadequate growth of formal employment, resulting in the growth of the urban informal sector, open urban unemployment and underemployment. The second set of challenges arises out of the inability of the urban physical and social infrastructure to grow in step with population, resulting in the deterioration of the quality of urban life. The former is identified as set of 'economic' ills, while the latter is set of 'social' ills of urbanisation. Many of these inadequacies are the result of inefficient and faulty management of cities, rather than population growth. These problems are visible in most cities in India, as in Maharashtra.

This chapter has seven sections. Section I enumerates characteristics associated with urbanisation. Detailed analysis of trends in the pattern of urbanisation in Maharashtra, at the state level, regional level and district-level is undertaken in Section II. The causes of growth of cities and consequences of rapid growth of population of cities are discussed in Section III. Section IV gives a brief review of the approaches to urban development adopted so far in the national and state level plans. Section V evaluates urban policy as it worked in Maharashtra. In the light of this evaluation, implications that emerge for future policy are considered in Section VI. Conclusions emerging from our analysis are given in Section VII.

SECTION I

Characteristics of Urbanisation

Economic Development

The level of urbanisation is regarded as an index of economic development. The two processes bear a high positive correlation. Urbanisation is related to the level of economic development measured, for want of a superior indicator, by per capita income. However, the relationship is not linear. When per capita income increases, urbanisation also increases though not as much. Economic growth leads to a shift in demand, and therefore, to a reallocation of resources—land, labour and capital—out of agriculture and into manufacturing and services. Till recently, cities in the developed countries (DCs) were based on industry but in the post-industrial age, they are dominated by services and yet no one considers them over-urbanised, a term that used to be applied to the Third World cities to emphasise their narrow industrial base.

Industrialisation and Density

An urban settlement is not just characterised by the relative importance of manufacturing and services but more importantly, by high density of population. Much of manufacturing is cheaper when produced on a large scale because of the economies of scale. Besides, there are external economies, ready availability of inputs, particularly, skilled labour, information and repair services, from which each producer profits when he is one of the many clustered in one location. People like to live near their place of work. Economies of scale and the cost of transport cause concentration of production and people in a specific location. Most services are produced on a small scale and require face-to-face contact of the producers with the customers and are, therefore, limited to the areas where people and production of goods is concentrated. The market for large-scale manufactures extends well beyond the boundaries of the city where it is located, to the rest of the country and at times, even abroad. Industrialisation leads to urbanisation but the latter does not necessarily lead to the former. However, bigger cities offer one precious advantage. Most businesses are subject to fluctuations, but swings in one line of production are often mitigated by swings in the opposite direction in another activity. Thus, a wage labourer is better off migrating to bigger rather than smaller cities, where he is likely to be more fully employed. All these factors increase the density of population in the cities.

Inequality and Urban Bias

The urban form or structure of cities in a country is determined by the nature of the society. The greater the inequalities in a society, the more unequal will be the urban structure. Egalitarian societies cannot produce cities. Cities cannot grow without a central power and mechanism to create a surplus, over consumption and concentrate it in urban areas. Such concentration is justified by the contribution that the cities make to national growth. In this sense, they are generative but their critics often regard them as parasites living on the surplus extracted from agriculture. Much of rural-urban differential in the standard of living in the less developed countries (LDCs) is often attributed to the urban bias of the planners and bureaucrats of these countries (Lipton, 1977). Many critics of the urban bias thesis would attribute it to sectoral rather than urban bias. They argue that the development strategy and policies, favoured industry against agriculture and the rich against the poor. The critics express their surprise at the urban bias thesis because they argue that the state legislatures and the union parliament in a country like India are dominated by rural rather than urban interest groups and this in fact, leads to their neglect.

Historical Evolution of Cities: Colonisation and Capitalism

Cities in the Third World have been shaped by colonisation and capitalism. India is no exception to this rule. Pre-colonial cities in India were interior cities but the British built new coastal cities. Calcutta, Bombay and Madras, not to mention New Delhi, grew in prestige as the British rulers lived in these cities in large numbers. The elite of provinces also shifted to the capital cities. A new hierarchy of cities reflecting the status hierarchy in the society came into being. The coastal cities were developed to handle the export-import trade with England. Consequently, they attracted many financial, commercial and trading firms. The growth of commercial capitalism soon gave rise to native industrial capitalism and the coastal cities increased their primacy in the region. Technological superiority enabled the Europeans to dominate the regional patterns of trade and the new cities served the interests of the mother country by dominating the hinterland through the hierarchy of cities. In the terminology developed in Latin America by the 'dependency school,' at the international level, Britain, the Centre, extracted surplus from India, the periphery; and at the regional level, the primate city became the Centre and the provincial towns, the Periphery. The theory predicts that over time the periphery would become poorer either absolutely or relatively, or perhaps both.

Technology, Globalisation and their Impacts on Cities

Advances in production, transport and telecommunications made possible by the application of computers and micro-electronics to these fields have annihilated distance and made decentralised production profitable. The world economy has changed in fundamental ways. A new international division of labour based on globally integrated production, spearheaded by the multi national corporations (MNCs) has dawned. Global production is serviced by global network of financial and producer services. A new concept of functional city system has been introduced to explain the recent changes in the world urban structure (Lo and Yeung, 1996). A functional city system is a network of cities that are linked, often in a hierarchical manner based on a given economic or socio-political function at the global or regional level. A collection of different functional networks of a city defines its external linkages with the world economy and its status within the world city system. A city grows in importance if it performs effectively and efficiently in a number of key functions, that another does not. The concept is claimed to be superior to the hitherto popular formulation of cities in core-periphery, dependency and linear relations. The boundaries between the core and periphery have become blurred. In the present borderless economy, acquisition and accumulation of functions defines the centrality and the role of the city in a world economy.

Globalisation and liberalisation have turned cities into junction points for movement of goods, capital and people and switch gears for transfer of information. Cities of not-too-distant a future would be producers of knowledge, research and development, innovations and inventions rather than of goods. The new phase of international division of labour, ushered in by globalisation and structural adjustment has led to a gradual decline of manufacturing in industrially advanced countries, hastening their transformation into service economies. Manufacturing has shifted to the new industrial economies (NIEs).

Earlier explanations of size, form and functions of cities based on dependency, centre-periphery, urban bias, Marxian and neo-Marxian paradigms are being questioned, modified or replaced by non-Marxian ones, drawing on the experience of the NIEs of Southeast Asia. Empirical verification of such paradigms is difficult, but need not deter us from devising policies to promote the benefits and reduce the evils of urbanisation. No single paradigm can claim a monopoly of solutions to such a complex issue as urbanisation. But, in order to deal with the problem we need to understand the emerging trends and pattern of urbanisation in Maharashtra.

SECTION II

Trends and Patterns of Urbanisation

An Overview of Urbanisation

Growing at 1.9 per cent per annum compound over the 1990s, India crossed the one billion mark and enumerated 1,027 million persons in 2001. So, almost 17 per cent or one sixth of the global population lived in India in 2001 (Registrar General, 2001a). Urban population increased at 2.6 per cent a year and improved its share in the total barely, by 2 percentage points, from 25.5 per cent to 27.2 per cent between 1991 and 2001. These urban dwellers lived in 5,161 cities/towns and were estimated at 285 million. Urban population is reported so far, for only 5,151 of them, which is 279.84 million (Registrar General, 2001b). Population living in urban India is indeed large, considering that 281.4 million lived in USA in 2000 (Registrar General, 2001a).

In all the censuses conducted in independent India, a larger share of Maharashtra's, compared to that of India's, lived in urban areas. In 1961, barely 17.8 per cent of India's, while 28.2 per cent of Maharashtra's lived in urban locations. Levels of urbanisation increased both in Maharashtra and India. In 2001, 27.8 per cent of India's while 42.4 per cent of Maharashtra's population was enumerated as urban (Director of Census Operations, Maharashtra, 2001b).

Till 1991, Maharashtra was the most urbanised state among the 16 large states of India. In 2001, with regard to the urban population, Maharashtra ranked second, with a share of 42.4 per cent, next to Tamil Nadu with a share of 43.9 per cent. Yet in absolute terms, Maharashtra's 41 million of urban population far exceeded Tamil Nadu's 27 million. These two states are closer to the world, with regard to the extent of urbanisation than India. According to the United Nations (1995), 45 per cent of the world population lived in cities in the mid-1990s.

Maharashtra's total population grew at 2.0 per cent a year compound over the 1990s, while the urban population grew much faster at 2.9 per cent a year compound. The total population in the state increased by almost 19 million, from 78 million in 1991 to 97 million in 2001, 10.5 million of this increase was in urban Maharashtra (Director of Census Operations, Maharashtra, 2001a, 2001b).

Components of Urban Growth: Natural Increase and Migration

Urban population in Maharashtra, as in India, grew faster than the total in the last 40 years from 1961. Rates of growth, both of total and urban population in Maharashtra had an edge over those in India. India's population in the post-Independence era has increased only through natural increase. International migration hardly contributed to India's population growth. As far as urban population in India is concerned, rural to urban migration has emerged as an important factor only in recent years. But it nevertheless is a secondary factor of urban population growth, next to natural increase in the last five decades (NIUA, 1998; Dyson, 2003). There are signs that interstate migration rates, both of out-migration from poor states and of in-migration into better off states have fallen in the recent past (Kundu and Gupta, 2000). While rates of so-called circulatory migration have declined, commuting has increased significantly (Visaria, 1997). But certain basic features of the overall pattern of interstate migration persist. People continue to move out of Uttar Pradesh and Bihar. They are attracted mostly to Delhi and Haryana in the north and in western India to Maharashtra and Gujarat; the two locations characterised by dynamic urban systems (Dyson, 2003).

Maharashtra has historically been an in-migrating state. Higher growth rate of Maharashtra's total population relative to that of India, in recent years, owes as much to natural increase as to in-migration from other states in India to Maharashtra (GoM, 2002). Most of the interstate migration is to urban Maharashtra. Apart from migrants from other states, those from rural Maharashtra too, flock to urban areas in search of employment. No doubt, given a higher incidence of contraceptive practice, the fertility levels are lower in urban than rural Maharashtra, but given the urban bias in accessibility to health infrastructure, mortality levels too, are lower in urban than rural Maharashtra. So, natural increase continues to be an important contributory factor of urban growth (IIPS, 2002). Between 1961 and 2001, urban population in Maharashtra grew at an average rate of 3.2 per cent a year compound rural population grew much slower, barely at 1.7 per cent a year. Growth of population, both urban and total, has slowed down over the decades (Registrar General 2001a; Director of Census Operations, Maharashtra, 2001a, 2001b).

Growth of Urban Units/Settlements and Population

Table 13.1 shows that barring the 1990s, in all the decades from 1961, the number of urban units/settlements grew faster in India than in Maharashtra. Between 1961 and 2001, the share of settlements in the country as a whole, declined from 10 per cent to 7.3 per cent, however, Maharashtra retained its share of a little over 14 per cent in the total urban population in India.

With nearly 44 per cent of the state's population living in urban areas, Tamil Nadu emerged as the most urbanised state in India in 2001. But 27.2 million urban dwellers in Tamil Nadu formed about 66 per cent of the urban dwellers in Maharashtra in 2001. In all the census years, the size of the urban population was smaller, while the number of urban units larger, in Tamil Nadu than in Maharashtra. The share of urban population in Tamil Nadu which was 11.5 per cent of the total urban population in India in 1961, declined to 9.5 per cent in 2001 (Director of Census Operations; Maharashtra, 2001b).

TABLE 13.1

Urban Units, Urban Population and Annual Rates of Growth in them, Maharashtra and India: 1961-2001

Year	*Maharashtra*		*India*	
	Number of Urban Units	*Population in Million*	*Number of Urban Units*	*Population in Million*
1961	266	11.2	2657	78.3
1971	289	15.7	3081	108.3
1981	307	22.0	3971	158.2
1991	336	30.5	4615	215.7
2001	378	41.0	5161	285.4
		Rates of Growth		
1961-71	0.8	3.4	1.5	3.2
1971-81	0.6	3.4	2.5	3.8
1981-91	0.9	3.3	1.5	3.1
1991-01	1.2	2.9	1.1	2.8

Note: Rates of growth are compound rates of growth per annum.

Source: Director of Census Operations, Maharashtra, 2001. *Provisional Population Totals Paper–2* of 2001 Rural-Urban Distribution of Population, Census of India 2001, Series–28, Maharashtra, Government Central Press, Mumbai. Statement S1, p.3. Registrar General, India, 2001.

Distribution of Urban Settlements and Population by Size-Class of Cities

Table 13.2 shows that in 1961, nearly 66 per cent of the urban population in Maharashtra lived in Class I cities that formed a little over 4 per cent of the state's urban settlements. Over the next four decades, the shares of Class I, II and III cities in the urban settlements increased and those of the other three size-classes declined. In 2001 share of Class I settlements was nearly 11 per cent while that of urban population living in them was nearly 80 per cent. All other size-classes of towns reported smaller shares of urban population in 2001 compared to 1961. Classes IV, V and VI lost their shares in both settlements and population.

Distribution of urban settlements and population in India followed a different pattern. The share of Class I

TABLE 13.2

Distribution of Urban Units/Settlements and Urban Population by Size-class of Settlements, Maharashtra: 1961–2001

Size Class	Urban Units/Settlements 1961	1971	1981	1991	2001
Class I	4.5	5.9	9.4	9.8	10.6
Class II	5.6	8.7	8.1	8.9	11.6
Class III	17.7	22.5	29.0	33.9	35.4
Class IV	33.5	33.9	32.6	30.4	27.0
Class V	33.1	24.2	15.6	13.7	13.2
Class VI	5.6	4.8	5.2	3.3	2.1
Total	**100.0**	**100.0**	**100.0**	**100.0**	**100.0**
Number	266	289	307	336	378

Population

Size Class	1961	1971	1981	1991	2001
Class I	65.8	70.7	75.3	77.8	79.7
Class II	6.9	7.4	5.9	6.5	6.7
Class III	11.4	10.6	11.0	10.4	9.4
Class IV	10.8	8.3	6.1	4.1	3.3
Class V	4.7	2.7	1.5	1.0	0.8
Class VI	0.5	0.3	0.2	0.1	0.1
Total	**100.0**	**100.0**	**100.0**	**100.0**	**100.0**
Number in Million	11.163	15.711	21.99	30.54	41.02

Note: Size-class of cities is as follows:

Class	Population
I	100000 and above
II	50000 - 99999
III	20000 - 49999
IV	10000 - 19999
V	5000 - 9999
VI	Less than 5000

Source: Director of Census Operations, Maharashtra; 2001b. Derived from data in Statement S5, p.10 and Statement S4, p.8.

TABLE 13.3

Rates of Growth of Urban Units/Settlements and Population in them by Size-class of Towns and Absorption of Decade Increase in Urban Population by Size Class of Towns : Maharashtra, 1961-2001

Size Class	Urban Units/Settlements 1961-71	1971-81	1981-91	1991-2001
Class I	3.5	5.3	1.3	1.9
Class II	5.1	0.0	1.8	3.8
Class III	3.2	3.1	2.5	1.6
Class IV	1.0	0.2	0.2	0.0
Class V	-2.3	-3.8	-0.4	0.8
Class VI	-0.7	1.3	-3.7	-3.2
Total	0.8	0.6	0.9	1.2

Population

Size Class	1961-71	1971-81	1981-91	1991-2001
Class I	4.1	4.0	3.6	3.2
Class II	4.1	1.2	4.2	3.2
Class III	2.7	3.7	2.7	2.0
Class IV	0.8	0.1	-0.5	0.7
Class V	-2.0	-2.4	-0.7	0.9
Class VI	-1.3	1.6	-3.5	-2.7
Total	**3.4**	**3.4**	**3.3**	**2.9**

Population Absorption

Size Class	1961-71	1971-81	1981-91	1991-2001
Class I	82.7	86.8	84.4	85.2
Class II	8.6	2.3	7.9	7.2
Class III	8.7	11.9	8.9	6.6
Class IV	2.3	0.3	-0.8	0.9
Class V	-2.1	-1.4	-0.3	0.3
Class VI	-0.1	0.1	-0.2	-0.1
Total	**100.0**	**100.0**	**100.0**	**100.0**
Number in millions	4.549	6.282	8.548	10.478

Source: Director of Census Operations, Maharashtra; 2001b. Derived from data in Statement S5, p.10 and Statement S4, p.8.

settlements in India was 4.5 per cent and accounted for 77.5 per cent of India's urban population in 1961 (NIUA, 1998). By 2001, the share of Class I settlements improved to 8.2 per cent but the share of population living in them declined to 61.5 per cent (Registrar General, 2001b). So, urban population growth was much more disbursed between cities/towns of different size classes in India than in Maharashtra, where it was concentrated in the largest size class.

Table 13.3 shows that irrespective of class, urban settlements grew at a slower pace in the 1990s than in the 1960s. The number of smaller towns in Class V and VI, in fact declined. Settlements in Class I and II increased faster in the 1990s than in the 1980s. The pace of urban growth itself has slowed down over years. However, in all the decades 83 per cent or more of the increase in urban population was absorbed by Class I cities. More importantly, over the 1990s, among the

Class I cities, nearly 88.2 per cent of the growth of urban population were absorbed by the million-plus cities and 6.8 per cent by cities with population between 1 to 5 lakhs. Population in cities with 5 lakhs up to 1 million in fact declined. So even among the large cities, the largest accommodated most of the increase in urban population during the last decade.

Restricting our comparison to population changes by size class of urban units in India with Maharashtra in the 1990s, we found that barring Class I, population in all size classes grew faster in India than in Maharashtra. Population living in Class I settlements increased at 2.1 per cent per annum in India, but much faster at 3.2 per cent in Maharashtra. Population in Class II and III increased at 3.8 per cent a year in the country, but slower at 3.2 per cent and 2.0 per cent a year respectively in Maharashtra.

More interesting was the pattern of growth in smaller towns with less than 20,000 inhabitants. Population in Class IV, Class V and Class VI cities, grew at 2.8 per cent, 3.5 per cent and 1.9 per cent a year respectively in India between 1991 and 2001. The corresponding growth rates in Maharashtra, were much lower, 0.7, 0.9 and –2.7 a year compound respectively.

It would be wrong to presume that people living in smaller cities in Maharashtra were migrating to larger ones. The observed pattern may result if cities grew in population size through natural increase much more than migration and graduated to the higher size-class. Given the lower levels of mortality in the state compared to the country, this process could probably be faster in Maharashtra than in India. The change could be attributed to another factor too. Some towns of the previous census may be declassified, while some new towns may be added or some may be merged with the adjoining urban units. The process changes the distribution of towns by size-class.

Maharashtra had 11 municipal corporations in 1991, 4 new were added over the 1990s. In 1991, only 3 corporations, Greater Mumbai, Pune and Nagpur, were million-plus cities. Together the 3 grew at 2.3 per cent per annum compound, slower than the growth of urban population of 2.9 per cent a year in the state in the 1990s. By 2001, 4 more cities, Thane, Kalyan-Dombivli, Nashik and Pimpri-Chinchwad joined the rank of million-plus cities in the state. The four together, grew at a rate, over 5 per cent a year compound to graduate to the class of million-plus cities in 2001. So, the flow of migrants was probably diverted to these 4 cities on the outskirts of Mumbai and Pune. Government of Maharashtra's efforts to disperse urban growth in the state by developing growth centres was successful though only partially.

To understand how the distribution of towns by size-class changed in Maharashtra during the last decade, we tried to trace the growth of each town identified in 1991 during the decade 1991-2001. The analysis confirms our earlier observation that changes in the distribution of towns by size-class in case of many towns was largely through demographic process. Growth of population automatically promoted many of them to the higher size-class. This was all the more true of larger towns. In the case of smaller towns, addition of new towns, de-classification of the existing towns was important factors along with upward shift to bigger size-class. Evidence of probable outmigration leading to movement of towns from bigger to smaller size class was there only for four towns in Maharashtra between 1991 and 2001. Change in the number of towns and population in the two smallest size groups was not the consequence of out-migration, but rather that of identification of some areas as urban and exclusion of some towns from the list of towns of 1991 as they failed to qualify as 'urban locations' in 2001.

Size Distribution of Class I Cities in Maharashtra

This raises the question of how equally or unequally the Class I cities are distributed. The knowledge that the city size distribution is unequal is not of much use to an urban planner. There is no norm or typical urban system that he could try to achieve. More nations have primate rather than non-primate cities and there are more countries with wide regional disparities than with equitable distributions of income.

Mumbai has always been a primate city of Maharashtra; but its primacy has declined over time. It accounted for 37.4 per cent of the state's urban population in 1981 but 29 per cent of it, in 2001. Mumbai's population increased at 1.9 per cent per annum compound in the 1980s, much slower than its annual growth rate of 3.8 per cent in the 1970s. Over the 1990s the growth rate decelerated further to 1.8 per cent a year compound. It would be wrong to attribute this deceleration wholly to either the market or the state. The market worked through the high price of land and labour discouraging new industry to locate in Mumbai and encouraging old industry to move out. On the other hand, it could be argued equally that the location policy of the state made Mumbai out of bounds for new large industry. The dispersal policy of the state is based on the assumption that concentration of large-scale industry causes concentration of other economic activity and hence that of population.

It may be pertinent to see how million-plus cities in Maharashtra compare with those in India. We restrict our comments to 2001, when there were 35 so-called million plus urban agglomerations and cities in India. Among them there were 27 million plus cities. Nearly, 73 million persons or 26 per cent of India's urban population lived in these 27 million-plus cities in 2001. Seven of them were located in Maharashtra. Together they had about 16.5 million inhabitants or 23 per cent of the population of all million-plus cities in the country. Greater Mumbai with a census count of 11.9 million was the largest city in India, accounting for 16 per cent of the population of 27 million-plus cities in the country. Managing large cities is a challenge but that of managing the largest among them, was indeed an enormous one.

Regional Growth and Equality

For census purposes, Maharashtra is divided into six divisions: Konkan, Nashik, Pune, Aurangabad, Amravati and Nagpur. These six divisions, for administrative purposes are grouped into three regions, the first three divisions, form rest of Maharashtra (RoM) region, Aurangabad forms Marathwada, while the last two together form Vidarbha Region. Table 13.4 shows that Rest of Maharashtra was the most urbanised region of the state, Vidarbha was in the second while Marathwada held the third place in all the three census years. Urban growth in Vidarbha has slowed down in the 1990s as the urban population in both, Amravati and Nagpur division, grew slower in the 1990s than in the 1980s (Director of Census Operations, Maharashtra, 2001b). In Marathwada, levels of urbanisation improved over the two decades, though the region continued to be ranked third on the basis of level of urbanisation in 2001. Even within RoM Region, Konkan, which includes Mumbai, Thane and Raigad, was the most urbanised division. Nearly 66 per cent of Konkan Division's population in 1981 and 75 per cent of it in 2001 lived in urban areas. Pune Division was relatively less urbanised than Konkan while Nashik was the least urbanised of the three divisions of RoM. Of these three, Pune experienced the fastest growth of urban population in the 1990s. Nearly, two-third of the Class I cities too were located in RoM Region (Director of Census Operations, Maharashtra, 2001b). The extent of urbanisation of a region depends on the extent of urbanisation of its districts. We shall see how levels of urbanisation changed in the districts of Maharashtra.

TABLE 13.4

Levels of Urbanisation (%) by Census Divisions and Regions, Maharashtra: 1981–2001

Census Division/Region	*1981*	*1991*	*2001*
Konkan Division	66.4	71.6	75.1
Nashik Division	22.1	25.6	28.2
Pune Division	30.5	32.3	37.5
Rest of Maharashtra Region	42.4	46.2	50.5
Aurangabad Division/ Marathwada Region	18.6	21.9	24.6
Amravati Division	22.2	25.0	26.5
Nagpur Division	29.7	35.0	37.1
Vidarbha Region	25.9	30.2	32.2

Source: Director of Census Operation, Maharashtra 1981 and 2001.

Urbanisation by Districts

Till 1981 there were 26 districts in Maharashtra. This number increased to 30 in 1991 and further to 35 in 2001. This increase in number of districts in the 1990s occurred, as in the past, through bifurcation of the existing districts in the state. Data relating to levels of urbanisation in these 35 districts in 1981, 1991 and 2001 are available. Two districts, Mumbai and Mumbai Suburban were wholly urbanised districts in all the three years. Gadchiroli was the least urbanised district in 1981, where only 2.43 per cent population lived in urban areas. In 1991, Sindhudurg became the least urbanised district in the state with 7.59 per cent of its population living in urban areas. In 2001, Gadchiroli, once again with 6.93 per cent of its population living in urban areas was the least urbanised district in the state.

The distribution of districts on the basis of urbanisation became far more equal over the two decades. The coefficient of variation declined from 85.00 per cent to 77.59 per cent between 1981 and 1991 and to 76.79 in 2001. This shows that equalising tendencies irrespective of whether they originated in the market or the state acted fairly well, in the pre-liberalisation period. But the equalising process has slowed down in the post-liberalisation era and is likely to continue in future if RoM, the most urbanised region of Maharashtra continues to be as attractive to investors in the future as it was in the past.

SECTION III

Causes and Consequences of Urbanisation and Problems of Growth of Cities

Causes of Urban Growth: Demographic, Economic and Social

Though most urban areas in Maharashtra grow largely through natural increase, rural to urban migration continues to be the second important component of urban growth. Apart from demographic factors, social and economic factors spur migrants from rural to urban locations. Some social factors include migration due to marriage, to access urban educational facilities, or to escape social discrimination, particularly among the socially deprived classes in India. However, most urban labour market studies reveal that more important than social, the economic causes are the push factors of migration from rural to urban locations in the state. Insecurity of employment resulting from intermittent employment, long spells of unemployment and lack of employment opportunities in the place of origin were some of the important determinants of such economic migration. These migrants came to urban areas in the hope of getting a job (Deshpande, 1979; Deshpande and Deshpande, 1998). More importantly, as in the past so also in the 1980s, most migrants to Maharashtra were attracted to Greater Mumbai (BMRDA, 1990). Analysis of the 2001 Census data confirms that the stream of net migration to the city has reduced considerably in the last two decades (Deshpande, 2003). Decline in the growth of urban population in the state could be the possible consequence of the slowing down of the growth of Mumbai's population.

Consequences of Urbanisation

Between 1991 and 2001, urban population in Maharashtra increased by about 10.5 million, 88 per cent of this increase (9.2 million) was in million-plus cities. Cities, big and small, are poorly managed, some more than the others. Consequently, the demand for unskilled labour falls much short of its supply, while the supply of infrastructure falls much short of its demand. The first deficiency causes higher unemployment in the cities than in villages. But as urban productivity is higher than rural, there are, proportionately to the population, fewer poor in the cities than in villages.

Urban Poverty

Rapid growth of cities and the absence of corresponding growth of employment opportunities is regarded as the root cause of growing urban poverty and unemployment in the developing countries. It is difficult to gather data relating to poverty in cities/towns. At the most, such data is available at state level though district level estimates are available for 1993-94 in Maharashtra. Table 13.5 shows that, the number of poor declined both in Maharashtra and in India, between 1977-78 and 1999-00. The decline was particularly steep in the 1990s. Further, the number of rural poor declined faster than urban poor, much more so in Maharashtra than in India. Poor in rural Maharashtra formed 9.25 per cent of the rural poor in the country in 1977-78; their share was 6.47 per cent in 1999-00. Share of urban poor in Maharashtra in the total urban poor in the country increased marginally from 14.55 per cent 15.36 per cent between 1977-78 and 1999-00. About 24 per cent, of the poor in Maharashtra lived in urban areas in 1977-78; their share nearly doubled and was 45 per cent in 1999-00. In India the corresponding increase was from about 20 per cent to barely 26 per cent. Urbanisation of poverty was much faster in Maharashtra than in India.

TABLE 13.5

Numbers of Poor and Incidence of Poverty in Maharashtra and India, from 1977-78 to 1999-2000

Year	*Poor in Million*					
	Maharashtra			*India*		
	Rural	*Urban*	*Total*	*Rural*	*Urban*	*Total*
1977-78	24.98	8.02	33.00	264.25	64.65	328.90
1983	19.38	9.71	29.09	251.96	70.94	322.90
1987-88	18.69	10.94	29.63	231.88	75.17	307.05
1993-94	19.33	11.19	30.52	244.03	76.34	320.37
1999-2000	12.51	10.29	22.80	193.24	67.01	260.25
	% Share of Poor in Total Population					
Year	*Maharashtra*			*India*		
	Rural	*Urban*	*Total*	*Rural*	*Urban*	*Total*
1977-78	63.97	40.09	55.88	53.07	45.24	51.32
1983	45.23	40.26	43.44	45.65	40.79	44.40
1987-88	40.78	39.78	40.41	39.69	38.20	38.86
1993-94	37.83	35.15	35.86	37.27	32.36	35.97
1999-2000	23.72	26.81	25.02	27.09	23.62	26.10

Source: Malhotra, 1997 for data of 1977-78, 1983, 1987-88 and 1993-98; Planning Commission, 2000, for data of 1999-2000.

Incidence of poverty differed between rural and urban areas in the two locations. In 1977-78 nearly 64 per cent of the persons in rural Maharashtra, while 53 per cent of them in rural India were poor. The share of urban poor was 45 per cent in India compared to 40 per cent in Maharashtra in 1977-78. Poverty declined perceptibly both in Maharashtra and India in the 1990s. Rural poverty ratio declined from 38 per cent in 1993-1994 to 24 per cent, in 1999-00 in Maharashtra. The corresponding decline was from 37 per cent to 27 per cent in rural India. Urban poverty declined too, from 35 per cent to 27 per cent in the state but from 32 per cent to 24 per cent in the country. Maharashtra carried a higher burden of urban poverty too relatively to that in the country in 1999-00.

Data on the incidence of poverty at district-level in Maharashtra is available only for 1993-94 for 30 districts of 1991 Census. Greater Mumbai was the only wholly urbanised district of the 30 districts in the state in 1991. Excluding Mumbai, among the 29 districts, the share of rural poor was the lowest, 4.94 per cent in Raigad and the highest, and 45.57 per cent in Dhule. Incidence of poverty was lower, in urban than rural areas in all districts, except Gadchiroli. Surprisingly, only 6.11 per cent of population in urban Gadchiroli was poor in 1993-94, as against 7.84 per cent in Mumbai, the richest district in the state. This casts doubts on the credibility of the data, especially for the poorer districts. The highest incidence of poverty was in urban Buldhana, where nearly 74 per cent of the population lived below the poverty line.

The share of poor in urban Maharashtra was 33.77 per cent in 1993-94. Only in 6 of the 30 districts, Mumbai, Thane, Raigad, Kolhapur, Pune and Ratnagiri urban poverty ratios were lower than the state average (GoM, 2002b). Curiously enough all these districts were in the more urbanised and developed RoM Region of the state; 4 of them were in the most urbanised Konkan Division. This suggests probably that urbanisation cannot and should not necessarily be equated with high incidence of urban poverty. High levels of economic activity had certainly helped in keeping urban poverty levels low in these 6 districts. Poverty continued to be high in districts where economic growth proceeded at a slow pace.

Unemployment

Urban Maharashtra continues to draw migrants from its rural hinterlands and from other states of India. Migrants are generally young men who come to Maharashtra in search of employment. Cities here do offer employment to many who enter the labour market, but excess supply of labour in relation to the demand for it results in high incidence of unemployment in urban labour markets.

Data on levels of unemployment are available from the National Sample Survey Organisation's (NSSO's) Employment Unemployment Surveys, undertaken every five years, from the late 1970s. The NSSO uses three reference periods: a year, a week and every day of the week, to capture seasonal and essentially intermittent nature of employment and unemployment that prevails in an agricultural country like India. Unemployment rates, defined as share of unemployed in the labour force, are reported for three statuses; usual status where the reference period is one year prior to the enumerator's visit to the household, current weekly status where it is a week, and current daily status where the activity status of an individual is recorded for every half day of the week. The last one is regarded as the most comprehensive measure of unemployment (GoI, 2001c).

Open unemployment is an urban rather than a rural problem, more severe in the larger cities. But as NSSO data are not available, neither at the district level nor for cities and towns, we compare the unemployment rates in Maharashtra with those in India.

Table 13.6 shows that irrespective of the location, unemployment rates were higher in urban than rural areas and higher among women than men in both the locations. This was not surprising. Urban unemployed

TABLE 13.6

Unemployment Rates (%) by Current Daily Status by Sex and Rural-Urban Residence, Maharashtra and India from 1977-78 to 1999-2000

Survey Year	Rural		Urban	
	Males	*Females*	*Males*	*Females*
Maharashtra				
1977-78	5.85	9.31	8.99	15.75
1983	6.25	7.23	9.05	10.44
1987-88	2.90	3.60	8.50	9.20
1993-94	4.60	4.00	6.00	7.80
1999-00	6.30	6.90	7.70	10.00
India				
1977-78	7.10	9.20	9.40	14.50
1983	7.50	9.00	9.20	11.00
1987-88	4.60	6.70	8.80	12.00
1993-94	5.60	5.60	6.70	10.50
1999-00	7.20	7.00	7.30	9.40

Source: GoM, 2002.

are more likely to be openly unemployed than rural, who are likely to be underemployed rather than openly unemployed. Higher incidence of unemployment among women relatively to men is due to employment discrimination against women in the labour market. Unemployment rates were lower in 1999-00 than in 1977-78 for men and women, in rural and urban areas in the two locations. However, the marginal increase in unemployment rates between 1993-94 and 1999-00 could be attributed to two factors. Firstly, it could be the net effect of a shift from own account work to wage employment where unemployment was likely to be open than disguised. Secondly, since most of the incremental wage employment was of informal and casual in nature, men and women were more likely to be openly unemployed now than in the past. Interestingly, barring a couple of exceptions, unemployment rates of men and women in Maharashtra were lower than the corresponding rates in India. So, Maharashtra continued to offer work to most of those who sought it.

Underemployment

Growing underemployment among those who are enumerated as workers is another economic evil associated with urbanisation. This is a consequence of the high share of self-employed among workers and preponderance of own account household enterprises. High incidence of self-employed in the workforce reflects the inability of the urban labour market to offer wage work to all those who seek it. Many are forced to take up petty trade or work in menial services where entry is relatively easy. Some may start their own enterprises or work in household enterprises as helpers. This results in high levels of underemployment that implies low productivity of labour so employed.

Based on an index used by the NSSO (1983), Table 13.7 gives estimates of underemployment by sex and rural-urban residence in Maharashtra and India. The data shows that irrespective of where they lived, women were more likely to be underemployed than men, more in rural than urban areas. However, men in India, both rural and urban, were subjected to marginally higher incidence of underemployment compared to men in Maharashtra. Not only did Maharashtra offer economic opportunities, but also the work offered in the state was more intensive than that offered else where in India.

Table 13.7 shows that in 1977-78, 5.7 per cent of the rural but 2.4 per cent of the urban men were underemployed in Maharashtra. The rates of underemployment declined till 1993-94 but increased marginally in 1999-00. The same pattern prevailed for men in India. Underemployment deepened among women; a higher proportion of women reported as workers by current weekly status, were underemployed in 1999-00 than in 1977-78 in both the locations.

TABLE 13.7

Index of Underemployment by Sex and Rural Urban Residence, Maharashtra and India from 1977-78 to 1999-2000

Survey Year	Rural		Urban	
	Males	Females	Males	Females
Maharashtra				
1977-78	5.7	13.9	2.4	5.1
1983	6.0	12.8	3.1	10.5
1987-88	0.6	5.7	1.9	2.4
1993-94	5.0	12.3	1.7	10.1
1999-2000	6.6	14.6	3.2	10.1
India				
1977-78	6.4	16.6	3.4	11.9
1983	5.8	12.8	4.0	10.1
1987-88	0.6	5.9	3.8	7.6
1993-94	5.1	18.0	2.9	13.7
1999-2000	6.3	19.4	3.7	13.3

Note: Index of Underemployment = (CWS-CDS)/CWS * 100 where CWS is the work participation rate by current weekly status and CDS is the work participation rate by current daily status.

Source: GoI, NSSO, Results of the Employment Unemployment Survey Rounds: 32nd (1977-78), 38th (1983), 43rd (1987-88), 50th (1993-94) and 55th (1999-2000), Central Sample.

Growth of Informal Sector

Rapid population growth is the main cause of excess supply of labour to urban labour markets, and is reflected only partly in open unemployment. In a situation where employment in the formal sector is shrinking, this excess labour is drawn into low productive jobs in manufacturing and service occupations in the informal sector. This sector mostly offers insecure, intermittent and low wage employment and being beyond the purview of most labour protective legislations, consists of such work, which is harmful to workers so employed. As a result many are often exposed to occupational health hazards.

Globalisation and liberalisation has further strengthened the process of informalisation of the workforce. As a result, some work done formerly in factories by the workers, is now done in homes informally. Work gets sub-contracted giving rise to contract workers who work from home. Secondly, to reduce non-wage costs, employers prefer employing 'flexi-workers' or non-regular workers comprising of casual, contract and female workers both, for manual work in factories and service occupations. Labour market studies confirm that female labour is often substituted for contract labour to increase this flexibility (Deshpande *et al.*, 1997). The concept of flexibility in the labour market has given rise to a new category of informal employment within the formal sector, often referred to as 'precarious' employment.

If we accept that workers informally employed consist of workers other than regular/wage salaried workers, then they would include self-employed and casual workers, where the former are in non-wage employment and the latter either belong to the 'precarious' category noted earlier, or are those who face uncertainties of intermittent wage employment. Self-employed together with casual workers give us a rough estimate of the share of informal sector employment among workers.

Table 13.8(a) gives such an estimate based on NSSO data. It shows that for the periods mentioned therein, the size of the informal sector comprising of self-employed and casual workers was larger in urban India than in urban Maharashtra. The size of the informal sector increased faster in urban India than in urban Maharashtra between 1987-88 and 1999-00. Among men in both the locations, informalisation was occurring through casualisation of labour indicating that wage work was increasingly available to men. However, more women were accepting self-employment in 1999-00 than they did earlier. This could be because of the freedom that self-employment offered to women to work from home, permitting them to combine work with housework. Alternatively women may have been forced to accept self-employment because they were unable to get wage work. Higher incidence of open unemployment among women suggests that second possibility was much more likely, than the first.

Table 13.8(b) gives yet another estimate of the size of the informal sector in urban Maharashtra, based on the data from Economic Censuses, undertaken in 1990 and 1998. Economic Censuses cover all enterprises and report employment in them. Hence, they exclude the self-employed in the economy. The estimated size of the informal sector based on this source is therefore smaller as it excludes the self-employed. Economic Censuses distinguish between own account enterprises (OAEs) that are essentially household enterprises that do not hire workers and other enterprises that hire at least one worker, which are called 'establishments'. The share of informal sector enterprises (OAEs) in total enterprises in urban Maharashtra increased from 54 per cent to 60 per cent between 1990 and 1998, and the share of

TABLE 13.8(a)

Estimate I: Share of Informal Sector of Employment by Sex in Urban Maharashtra and Urban India, from 1987-88 to 1999-2000

	Maharashtra					
Year	*Males*			*Female*		
	Self-employed	*Regular**	*Casual*	*Self-employed*	*Regular**	*Casual*
1987-88	32.4	55.0	12.6	26.3	42.9	30.8
1993-94	36.4	53.0	10.6	29.2	46.0	24.8
1999-00	32.9	54.1	13.0	32.7	44.4	22.9
	India					
Year	*Males*			*Female*		
	Self-employed	*Regular**	*Casual*	*Self-employed*	*Regular**	*Casual*
1987-88	41.0	44.4	14.6	39.3	34.2	26.5
1993-94	41.1	42.7	16.2	36.4	35.5	28.1
1999-00	41.2	41.9	16.9	38.4	38.5	23.1

Note: * regular wage/salaried workers.

Source: GoI, NSSO, Results of the Employment Unemployment Survey Rounds: 43rd (1987-88), 50th (1993-94) and 55th (1999-2000), Central Sample.

TABLE 13.8(b)

Estimate II: Share of Informal Sector of Enterprises and Employment in Enterprises in Urban Maharashtra: 1990 and 1998

Total (in thousand)	*Own Account Enterprises (a)*	*Establishments Enterprises (b)*	*Total Enterprises (a) + (b)*	
1990	714 (54.3)	602 (45.7)	1316 (100.0)	
1998	969 (59.8)	652 (40.2)	1621 (100.0)	
Total Employment (in thousand)	*In Own Account Enterprises*	*In Establishments*	*Labour That is Not Hired in Establishments*	*In All Enterprises*
	(a)	(b)		(a) + (b)
1990	998 (16.3)	5115 (83.7)	554 (9.1)	6113(100.0)
1998	1305 (19.3)	5452 (80.7)	970 (9.9)	6757(100.0)

Source: GoM, 2002. Economic Survey of Maharashtra State, 2001-2002, Directorate of Economics & Statistics, Planning Department, Mumbai. Derived from data in Table Nos. 60 and 61.

employment in them increased from 16.3 per cent to 19.3 per cent. If we add the number of workers who worked in establishments, but were not hired workers to these, 25.4 per cent of the workers worked in the informal sector in urban Maharashtra in 1990. Their share increased to 29.2 per cent by 1998.

Informal employment increased in the urban sectors of the economy both in the state and the country. The only solace was that casualisation, between both men and women in India were occurring at higher average real wage (Deshpande and Deshpande, 2002). Though, data on comparable average wages in Maharashtra is not available, it is possible that average real wages of casual workers might have increased in the state as well as in the country between 1993-94 and 1999-00. Steeper decline in poverty ratios in rural rather than urban Maharashtra supports indirectly, our claim that average casual wage is likely to have increased over the 1990s in Maharashtra as in India.

Consequences: Inadequate Access to Amenities

Housing: Growth of Slums

Proliferation of slums and squatter colonies in large cities show the apathy of the urban elite to the living conditions of the poor. When conditions of housing are generally poor as in India, slums are difficult to define and identify. Generally, they are defined with reference to environmental and structural deficiencies, however, these definitions and estimates of the slum population differ between the agencies collecting such data.

In 2001 Census, slum areas were defined as follows. Slums included: a) all areas notified as 'slums' by state/local government and union territory (UT) under any Act; b) all areas recognised as 'slums' by state/local and UT administration which had not been formally notified as 'slums' under any Act; and c) a compact area of at least 300 population or about 60-70 households of poorly built congested tenements, in unhygienic environment usually with inadequate infrastructure and lacking in proper sanitary and drinking water facilities. Based on this definition slum population was enumerated separately in urban Maharashtra in 2001 (Director of Census Operations, Maharashtra, 2001c).

A little over 10.6 million persons lived in slums in 62 out of the 65 urban units in Maharashtra in 2001. Three urban units, Cantonment Boards of Pune and Kirkee and Karad Municipal Council did not report slums. Slum population by size arranged in descending order, in 30 of these 62 cities is reported in Table 13.9. Nearly 93.4 per cent of the slum dwellers in 62 urban units in Maharashtra lived in these 30 cities, almost 55

TABLE 13.9

Magnitude and Share of Slum Population* in the Total Slum Population in Maharashtra and within the Population of the City in 30 Cities: 2001

City	*Slum Pop. Number*	*Total Population Number*	*Share in Slum Pop. in the State*	*Share in Population of the City*
Gr.Mumbai	5823510	11914398	48.9	54.6
Nagpur	726664	2051320	35.4	6.8
Pune	531337	2540069	20.9	5.0
Thane	420276	1261517	33.3	3.9
Amravati	232619	549370	42.3	2.2
Solapur	231420	873037	26.5	2.2
Malegaon	212577	409190	52.0	2.0
Nashik	142234	1076967	13.2	1.3
Navi Mumbai	138621	703947	19.7	1.3
Aurangabad	136276	872667	15.6	1.3
Akola	135009	399978	33.8	1.3
Pimpri Chinchwad	129357	1006417	12.9	1.2
Bhiwandi	111304	598703	18.6	1.0
Dhule	92718	341473	27.2	0.9
Nanded-Waghala	82715	430598	19.2	0.8
Kamptee	78854	84340	93.5	0.7
Parbhani	76324	259170	29.4	0.7
Beed	74283	138091	53.8	0.7
Latur	71040	299828	23.7	0.7
Kolhapur	67462	485183	13.9	0.6
Achalpur	66790	107304	62.2	0.6
Ambarnath	64195	203795	31.5	0.6
Jalgaon	62696	368579	17.0	0.6
Jalna	56157	235529	23.8	0.5
Ullhasnagar	53717	472943	11.4	0.5
Chandrapur	50795	297612	17.1	0.5
Ballarpur	49298	89995	54.8	0.5
Bhandara	46271	85034	54.4	0.4
Yavatmal	43232	122906	35.2	0.4
Gondiya	38942	120878	32.2	0.4
Maharashtra*	**10644605**	**33803460**	**31.5**	

Note: Slum population arranged in descending order in 30 of the 62 cities/towns in 2001 is reported in the Table above.

*Data relate to the slum population, total population in Class I and Class II cities in Maharashtra in 2001.

Source: Director of Census Operations, Maharashtra, 2001.

per cent of them lived in Greater Mumbai alone. Nagpur had the second largest number but they formed barely 7 per cent of the slum dwellers in the State. Their respective shares in other million-plus cities were lower. Together, 6 of the 7 million-plus cities accounted for nearly 73 per cent of the slum population living in the 62 cities of Maharashtra.

Impact of slum population on the quality of life in the cities is often assessed by deriving share of slum population in city's population. Slum dwellers in the State were concentrated in Mumbai, their share in city's population of 11.9 million was alarmingly high, nearly 49 per cent. The corresponding share in a small city like Kamptee, with barely 84 thousand dwellers in 2001, was enormous, nearly 94 per cent. This reflects, probably, the poor state of housing stock in Kamptee. In 14 of these 30 cities, the share of slum population in the city's population was higher than the state average of 31.5 per cent. Five of them were Class I cities of which, three were million-plus cities of Mumbai, Nagpur and Thane and two, were the municipal councils of Yavatmal and Gondiya with more than 120 thousand residents in 2001. Four were Class II cities with a population between 50 and 99 thousand, three had a population between 20 and 49 thousand, while two had less than 20 thousand residents. The share of slum population in the city's population was the lowest, 11.4 per cent in Ulhasnagar. Despite being million-plus cities, in both Pimpri Chinchwad and Nashik, barely 13 per cent of the city dwellers resided in slums in 2001, reflecting relatively better housing conditions than other million-plus cities.

Being the richest district in the state, on the basis of per capita income, Mumbai has always attracted migrants from the rest of Maharashtra and other states in India (Deshpande and Deshpande, 1991; CRD, 1996; GoM, 1998). Though, this growth of population was always accompanied by increase in real per capita incomes in this prosperous city; however, the supply of formal housing failed to increase along with the population. Scarcity of land in relation to the growing demand for it resulted in the skyrocketing prices of land over time. Legal interventions, especially the Rent Control Act, 1948 and Urban Land (Ceiling and Regulation) Act, 1976, further distorted Mumbai's land market (Deshpande and Deshpande, 1991). The city failed miserably to provide affordable housing to the poor who migrated to Mumbai for sheer survival. Since affordable housing was not available, many squatted on open lands owned by private individuals and local, state and central governments. This was the main cause of proliferation of slums in the city over time (GoM, 1998).

2001 Census data shows that the process of migration and slum formation has been initiated in Nagpur, Thane and Pune, though the problem was yet not as severe. Slum dwellers in Nashik and Pimpri-Chinchwad too, were fewer. Their shares in city population were low suggesting probably that the poor could still afford formal housing in these cities. High shares of slum population in medium sized cities like Kamptee, Achalpur, Ballarpur and Bhandara and smaller cities like Malegaon, Amravati and Akola suggest that housing in these cities, in general, was of a poor quality and its supply had probably failed to grow, with growth of population.

Amenities in Slums

Housing conditions of persons living in urban locations and the amenities enjoyed by them are far from satisfactory while those of persons living in slums are known to be abysmal. Given the high concentration of slums in Mumbai, one wonders how the living conditions in slums in Mumbai compare with those in the rest of urban Maharashtra. NSSO's 49th Round (1992-93), gives valuable insights on this aspect of urban living in Maharashtra. In 1992-93, 37 per cent of the households in Mumbai lived in squatter settlements, undeclared and declared slums compared to 20 per cent in urban Maharashtra excluding Mumbai. Seven per cent of the households lived in undeclared slums in both the locations. About 13 per cent of the households in the rest of urban Maharashtra lived in declared slums; in Mumbai their share was more than twice as high, 27 per cent. Squatters formed 2 per cent of all households in Mumbai while their share in other cities was barely 0.2 per cent.

Housing stock in Mumbai was much older than that in the rest of urban Maharashtra. More importantly, barely 40 per cent of the houses built in the 1980s in Mumbai, and 67 per cent of them built, elsewhere in urban Maharashtra could be considered as 'good' and 'satisfactory' for living. In the absence of supply of good/satisfactory houses, newcomers to Mumbai in the 1970s and 1980s were probably forced either to squat or to encroach open places. These squatter settlements eventually became slum pockets over time.

Slum households in Mumbai, compared to their counterparts elsewhere in urban Maharashtra, were more likely to be housed in *pucca* and semi *pucca* structures. As against 41.8 per cent of all households in Mumbai, barely 10.8 per cent of the households in other urban areas in Maharashtra had underground drainage. About 2.1 per cent of the slum households in Mumbai reported underground drainage facility. Slum households in Mumbai had better access to garbage disposal arrangement than those living in the rest of urban Maharashtra. An overwhelming majority of 80.7 per cent, of slum households in Mumbai had electrically lighted. Share of such households in the other part of state was lower, only 63.5 per cent in urban areas other than Mumbai. Households living in slums in Mumbai thus were much better off than those in other urban areas of Maharashtra. The most important amenity that they lacked were toilets, which obviously were far too few in relation to their needs in slums and squatter colonies. Hence, their availability did not mean accessibility. This data assures us that though the growth of slums was not an inevitable consequence of urbanisation, it was one of the failures of urban management, that ignored supply of housing affordable to the poor (GoM, 1998).

Housing in Urban Maharashtra and Urban India in 2001

Housing conditions and amenities available to residents differ in urban areas of Maharashtra and urban India. Data culled out from the Housing Tables of 2001 Census recently published by the Registrar General (2001c) for the two locations are reported in Table 13.10.

Almost 80 per cent in urban Maharashtra and 77 per cent in urban India were used only for residential purposes. Nearly two-thirds of the households considered their houses to be in good condition and almost a third thought that they were in a liveable condition in both the locations. Only 3 per cent of the households stated that they considered their houses to be in a dilapidated state! This undoubtedly reveals that the poor state of housing in the country in general, makes most households accept whatever shelter they have. Compared to households in urban India, a smaller share of households in urban Maharashtra, were likely to use 'non-permanent' materials for their dwellings. Nearly 47 per cent of the households in urban Maharashtra and 35 per cent in urban India were housed in one-room tenements. The share of two roomed tenements was marginally higher in urban India.

TABLE 13.10

Housing and Amenities in Urban Maharashtra and Urban India: 2001

(Per Cent)

Characteristic of Housing/ Amenity	*Urban Maharashtra*	*Urban India*
Housing		
1. Purpose for which the Housing Unit was Used		
Residential	79.3	77.3
Residential Cum Other Use	2.1	2.8
2. Condition of the House Used as Residences		
Livable	34.2	32.2
Dilapidated	3.0	3.7
3. Households Living in Houses with		
a) Material of the Roof		
i) Grass, Bamboo etc.	2.2	7.0
ii) Plastic, Polythene etc.	1.2	0.8
b) Material of the Wall		
i) Grass, Bamboo etc.	2.1	3.9
ii) Plastic, Polythene etc.	0.8	0.4
iii) Mud, Unburnt Bricks	12.6	12.8
iv) Wood	1.6	0.9
c) Material of the Floor		
i) Mud	13.9	13.9
ii) Wood/Bamboo	0.2	0.4
4. Type of Structure in which Households Lived		
Permanent	81.6	79.2
Rest	18.4	20.8
5. Number of Rooms in which Households Lived		
i) No Exclusive Room	3.9	2.3
ii) One Room	46.7	35.1
iii) Two Rooms	26.9	29.5
6. Number of Rooms by Nature of Ownership		
a) Owned	67.2	66.8
i) No Exclusive Room	3.5	2.0
ii) One Room	41.3	29.2
iii) Two Rooms	27.9	29.3
b) Rented	28.5	28.5
i) No Exclusive Room	4.3	2.8
ii) One Room	57.6	46.9
iii) Two Rooms	25.4	30.4
c) Other	4.3	4.7
i) No Exclusive Room	6.6	3.7
ii) One Room	58.3	46.8
iii) Two Rooms	20.8	28.1
Amenities		
1. Water Supply		
a) All Sources		
i) Tap	89.2	66.7
ii) Hand Pump	4.5	16.2
b) Within Premises		
i) Tap	49.7	94.4
ii) Hand Pump	8.3	1.7
c) Near Premises		
i) Tap	80.3	59.7
ii) Hand Pump	10.9	23.3
d) Away from Premises		
i) Tap	54.7	41.7
ii) Hand Pump	15.9	22.3

Contd. ...

Contd. ...

Characteristic of Housing/ Amenity	*Urban Maharashtra*	*Urban India*
2. Source of Lighting		
i) Electricity	94.3	87.6
ii) Kerosene	5.1	11.6
3. Bathroom within Premises	81.5	70.4
4. Latrine/Drainage		
No Latrine	41.9	26.3
No Drainage	12.4	22.1
5. Households without Separate Kitchen	17.6	24.1
6. Fuel Used for Cooking		
i) Firewood	9.9	22.7
ii) Crop Residue	1.2	2.1
iii) Cowdung cakes	0.3	2.0
iv) Coal/Charcoal	0.5	4.6
v) Kerosene	30.0	19.2
vi) LPG	57.0	48.0

Source: Registrar General of India, 2001b.

Access to Amenities

Water Supply: Availability and Accessibility

Availability of piped water, within and outside the premises and from wells is considered as access to potable water (NIUA, 1998). Nearly 9 of every 10 households in urban Maharashtra, but only about 7 of 10 in urban India were supplied drinking water through taps. Provision of water through hand pumps was more common in urban India than in urban Maharashtra.

However, the quantity and quality of water available across the cities and households within a city differs substantially. Government of India has approved norms of adequacy that depend on the population of the city. Availability of 70 litres per capita per day (lpcd) is considered adequate for town of under 20,000 population; of 100 lpcd for one of 20,000 and more but not exceeding 60,000; of 125 lpcd for a town with population between 60,000 and 100,000 and of 150 lpcd for a city with population exceeding 100,000 (GoM, 1995). The lack of access to drinking water at the city level can be realised from the grim reality of Class A and Class B municipal towns in Maharashtra in the mid-1990s. Only 4 of the 21 Class A municipalities and 9 of the 47 Class B municipalities could meet the norms of 150 lpcd and 125 lpcd appropriate to them (GoM, 1995). The reality is likely to be grimmer because the figures of total supply of water are the latest available, whereas those of population used to obtain per capita availability, relate to 1991.

The situation had not changed considerably in Class I cities in the late 1990s. Only in 3 of the 27 Class I cities identified in 1991 Census in Maharashtra were supplied 200 lpcd, much more than 150 lpcd, approved by the norms of adequacy. In 6 of the 27 Class I cities, water supplied per capita was less than 100 lpcd, while in 19 others, it was between 100-200 lpcd (GoI, CPCB, 2000). Even if we assume that in half of the 19 Class I cities, municipal authorities could attain the norm of 150 lpcd, in only 12 to 13 of the 27 Class I cities of 1991 Census the norm of adequate water supply was attained in 2000.

Access to Electricity, Bathrooms, Toilets, Drainage and Other Amenities

Ninety four per cent of the urban households in Maharashtra, and 88 per cent of them in India reported electricity as a source of lighting. Seven of every 10 households in urban India and 8 of every 10 in urban Maharashtra had bathrooms within the house. But almost 42 per cent of the households in urban Maharashtra did not have latrines. Their corresponding share was lower, 26.3 per cent, in urban India. Households in urban Maharashtra were better provided with drainage than those living in urban India. Finally, data on fuel used for cooking assures us that the use of traditional type of materials was more common among households living in urban India than in urban Maharashtra.

This overview confirms that in Maharashtra, the urban dwellers were better housed and had access to most urban amenities compared to those who lived in urban India. But urban households in Maharashtra had higher availability and accessibility to all amenities except latrines compared to those living in urban India. Having seen the impact of population growth on urban living conditions we shall turn to examine the policies of urban development pursued in India and Maharashtra after independence.

SECTION IV

Policies of Urban Development in India

Approaches to Urban Development in the National Plans

Urban development did receive attention in all the Five Year Plans of the Government of India. However, urban policy was based on the prevailing perceptions of the process of urbanisation and growth of large cities. That urbanisation is an inevitable consequence of industrialisation, which accompanies economic development, was acceptable to our planners. Further, it leads to the growth of large cities was also a reality that they could not deny. But, growth of population in cities was held responsible for many of the city level problems that in fact emerged because cities were managed inefficiently. In the process, the policy makers overlooked the fact that large cities contribute to development and tend to enjoy agglomeration economies. As a result, all plans except the Tenth, fail to take cognisance of the role cities play in economic development.

The summary of the national urban policy framework as it was conceptualised is as follows:

- Balanced urban growth and regional development were both accorded a high priority in all the Plans.
- Urgent need to prevent further growth of population in the large cities too is emphasised in all the Plans.
- Dispersal of population away from bigger cities was to be achieved by planning a spatial dispersal of economic activity to the backward districts and by developing small and medium towns. New industries were to be established away from large, congested cities. The basic instrument of this policy was industrial location policy that diverted industries to backward regions/districts. The policy was expected to bring about dispersal not only of industry, but also of employment and population and thereby bring about balanced regional development.
- The regional plans formulated by the regional authority were to be implemented by the local bodies. It was, therefore, necessary to strengthen urban local bodies and make them self-financing in the long run. There was a critical need to augment resources at local level by speedy assessment and collection of existing taxes, their timely upward revision, broadening the base of taxation, levying betterment taxes and charging stamp duties on sale or conversion of land to more productive uses.
- Later plans accepted that since growth of large cities could not be prevented, efforts were needed to augment civic services in metropolitan cities.
- The need to address urban policy in relation to the problem of poverty, unemployment and underemployment in cities and the informal sector is recognised. So urban poverty alleviation schemes like The Nehru Rozgar Yojana (NRY), Urban Basic Services Programme (UBSP), Environment Improvement of Urban Slums (EIUS), Prime Minister's Integrated Urban Poverty Eradication Programme (PMIUPEP) were undertaken at different points of time by the Central Government. They were merged into the Swarna Jayanti Shahari Rozgar Yojana (SJSRY) in 1997.
- Following the recommendations of the NCU and the Planning Commission, the Mega-city Scheme was introduced in 1992 for infrastructure improvements of metropolitan cities. The main objective of the scheme was to prepare the local governments to use infrastructure finance and market instruments to fund their capital investments. The scheme was restricted to Kolkata Mumbai, Chennai, Hyderabad and Bangalore.
- An important legal intervention, Constitution (74th Amendment) Act, 1992 was enacted during the Eighth Plan period, prescribing an institutional framework for urban governance. The Act envisaged that elected municipal governments would remain at the helm of civic affairs, including planning and provision of infrastructure and services.
- Due attention was given to the housing for urban poor. It was recognised that in the context of urban housing, both, the law and its practice remained heavily weighted against the urban poor. There was a need for an equitable urban land policy to assist the poor in their access to land for shelter. In practice, land use was largely, regulated by markets or public authorities, both mostly excluded the poor.
- The Tenth Plan, unlike the earlier ones, explicitly states that urbanisation would be a key determinant of economic growth in future and accepts the crucial role that cities are likely to play in the economic development of the country. Broad-based reforms in the urban sector are visualised since cities would act as engines of growth and contribute to economic development.
- It is emphasised that cities not only provided higher standard of amenities to the residents but were also instrumental in developing rural hinterlands. They provided ready market for goods

produced in the rural sector and supplied urban products to the rural residents.

- To help the cities play this role, reforms in land and housing policy and of pricing of utilities were to be undertaken, mainly to augment the resources of the ULBs. This could help ULBs maintain civic services adequately and expand urban infrastructure in step with the growing needs. Hence, a vigorous programme of upgrading urban infrastructure and services forms an integral part of the Tenth Plan.
- The Plan admits that the urban land policy based on rigid development plans that regulated land use, through zoning, had failed miserably. Urban development authorities set up to implement these land use plans, failed to meet the growing needs of housing, which resulted in unauthorised colonies, of which slums was the most extreme form.
- Nearly 90 per cent of the housing shortage pertained to the weaker sections. The formal sector had failed to provide housing to the poor. All policies of allocation of land, extension of funding assistance and provision of support services, had to be diverted to increase the supply of affordable housing for the poor.
- Problem of housing slum dwellers had to be dealt separately for which land had to be provided at affordable prices. Future proliferation of unauthorised settlements had to be prevented and there was a need to regularise the existing ones through a pragmatic policy. IA scheme of housing with Central assistance started in the Ninth Plan, Valmiki Ambedkar Awas Yojana (VAMBAY), which had a combination of subsidy and loan, to provide immediate benefit to the most disadvantaged urban dwellers could be pursued in all cities.
- There was a need to finalise the National Slum Policy drawn up by the Department of Urban Employment and Poverty Alleviation in 1999. Basic data on slums and civic amenities provided in these settlements was weak; firstly, because no widely accepted definition of a slum was available and secondly, because the urban authorities did not have a proper listing of slum settlements in the towns.
- Slums were often regarded as an inevitable consequence of the continuing migration of unskilled workers; the reality was that most of them were permanent residents who had lived in these locations over generations. The new Slum Policy aimed at changing attitudes of the authorities and people at large towards slum dwellers by creating awareness to their problems. The focus on slums was expected to help planners realise the multi-dimensional view of urban poverty.

Urban Development Schemes in Maharashtra

The governments in Maharashtra welcomed urbanisation as a progressive and desirable development, only if it took place in a well-planned manner. Mumbai, the state's capital was particularly affected by the urban problems of haphazard urban growth, shortages of housing, drinking water, electricity, schools, hospitals and other social facilities. Mumbai was looked upon as 'miniature India' and its special problems find mention in most of the state plans. The urban development policy in Maharashtra was based on the objectives of economic growth with equity across regions, districts and even cities and for the poor within each city. To achieve this goal, the state pursued three types of policies.

- First, there were policies that were pursued to correct regional imbalance in development. Programmes were designed to promote regional equity and bring about the development of backward districts.
- To achieve this objective, industries were to be set up in the backward districts by pursuing a conscious policy of industrial location. Accordingly, setting up industries in large cities was banned. Monetary and fiscal incentives were offered to entrepreneurs locating their units in the backward districts.
- As urban growth was haphazard in the past, the second set of policies was addressed to balanced urban growth. This was to be attained by growth of small and medium towns and of growth centres that could either reduce migration to large cities or divert it to these new urban centres. New towns were set up and physical infrastructure in small and medium towns was improved to attract industries. The policy could be expected to create employment in these towns and thereby check migration to bigger cities. Development of Thane, Kalyan, Dombivili, Navi Mumbai and more recently Pimpri-Chinchwad

was undertaken to relieve the population pressure on Mumbai and Pune.

- Special institutions like CIDCO, and MMRDA were created and were given the responsibility of regional development. CIDCO was responsible for acquiring land, planning and implementing the entire township of Navi Mumbai and recently been given responsibility of many other towns in the state. MMRDA was, till recently a planning body responsible for preparing regional plans. Apart from these two, new institutions were created for diverting industries and provide them infrastructure and finance.
- Maharashtra Housing and Development Authority (MHADA) was created specially for providing urban housing. Government was required to help MHADA acquire land. It planned to build houses in towns with the funds obtained from Housing and Urban Development Corporation (HUDCO)/ Life Insurance Corporation (LIC)/General Insurance Corporation (GIC) and open market borrowing (OMB). The programme was also to be funded from advanced contributions of the prospective allottees.
- The third set of policies was designed to promote the access of the poor to the urban services. Slum improvement and clearance policy evolved in mid-1970s and environmental improvement programmes, implemented in urban Maharashtra formed part of this policy package. Dalit Vasti Sudhar Yojana was started by the government in the mid-1990s on 100 per cent grant basis to improve civic amenities in urban localities that housed largely scheduled castes. For helping the urban poor Swarna Jayanti Shahari Rozgar Yojana is implemented in Maharashtra since 1997.
- The Tenth Plan of the Government of Maharashtra observes, that population growth was the root cause of city-level problems of unemployment, poor quality of life and deterioration in the urban infrastructure resulting in poor living conditions and environmental degradation. A comprehensive policy was needed to tackle these problems. There was a need to strengthen urban local bodies (ULBs) for these purposes.
- Recognising the crucial role, Mumbai is likely to play with the liberalisation of the Indian economy, Mumbai mega-city development is contemplated in the Tenth Plan. The Tenth Plan has provided Rs.800 crores for the scheme under the following heads: for developing commercial complexes and technology park, urban land development and renewal, water supply, sanitation and public health, transport and related infrastructure and institutional development and technical assistance. MMRDA would act as the coordinating and monitoring agency while the scheme would be executed as noted earlier by BMC, BEST, CIDCO, TMC, KMC and NMMC.
- The state assisted scheme of Environmental Improvement in Slums, is replaced by, National Slum Improvement Programme. All municipal corporations and municipal councils to be covered under the scheme are to provide not only the basic amenities but also the social infrastructure of primary, adult, and non-formal education, child-care, health care and entertainment. The scheme envisages helping the poor either to build or improve their own houses, for which assistance of at least 10 per cent would be provided.
- The long list of the programmes planned and implemented by the Central and state government bear testimony to their concern for growth and equity across regions and cities and for the poor within a city. This is not the place for evaluating each and every programme individually. We shall restrict ourselves to reviewing programmes pursued in Maharashtra by grouping them according to the main objective that they were designed to serve. As noted earlier, there are programmes designed to promote regional equity, others to reduce the imbalance in the city size distribution, and still others to promote the access of the poor to the urban services. Some overlapping between them is unavoidable as some schemes may serve more than one objective. We shall look at the actual outcomes to see how far they could attain the objectives set forth by the policymakers. However, the assessment cannot be strictly quantitative because data required for it are not available.

SECTION V

Urban Policy at Work in Maharashtra

Urban policy is more an art than an applied science. The data set, available to governments that frame the policy is inadequate to provide simple solutions to the problems they face. All governments are subject to diverse pulls and pressures from interest groups comprising of business, managerial and political interests. Moreover, all governments, local, regional and national, that frame and implement urban policies are torn by conflict between efficiency and equity.

Misapprehensions about Urbanisation

In a predominantly rural economy like India, where over 70 per cent of the population lived and worked in rural areas even in 2001, it is not surprising to find widespread misconceptions, misapprehensions and misinformation about urbanisation in general and that of growth of large cities in particular. Even in a highly urbanised state like Maharashtra, 59 per cent of the population lived in rural areas in 2001. Universally, urbanisation is correlated with economic development and Maharashtra is no exception. In Maharashtra urban population grew faster than the total but both these rates have decelerated over the last two decades. Contrary to general impression, there is no evidence of urban explosion and much less of explosion of Class I cities in Maharashtra. Rather population of all urban units in the state, irrespective of city-size was growing slower in the 1990s than in the 1980s.

There is yet another misconception about urbanisation. It is often pointed out that distribution of urban populations by size-class of towns in Maharashtra is skewed, and worse still, it is becoming more so over time. Data presented earlier lend substance to the fear but only apparently. As Mills and Becker (1986) observe, it is difficult to imagine an economic growth process that would not lead to an increase in share of urban population living in cities of at least modest size. As a country urbanises, not only do its cities grow—though typically less rapidly than the urban population—but also the number of cities in excess of the threshold size also increases. In Maharashtra number of Class I cities increased from 27 to 34 between 1991 and 2001. Municipal corporations having million-plus population increased from 3 to 7 during the decade. Just over 13 million persons lived in these 3 corporations in 1991, where as 21.2 million lived in 7 of them in 2001. Their share in Maharashtra's urban population increased from about 43 per cent to 52 per cent between 1991 and 2001. But the share of population in Greater Mumbai in the state's urban population, declined from 32 per cent in 1991, to 29 per cent in 2001. So this pattern of urbanisation was a consequence of the steady economic growth that occurred in the state, at least till mid-1990s.

More than one reason can be attributed to condition in which Maharashtra's premier city, Mumbai is at present. The most important of them was the misconception about urbanisation and growth of cities we noted earlier. These misconceptions played a major role in deciding the urban policy framework in Maharashtra. The influx of refugees after partition and the economic migration after the 1950s in the wake of the fast growth of engineering and chemical industries in Mumbai was not accompanied by adequate investments in Mumbai's civic infrastructure. This imbalance was interpreted 'wrongly' as evidence of Mumbai having grown beyond its 'optimum' size. Experience shows that growth of industry has led to influx of migrants, which in turn was likely to increase population in Mumbai. Hence, the Barve Study Group recommended banning of new industrial units, barring few exceptions, in the Island City and the suburbs (GoM, 1961b). The Gadgil Committee (1965) deplored the lax implementation of the Barve Group's recommendations and suggested shifting of economic activity particularly heavy industry out of Greater Mumbai. This was justified further on the basis of equity because the process was expected to bring about development of backward regions of Marathwada and Vidarbha.

Fortunately, the state government did not go as far in their Industrial Location Policy (ILP) of 1975 but continued the ban on location of new and expansion of old large and medium industrial units in Mumbai. These restrictions were relaxed in 1993 in case of non-polluting high-tech industries, when it was realised that as a result of the ILP, industry did not move either to the rest of the Mumbai Metropolitan Region (MMR) or to the backward regions of Maharashtra but rather to other states of India (BMRDA, 1995). For the last two decades or more the urban policy in Maharashtra instead of helping labour, management and entrepreneurs to increase their productivity and creativity, was directed to prevent growth of income and employment explicitly in large and medium industries and implicitly in the economy of Mumbai. To achieve this objective of industrial dispersal with equity and to reduce regional disparities, various policies were used. In what follows, we will first examine the policy options Maharashtra had, the policy instruments and institutional framework was created in the state to achieve the policy goals.

Strategies and Schemes to Reduce Regional Disparities

Reducing regional disparities in development has been the major objective of state policy in Maharashtra, ever since the state was formed in 1960. Many strategies have been used the world over to reduce regional disparities in income and employment. Prominent among them include employment deconcentration or dispersal of jobs and more efficient and equitable metropolitan expansion. Most of the schemes of balanced regional development formulated by the state were of this nature.

Employment Deconcentration or Dispersal of Jobs through Industrial Dispersal Policies

The Indian Constitution assures every citizen the fundamental right to carry on his/her trade or profession in any part of the Indian Union. Constrained by this Constitutional provision and convinced by the impossibility of preventing people from migrating to prosperous locations, the central and the state governments in independent India implemented a two-pronged strategy to reduce and/or to divert migration flows to urban locations. The state government used industrial licensing policy to disperse industry regionally. In addition, financial incentives were offered to attract industries to backward regions. The ban and positive incentives formed one prong of the strategy, the other being adoption of schemes to alleviate rural poverty and unemployment often identified as the major cause for rural-urban migration.

The policy of dispersing industry regionally includes measures like discouraging new economic activities from being located in the large cities. Such discouragement may take the form of a ban on location of new industrial units in the large cities or incentives to locate in smaller cities or backward regions. Existing units may be offered incentives to shift to socially preferred locations and new cities may be constructed. The policy maker wants to control the growth of large cities, usually located in the prosperous region and to stimulate the growth of cities in the backward regions. The policy if successful is likely to disperse employment too, which is concentrated generally in large cities.

An instrument most widely used to bring about such deconcentration is the growth-centre policy. A growth-centre consists of an urban complex that includes a few dynamic growth industries. These industries are expected to stimulate the growth of ancillary industries and help the emergence of specialised services and skilled labour. The 'concentrated deconcentration' in the form of growth-centres prevents dissipation of the economies of agglomeration, that dissipation which accompanies other measures of regional dispersal. Policies for spatial deconcentration also include policies to transform rural economy and thereby slowing down the rate of urban growth, policies to limit large cities through control of migration and stimulating the growth of intermediate towns and building new cities. These measures are expensive and difficult to implement. Hence, the most commonly used instrument is a policy package of incentives to industry to locate in identified backward regions.

More Efficient and Equitable Metropolitan Expansion

Those who argue for dispersal policy because large cities suffer from many diseconomies or negative externalities, confuse size with bad management. Most amenities and services of infrastructure in Indian cities are not charged according to their marginal cost. This results in subsidising the rich at the cost of the poor. Much of the air pollution in big cities of India is caused by transport system in which personalised motor transport has gained in popularity over public transport through wrong pricing of fuel and road space. Slums have proliferated and land prices skyrocketed because of Rent Control And Urban Land Ceiling Acts. Much of the growth of organised crime in big cities is the side effect of prohibition, import bans and high import tariffs, mistaken interventions in the land market, neglect of police and judiciary and criminalisation of politics all of which has very little to do with size of cities.

Despite all the urban evils, the bigger cities in India offer a higher quality of life as indicated by lower levels of mortality and fertility, greater gender equality, less social discrimination, higher levels of literacy and human resource development and easier access to amenities such as safer drinking water, health and sanitation not to mention employment and income. Fears of unbridled urbanisation in Maharashtra have been misplaced as is evidenced by the deceleration of urban growth in the 1980s and the 1990s, much more, in the growth of large cities. This is not to say that all is well with big cities and much less to say that the state give up the dispersal policies. The essential point is that cities can be managed efficiently and equitably and when they are, the tendencies for dispersal are set in motion without elaborate interventions (Deshpande and Deshpande, 1991).

Institutional Framework Created: How did it Work?

Though Maharashtra was formed in 1960 as the Marathi-speaking state, its linguistic homogeneity was marred by uneven regional development. So Maharashtra made regional balance an integral part of its development policy. Corporations such as the Maharashtra Industrial Development Corporation (MIDC), Maharashtra State Finance Corporation (MSFC), and the State Industrial and Investment Corporation of Maharashtra Limited (SICOM) were created to attain this objective. The MIDC provides the basic infrastructure and the MSFC and the SICOM provide term finance to medium and large-scale industries and offer to entrepreneurs a package of services ranging from project design to its implementation. Besides, SICOM and the Regional Development Corporations offer attractive monetary and fiscal incentives to entrepreneurs and persuade them to locate the industry in their regions. Based on the data available, we can evaluate the success achieved so far in developing the relatively backward areas industrially.

In the absence of any other objective criterion to decide what constitutes equitable distribution, the best we can accept is the distribution of population as the standard for comparison. In 2001, rest of Maharashtra (including Mumbai) had 62.6 per cent, Marathwada 16.1 per cent and Vidarbha 22.3 per cent of the state's population. If equity is the objective, we could expect the shares should conform to this distribution.

Compared to the share in population, RoM in 1995 accounted for 81 per cent of the industrial projects and 73 per cent of the total investment in Maharashtra. The region also employed nearly 79 per cent of the industrial workers in the state. Six districts, Raigad, Thane, Pune, Ratnagiri, Nagpur and Chandrapur accounted for almost two-thirds of the state's total investment in that year. Four of these six were in RoM. Seven districts, that together had less than half a per cent of the state's investment; were Beed, Parbhani, Osmanabad, Jalna and Latur in Marathwada and Buldhana, Akola in the Vidarbha Region. In the case of projects that involved foreign direct investment, RoM had the lion's share of 85.3 per cent of both projects and investment. Also 81 per cent of the total investment of Rs. 32,400 crore in the state was in the districts of Konkan, Pune and Nashik (MEDC, 1995).

Of the units assisted by the MSFC, 62 per cent were located in the RoM, they accounted for 74 per cent of the loans sanctioned and disbursed by the MSFC. The share of RoM in the units assisted, loans sanctioned and disbursed by the SICOM was also disproportionate to the region's population share.

The pattern of regional investment has not changed in the subsequent period. In 2001, Konkan Division accounted for 25.6 per cent of Maharashtra's population. Mumbai and Konkan together, accounted for 47.5 per cent of the total investments in the state in 2002. Amravati had 10.2 per cent of state's population but could attract only 0.4 per cent of the state's total investments. Nashik and Aurangabad both had a little over 16 per cent of the state's population but their shares of the state's total investments were abysmally low, 1.01 per cent and 2.3 per cent respectively. Nagpur and Pune had fared slightly better than the other divisions in attracting investments. Nagpur could get 7.6 per cent while Pune 9.2 per cent of the total investments, though based on their shares in population, these shares should have been 11 per cent and 21 per cent respectively (MEDC, 2002). So regional disparities in investment persisted, despite the efforts of the government to disperse industry regionally to achieve equity.

The institutional structure created after the formation of the state and the dispersal policy followed since then had not changed the regional imbalance in industrial development materially till mid-1990s. A more sympathetic assessment would credit the policy with success in preventing its worsening.

Schemes to Promote Balanced City-Size Distribution

Distribution of urban population by city-size was skewed in 1961. Schemes addressed to integrated development of small and medium towns, development of new towns and growth centres was expected to produce an equitable city size distribution. Though no attempt was made to control migration to large cities directly, the IDSMT scheme, which aimed at stemming the flow of migration, has been in operation since the Sixth Plan. It was expected that the scheme would accelerate economic growth and employment generation in these towns and help reduce migration to big cities. Unfortunately, in the absence of relevant data for each city, it is not possible to say whether IDSMT Scheme could stem migration flows from smaller to larger urban units.

In recent literature on city-size distribution, a distinction is made between desirability of limiting the growth of large cities and the feasibility of doing it. It is argued that, in mega-cities like, Mumbai, the diseconomies of scale far exceed the economies. Therefore, such cities should not be allowed to grow further. Unless the Indian Constitution is suitably amended, migration to cities cannot be stopped and it is doubtful if it could be even after the amendment. Most of the large cities in India grew more by natural increase than by migration and the young entrants to the labour markets in these cities need employment much the same way, as do young entrants elsewhere in the country. Employment cannot be generated without investment, which in turn, has to include that in housing and related infrastructure and in transport to help people commute to places of work. If it is difficult to control migration into large cities, it is far more difficult to make people move out of them. As a result, the historically established city-size hierarchy defies state intervention to alter it and the success, if any, tends to be tardy.

Another reason for the tardy success is that the city-size distribution is influenced by many policies besides those that are directly addressed to altering it. These other policies include strategies of industrialisation, such as import-substitution or export promotion, heavy-industry-first or light-industry-first, agriculture *versus* industry, pricing of foreign exchange, factors of production and agricultural products, base-point pricing, pricing of land and urban services, etc. Quite a few of these policies ran counter to those that were pursued to create an even pattern of urban growth (Deshpande and Deshpande, 1991). Emphasis on agriculture, small industry, export of agricultural products and above all pricing of agricultural goods closer to the international prices would have probably led to a prosperous agriculture and a more balanced urban structure. If such basic goods as steel, cement, coal and other mineral products were not made available at uniform prices all over India, regions where they were produced or mined would have been industrialised and Mumbai-Pune belt might not have been as congested as it is today. If land, food, housing, water, electricity, urban transport were not subsidised in Mumbai, many industries currently located in Mumbai would have been located elsewhere. The textile mills were exempted from the scope of the location policy and many industries wanting to move out of Mumbai are not allowed to do so to avoid hardship to workers in Mumbai.

Thus, the fault may not lie in the policy package. It may be that far too much was expected of it or that too few resources were provided for the purpose. More importantly, to succeed, the policy package needed to be complemented by measures to improve incomes and productivity in agriculture in the relatively backward regions. Along with irrigation, transport, credit, storage and elimination of middlemen and more egalitarian land ownership, increase in agricultural productivity requires different kind of cities called agropolises (Friedman and Douglass, 1976), which not only provide the market for farm produce but also process it for export to wherever it is demanded. In Europe, there were 16 villages to a city in 1970. In Maharashtra there were 133 in 1971 but even in 2001 there were 115 villages for every town in 2001 (Director of Census Operations, Maharashtra, 2001a). Though further breakup by regions is not available the concentration of million-plus as well as Class I cities in RoM suggests that cities in Marathwada and Vidarbha may have to cater to many more villages than those in RoM. Yet development of agropolises is an option worth considering rather than depending entirely on industry for development of backward districts, all the more because the basic infrastructure for industrial development may not be there in many of these districts.

Agriculture employed, a major proportion of the rural workforce in Maharashtra, in 2001. Cultivators together with agricultural labourers formed nearly 73 per cent of the male and 89 per cent of the female rural workers in 2001 (Director of Census Operations, 2001d). Share of main workers so employed was 76 per cent among rural men and 94 per cent among rural women in Maharashtra in 1991 (Registrar General, 1998). These data are not strictly comparable as those for 2001 include marginal workers while data for 1991 exclude them. But since incidence of marginal work is likely to be more common in a seasonal activity like agriculture, we could safely conclude that some workers, especially men, who were employed in agriculture may have found their way to rural non-farm sector in the 1990s. The process had been initiated among rural men between 1981 and 1991. During the 1980s, 36 per cent of the new entrants to rural male workforce had entered the rural non-farm sector. Rural men had moved out of livestock, household industry and construction. Almost 10 per cent each found their way to non-household manufacturing and trade and almost 12 per cent entered services (Deshpande, 1996). It is not possible to know the pattern of rural labour absorption by sectors in the 1990s, since the relevant data are yet to be published. Pattern of absorption in the 1980s shows that a large share of the incremental male workforce in rural Maharashtra entered the tertiary sector rather than the secondary sector. The process could be expected to continue over the 1990s. If so, growth of tertiary sector also holds some promise of future expansion.

The plan documents of the central and state governments mention high priority being given to urban development and regional balance. The responsibility of securing development and balance is vested in the urban development department. Though the extent of urbanisation has increased substantially over time in India and Maharashtra, the allocation for urban development as a share of total plan outlay have remained very meagre. For instance, though 40 per cent of Maharashtra's population live in towns, the allocation to urban development was barely 4 per cent even in the Eighth Plan and has not increased in the subsequent plans. No wonder then the achievement fell short of the target plan after plan. Time is now to pause and consider if we are not spending too little on too many schemes.

Globalisation and liberalisation of the economy do offer the backward regions a chance to develop fast under certain conditions. Liberalisation of agriculture could help the middle peasantry to improve incomes through a favourable shift in price terms of trade. This will create pressures for increasing the productivity of land, diversification of agriculture, growth of agro-processing industry and increase the ability to pay for the services of infrastructure needed for greater production. A government constrained by shortage of resources is more likely to respond to actual than potential demand for infrastructure. New opportunities of public-private partnership open up. Under the liberal regime production of goods and services, is guided solely by the market. Hence, it is likely to be more efficient than when it is subsidised and depends on not-too-public-minded government machinery for the supply of inputs. This is not the place to debate the relative virtues of planning based on the dominant producer role assigned to the public sector and that based on the facilitator role played by it in a largely market driven economy integrated in the world economy. Continuation of the industrial dispersal policy with a liberalised agriculture may reduce the danger of such an undesirable occurrence in the state.

Equity and Efficiency within a City: Improving Access of Urban Poor to Amenities

The government tried to improve the access of the poor to urban services. The schemes included programmes of slum improvement, provision of basic services such as drinking water, toilets, garbage disposal and social services such as primary education and health. The state tried to provide subsidised housing to low income and middle income groups. It implemented the SJSRY to alleviate poverty. Adequately funded, many of the programmes promoting equity contribute to increasing efficiency. Ambitious development plans were formulated but not much was done to raise the revenues to implement them. Consequently, the development plans resembled castles in the air unrelated to the dismal ground realities of urban life. Much the same was true of regional plans. Assets created by the planned investments were not maintained properly. There was very little participation of the citizens in planning and much less in its implementation.

It was hoped that the 74th Amendment of the Constitution in 1992 would go a long way in correcting many of the deficiencies of the top-down approach to planning. The municipal corporations and councils were now responsible for social and economic development including alleviation of poverty. They had to prepare an environmental status report and they needed resources to carry out these functions. Being recognised as the third tier of the government, they have to be assured funds to undertake the investments. The amendments are hailed as a big and a right step in democratic decentralisation. Much will depend on how quickly the privileged classes accommodate the challenges from below.

The amendment is unlikely to be of much help in the short term or even the medium term. The elected councillors and municipal officers would need to be trained in planning for social and economic development and poverty alleviation. Training is also necessary in methods of raising resources by levying taxes, and service charges that would cover the marginal cost of providing the services. Local bodies led by statesmen with foresight would do well and prosper, whereas those led by myopic politicians would suffer. Democratic decentralisation offers no assurance of regional equality.

SECTION VI

Impact of Urban Policy and Implications for Future

We tried to see how far the urban policy could achieve the specific objectives it set forth. This evaluation is necessary all the more because in the era of liberalisation, the state would not be able to pursue many of these policies with the same vigour as it did in the past.

Development of Backward Regions and Primacy of Large Cities in their Respective Regions

Balanced regional development was one of the most important objectives of state policy in Maharashtra. But despite the effort to disperse industry to backward regions, most of it remained on the periphery of Mumbai and Pune. To avail themselves of the incentives provided by the state some industrial development did occur in Marathwada and Vidarbha but even there the industry has remained mostly within their primate cities and at the most on their fringes.

Aurangabad and Nagpur, the former much more than the latter, enjoy much greater primacy in Marathwada and Vidarbha than Mumbai in the rest of Maharashtra. This was so because in RoM there are other cities like Thane, Kalyan, Navi Mumbai, Pune and Nashik that grew since industry was not allowed to be located in Mumbai. This is brought out in Table 13.11.

Though these data relate to 1991, the distribution of investment that emerged over the 1990s across regions suggests that the pattern is not likely to have changed in the subsequent period. To avoid further concentration in these districts, the dispersal policy applicable to Mumbai should be extended to Aurangabad and Nagpur. Experience of Mumbai shows that if industry is not allowed to locate at its best location, it moves to the nearest second best site which has the basic infrastructure in place. Thus, it would be necessary to see that it does not happen.

TABLE 13.11

Regional Primacy of Mumbai, Aurangabad and Nagpur in 1991 (Per Cent Shares of Cities in Regional Totals of Respective Variables)

City	*Population*	*Factories*	*Employment*	*Working Capital*	*Value of Output*	*Value Added*
Mumbai	51.2	73.97	73.13	16.97	57.05	56.46
Aurangabad	17.3	37.10	52.50	64.70	63.50	78.40
Nagpur	18.9	37.63	46.39	47.39	45.15	43.24

Note: Excepting population, which relates to 1991, other variables relate to 1991-92.

Source: GoM, 1997.

Mumbai has always dominated and continues to dominate Maharashtra's economy even now. The question is why does this primacy continue? The answer is to be found not only in the higher per capita incomes but also in the higher productivity of labour and capital in Mumbai relatively to the state and the country. Estimates available for the 1980s indicate that the net national product (NNP) per capita and per worker in Mumbai was more than twice as high as that in the rest of Maharashtra excluding Mumbai. A worker in Mumbai was more productive than his counterpart elsewhere in Maharashtra. In the mid-1980s, value added by manufactures per worker in Mumbai was 1.84 times that added per worker in the rest of Maharashtra excluding Mumbai. The higher productivity of a worker in Mumbai was all the more creditable because it was provided as much equipment to work with, as a worker in the rest of the state. But a rupee of fixed capital invested in Mumbai in the mid-1980s produced 2.5 times the value added as that invested in the rest of Maharashtra (Deshpande and Deshpande, 1993). Curiously enough, this was so even after the ILP had prevented further growth of manufacturing in Mumbai!

Impact on Per Capita Incomes: By Regions and Districts

Level of urbanisation is regarded as one of the indicators of economic development. However, economic development is difficult to measure with one single criterion. Per capita income, share of population below poverty, and levels of unemployment are some of the indices commonly used to assess levels of economic development in an economy. It would be interesting to see how the administrative regions and districts compared in terms of these indices. Estimates of households below poverty line at district level are available only for 1993-94 and do not help in making comparisons. Data on incidence of unemployment too are not available at district level. So we shall see how per capita incomes differed between regions and districts that were at different levels of urbanisation. More importantly we shall see how they changed over the 1990s.

Indicators and Backlog Committee (1997) reported per capita incomes averaged for three years 1989-90, 1990-91 and 1991-92 for 30 districts as of 1991 and 3 regions. The average per capita income for Maharashtra including Mumbai was Rs. 7107. It was 13 per cent lower, Rs. 6193, if Mumbai were excluded. Regional disparities in incomes were wide. RoM had per capita income that was higher than the state average, by 17.5 per cent, if state per capita income including Mumbai were considered, but only 13.8 per cent higher, if state income excluding Mumbai were considered. Vidarbha ranked second with per capita income of Rs. 5358, which was 75.4 per cent of the state's per capita income including Mumbai and 86.5 per cent of it excluding Mumbai. Marathwada had the lowest per capita income of Rs. 4738, 66.7 per cent and 76.5 per cent respectively of the income per capita for Maharashtra including and excluding Mumbai.

Disparities in incomes at district level were wider. Mumbai had the highest per capita income of Rs. 13453, 3.58 times that for Gadchiroli, the poorest district with per capita income of Rs. 3755. Mumbai's per capita income was 1.89 times higher if the district were included to calculate the state's per capita income and it was 2.17 times higher if the district income was excluded for calculating State's per capita income. Only 5 of the 30 districts reported per capita incomes higher than the state per capita income inclusive of Mumbai. They were Greater Mumbai, Thane, Raigad, Pune and Nagpur. If we were to exclude Mumbai while considering state per capita income, 3 more districts Kolhapur, Aurangabad and Chandrapur could enter this group. In other words, 22 of the 30 districts had incomes that were lower than the state average, if Mumbai was included or excluded for deriving this average. Of the 5 districts with higher than average income (including Mumbai) 4 were in RoM, only 1 was from Vidarbha. If we were to consider state per capita average income excluding Mumbai, of the 8 districts, 5 were from RoM, 2 from Vidarbha and only 1 was from Marathwada (GoM, 1997).

The levels of income increased over the 1990s but income disparities had widened, though marginally, both between regions and districts. Per capita income of Maharashtra including Mumbai was Rs. 22,763 in 1998-99 at current prices, that excluding Mumbai was nearly 16.7 per cent lower at Rs. 19,506, indicating that Mumbai's income had increased faster than that in the rest of the state in the intervening period. RoM continued to be the richest region. Per capita income in RoM including Mumbai was Rs. 26,864, 18 per cent higher than that in the state. RoM's income excluding Mumbai of Rs. 21,915 however, was only 12.4 per cent higher than the per capita equivalent in the state indicating that incomes outside the region were picking up. Per capita incomes in Vidarbha increased faster than in Marathwada. Vidarbha's per capita income, Rs. 18,272 in 1998-99, was 80.3 per cent of the state per capita income including Mumbai, in the early 1990s this ratio was 75 per cent. This was equivalent to nearly 94 per cent of state's income per capita excluding Mumbai, in 1989-92 this ratio was 86 per cent. This was not so with Marathwada, where the per capita income of Rs. 14,559, was 64.0 per cent and 74.6 respectively of the state per capita income including and excluding Mumbai in 1998-99. The corresponding ratios were 66.7 per cent and 76.5 per cent in the early 1990s. So, Marathwada was worse off in the late than the early 1990s.

This was true of district incomes too. Mumbai with an income of Rs. 45,471 per capita was the richest district in the state in 1998-99. This per capita income was almost twice as high as of an average Maharashtra if Mumbai were included, while calculating the latter, but was 2.33 times as high if Mumbai were excluded while deriving it. Dhule was the poorest district with a per capita income of Rs. 11,789, that was barely 26 per cent of the per capita income of Mumbai. In 1989-1992, Gadchiroli, the poorest district, had an income that was 28 per cent of that of Mumbai's. Despite efforts to contain Mumbai's growth, incomes had risen in this megacity. The same 5 of the 30 districts, Mumbai, Thane, Raigad, Pune and Nagpur reported higher than the state per capita income including Mumbai. Thane, however, ranked second now instead of third as in the past and Nagpur had an edge over Pune and ranked fourth. If we were to compare district incomes with state's derived by excluding Mumbai, five more could be added to this list. They are Sindhudurg, Nashik, Sangli, Kolhapur and Chandrapur. Eight of these 10 districts are in RoM, and two in Vidarbha; none in Marathwada (GoM, 2001).

Not only was RoM the most urbanised and the richest of the three regions of the state but over the 1990s, districts of RoM fared relatively better than those in Marathwada, the least urbanised region in the state. Even within RoM, Konkan, the most urbanised division, had done better than the other two divisions, Pune and Nashik. Of the five districts of Konkan division, barring Ratnagiri, the other four Mumbai, Thane, Raigad and Sindhudurg had per capita incomes higher than state per capita income excluding Mumbai in 1998-99. Pune division had three such districts, while Nashik had only one such district. So, even within RoM, the rich division had become richer as investments had a tendency to get concentrated in these better off districts. The policies pursued to attain regional balanced development met with limited success. As a result, the income inequalities between districts were wider in the late than early 1990s.

New Schemes and their Impacts

Valmiki Ambedkar Awas Yojana (VAMBAY) scheme has been initiated by the Government of India mainly for the construction/upgradation of houses and community toilets (Nirmal Bharat Abhiyan: NBA) for persons belonging to economically weaker sections of society residing in slum type hutments. The scheme consists of a GoI subsidy of Rs. 20000 per unit of house and community toilet and the rest amount of the project cost is to be borne by the beneficiary or the executing agency. Under this scheme, Maharashtra has received Rs. 845.6 lakhs to cover 328 houses and 3900 toilet seats by sanctioning HUDCO loans and other types of loans/grants. Some activities such as rehabilitation of the slum dwellers in Kamgar Putla in Pune district who lost their homes during monsoon floods of the year 1997 are to be carried out.

Urban Reforms Incentive Fund (URIF), in order to deal with ever growing urban problems, an Urban URIF with an initial outlay of Rs. 500 crore has been set up to provide reforms linked assistance to the states. Thirteen states and three union territories have so far signed a Memorandum of Agreement with the Centre for availing assistance under URIF. The seven reform areas covered by URIF include rationalisation of stamp duty, revision of municipal laws in line with a model legislation prepared by the Ministry, reform of Rent Control Laws and repeal of Urban Land Ceiling Act. Maharashtra is one of the signatory of aforesaid Memorandum of Agreement. However, no significant study on the impacts of this scheme is found in the recent literature.

Lessons Learnt for Future Policy

This analysis has an important implication for policy in the future. Government of Maharashtra had set before it balanced regional development as the goal to be achieved through planning. To achieve this goal, special efforts were necessary since these regions were starved of industry. The policy prescription that followed was to take industry to these regions. Not only was the urban policy formulated with this specific objective, the government even set up institutions to help this process. The ILP was the main policy instrument that was used almost over four decades. By restricting growth of industry in Mumbai, the government could, at the most, take it to its adjoining districts not very much beyond them. Given the institutional set up, especially of MIDC, MSFC and SICOM, the ILP could set up industries in few districts of Vidarbha and Marathwada. But the primacy of Nagpur in Vidarbha and Aurangabad in Marathwada suggests that even in the late 1990s other districts in these regions continued to be industrially backward. Despite the changes in the ILP in 1993, income inequalities between regions and districts widened over the 1990s.

There is a natural tendency for new industries to locate either in areas where industries already exist or in areas nearby to take advantage of agglomeration economies that emerge in the process. In India, total factor productivity, productivity of labour and capital taken together, increases with city size. The Class I cities are about 23 per cent more productive than Class IV cities. Within Class I cities, going from a city of 100,000 to one of 2000000 results in a 31 per cent efficiency gain (Shukla, 1988). Maharashtra could not have been an exception to this rule. Probably this explains only partly why RoM continued to develop with or without Mumbai! The region had the largest share of Class I cities and 6 of the 7 million-plus cities in 2001. If this were so, the policy of industrial dispersal, so far pursued would have to be reconsidered and suitably changed.

The other important implication is that, though the government institutions provided infrastructure in the industrial estates, probably it was inadequate and also of a poor quality, most probably both, than what it was available in RoM. So the backward districts failed to lure industry towards them.

Regional inequalities increased in Maharashtra in the post-reform period despite the efforts of the government to reduce them through its industrial dispersal policy. The process was likely to accelerate in future unless we try to lay emphasis not on manufacturing alone but try to develop both agriculture and the rural non-farm sector in the backward districts.

Productivity, City Size and Agglomeration Economies

That economic growth of a country or a region contributes to the growth of cities that in turn leads to urbanisation is well recognised. But its inverse, as a country or a region urbanises some cities grow faster and contribute to economic growth is not true. Maharashtra offers a prospective migrant a wide choice of city sizes to move to and it is not for nothing he migrates to the bigger of them. Even the beggars are aware of the higher productivity in larger cities and flock to these cities in preference to the smaller ones. Labour migrates to large cities too. Agglomeration of commercial undertakings located in close proximity to one another enhances efficiency of communications especially in societies like India where telecommunications are costly. The higher productivity in Maharashtra is reflected in higher wage rates in Mumbai and also in the higher per capita municipal revenues in contrast to smaller towns (Deshpande and Deshpande, 1991; 1993; Crook, 1993).

This awareness-led National Commission on Urbanisation (NCU, 1988) recommended that Mumbai along with other three metros should be granted national status. NCU felt and rightly so that these cities were generators of wealth and if they were to collapse the economy of the country would receive a grievous blow. Noting that much of the industrial machinery in Mumbai, Kolkata and Chennai was obsolete and the social and physical infrastructure totally inadequate, the Commission felt that topmost priority had to be given to save the national cities and help them in reviving their economies.

With globalisation and liberalisation this perspective changes slightly. The question now is not one of helping a city like Mumbai to revive, but one of helping it to thrive and benefit not only itself but also the state and the country at large. Great future lies ahead for Mumbai as it can play an important role in integrating India with the global economy. Globalisation would bring along with it changes in Mumbai's economy and in rest of Maharashtra's. Going by international experience, much of the industrial activity that would be exposed to international competition would shift to the cheaper hinterland of Mumbai. The city will become as noted earlier a junction-point and a switchgear transferring people, commodities, capital and information to national and international destinations (Deshpande and Deshpande, 1993). Mumbai has the potential to become an important financial centre in Asia, and possibly in the world when India becomes a fully open economy (Harris, 1992). Mumbai will not be able to play this role unless its physical and social infrastructure, 'disastrous' in comparison to her competitors' abroad, is modernised and augmented. The urban policy of the national and state government in future would have to recognise the role Mumbai would have to play as a global city.

Policy Recommendations

- Urbanisation being a state subject, the state government need to prepare state urbanisation strategies, its implementation priorities, etc. The goals of urban agenda involves a host of broad sub sectors development, like sustainable provision/ expansion of urban infrastructure facilities: water supply, sanitation, environment planning, transport infrastructure, creating an enabling legal, financing, regulatory framework for housing, land acquisition/development, township development, poverty alleviation, research/training, database, strengthening of urban local bodies (ULBs)/ capacity building of ULB personnel, etc.
- A reliable database needs to be created on a continuous updating basis. Level of urbanisation basically depends upon the density of population, level of economic development, etc. The reforms in the urban sector should comprise enhancing the flow of investment to the critical sectors of urban infrastructure as also creating a facilitating process for speeding up the growth of new economic activities as well as expansion in existing ones. Urban upgradation encompassing housing, social, physical, economic environment, amenities and services including integrated transport system has to be recognised as part of state development process.
- Housing is one of the important basic needs of people along with food and clothing. It is important not only as it caters to the basic needs of the society but also because it characterises the place in terms of social ecology, living standards, etc. Homelessness has specially been observed with respect to the vulnerable sections necessitating the need to programme appropriate schemes to increase the availability of affordable housing to economically weaker sections and low income group which in turn leads to facilitating allocation of land, extension of funding assistance, provision of support services, etc. It should be the government's endeavour to guarantee conditions under which the poor and the disadvantaged will be able to secure adequate housing in healthy environment. Thus, an important concern of the government will be to provide policy framework and legislative, fiscal and financial system that would put into effect the enabling role of the government in the housing delivery system. There is also a need to introduce separate housing scheme for persons living below poverty line in urban areas.
- The state should effectively carry out the implementation of the 74th Constitution Amendment Act, 1992 and take initiatives of improvements to overcome structural deficiencies in the way of augmentation of revenue from sources like property tax, trade/commerce license fees, etc. and from other sources, like street tax, change of land use, municipal bonds, etc. More importantly, it should identify areas of levy/ collection of taxes in the from of land/building/ house tax, profession/vocation tax, composite levies; municipal rental property tax, road development fund, etc., as also cost effective collection mechanism to eliminate backlog. In other words, to counter the severity of urban problems, the modes of solutions have to be

coherent, comprehensive to address to the local situations.

- Urban poverty has emerged as a complex, multidimensional phenomenon. However, in order to meet individual's needs, programmes need to cater to all types of vulnerabilities on a proper assessment of possible forms of poverty in a given context. Innovative areas of employment also need to be explored to suit the state conditions. As far as planning process is concerned, community based development, municipality/district/state level plans could be strengthened. Since urban poverty is a growing or persistent phenomenon, there will be a continuous need to gather information on the levels of poverty, relative income inequalities, etc. and to study the composition of its manifestations. There is a definite case for preparation of well documented case studies of success/failures, reasons thereof spelling out clear cut steps, initiatives, etc.

SECTION VII

Conclusions

Although Maharashtra is a highly urbanised state levels of urbanisation were uneven across regions and districts within the state. Urban population in Maharashtra grew faster than the total but not alarmingly so. It grew slower in the 1990s than in 1980s, and in all cities irrespective of the size-class. A disproportionately large share of the state's population lived in Class I cities, much more so over time. This was the natural outcome of economic growth. Tendencies towards equalisation of the extent of urbanisation and urban growth were in operation across districts and regions but operated much too slowly to satisfy the protagonists of regional equality.

It is difficult to attribute equalisation to either the state or the market. Perhaps both could share the credit. The Government of Maharashtra followed an elaborate industrial policy to disperse industry to reduce regional disparities. These measures succeeded more in dispersing industry within the rest of Maharashtra region than outside it. The failure is not surprising to students of regional economics. Apart from lack of commitment from appropriate governments, too much is often expected of the policy package and too little is provided for implementing it. For the measures to succeed, the policy package needs to be complemented by measures to improve agricultural productivity in the relatively less developed regions. Development of agriculture would require provision of more irrigation, transport, credit and storage facilities to the farmers.

Globalisation and liberalisation hold some promise and pose some dangers for the backward regions. Liberalisation of agriculture offers opportunities to improve incomes for the middle peasantry. Accompanied by the development of agro-processing industry, the emergence of sizable market may induce domestic and foreign investors to go to these regions. All the more if a liberal dispersal policy accompanied liberalisation. The dangers are that if the basic infrastructure of power, transport and communication did not improve in the backward regions, liberalisation would not help them to industrialise or urbanise.

The 74th Amendment to the Constitution is a big step towards democratic decentralisation. However, it is unlikely to bring about even urban development in the short to medium term. Cities have to function efficiently and equitably. Liberalisation forces cities to specialise nationally and globalisation forces them to specialise internationally. Cities have to find out their comparative advantages and concentrate on exploiting them. Availability of an efficiently managed physical and social infrastructure services helps reduce private costs and makes private industry nationally and globally competitive. Innovative ways of forging public-private partnerships need to be explored and experimented with. The NGOs could play an important role in the partnerships.

Efficiency and equity are not irreconcilable always and everywhere. Improvement in the access of the poor to the social, economic and civic infrastructure would improve their efficiency, incomes and ability to pay for civic services. Intra-city equity is as important as inter-regional equity. We hope that the 74th Constitutional amendment would go some, if not all the way, in promoting intra-city equity and make cities not only economically more efficient but also socially more liveable.

Chapter 14

Employment

Introduction

'Ability to perform some useful work' is more often than not, the only resource endowment that a labourer commands. Any individual's status in the employment market depends on 'skills' or capabilities, knowledge of the market for employment, mobility, expected level of remuneration and willingness as well as the ability to diversify skills. Employment enables in equipping/endowing the person with purchasing power, self-respect and social recognition. Hence, it is one of the most critical indicators of development. But compared to other economic indicators, like income or investment, it changes much slowly. In many LDCs, sectoral composition of employment changes as slow as some other concomitant development features such as the literacy rate. Employment is 'derived demand for labour' i.e. it depends on the demand for goods produced, as well as the availability of other supplementary inputs a like machinery, raw materials and 'skills', required to handle the materials and machines/tools. Hence, additional anticipated demand for the product and warranted 'investment' (i.e. additional stock of capital) for the same are crucial determinants of employment. Technical changes, often aimed at reducing at least some of the inputs per unit of output, are other long-term factors that overshadow the pace and composition of employment.

The first simple approximation of 'employment' is "number of persons reported to be engaged in 'some' gainful activity" as reported in the census. This can be further disaggregated by the nature of economic activity in which they are employed i.e. sector, type of ownership under which they are employed or their age/sex composition or location of employment (e.g. by regions or rural/urban). We now present the data on total number of workers, i.e. main and marginal based on three successive censuses (Table 14.1).

TABLE 14.1

Employment Scenario in Maharashtra

Activity	*1981*	*1991*	*2001*
Total Workers	**26718230**	**33910366**	**42053330**
Main	24301793	31006109	35670836
Share in Total	90.96	91.44	84.82
Marginal	2416437	2904257	6382494
Share in Total	9.04	8.57	15.18

Sources: Census of India (1981, 1991 and 2001).

It may be observed that in the last decade, the proportion of 'marginal workers' in 'total workers' has increased by 6.49 percentage points. This implies that the number of persons registered to be employed for 'some time' in 'some activity', also including those, who are engaged in addition to their 'main activity', has gone up. This may be due to the inadequacy of the 'main employment', emergence of new work opportunities that are seasonal or temporary in nature, or perhaps a reflection of redeployment of the existing workforce in a new or different activity. The Census questions, which elicit this information, are usually unhelpful to hazard a guess about the underlying process at work. We may now look at the decomposition of total workers by major type of economic activity. This is presented in Table 14.2.

As the Table 14.2 shows, the proportion of cultivators has declined by 2.31 and 4.25 percentage points between 1981 and 1991 and 1991 and 2001 respectively, while the proportion of agricultural labourers has remained more or less stable at 26.85 per cent. In 2001, share of 'other workers' has gone up to 42.1 per cent and there is a marginal improvement in household industry workers. 'Other workers' category consists of very different and heterogeneous types of

TABLE 14.2

Per Cent Composition of Workers by Major Economic Activity

Activity	*1981*	*1991*	*2001*
Cultivators	8535910 (35.12)	10172108 (32.81)	12009903 (28.56)
Agricultural Labourers	6470855 (26.63)	8313223 (26.81)	11290945 (26.85)
Household Industry Workers	620506 (2.55)	498431 (1.61)	1046149 (2.49)
Other Workers	8674522 (35.69)	12022347 (38.77)	17706333 (42.10)
Total	**24301828 (100.00)**	**31006109 (100.00)**	**42053330 (100.00)**

Note: Figures in the parentheses represents column percentages.

Source: Primary Census Abstract—1981, 1991c and 2001.

TABLE 14.3

Activity-wise Employment and their Percentage to Total for Year 1991 and 2001 in Maharashtra State

Activity	*1991*	*Per Cent to Total*	*2001**	*Per Cent to Total*
Agricultural Labourers	9532101	27.54	11290945	26.85
Cultivators	11542964	33.35	12009903	28.56
Agri., Hunting, Foresting and Fishing	608609	1.76	1284095	3.05
Total Agriculture & Allied Activities	21683674	62.64	24584943	58.46
Mining & Quarrying	87001	0.25	107675	0.26
Household Industries	559515	1.62	1046149	2.49
Manufacturing	4124988	11.92	4337708	10.31
Total Manufacturing	**4684503**	**13.53**	**5383857**	**12.80**
Electricity, Gas & Water	171143	0.49	180493	0.43
Construction	249120	0.72	335896	0.80
Wholesale & Retail Trade Restaurant	2314818	6.69	3527352	8.39
Transport, Storage & Communications	899319	2.60	1305446	3.10
Total Retail Trade and Transport	3214137	9.29	4832798	11.49
Financing, Insurance Real Estate & Business Services	745883	2.15	1226203	2.92
Community Social & Personal Services, Other	3779129	10.92	5401464	12.84
Total Services	**4525013**	**13.07**	**6627667**	**15.76**
Total	**34614591**	**100.00**	**42053331**	**100.00**

Note: * Total of 'other workers' from Census 2001 were distributed over other sectors by using the sectoral shares as available from EC 1998.

Source: Census of India, Primary Census Abstract 1991d, 2001. *Economic Census, Maharashtra State Employment Review.*

work opportunities. We need to probe a little further to spell out the rise in 'other workers,' We may look at more detailed activity-wise employment (Table 14.3).

There is a decline of 4.18 percentage points in the share of agriculture and allied activities. The fall is more pronounced in the case of cultivators. The share of forestry and fishing has registered an impressive rise. Though the number of workers in 'manufacturing' as well as in the mining and quarrying has increased, their shares have fallen. The rising share of the tertiary sector is a well-known characteristic of development and that has been experienced in Maharashtra.

This is evident from absolute numbers as well as shares of the tertiary activities. To emphasise the same we present in Table 14.4 data on employment in 'shops', 'commercial establishments' and 'restaurant', 'theatre', etc., separately which indicates the rapid growth of these service sectors.

TABLE 14.4

Employment in Shops and Commercial Establishment in Maharashtra

(in '000)

Year	*Shops*	*Commercial Establish-ments*	*Restaurant, Theatres, etc.*	*All Establish-ments*
1988	454	909	199	1561
1993	503	119	213	835
1995	540	1216	219	1975
1997	540	1266	240	2046
1998	570	1369	245	2184

Source: GoI (various issues), Indian Labour Statistics.

Regional Profile of Employment

We may now look at the regional distribution of workforce. We will first look at the distribution of workers by urban and rural areas. As Table 14.5 shows, nearly one-third of the workers are in urban Maharashtra and the rest two-third are in rural

TABLE 14.5

Distribution of Workforce by Rural and Urban Areas

(Figures in Lakh)

Activity	*1991*			*2001*		
	Total	*Rural*	*Urban*	*Total*	*Rural*	*Urban*
Total	**339.10**	**240.33**	**98.77**	**420.53**	**281.07**	**139.47**
Main	310.06 (91.44)	213.81 (88.96)	96.25 (97.45)	356.71 (84.82)	227.52 (80.95)	129.19 (92.63)
Marginal	29.04 (8.56)	26.53 (11.04)	2.52 (2.55)	63.82 (15.18)	53.55 (19.05)	10.28 (7.37)

Note: Figures in parentheses indicates percentage.

Source: Census of India (1991 and 2001).

Maharashtra. Notably, both rural and urban areas have experienced great rise in number of marginal workers. The rise is faster in urban areas. The rate of growth of 'main workers' in urban areas is almost five times the rate observed in rural areas.

TABLE 14.6

Compound Annual Growth Rates of Main and Marginal Workers

Activity	*Total*	*Rural*	*Urban*
Total	**2.18**	**1.58**	**3.51**
Main	1.41	0.62	2.99
Marginal	8.19	7.28	15.11

Historically, Maharashtra consists of five different regions (Konkan, Khandesh, Western Maharashtra, Marathwada and Vidarbha) each with a distinct historical background, heritage and economic institutions. Nature of economic resources and opportunities as well as the characteristics and level of economic development in these regions are disparate. Regional imbalance in growth and development is a sensitive and burning issue in Maharashtra. The districts in these five distinct regions fall into seven administrative divisions including Brihan Mumbai.

Table 14.7 provides the classification of workers by major economic activity. Differences in the nature of occupations are stark. Mumbai has 97.1 per cent in other workers and Amravati division has only 23 per cent in this category. The 'other workers' reflect diminished dependence on agriculture. The share of this category of workers is above the average in case Brihan Mumbai and Konkan, while in Pune region it is fairly close to average. In the remaining regions 'dependence on agriculture' is obvious. If we take all regions together Pune division accounts for 21.6 per cent total labourers followed by Nashik (16.9 per cent) and Aurangabad (16.2 per cent). Tables 14.8 and 14.9 give data for males and females separately.

Employment by Types of Organisation

There are several organisational forms or types of economic activity. Given the availability of secondary data we can distinguish the organisational type by ownership (public and private), nature of legal recognition or regulation (e.g. registered/unregistered also called organised/unorganised) and by size large/small. In the Table 14.10, we present data on employment in public and private sector for a period 1987-88 to 1999-00. The 'public sector' is subdivided in central, state and 'quasi government', which are further subdivided by central, state and local bodies. The private sector is subdivided in large and small establishments. The enterprises covered here are the core of organised sector employment.

TABLE 14.7

Region-wise Workers Classification (Persons) as per Census 2001

Region	*Total Workers Main & Marginal*	*Cultivators*	*Agri. Lab.*	*Household Industry Workers*	*Other Workers*
Br. Mumbai	4527926	1693	1446	127708	4397079
Konkan	5354903	1257461	705598	127458	3264386
Nashik	7121368	2478143	2453069	163493	2026663
Pune	9082980	3330978	1801187	298092	3652723
Aurangabad	6805770	2641880	2423441	114346	1626103
Amravati	4434546	1148751	2219094	56494	1010207
Nagpur	4725837	1150997	1687110	158558	1729172
Maharashtra	**42053330**	**12009903**	**11290945**	**1046149**	**17706333**
	Activity-wise Zonal Distribution				
Br. Mumbai	100.0	0.0	0.0	2.8	97.1
Konkan	100.0	23.5	13.2	2.4	61.0
Nashik	100.0	34.8	34.4	2.3	28.5
Pune	100.0	36.7	19.8	3.3	40.2
Aurangabad	100.0	38.8	35.6	1.7	23.9
Amravati	100.0	25.9	50.0	1.3	22.8
Nagpur	100.0	24.4	35.7	3.4	36.6
Maharashtra	**100.0**	**28.6**	**26.8**	**2.5**	**42.1**
	Zone-wise Activity Level Distribution				
Br.Mumbai	10.8	0.0	0.0	12.2	24.8
Konkan	12.7	10.5	6.2	12.2	18.4
Nashik	16.9	20.6	21.7	15.6	11.4
Pune	21.6	27.7	16.0	28.5	20.6
Aurangabad	16.2	22.0	21.5	10.9	9.2
Amravati	10.5	9.6	19.7	5.4	5.7
Nagpur	11.2	9.6	14.9	15.2	9.8
Maharashtra	**100.0**	**100.0**	**100.0**	**100.0**	**100.0**

Sources: Census of India (2001).

From 1987-88 to 1996-97, there is a steady rise in employment in all the major subcategories. From 1997-1998 onwards the employment in all segments except private small enterprises have declined. This fall, in the case of public sector may be due to the fiscal crunch leading to restrictions on filling upon vacant posts. In the case of private large size enterprises, this may be due to the business cycle (the enduring recession from 1998 to 2000) and restructuring measures taken up in response to it (e.g. voluntary retirement schemes introduced in some large enterprises). The employment in small enterprises has experienced a fall immediately after 1997 and a subsequent recovery in later years.

However, except for the declining trends, the rates of growth of all these categories are similar and close. Hence, the composition (in terms of per cent shares) does not show very drastic shifts. Notably, the share of

TABLE 14.8

Region-wise Workers Classification (Male) as per Census 2001

Region	*Total Workers Main & Marginal*	*Cultivators*	*Agri. Lab.*	*Household Industry Workers*	*Other Workers*
Br. Mumbai	3781749	1353	995	84313	3695088
Konkan	3675366	580770	303892	68847	2721857
Nashik	4255136	1414069	1061424	85408	1694235
Pune	5623045	1824397	741751	135553	2921344
Aurangabad	3992246	1519592	1051314	58114	1363226
Amravati	2698417	734460	1061026	34614	868317
Nagpur	2898805	691118	708391	73762	1425534
Maharashtra	**26924764**	**6765759**	**4928793**	**540611**	**14689601**
	Percentage to Total Workers				
Br. Mumbai	100.0	0.0	0.0	2.2	97.7
Konkan	100.0	15.8	8.3	1.9	74.1
Nashik	100.0	33.2	24.9	2.0	39.8
Pune	100.0	32.4	13.2	2.4	52.0
Aurangabad	100.0	38.1	26.3	1.5	34.1
Amravati	100.0	27.2	39.3	1.3	32.2
Nagpur	100.0	23.8	24.4	2.5	49.2
Maharashtra	**100.0**	**25.1**	**18.3**	**2.0**	**54.6**
	Percentage to State				
Br. Mumbai	14.0	0.0	0.0	15.6	25.2
Konkan	13.7	8.6	6.2	12.7	18.5
Nashik	15.8	20.9	21.5	15.8	11.5
Pune	20.9	27.0	15.0	25.1	19.9
Aurangabad	14.8	22.5	21.3	10.7	9.3
Amravati	10.0	10.9	21.5	6.4	5.9
Nagpur	10.8	10.2	14.4	13.6	9.7
Maharashtra	**100.0**	**100.0**	**100.0**	**100.0**	**100.0**

Source: Census of India, 2001.

TABLE 14.9

Region-wise Workers Classification (Females) as per Census 2001

Region	*Total Workers Main & Marginal*	*Cultivators*	*Agri. Lab.*	*Household Industry Workers*	*Other Workers*
Br. Mumbai	746177	340	451	43395	701991
Konkan	1679537	676691	401706	58611	542529
Nashik	2866232	1064074	1391645	78085	332428
Pune	3459935	1506581	1059436	162539	731379
Aurangabad	2813524	1122288	1372127	56232	262877
Amravati	1736129	414291	1158068	21880	141890
Nagpur	1827032	459879	978719	84796	303638
Maharashtra	**15128566**	**5244144**	**6362152**	**505538**	**3016732**
	Percentage to Total Workers				
Br. Mumbai	100.0	0.0	0.1	5.8	94.1
Konkan	100.0	40.3	23.9	3.5	32.3
Nashik	100.0	37.1	48.6	2.7	11.6
Pune	100.0	43.5	30.6	4.7	21.1
Aurangabad	100.0	39.9	48.8	2.0	9.3
Amravati	100.0	23.9	66.7	1.3	8.2
Nagpur	100.0	25.2	53.6	4.6	16.6
Maharashtra	**100.0**	**34.7**	**42.1**	**3.3**	**19.9**
	Percentage to State				
Br. Mumbai	4.9	0.0	0.0	8.6	23.3
Konkan	11.1	12.9	6.3	11.6	18.0
Nashik	18.9	20.3	21.9	15.4	11.0
Pune	22.9	28.7	16.7	32.2	24.2
Aurangabad	18.6	21.4	21.6	11.1	8.7
Amravati	11.5	7.9	18.2	4.3	4.7
Nagpur	12.1	8.8	15.4	16.8	10.1
Maharashtra	**100.0**	**100.0**	**100.0**	**100.0**	**100.0**

Source: Census of India, 2001.

TABLE 14.10

Distribution of Employment in Public Sector and Private Sector

Year	*Public Sector Establishments*						*Private Sector Establishments*			*Total*
	Central Govt.	*State Govt.*	*Quasi Government Central*	*Quasi Government State*	*Quasi Government Local*	*Total Public Sector*	*Large*	*Small*	*Total Private Sector*	
1987-88	486600	486900	406200	244700	572000	2196400	1278000	75100	1353100	3549500
1990-91	481100	509300	424700	266900	599600	2281600	1291800	74100	1365900	3647500
1995-96	478000	531500	405300	275300	652900	2343000	1438300	81100	1519400	3862400
1996-97	447700	527900	424200	267200	679300	2346300	1453800	82100	1535900	3882200
1997-98	432800	531200	416400	268100	683000	2331500	1437600	79000	1516600	3848100
1998-99	427400	522300	412700	263900	679100	2305400	1423900	80800	1504700	3810100
2000-01	423800	518300	412100	262100	673600	2289900	1388700	81200	1469900	3759800

Source: GoI, (various issues), *Statistical Abstract of India.*

the central government has declined from 13.79 per cent in 1987-88 to 11.27 per cent in 2000-01. Similarly, share of large private enterprises has gone up in the first seven years (35.42 per cent to 37.42 per cent) and declined by 0.28 per cent points by the end of decade (36.94 per cent).

It is well known that the size of the registered and organised sectors in India is relatively small. Rest of the economic entities fall in the category called unorganised or informal sector. In the case of the manufacturing sector the definition of organised or formal is crisp. All the enterprises requiring registration under Factory Act, 1948 are called 'organised and formal.' In other sectors, such crisp definition is not available. Nonetheless, we attempted approximation of formal-informal segregation by using the data from Economic Census. EMI enterprises are roughly, the organised and formal sector establishments and Economic Census entities are taken to be informal sector enterprises. These are presented in Table 14.11. There are some remarkable changes. Employment in all sectors of EC has increased. The number of establishments and employment in agriculture has increased very rapidly and its share in EC has increased from 5.96 per cent to 9.27 per cent. Similarly, the shares of wholesale trade, transport storage and communication, finance and insurance and community and social and personal services have improved.

On the other hand, the share of the formal segment, as approximated by EMI employment, in total employment has fallen from 29.44 in 1991 to 25.68 in 2001. In all sectors except electricity, gas and water supply, share of the formal segment has declined. The secular fall in share of formal sector and impressive rise in case of informal sector is noteworthy. Like growth in marginal workers discussed above, this trend too reflects an increased flexibility, seasonality and perhaps rises in 'footloose labour' as against the fall in the 'entrenched labour'. A part of the decline in the entrenched, organised labour may be due to restructuring prompted by adjustment to cyclical fluctuations as well as changes in 'perceptions of or about, changed business environment (e.g. de-reservations in small sector, reduction in import duties, changes in patterns of ancillarisation). It may be noted that there have been no major changes in labour legislations (e.g. Industrial Disputes Act or Payment of Wages or Bonus Act) and no other labour market reforms have been implemented. Yet, there is significant fall in the number of industrial disputes and number of man-days lost in industrial disputes (Table 14.12).

TABLE 14.11

Distribution of Employment into Formal and Informal Sectors, and their Percentage to Total Employment for Year 1991 and 2001

Activity	*1991*						*2001*					
	EC	*Per Cent*	*EMI*	*Per Cent*	*Total*	*Per Cent*	*EC*	*Per Cent*	*EMI*	*Per Cent*	*Total*	*Per Cent*
Agri., Hunting, Foresting & Fishing	546042	5.96	62567	1.64	608609	4.69	1219997	9.27	64098	1.41	1284095	7.25
Mining & Quarrying	43710	0.48	43291	1.13	87001	0.67	55671	0.42	52004	1.14	107675	0.61
Manufacturing	2862226	31.25	1262762	33.04	4124988	31.78	3033976	23.06	1303732	28.67	4337708	24.50
Electricity, Gas & Water	57315	0.63	113827	2.98	171143	1.32	38993	0.30	141500	3.11	180493	1.02
Construction	99217	1.08	149903	3.92	249120	1.92	172627	1.31	163269	3.59	335896	1.90
Wholesale & Retail Trade & Restaurants, Hotels	2237175	24.43	77644	2.03	2314818	17.83	3436647	26.12	90705	1.99	3527352	19.92
Transport, Storage & Communications	377996	4.13	521323	13.64	899319	6.93	685024	5.21	620422	13.64	1305446	7.37
Financing Insurance, Real Estate & Business Service	481938	5.26	263946	6.91	745883	5.75	845242	6.42	380961	8.38	1226203	6.93
Community Social & Personal Service	2452723	26.78	1326406	34.71	3779129	29.11	3670814	27.9	1730650	38.06	5401464	30.51
Total	**9158342**	**100.0**	**3821669**	**100.0**	**12980011**	**100.0**	**13158993**	**100.0**	**4547341**	**100.0**	**17706334**	**100.0**
Formal (EMI), Informal (EC) Per Cent to Total	70.56		29.44		100.00		74.32		25.		100.00	

Note: Total of 'Other workers' from Census 2001 were distributed over other sectors by using the sectoral shares as available from EC 1998.

EMI-Formal Sector. EC-Informal Sector.

Source: GoM (*Maharashtra State Employment Review*) and GoM (*Economic Census*).

TABLE 14.12

Industrial Disputes (Central and State Sphere)

Year	Number of Disputes	Number of Man-days Lost
1991	173	3303673
1992	170	3244528
1993	176	2771002
1994	147	2362678
1995	112	1718734
1996	80	1822704
1997	48	1301960
1998	35	933799

Source: GoI (various issues), *Indian Labour Statistics.*

Thus, the decline in the share of 'formal sector' employment cannot be directly attributed to so-called labour reform policy measures. At the same time, as earlier pointed out, the employment in 'small enterprises' in the 'core' organised sector has not fallen but improved somewhat. Business sectors as well as unions seem to have sensed the change in the milieu. Business units seem to be able to restructure more quickly and perhaps with less of additional investment and labour. These efficiency improvements are welcome and desirable. At the same time, they are inevitably reflected as the socalled 'jobless growth' in the organised sector.

Employment: Perspective Based on Census and NSS Data Together

Our description so far has been mostly based on census data. Census data have many limitations. In particular, census queries are not intended to probe deeper into the various aspects of economic activity. We, therefore, combine population data from census with the NSSO data on 'employment/unemployment' and few other aspects of employment. We do recognise that NSSO data too suffers from some limitations and similarly, combining these two sources results in some problems. As the Central sample data were not available, we have used State sample data. Estimates from these samples may (and do) widely differ. Hence, we have avoided their 'combined and conjunctive' use for further quantitative estimation.

We present in Table 14.13 the estimates of workforce based on census and NSSO rounds pertaining to years 1987-88, 1993-94, and 1999-2000. The procedure that we applied is as follows: the NSSO rounds provide work-participation rates, for rural males, rural females, urban

TABLE 14.13

Workforce in India, Maharashtra and Other States Based on Census Population and NSS WPR: Total

(Figures in Lakhs)

States	Regions	1987-88			1993-94			1999-2000		
		Male	Female	Total	Male	Female	Total	Male	Female	Total
India	Rural	1608	909	2517	1873	1039	2912	2042	1066	3108
	Urban	518	138	656	641	171	812	766	186	952
	Total	2126	1047	3174	2514	1210	3724	2808	1252	4060
Maharashtra	**Rural**	**126**	**104**	**230**	**141**	**119**	**260**	**152**	**119**	**271**
	Urban	**72**	**20**	**92**	**93**	**26**	**119**	**113**	**26**	**139**
	Total	**198**	**124**	**322**	**234**	**145**	**379**	**265**	**145**	**410**
Andhra Pradesh	Rural	138	107	244	162	130	292	172	132	304
	Urban	41	17	57	54	19	73	63	21	84
	Total	178	123	302	216	150	366	235	153	389
Karnataka	Rural	84	55	139	99	69	168	108	67	175
	Urban	33	12	45	42	13	55	49	15	64
	Total	117	67	184	141	82	222	157	82	238
Gujarat	Rural	74	48	122	83	54	137	92	61	153
	Urban	34	7	41	43	10	53	51	12	63
	Total	108	55	163	126	64	190	143	73	216
Labour Force in	Maharashtra									
Maharashtra	Rural	130	107	237	148	123	272	162	128	290
	Urban	79	22	101	99	28	127	123	29	152
	Total	209	130	338	247	152	399	285	157	441

Source: NSSO, 43rd, 50th, 55th Round; Census of India, 1991c, 2001.

TABLE 14.14

Workforce (Based on Census Population and NSSO WPRs): Rural

(Figures in Lakhs)

State/Union Territory	1987-88			1993-94			1999-2000		
	Male	Female	Persons	Male	Female	Persons	Male	Female	Persons
All India	1608	909	2517	1873	1039	2912	2042	1066	3108
Maharashtra	**126**	**104**	**230**	**141**	**119**	**260**	**152**	**119**	**271**
Andhra Pradesh	138	107	244	162	130	293	172	132	304
Karnataka	84	55	139	99	69	168	108	67	175
Gujarat	74	48	122	83	54	137	92	61	153

Source: NSSO 43rd, 50th, 55th Round; Census of India, 1991c, 2001.

TABLE 14.15

Workforce (Based on Census Population and NSSO WPRs): Urban

(Figures in Lakhs)

State/Union Territory	1987-88			1993-94			1999-2000		
	Male	Female	Persons	Male	Female	Persons	Male	Female	Persons
All India	518	138	656	641	171	812	766	186	952
Maharashtra	**72**	**20**	**92**	**93**	**26**	**119**	**113**	**26**	**139**
Andhra Pradesh	41	17	57	54	19	73	63	21	84
Karnataka	33	12	45	42	13	55	49	15	64
Gujarat	34	7	41	43	10	53	51	12	63

Source: NSSO 43rd, 50th, 55th Round, Census of India, Primary Census Abstract, 1991c, 2001.

males, and urban females separately (Round No. 43, 50 and 55). These were used to derive total workforce based on total population of these four sub-categories. Total population of these four categories were arrived at using the projection method and estimates by the Registrar General.

The workforce participation rates (WPR) of Maharashtra are fairly close to all India WPRs in case of rural and urban males as well as urban females. WPRs for rural females in Maharashtra are significantly higher than 'all-India' in all the three rounds. Generally, WPRs of the two adjacent states, Andhra Pradesh and Karnataka, (except for rural and female WPRs in Karnataka) are higher than that of Maharashtra and that of Gujarat are slightly lower than Maharashtra. It is important to observe that WPRs in all sub-categories (RM, RF, UM, UF) are falling except for the small rise in 50th Round. WPRs variations occur due to the difference between the rate of growth in size of work force and total population. As total population may be changing due to many non-comparable sources or their variable vigour and strengths of these sources (e.g. migration), we may compare rates of growth of labour force itself, growth rates of labour force by

TABLE 14.16

Work Participation Rates (Per Cent) in India, Maharashtra and Other States

States	Region	WPR 1987-88		WPR 1993-94		WPR 1999-00	
		M	F	M	F	M	F
India	Rural	53.9	32.3	55.3	32.8	53.1	29.9
	Urban	50.6	15.2	52.1	15.5	51.8	13.9
Andhra Pradesh	Rural	59.5	47.0	63.1	52.1	60.5	47.8
	Urban	50.3	21.5	54.4	19.9	51.1	17.8
Karnataka	Rural	56.8	37.7	60.4	43.0	59.5	38
	Urban	49.4	19.6	54.2	18.1	54.5	17.8
Maharashtra	**Rural**	**54.6**	**46.2**	**55.1**	**47.7**	**53.1**	**43.4**
	Urban	**49.6**	**15.9**	**52.6**	**16.9**	**53.2**	**13.7**
Gujarat	Rural	55.9	38.1	57.4	39.6	58.4	41.3
	Urban	51.0	11.2	53.5	14.2	53.6	13.5

Source: NSSO, NSS 43rd, 50th, 55th Round.

TABLE 14.17

Growth Rates of Employment between NSSO Rounds

State/Union Territory	*Region*	*CAG for 1987-1988, 1993-94*		*CAG for 1993-1994, 1999-00*	
		Male	*Female*	*Male*	*Female*
India	Rural	3.10	2.71	1.74	0.52
	Urban	4.35	4.35	3.62	1.70
Andhra Pradesh	Rural	3.30	4.13	1.23	0.26
	Urban	5.99	2.88	3.04	2.17
Karnataka	Rural	3.26	4.66	1.69	-0.55
	Urban	5.07	1.56	3.25	2.84
Gujarat	Rural	2.32	2.44	2.13	2.51
	Urban	4.59	8.66	3.63	2.58
Maharashtra	**Rural**	**2.35**	**2.63**	**1.41**	**0.07**
	Urban	**5.08**	**5.49**	**4.09**	**-0.07**
Maharashtra*	**Rural**	**2.42**	**1.04**	**0.89**	**-2.92**
	Urban	**4.65**	**4.17**	**4.19**	**1.81**

Note: *These growth rates are based on figures of workforce taken from Directorate of Economics and Statistics.

Source: NSSO, NSS 43rd, NSS 50th, and NSS 55th Rounds, GoI 1981 and 1991.

subcategories across adjacent states as well as all India. These reveal a similar pattern albeit with some notable divergences. Growth rates for Maharashtra for all sub-categories (RM, RF, UM, UF) are lower than 'All India'. In the case of urban females the growth rate between 50th and 55th Round is negative (-0.07%. p.a.).

The WPRs that we have described so far are crude WPRs and these are not age-specific. In the course of development, various processes can lead to fall in age-specific WPRs, which may result in crude WPRs to fall. (e.g. the proportion of child labour will fall; younger generation will enter labour force after attaining better training; and the requirement to work for earning livelihood for the old aged worker may also diminish due to better family/social support or higher savings). In Table 14.18, the ratio of 'persons attending education' (code 91 in NSSO data) to 'total of not in labour force' (code 91-99) is presented. It may be noted that 'attending education' happens to be the major reason for 'not being in labour force'. As per successive NSSO rounds (i.e. 37th, 43rd, 50th Round) participation of child labour (age group 5 to 14) has been consistently falling (Table 14.18).

The fall is significant in the case of urban male children (3.05 in 1977-78 to 0.92 in 1993-94) followed by rural male children (10.59 in 1977-78 to 3.10 in 1993-94). Decline in WPRs of female child labour is slower (from 10.35 to 4.35 in rural and 2.12 to 1.11 in urban). Labour participation rates for age groups 15-29 also indicate fall. WPRs in rural males of age 15-29 have fallen from 85.93 to 72.36 and 71.09 to 63.72 for urban males. One can notice a somewhat lower fall in the case of urban as well as the rural female labour force. One may reasonably speculate that the potential male workers in this age group seem to join the labour force somewhat late because many of them may be acquiring more training or investing more years in education.

TABLE 14.18

Labour Force Participation Rates for Younger Groups (Age 5-14 and 15-29)

(Per Cent)

Year	*Age Group*	*Rural*		*Urban*	
		Male	*Female*	*Male*	*Female*
1977-78	5-14	10.39	10.35	3.05	2.12
	15-29	85.93	67.54	71.09	22.29
1983	5-14	9.59	10.29	3.04	2.09
	15-29	80.28	64.9	72.47	18.75
1987-88	5-14	6.63	7.69	1.91	1.30
	15-29	78.04	61.8	67.21	16.23
1993-94	5-14	3.10	4.35	0.92	1.11
	15-29	72.36	53.26	63.57	16.58

Source: GoM, 2002a.

TABLE 14.19

Ratio of Man-days under 'Attend Education' to Man-days under 'Not in Labour Force'

Usual Activity Status		*1993-1994*				
		SR1	*SR2*	*SR3*	*SR4*	*Combined*
Rural	Males	61.26	60.71	62.39	58.93	60.83
	Females	34.09	34.52	37.37	34.43	35.08
Urban	Males	69.25	65.38	65.49	65.61	66.43
	Females	31.62	30.51	31.42	31.73	31.32
Usual Activity Status		*1999-2000*				
		SR1	*SR2*	*SR3*	*SR4*	*Combined*
Rural	Males	67.70	62.88	65.93	63.89	65.22
	Females	33.33	34.39	35.94	33.58	34.37
Urban	Males	64.50	65.71	62.42	64.08	64.07
	Females	31.02	28.70	30.24	31.06	30.27

Source: NSS State sample, Directorate of Economics and Statistics.

It may as well be because of the preparedness of the family or parents to support them for a longer period without forcing them to join the workforce. There is a tendency to report household work as the primary engagement, which causes greater reporting in the '92-99' category of NSS response.

We may now turn to another important aspect of the employment. How many people reported to be part of the labour force do not get employment? In Table 14.20 below, we present the estimates of unemployment by 'current daily status'.

TABLE 14.20

Unemployment Rate (Current Daily Status) Maharashtra

(in Per Cent)

Survey Period	*Rural*			*Urban*		
	M	*F*	*P*	*M*	*F*	*P*
1972-73	7.80	12.7	NA	NA	NA	NA
1977-78	5.85	9.31	NA	8.99	15.75	NA
1983	6.25	7.23	NA	9.05	10.44	NA
1987-88	2.90	3.50	NA	8.50	9.20	NA
1993-94	4.60	4.00	4.30	6.00	7.80	6.3
1999-00	6.30	6.90	6.50	7.70	10.00	8.10

Note: M=Male, F=Female, P=Person.

Source: MHDR, NSSO 55th Round.

The incidence of unemployment has varied widely. Beginning from 1972-73 up to 1987-88 the rural as well as urban unemployment rates have fallen. Generally, unemployment rates have been rising over the years (there are small but noticeable dips as well e.g. 1987-88 show decline in the rural unemployment rate) however, there is a rise in unemployment rates for all categories between 1993-94 and 1999-00. These estimates must be taken with all the customary caution and caveats applicable to the NSS method of eliciting response and measuring employment and unemployment.

We have estimated the 'number of workdays' worked per worker per year using the current daily status for 'principal plus subsidiary workers'. This results in very high figure of 355 and 359 days for the rural male and female respectively and 347 and 339 for the urban male and female respectively. These estimates would differ if one uses weekly status data. As similar data by weekly status are not available from NSSO we cannot prepare any alternative comparable estimate of this aspect. These number of days worked per worker per person are on very high side. This high level reported is due to the following reasons. Firstly, this data from 'state sample' relates to 'principal and secondary workers' together (i.e. 'principal plus secondary workers' combined). Secondly, even a part of the day worked is taken to be 'a day worked' as per the NSS method of enumeration and counting (Table 14.21).

TABLE 14.21

Per Person Number of Days Worked in a Year

Year	*Region*	*Sex*	*Combined*	*SR 1*	*SR 2*	*SR 3*	*SR 4*
1993-1994	Rural	M	358	88	88	89	88
		F	361	88	90	89	89
	Urban	M	350	86	86	86	88
		F	347	83	87	86	85
1999-2000	Rural	M	355	86	89	88	88
		F	359	87	89	89	89
	Urban	M	347	85	85	86	86
		F	339	82	83	84	85

Notes: Per Person number of days worked in a year are estimated as estimated person days of status 11-72 divided by estimated person days of status 11-82 multiplied by 365.

M=Male, F=Female.

Sources: NSSO, NSS 50th and 55th Rounds, Directorate of Economics and Statistics.

Whatever employment is reported to be available, does it fluctuate across seasons or months? For example, it is generally believed that seasonal fluctuations in production activity in agriculture would cause employment to fluctuate in a similar manner (if not with similar magnitude and force). A partial reflection of this is found in higher wage rates for agriculture operations that experience 'peaking'. Do such or similar fluctuation occur in unemployment rates and wage rates in other non-agricultural sectors? There is no regular and extensive data available to form a reasonable judgement.

TABLE 14.22

Table Indicating Unemployment Rates by Sub-Rounds

Usual Activity Status		*1993-1994*				
		SR1	*SR2*	*SR3*	*SR4*	*Combined*
Rural	Males	0.72	0.91	0.93	1.28	0.96
	Females	0.26	0.25	0.48	0.00	0.25
Urban	Males	3.88	3.09	4.62	2.12	3.43
	Females	6.72	2.99	4.26	3.28	4.26
Usual Activity Status		*1993-1994*				
		SR1	*SR2*	*SR3*	*SR4*	*Combined*
Rural	Males	2.05	0.75	0.93	1.53	1.32
	Females	0.96	0.65	0.30	0.31	0.63
Urban	Males	4.87	5.21	3.99	3.98	4.47
	Females	8.08	8.00	6.20	5.17	6.31

Source: NSS State Sample, Directorate of Economics and Statistics.

Yet as a partial measure, we have attempted to judge this issue by examining the sub-round data on unemployment rates and wage rates of casual labourers in agriculture. Except for some minor fluctuations no regular cyclical or strong seasonality can be asserted. The data that we used for this purpose pertain to state sample. Hence the reported rates also differ from central sample.

TABLE 14.23

Average Wage Earnings per Day Received by Casual Wage Labourers by Age Group, Type of Operation by Sex and Sub-Round

Year	*Region*	*Sex*	*Sub R1 July-Sep.*	*Sub R2 Oct.-Dec.*	*Sub R3 Jan.-Mar.*	*Sub R4 Apr.-Jun.*	*Combined*
1993-1994	Rural	M	18.93	19.38	20.95	21.92	20.32
		F	13.25	12.98	20.73	14.18	15.50
	Urban	M	21.61	27.57	25.56	20.46	23.85
		F	14.65	14.93	20.55	17.59	17.11
1999-2000	Rural	M	39.74	38.89	39.95	43.31	40.41
		F	28.89	29.91	28.13	33.44	30.05
	Urban	M	58.37	63.08	46.81	60.36	55.81
		F	28.23	40.73	39.91	25.71	33.81

Sources: NSS State sample, Directorate of Economics and Statistics.

TABLE 14.24

Real Wage Rate at 1993-94 Prices

Year	*Region*	*Sex*	*Sub R1 July-Sep.*	*Sub R2 Oct.-Dec.*	*Sub R3 Jan.-Mar.*	*Sub R4 Apr.-Jun.*	*Combined*
1993-1994	Rural	M	18.93	19.38	20.95	21.92	20.3200
		F	13.25	12.98	20.73	14.18	15.5000
	Urban	M	21.61	27.57	25.56	20.46	23.8500
		F	14.65	14.93	20.55	17.59	17.110
1999-2000	Rural	M	24.23	24.06	25.22	28.13	25.3342
		F	17.62	18.50	17.76	21.72	18.8392
	Urban	M	37.81	41.63	31.12	40.21	36.8187
		F	18.29	26.88	26.53	17.13	22.3050

Notes: M=Male, F=Female.

Source: NSS State sample, Directorate of Economics and Statistics, Economic Survey of Maharashtra, 1993-94, 1999-00.

Two important observations that can be made from the data presented in the above tables. Firstly, the wage rates appropriately deflated by CPI for rural Maharashtra published by Directorate of Economics and Statistics show that real wages of casual labourers have improved. The growth is more pronounced in the case of urban male wage rate (combined) (7.23 per cent p.a.) followed by rural male real wage rate (combined) that grew by 4.36 per cent per annum.

TABLE 14.25

Growth Rates of Real Wages between NSSO Rounds 1993-94 and 1999-00 (Based on Real Wages at 1993-94 Prices)

Region	*Sex*	*Sub R1 July.-Sep.*	*Sub R2 Oct.-Dec.*	*Sub R3 Jan.-Mar.*	*Sub R4 Apr.-Jun.*	*Combined*
Rural	M	4.20	3.67	3.14	4.24	3.74
	F	4.86	6.09	-2.55	7.36	3.31
Urban	M	9.77	7.11	3.34	11.92	7.51
	F	3.77	10.30	4.35	-0.44	4.52

Notes: M=Male, F=Female.

However, there is negative growth recorded by sub-round-to-sub-round comparison for rural female in 'sub-round 3' and urban female in 'subround 4'.

As Table 14.26 shows the female wages are usually 25 to 28 per cent lower than male wages. The variations across sub-rounds show much greater inequalities. For example, sub-round 2 of 1993-94 rural areas ratio was as low as 0.54 and for urban areas sub-round 4 of 1999-00 was even lower i.e. 0.43.

TABLE 14.26

Ratio of Wages for Females to Wages for Males

Year	*Region*	*Sub R1 July-Sep.*	*Sub R2 Oct.-Dec.*	*Sub R3 Jan.-Mar.*	*Sub R4 Apr.-Jun.*	*Combined*
1993-1994	Rural	0.70	0.67	0.99	0.65	0.76
	Urban	0.68	0.54	0.80	0.86	0.72
1999-2000	Rural	0.73	0.77	0.70	0.77	0.74
	Urban	0.48	0.65	0.85	0.43	0.61

Source: NSS State sample, Directorate of Economics and Statistics.

We may also contrast the wages as earned by casual labourers to daily wage earnings of worker employed in organised manufacturing sector. In 1993-94 the daily wage received by organised manufacturing sector (Rs. 115.7 per day) was 5.53 times higher than that of casual labourer (Rs. 18.20 per day.) Similarly, in 1999-2000, the daily wage received by organised manufacturing sector was Rs. 157.49 as against the casual wage labourer earned Rs. 36.49 per day. Thus, inequality as measured by ratio of the daily wage earnings has reduced. We may also compare the wage received on EGS, which are usually distress minimum wages available under scarcity work. Here we have nearly equal levels in 1993-94: i.e. Rs. 18.20 per day for 'casual labour' as against 18.84 for EGS work. However, wage rate for 'casual labourer' is higher

TABLE 14.27

Economic Status of Persons Categorised 'Available for Work but Not-Working' for each MPCE Class per 1000

(a) In Urban Areas

MPCE Class	*1999-2000 Urban* F	M	P	*MPCE Class*	*1993-1994 Urban* F	M	P
< 300	0	7	4	< 160	0	14	8
300-350	5	5	5	160-190	0	8	4
350-425	7	20	13	190-230	0	10	5
425-450	3	12	8	230-265	3	10	6
500-575	6	24	16	265-310	0	12	6
575-665	5	34	20	310-355	9	27	18
665-775	10	32	22	355-410	6	26	16
775-915	4	19	12	410-490	5	22	14
915-1120	11	33	23	490-605	9	27	19
1120-1500	10	30	21	605-825	11	17	14
1500-1925	13	23	18	825-1035	5	7	7
1925 <	11	13	12	1035<	5	10	8
All Classes	**7**	**23**	**16**	**All Classes**	**6**	**18**	**12**

Source: NSS State Sample, Directorate of Economics and Statistics Department.

(b) In Rural Areas

MPCE Class	*Urban* F	M	P	*MPCE Class*	*Urban* F	M	P
< 225	5	2	3	<120	0	0	0
225-255	0	0	0	120-140	0	0	0
255-300	5	3	4	140-165	0	2	1
300-340	2	7	4	165-190	0	0	0
340-380	0	3	2	190-210	0	3	2
380-420	1	6	3	210-235	0	4	2
420-470	1	9	6	235-265	1	9	5
470-525	3	7	5	265-300	0	4	2
525-615	0	10	5	300-355	1	6	3
615-775	2	14	8	355-455	1	3	2
775-950	0	10	5	455-560	2	9	6
950 <	7	11	9	560<	4	10	7
All Classes	2	7	5	All Classes	1	5	3

Source: NSS State Sample, Directorate of Economics and Statistics Department.

(Rs. 36.49 per man- day) than the EGS wage rate (Rs. 28.81 per man-day).

The unemployment rates differ by consumer expenditure classes and exhibit some interesting though not very surprising patterns. Availability of work will not always be responded to by taking up the work 'as' and 'as and when available'. This may be partly due to level of remuneration expected, partly because compulsion to work may not be stringent (a variant of voluntary unemployment). Thus, seeking work and accepting available work may be higher in lower income classes and this would result in lower unemployment rates in lower income classes and higher income classes would have relatively higher rate of unemployment. Available data does not permit us to have unemployment rates across income classes. However, we may use consumer expenditures as proxy for income and examine the rate of unemployment. These are available for years 1993-94 and 1999-00. These have been tabulated in the Tables 14.27 and Figures 14.1.

The hypothesis mentioned above is only partially supported. Data do not show linear rise in unemployment rate as consumer expenditures rise. There are marked dips and rises or breaks in the middle or mid-upper classes of expenditure group. If we plot consumer expenditures against rate of unemployment, it exhibits a parabola like shape in the case of urban male workers. Generally, the unemployment rates for expenditure classes are uniformly lower among females than males reflecting greater compulsion to work as and when available irrespective of the expenditure class.

FIGURE 14.1

Unemployment Rates by MPCE Class per Thousand Urban

(a) 1993-94

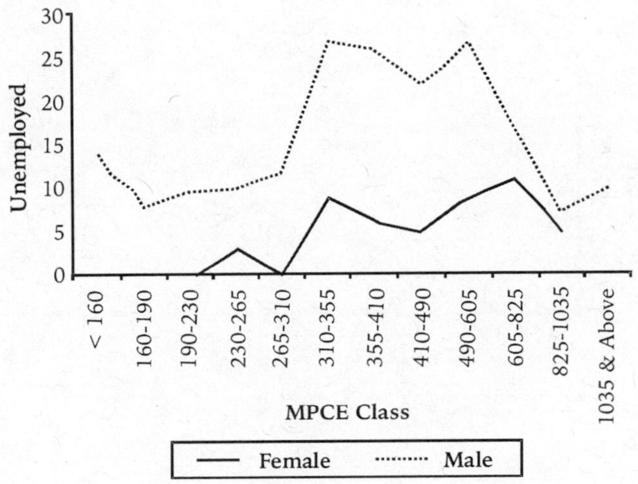

(b) 1999-2000

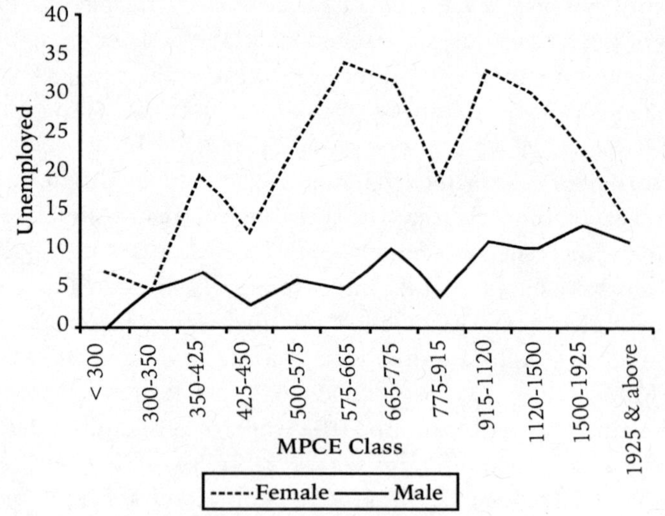

FIGURE 14.2

Unemployment Rates by MPCE Class per Thousand: Rural

(a) 1993-1994

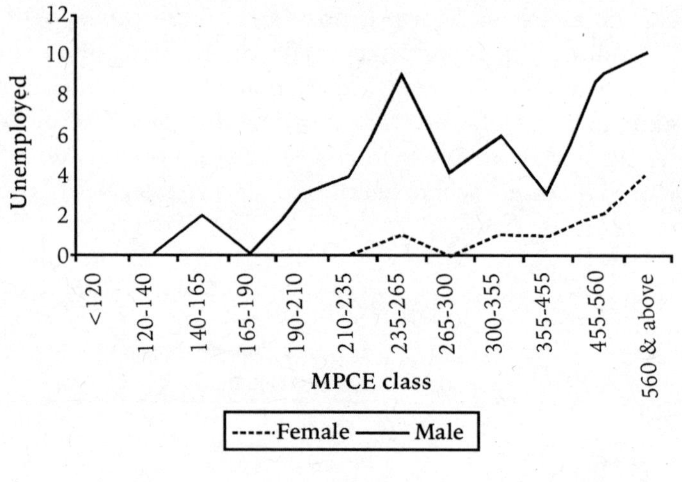

(b) 1999-2000

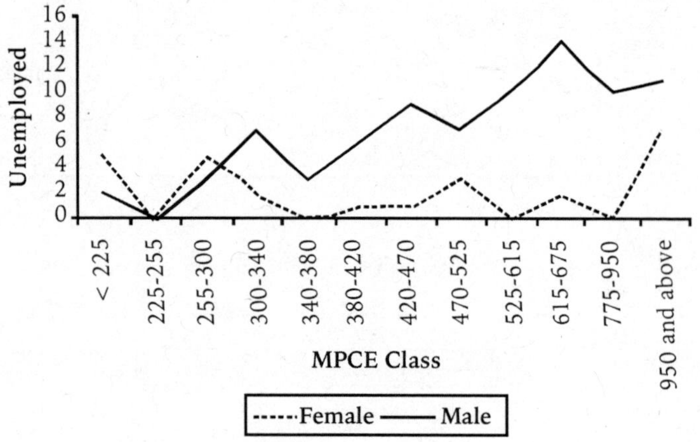

The unemployment rates for SC/ST and OBC are presented in Table 14.28, it may be remarked that the unemployment is markedly higher among these social categories. Unemployment in these social groups is uniformly higher in urban areas.

TABLE 14.28

Number of Persons Unemployed per Thousand Persons according to the Current Daily Status for Maharashtra and India (1999-2000)

Particulars	*Rural*				*Urban*			
	MS		*India*		*MS*		*India*	
	M	*F*	*M*	*F*	*M*	*F*	*M*	*F*
ST	28	25	30	15	38	18	37	11
SC	51	38	50	21	64	15	52	12
OBC	29	23	32	14	48	11	40	13

Notes: M - Male; F - Female.

Source: NSSO Report, 55th Round, September 2001.

Employment Guarantee Scheme (EGS): Overview and Appraisal

Much before the rediscovery by modern economists, the British colonial administration did recognise that real and essential nature of drought and famine lies in 'scarcity of work' rather than 'scarcity of food'. This awareness is reflected in its 'scarcity code'. EGS in Maharashtra was 'designed' to ensure availability of work for those who lacked it and demanded for the same and that too within radius of five kilometres provide number of workers demanding work were at least 50. The 'work' to be provided was designed to be labour intensive. Imposing the condition that at least 60 per cent of the total expenditure would be on wages ensures this. Moreover, 'work undertaken' should be a part of capital or asset forming expenditure programmes. All these three characteristics (work on demand with or without drought, labour intensity of work undertaken and asset creation through such works) were supposed to be distinguishing feature of the scheme that made them appear distinct from the much familiar 'scarcity works' undertaken by colonial administration. EGS was envisaged as a continuously ongoing scheme with or without drought/famine. Professional tax was levied as earmarked or 'tagged tax' to finance the expenditure needed for the provision of work on demand. In between this programme was modified to fit in the food for work programme. This was more due to the 'financial availability' as per central plan provisions. The payment of wages partly in kind i.e. foodgrain and partly in cash is not usually favoured by labourers. In particular, when they are expected to work for a continuously for longer number of days on EGS, they end up cumulating lot more grain than they hope to and manage to hold. Moreover they loose the choice of foodgrain (e.g. Sorghum rather than wheat), the quality and variety. They make up the short fall in cash wages by often reselling the grain received as wages at whatever (often unfavourable) price that is reigning in the local market. This perhaps depresses the effective wage received.

The 'Administration' has had uneven experiences in operating this scheme. After the initial few years of operation, it became increasingly difficult to locate and 'carve out and fit in' works that could meet the labour-intensity criterion. Notably, since late eighties and beginning of the nineties, a variety of works were permitted and fitted into EGS ambit. The expansion was significant and now includes soil conservation, land-levelling, bunding on private lands, horticultural and forestry plantations. The employment i.e. number of man-days generated through this programme has been shown in Table 14.29.

TABLE 14.29

EGS Performance in Maharashtra: 1993-94 to 1999-2000

Year	*Total Expenditure in Lakh Rs.*	*Employment Generated in Lakh Man-days*
1993-94	30855.25	983.99
1994-95	32607.14	942.05
1995-96	38971.39	970.16
1996-97	30281.14	901.14
1997-98	30468.48	900.06
1998-99	40884.76	918.59
1999-00	45585.89	949.39
2000-01	54085.35	1112.26
2001-02	89265.06	1616.95

Source: Monthly Progress Reports of EGS, Dept. of Planning, GoM.

It is evident from Table 14.29 that the total number of man-days generated under this scheme has been more or less stable at an average of 938 lakh man-days per year. During last two years i.e. 2000-01 and 2001-02 this has risen to 1122.26 and 1616.95 lakh man-days respectively. This sudden surge is due to drought condition in several districts. There are nearly 85 permanently drought stricken blocks or *talukas* in Maharashtra. Many of them also constitute the pockets of poverty or 'work and income scarcity'. It may be noted that Aurangabad division accounts for, on an average, one-third of the expenditure and man-days generated through EGS. In addition to the incidence of poverty and work scarcity, there are some other equally (perhaps more important) additional factors that affect the performance of EGS across districts. Some districts have a more active political leadership and greater awareness about the scheme. This results in a better 'organised demand for work' and administration is rendered more alert and responsive. On the other hand, part of the difference also lies in *suo motu* preparedness and keenness of administrative leadership to implement the schemes available in imaginative and enthusiastic manner.

Again, if we use a suitable deflator, the real wages in the EGS have slightly gone up. EGS wages are statutorily fixed as equal to minimum wage rates for agricultural labourers in class three towns and drought prone areas. Thus, the revision usually (though not always) keeps pace with the rise in CPIAL. However, EGS wages are likely to have grown slower than wage rates of casual labour prevalent in the market. For example, EGS wages were approximately Rs.18 to 19 per man-day in 1993-94.

This is almost equal to the rural causal agricultural labour wage rate. However, the EGS wages per day work out to be Rs. 28 to 29 per man-day, as against market-wage rate of a 'casual agriculture labourer' of Rs. 36. However, the wage rate level need not be the only primary determinant of EGS attendance. It is the relative scarcity of work and availability of work during a particular season at a particular place. It is further conditioned by the organisational requirement of minimum number of workers to be available and demanding work. These organisational conditions generally explain the role played by 'labour contractors'. They are officially forbidden to be part of the EGS but they happen to be the real promoters and *modus operandi* managers of labour societies. Mobilisation of workforce to meet the attendance needed at the worksites is in some place facilitated by politically alert leadership or unions/organisation of workers. Estimation of the actual feasible labour attendance and materialising of the same, carving out the work components in different admissible categories of development expenditure are some of the critical problems in operating this scheme.

TABLE 14.30

Expenditure and Employment through EGS by Districts and Divisions

Year	*Region*	*Total Exp. (Lakh Rs.) (a)*	*EGM*	*% to Total (a)*	*% to Total (b)*	*Estimated Wage*
1993-1994	Konkan	2426.18	70.36	7.86	7.15	20.69
	Nashik	4952.77	155.61	16.05	15.81	19.10
	Pune	5767.11	194.78	18.69	19.79	17.8
	Aurangabad	9645.11	308.41	31.26	31.34	18.86
	Amravati	3164.64	97.80	10.26	9.94	19.41
	Nagpur	4899.43	165.76	15.88	16.85	17.73
	Maharashtra	**30855.25**	**983.99**	**100.00**	**100.00**	**18.81**
1995-1996	Konkan	3411.02	79.36	8.75	8.18	25.79
	Nashik	5928.47	150.28	15.21	15.49	23.67
	Pune	9522.38	272.12	24.43	28.05	20.99
	Aurangabad	12852.74	311.36	32.98	32.09	24.77
	Amravati	3325.99	73.24	8.53	7.55	27.25
	Nagpur	3930.79	83.80	10.09	8.64	28.14
	Maharashtra	**38971.39**	**970.16**	**100.00**	**100.00**	**24.10**
1997-1998	Konkan	3771.19	99.6	12.38	11.07	22.72
	Nashik	4364.22	124.78	14.32	13.86	20.98
	Pune	4370.69	112.71	14.34	12.52	23.27
	Aurangabad	9616.99	313.12	31.56	34.79	18.43
	Amravati	3096.62	92.72	10.16	10.30	20.04
	Nagpur	5247.77	156.13	17.22	17.35	20.17
	Maharashtra	**30468.48**	**900.06**	**100.00**	**100.00**	**20.31**
1999-2000	Konkan	6490.03	136.61	14.24	14.39	28.50
	Nashik	7428.89	148.50	16.30	15.64	30.01
	Pune	3610.35	72.80	7.92	7.67	29.75
	Aurangabad	15538.22	329.24	34.09	34.68	28.32
	Amravati	5130.12	109.66	11.25	11.55	28.07
	Nagpur	7388.28	161.58	16.21	17.02	27.43
	Maharashtra	**45585.89**	**949.39**	**100.00**	**100.00**	**28.81**
2000-2001	Konkan	6346.84	134.43	11.73	12.09	28.33
	Nashik	10466.20	217.22	19.35	19.53	28.91
	Pune	4930.31	96.48	9.12	8.67	30.66
	Aurangabad	18582.61	384.89	34.36	34.60	28.97
	Amravati	6391.55	131.72	11.82	11.84	29.11
	Nagpur	7367.84	147.52	13.62	13.26	29.97
	Maharashtra	**54085.35**	**1112.26**	**100.00**	**100.00**	**29.17**
2001-2002	Konkan	8806.03	162.23	9.87	10.03	32.57
	Nashik	15794.73	285.45	17.69	17.65	33.20
	Pune	7877.02	141.11	8.82	8.73	33.49
	Aurangabad	35604.09	647.18	39.89	40.02	33.01
	Amravati	9766.74	177.40	10.94	10.97	33.03
	Nagpur	11416.45	203.58	12.79	12.59	33.65
	Maharashtra	**89265.06**	**1616.95**	**100.00**	**100.00**	**33.12**

Note: EGM- Employment generated man-days in lakh.

Source: Monthly Progress Reports of EGS, Department of Planning, GoM.

Policy Issues

Employment has its own evolutionary concomitant and determinant factors. In registered manufacturing sector elasticity of employment (measured as number. of workers as well as man-days worked) with respect to manufacturing SDP is 0.14. Elasticity estimate with respect to 'gross capital formation' is also of a similar magnitude. These estimates indicate the historical response rate of employment with respect to concomitant and contemporaneous factors like output and investment. As Report of the Steering Committee on Labour and Employment for the Tenth Five Year Plan (Chairman: S. P. Gupta) has argued, the principal source that will generate additional employment will not be large enterprises organised sector. The informal and tiny small and medium size establishments hold better promise of employment growth. The patterns of employment growth in formal and informal segments discussed earlier support this judgement. However, it may be pointed out that the relationship between 'informal' and 'formal' could be complementary as well as competitive. In sectors, where scale economies are not important in production but economies of size and scale do matter in trading and marketing (transport, distribution networks, brand building, etc.), small and tiny would be the 'procurement centres' for large enterprises. On the other hand, in many local and regional markets small and medium enterprises will be able to effectively compete and survive with large sized producers. Moreover, it should be emphasised that the role of the government and efficacy of the government assistance schemes in promotion of the SMEs or informal segment enterprises will be limited. Several of the factors that influence the success of SMEs or informal segment entities are not amenable to easy monitoring, replication, assistance and/or regulation. Government agencies engaged in training, information services, and markets intelligence or market building may be helpful in providing appropriate policy responses. However, the schemes involving subsidies, may be infeasible and/or undesirable in the present precarious fiscal situation. Moreover, these are not likely to be very effective or capable of any significant push or impact on employment.

There are some other policy measures that deserve consideration. The experience of Western Maharashtra districts suggest that diversification of agriculture raises absorption of labour and affords better employment potential. For this purpose, introduction of new crop-mix (as well as varietal diversification) in arid regions and increase in protective irrigation wherever feasible is very crucial. Similarly, the government should consider reform of agricultural marketing to allow direct marketing by farmers' companies and societies and amend laws to accommodate this possibility. In the manufacturing sector, emphasis should be on food processing industries and investments in post-harvest infrastructure should be focused. Both of these afford considerable growth of employment opportunities in storage handling and transport. It will be necessary to overhaul and upgrade the system of ITIs by handing over their management to private business houses and other bodies under joint management MoUs. In the service sector policy efforts and investments by the state are most needed in strengthening tourism and transport. Thus, to summarise diversification of agriculture, post-harvest operations and storage, food processing, packaging, tourism, primary education, other services would be the thrust areas of employment growth. These areas compare well with the nature of thrust areas identified by the Gupta Committee Report.

Apart from the policy initiatives mentioned above, the ability of the government to influence the volume of employment available is generally limited. There are three principal ways in which the government can hope to have an effect on employment: (i) government can raise the demand for goods and services with the hope that multiplier effect will enhance employment; (ii) it can strengthen and support specific sections or activities in anticipation of market trends and bolster the market trends. This also includes regulatory efforts to promote as well as prohibit some of the practices e.g. child labour, discriminatory wages, bonded labour; and (iii) it can increase demand for labour by undertaking works that are socially productive and useful.

Presently, the Government of Maharashtra has been operating one or the other expenditure programme that fits into the types of policy interventions mentioned above. Government's 'development expenditures on capital account other than repayment of loans' is a measure of new additional demand directly induced by government budgetary activity. Ability to raise these expenditures depends on the plan schemes, burden of past debt and credit rating. It is well known that 1997 onwards, the financial ability of state governments has weakened. Maharashtra is no exception. Out of total expenditures 'development expenditures' account for 55 per cent. One can at best hope more economic application of resources (without time overruns and overshooting of expenditures) resulting in better and greater effective availability of resources. This is an onerous serious constraint. Lack of saving, inability to attract FDI, high cost of power, high cost of credit, poor and unreliable infrastructure unimaginative and mindless regulations, untargeted non-merit subsidies are the well-known factors that have caused retardation of output and employment opportunities. Given fiscal constraints, incremental improvements in the existing capacity would be the best that one can hope.

Plan programmes include several promotional measures aimed at enhancing skills, training for commencing and conducting the business e.g. TRYSEM. There are no credible studies that evaluate the efficacy of these programmes. State's spending on education and training has been a crucial factor. Given the faster rise in service sector one expects more growth of labour and skill intensive job opportunities. Availability of training and educational facilities will be one of the long-term factors that would condition the supply response of the labourers. Administrative flexibility and market orientation of pre-existing training and educational institutions will become even more crucial. Relatively low 'work participation rates' in urban areas need further exploration. We need further understanding and insight about the factors that influence the WPRs.

EGS has been operative for a long period. As pointed earlier, the objective in EGS design was to overcome the scarcity syndrome of providing 'work' in drought years. Instead it hoped to establish permanent organised programme of productive works that can provide for employment for whosoever demands for it at any period of any year. There are several difficulties in running the scheme. Most notable among them are two fold. Firstly, labourers do not have the propensity to migrate for work, even temporarily, away from their normal residential place. In some districts, it has been found that willing migrants from adjacent states have attendance that is more frequent on EGS works. Given the 'radius limitation' on place of work and type of works (labour intensity criterion) administration is constrained in responding and realigning the resources quickly. We did not find strong evidence suggesting that EGS causes labour scarcity and artificial upward push in wages. As NSS data on casual wages of agricultural labourers indicate that EGS wages may in fact be little lower than market rates. Thus, EGS perhaps provides, effective floor to rural or agriculture wage rates. However, availability of EGS works opportunities is very uneven across districts. The rise in 'casual labour wage rate in agriculture' must have been due to few other factors as well. Hence, upward trend in agriculture wage rate cannot be attributed to EGS alone.

Again as pointed out earlier, success of the programme depends on 'scarcity of work', political awareness and administrative enthusiasm and alertness. In this sense the EGS has yet to come out of the scarcity syndrome completely. Nonetheless, when favourable factors exist, this scheme has been the only effective programme against unemployment that government has been able to administer. It is a self-targeting scheme that provides for work and income. Compared to many other anti-poverty programmes it is perhaps 'less wasteful' and 'better targeted'. Due to inadequate and untimely precipitation, the demand for EGS works went up by nearly 15 per cent in last two years. In the drought prone areas of more developed districts like Pune also the attendance on EGS work has surged. Surprisingly, no such 'natural buoyancy in the demand for work' has been noticed in the poorest of the districts. This underlines the importance and relevance of political awareness and administrative responsiveness. Only if both of these factors work in a conducible way this scheme appears to be a tenable intervention. Yet, it should be pointed out that EGS cannot be the principal programme against unemployment. It cannot tackle more than 30 per cent of the unemployment even if one assumes very low unemployment rate of 3 per cent. The additional employment needed to eliminate rest of the unemployment must come from growth of the economic activity itself. Therefore, provision of better growth enhancing and 'investment-friendly' policy environment, prudent tax and fiscal regime, reliable and affordable infrastructure turn out to be the principal factors, and no one else but the government can provide these.

Chapter 15

Water and Environment

Introduction

Maharashtra is one of the most industrialised and populated states in India. This makes concerns for environmental degradation in Maharashtra far more serious than those in the other states in the country. In fact, Maharashtra is among the foremost states that encountered the problems of environmental pollution and also took action to tackle them (GoM, 2003b).

The problems of water resources in the state are related to both depletion and pollution. While the issues in rural areas are lack of water supply infrastructure and difficult access to safe water, in urban areas, the ever-increasing demand, inadequate and sub-standard quality of services are endemic. High levels of indoor and ambient air pollution are of serious concern in the state. Industries and vehicles are major man-made sources of ambient air pollution, and low quality of fuels, create indoor air pollution. Noise level, particularly, in urban regions are at alarming stage. Solid waste problems, due to concentration of population and wasteful consumption patterns, are more obvious in urban areas. Inefficient solid waste management (SWM) has led to significant land degradation. Growing demand for fuel, fodder, agricultural and industrial production is fast depleting forest and biodiversity, resulting in the loss of genetic diversity in the region.

Thus, almost all of the natural and environmental resources in the state are under stress due to anthropogenic activities. Major sectors identified in this chapter are–Water Resources, (including water supply and sanitation, freshwater pollution and coastal pollution), Air Pollution, Noise Pollution, Solid Waste Management, Land Degradation, Forests and Biodiversity, Climate Change Issues, Trade and Environment linkages, Environmental Education and Environmental Policy. The objective is to review the state of each sub-sector and, based upon the analysis of available data and information, suggest measures for an efficient environmental management.

Water Resources

The quantity of inland water resources in Maharashtra accounts for only 4.93 per cent of the total availability in India. Since the state houses more than 9 per cent of the country's population, per capita water availability in the state is lower than the national average. Rivers and lakes are the main sources of surface water, but water flow of two major river basins in the state (Krishna and Godavari) is much below the national average. While the average annual surface water potential for an Indian river is 1,869 km^3 per year, it is only 110.54 km^3 per year for the Godavari basin and 78.12 km^3 per year for the Krishna basin (MoWR, 2003).

The distribution of annual rainfall is highly uneven with Konkan region receiving as high as 2500 mm and Marathwada as low as 800 mm of rainfall per annum. The precipitation is concentrated between the months of June and September, particularly in the Konkan and Sahyadri regions. About 90 per cent of the land in the state has basaltic rock, which is non-porous and prevents rainwater percolation into the ground and makes the area drought-prone. Most of the districts (19 out of 35) show fall in the groundwater level during the post-monsoon period over 20 cm per year and it has continued for about last 20 years (1981-2000). In 2001, drought-affected about 20,000 villages in 23 districts, 28.4 million people and 4.5 million hectares of crops. Several districts including Ahmednagar, Dhule, Sangli, Satara, Solapur, Beed, Osmanabad, Latur, Nashik have been affected by severe water scarcity (GoM, 2003c).

However, lack of water management, rather than natural scarcity of water, is the main reason for drought. Since 1960, government has spent over Rs.16,000 crores on rural water supply and yet there are around 20,000 drought affected villages and 45 million people without safe and secure water. The reasons for problems being perpetual appear to be as follows. Firstly, political interests connected to the sugar baron lobby have resulted in accelerated growth of sugarcane, a highly water intensive crop, cultivated in areas, which get lesser rainfall than even the desert state of Rajasthan. Sugarcane crop is grown only on 3 per cent of the irrigated area, but it consumes almost 70 per cent of the water consumed by all crops. Secondly, mismanagement of the resources by state authorities is responsible for the water scarcity. Though Maharashtra has the largest number of dams in the country, only 17 per cent of its agricultural land is irrigated. Despite ample resources and water related schemes, government regulations are such that problems do not have solutions. For example, if any farmer wants to replace a defective pump for his bore well, the regulation requires that replacement of the pump and bore well should be done together (Martyris, 2003).

Water Supply Scenario

Safe and regular water supply is a necessary aspect of development, but wide disparities exist in water supply in urban and rural areas of the state. As far as urban population is concerned, all 247 urban centres have piped water supply schemes for drinking, though the supply of water is not adequate as per the standard laid down by the Government of India. Similarly, the coverage of rural population with adequate public drinking water supply is about 70 per cent (GoM, 2003c).

Maharashtra was the first state to prepare a White Paper on Water and Sanitation in June 1995, following which the GoM established a separate department for water supply and sanitation for better coordination of the sector. As per the policy approved by the state government, the water supply and sanitation department (WSSD) implements the programmes for provision of drinking water supply services through the Maharashtra Jeevan Pradhikaran (MJP), the Groundwater Survey and Development Agency (GSDA), and the *zilla parishads* (ZPs). The MJP is responsible for the design and construction of water and wastewater schemes in urban and rural areas and mobilisation of resources on behalf of the local bodies.

Considering the need for sectoral reforms, in January 2000, the GoM established the Sukthankar Committee to prepare a road map for improved provision of water and sewerage services in rural and urban areas. Subsequently, the WSSD has, with the inputs from the Committee, undertaken several positive steps, which include extensive consultation workshops for rural water supply and for introduction of sector reforms, improved groundwater management, introduction of efficiency improvement and private sector participation (PSP) in the urban water supply sector. The GoM has also introduced a sectoral reforms package for rural water supply along the lines of GoI guidelines and restructured the urban capital grants programme to provide incentives for efficiency improvement.

In order to achieve substantial and far-reaching reforms in the water sector, the Committee strongly recommended the establishment of an independent Maharashtra Water and Wastewater Regulatory Commission (MWRC). The MWRC would be responsible for regulating both water supply and wastewater disposal services. However, sanitation aspects such as solid waste management and low cost sanitation are proposed to be excluded from the purview of the MWRC (GoM, 2003b).

Urban Situation

The share of urban population in Maharashtra is about 42.4 per cent as against a national average of 27.8 per cent (GoM, 2003b). Mumbai, Pune and Nagpur are among the 15 most populous agglomerations in India. Therefore, satisfying the basic needs of water and sanitation poses a challenge for the authorities. Data from MJP show that the water supply levels in urban areas are inadequate as only 15.3 per cent local bodies satisfied the norms of per capita water consumption. The disparity in the amount of water supply in various urban centres as well as within different areas of a city is very striking. For example, though Mumbai has a maximum water supply of 200 lpcd, on an average, the supply in different areas of the city is very much skewed. While slum areas of Mumbai are not getting even 90 lpcd, the well-off areas receive as high as 300-350 lpcd (GoM, 2003d). Water quality is also not very satisfactory and, on an average, in 2000-01 Mumbai showed the highest contamination at 15 per cent compared to Pune (1.3 per cent), Nashik (1.08 per cent), Navi Mumbai (9.26 per cent) and Thane (4 per cent). The main reasons for high level of contamination are inappropriate sanitation, absence or inadequate dose of the disinfectant and recontamination in the distribution network (PHD, 1999; NEERI, 2002).

Over use and misuse of water can be observed in various human activities. Due to intermittent water supply system, it is the normal practice of every household to store more water than needed. When fresh water is to be stored, the old stock of the previous day is just thrown away to empty the containers. Unnecessary keeping the water tap running, while bathing, shaving and so on, is a common feature. Excessive use of water for gardening not only spoils the plants but also results in wastage. Leakage from water mains, feeder lines and public and private taps is a common and neglected phenomenon. It is estimated that, on an average, for domestic use about 20-50 per cent water is wasted in urban areas such as Mumbai (IDFC, 2003).

Rural Situation

About 64 per cent of villages and 72 per cent of *wadis* (hamlets) have a per capita water supply of more than 40 lpcd with duration of supply varying from one to three hours per day (data as of April 2002). A majority of the rural piped water supply schemes does not supply water at designed pressure. At various retail delivery points, pressure is almost negligible and consumers have to wait for an inordinately long time to fill their vessels. Even in the cases where water is available, the quality of drinking water is not satisfactory. Limited surveys conducted in rural areas show that average bacteriological contamination is 32 per cent and in some rural areas of Pune district it is as high as 66 per cent.

In rural areas, effective and sustainable management of water resources and proper maintenance of water supply infrastructure are the key issues. And therefore, many rural water supply and sanitation schemes have been initiated in the state. The Government of Maharashtra implements the rural water schemes through two main programmes, namely, the Accelerated Rural Water Supply Programme (ARWSP) funded by the Government of India and the Minimum Needs Programme (MNP). It is obligatory on the part of the state to provide, under MNP, funds at least on a matching basis in relation to the Central allocation for the ARWSP. Specific projects are also funded with the financial assistance made available by the World Bank and bilateral funding agencies (GoM, 2003b).

All new programmes based on the new policy of community-led demand-driven principles, namely Government of India sponsored Sector Reform Programme, Swajaldhara Programme, Prime Minister's 15 August Special Programme, PMGY Programme, World Bank aided Jalswarajya Project and even any new schemes in ARWSP and MNP are planned and implemented at *gram panchayat* level. Thus, planning, implementation, operation and maintenance of the programmes are now entrusted to the villages.

Recently, the GoM has launched Sant Gadgebaba Urban Cleanliness Drive and Jawaharlal Nehru Clean City Campaign, which is one of its revolutionary programmes. Sant Gadgebaba Clean Village Campaign, initially implemented in rural areas, has received wide popularity in a very short span. And the favourable response has resulted in its espousal in urban areas from November 2002 onwards. Many organisations participate in this campaign and the best performers are suitably rewarded. However, the main hurdle in continuation of campaign is availability of funds. The campaign needs an estimated amount of Rs. 10 crore that includes prize distribution costs of Rs. 731 lakhs and other expenses including publicity and propaganda costs of Rs. 269 lakhs. It was decided that the provision for Rs. 10 crore per year will be made by MHADA and the funds will be handed over to the state government. But, as of November 2002, MHADA has been able to provide only 10 per cent of the total amount (GoM, 2003c).

As of March 2001, MJP, the main implementing agency for ARWSP, revealed that there were 4,390 schemes sanctioned for execution, of which only 1,474 schemes were completed, and 1,666 were in progress, which require huge funds for completion (CAG, 2000-01).

Status of Sanitation

Sanitation facilities in both urban and rural areas of state are highly inadequate. According to the 54th Round of the NSS (1999), about 46 per cent of the population in Maharashtra had access to sanitation facilities.

In rural areas, as of 1997, only 6.25 per cent of the rural population had provision of sanitation, which due to government initiative, increased to about 20 per cent by 2002 (GoM and WSP-SA, 2002). Despite a subsidy programme of the state government providing 87.5 per cent of the cost for the construction of toilets between 1997 and 2000, it was found that 57 per cent of the toilets constructed under this programme were not being used. Thus, mere provision of facilities has proved insufficient to solve the problems of rural sanitation. And, the concept of total hygiene and creating awareness among the rural masses is essential.

In urban areas, about 84 per cent of the urban population, as per the 54th round of the NSS, has access to sanitation facilities as compared to Kerala (95 per cent), Punjab (85.2 per cent) and West Bengal

(84.8 per cent). The amount of wastewater generation in major towns of Maharashtra (Table 15.1) shows that the domestic sector accounts for a predominant share. Very few towns have properly planned sewerage systems. While in Konkan and Western Maharashtra regions, about 45 per cent of the local bodies have underground drainage (UGD); in Marathwada and Vidarbha regions this figure is only 23.5 per cent. Even if a particular region or city has UGD, it is not necessary that the whole area under region or city must be covered. In Sangli-Miraj-Kupwad (SMK) Municipal Corporation, for example, only 51 out of the 68 wards have UGD facility with some wards being only partially covered. Consequently, about 99 per cent of the sewage generated by the municipal councils and over 50 per cent of sewage discharged by municipal corporation goes untreated. In many cases, the sewage treatment plants (STPs) constructed long back for a much less capacity are overloaded now. Thus, possibility of the untreated sewage discharged into the rivers is high, which pollutes drinking water sources of many towns downstream.

TABLE 15.1

Wastewater Generation in Maharashtra (2001-02)

Region/City	*Wastewater Generation (MLD)*	
	Sewage	*Effluent*
Konkan		
Mumbai	2271.00	240.0
Navi Mumbai	143.52	-
Thane (2001)	160.00	0.03
Pune		
Pune	265.00	-
Sangli-Miraj-	(sewage and effluent)	
Kupwad	48.645	
Nashik		
Nashik	160.0	29.39

Source: Environmental State Reports of various MCs (2001-03).

The data on wastewater collection is insufficient and is available for only three cities i.e. Mumbai, Nagpur and Pune. A study by CPCB in 2000 showed that though 83 per cent of wastewater was collected in Maharashtra (Class I and Class II cities), only 13.3 per cent was actually treated (UNEP, 2001).

Fresh-water Pollution

Various water supply sources such as rivers and lakes in the state are under the threat of getting contaminated due to over-abstraction of groundwater and also due to other man-made interventions like excess use of fertilisers (mostly urea), mixing of untreated effluent in drinking water resources and industrial pollution. Based upon the information from Maharashtra Pollution Control Board (MPCB), Comptroller and Auditor General (CAG) report observed that the aggregate sewage discharged by 219 councils was 1,050 MLD (as on March 2000), out of which only 14 MLD was adequately treated and the remaining 1,036 MLD (almost 99 per cent) was discharged untreated. Only three municipal councils of Lonavala, Ahmednagar and Pandharpur undertook some treatment before discharging the wastewater into the rivers (ToI, 2002).

Analysis of the data from sub-regional offices of MPCB and department of environment, GoM shows that effluents from many of the industries in Thane, Raigad, Kolhapur and Sangli have a very high BOD load. Out of 9,135 industries only 4,657 (about 51 per cent) were providing wastewater treatment facilities. Many of the districts such as Akola, Buldhana, Nagpur and Nashik have very low performance in terms of industrial wastewater treatment as only 2 to 8 per cent of industries were providing treatment facilities. Even in the Konkan region, less than 50 per cent of industries have treatment facilities. However, the data show that almost all industries (more than 95 per cent) having treatment facilities were able to treat their effluent despite the fact that very few districts had satisfactory CETP facilities.

River Pollution

Of the total wastewater and solid waste released into Godavari river basin, Maharashtra's share is 40.5 per cent and 42 per cent, respectively. Most of the industrial activities are located in Aurangabad and Nashik districts and distillery units are the largest polluters in the state followed by pharmaceuticals, leather, pulp and paper and pesticide units. Nashik is the most polluting city in terms of both wastewater and solid waste generation. Hingoli is a major contributor of wastewater and Ahmednagar accounts for about 17 per cent of solid waste generation. The stretch from Nashik to Nanded is particularly polluted with wastewater contributed from domestic and industrial sources.

The share of Maharashtra in wastewater and solid waste released into the Krishna river basin forms only 2 per cent and 3 per cent, respectively. Satara accounts for the largest share and releases about 32.5 per cent and 22.9 per cent of wastewater and solid waste, respectively, followed by Karad. Hence, the stretch of the river from Karad to Sangli is highly polluted due to release of effluents, mainly from sugar industries and distilleries.

Tapi River Basin within Maharashtra receives about 46.3 per cent and 42.4 per cent of total wastewater and solid waste discharged into it, respectively. Jalgaon and Dhule account for the largest share of wastes released into Tapi within the state. Industrial effluents coupled with sewage make the river highly polluted during the summer months when river flow is the least. Kolhapur city discharges about 81 MLD of municipal wastewater into the Panchaganga river. The municipal STP set up in 1976 has a capacity of 29.8 MLD and is grossly inadequate. As a result, the remaining wastewater gets discharged into the river without any treatment. Moreover, only primary treatment is given, which is insufficient for satisfying prevailing river water standards. Obsolete machinery with poor upkeeping has added to the pollution in the river (Deshmukh *et al.,* 2003).

Thus, continuous flow of untreated or partially treated wastewater into the rivers has degraded their water quality considerably. Based on the CPCB guidelines majority of the rivers in Maharashtra fall in the 'D' category with respect to BOD (i.e. they can neither be used as drinking water source nor for outdoor bathing). The water is capable of propagating wildlife and can be used for irrigation, industrial cooling and controlled waste disposal. Data show that since 1994, most of the rivers have been in the 'D' category, while the desired category is 'C' (which refers to drinking water source after conventional treatment or higher). The results obtained from the regional offices of the MPCB indicate that out of 98 monitoring stations, 40 stations show deterioration in river water quality. The state classification of rivers is designated as A-I, A-II, A-III and A-IV in decreasing order of water quality. Accordingly, the overall water quality of rivers observed in the state is more or less within the limits of A-II class, i.e, water to be used only after conventional treatment.

Lake Pollution

The Lonar saltwater lake in Buldhana, located in the world's oldest meteoric crater, is coming under threat as a result of unchecked sewage flow. There has been an increase in the water level in the lake, decreasing its salinity levels. Such changes could also affect the ecosystem, which is unique to the area. For example, three rare spider species and two scorpion species belong to this area (Gokhale, 2003). Similarly, the Powai lake in Mumbai is also under stress as a result of wastewater flowing from nearby slums, industrial and residential complexes and silting problems. This has been included, along with 21 other urban lakes, in the National Lake Conservation Programme (NLCP) of the Ministry of Environment and Forests (MoEF), Government of India (GoI) started in 1995. In Pune, three lakes namely, Katraj, Pashan and Model Colony lakes, are also being included in the NLCP.

Coastal Pollution

Natural beauty and availability of livelihood resources have resulted in concentration of population in coastal areas. However, people perceive the ocean as a bottomless pit, which can accumulate and assimilate unlimited quantity of pollutants, and therefore, they go on releasing waste into it, causing harm to marine

FIGURE 15.1

Share of Maharashtra in Generation and Collection of Municipal Wastewater (mld) Among Important Coastal States in India

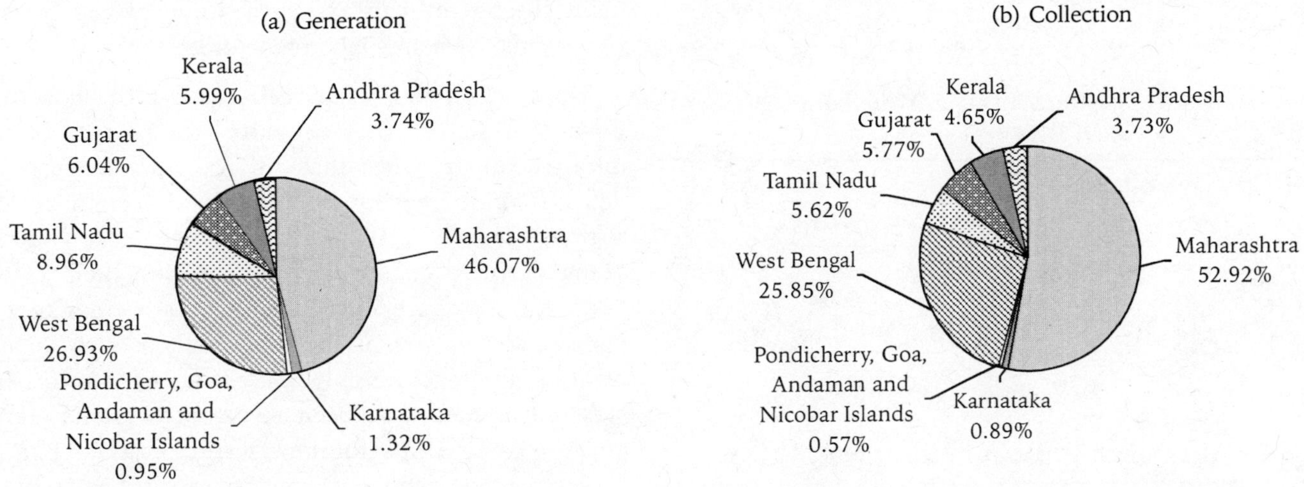

Source: CPCB (2002a).

ecosystem. Maharashtra leads both in generation and collection of wastewater among all coastal states in India. It generates about 46 per cent of the total wastewater generated by all coastal states in India and collects about 52.9 per cent of its generated wastewater as shown in Figure 15.1.

In fact, in terms of all parameters including supply of water, wastewater generation, wastewater disposal into the sea, both treated as well as untreated, Maharashtra ranks first among all the coastal states in India. About 3000 million litres of wastewater is discharged into the sea in Mumbai alone. The CAG report noted that the seawater in Mumbai is highly polluted and unfit for bathing, water sports and commercial fishing (ToI, 2002). The Coastal Regulation Zone (CRZ) needs to be properly implemented as they are of vital importance in preventing the coastal pollution.

Effects of Water Pollution

Many regions in the state receive poor water quality in terms of physical, chemical and bacteriological parameters. As many as 875 and 1183 villages, spread over 28 districts, are affected by excess iron and fluorides, respectively. Of all water resources, about 7 per cent had fluoride problem, 8.2 per cent nitrate contamination and about 3 per cent had iron problem. Most of these villages are located in Sindhudurg, Ratnagiri, Raigadh, Thane, Solapur, Nagpur, Chandrapur, Yavatmal, Nanded and Ahmednagar districts.

Chemical and bacteriological contamination of groundwater has severe and serious health hazards as can be seen from the number of cases on various ailments reported from rural areas during 1999-2002 (Table 15.2). Reports from PHD show that, on an average, 1.2 million people are affected every year and about 350 people die of bacteriological contamination in drinking water. However, the trend analysis of attacks and deaths, due to water borne diseases, between 1997 and 2002 indicate progressive decline (PHD, 2002). This is due to increased availability of clean drinking water and health services provided by GoM under various programmes.

TABLE 15.2

Year-wise Attacks and Deaths Due to Waterborne Diseases in Rural Areas

Disease	*1999-2000*		*2000-2001*		*2001-2002*	
	Attacks	*Deaths*	*Attacks*	*Deaths*	*Attacks*	*Deaths*
Gastro	65067	68	82479	128	67295	119
Diarrhoea	1023194	18	1146395	31	1104841	16
Inf. Hepatitis	16159	289	13343	197	12066	142
Typhoid	13079	3	15438	5	13320	7
Cholera	348	1	1043	4	1326	3
Total	**1117847**	**379**	**1258662**	**365**	**1198848**	**287**

Source: PHD, GoM (2002).

The records during 1995-2002 in a hospital in Mumbai show that, on an average, about 50 per cent of the cases are related to water borne diseases like gastro (diarrhoea), enteric fever (typhoid) and hepatitis B (jaundice). The effects of these diseases are more prevalent among children below 12 years of age. Seasonal variation of incidence of diarrhoea remains constant over the years or stable during the pre-monsoon and post-monsoon periods, but there is a sharp increase in the cases during the monsoon season. This indicates the possibility of mixing of sewage with water supply sources and supply mains (Sharma, 2002).

Governance in Water and Sanitation

Water tariff levels are uniformly low in almost all districts of Maharashtra. To break even, in terms of just maintenance expenses and staff salaries, the urban local bodies (ULBs) will probably need to charge 2 to 2.5 times their current tariffs. It must be highlighted that BMC, has had, a historically healthy surplus, in water and sewerage account. However, in other MCs, the cost recovery is lesser than the operation and maintenance expenditure. Deficits of local bodies on the water supply and sewerage account have been as high as 95 per cent in Nagpur and as low as 17 per cent in Sangli-Miraj-Kupwad (SMK), as per the data for 1999-00. The main reason for this is the attitude of the people to view water as a free gift of nature.

However, it has been realised that the government does not have the capacity to invest in huge infrastructure projects that are necessary to sustain the demand of increasing population, especially in urban regions. Hence, private sector participation (PSP) is being actively encouraged in services such as water supply, sewerage and solid waste management. Maharashtra is one of the foremost states to undertake reforms in water supply and sewerage services. The state government has been giving both grants and loan guarantees to ULBs for new water projects. But these projects have been suffering from problems of poor operations and maintenance (O&M), inefficient customer service, water leakage, unauthorised connections, theft, and low energy conservation of existing systems.

Unaccounted-for-water (UFW), which is the difference between amount of water supplied and water sold, ranges as high as 50 to 65 per cent in the state. As a part of the reform process in the SMK Municipal Corporation, PSP is being undertaken in the area of water and sewerage, accounting reforms, energy and water leak detection audits, solid waste management, resource mobilisation and improved service access to the poor (FIRE (D), 2002). While data on actual leakage levels do not exist, in most cases, they are estimated to be in the range of 40 to 55 per cent.

However, due to lack of success of PSP, there are also opinions against the privatisation of water resources. For example, of the six first generation privatisation projects taken up, four have been abandoned. Pune, which was the first city to undertake PSP in its water and sewerage project, had to cancel it due to political pressure (Das, 2002). Since private participation is for a profit motive, it is bound to push up prices, which will create social inequities, as water is a necessity of life. Further, private companies are prompt in disconnecting the supply on non-payment of bills, which can be a crucial issue in a developing country like India. The main motive for bringing in PSP in the water sector is for investment purposes but, due to low possibility of returns in water sector, this may not happen similar to other infrastructure projects (Dharmadhikary, 2003).

On the other hand, there is some scope for people's participation and small-scale private initiatives (SPI) as there have been some success stories on this account. In Kolhapur district, the water mandal of four villages has maintained its own multi-village piped water supply scheme for 19 years and has an operating revenue surplus of Rs. 37,000 (WSP and DFID, 2000). Further, even people who could not afford a private connection were able to access public stand posts where water was provided free. The reasons for the success were mainly the able leadership and transparency in operations. Despite the fact that the spread effect of this concept has been non-existent, the lessons to be learnt are many. Such system of management could help to overcome the fiscal problems of government organisations as well as ensure sustainable use of water resources.

Even in urban areas, involving community groups in handling water supply through private-public partnerships may be viable. City and Industrial Development Corporation (CIDCO), in Navi Mumbai, have had some success in privatisation of urban infrastructure. This includes maintenance of sewerage pump, water pumps, meter reading and billing, maintenance of parks and gardens, collection of CIDCO's service charges and so on (Suresh, 2002).

In addition, there have been efforts by external agencies like the Department For International Development (DFID) and United States Agency for International Development (USAID) in collaboration with ULBs and rural communities to establish a setup for water management, which makes the system sustainable. USAID is working with various ULBs in Maharashtra. A study conducted by USAID in Kolhapur revealed that water could be saved up to 12,414 m^3 per day, and electrical energy consumption up to 666,029 units per year, leading to an estimated revenue savings up to Rs. 231 million with an average payback period of approximately one year (USAID, 2001).

Air Pollution

Both ambient and indoor air pollution levels have reached an alarming stage in Maharashtra. Major sources of ambient air pollution are industries, power plants and motor vehicles emitting high levels of sulphur dioxide (SO_2), nitrogen dioxide (NO_2), carbon monoxide (CO), suspended particulate matter (SPM) and numerous other pollutants. Indoor air pollution is the result of low quality fuels such as wood, coal, kerosene, etc., being used in rural and urban poor households.

Ambient Air Pollution

High level of SPM is a cause of serious concern in most cities in the state with Solapur and Mumbai showing much higher levels than other cities. In fact, if necessary precautionary measures to curb the air pollution are not taken, then in the near future, Mumbai may stand among one of the most polluted cities in the world. Nashik, Nagpur and Solapur have shown increasing SPM levels during 1997 and 2001. Thane is the only city, which has shown some decline in the SPM levels during the same period but the levels are still above the prescribed standards of CPCB. The reasons for improvement are introduction of new vehicles with low emissions, overall improvement in road conditions and reduced congestion. Table 15.3 shows observed levels of air pollution parameters for some major locations in Maharashtra during 1997-2004.

Time series data availability on pollution parameters is scarce and as shown in Table 15.4, only three towns

TABLE 15.3

Major Air Quality Parameters for Selected Locations in Maharashtra during 1997-2004 ($\mu g/m^3$)

Parameter	*Year*	*Location*									
		Thane	*Nashik*	*Nagpur*	*Chandrapur*	*Solapur*	*Mumbai*	*Dombivali*	*Aurangabad*	*Ambernath*	*Pune*
	1997-98	13-40	5-24	4-40	18-43	16-21	6-51	29	12.62	28	49.15
	1998-99	9-35	7—38	6-48	24-54	13-17	12-46	24	-	49	-
	1999-00	10.8-14.5	6.5-37.4	5.5-31.8	16-33	17.9	9-43	34	-		43.46
SO_2	2000-01						7-26			37.27	
	2001-02	19.2-22.4	11.1-29.8	9.5-10.1	-	19.5-46.27	7-25	-	-	-	36.5-44.36
	2002-03						14-40			28.02	
	2003-04	6-70	17.1-58.3	6.1-29.3	-	-	11.2- 14.2	-	14.8- 15.1	-	8.4-35
	1997-98	34-41	15-34	16-55	29-53	35-47	22-80	66	8.71	20	58.1
	1998-99	23-32	9-37	9-52	29-53	25-45	19-49	31	-	36	-
NO_2	1999-00	20.1-25.9	13.8-21.9	12.4-52.8	28.2-54.2	45-45.6	18-46	37.4	-	40.5	58.43
	2000-01						14-69			75.73	
	2001-02	50.2-75.6	58-94.3	169.7-194.7	174.8-214	179.5-200.7	16-57	94.3	-	66.49	48.4-101.7
	2002-03						24-96			159.8	
	2003-04	6.5-27	16.7-55.8	18.4-69.6	-	-	45.8-107	-	14.8-15.8	-	11.8-47.5
	1997-98	150-343	159-199	114-133	116-132	229-314	166-441	211	673	203	310.5
	1998-99	141-179	143-190	146-161	172-181	222-247	162-356	124	-	217	-
	1999-00	-	-	163.83	-	-	108-424	-	-	-	199
SPM	2000-01						148-373			252.15	
	2001-02	-	-	-	-	-	120-390			185.33	61-27.37
	2002-03						172-463			190.48	
	2003-04	201.6-3621*	163.19-839#	80.1-1114.3♦	-	-	-	-	40.5-181.7	-	102.7-440.2

Note: 3621* indicates dumping site, 839# indicates commercial area, 1114.3♦ indicates industrial area.

Source: MPCB (2002), MASHAL (1998), *http://mpcb.nic.in.*

TABLE 15.4

Trends in Air Quality for Three Major Cities in Maharashtra during 1990-2004

Year	*Parameter Concentration Expressed in Annual Average ($\mu g/m^3$)*								
	SO_2			*NOx*			*SPM*		
	Mumbai	*Pune*	*Nagpur*	*Mumbai*	*Pune*	*Nagpur*	*Mumbai*	*Pune*	*Nagpur*
1990	18	13.85	9.05	40	36.60	9.05	243	223.00	205.00
1991	28	17.05	8.25	45	22.05	16.70	279	197.50	248.50
1992	26	-	9.40	48	17.10	20.70	309	-	186.50
1993	26	27.80	7.95	49	39.00	14.50	224	179.50	130.50
1994	27	-	6.10	43	-	12.60	275	-	184.50
1995	24	22.55	8.25	43	23.45	13.60	291	140.00	179.00
1996	23	41.50	7.75	39	41.50	16.90	325	210.50	181.50
1997	24	53.10	9.05	36	61.10	18.55	272	276.50	140.00
1998	23	49.15	7.20	40	58.10	15.45	254	310.50	143.50
1999	26	-	-	39	-	-	255	-	-
2000	20	43.46	7.23	42	58.43	20.16	251	199.00	163.83
2001	17	-	-	45	-	-	240	-	-
2002	28	-	-	57			245		
2003	13.15	20.47	15.26	61.45	35.77	34.84	-	263.43	290.67

Source: Calculated from CPCB (2000), CPCB (2002:b), Phatak (2002) and MPCB (2003-04).

TABLE 15.5

Comparison of Air Quality Parameters in Metro Cities and Some Towns of Maharashtra (2000-04)

City	*Combined Site Average of Mean of Annual Averages (µg/m³)*															
	SO_2				*NOx*				*SPM*				*RPM*			
	2000-01	*2001-02*	*2002-03*	*2003-04*	*2000-01*	*2001-02*	*2002-03*	*2003-04*	*2000-01*	*2001-02*	*2002-03*	*2003-04*	*2000 - 01*	*2001-02*	*2002-03*	*2003-04*
Delhi	16.5	13.3	13.2	10.6	41.5	28.9	35.1	39.0	312.0	334.5	441.5	374.0	123.4*	519#	-	-
Kolkata	25.3	21.9	13.3	18.1	44.2	86.7	96.4	83.3	285.0	319.0	320		149.5	145.3	-	-
Chennai	15.1	20.7	40.0	19.8	14.1	21.0	20.7	34.5	85.7	96.8	156.0	170.8	71.6	83.0	-	-
Bangalore	18.9	19.6	14.6	12.8	32.4	22.4	23.1	29.7	120.0	121.0	126.0	146.0	-	89.66	-	-
Ahmedabad	9.0	11.2	10.0	18.7	35.2	45.9	42.1	28.0	-	366.0	344.0	311.0	163.3	229.5	-	-
Hyderabad	12.0	11.7	6.7	5.4	29.3	32.5	27.0	29.5	199.0	159.3	187.0	181.3	127.1	98.0	-	-
Mumbai	11.8	12.9	9.7	7.4	31.1	27.3	17.8	22.5	-	220.0	226.0	227.0	249.0	277.0	314.0	254.0
Nagpur	9.3	8.8	8.7	6.5	21.1	14.7	12.9	20.8	-	133.0	233.0	219.0	178.0	121.0	-	-
Solapur	18.9	19.4	20.1	19.9	45.8	46.4	47.3	45.3	390.0	403.0	407.0	396.0	177.5	192.0	-	-

Note: *24 hourly average at traffic junctions; #24 hourly average in industrial areas.

Source: CPCB (2000), (2001:a) and *http://cpcb.nic.in*

have the data for the past 10 years. The trends show that SO_2 levels are declining due to the use of clean fuels by industries, NOx levels are increasing due to rise in vehicle population and SPM levels are fluctuating without any definitive trend and due to various reasons.

Table 15.5 compares ambient air pollution levels in Indian metro cities with some towns of Maharashtra during 2000-04. Accordingly, SPM levels in major cities of Maharashtra are either comparable or lower than other places. But concentration of respirable particulate matter (RPM) is higher than other towns. RPM levels in mumbai, Nagpur and Solapur, both in 1999 and 2000, were found more than acceptable levels. RPM constitutes a major fraction of SPM in Nagpur but in Mumbai and Solapur, the share of RPM is reasonably less. In order to mitigate the adverse effects of RPM, the GoI has taken several steps, which apply to Maharashtra also. These include mandatory use of CNG, low sulphur diesel, phasing out of old vehicles, guidelines for various industrial units, etc.

Indoor Air Pollution

High levels of pollution within houses and premises have severe repercussions on the health of women, children and aged people. However, this has been a highly neglected area in the state as access to clean fuels like LPG is limited in rural areas. Recently, some efforts have been made to provide clean fuels in rural areas. As a part of the Community Biogas Plant (CBP) the state has installed 448 plants and, by 2001 end, could achieve only 20 per cent of its target for 2001-02.

The Maharashtra Energy Development Agency has installed three Institutional Biogas Plants (IBPs) in Sangli district and one in Mumbai for kitchen wastes during 2001-02. The National Programme on Improved *Chulhas* (NPIC) aims at satisfying the requirements of a good *chulha*. However, the state has achieved only 37.3 per cent of its targets under the NPIC programme, compared to Tamil Nadu and West Bengal (100 per cent). NCAER conducted a study in 2001-02, for evaluating the performance of NPIC programme in various states which revealed that in Maharashtra 56.2 per cent of the *chulhas* were working and in use, 11.8 per cent were working and not in use and 23 per cent were dismantled.

Maharashtra received the first place under the National Project on Biogas Development (NPBD) programme for 2001-02. As a part of the NPIC programme the Appropriate Rural Technology Institute (ARTI), Pune is the Technical Back up Unit (TBU) for Maharashtra and designs improved stove technologies. It also conducts indoor air pollution assessment of traditional stoves *vis-à-vis* improved stoves. ARTI has trained traditional potters to build these improved *chulhas*, which have had a strong impact in Sangli, Satara and Kolhapur as it enabled easier access to *chulhas* in rural areas. A survey conducted by an NGO, in a village of Raigadh district, revealed that PM_5 and CO were reduced by as much as 54 per cent in the kitchen due to the use of improved *chulhas*.

Effects of Air Pollution

Limited studies carried out in the state have shown that high levels of SPM, NOx and HC were causing high incidence of respiratory diseases like tuberculosis, cardiovascular diseases and asthma. The SPM levels reported in Mumbai range between 160 $\mu g/m^3$ and 280 $\mu g/m^3$ of which about 60 to 70 per cent are RPM. Higher levels of RPM are responsible for various health problems in the state. A study in Chembur area of Mumbai indicates that for every 10 $\mu g/m^3$ increase in SO_2 concentration, the social costs could exceed Rs. 100 million, which include only dyspnea and mortality effects. The loss of rent not including property values, could amount to Rs. 1 million per year and the cumulative loss in property value due to each 100-unit increase in SPM concentration could be around Rs. 2000 million (IDR, 1999). In addition to health effects, air pollution also has several other effects such as reduction in visibility, spoiling of buildings, damage to material and machines, and effects on vegetation and animals. These are yet to be estimated for the state and detailed studies in various regions of Maharashtra are required on the economic damage of air pollution.

Monitoring and Abatement

Monitoring results at National Ambient Air Quality Monitoring (NAAQM) stations in Maharashtra for the period 1997-98 to 2000-01 revealed that out of 26 stations, monitoring is not being carried out at 7 stations. The results of air quality parameters were found within limits at 8 stations. Monitoring air quality within Mumbai city is mainly the responsibility of the BMC. But National Environmental Engineering Research Institute (NEERI) also conducts monitoring at some locations. MMRDA, in some project based studies, also collects data on carbon monoxide (CO), particulate matter less than and equal to 10 μm i.e. PM_{10}, lead and ozone. However, monitoring results of NEERI were not available with the MPCB. Many times, it is reported that the mobile monitoring vans were not functioning satisfactorily and the mandatory 104 measurements every year, required as per the CPCB guidelines, are rarely complied with, except in Mumbai. As per records of MCGM (Shrivastava and Kunte, 2003), its mobile monitoring van is in excellent condition and it is analysing more than 150 samples per year (156 samples during 2002-03). However, overall status of air monitoring in the state is not satisfactory (CAG, 2000-01).

As per records of MPCB and GoM, most of the industrial estates in Konkan and Pune (90 to 100 per cent) have provided air pollution abatement facilities, whereas in Nagpur and Nashik region, the provision of facilities for controlling air pollution is highly unsatisfactory. In Amravati region, the number of industries providing abatement facilities ranges from 75 per cent to 100 per cent. One reason for less number in Nagpur and Nashik could be that only few industries have air polluting potential.

Noise Pollution

Noise pollution is an unwanted sound that is produced by various natural or man-made sources such as oceans and construction and industrial activities. Noise can have many adverse effects like hearing impairment, sleep disturbance, reduced performance, annoyance and harming physiological functions. There are several legislations relating to noise pollution including Noise Pollution (Regulation and Control) Rules, 2000. As a safeguard against harmful noise levels, the CPCB has specified noise standard for various categories of areas such as silence or sensitive (40-50 dB), residential (45-55 dB), commercial (55-65 dB) and industrial (70-75 dB), where lower range in parenthesis is for night and upper range is for daytime noise levels.

In Maharashtra, noise levels in many towns exceed standards in all categories of areas, for both day and night, by wide margins, mainly due to industrial and vehicular noise. The noise levels are much higher during festival times like *Ganeshutsav* and *Navratri*. In sensitive areas, even the higher end of the noise level exceeds acceptable standards (CSO, 2001). In Mumbai, aircraft noise is a major source of noise pollution generated during landing, take-off and ground operations of aircrafts. Night time noise levels are particularly higher in Mumbai than in other cities, mainly because several activities in the city take place on a round-the-clock basis.

Some data for residential areas indicate that Thane had an average figure of 62 dB(A), while Navi Mumbai and Nashik were higher at 69.9 dB(A), and 81 dB(A), respectively in 2000-01 (TMC, 2001; NMMC, 2000-01; NMC, 2001-02). Aurangabad had a noise level of 67.9 dB(A) in 1998 (MASHAL, 1998). Obviously, these figures are much above the limits prescribed for residential areas. Records of MPCB for industrial regions show that except for one industrial estate in Thane, where the sound levels are very high at 245 dB, they are within specified limits in other industrial areas.

Solid Waste Management

Solid waste management (SWM) in Maharashtra, particularly in major towns, is highly inefficient at all stages, i.e., collection, transportation, treatment and disposal. There are several crucial environmental, economic and social issues involved in SWM and that are to be addressed in the case of municipal solid waste (MSW), hazardous waste (HW) and biomedical waste (BMW).

FIGURE 15.2

Solid Waste Generation in Major Regions of Maharashtra (2001-2002)

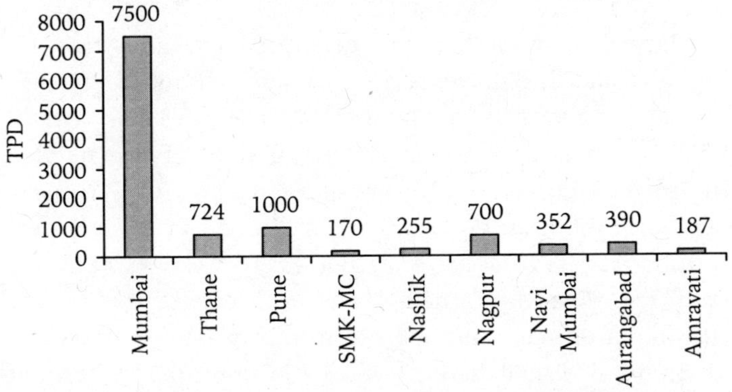

Source: Compiled from Environment Reports of various MCs (1999-2002).

Municipal Solid Waste

Maharashtra generates over 16,000 tonnes per day (TPD) of MSW of which around 50 per cent is generated in three cities (Mumbai, Pune and Thane) only (Figure 15.2). Per capita solid waste generation in urban Maharashtra is between 0.4 and 0.5 kg per day. Compared to other metro cities in India as well as in Maharashtra, MSW generation is highest in Mumbai and city alone generates about 7,500 TPD followed by Pune at 1000 TPD and Thane at 724 TPD (TMC, 2001; Shrivastava and Kunte, 2003).

Composition of MSW differs in various regions of Maharashtra as shown in Figure 15.3 for 6 major cities. Although authentic data on solid waste composition are not available, some MCs maintain proper records. Data for Mumbai show that city's MSW has about 63 per cent non-biodegradable waste and 37 per cent biodegradable wastes. These figures for Nagpur are 65 per cent and 35 per cent, respectively. The share of biodegradable waste is more than 50 per cent for all the cities other than Mumbai. In Pune, about 95 per cent of solid waste is either biodegradable or recyclable and for Navi Mumbai it was almost 100 per cent. For Nashik about 73 per cent is biodegradable and for Thane, mixed garbage accounted for 63 per cent, which could not be classified into any category. Mumbai's

FIGURE 15.3

Composition of Solid Waste in Major Cities of Maharashtra

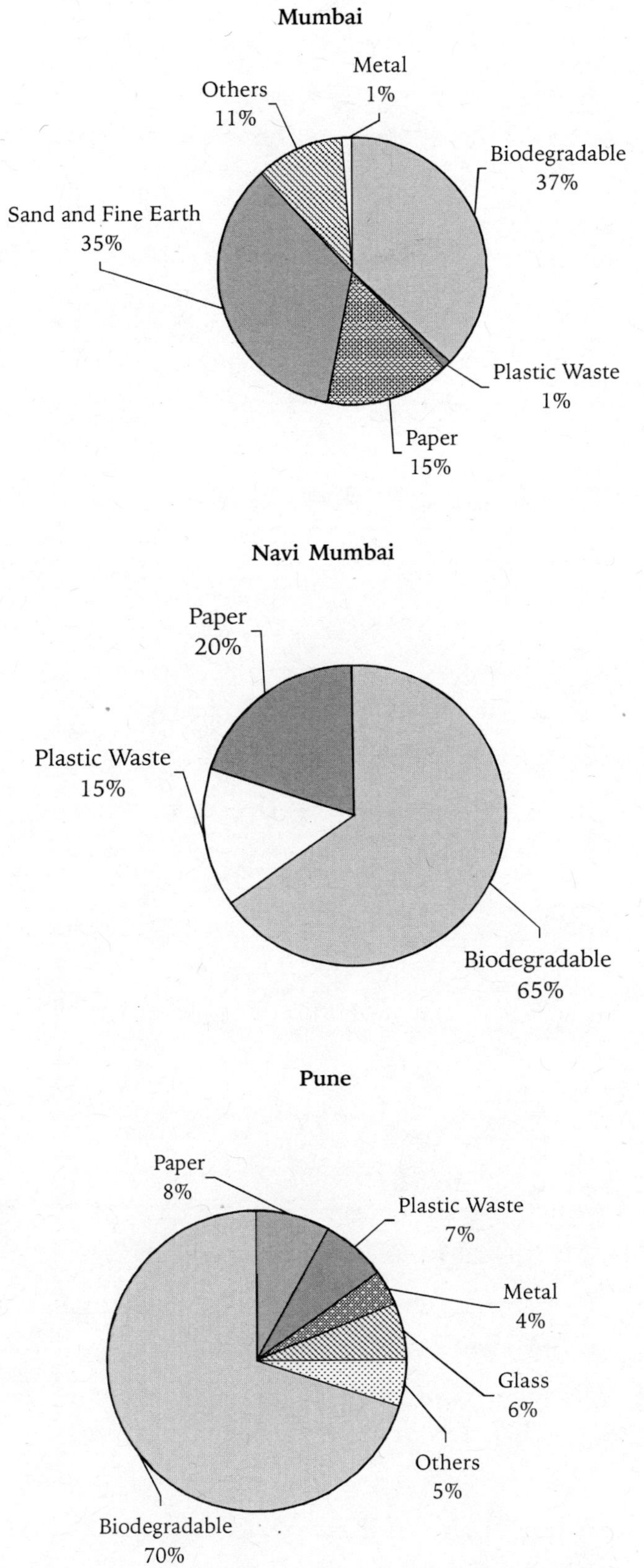

Contd...

Contd....

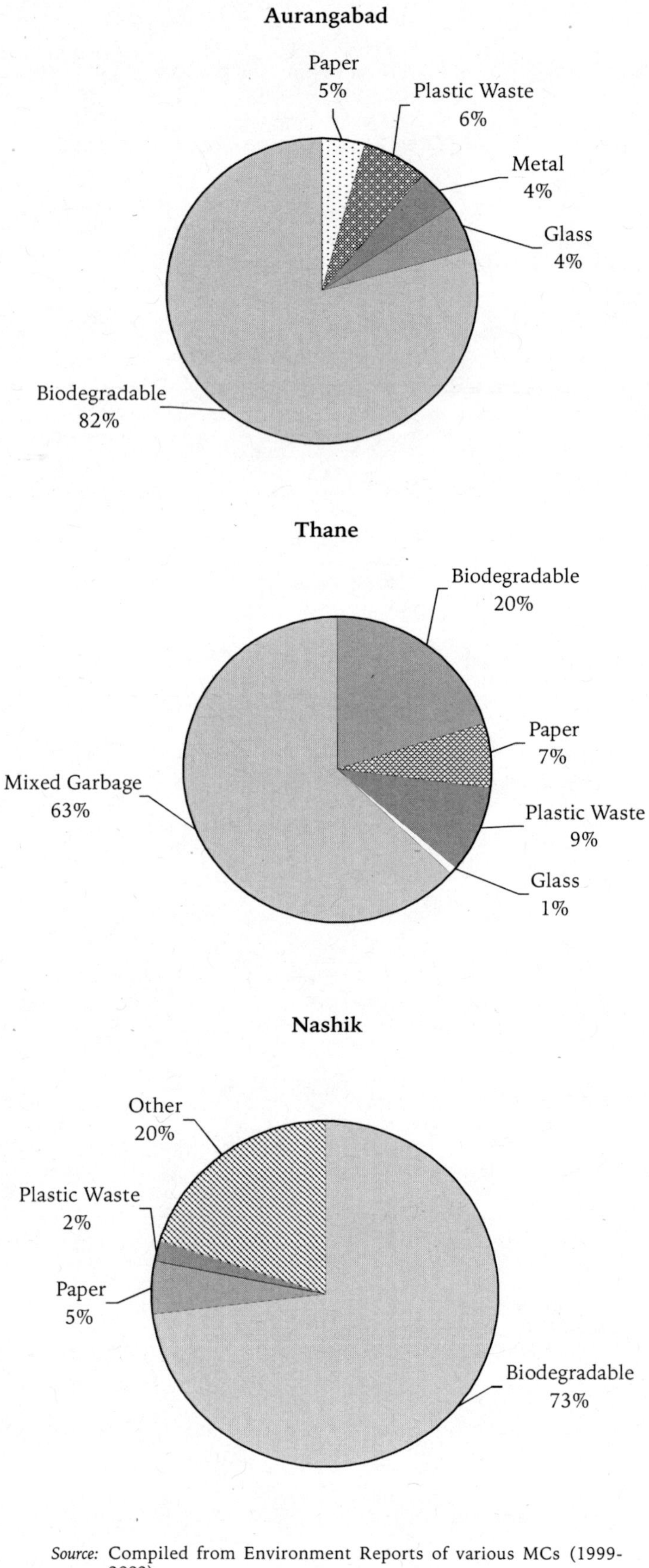

Source: Compiled from Environment Reports of various MCs (1999-2002).

clearing efficiency of solid waste is about 86.2 per cent, which is the highest among all the major cities in Maharashtra, followed by Thane's at about 57 per cent (CSO, 2001). The high content of biodegradable and recyclable wastes provide ample opportunities for more efficient and resourceful waste management. However, despite some limited efforts of composting and power generation, alternative solutions of SWM have not been very successful, mainly due to their high cost.

Hazardous Waste

Hazardous wastes (HW) generated by industries are highly toxic and have serious repercussions on health. The state accounts for about 21 lakh tonnes per year of HW, which is about 50 per cent of total HW generated in India. Despite Maharashtra being the largest generator of hazardous waste in the country, very few industrial estates have provided for HW treatment facilities. Thane, Ratnagiri and Raigad are generating the maximum amount of hazardous waste. This waste is dumped either without or with improper treatment causing health hazards and environmental pollution. Despite the commissioning of a sanitary landfill and incineration facility at Taloja, the industries are unwilling to pay for the treatment cost.

Biomedical Waste

Maharashtra contributes to the largest share of biomedical wastes (BMW) among all states at about 31 tonnes per day, which is about 60 per cent of total BMW generated in India. As can be seen from the Figure 15.4, the Konkan region accounts for 45.40 per cent of the BMW generation, with Mumbai's share being the largest, while Pune and Nagpur account for 18.13 per cent and 11.21 per cent, respectively. Despite the Biomedical Waste Rules coming into effect, the major hospitals in Nagpur and Wardha were not following them (Sarkar, 2000).

Various MCs and MPCB have taken steps to specially handle medical waste. For instance, BMC allocated one acre of land near Deonar dumping site for handling of BMW. The site is made inaccessible to ragpickers and guarded from foraging animals. Many of the hospitals have been asked to set up their own incinerators and were also advised to have shared treatment facilities. In 2002, MPCB served notices to 62 hospitals, which were responsible for generating 75 per cent of the total medical waste, under the Waste (Management and Handling-II Amendment) Rules, 2000. These hospitals have to now comply with the

FIGURE 15.4

Region-wise Generation of BMW

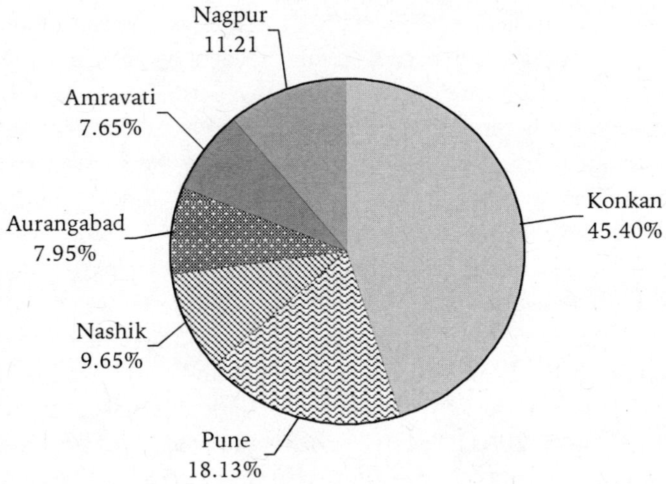

Source: Data from MEDC (2001).

requirements of these rules, else, will have to face prosecution (Dutta, 2002a).

Thane Municipal Corporation (TMC) is seeking help of private parties for setting up a common biomedical waste facility on a build-own-operate-and-transfer (BOOT) basis. Hospitals in TMC region will be charged either on per bed basis or lumpsum amount per year as all infrastructure facilities like land, water and electricity for common treatment plant will be provided by TMC (Holla, 2002).

The major hurdle in handling the BMW is the high cost of disposal and treatment, which may result in unethical practices being adopted by hospitals. For example, in 2001, 214 municipal hospitals and 211 private health care institutes out of about a total of 1,340 institutes in Mumbai have entered into a MoU with BMC to send their infectious waste to a common facility. However, the BMC authorities feel that after the billing system has been introduced, hospitals are sending less quantity of wastes to treatment facility. While the hospitals in Mumbai used to send 17 TPD of BMW in 2001, it is reduced to as low as 1.5 TPD in 2002 which is a serious concern. Other problems are lack of trained manpower and low level of awareness among hospitals regarding hospital waste management, as largely felt by field officers of MPCB.

Health and Other Effects

There are several environmental and socio-economic implications associated with solid waste in Maharashtra. Uncontrolled and open dumping of waste on land attracts rodents, insects, etc., and creates highly unhygienic conditions. Excessive dumping and land filling with waste deteriorates the quality of land and also the groundwater gets polluted due to leaching of hazardous substances. Solid wastes released directly into water bodies are highly polluting. Thane-Belapur industrial belt in Navi Mumbai creates more than 100 TPD of solid waste, most of which is highly toxic. The water bodies such as the Ulhas River have registered high levels of mercury and arsenic. This could be due to unauthorised dumping of solid waste in the river.

Indiscriminate burning of waste releases toxic fumes, which have serious health effects. Plastic waste sorted out from MSW by ragpickers is recycled without proper technology giving rise to highly toxic fumes. It is reported that burning of waste at the Deonar dumping ground in Mumbai caused sickness among nearby residents. This resulted in a public interest litigation forcing BMC for some improvement (ToI, 2003). Further, the opportunity cost of the land used for dumping of waste is not considered, which could be very high in cities like Mumbai.

Social dimension, in the form of the involvement of informal sector in SWM, is worth mentioning. Some studies have revealed that this system works very efficiently through a chain of waste (rag) pickers, waste buyers and wholesalers. Mumbai has several thousands of rag pickers having solid waste collection as their primary source of income. Most of these ragpickers have migrated from other places in Maharashtra and nearby states and adopted waste collection as their profession. Ragpicking has both positive and negative aspects. On the one hand, it is a source of income and employment for the migratory labour. They form an important part of SWM in the city by segregating recyclables from the waste, which is not done by municipality workers. On the other hand, these ragpickers are exploited by the middlemen and get paid much lesser than the market rate for their recyclable wastes. They are also not aware about the unhygienic conditions that they are working in and the harmful effects of the toxic waste that they are dealing with (Sharma *et al.*, 1997).

Steps by Authorities

Maharashtra has taken the lead in the country for adopting eco-friendly disposal of waste as six MCs in the state have decided to put up MSW power plants. The first MSW power plant in the country using 500 TPD of waste and with 5 MW generating capacity came up in Nagpur in 2000. Power plants of varying capacity have been planned at Mumbai, Pune, Kalyan, Solapur and Pimpri-Chinchwad. Most of these plants were conceived on a build-own-operate (BOO) basis, wherein the MCs have agreed to provide garbage free of cost at the site of the power plant. The land for the privately owned power plant was provided on lease at a nominal charge of Re. 1 per km^2 per year. The central and state governments, on their part, have provided a number of incentives to such plants like interest subsidy, assured power purchase, 100 per cent income tax depreciation and protection from foreign exchange fluctuations (Vaidya, 2000).

Community groups have been involved in management of solid waste in many cities. Treatment and disposal of solid waste by vermiculture composting has become an important method. In Mumbai, as a result of BMC's efforts to ensure segregation of dry and wet waste, as many as 12,500 odd residential societies are now segregating their waste at source and 45 vermiculture sites are converting the wet garbage into compost (ToI, 2003a). However, one recent survey revealed that 60 per cent of the housing societies did not segregate waste. On one hand, people showed a lack of willingness and awareness and, on the other hand, BMC officials did not provide the necessary infrastructure to do so (Moitra and Ramachandran, 2003). In order to handle the solid waste in urban areas, some of the projects have been put up for PSP, thus, changing role of authorities from governance to facilitation. However, some incidences of mismanagement by private contractors have been reported such as while contracts were given for 4,000 TPD collection, in reality only 2,500 TPD waste was collected, causing huge losses to the BMC (Sen, 2003).

Forests and Biodiversity

State of Forests

There are six forest types in the state, namely, Tropical Semi Evergreen, Tropical Moist Deciduous, Tropical Thorn, Subtropical Broadleaved Hill and Littoral and Swamp Forests. Deciduous forests can be found in Nashik and Thane districts and the 'Mawal' strip. Raigad, Ratnagiri and Sindhudurg districts, though capable of producing semi-evergreen trees have predominantly deciduous trees due to human interference. Evergreen forests can also be found in Ahmednagar, Pune, Satara, Sangli and Kolhapur districts (Ghate, 2003).

Maharashtra has a total geographical area of 30.77 million hectares. As per the assessment by the Forest Survey of India, state's forest cover accounted for 15.17 per cent of the total geographical area in 1997, which has increased to 20.13 per cent in 1999 (FSR, 1999 and 2001). Thus, as per FSR (2001), the forest cover in the state is marginally higher than the average forest cover in India (19.39 per cent). However, the state is still lagging far behind the target of 33 per cent forest cover envisaged by the GoI in the country. Maharashtra's actual forest cover in the 1970s was 40700 km^2, which was reduced to 30740 km^2 in 1980-1982 but increased to 47482 km^2 by 2001. This trend is visible in the case of both dense as well as open forest area. However, the area under dense forest cover in Maharashtra has increased by 2991 km_2 between 1997 and 1999 and 4173 km^2 between 1999 and 2001. In both the assessments (1999 and 2001), Maharashtra showed the greatest increase among all the states in India (FSI, 2000 and 2002; GoM, 2003d).

The increase in dense forests is due to the conversion of open forests, scrub and non-forest areas to dense forests. The net decrease of 16 km^2 of mangroves is on account of degradation on one hand and conversion from non-forest area to mangrove on the other. None of the seven hilly districts in the state (Raigadh, Kolhapur, Nashik, Pune, Satara, Sindhudurg and Ratnagiri) have a forest cover of more than the required one of 66 per cent. Sindhudurg has the largest area under forest cover at 45.67 per cent followed by Raigarh at 31.99 per cent (FSI, 2002).

The major reasons for depletion and degradation of the forests are rapid urbanisation, industrialisation, construction of big dams, use of forestlands for rehabilitation purpose etc. In addition, the state is facing an acute problem of water shortage. Average rainfall in the state is much less as compared to other parts of the country, therefore, much attention is required for water harvesting as well as protection, preservation and development of catchment areas. Lack of attention on forestry sector is creating havoc in various components of entire ecosystem including water, air and soil. The Forestry sector is among the least priority sectors as the state's plan and non-plan budget reflect. The total plan of the state is Rs. 13,000 crores where as funds allotted for forests is only Rs. 30 crores and on Non-plan side provision for the state is Rs. 55,000 crores where as for the forests it is only Rs. 300 crores. This is approximately 0.1 per cent of total budgetary provision of the state (GoM, 2003c).

Mangroves are specialised coastal plants that have tremendous ecological and socio-economic significance,

FIGURE 15.5

Forest Cover in Major Regions of Maharashtra

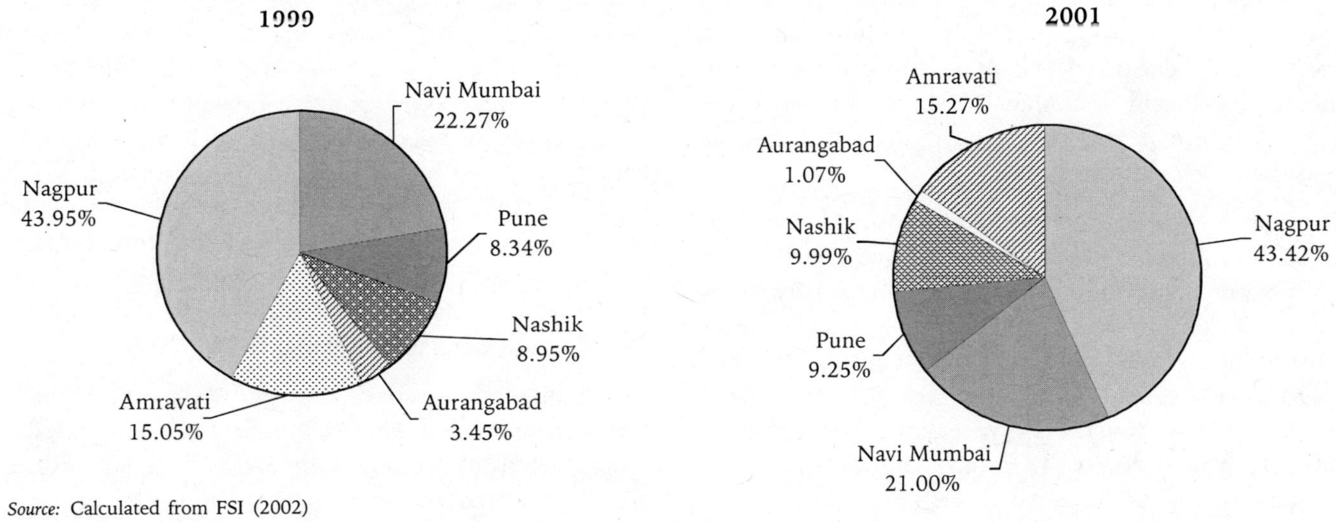

Source: Calculated from FSI (2002)

but are being threatened by encroachers and developers. The area under mangroves in Maharashtra was 200 km^2 in 1972-1975, which was reduced to 108 km^2 in 1997 but increased to 118 km^2 in 2001. According to MMRDA, the mangrove areas in Mumbai have shown significant increase since 1991. However, this claim is under some contention, as the maximum numbers of reclamations have taken place between 1991 and 1997 (Singh, 2003).

As shown in Figure 15.5, in 1999, the Nagpur division had the largest share of forest cover in Maharashtra (41.95 per cent) followed by Navi Mumbai at 22.27 per cent. Aurangabad region has the least forest cover at 3.45 per cent. In 2001, while Nagpur, Pune, Nashik and Amravati showed some increase, Aurangabad and Navi Mumbai showed a decline in their forest cover.

About 5 per cent of Maharashtra's geographical area is declared as protected area. The state has 5 national parks, 36 wildlife sanctuaries, 40 forest parks and two tiger reserves named Melghat and Tadoba and a wetland of national importance, called Ujni, in Solapur. About 36 per cent of the villages in Maharashtra have forests as a recorded land use, which is inhabited by 19.04 million people.

The number of villages having forest area of less than 100 ha, between 100-500 ha and more than 500 ha are 52 per cent, 37 per cent and 11 per cent, respectively, which indicate the problem of encroachment. On the forestland, there are two types of encroachment. First is done by the local inhabitant, specially tribal for cultivation and to meet their livelihood, second is done by forest mafia mainly in and adjacent to the city area for construction of building, farm houses, etc. The state government has appointed the committee at district and state levels to monitor and supervise the removal of encroachments on the forestland.

Joint Forest Management

Having a large tribal population, forests have an extremely important role to play in the economy of Maharashtra. In pursuance of National Forest Policy 1988, Government of Maharashtra declared its intentions of going ahead with Joint Forest Management (JFM) in degraded and dense forests. JFM in the state envisages people's participation for protection, development and preservation of forest. Through JFM, not only the task of protection and preservation of forest ecosystem is taken, but it also generates employment in tribal areas and enhances the livelihood means of the weaker section of the society who live in and around forest areas. In the state about 15,000 villages are in and around forest area covering more than 34,000 km^2 forest area. About 4,100 JFM committees have been established and up to March 2004, JFM Committees will cover all the forest fringe villages (GoM, 2003d). There are many NGOs in the state involved in activities such as increasing forest cover and development of the tribal areas at the grass-root level. Government authorities could support their efforts.

Biological Diversity

The Western Ghats region in Maharashtra falls among the most important biogeographic zones of India, as it is one of the richest centres of endemism.

Due to varied topography and microclimatic conditions, some areas within the region are considered to be active zones of speciation. About 1,500 endemic species of dicotyledonous plants are reported from the Western Ghats. However, due to increased anthropogenic activities, Matheran, Panchgani and Mahabaleshwar are the three hilly sites in the state, which have been declared as ecosensitive zones by the MoEF.

Damage due to encroachment into national parks for commercial and poaching activities has not been given due attention. Some of the important biodiversity spots adversely affected by human activities in the state are as follows (Sehgal, 2002). Bhimashankar Sanctuary in the Western Ghats (Pune District) is well known for the Giant Squirrel it houses. However, tourism projects, construction of roads through the forests and development projects designed to cater to the pilgrims' needs may harm the existing habitats. Sanjay Gandhi National Park (Mumbai) is heavily encroached by slumlords and, being a water catchments forest area, encroachment is indirectly threatening the water security of Mumbai. Despite the court's order to rehabilitate the slum inhabitants, the authorities have not taken any substantial action, due to political patronage to the slum inhabitants. Other encroachers in the park are tourists, temple visitors, politically connected individuals and illegal liquor distilleries, which use trees as fuel wood. Timber factories are not regulated sufficiently and, contrary to the Supreme Court's orders, they carry on their activities resulting in large-scale cutting of trees.

Gautala Autaramghat Wildlife Sanctuary (Auranagabad), which is the home to the sloth bear, barking deer, wild boar, *nilgai* and leopard is denotified due to commercial interests. However, a local organisation, Nisraga Mitra Mandal, intervened and a stay-order from the court was obtained. Similarly, Kalsubai-Harishchandragadh Sanctuary was denotified in order to construct the Ghatkar Pump Storage Project, which may be detrimental to the sanctuary.

Reduction in tiger population over the last decade is a matter of serious concern. The crucial reason for this is believed to be the contradiction between wildlife protection and revenue earning activities of the forest department (India Jungles, 2003). Melghat Tiger Reserve is being disturbed by Chikaldhara Pump Storage Project, which may drown large areas of the forests, lead to the construction of roads and disturb the tiger reserve substantially. Further, the government is planning to denotify 500 km^2 of the forests for construction and commercial activities, which would adversely affect the flow of Sipna, Dolnar and Tapi rivers. This may adversely affect the supply of water to the downstream communities. In Tadoba Tiger Reserve, a large tract of forests supplies coal to the Nippon Denro Ispat's thermal power project. This proposal threatens a large variety of species of trees such as Teak, Lohara, Baranj and Bandar blocks of forests. Further, this mining area is very close to the Tadoba-Andheri Reserve, which will harm the tiger habitats and the forest reserves. Other animals such as rhinoceros, elephant, lion and brown antlered deer are not seen in the state since 1993 though they were found earlier (CSE, 1999).

Wildlife conservation strategy, 2002, has highlighted the importance of encroachments and suggested that illegal activities from within forestlands and protected areas should be removed. Fully tapping the potential in wildlife tourism and at the same time taking care that it does not have adverse impact in wildlife and protected areas. The revenue earned from increased tourism should be used entirely to augment available resources for conservation. People should be encouraged to take up afforestation and conservation in new areas.

Land Degradation

It refers to the loss in land productivity due to human activities such as demographic pressure, socio-economic activities, land use change, etc., resulting in depletion of essential crop nutrients, water logging and salinity. While in India, about 48 per cent and 44 per cent of all canal command area is water logged and saline, in Maharashtra, these figures are as high as 88 per cent and 100 per cent, respectively. Maharashtra soils are not only deficient in phosphorous (P) and potassium (K) but also in nitrogen (N), mainly because farmers in rainfed areas use very little fertilisers.

In fact, Maharashtra soils show the greatest deficiency compared to other states in the country, thereby, causing the negligence of agriculture sector. Further, excessive use of water for irrigation also leads to increasing salinity of soils. For example, in the Kolhapur region, due to the location of sugar mills, farmers started cultivating sugarcane, which is a highly water intensive crop. However, region's fine-grained black soils do not allow penetration of water, leading to continuous build up of salt levels. It is estimated that salt content of soils increases by 20 to 25 tonnes per hectare after a single crop of sugarcane is grown. Increase in salinity also reduces the yield of sugarcane on the same land in successive years (Jayan, 2003).

Environmental Education

Promotion of Environmental Education (EE) among people is of utmost importance for making them understand their relationship with the nature. The MoEF has initiated several programmes in the country such as National Environment Awareness Campaign (NEAC), Eco-Clubs (National Green Corps), Global Learning and Observation to Benefit the Environment (GLOBE) and mass awareness through the electronic media. In Maharashtra, environmental concepts have been included in school syllabi. In fact, there are many formal education centres, which teach environment as a part of the course curriculum both at school and higher levels. In the case of informal education, several NGOs are involved in promoting the schemes of MoEF and GoM.

Environmental Education in the state is also boosted through the efforts of international organisations, like, India Canada Environmental Facility (ICEF) and World WildLife Fund for Nature (WWF). About 231 nature clubs (NCs) have been established under ICEF-WWF programmes in the state. Of this 102 are located in the Konkan region, 77 in the Pune region and 52 in the Nagpur region. The Environment Department, GoM has also established about 200 nature clubs in the state. Activities of NC's include seminars, exhibitions, essay writing and poster competition, SWM, anti-plastic campaigns, etc. The students go to rural areas and demonstrate the advantage of cleanliness and upkeep of environment to the villagers. It was found that generally the participation rate in schools was low because a fee was charged from student members to join NC under ICEF-WWF programme, which they could not afford (Sharma *et al.*, 2002; Warade, 2003).

Some Relevant International Issues

Two of the international issues of importance for Maharashtra could be global warming and climate change and trade and environment linkages as they may have significant impact on the future development of the state.

Possible Impact of Climate Change

For a coastal state like Maharashtra, climate change has severe implications. Preliminary estimates show a substantial negative impact on the state affecting its agriculture productivity, water resources, coastal activities, and health of people. The coastal regions are agriculturally fertile and a rise in sea level will make them highly vulnerable to inundation and salinisation. Coastal infrastructure, tourist activities and onshore oil exploration are also at risk. For example, Mumbai's northern suburbs like Versova Beaches and other populated areas along tidal mud flats and creeks are vulnerable to land-loss and increased flooding. Beyond actual inundation, rising sea levels will also put over 1.3 million people of the state at a risk of flooding. This will displace a large number of people and result in rapid landward urbanisation, straining resources and putting more pressure on civic amenities. Further, it will also increase seawater intrusion into freshwater resources, thus, reducing the available freshwater supplies. The dominant cost, as indicated is land loss, which accounts for 83 per cent of all damages. In present value terms, the damage could be as high as thousands of billions of rupees (Sharma, 1998c; TERI, 2002).

Trade and Environment

It refers to how trade affects the environment and *vice versa*. In Maharashtra, many export-oriented industries, producing goods for foreign consumers, are responsible for the deteriorating local environment. At the same time, there are several non-tariff trade barriers, such as product and process standards and packaging requirements adopted by importing countries, which may hinder the state's export to these countries. Some of the industries affected by these regulations could be textiles, leather, and agriculture and food products.

Some studies have shown that trading of waste paper has more positive effects on the environment as its use for the production of new paper reduces the pressure on primary resources. The Western Ghats region in the state is rich in biodiversity and has several unique species of flora and fauna. The Convention on International Trade in Endangered Species of Wild Life and Fauna (CITES) agreement stresses on the need to prevent illegal trade of endangered species, to prevent their extinction. In Maharashtra, the Black Buck is regarded as one such species and efforts are required to protect it (Sharma, 1995; Sharma *et al.*, 1997).

Efficacy of Environmental Regulations

The environmental laws and policies regulate all aspects of the environment; starting right from identification of the problem to its solution. Maharashtra is one of the leading states in the country, enforcing such legislations. Since the state does not have its own 'water or forest policy', the National Forest Policy and National Water Policy apply by default. However, steps are being taken to formulate a state-specific water policy, involving a shift from supply driven to demand-driven wherein the government would play the role of a facilitator rather than that of a provider. There is also a proposal to create Maharashtra Water and Waste Water Regulatory Commission (MWRC) and Maharashtra Water Resource Planning and Regulatory Authority (MWRPRA) for the independent fixation of service standards and tariffs and other allied issues (Khatua, 2002).

Role of Authorities

The Environment Department, GoM, MPCB and various MCs are involved in administration of environmental regulations. MPCB monitors air and water quality, solid waste management, noise pollution, and conducts environmental awareness and training programmes. There are 33 water quality stations monitored under MINARS and 5 stations under GEMS, the results of which are sent to the Central Laboratory in Belapur for analysis. MPCB has also established 13 monitoring stations along the sea coast of Mumbai to monitor the effect of pollutants on sea water on monthly basis. In November 1995, the state was declared as 'air pollution control area'. MPCB observes the extent of air pollution throughout the state by using 51 air monitoring stations covering 19 different areas. Within cities MCs have set up their own monitoring stations. In addition, regular monitoring and assessment of air pollution caused by stacks emissions from industries is conducted. Stack samples are analysed for parameters such as sulphur dioxide, nitrogen oxides, and total particulate matter etc., as per the requirements of the Air Act of 1981.

The MPCB has divided the industries into red, orange and green categories based on their pollution potential, in decreasing order. The industries, which are in the red category, are subjected to more frequent monitoring activities. Any industry, operation, process, or an extension and addition thereto, which is likely to generate any kind of pollution, will have to obtain the consent of the MPCB under the provisions of various Acts. There are three types of consents issued, namely, Consent to Establish, required before the actual commencement of the works for establishing the industry/activity; Consent to Operate, needs to be taken before the actual commencement of production including trial production, and it is valid for certain duration and Renewal of Consent to Operate for renewing the consent after expiry of the period mentioned in the consent to operate. The consent application is very comprehensive and requires detailed information regarding location, functioning and environmental management of the industry.

The MPCB prescribes certain mandatory conditions and standards so that pollution parameters are not exceeded by the industries. These are based on the industry type, raw materials used, processes involved, qualities of waste generated and overall environmental conditions in which the industry exists. When a particular industry has failed to comply with these conditions, action is taken against it. MPCB is also involved in research activities to improve its performance and taking policy decisions so as to improve overall environment quality in the state.

As far as watersheds are concerned, an important element of long-term sustainability is to forge linkages with permanent institutions in the area. Efforts will be made to strengthen linkages between watershed community organisation and *Panchayat Raj* Institutions (PRI). Since PRIs are in varying degrees of administrative effectiveness in the states, the latter are likely to follow different mechanisms for linkages between the watershed institutions and the PRIs. Wherever possible *panchayats* should be encouraged to undertake direct implementation of the Watershed Project. Elsewhere linkages should be forged between the *panchayats* and the watershed communities. Some of the mechanisms being adopted at present include: (i) provision of nominating two representative of the Village *panchayat* into the Watershed Committee of which one is a woman; (ii) declaring Watershed Committee as a sub-committee of the Land Management Committee under the Panchayat Raj Act.

For some schemes such as Drought-prone Areas Programme (DAP) and Desert Development Programme (DDP), *Panchayati Raj* Institutions have been assigned very active role at the district, block and village. The state governments have been authorised to empower the *zilla parishads* to discharge all functions of the District Rural Development Agencies (DRDAs) for planning and development of the watershed projects. In that capacity, the *zilla parishads* will select the watershed projects and the project implementation agencies, approve watershed committees and monitor and review the implementation of the programme.

The *panchayat samitis* have been given the right to monitor the implementation of the programme at the block level and give guidance for integration of other area development programmes. At the village level, the *gram panchayat* is to be fully involved in mobilising the community, training, dovetailing of other programmes and maintenance of common property resources such as pasture lands, fisheries tanks, plantation, etc. The *gram panchayat* has been entrusted with the task of monitoring the implementation of the programme. In addition to the above-mentioned functions, the *Panchayati Raj* Institutions are also entitled to take on the responsibility of planning and development of a cluster of watershed projects. In the capacity of a Project Implementation Agency, the *zilla parishad/ panchayat samiti/gram panchayat* concerned shall be subjected to the complete discipline and control of DRDA as any other PIA. They will have to constitute Watershed Development Team on the same lines as any other PIA and shall accordingly be entitled to demand and receive the prescribed administrative cost for each project.

For example, Ralegaon Siddhi Project, covering four watersheds in geographical area of about 892 hectares in Maharashtra, is one of the success stories. In a total project outlay of Rs. 112.75 lakh, the state government contributed Rs. 52.75 lakhs, Rs. 47 lakhs was borrowed from banks, Rs. 11 lakhs was put together by villagers through *shramdan* and the remaining Rs. 2 lakhs was raised from other sources. Result of the initiative: a series of checkdams, cemented *bandharas,* and *nullah bunds* have been built at strategic locations. All these increased the infiltration of harvested water and recharged groundwater. Today Ralegaon Siddhi has 2 percolation tanks, 30 *nullah bunds,* 85 wells, and 8 borewells all of which are viable right through the year. Farmers now grow two or three crops every year including fruits and vegetables. All the soil and water conservation structures were built through community action. The villagers have stopped grazing their animals on common lands; instead, they have switched to other ways. To take care of equitable distribution of water, they have formed associations called Pani Puravatha Mandals. The success story owes much to leadership of Shri Anna Hazare who turned a once poverty stricken Ralegaon Siddhi into a self-sufficient village. It is the people's participation that gave it all element of sustainability.

Reasons for Underperformance

Although, responsible authorities in Maharashtra follow the rules and regulations prescribed under the various Acts of the MoEF, the performance of the state on environmental fronts is far from satisfactory. There are several reasons for not achieving desired results and some of them are summarised as follows:

Problems from Authorities

- Multiplicity of authorities responsible for environmental sector is a serious problem in the state. The Department of Environment, MPCB and MCs are jointly responsible for environmental management. Recently, the Traffic Police Department is also involved in PUC checking. However, neither the common man nor many industries know the exact role of each of the authorities. Often, there are conflicts in carrying out the duties and sharing of data and information.
- Mismanagement of resources, rather than lack of resources, seems to be one of the main reasons for the underperformance of the environment sector. For example, in many MCs, a large number of their fleet of vehicles for waste collection is under repair, the timings of waste collection are inconvenient; and there is a lack of efforts from local authorities to educate people to manage their waste.
- Some of the MCs are taking steps to adopt efficient SWM but have not planned it properly. For example, they have planned to increase waste collection points and also ordered for several new waste collection bins but they are the same as old ones and not meant for segregated waste.
- Absence of a central database or environmental information system makes it difficult to track the defaulters. The officials are reluctant to reveal data and information to researchers or to the public, thus making it difficult to analyse the changes in the quality of the environment. Further, the findings of different agencies are too inconsistent, and therefore, analysis results could not be certain.

Problems from the Public

- There is a general lack of civic sense and willingness to play a constructive role in improving th environment problems is the state's responsibility and they do not have any role for themselves in it.
- In many cases, lack of awareness and education among masses about the environmental issues is the main reason for deteriorating conditions.

- Misuse or overuse of resources is a predominant reason for waste of natural resources. For e.g., a recent finding in Mumbai indicates that about half of the water provided to citizens is used inefficiently for non-potable purposes such as showering, brushing teeth, toilet flushing, shaving and car washing, etc. (IDFC, 2003).
- Even among the elite and educated class, "not in my backyard and throw away" attitude is damaging as although it can clean their own premises/establishments, it is harmful for their surroundings.
- Some of the environmental regulations are stringent and the technology to meet them is quite expensive. Hence, the defaulters try to circumvent the regulations, thus increasing the possibility of the use of unethical practices.
- Emerging environmental extremism in the state is a serious issue as, at times, it halts important development projects under the disguise of environmental damages due to the project.

Gaps in Existing Policies

- The existing environmental policies are lacking in some technical and other aspects. For example, surface water pollution due to washout of air pollutants and groundwater pollution through leaching of toxins from solid waste dumpsites, find no mention under regulations.
- The provisions for controlling the waste of a mine, quarry or a major construction site, which may be washed by rain into a water stream, are not sufficient.
- It is difficult for people to proceed against the polluter without prior sanction of the pollution board. This increases chances of collusion of defaulter with pollution authorities. Prosecution is difficult under the Environment Act, as polluters cannot be prosecuted for want of knowledge on their part.

Conclusions and Recommendations

Maharashtra, being a highly industrialised and populated state of India, has enormous environmental problems, which need urgent attention. All sub-sectors of environment i.e. water and wastewaster, air pollution, solid waste, forest and biodiversity, etc., require an efficient management.

Based upon the analysis of available data, information and personal interaction with the authorities, following suggestions could be helpful for improving environmental conditions and achieving sustainable development in the state.

Water and Wastewater

Educating all stakeholders, including commons, authorities responsible for distribution and policy makers, through mass awareness, media, training programmes, etc. could reduce the problems of wastage of water. Steps should be taken to create awareness about the importance of this natural resource so as to reduce the wastage of water at every stage.

- Improvement in rural water supply will require major institutional reforms as follows: adopting demand responsive approach (DRA) for service provision and the use of participatory process; empowering local institutions *(zilla parishads* and *gram panchayats*) and user groups (village water committees) to assume the lead role in decision making and operations; and ensuring financial viability of rural water supply through the DRA and an appropriate regulatory framework.
- Most of the MCs are making loss due to low charges for water. The structure of water tariff should be such that it ensures recovery of production cost. Demand side management, conservation and increasing the water tariffs for various uses will also discourage the users to misuse or overuse water.
- The scope exists to save as much as about 20-50 per cent of water if simple conservation measures are used in daily routine activities such as using water in a glass instead of use of running tap for shaving, using a bucket rather than hose for car washing etc. (IDFC, 2003).
- Regulating exploitation of groundwater resources and at the same time strengthening the sources through community initiative programmes like Shivkalin Pani Sathwan Yojana in rural areas and innovative programmes such as Aquifer Management Pilot Programme, which has been included in the World Bank aided Jalswarajya Project should be encouraged and their proper implementation must be ensured.
- Rainwater harvesting, a traditional art in water scarce areas of India, could be revived as a potential way to meet the water demand both in

rural and urban areas. Many parts of Maharashtra receive heavy rainfall during the monsoon season and this water could be trapped in underground constructed reservoirs, tanks, etc. and used for various purposes other than drinking. Some of the MCs have made rainwater-harvesting compulsory for all new building proposals. This could be extended to all parts of Maharashtra and for existing buildings. It will also be useful for ground water recharge, through borewells and inundation tanks, particularly in areas of scanty rainfall.

- Focusing on quality of water is essential as polluted water is causing several diseases in the state. Improving the conditions of water supply lines will reduce leakages and recontamination of water, and hence, would save water and reduce water related health hazards. Checking of water contamination at service connections, preventing mixing of sewage and drainage with water supply, cleaning storage and overhead tanks, repairing deteriorating internal lining of water mains and stopping seepage of surface water into mains through joints etc. are necessary. Some simple measures such as water boiling, using clean vessels, etc. could help in reduction of water borne diseases.
- Public cooperation is needed in not polluting the water resources by actions such as idol immersion, dumping of material used for worshipping like leaves and flowers during various festivals such as Ganapati, Navratri and Durga celebrations. This again, requires generating awareness among masses and their willingness to improve the conditions.
- Treatment of wastewater for reuse in irrigation and campaign for sensitisation of the community in urban areas programmes such as Sant Gadge Baba Sanitation Campaign should be encouraged.
- Surface water resources such as rivers and lakes need special attention in terms of both their usefulness and aesthetic appeal. Stress should be on cleaning and restoration of these resources, identifying sources of pollution and diverting them to other areas, and desilting of resources for increasing the capacity, etc.
- Some of the resources such as Lonar Salt Lake should be given special status and priority for carrying out the conservation and pollution prevention activities.
- The steps taken by GoM such as policy for restricting the location of industries along the riverbank according to the pollution potential of the industry could bring fruitful results in preventing river water pollution. Distillery units are of major concern in terms of environmental pollution. Therefore, it is essential to restrict their further development in these regions and existing ones should be asked for providing additional treatment facilities.
- There is an urgent need for regulations to address the issue of sustainable use of groundwater resources as their overexploitation has resulted in depletion in many areas of the state.
- Maharashtra, being a coastal state, needs special care to keep its beaches and other public places clean. This may result in boosting the flow of tourists to the state and improve its economy. Coastal biodiversity has special ecological significance and mangroves, saltpans and marine resources should be protected for sustainable development of coastal areas.
- Conventional treatments for municipal wastewater could be accompanied by low cost methods such as disposal of wastewater into constructed wetlands, particularly in areas where land prices are low. In rural areas, it can be treated using the duckweed-based system. Aerated lagoons, successfully tried in some areas could also be extended to other regions. In urban areas, adopting in-house wastewater recycling by housing societies, industrial premises and other establishments could reduce the load on conventional municipal systems.
- While major industries can take care of their effluents, small and medium level firms, due to high cost, find it difficult to treat their wastewaters to meet the prescribed standards. Accelerated and improved concept of CETPs, both in terms of technology and management, could be beneficial for such firms.
- Municipal wastewater, after proper treatment, could be used for irrigation purposes. This would be beneficial for areas with water scarcity and will also provide necessary nutrients for crops, thereby reducing the use of chemical fertilisers.

Air Pollution

Air pollution could be curbed substantially by controlling pollution from vehicles and industries.

- Programmes directed towards educating the public about measures for curbing vehicular pollution like avoiding idling, maintenance of vehicles, etc. through mass media should be launched. Industries should be asked to internalise the cost of environmental pollution into their economic accounts. In rural areas, cheap availability and easy access to clean fuels such as LPG will reduce the risks of indoor air pollution, especially among women and children.

- In order to achieve an effective abatement of air pollution, source identification and apportionment of pollutants is necessary. Approaches such as source models, receptor models, etc. can reveal both qualitative and quantitative contributions from all major sources in the study area. These techniques could be very effective in policy formulation and enforcement as they make it easy to identify the major culprits (sources) causing the pollution and focus on abatement measures for them. Some of such studies on source apportionment of aerosols in Mumbai were conducted in early nineties and have also been started recently by MMRDA (Sharma, 1994; Sharma, 1998b; Shrivastava and Kunte, 2003).
- Improvement in road infrastructure and traffic management is the key to reduce vehicular pollution. Construction of structures facilitating smooth traffic flow such as flyovers and subways are required in urban areas. Convenient and cheap mass transport schemes should be encouraged to reduce private traffic and congestion on the roads. Clean fuels such as low sulphur diesel, CNG, LPG or ethanol-blended fuels require large-scale introduction for use in automobiles.

Solid Waste

- An efficient SWM would include the safe and hygienic collection, transport, treatment and disposal of all categories of waste i.e. MSW, industrial waste and BMW. Policy for SWM should be framed using the principle of the 4 Rs i.e. reduce, recover, reuse and recycle. In fact, only 10-12 per cent of waste in general is of high risk, which could be separated at source in order to prevent it from getting mixed into the MSW.
- Some of the MCs in the state have already asked housing societies for source separation of waste, which will help in managing biodegradable and recyclable waste. Similarly, individual premises could be asked to increase vegetation cover such as plantation, gardening, etc. Vermiculture and composting at housing society level should also be promoted. However, despite the month long awareness programme by BMC, a survey revealed that 60 per cent of the housing societies did not segregate waste. On one hand, people showed a lack of willingness and awareness and on the other hand BMC officials did not provide the necessary infrastructure to do so (Moitra and Ramachandran, 2003).
- Use of innovative technologies, such as waste-to-energy, waste-to-building-material, waste-to-manure, etc. could be of double benefit as these not only manage the waste in a scientific way but the end products may fetch revenue for the resource crunched state.
- Creating awareness among workers and adopting low waste manufacturing processes could minimise quality of industrial waste occupational hazards among workers. Encouraging common hazardous waste management facilities for industries, and adopting better manufacturing processes can also manage waste.
- Social issues associated with SWM are to be tackled in an appropriate manner. Problems related to the health and exploitation of informal waste pickers and health of MC's staff. These could be solved to a great extent by educating them about the adverse impacts of MSW on health and providing them with preventive measures such as gloves, masks, etc. Ragpickers could also be provided with photo identity cards, which they can show to various housing societies/households and collect source separated waste from them.

Miscellaneous Issues

- Norms for noise pollution could be met by restricting the use of loud speakers during festivals (like Ganeshutsav, Navaratri, etc.), marriages and other events. Banning blowing of horns at traffic junctions is also needed, particularly in urban areas with high traffic density. Green belts surrounding industrial estates would also be helpful. Keeping in mind the vast area (almost 9,000 sq.km.) covered by bamboo in the state and its various uses, a policy should be devised to cater rural needs of the state. Use of this species as a means of employment generation by training artisans for creating quality handicraft and utility items for market may be explored. A well-planned discussion between the State Forest Department and various communities (bound to be affected from JFM) should determine Joint Forest Management (JFM). This will empower communities in deciding the structure of the forests in their neighbourhood. A specific scheme incorporating above viewpoint may be considered in the State Plan for implementation of JFM.

- Energy saving measures and the promotion of renewable energy will have long lasting impact on the environment. Steps such as installation of solar water heaters, photovoltaic systems for garden and street lighting, use of compact fluorescent lamps, energy conserving building design, energy audits for industries and energy conservation campaigns are required to be taken. Use of wind energy in the state has been started but requires proper cost-benefit analysis for further promotion.
- The role of NGOs and Community participation in expanding activities of JFMs is very important, as it would lead to increase in forest cover and development of the tribal areas. Hence, such initiatives at the grassroot level should be promoted and supported by both state and central governments and local people.
- To achieve the goal of 33 per cent tree cover in the state, a massive afforestation programme, with the help of other departments such as Public Works, Irrigation, School Education, Environment and Urban Development, etc. should be initiated.
- Integrated environmental management of slum areas especially in larger cities like Mumbai, Thane, Pune, etc. are of utmost importance. Many of these settlements are unauthorised and are plagued with the problems of congestion, unhygienic conditions and pollution related diseases. Improving conditions of slums requires collaboration among all stakeholders, i.e., public, government, NGOs, etc. Programmes such as Slum Redevelopment Scheme could only be useful when people are more aware of hygienic conditions and, in addition to incentives of free housing, they are also persuaded to shift to these tenements and not to sell them.
- For an overall better management of the environment, a system of incentive and punishment should be introduced. Achievers of pollution norms should be rewarded and defaulters should be penalised to discourage them from further lapses.
- Although research for innovations in ecology and environmental issues is the need of the hour, for a financially troubled state, repetition of the same kind of research is a sheer wastage of funds and could be avoided. Instead, action-oriented projects that practically bring change in the society should be promoted.
- Recently, use of public interest litigations (PILs) by NGOs, CBOs and individuals have drastically increased. While some of these are justified, others might just come up without having adequate information about the concerned project and retard the development activities. Hence, it becomes important to enhance public consultation and impart information, in general, as this would help in avoiding confrontation during project implementation stage and would make project feasible with the public support. Restricting unnecessary use of PILs is required so that they do not halt the development project of public interest. People should be given a reasonable time to put their views before commencement of activities and, after that no one should be permitted to obstruct the work.
- Conflicts between regulations of Central and state governments, which affect development plans of the state government, should be avoided. One such example could be of the CRZ regulations of the Central government and the Slum Redevelopment Scheme of the state government. Another recent example is the proposal of state government to increase the capacity of the Vaitarna Lake so as to have more water for Mumbai, which was turned down by MoEF on the grounds that it was harmful for the flora and fauna of the region that would be submerged due to an increase in the height of the Vaitarna Dam. Such conflicts can be reduced by making state level committees of experts who have done substantial work in the area of conflict. They would be able to convince the authorities regarding the positive and negative aspects of the concerned issues. Handling the issues related to encroachment, biodiversity conservation and forest offences needs capacity building and higher

investment. Forest management planning and protection need to be reinforced through appropriate HRD activities and adequate infrastructure. Recent trends for dealing with anthropogenic impact on biodiversity include village eco-development for which models are now available in the India Eco-development Project of MoEF and project was funded by UNDP in 1994. The main objective of the Project is to conserve biodiversity through eco-development and aims at Improved Protected Area Management (IPAM), Village Eco-development and Eco-development support. The Project also envisages preparation of future biodiversity projects covering a larger number of protected areas. The India Eco-development project is being implemented in seven areas, namely Buxa, Palamau, Nagarhole, Periyar, Pench, Ranthambore, tiger reserves and Gir National Park to conserve biodiversity through eco-development.

- Many of the public actions like spitting, urinating and defecating openly not only indicate uncivilised behaviour, but also create unhealthy conditions. Such actions can be stopped only by the cooperation of the public and stringent action by authorities.
- Capacity building is required in all areas of environment such as education, science and technology, economics and policy, social dimension, etc. Environment Education (EE) efforts, particularly in schools of rural and poor urban areas, are required to be accelerated. Care should be taken to encourage the students to join the EE programmes such as NCs, campaigns, trainings, nature trails, etc., with as far as possible, no financial contribution from children's side.

Chapter 16

Conclusions and Policy Recommendations

The preceding discussion gives a detailed account of the major development sectors of Maharashtra. The present scenarios of these sectors and main findings have been discussed, highlighting the successes and failures on each front. Based upon the findings of each sector in the state, overall conclusions and policy recommendations are suggested as follows.

Overall Conclusions

Based on the analysis of available data, information and subsequent findings of each chapter, overall conclusions are listed as follows:

- Maharashtra has good physical, social and financial infrastructure and a relative abundance of entrepreneurs. It is the most industrialised; the second most urbanised and, judged by the per capita income, the third richest state in India. However, weak agro-climatic conditions and low irrigation potentials and their utilisation in the state have resulted in low agricultural yields. Maharashtra spends a small share of its GDP on health and education. The social, economic, cultural and political climate in the state is responsible for lags in overall human development. Coalition politics and the coalition government, in recent years, have given an unfocused approach to key elements of institutional and policy reforms.
- Since 1997, the financial ability of all state governments has weakened and Maharashtra is no exception to this. Decline in receipts, apart from poor own tax and non-tax revenue, along with steady decline in the central transfers has put the state finances on a critical path. Analysis of state's current fiscal situation indicates that if the GoM does not undertake any significant fiscal reforms, the current fiscal situation may become unsustainable. The state is already unable to cope up with the high levels of debt and deficits.
- Though the major population of Maharashtra resides in rural areas, with agriculture as the dominant source of livelihood, the growth rate of this sector is very low. Public investment in agriculture is reported to be almost stagnant. The slowing down in the growth of work animals has been concomitant with the expansion of milch animal population in Maharashtra, which showed over 53 per cent growth between 1956 and 1997. Inadequate infrastructure and lack of flow of information technology have been cited as the major barriers for better market integration in the existing marine fish markets of India.
- Many of the irrigation projects started in different plan-periods have not been completed in time, which has resulted in cost overruns besides delaying water supply to farmers. Projections indicate that demand for irrigation water in the state is expected to increase by 182 per cent between 1996 and 2030. The investment required to create one hectare of irrigation under the MMI sector has increased by about 17 times between the Third and Eighth Five-Year plans in the state. This is partly due to inadequate allotment of funds required for completion of the projects. The ratio of potential utilised to the total potential created in irrigation, especially in MMI sector, is abysmally low in the state, as compared to the national average, due to inadequate allocation of funds required for constructing main and sub-canals. Area under micro-irrigation has increased phenomenally (about 65 per cent/annum) since 1986. Despite this, drip-irrigated area accounted for just 4.97 per cent of the net irrigated area as of 1999-00.

- The GoM followed an elaborate industrial policy to disperse industry and thereby reduce regional disparities within the state. However, this has not yielded the desired result and it is the time to have a fresh look at the policies, programmes and industrial setup for promotion and the long-term viability of the industrial sector in the state.

- The ratio of bank credit to infrastructure financing to the total bank credit was a meagre 2 per cent in 1998 and even in 2002 it was just about 6.5 per cent. Though Maharashtra's per capita consumption of power is high when compared to that for all India, the problem of regular supply of power across all the regions of the state is yet to be tackled. High T&D losses, poor maintenance, poor monitoring of consumption and distortions in pricing of electricity have adversely affected the growth of power sector and also the profitability of MSEB. Industries in the state have also been disadvantaged, while competing in the global market place, directly as a result of the irregular power supply at a high cost. Rural road network is better in Maharashtra than in other states, but urban regions, both in terms of quality of roads and road length, are not satisfactory. In terms of teledensity, Maharashtra falls among top states but the teledensity is skewly distributed. Low tariffs, poor service coverage, contaminated water supply, lack of accounting norms, deficient institutional arrangements, etc. are the problems of water supply, particularly in urban areas of the state.

- Most of the PSUs in Maharashtra are in a financially vulnerable position and continue to depend on the grants and support from the government. Further, delays in the finalisation of the accounts of the PSUs, as well as inefficient practices of some of the PSUs have resulted in severe losses to the government. There are at least 30 units, where restructuring can take place immediately. Several of these 30 units operate on low efficiency and high cost basis. The government could easily merge some of them and form a single corporation. State's restructuring and privatisation agenda is gaining momentum, but very slowly. If accelerated and enforced properly, privatisation and restructuring will provide a good deal of revenues to the state government and also make the PSUs commercial entities in the true sense of the term.

- In 2000, for the first time, the *World Human Development Report* affirmed that the enjoyment of human rights is an integral part and a necessary condition for human development. The development of the weaker sections, co-terminus with their emancipation, may pose major challenges in Maharashtra in the coming decades.

- Maharashtra, with its rich cultural heritage and natural beauty, boasts traditional age-old handwoven and handcrafted articles along with the advanced technology in the state. Handlooms and handicrafts have the potential to provide gainful employment to thousands of weavers and craftsmen with minimum financial investment in the state.

- Increasing public demands for better quality of services are posing major challenges for governance in the state. There are age-old legislations that still hold well. It is indicated that there are about 400 obsolete laws in the country which were formulated ages ago, have ceased to have any relevance in present times, and thus, are not conducive to the development of the state.

- Developmental intervention, over the years, has brought about a marked reduction in poverty and illiteracy in the state. Specifically, the gap between rural and urban poverty and rural and urban illiteracy has declined. With respect to primary education and electricity too, the state has performed well. Special programmes such as EGS, IAY, SGSY, etc. have helped in tackling problems of rural employment and poverty, to some extent. The PRIs helped the emergence of leadership and contributed for the improvement of quality of rural life.

- The primary strength of tourism in Maharashtra is Mumbai. In addition to being the commercial and entertainment capital of the country, Mumbai is now planning to be a top urban tourist destination. The city houses many famous tourist spots such as the Gateway of India, museums, shopping malls, Bollywood, amusement parks, beaches and the international airport that brings around 26 per cent of international tourists to India. The weaknesses of tourism in Maharashtra include long haul tourist dependence, Mumbai's host ambience and its poor connectivity to various within state destinations, dependence on business tourism, lack of innovation, information availability and quality human resources. The opportunities for the state's tourism are based on domestic tourism, proximity to economically growing ASEAN countries, growth in cultural tourism, business tourism and MICE market and the international airport that is being planned at Goa, just a few kilometres away from the high tourism potential district of Sindhudurg. The threats to tourism are the perception of tourists about various aspects, global and national effects, safety and security issues in Mumbai, economic situations at source market and competition from other Indian states.

- Although Maharashtra is a highly urbanised state, levels of urbanisation are uneven across regions and districts. Policies towards equalisation of the extent of urbanisation and urban growth were in operation but implemented too slowly to satisfy the protagonists of regional equality. While globalisation and liberalisation hold some promises, they also pose some danger for the backward regions of the state. Urban poverty has emerged as a complex, multidimensional phenomenon. However, in order to meet individual's needs, the programmes need to cater to all types of vulnerabilities on a proper assessment of possible forms of poverty in a given context. Homelessness has specially been observed, with respect to the vulnerable sections, necessitating appropriate schemes to increase the availability of affordable housing to economically weaker sections and low income group, which, in turn, leads to facilitating allocation of land, extension of funding assistance, provision of support services, etc.
- In the registered manufacturing sector, the elasticity of employment with respect to manufacturing SDP is 0.14. Elasticity estimate with respect to 'gross capital formation' is also of a similar magnitude. The informal and very small and medium size establishments hold better promises of employment growth. Lack of savings, inability to attract FDI, high cost of power, high cost of credit, poor and unreliable infrastructure, improper regulations and untargeted non-merit subsidies are the well-known factors that have caused retardation of output and employment opportunities in the state. EGS perhaps provides effective floor to rural or agriculture wage rates. However, availability of EGS works opportunities is very uneven across districts.
- There is a lack of desired attention towards the environmental management in the state. In general, public cooperation and coordination among concerned authorities is not satisfactory. Both quantity and quality of water are not up to the mark and wide disparity exists in the amount of water supplied in different areas. Per capita water availability in the state is lower than that at national level. Wastage of water in a common feature and it is as high as 50 per cent due to misuse, overuse and leakage during various stages of water supply system. Similarly, sanitation facilities, in both urban and rural areas are highly inadequate. Various programmes on water supply and sanitation, initiated by the GoM have met with only a limited success. While high levels of SPM and RPM from industries, transportation and construction activities are the major causes of concern in urban areas, the low quality of fuel used in rural areas is responsible for indoor air pollution. Higher levels of RPM are responsible for various health problems in the state. Noise levels in many towns exceed standards in all categories of areas, for both day and night, by wide margins, mainly due to industrial and vehicular noise.
- Proper treatment and disposal of wastewater and solid waste are lacking. As high as 99 per cent of sewage from municipal councils and 50 per cent of that for municipal corporations goes untreated and eventually finds its way into various water bodies. Continuous flow of untreated or partially treated wastewater into the rivers has degraded their water quality and they can neither be used as drinking water source nor for outdoor bathing. Millions of people in the state, especially, children, get affected due to water borne diseases. Only 10-12 per cent of total waste generated is of high risk, which could be separated at the source in order to prevent it from getting mixed into the MSW. However, despite some policy initiatives from ULBs, most of the housing societies do not segregate waste and the main reasons for this are lack of willingness, poor awareness and civic sense among people and lack of necessary infrastructure provided by the authorities. Use of non-conventional energy such as wind energy in the state has been started but it lacks proper cost-benefit analysis for further promotion.

Policy Recommendations

In order to plan an appropriate strategy for future development of the state, the following policy recommendations are suggested.

- To grow at a sustainable rate of 8 to 10 per cent per annum, over the decade 2002-2012, and for overall human development, the state should concentrate on manufacturing, infrastructure and services sectors. Agriculture and allied sectors, being the priority sectors in the future growth of the state, should be given due emphasis and necessary measures need to be taken for streamlining the credit flow in these sectors.

- Since the current fiscal policy stance is unsustainable, a fiscal correction is a must to achieve a sustainable fiscal policy regime. Three major areas of reforms could be—enhanced resource mobilisation effort, expenditure restructuring and an interest cost minimising debt management policy.

- Medium-term framework resource mobilisation effort of GoM would need to concentrate on both own tax and non-tax revenues. This would entail reforms involving areas of tax policy and tax administration. Introduction of state-level VAT would be one such step in the area of tax policy. This would reduce problems of double taxation of commodities and multiplicity of taxes, resulting in cascading tax burden. This would also reduce or eliminate artificial manipulation with the tax base, ensuring better compliance.

- For a better tax administration, the present system would require to be revamped with an improved computerisation with facility to prepare a large database and its retrieval system. Tax audit can be done on the basis of third party information system provided by such computerised database.

- With regard to non-tax revenues, user charges for all non-merit services would need to be linked to the cost. For merit goods, such as primary education and basic health care facilities, this norm may not be applied.

- There is also sufficient scope for increasing the earnings in the form of interest, dividends and profits. The government must bring out a proper disinvestments policy for withdrawing from the sectors, which can be considered to be non-core areas. Proceeds of such disinvestments can be used to finance the high cost debts by introducing large-scale debt swap.

- On the expenditure side, any reform would be limited given the committed liabilities nature of the expenditure items, like interest payment, pension and salaries and wages. One way of reducing the salary payments is to go for reduction of the number of state government employees. It can be suggested that the reduction in numbers can be 2 per cent per annum. This is so because average natural attrition rate is 2.8 per cent per annum. But such reduction should not affect the delivery of critical services. Arresting the growth of pension would not be an easy task. New initiatives in this regard should be taken which could be in terms of introduction of 'Funded Pension Schemes' for the new employees.

- Rapid reduction in the debt-servicing obligation both by reducing the fiscal deficit and also by a reduction in the cost of debt servicing is another area of focus. In the prevailing low interest rate regime, an active debt management policy should try to alter the high cost debt structure to low cost, through large-scale retiring of expensive debt introducing debt swapping. State public sector enterprises need to function on commercial lines, and should provide adequate return on capital invested.

- For better contingent liabilities management, rationale for extending guarantees should be carefully examined and underlying risks documented. For better cash management, treasury operations should be fully computerised and access to overdraft with RBI be reduced, if not eliminated.

- The government may have to reformulate its policies and priorities to create an environment suitable for agricultural growth. Improvement in agricultural productivity and diversification of the traditional patterns of horticulture, animal husbandry, etc., is required. Equally important is the need to promote rural non-farm employment so that the burden on the agricultural sector is reduced. Growth in both of these sectors will generate more rural income, stimulate consumer demand and give a boost to other economic sectors. The GoM should withdraw its support to the cooperative sugar mills and in the cotton sector. It should also phase out the monopoly procurement scheme. Allied activities, which provide supplementary and complementary employment and also add to the income of the farmers, must be promoted. Offshore fishery resources should be promoted through introduction of newly designed fuel-saving multiday mechanised fishing vessels, deep sea fishing vessels, and production of both marine inland fisheries from reservoirs and culture fisheries to increase the overall fish production. There is a need to educate fishermen and disseminate to them the information about mechanised fishing techniques and efficient marketing of fish-catch.

- The GoM must reform the APMC Act, 1963 so as to allow private parties to develop agricultural markets in the state as this would facilitate the creation of more markets and improve market infrastructure. Private sector investment in agro-processing, use of IT for dissemination of information to farmers and upgradation of knowledge, skills and communication capacity of extension personnel will help in increasing the agricultural performance. To rejuvenate rural credit delivery system, high transaction costs and poor repayment performance need to be tackled. In order to fully capitalise on exports, it is necessary to invest in post-harvest technology and ensure that there are no infrastructure bottlenecks. In addition, technical measures for maintaining food quality and sanitary and phytosanitary requirements are required.
- While no single strategy is going to solve the problem of water scarcity, there is an urgent need to formulate appropriate strategies to reduce the demand for water in the irrigation sector. On the whole, the state must plan to use water judiciously, reduce its intervention in sensitive crops like cotton and sugarcane, capitalise on its horticultural and floriculture sectors, promote allied activities, strengthen rural infrastructure and encourage private sector participation and investment in agriculture. Policies on water resource development and management should be different for water surplus and water scarce basins. The state should also study the feasibility of transfer of water from water surplus basins to water scarce basins. To compensate for the inequality in the distribution of surface irrigation, more investment must be made on minor irrigation and watershed development programmes in those districts, which have less area under surface irrigation.
- Priority must be given to bridge the gap between irrigation potential created and actual area under irrigation. Constructing community wells, increased use of drip irrigation and better utilisation of available groundwater may ease this problem. Watershed development is very necessary to stabilise the carrying capacity of land and water resources in rainfed areas. Irrigation policy should be focused on completion of ongoing projects. Massive Watershed Development Programmes (WDPs) must become central, and not marginal. The GoM should seek to involve *Panchayat Raj* Institutions in both implementation and maintenance of projects under WDPs. Proper coordination between departments that are operating WDPs is needed. The state must also make full utilisation of resources available from NABARD's RIDF facility.
- Since irrigation sector of Maharashtra is the largest in India, it is essential to establish a Water Regulatory Authority (WRA), similar to State Electricity Regulatory Commission (SERC), to manage and suggest strategies for improving the performance of irrigation sector as well as to solve all water related disputes within the state. Water rates for different uses and working expenses needed to maintain the sector should be approved by the WRA. In order to increase the collection of water revenue, a two-part tariff structure can be introduced, wherein all land owners within the command area should pay a flat annual membership fee, on a per hectare basis, which entitles them to claim water, and a variable fee linked to the actual extent of service used by each member.
- Department of Industries should evolve suitable schemes and activate its district centres to adopt new management techniques for quality improvement, cost reduction, improved productivity and operational efficiency. Sick small-scale units and non-BIFR units should be rejuvenated. For industrial development in the backward regions of the state, better institutional support should be provided. Film industry should be supported and promoted, particularly to make it competitive in the global markets. In view of the growing concerns for the environment, industrial pollution

should be tackled and clean technologies should be promoted to minimise damage to environment.

- The infrastructure facilities especially power, ports and road network should be improved. The provision of most of the infrastructure services involves the Central Government, the state government and the local bodies. A proper integration of roles, responsibilities and obligations of these layers of the governments is required. Accelerated Power Development Reform Programme (APDRP) can be treated as a model, which provides efficiency-based incentives to states. Similarly, other incentive schemes should be devised for the efforts of the state in providing various infrastructure services and promoting efficiency. There is an urgent need to develop centre-state cooperation and private sector participation in the development of infrastructure. Private sector participation can take various hybrid forms including responsibility of construction, transient ownership, operation, and leasing and ultimate ownership. Privatisation can also act, as a substitute for the lack of political will to implement tariff rationalisation by the state utilities. Privatisation in distribution of power and water can help in reducing T&D losses, leakages and thefts and improve financial position of SEBs and ULBs.
- Removal of anomalies in tariff policies both across various infrastructures services (inter-services) and also within the same service (intra-service) needs to be carefully looked into. Some of the infrastructure schemes, such as construction of roads can be integrated with the employment and income generation programmes to help in alleviation of poverty. One of the most contentious issues in development of infrastructure in the state pertains to the land acquisition and displacement of PAP. The state should ensure proper compensation packages to the PAP to ensure development of infrastructure with a less inhuman face.
- Technical and conceptual capabilities, which can provide impetus to the functioning of the organisations, are the needs of the hour in the programme of restructuring and reformulation of the public sector undertakings in Maharashtra. Outright sale of the equities of the public sector enterprises may not evoke much response in the absence of a clear-cut portrayal of the role of the state as well as the enterprise in the industry and the economy in which the firm operates. Unit-specific disinvestment strategy would go a long way to improve the efficiency and revenue generation capacity of the enterprise. The state needs to make a clear distinction between public corporations and cooperatives in the manner in which it proceeds for disinvestment. Since public sector cooperatives have a welfare maximisation criterion, it would be difficult to formulate a disinvestment policy in these cases.
- Human and social capital should be strengthened to generate initiatives in governance that dovetail development with local conditions and emancipate people. Building technical capacities that equip people to create employment opportunities in their local environment is necessary. Political parties and trade unions with the help of NGOs and others should try to resolve human development issues and empowerment of women. Diversification of skills enhancement is required to ensure wider employment choices and opportunities in the state. A statutorily enforceable time-bound, Universal Food and Nutrition Security Action Plan should be formulated with committed resource allocation for near universal PDS.
- A Comprehensive Resources and Sustainable Livelihoods Action Plan with specified actionable programmes should be targeted to ensure one guaranteed dignified year-long livelihood for every family through vigorous promotion of sustained agriculture and micro-enterprises, re-oriented EGS, and integrated livelihoods with forest conservation. The Plan must include a comprehensive package of training in entrepreneurial and technical skills, the creation of employment opportunities in the local environment, financial and technical inputs, lab to land linkages, development support and the effective implementation of land-laws to provide inalienable land rights to SCs and STs.
- A comprehensive Health Assurance Programme should be implemented including a Universal Health Insurance Scheme, a special tribal health policy, strengthening and extension of primary health care with assured budgetary allocations, and social audit of public and private health centres. An Education Assurance and Action Programme linked to livelihoods should be implemented with inclusion of livelihoods (vocational and entrepreneurial) streams from VIII

standard and open schools-cum-community polytechnics. The programme should also include multiple entry points in academic institutions with bridge examinations, consolidation of literacy with functional and entrepreneurial skills, and qualitative improvement in teaching methods.

- Community participation and leadership in the local self-governance should be strengthened through capacity building of *Panchayati Raj* functionaries and *gram sabha* members. This is required to manage natural resources and implement PESA effectively, empower women's *panchayats* and transfer financial powers to *panchayat samitis* and *gram panchayats*. Policies should be implemented through formulation of supportive rules, regulations and procedures including monitoring of functionaries and welfare schemes by *gram sabha*, continuation of subsidies for social sector, extension of reservation policy (with preference to first generation beneficiaries) to private sector and underprivileged among minorities. Persons with disability should be given equal access to technical, professional and higher education, provided with livelihood security, and should be empowered to participate in the institutions of local self-governance.
- The tradition and richness of the handmade textiles and handicrafts must survive along with technological advancements in order to bring an economic balance and maintain job opportunities in rural areas. Developing a good marketing network can give a push to the accumulated inventories and augment the modern development of the handlooms and handicrafts sector. Revamping of the Handloom Corporation will provide a major thrust to the sector. Developing and exploiting the inherent skills in producing consumer-oriented merchandise, with design and quality intervention and marketing in the right environment, would better sustain this sector.
- In governance, a systemic change starting with electoral reforms and system improvements is recommended. Electoral reforms will have to start with process improvements like prevention of polling irregularities, arresting and reversing criminalisation and checking abuse of unaccountable money power. Systems improvement should include reforms in political parties. Report of various committees on reforms should include public opinion and a time frame should be set for the implementation of any report after it is submitted. Repeal of old and obsolete legislation is necessary. The State Law Commission should tackle the task of identifying obsolete laws as quickly as possible. Administrative reforms are necessary to improve the efficiency and transparency of government functioning and service delivery. Public private participation (PPP) can promote good governance. This system has been tried out successfully for the registration of documents and can be used in the PDS and other activities.
- Once the Legislature passes the Appropriation Bill, (already passed by the Centre in August 2004) expenditure should be totally in accordance with the appropriation. The police authorities should become instruments for upholding the Rule of Law. For making this effective, they need to be insulated from any political interference in their operational matters. The police should also be made accountable to the law.
- Maharashtra has taken several good initiatives for e-governance. For instance, SETU is for the issue of various types of certificates and SARITA is for registration. Quality in government services can be improved by integrating the Citizen's Charter and information technology initiatives under a holistic umbrella. There should be a proper monitoring of the citizens' charters, preferably by an NGO, and they should be easily available without any difficulty and should be given a wide publicity. The institution of *Lok Ayukta* should be made more transparent to the public.
- For integrated development of villages, measures need to be taken to expand the medical and transport facilities, post and telegraph services, market and *pukka* roads to a large number of villages. Special attention is required for Vidarbha region, which is lagging behind. Devolution of more power to the *gram sabha* with greater accountability and transparency at all levels could enhance the people's participation and empowerment.
- The *panchayats* should be endowed with adequate responsibilities and necessary powers in the area of financial administration so as to ensure their autonomy in the decision making process at local levels. In addition to funds allotted for the centre-sponsored schemes, financial assistance could be provided to the *panchayats* to undertake development programmes as per the local

requirement. Efforts could be made to provide certain percentage of grants to the *gram panchayats* as untied grants, subject to the broad guidelines under which such untied funds could be utilised. Authorisation to *panchayats* to levy and collect appropriate taxes, duties, tolls and fees, making such amendments which are in consonance with the provisions of Article 243H of the Constitution and recommendations of the State Finance Commission should be considered.

- Tourism development requires removal of information barriers, intelligent decision making process and information about Maharashtra's present key markets, their spending patterns, future interests and economic conditions. A long-term standard system of tourism data collection and analysis with the help of Ministry of Tourism, the GoI and the GoM should be developed. Also, sustainable tourism guidelines, policies and standards that would help in development of eco-friendly destinations such as Sindhudurg beach destination and wildlife destinations in Vidharba should be framed. Sustainable Tourism Destination Plans for some specific places should be undertaken in the short term and encourage private sector participation by adequate promotion of such destinations in Maharashtra.

- Implementation of Tourism Satellite Account is needed in cooperation with WTO and WTTC, India to promote investment in the tourism sector at grassroot level e.g. development of micro-enterprises to promote rural tourism. A high level of professional education and training at all levels of the tourism industry is needed. This will consider the levels and targets for future demand by improving quality of services. It will also include increasing the tourism awareness of the people of Maharashtra and encouraging young people to engage in tourism courses and undertake tourism as a profession. Maharashtra's religious destinations attract tourists from all over India and abroad. Improving the environment and ambience of such religious destinations should be undertaken.

- The goal of the urban agenda involves development of a host of broad sub-sectors like sustainable expansion of urban infrastructure facilities such as water supply, sanitation, environment planning, transport infrastructure, creating an enabling legal, financing, regulatory framework for housing, land acquisition and development, township development, poverty alleviation, research and training, strengthening of urban local bodies (ULBs) and capacity building of ULB personnel, etc.

- Enhancement in the flow of investment to the critical sectors of urban infrastructure, creating a facilitating process for speeding up the growth of new economic activities and expansion of the existing ones is suggested. Urban upgradation encompassing housing, social, physical and economic environment, amenities and services, including integrated transport system, have to be recognised as part of state development process. An important concern of the government should be to provide policy framework and legislative, fiscal and financial system that would put into effect the enabling role of the government in the housing delivery system.

- Innovative areas of employment are required to be explored to suit the state conditions. Diversification of agriculture and protective irrigation will provide better employment potential. This may need reforms in agricultural marketing to allow direct marketing by farmers' companies and societies and amending laws to accommodate this possibility. Government can raise the demand for goods and services with the hope that the multiplier effect will enhance employment. Given the fiscal constraints, incremental improvements in the existing capacity would be the best that one can hope. Government agencies engaged in training, information services, market intelligence and market building would be helpful.

- Maharashtra has several environmental problems, which need urgent attention. The state leads in industrial and economical growth, which generates high levels of pollution, and at the same time, it also houses India's best bio-diversity hotspots, sanctuaries and national parks. Therefore, very balanced strategies are needed to solve the current environmental problems and prevent future ones. Environmental awareness and education need a significant capacity building among all stakeholders of environment, including commons, authorities and policy makers, through media, training programmes, camps, etc. Increased role of NGOs and community in sustainable environmental management is the need of hour.

- Water conservation measures such as rainwater harvesting and sustainable use of groundwater resources would reduce problems of shortage of water. Demand-side management and rationalising the water tariffs for various uses will discourage the users to misuse or overuse water. Reuse and recycling of municipal wastewater should be encouraged. After proper treatment, wastewater could be used for irrigation purposes. This would be beneficial for areas with water scarcity and will also provide necessary nutrients for crops, thereby reducing the use of chemical fertilisers. Conventional treatments for municipal wastewater accompanied by low cost treatment methods, such as disposal of wastewater into constructed wetlands, in-house wastewater recycling by housing societies and other establishments, etc. would reduce the load on conventional municipal systems. Accelerated and improved concept of CETPs, both in terms of technology and management, would be beneficial for industrial areas.
- Alarming levels of air pollutants and health problems associated with them indicate the need for an urgent action for improvement of vehicle design, use of clean fuels, improvements in road infrastructure and better traffic management. Promotion of mass transport by improving the condition of existing mass transport system, encouraging private car pool, etc. will reduce air pollution to a great extent. Encouragement of renewable energy and non-conventional energy sources, innovative technologies, bio-fuels, energy audits, energy campaigns, etc. will have long lasting positive impact on the environment.
- Policies for SWM should be framed using the principle of the four Rs i.e. reduce, recover, reuse and recycle. Source separation of waste should be encouraged so that mixing of waste is avoided and segregated waste could be utilised in a meaningful way. Housing societies should be encouraged to go for vermi-composting, kitchen garden techniques, etc. Similarly, promotion of common hazardous waste collection, treatment and disposal facilities for industries is required. Strict enforcement of policies is necessary to prevent deforestation and encroachment on forestland and other areas of public interest. Coastal biodiversity and marine resources should be protected for sustainable development of coastal areas of the state. Last but not the least, conflicts between the regulations of central and state governments, which affect development plans of the state, should be avoided.

References

Abbie *et al.* (1982). "Economic Returns to Investment in Irrigation in India", *World Bank Staff Working Papers No. 336*, The World Bank, Washington D.C.

Acharya, Sarathi (1990). *Maharashtra Employment Guarantee Scheme: A Study of Labour Market Intervention*, ILO-ARTEP, Delhi.

Agarwal, Nikita (2003). "From Line to Online", *rediff.com*.

Aggarwal, Suresh Chand (2002). "Productivity in Public, Joint and Private Sectors of Indian Industry: An Assessment of Relative Performance in Pre and Post Reform Periods", *Journal of Indian School of Political Economy*, April-June, pp. 235-50.

Agnihotri, V.K. (2002). "Keynote Address", *International Workshop on Good Governance*, New Delhi, *http://persmin.nic.in/arpg/gg2000.htm*, June 6, 2003.

Ahluwalia, Harjeet (2003). "Infrastructure Development", *Employment News*, 27 (51), March 22-28.

Ahluwalia, Isher Judge (1985). *Industrial Growth in India: Stagnation since the Mid-Sixties*, Oxford University Press, Delhi.

Ahluwalia, Montek S. (2002). "State-level Performance under Economic Reforms in India" in Anne O. Krueger (Ed.), *Economic Policy Reforms and the Indian Economy*, OUP, New Delhi.

Aikara, J. (1996). "Inequality of Educational Opportunities: The Case of Scheduled Castes in India", *Journal of Educational Planning and Administration*, X, (1), pp. 1-14.

AIMA News (2002). A bi-monthly newsletter of All India Management Association, 6(6), November-December .

———. (2003). A bi-monthly newsletter of All India Management Association, 6 (1), January-February.

Annual Report (2001-2002). Export Promotion Council for Handicrafts, under the aegis of Development Commissioner, Ministry of Textiles, Government of India.

———. (2001-2002). Khadi and Village Industries Commission, A Premier Organisation for Rural Industrialisation-Report prepared by the Directorate of Economic Research.

Anshuman, Ravi, V. (2003). "Disinvestments of PSUs: Leaving Money on the Table", *Economic and Political Weekly*, March 8, pp. 949-54.

Apte, J.S. (2002). "Grameen Vikas Karyakramache Ardhashatak", *Loksatta*, 2nd October.

Aram, Arul I. (2002). "E-Governance-Towards the Global Village", *www.inomy.com/egovernance/gover1.asp*, June 8.

Bagchi, Amiya Kumar (1970). "Long-Term Constraints on India's Industrial Growth, 1951-68", in Robinson, E.A.G. and Kidron Michael (eds.).

Bagchi, S.K. (2000). India Watch Monograph Series Natural Resource Management–Western Region, Uplabdhi-Trust for Development, New Delhi.

Bajpai, Nirupam and Jeffrey D. Sachs (1996)." Trends in Inter-State Inequalities of Income in India", *Development Discussion Paper No. 528*, Harvard Institute for International Development, Harvard University.

———. (1999). "The Progress of Policy Reform and Variations in Performance at the Sub-National Level in India", *Development Discussion Paper No. 730*, Harvard Institute for International Development, Harvard University.

Balakrishnan, S. (2003). "Many Major Issues Confront Shinde", *Times of India*, Mumbai, May, 27.

Bang, A. (1983). "Rojgar Hami Yojanebabat Gawai Samiteeche Nishkarsh Va Aapan", *Hakara*, Year 4, No. 1 (Jan.-March) (Marathi).

Baradhan, Pranab K. (2003). "Political Economy and Governance: Issues in the Indian Economic Reform Process", The Australia South Asia Research Centre K.R. Narayanan Oration, The Australian Natural University, Canberra.

———. (1997). "Corruption and Development: A Review of Issues", *Journal of Economic Literature*, 35.

Baru, Sanjaya (2002). "Why Maharashtra Isn't a Malaysia", *Financial Express*, Mumbai, October 25.

Basak, Asoke (2002). "Infrastructure Summit 2002", MEDC, *www.medcindia.org* February 28.

Baviskar, B.S. (2002). "Including the Excluded: Empowering the Powerless Case Studies of Panchayati Raj in Maharashtra", Paper Presented in a Workshop at Institute of Social Sciences on 12-13 September, New Delhi.

Bedi, K., P.J. Singh and S. Srivastava (2001). *Government New Governance Opportunities for India*, Sage, New Delhi.

Behura, Debdutt and Pradhan, Durga Charan (1998). "Cointegration and Market Integration: An Application to the Marine Fish Markets in Orissa", *Indian Journal of Agricultural Economics*, 53, (3), pp. 344-350.

Besley, Timothy and Robin Burgess (2002). "The Political Economy of Government Responsiveness: Theory and Evidence from India", *Quarterly Journal of Economics*, V 117(4).

Bhagwat, V. (2001). "Engendering the Curriculum and Developing a Curriculum on Gender: A Tightrope Walk", Paper presented at the curriculum and Research Workshop, IIAS, Shimla.

———. (2002). "Women's Studies in the University: Engagements and Disruptions", *Indian Journal of Gender Studies*, 9(2), Sage Publication, New Delhi.

Bhalla, Shiela (2000). "Behind Poverty: The Qualitative Deterioration of Employment Prospects for Rural Indians", *Working Paper No. 7*, Institute for Human Development.

Bhalla, G.S. and Gurmail Singh (2001). *Indian Agriculture: Four Decades of Development*, Sage Publications, New Delhi.

Bhandari, Chitra (1993). "All Women Panchayats of Maharashtra", *Peoples Action*, 8(2).

Bhat, K.S. (1974). "Panchayati Raj Administration in Maharashtra", *Popular Prakashan*, Bombay.

Bhatkar, R. (2003). "Bilgaon: Navya Bhavishyachi Nandi", *Sakal* (daily) March 9, (Marathi), Mumbai.

Bhatnagar, Subash and Schware (eds.) (2000). *Information and Communication Technology in Rural Development*, Thousand Oaks, CA, Sage.

Bhatnagar, Subash (2000). "Information Technology and Development: Foundation and Key Issues."

Bhosale, B.V. (2003). *Chairmakers in Transition*, Nurali Prakashan Company, Mumbai.

Bhushan, Prashant (2002). "India Approves Freedom of Information Law, Freedom of Information Bill, National Campaign Committee for the People's Right to Information", *www.freedoninfo.org*.

BMRDA (1995). Draft Regional Development Plan for Bombay Metropolitan Region, Bombay Metropolitan Region Development Authority, Bombay.

Bokil, M. (1995). "Bhatkya Vimukthanchi Loksankhya Nemki Keethi", *Sakal Weekly*, Oct. 21.

———. (2002). "De-notified Nomadic Tribes—A Perspective", *Economic and Political Weekly*, 37, (2), pp. 148-154.

———. (2002). "Grameen Vikasneetee", *Manthan*, pp. 5-11.

———. (2002). Tribal Communities and Sustainable Livelihood: Lessons From Bordi, *Journal of Rural Development*, 21(2), pp. 163-186, Hyderabad, NIRD.

Bokil, M.S. (1996). "Privatisation of Commons for the Poor Emergence of New Agrarian Issues", *Economic and Political Weekly*, 31 (33).

Borwankar, C. Meera (2003). "Good Governance – Maharashtra Police Perspective", Presentation at the *Workshop on Governance: The Maharashtra Experience*, jointly by JBIMS and IIPA, at Jamnalal Bajaj Institute of Management Studies Mumbai on April 28.

Brara, Alok (2003). "State Initiatives in Infrastructure Development", India Infrastructure, 50 (6).

Brenda Gael McSweeney (2002). UNDP representative, Cited Mark Malloch Brown, Address at the Launch of the *Maharashtra Human Development Report*, Mumbai, June.

Brewer, J. *et al.* (1999). *Irrigation Management Transfer in India: Policies, Processes and Performance*, Oxford and IBH Publishing Company, New Delhi.

Burange, L.G. (1999). "Industrial Growth and Structure Manufacturing Sector in Maharashtra", *Economic and Political Weekly*, February 27-March 5.

Business Council (1999). *Changes in Leisure Time : The Impact on Tourism.*

Business Standard (2003). "Maharashtra Cabinet Kicks of Discussion on Information Bill", Mumbai, March 11.

Business Standard (2003). Mumbai, February 25.

CAG (2000-01). *Maharashtra Civil Report*, Comptroller and Auditor General of India, New Delhi.

———. (2001-02). *Maharashtra Civil Report*, Comptroller and Auditor General of India, New Delhi.

———. (2001). *Overview of Government Companies and Statutory Companies*, Comptroller and Auditor General of India, New Delhi.

———. (1981). *Primary Census Abstract*, Series-14, Maharashtra, Registrar General, New Delhi.

Census of India (1991a). *Aging Population of India An Analysis of the 1991 Census Data*, Registrar General, New Delhi.

———. (1991b). *State Profile 1991 India*, The Controller of Publications, Registrar General, New Delhi.

———. (1991c). *Maharashtra Primary Census Abstract*, Series-14, Registrar General, New Delhi.

———. (1991d). *Primary Census Abstract*, Registrar General, New Delhi.

———. (2001a). *Provisional Population Totals*, Paper-3 of 2001, Series-28 Maharashtra, Distribution of Workers and Non-Workers, Registrar General, New Delhi.

———. (2001b). *Provisional Population Totals*, Paper-1 of 2001, Series-1, India, Registrar General, The Controller of Publications, New Delhi.

Central Electricity Authority (2000). *Sixteenth Electric Power Survey of India*, Central Electricity Authority, Ministry of Power, Government of India, New Delhi.

Center for Research and Development (1996). *Socio-economic Review of Greater Bombay 1994-95*, Mumbai.

Chakrabarty, G. and P.K. Ghosh (2002). Report No. 4 - *Human Development Profile of Scheduled Castes and Scheduled Tribes in Selected States – A Bench Mark Survey*, NCAER, New Delhi.

Chand, Ramesh (2001). "Emerging Trends and Issues in Public and Private Investments in Indian Agriculture: A State-wise Analysis", *Indian Journal of Agricultural Economics*, 56(2), pp.161-184.

Chandrasekhar, C.P. (1988). "Aspects of Growth and Structural Change in Indian Industry", *Economic and Political Weekly*, Special Number, November, 23, (45-7), pp. 2359-70

Changes in Leisure Time (1999). "The Impact on Tourism", *Leisure Time*.

Chatterjee, S.K. (2000). "Educational Development of Scheduled Castes: Looking Ahead", Gyan Publishing House, New Delhi.

Chaturvedi, A.N. (1985). "Waste Land Afforestation", *The Indian Forester*, 111, (11), pp. 919 - 926.

Chaudhuri, B. (1992). "Tribal Transformation in India", *Tribal Studies of India* Series, Vol. II, Inter-India Publication, New Delhi.

Chelliah, R.J. and Narain Sinha (1982). "State Finances in India: The Measurement of Tax Effort of State Governments, 1973-1976", *The World Bank Staff Working Papers*, No. 523.

Chelliah, R.J., P.K. Aggarwal, M.C. Purohit and R.K. Rao (2001). *Primer on Value Added Tax*, National Institute of Public Finance and Policy, New Delhi.

China National Tourism Administration (1999-2005). Beijing, China (Translated) in Plan of Action For Sustainable Tourism Development in "The Asian and Pacific Region" (1999-2005), A Progress Report.

CMIE (2003). "Infrastructure", Centre for Monitoring Indian Economy Pvt. Ltd., Mumbai.

Compendium of Textile Statistics (2002). Office of the Textile Commissioner, Ministry of Textiles, Government of India, Mumbai.

Cook, Richard and James Manor (1998). Democracy and Decentralisation in South Asia and West Africa, Participation, Accountability and Performance, Cambridge University Press, Cambridge.

CPCB (2000). "Air Quality Status and Trends in India", Central Pollution Control Board, Ministry of Environment and Forests, NAAQMS/14/ 1999-2000, Delhi.

———. (2001). Respirable Particulate Matter and its Health Effects, Central Pollution Control Board, Ministry of Environment and Forests, NAAQMS/19/2001-2002, Delhi.

———. (2002a). "Municipal Sewage Pollution along Indian Coastal Waters", Central Pollution Control Board, Ministry of Environment and Forests, CPOCS/27/2002-2003, Delhi.

———. (2002b). "National Ambient Air Quality Standards", Central Pollution Control Board, Ministry of Environment and Forests, NAAQMS/22/ 2001-02, Delhi.

———. (1999-2004). "Ambient Air Quality in India", National Air Quality Monitoring Programme (NAMP), Central Pollution Control Board, Ministry of Environment and Forests, Delhi.

Crook, Nigel (1993). *India's Industrial Cities Essays in Economy and Demography*, OUP, New Delhi.

CSE (1999). *State of India's Environment*, The Citizen's Fifth Report, Part II Statistical Base, CSE, Delhi.

CSO (2001). *Compendium of Environmental Statistics 2000*, Central Statistical Organisation and Government of India, New Delhi.

CWC (1998 and 2000). *Water and Related Statistics*, Central Water Commission, Ministry of Water Resources, Government of India, New Delhi.

Da Cunha, Gerson (2002). "Our Cities the promise and the Plight", *Human Scape*, Vol 1 X, Issue X.

Dahiwale, S.M (1995). "Consolidation of Maratha Dominance in Maharashtra", *Economic and Political Weekly*, 30 (6), pp. 336-342.

———. (2000). "Identifying 'Backwardness' in Maharashtra", *Economic and Political Weekly*, 35 (37), pp. 3293 – 3297.

———. (2003). "The Political Mobilisation of Backward classes in India: An Overview", Submitted to *Man and Development*, March.

Dalvi, S. and Bokil, M (2000). "In Search of Justice: Tribal communities and Land Rights in Coastal Maharashtra", *Economic and Political Weekly*, 35,(32), pp. 2843-2850.

Dantwala, M.L(1978). *Some Neglected Issues in Employment Planning: Dilemmas of Growth—The Indian Experience*, Sage Publications, New Delhi.

Das, Anjana and Jyothi Parikh (2000). "Making Maharashtra State Electricity Board Commercially Viable", *Economic and Political Weekly*, 1 April.

Das, Binayak (2002). "Shut and Dried", *Down to Earth*, Centre for Science and Environment, September 15th, New Delhi.

Datar, C. (2003). *Status of Women in Maharashtra – An Update, Unit for Women's Studies*, TISS, Mumbai.

Datt, Gaurav and Martin Ravallion (1991). *Impacts on Time Allocation and Poverty of Public Works in two Maharashtrian Villages*, Welfare and Human Resources Division, World Bank, Washington DC.

Dave, Uttam (2002). "Dimensions of Domestic Tourism", Pacific Asia Travel Association (PATA).

Deaton, Angus (2003). "Regional Poverty Estimates for India, 1999-2000", Research Programme in Developmental Studies, Princeton University, *www.princeton.edu/~deaton*

Department of Secondary and Higher Education (2001). *Scheme of Community Polytechnics - Norms and Guidelines*, Govt. of India, New Delhi.

Desai, Vasant (1990). *Panchayati Raj- 'Power to the People*, Himalaya Publishing House, Bombay.

Deshmukh, S.K, K.G. Hiraskar, S.V. Lipare and A.B. Ayare (2003). "Municipal Wastewater Management and River Pollution: Strategy for Techno-Economic Feasible Treatment", Report submitted to IGIDR under EMCAB Project.

Deshmukh, Smita (2003). "Worried BMC to Impose 10 pc Water Cut", *Times of India*, April 2, Mumbai.

Deshpande, R.S. and A. Narayanamoorthy (1999). "An Appraisal of Watershed Development Programme Across Regions in India", *Artha Vijnana*, 12(4), pp. 315-415.

Deshpande, Sudha and Lalit Deshpande (1991). "Problems of Urbanisation and Growth of Large Cities in Developing Countries, A Case Study of Bombay", *WES Research Working Paper No. 177*, ILO, Geneva.

———. (1993). Memorandum submitted to the Tenth Finance Commission on behalf of Brihan-Mumbai Mahanagarpalika, Mumbai.

———. (2002). *Reforms and Labour Market in India*, in Institute of Applied Manpower Research, Reforms and Employment, Concept Publishing Company, New Delhi.

Deshpande, Lalit (1979). *Bombay Labour Market*, Department of Economics, University of Bombay, Mumbai, *Mimeo.*

Deshpande, R.S. and A. Narayanamoorthy (2001). "Issues before the Second Irrigation Commission of Maharashtra", *Economic and Political Weekly*, 36(12), pp. 1034-1043.

Deshpande, R.S and N. Rajasekaran (1995). *Impact of National Watershed Development Project for Rainfed Areas in Maharashtra*, Gokhale Institute of Politics and Economics, Pune, Maharashtra.

Deshpande, R. S and V. Ratana Reddy (1990). "Social Dynamics and Farmers' Society. A Case Study of Pani Panchyat", *Indian Journal of Agricultural Economics*, 45(3), pp. 355-361.

———. (1991). "Watershed Development Approach in Fragile Resource Region: An Analytical Study of Maharashtra", *Mimeograph Series No. 33*, Gokhale Institute of Politics and Economics, Pune, Maharashtra.

Deshpande, Sudha (1996). "Changing Structure of Employment in India, 1981-1991", *Indian Journal of Labour Economics*, 39, (4), October -December.

———. (2003). "Migration to Mumbai: What Do the Census Data Show?" ,translated in Marathi, *Loksatta*, June 4- 6.

Deshpande, Sudha and Ashish Deshpande (1998). "Impact of NEP on Working Women in Slums in Mumbai", Report of the Research Project funded by the Department of Women and Children, Ministry of Human Resource Development, Government of India.

Deshpande, Sudha, Guy Standing and Lalit Deshpande (1997). *Labour Flexibility in a Third World Metropolis, A Case Study of Bombay*, Commonwealth Publishers, New Delhi.

Dharmadhikary, Shripad (2003). "Privatisation not the Answer", *The Hindu*, January 28th.

Dholakia, B. (1978). "Relative Performance of Public and Private Manufacturing Enterprises in India: TFP Approach", *Economic and Political Weekly*, February 25, pp. M4-M11.

Director of Census Operations, Maharashtra (2001a). "Provisional Population Totals Paper-1 of 2001", *Census of India 2001*, Series–28, Maharashtra, Government Central Press, Mumbai.

———. (2001b). "Provisional Population Totals Paper-2 of 2001, Rural-Urban Distribution of Population", *Census of India 2001*, Series–28, Maharashtra, Government Central Press, Mumbai.

———. (2001c). *Population Data with Data on Slum Population in Urban Units*, Government of India Press, Nashik.

———. (2001d). "Provisional Population Totals Paper-3 of 2001 Distribution of Workers and Non-workers", *Census of India 2001*, Series–28, Maharashtra, Government Central Press, Mumbai.

Directorate of Education (1994-95). *Education at a Glance*, Pune, Maharashtra State.

Dr. Ambedkar Sanshodhan Va Prashikshan Sanstha (1998). *Samaj Kalyan Vikas Yojana*, Pune, Government of Maharashtra.

Draft Report of the Sub-Group on Handicrafts for Tenth Five-Year Plan (2002-2007). Office of the Development Commissioner (Handicrafts), Ministry of Textiles, Government of India.

Dreze, J. (1990). "Poverty in India and IRDP Delusion", *Economic and Political Weekly*, 25, (9).

Dutta, Rita (2002a). "MPCB to Serve Notices to 62 hospitals", *Express Healthcare Management*, August 16 to 31st Issue, Indian Express Group, Mumbai.

———. (2002b). "MPCB is Short of Manpower to Look into BMW issue", *Express Healthcare Management*, August , Indian Express Group, Mumbai.

Dyson, Tim (2003). "India's Population: Past, Present and Future", *Pravin Visaria Memorial Lecture*, March 4, Ahmedabad.

Easter, K.W. (2000). "Asia's Irrigation Management in Transition: A Paradigm Shift Faces High Transaction Costs", *Review of Agricultural Economics*, 22 (2), pp. 370-388.

Economic Times (2002). Business Travel News "Tax Responservice", March 18.

———. (2003). Editorial, "For Speedy Justice", Mumbai Edition, May 15.

FAI (2002). *Fertiliser Statistics: 2001-02*, Fertilisers Association of India, New Delhi.

FIRE (D) (2002). "Project Notes: State Incentives to Increase Efficiencies in Urban Water Supply in Maharashtra", Indo-Us Financial Institutions Reform and Expansion Project - Debt Market Component, *www.indiaurbaninfo.com/niua/projectNo. 28.pdf* , March 28.

———. (2002). "State Incentives to Increase Efficiencies in Urban Water Sector in Maharashtra", FIRE (D), Note No: 28, New Delhi.

Florence, P. Sergent (1948). *Investment, Size and Location of the Plant*, Cambridge University Press, Cambridge.

Ford Foundation Report (2001). *Hidden No More - Seeking Equal Treatment, India's Dalit People Speak Out*, Ford Foundation, pp. 9-10, New Delhi.

Friedman, J.P. and M. Douglass (1976). "Agropolitan Development: Towards a New Strategy for Regional Planning in Asia", in UNCRD, pp. 333-87.

FSI (2000). *State of Forest Report 1999*, Forest Survey of India, Ministry of Environment and Forests, Dehradun, India.

———. (2002). *State of Forest Report 2001*, Forest Survey of India, Ministry of Environment and Forests, Dehradun.

Gadgil, D.R. (1948). "Economic Effects of Irrigation: Report of a Survey of the Direct and Indirect Benefits of the Godavari and Pravara Canals", *Publication No. 17*, Gokhale Institute of Politics and Economics, Pune, Maharashtra.

Gandhi, Vasant P. and N.T. Patel (2001). "The Impact of WTO on Agricultural Inputs", in Dutta and Deodhar (co-ordinators) *Implications of WTO Agreements for Indian Agriculture*, Centre for Management in Agriculture, IIM, Oxford and IBH Publications, New Delhi.

Gavaskar, M. (2000). "Human Rights and Uncivil Society, Dalit — Savarna Divide in Borgaon", *Journal of Human Rights*, 4(1 and 2).

Gayakwad, J. (1990). "Maharashtrateel Adivasee: Sankhyatmak Goshwara" (Marathi), *Hakara*, Jan-June, Year II, Issue I and II.

Ghate, Utkarsh (2003). "Biodiversity Hotspots Conservation Programme Western Ghats of Maharashtra", RANWA, Pune.

Gill, K.P.S. (2001). "Freedom from Fear - Politics and Governance - Bad Policemen, Bad Politicians", *Hindustan Times*, Delhi, August 17.

Godbole, M.D. (2001). *Committee Report on Good Governance*, a one man Committee of Dr. M.D. Godbole appointed by Government of Maharashtra.

Godbole, J. (1981). "Dhangarala Dhattura Shaharwasiyanna Malida!", *Hakara*, No. 3, July-Sept.

Godbole, M. (2000). "Electricity Regulatory Commissions-Empowerment of Consumers", *Economic and Political Weekly*, 22 January.

———. (2002). "Maharashtra Human Development: Some Issues", *Economic and Political Weekly*, 37 (42), pp. 4256- 4268.

Godbole, Madhav (1999). *Report of the Committee on Cooperative Sugar Factories in Maharashtra*, Mumbai.

———. (2001). "Making State Budgets Transparent and User-Friendly", *Economic and Political Weekly*, April 12, pp. 1349- 1358.

———. (2002). "Manavi Vikasacha Khara Chehra", *Loksatta*, 20th October.

GoI (1961, 1971, 1981, 1991, 2001). *Census of India*, Various Issues for Maharashtra, Government of India, New Delhi.

———. (1972). *Report of the Second Irrigation Commission -1*, Ministry of Irrigation and Power, Government of India, New Delhi.

———. (1983). *Report of the Third Quinquennial Survey on Employment and Unemployment Survey Results*, Maharashtra, National Sample Survey Organisation, Department of Statistics, New Delhi.

———. *National Water Policy*, Ministry of Water Resources, Government of India, New Delhi.

———. "A Note on the Third Quniquennial Survey on Employment Unemployment", in *Sarvekshana*, National Sample Survey Organisation, VXI(4), Issue No. 35, April.

———. (1988). *Report of the National Commission on Urbanisation*, Ministry of Urban Development, New Delhi.

———. (1990). *Employment and Unemployment in India*, NSS 43rd Round (July 1987-June 1988) National Sample Survey Organisation, Department of Statistics, New Delhi.

———. (1990a). Results of the Fourth Quinquennial Survey on Employment and Unemployment (All India), NSS 43rd Round (July 1987-June 1988), *Sarvekshana* Special Number, National Sample Survey Organisation, Department of Statistics, Ministry of Planning, New Delhi.

———. (1992). *Eighth Five-Year Plan*, Planning Commission, New Delhi.

———. (1992a). *Report of the Committee on Pricing of Irrigation Water*, Planning Commission, Government of India, New Delhi.

———. (1992-93). 49th Round on Housing, National Sample Survey Organisation, Maharashtra State Sample (Unpublished Tables).

———. (1993). "Report of the National Commission for Schedule Castes and Scheduled Tribes", *First Report*, 1992-93.

———. (1994-95). *Second Annual Report* (Financial Year 1994-95), Government of India, New Delhi.

———. (1994-95a). *Second Annual Report*, National Commission for Minorities, 1997, Government of India, New Delhi.

———. (1996). *The India Infrastructure Report: Policy Imperatives for Growth and Welfare, Expert Group on Commercialisation of Infrastructure Projects*, National Council of Applied Economic Research, New Delhi.

———. (1997). *Employment and Unemployment in India, 1993-94*, Fifth Quinquennial Survey (July 1993-June 1994), National Sample Survey Organisation, NSS 50th Round Department of Statistics, New Delhi.

———. (1997a). *Ninth Five Year Plan: 1997-2002*, Vol. II, Planning Commission, Government of India, New Delhi.

———. (1998). *Household Capital Expenditure during 1.7.91 to 30.6.92*, Debt and Investment Survey, NSS 48th round, NSSO, Department of Statistics, Ministry of Planning and Programme Implementation, Government of India, New Delhi.

———. (1998a). *Statistical Abstract of India*, Central Statistical Organisation, Department of Statistics and Programme Implementation, Government of India, New Delhi.

———. (2000). *Draft National Tourism Policy of India*, Government of India.

———. (2000a). *Gramin Bhartache Parivartan Parivartanasathi Karyakram*, Ministry of Rural Development.

———. (2000b). *Status of Water Supply and Wastewater Generation, Collection, Treatment and Disposal in Class I Cities*, Central Pollution Control Board, Ministry of Environment and Forests, New Delhi.

———. (2001a). *Blueprint for Power Sector Development*, Ministry of Power, Government of India, New Delhi.

———. (2001b). *Report of the Expert Group Settlement of SEB Dues*, Ministry of Power, Government of India, New Delhi.

———. (2001c). *Employment and Unemployment Situation in India, 1990-2000 Part I*, NSS 55th Round (July 1990-June 2000), National Sample Survey Organisation, Ministry of Statistics and Programme Implementation, New Delhi.

———. (2001d). Amendments in the Guidelines of Swarnajayanti Gram Swarojgar Yojana, District Rural Development Agency, Ministry of Rural Development, Pune.

———. (2001e). Dept. of Secondary and Higher Education-2001, Scheme of Community Polytechnics -Norms and Guidelines, New Delhi.

———. (2001f). *Disinvestment Commission Report*, Government of India, New Delhi.

———. (2001g). *Employment and Unemployment in India, Key Results*, NSS 55th Round (July 1999-June 2000) National Sample Survey Organisation, Department of Statistics, New Delhi.

———. (2001h). *Provisional Population Totals*, Paper 1 and 2 of 2001, Maharashtra Census of India, 2001.

———. (2001i). Report of the Working Group on Watershed Development, Rainfed Farming and Natural Resource Management for the Tenth Five Year Plan, Planning Commission, Government of India, New Delhi.

———. (2002a). *Tenth Five Year Plan: 2002-2007*, Various Volumes, Planning Commission, Govt. of India, New Delhi.

———. (2002b). *National Human Development Report 2001*, Oxford University Press, New Delhi.

———. (2002c). *Annual Report on The Working of State* Electricity Boards & Electricity Departments, *2001-02*, Power & Energy Division, Planning Commission, New Delhi , *http://planningcommission.nic.in*.

———. (2002d). "Structure of APDRP, Reform Framework and Principles Of Financial Restructuring of SEBs", Report of the Expert Committee on State-Specific Reforms, Ministry of Power, New Delhi.

———. (2002e). "Structure of APDRP, Reform Framework and Principles of Financial Restructuring of SEBs", Report of the Expert Committee on State-Specific Reforms, Ministry of Power, New Delhi.

———. (2002f). Maharashtra Infrastructure Summit, organised by and collaboration with MEDC and other prominent Chambers of Commerce and Industry, Mumbai, November.

———. (2002g). Annual Report on The Working of State Electricity Boards and Electricity Departments, *2001-02*, Power and Energy Division, Planning Commission, New Delhi (1st March, 2003).

———. (2002h). *National Water Policy*, Ministry of Water Resources, Government of India, New Delhi.

———. (2002i). *Planning Commission Strategy*, Government of India.

———. (2002j). *Swarnajayanti Gram Swarojgar Yojana: A Brief Review*, Ministry of Rural Development.

———. (2002k). Report of the National Commission on Labour, Ministry of Labour, Government of India.

———. (2003a). *Agricultural Statistics at a Glance: 2002*, Directorate of Economics and Statistics, Ministry of Agriculture, Government of India, New Delhi.

———. (2003b). *Annual Report, 2002-2003*, Department of Telecommunications, Ministry of Communications and Information Technology, New Delhi

———. (2003c). *Rating of State Power Sector*, Minisrty of Power, Government of India, (17th April, 2003).

———. (2004). Report of Task Force on Micro Irrigation, Ministry of Agriculture, GoI, New Delhi.

———. (2005). A White Paper on State-Level Value added Tax, Government of India, 2005.

Gokhale, Madhav (2003). "A Lake's Death by Drowning", *Indian Express*, March 9th, Mumbai.

Goldar, Bishwanath (2000). "Employment Growth in Organised Manufacturing in India", *Economic and Political Weekly*, 1 April, 35, (14), pp. 1191-5.

GoM (1961). *Report of the Committee on Democratic Decentralisation*, (V.P. Naik Committee), Bombay.

———. (1961a). *Report of the Study Group on Greater Bombay*, Government Central Press, Bombay.

———. (1962). *Report of the Irrigation Commission of Maharashtra*, Government of Maharashtra, Bombay.

———. (1965). *Report of the Committee Appointed for Regional Plans for Bombay-Panvel and Poona Regions*, Government Central Press, Bombay.

———. (1971). *Report of the Evaluation Committee on Panchayati Raj*, (L.N. Bongirwar Committee), Bombay.

———. (1984). *Report of the Fact Finding Committee on Regional Imbalance*, Planning Department, Bombay.

———. (1986). *Panchayati Raj Evaluation Committee Report*, (P.B. Patil Committee), Bombay.

———. (1995). *White Paper on Water Supply in Maharashtra*, Mumbai.

———. (1996). "Urban Development, Urban Housing and Urban Transport" *Approach Paper to the Ninth Five Year Plan*, Working Group of the State Planning Board, November.

———. (1996a). *Udyog Mitra 1996 Maharashtra*, The Corporate State Industrial Statistics as on 31-3-1996, Department of Industries, Mumbai.

———. (1997). "Relative Levels of Development, Backlog and Removal of Regional Imbalances", *Report of the Indicators and Backlog Committee*, Vol. I, Mumbai.

———. (1998). "Report of the Committee Appointed by the Government of Maharashtra for Evaluation of Land Reforms", published in *Journal of Indian School of Political Economy*, Vol. X, Jan-March.

———. (1998a). *Socio-economic Review of Brihan Mumbai 1996-97*, Directorate of Economics and Statistics, Centre for Research and Development, Department of Planning, Mumbai.

———. (1999). *White Paper on State's Finances*, Government of Maharashtra.

———. (1999a). *Handbook of Basic Statistics of Maharashtra State*, Directorate of Economics and Statistics, Government of Maharashtra.

———. (1999b). *Maharashtra Water and Irrigation Commission Report*, Government of Maharashtra, Mumbai.

———. (1999-00). National Sample Survey (State Sample), Directorate of Economics and Statistics, Planning Department, Mumbai.

———. (2000). Valluri Committee's Report on "Monopoly Cotton Procurement Scheme", Mumbai.

———. (2000-2001). *Performance Budget: Social Welfare, Culture and Sports* ,Department, Government Press, Wai.

———. (2001). *District Domestic Product of Maharashtra 1993-94 to 1998-99 (Base Year 1993-94)*, Directorate of Economics and Statistics, Mumbai.

———. (2001a). *Report of the Energy Review Committee* (Part 1 and 2), Mumbai.

———. (2001, 2002 and 2003). *Economic Survey of Maharashtra*, Department of Economics and Statistics, Planning Department, Government of Maharashtra, Mumbai.

———. (2001-2002). *Annual Plan 2001-2002*, Part -I, II, III, Planning Department, Govt. of Maharashtra, Mumbai.

———. (2002a). *Tenth Five Year Plan Vol.I and Vol II*, Govt. of Maharashtra, Planning Department, Mumbai.

———. (2002b). *Human Development Report Maharashtra*, Planning Department, Mumbai.

———. (2002c). *Economic Survey of Maharashtra 2001- 02*, Directorate of Economics and Statistics, Planning Department, Mumbai.

———. (2002d). *Women and Men in Maharashtra-1998*, Directorate of Economics and Statistics, Planning Department, Mumbai.

———. (2002e). *First Report of the Maharashtra State Minorities Commission*, Government of Maharashtra.

———. (2002f). *Sixteenth All India Livestock and Farm Equipment Census-1997: Maharashtra State*, Department of Animal Husbandry, Maharashtra State, Pune.

———. (2002g). Administrative Reforms Committee, headed by D.M. Sukthankar, December.

———. (2002h). Directorate of Economics and Statistics, Mumbai.

———. (2002i). *Malnutrition Related Deaths of Tribal Children in Nandurkar District of Maharashtra*, Pune, Tribal Reseach and Training Institute.

———. (2002j). Personal Communication with Department of Environment, Government of Maharashtra, Mumbai.

———. (2002k). *Tenth Five Year Plan: 2002-2007 and Annual Plan, 2002-2003*, Maharashtra State, Planning Department, Government of Maharashtra, Mumbai.

———. (2002l). "Maharashtra Power Sector Reforms", *White Paper*, Department of Industries, Energy and Labour, Mumbai.

———. (2002m). Principles of the Maharashtra Infrastructure Development and Support Act (MIDAS), Maharashtra Infrastructure Summit, Mumbai.

———. (2002n). *Human Development Report Maharashtra 2002*, Government of Maharashtra, Mumbai.

———.(2002o). Mahila va Bal Vikas Doran Aani Nirnay, 1975 to Jan. 2002, Ek Drustikshep (Marathi), Pune: Yashwantrao Chavan Vikas Prashashan Prabodhini.

———. (2003). *Report of Regional Consultations*, Government of Maharashtra, Mumbai.

———. (2003a). *Economic Survey of Maharashtra: 2002-03*, Department of Economics and Statistics, Government of Maharashtra, Mumbai.

———. (2003b). Directorate of Economics and Statistics, 2003, *Statistical Abstract of Maharashtra State 1995-96 and 1996-97*, Government of Maharashtra, Mumbai.

———. (2003c). *Report of the Committee appointed by the Government of Maharashtra to prepare an Action Plan for Agricultural Progress in Maharashtra*.

———. (2003-2004). *Performance Budget 2003-04*, Higher and Technical Education Department, Government of Maharashtra, Mumbai.

———. (2003-2004). *Implementation Various Schemes for the Welfare of Backward Class*, Department of Social Justice, Dept. of Social Justice, Mumbai.

———. (2004). *Economic Survey of Maharashtra*, Department of Economics and Statistics, Planning Department, Government of Maharashtra, Mumbai

———. (Various Years). *Season and Crop Report*, Commissioner of Agriculture, Pune, Maharashtra.

GoM and WSP-SA (2002). Background Note for Workshop on "Strategy Building for Rural Sanitation in Maharashtra", Pune, August 22nd to 24th.

GoM (1993-94). National Sample Survey (State Sample), Directorate of Economics and Statistics, Planning Department, Mumbai.

GoM: Rural Development and Water Conservation Department, Watershed Development Programme in Maharashtra (unpublished material).

Goswami, P.R. (2001). "Literacy, Information and Governance in Digital Era: Indian Scenario", winning paper at the second international paper competition for the best papers on *Information in a Networked World: The Developing World Perspective*, American Society for Information Science and Technology, (ASIST), Special Interest Group/International Information Issues (SIG/III).

Gramin va Advasi Vikas Sanstha (2000). *Adivasi Sanvad*, No. 6, Oct.-Dec. Guidelines, Babasaheb Ambedkar Hastshilp Vikas Yojna, (AHVY)-Office of the Development Commissioner (Handicrafts), Ministry of Textiles, Government of India, West Block VII, R.K. Puram, New Delhi.

Gulati, Ashok and Seema Bathla (2002). "Capital Formation in Indian Agriculture, Trends, Compositions and Implications for Growth", *Occasional Paper No: 24*, National Bank for Agricultural and Rural Development (NABARD), Mumbai.

Gulati, Ashok and Kelly Tim (1999). *Trade Liberalisation and Indian Agriculture*, Oxford University Press, New Delhi.

Gulati, Ashok and Seema Bathla (2002). "Institutional Credit to Indian Agriculture: Defaults and Policy Options", *Occasional Paper-23*, National Bank for Agricultural and Rural Development, Mumbai.

Gulati, Ashok *et al.* (1994). "Major and Medium Irrigation Schemes: Towards Better Financial Performance", *Economic and Political Weekly*, 29(26), A72-A79.

Gupta, S.P. (2002a). Report on the Steering Committee on Labour and Employment for 10th Five Year Plan (2002-2007).

———. (2002b). Report of the Special Group on Targeting Ten Million Employment Opportunities per year over the 10th Plan Period.

Guru, G. (1995). "Gowari Tragedy — Crisis of Maratha Hegemony", *Economic and Political Weekly*, 30 (6), pp. 303-304.

———. (1991). "Dalit Killings in Marathwada", *Economic and Political Weekly*, pp. 2926- 2930.

Handicrafts Schemes for 10th Plan-Officer of the Development Commissioner (Handicrafts), Ministry of Textiles, Government of India.

Haribakthi, Sailesh (2003). "Haribakthi Cheers Indo-Pak Trade Moves", *Financial Express*, Mumbai, May 8.

Harris, Nigel (1992). "Bombay in a Global Economy: Structural Adjustmant and Role of Cities", Paper presented at the Workshop on *Evolving Cultural Identity of Bombay, XIXthe and XXth Centuries*, at S.N.D.T Women's University, Bombay, 16-19th December.

Health Department (2000-01). *Performance Budget—Medical, Public Health and Employees Insurance Scheme*, Government of Maharashtra, Mumbai.

Hindu Report (2000). "Plea for More Financial Powers to States", *The Hindu*, Chennai Wednesday, May 10.

Holla, Usha (2002). "TMC-NGO Waste Management Facility to be Inaugurated Soon", *Express Healthcare Management*, May, Indian Express Group, Mumbai.

Humanscape (2002). "The Plight of Dalits", *Humanscape*, Dec. pp. 28-29.

ICTs' (2001). "ICTs in Rural Poverty Alleviation", *Economic and Political Weekly*, 36(11), pp. 917-920.

IDFC (2003). "How Much Water Can you Save?", A Feature by Ajay Narayanan, *Times of India*, 4th August.

IDR (1999). *India Development Report* (ed.), Oxford University Press, New Delhi.

———. (1999). "Air and Water Quality, New Initiatives", *India Development Report*, Oxford University Press, New Delhi.

IHR (2000). *India Hotel Report, 2000*.

IIR (2003). "Maharashtra: A Statistical Profile", *India Infrastructure Report 2003*, Network and Oxford University Press.

Ilaiah, K. (2001). *Sameeksha: Rethinking Development, Mumbai: PMIR Students' Council*, The Tata Institute of Social Sciences.

Inamdar, N.R. (1970). "Functioning of Village Panchayats", *Popular Prakashan*, Bombay.

———. (1985). *Panchayati Raj in Maharashtra: A Comparative Perspective, in Panchayati Raj Institutions*, Silver Jubilee Commemorative Volume, GoM, Bombay.

INCID (1994). *Drip Irrigation in India*, Indian National Committee on Irrigation and Drainage, New Delhi.

India Jungles (2003). "Maharashtra Tigers in Trouble" by Jayan, T.V in 'Field Day,' *Down to Earth*, Centre for Science and Environment, January 31, New Delhi.

Indian Social Institute - A Centre for Research, Training and Action for Social and Economic development-Training programmes 2003, 10 Institutional Area, Lodhi Road, New Delhi.

Institute of Applied Manpower Research, (Various Issues), *Manpower Profile India*, New Delhi.

Institute of Social Sciences (2000). *Status of Panchayati Raj in India*, Concept Publishing Company, New Delhi.

International Federation of Red Cross and Red Crescent Societies (2001). *World Disaster Report — Focus on Recovery*, Jeniva, International Federation of Red Cross and Red Crescent Societies.

Irrigation Department (1999). *Maharashtra Water and Irrigation Commission Report*, Vol. I, Government of Maharashtra, Mumbai.

Iyer, R.C. (2003). "The Role of the Institution of Lok-Ayukta in Preparing Better Governance", Presentation at the Workshop on *Governance: The Maharashtra Experience*, Jointly by JBIMS and IIPA, at Jamnalal Bajaj Institute of Management Studies, Mumbai on April 28.

Iyer, Ramasamy, R. (2003). *Water: Perspectives, Issues, Concerns*, Sage Publications, New Delhi.

Jadhav, Narendra (2002). *Special Session on Infrastructure Financing, Maharashtra Infrastructure Summit 2002*, organised by the GoM in collaboration with MEDC and other prominent Chambers of Commerce & Industry in Mumbai on the 10th, 11th, & 12th November, at Hotel Taj Mahal, Mumbai, *http://www.medcindia.org/cgibin/ index.htm*.

Jain, L.C (2000). "DAM vs. Drinking Water Exploring the Narmada Judgement", *Parisar Prakasham*, Pune.

Jain, R. (2002). "Surmountring Stalemates: Muslims and Schooling", in Jha, J. and Jhingram, R., *Elementary Education for the Poor and other Deprived Groups*, New Delhi, Centre for Policy Research, (A memeographed report).

Jare, Ramesh and Santosh Kumar (2001). "Motion of No-Confidence Against Sarpanchs", in Tuljapur Taluka, *A Study Report*, Rural Campus, Tata Institute of Social Sciences, Mumbai.

Jha, Prem Shankar (2002). "From Democracy to Kleptocracy", Extracts from the Affidavit Submitted to the Venkatswamy Commission, *Manushi*, Issue 128.

Jogdand, P.G. (2000). "Human Rights Violation of the Dalits: An Inquiry into Indian Social Reality", *Indian Journal of Human Rights*, 4, (142), pp. 121-136.

———. (ed.) (2000). *New Economic Policy and Dalits*, Rawat Publications, Jaipur and New Delhi.

John, S. (2002). *Struggle for Survival*, Pune: National Centre for Advocacy Studies.

Joshi, P.D. (1998). *Changing Pattern of Consumption Expenditure in India and Some Selected States* (Sarvekshana Analytical Report No. 2), NSSO, Mumbai: Reserve Bank of India.

Joshi, P.K. and A.K. Agnihotri (1983). "Ex Ante Assessment of Afforestation for Fuelwood on Waste Lands – A Multi – Objective Programming Approach", *Indian Journal of Agricultural Economics*, 38, (3), July – September, pp. 308-316.

Kakodkar, Anil (2002). Nuclear Power in India: An Inevitable Option for Sustainable Development of a Sixth of Humanity World Nuclear Association Annual Symposium, London.

Kanmony, C.J. (2003). "Education After Globalisation", *Kisan World*, Feb., pp. 30- 32, Chennai.

Katakam, Anupam (2002). "The Warana Experiment", *Frontline*, 19, (01).

Keniston, Kenneth (2001). "Grassroot ICT Projects in India", International Federation for Information Process Working Group, *Social Implications of Computers in Developing Countries*, 11(3).

Kerr, John (2002). *Watershed Development Projects in India: An Evaluation*, Research Report-127, International Food Policy Research Institute, Washington D.C., U.S.A.

Khandewale, S. (2003). "Maharashtrachi Vittiya Sthiti Va Upay: Jagathik Bankecha Ahaval", *Aajacha Sudharak*, April-May,(Marathi).

Khanna, B.S. (1994). *Panchayati Raj in India (Rural Local Self Government: National Perspective and State Policies)*, Deep and Deep Publications, New Delhi.

Khatua, B.C. (2002). *Water Supply and Sanitation*, Maharashtra Infrastructure Summit 2002, MEDC, Mumbai.

Khullar, Mukesh (2003). "E-Governance Initiatives in Maharashtra", Presentation at the Workshop on *Governance: The Maharashtra Experience*, Jointly by JBIMS and IIPA, at Jamnalal Bajaj Institute of Management Studies, Mumbai on April 28.

Krishanaraj M., A. Kanchi (2003). Employment Guarantee Scheme — An examination of the Administraive Mechanism, Implications for Women (Monograph), Mumbai: RCWS, S.N.D.T University, 2003.

Krishna Kumar, T. (1996). "Management of Development in the Newly Emerging Global Economic Environment", *Economic and Political Weekly*, 31 (25), pp. 1598-1605.

Krishnaraj, M. (1980). *Approaches to Self-reliance for Women: Some Urban Models*, Mumbai, RCWS, S.N.D.T.

———. (1987). *Development Perspective for Women*, Mumbai, RCWS, S.N.D.T.

———. (1987a). *Women Workers in Readymade Garment Industry*, Mumbai, RCWS, S.N.D.T.

Krishnaraj, M. and J. Deshmukh (eds.) (1993). "Macro Data", *Gender in Economics: Theory and Practice*, Aganta Publications, Delhi.

———. (1989). *Women in Handicrafts — An all India Study for Database and Policy Analysis*, Mumbai: RCWS, SNDT.

Kruegar, Anne, O. (ed.) (2002). *Economic Policy Reforms and the Indian Economy*, OUP, New Delhi.

Kshirsagar, K.G. and Deepak Shah (2002). "Flow of Credit to Small and Marginal Farmers in Maharashtra", AERC study report, Gokhale Institute of Politics and Economics, Pune.

Kulkarni S. (2002). "Women and Malnutrition- Malnourished Women in Maharashtra", *Humanscape*, Dec., pp. 14-17.

Kumar, A. and B. Jojo (2004). "Evaluation Study of the Umbrella Scheme to Promote Voluntary Action for Persons with Disabilities" - Draft unpublished mimeograph.

Kumar, Davinder (2001). "Who's Immune to this Disease?" Joint Action Committee Kanpur (JACK), 22nd Jan.

Kundu, A. and S. Gupta (2000). "Declining Population Mobility, Liberalisation and Growing Regional Imbalances, the Indian Case", in Kundu, A. (ed.) *Inequality, Mobility and Urbanisation*, Indian Council of Social Science Research, Manak Publications, New Delhi.

Kurien, N.J. (1987). "IRDP: How Relevant is it?" *Economic and Political Weekly*, 22(5).

Lahiri, Ashok (2002). "Sub-National Public Finance in India", *Economic and Political Weekly*, April 29.

Lahiri Ashok *et al.* (2001). *Study of Maharashtra's Finances*, National Institute of Public Finance and Policy (NIPFP), New Delhi.

Lahiri S., B. Choudhary, N. Singh and H. Singh (2002). Alternative Economic Survey 2001- 02. Economic Reforms: Development Denied, Rainbow Publications, New Delhi.

Laveesh, Bhandari and Dripto Mukhopadhayay (2000). *Industrial Corridors in India*, National Council of Applied Economic Research, New Delhi.

Leni (2003). "Nature: Gendered Concern", *Humanity Today*, Jan.-Feb., pp. 40-43, Mumbai: Human Rights Watch Cell.

Levy, V. (1987). "On Estimating Differentials Between Public and Private Sectors in a Developing Economy – Iraq", *Journal of Comparative Economics*, 5, pp. 235-50.

Lieten, G.K. (1996). *Development, Devolution and Democracy Village Discourse in West Bengal*, Sage Publications, New Delhi.

Lipton, Michael (1977). *Why Poor People Stay Poor: Urban Bias in World Development*, Harvard University Press, Cambridge, Mass.

Lo, Fu-chen and Yeung, Yue-man (1996). "Introduction", in Lo, Fu-chen and Yeung, Yue-man (Eds.), *Emerging World Cities in Pacific Asia*, United Nations University Press, Tokyo, Japan.

Mahajan, U. (2002). *Nyayasathi Ladha: Vachal Eka Dashkachi, Sarvahara Jan Andolan, 1990-2001*.

Mahapatra, Richard (2001). *Down to Earth*, CSE, New Delhi, pp. 30 - 34.

Maharashtra State Commission for Women (1997). *Status of Women in Maharashtra: A Situational Analysis, 1981-95*, Mumbai.

Maharashtra State Social Welfare Advisory Board Annual Report (2000-01 and 2001-02). Government of Maharashtra, Mumbai.

Mahbub ul Haq Human Development Centre (2002). *Human Development in South Asia 2001, Globalisation and Human Development*, New York, Oxford University Press.

Majumdar, S.K. (1995). "Public, Joint and Private Sectors in Indian Industry", *Economic and Political Weekly*, November 30, pp. M46- 53.

Malhotra, N. and N. Rizvi (1997). *Source Material on Education of Scheduled Castes and Scheduled Tribes*, Delhi, Anamika Publications.

Malhotra, Rajeev (1997). "Incidence of Poverty in India: Towards a Consensus on Estimating the Poor", in *The Indian Journal of Labour Economics*, 40(1).

Mallik, R.M. (2002). "Capacity Building of Panchayati Raj Institutions in Rural Development: A Case Study of Orissa", *Occasional Paper –25*, Mumbai: NABARD.

Mandlekar, V.B. (1991). "Panchayati Raj in Maharashtra", Ph.D Thesis submitted to the University of Bombay, Bombay.

Mane L. (1997). *Vimuktayan: Maharashtraatil Vimukta Jamati — Ek Chikitsak Abhyas* (Marathi), Mumbai, Yashwantrao Chavan Pratishthan.

Mani, Sunil (2003). "Deregulation, Entry of MNCs, Public Technology Procurement and Innovation Capability in India's Telecommunications Equipment Industry", *http://www.intech.unu.edu/whoswho/rese arch/mani-biography.htm*.

Martyris, Nina (2003). "Its Not of Funds that Stems the Water Flow", *Times of India*, 9th March, Mumbai.

MASHAL (1998). *Environmental Status Report: 1997-98,* Aurangabad Municipal Corporation, MASHAL, Pune.

———. (2001-02). *Environmental Status Report: 2001-02 of Sangli-Miraj-Kupwad* ,Municiapal Corporation, MASHAL, Sangli.

Mathew, George (1994). *Panchayati Raj From Legislation to Movement*, Concept Publishing Company, NewDelhi.

———. (2001). 'Maharashtra's Gram Sevak Raj', *The Hindu*, August 13.

Mathur, Mukesh P. (2003). "Panchayati Raj Institutions and the State Finance Commissions-Report', *India Infrastructure Report 2003*, Oxford University Press, New Delhi.

MAVIM (2002). Towards Empowerment—Documenting Success Stories from Maharashtra Rural Credit Programme (MRCP) 1994-2002, Government of Maharashtra, Mumbai.

MCGM (2001-2002). *Environment Status of Brihan*, Mumbai Municipal Corporation, 2001- 2002, MCGM, Mumbai.

MEDC (1988). *Industrial Maharashtra Facts, Figures and Opportunities*, MEDC, Mumbai.

———. (1995). "Foreign Direct Investment in India Performance, Prospects and Challenges", *MEDC Monthly Economic Digest for Business Executives*, Special Number, Maharashtra Economic Development Council, January.

———. (1998). *Industrial Opportunities in Maharashtra*, MEDC, Mumbai.

———. (2000). "Four Decades of Maharashtra – A Profile", Maharashtra Economic Development Council and Yashwantrao Chavan Pratisthan, Mumbai.

———. (2001). *Social Infrastructure in Maharashtra*, Maharashtra Economic Development Council, Mumbai.

———. (2002). "Maharashtra Economic Development Council (MEDC)", *Monthly Economic Digest for Business Executives*, XXXII(2), December.

———. (2002a). "Project Profiles", Maharashtra Infrastructure Summit, Maharashtra Economic Development Council, Mumbai.

———. (2002b). "Success Saga Maharashtra", *Maharashtra Infrastructure Summit*, Maharashtra Economic Development Council, Mumbai.

Mills, Edwin S. and Becker Charles, M. (1986) *Studies in Indian Urban Development, A World Bank Research Publication*, Oxford University Press, Washington D. C.

Ministry of Tourism (1999-2005). Turkey (Plan of Action for Sustainable Tourism Development, (PASTA) Plan 1999-2005, A Progress Report).

Minority of Human Resources Development (2002). Education of Scheduled Castes and Scheduled Tribes–1991-92 to 1993-94, New Delhi, Government of Maharashtra.

Mishra, R.K. and B. Navin (2002). "Privatisation Practices in States", in *Restructuring of State Level Public Enterprises*, Mittal Publications, New Dellhi.

Mishra, R.K. and K.S. Bhat (2003). *Privatisation*, New Delhi, Vikas Publishing House, pp. 4-10.

Mitra, Subrata K. (2001). "Making Local Government Work: Local Elites, Panchayati Raj and Governance in India", in *The Success of India's Democracy*, Atul Kohli (ed.), Cambridge University Press, Cambridge.

MNES (2003). Website of Ministry of Non-Conventional Energy Sources.

Mohanty, Bidyut (1995). "Panchayati Raj, 73rd Constitutional Amendment and Women", *Economic and Political Weekly*, 30(52), pp. 3346-3350.

Moitra, Aheli and Jyotsna Ramachandran (2003). "Dry or Wet? It's all Garbage for them", *The Indian Express*, May 8, Mumbai.

Moni and N. Vijayaditya (2003). "Convergence and E-Governance: National Informatics Centre - An Active Catalyst and Facilitator in India", Report submitted to the Planning Commission Working Group on Convergence and E-Governance for the formulation of the Tenth Five Year Plan, New Delhi.

Morris, Sebastian (2001). "Issues in Infrastructure Development Today: The Interlinkages", *India Infrastructure Report: Issues in Regulation and Market Structure Network*, Oxford University Press, New Delhi.

MoWR (1999). Report of the Working Group on Water Availability for Use, National Commission for Water Resources Development Plan, Ministry of Water Resources, Government of India, New Delhi.

———. (2003). Website of Ministry of Water Resources, *http://wrmin.nic.in*.

MPCB (2002). Maharashtra Pollution Control Board, Mumbai.

———. (2003-04). "Region-wise Ambient Air Quality Status for the Year 2003 – 2004," Maharashtra Pollution Control Board, *http://mpcb.mah.nic.in/envtdata/airregio nwise.php*, Mumbai.

Mujumdar, N.A. (1998). "Credit Support to Priority Sectors: A Macro Perspective", *Economic and Political Weekly*, XXXIII(4), January 24, pp. 147-150.

———. (1999). "Reviving Rural Credit", *Economic and Political Weekly*, June 19-25, pp. 1577.

———. (2000). "The New Architecture of the Rural Credit System", Professor M.L. Dantwala Monograph Series Monograph No. 1, Department of Economics, University of Mumbai, Mumbai.

———. (2002). "Rural Development: New Perceptions", *Economic and Political Weekly*, Sept- 2002.

Mungekar, B. (2003). *The Economy of Maharashtra: Changing Structure and Emerging Issues*, Dr. Ambedkar Institute of Social and Economic Change, Mumbai.

Muricken, A. (ed.) (2002). *VIKALP* -Alternatives, "Threats to Democracy," Special Issue, X.(3), Mumbai, Vikas Adhyayan Kendra.

Murthy, Narayana. N.R. and Raju, Sandeep (2002). "Comment" on Saxenian Annlee's Paper "Banagalore: The Silicon Valley of Asia?" in Kruegar, Anne, O. (Ed.), *Economic Policy Reforms and the Indian Economy*, UP, New Delhi.

Nagraj, R. (2000). "Organised Manufacturing Employment", *Economic and Political Weekly*, 16 September, 35(38), pp. 3345-8.

Naib, Sudhir (2003). "Partial Divestiture and Performance of Indian Public Sector Enterprises", *Economic and Political Weekly*, July 19, pp. 3088-93.

Naik, Gopal *et al.* (2002). *Assessing the Impact of Irrigation Management Transfer: Case Studies from Maharashtra*, Oxford and IBH Publishing Company, New Delhi.

Nair, K.N. and A.C. Das (1990). "Cattle Breeding Technology and Drought Power Availability: An Unresolved Contradiction", in *Resources, Institutions and Strategies: Operation Flood and Indian Dairying*, Martin Doombos and K.N. Nair (eds.), Sage Publications, New Delhi.

Nalinakshan, K. (2002). "Maharashtra Infrastructure Summit 2002", MEDC, *www.medcindia.org*, February 28.

Narayan, Jayaprakash (2003). "Making Elected Representatives Accountable," Proceedings of Seminar on *Getting the Governance Indians Deserve*, organised by ASSOCHAM, BCCI and IMC on 25 March, published by IMC, Mumbai.

Narayana, J. (2002). "Civil Society and Indian Transformation", *Liberal Times*, X, pp. 24-25.

Narayana, K.S. (2003). "The Difficult Art of Governance", *Deccan Herald*, Sunday, January 19.

Narayanamoorthy, A. (1995). "Status of India Irrigation", *Man and Development*, 17(4), pp. 49- 56.

———. (1996). "Evaluation of Drip Irrigation System in Maharashtra", Mimeograph Series No. 42, Gokhale Institute of Politics and Economics, Pune, Maharashtra.

———. (1997). "Economic Viability of Drip Irrigation: An Empirical Analysis from Maharashtra", *Indian Journal of Agricultural Economics*, 52 (4), pp. 728-739.

———. (2001a). "Irrigation and Rural Poverty Nexus: A Statewise Analysis", *Indian Journal of Agricultural Economics*, 56 (1), pp. 40-56.

———. (2001b). *Impact of Drip Irrigation on Sugarcane Cultivation in Maharashtra, Agro-Economic Research Centre*, Gokhale Institute of Politics and Economics, Pune, Maharashtra.

———. (2002). "Indian Irrigation: Five Decades of Development", *Water Resources Journal*, 212, pp. 1-29.

Narayanamoorthy, A. and Kshirsagar, K.G. (2000). 'Rapid Impact Evaluation of NWDPRA", in *Maharashtra*, Agro-Economic Research Centre, Gokhale Institute of Politics and Economics, Pune, Maharashtra.

National Commission for SC and ST (1993). *Report of the National Commission for Scheduled Castes and Scheduled Tribes 1992 to 1993*, New Delhi, Government of India.

National Council of Applied Economic Research, *Human Development Report*-West and Central India New Delhi, Oxford University Press.

National Institute of Rural Development (1999). *Indian Rural Development Report 1999*. National Institute of Rural Development, Hyderabad, India.

International Institute for Population Sciences (1994). *National Family Health Survey (1994), Maharashtra: 1992-93*, Pune, Mumbai.

———. (2002). *National Family Health Survey (NFHS-2)* Maharashtra, 1998-99 Mumbai.

Nayyar, Deepak (ed.) (1994). *Industrial Growth and Stagnation- The Debate in India*, Oxford University Press, Delhi.

Nederveen, P.J. (1996). "Globalisation and Culture- Three Paradigms", *Economic and Political Weekly*, 31 (23), pp. 1389-1893.

NIRD (2000). *India Rural Development Report 1999*, Regional Disparities in Development and Poverty, NIRD, Hyderabad.

NIUA (1998). "India's Urban Sector Profile", National Institute of Urban Affairs, *Research Study Series*, No. 61, New Delhi.

NMC (2001-02). *Environment Status of Nashik Municipal Corporation, 2001-2002*, NMC, Maharashtra.

NMMC (2001-02). *Environment Status of Navi Mumbai Municipal Corporation, 2001-2002*, NMMC, Navi Mumbai.

NSSO (1990). *An Economic Profile of Some Major Tribes of India, July 1988- June 1989*, Govt. of India, 44th Round, NSSO, New Delhi.

———. (2001). *Employment and Unemployment Situation in India, Part I, July 1999-June 2000*, Ministry of Statistics and Programme Implementation, 55th Round, NSSO, New Delhi.

Omvedt, Gail (1990). "Women, Zilla Parishads and Panchayt Raj Chandwad to Vitner", *Economic and Political Weekly*, 25, (31), pp. 1687- 1690.

Oommen, T.K. (2001). *Understanding Indian Society: The Relevance of Perspective from Below*, Dept. of Sociology, Pune.

Padhmanaban, R. (1998). "Financial Worries, Maharashtra Faces a Difficult Financial Situation", *Frontline*, 15 (20).

Pande, D. (1993). *Migrant Labour and Tender Dimensions -A Microanalysis of Gender Differences in Migrant Workers*, Mumbai: RCWS, S.N.D.T.

Pankaj, M. (2003). "Kavali Pangal Rokhanara Ankur", *Sakal*, 30 March (Daily), (Marathi), Mumbai.

Parikh, Kirit and R. Radhakrishna (eds.), (2002). *India Development Report*, Oxford University Press, New Delhi.

Patel, R.K. (1993). "Present Status and Promise of Dairying in India", *Indian Journal of Agricultural Economics*, 48, pp. 11-33.

Patil, L.R. (2003). "Jagatik Vyapaar Sanghatnes Amerikecha Suroong", *Loksatta*, 9th March, p. 5 (Marathi).

Patil, R.B. (2002). "Panchayati Raj in Kolhapur District (Maharashtra)", Paper Presented in a Workshop at Institute of Social Sciences on 12-13 September, New Delhi.

Paul, Samuel (2002). "Holding the State to Account: Citizen Monitoring in Action", Action Aid Karnataka Projects–Books for Change, Bangalore, India.

Performance Report (2001-2002). Office of the Development Commissioner (Handicrafts), Ministry of Textiles, Government of India.

Pethe, A., Ajit Karnik and Dilip Karmakar (2003). "Finances of Urban Local Bodies in Maharashtra: A Statistical Profile", Chapter 8.4 in *India Infrastructure Report 2003*, 3i Network and Oxford University Press.

Pethe, Abhay (2003). *Infrastructure Development Report*, Mumbai.

Phadke, Y.D. (1997). "Visavya Shatakatil Maharashtra", Vol. 5, (Marathi), *Shrividya Prakashan*, Pune.

Phatak, V.K. (2002). "Air Quality Management in Mumbai, Mumbai Workshop: Urban Air Quality Management", MMRDA, Mumbai.

Pieterse, J.N. (1996). "Globalisation and Culture — Three Paradigms", *Economic and Political Weekly*, June 8, pp. 1389-1393.

Prabhakara, S. and H.G. Shankara Murthy (1994). "Economics of Mechanised Fishing Boats in Coastal Karnataka", *Agricultural Situation in India*, 49, (1), pp. 15-18.

Prabhu, K.S. (1992). "Regional Dimensions of Human Development in India: Implications for the Eighth Plan", mimeo, Paper presented at the seminar on April 16, *Issues Pertaining to the Eighth Plan*, University of Mumbai.

Prabhu, K.S. and S. Chatterjee (1993). *Social Sector* Expenditures *and Human Development: A Study of Indian States*, Department of Economic Analysis and Policy, Reserve Bank of India, Mumbai.

Prabhu, K.S. and S. Kamadar (1996). "On Defining Poverty from a Human Development Perspective: Some Preliminary Notes", Paper presented at the National Conference on State Level Human Development Reports, 30th November to 1st December, Bhopal.

Prabhu, K.S. and P.C. Sarkar (1998). *Financing Human Development in Indian States: Trends and Implications" (1974-75, 1995- 96)*, University of Mumbai.

Premchand, A. (1993). *Public Expenditure Management*, IMF.

Puhazhendhi, V. and B. Jayaraman (1999). "Rural Credit Delivery: Performance and Challenges Before Banks", *Economic and Political Weekly*, January 16, pp. 175-182.

Purav, P. (Ed.) (1996). *Annadatree* (Marathi), Mumbai, Annapurna Mahila Mandal.

R., Venkatesan and Sonalika Varma (1998). *Policy Competition Among States in India For Attracting Direct Investment*, National Council of Applied Economic Research. New Delhi

Radhakrishna R. (2005). "Food and Nutrition Security of the Poor: Emerging Perspectives and Policy Issues", *13th Dr. L.T. Lakdawala Memorial Lecture*, Gujarat Institute of Development Research, Ahmedabad, India.

Raghavan, R.K. (2000). "A Case Study on Crime", *Frontline*, 17 (13).

Rajasekaran, N. (1998). "Land Reforms in Maharashtra: A Regional Analysis", *Review of Development and Change*, III(2), July- December.

Rakesh, Mohan (2002). "Small-scale Induatry Policy in India: A Critical Evaluation", in Anne, O Kruegar, (ed.), *Economic Policy Reforms and the Indian Economy*, OUP, New Delhi.

Ram Mohan, T.T. (2003). "Strategic Sale versus Public Offer: Dispelling Myths" ,*Economic and Political Weekly*, July 12, pp. 2969-76.

Ramchandraiah, C. (2003). "Information Technology and Social Development", *Economic and Political Weekly*, 38 (12 and 13), pp. 1192-1197.

Ranganathan, V. (2003). Introductory Remarks at the Workshop on "Governance: The Maharashtra Experience," Jointly by JBIMS and IIPA, at Jamnalal Bajaj Institute of Management Studies Mumbai, 28th April .

Ramaswamy, V.S., Namakumari (2002). *Marketing Management, Planning Implementation and Control, The Indian Context* 3rd edition.

Rao, Hanumantha (2003). "Reform Agenda for Agriculture", *Economic and Political Weekly*, 15th February, pp. 615-620.

Rao, M. Govinda (2002). "State Finances in India: Issues and Challenges", *Economic and Political Weekly*, August 3.

Rao, V. (2000). "Reflection from Tribal Development", *Journal of Rural Development*, 20, (1), pp. 87-97.

Rastogi, Anupam B. (2002). "Infrastructure Sector in India, 2000-01", Sebastian Morris (ed.), *India Infrastructure Report 2002, Governance Issues for Commercialisation*, Oxford University Press, New Delhi.

———. (2003). "The Infrastructure in India, 2001-02", in Sebastian Morris (ed), *India Infrastructure Report 2003*, 3i Network, Oxford University Press, New Delhi.

Rath, N. (1985). "Garibi Hatao: Can IRDP Do It?" *Economic and Political Weekly*, 20, (6).

Rath, Nilakantha (1997). "A Note on Approach to Irrigation in Maharashtra", Paper presented at the *Workshop on Economic Problems of Water*, organised by the Second Irrigation Commission of Maharashtra and Marathi Economic Association, Sangli, Maharashtra, May 14-15.

Rath, Nilakantha and A.K. Mitra (1989). "Economics of Irrigation in Water-Scarce Regions: A Study of Maharashtra", *Artha Vijnana*, 31 (1), pp. 1-129.

Rath, S. (2003). "Grape Cultivation for Export- Impact on Vineyard Workers", *Economic and Political Weekly*, 38 (5), pp. 480- 489.

Ravallion, M., Gaurav Dutt and S. Chaudhuri (1993). "Does Maharashtra's Employment Guarantee Scheme Guarantee Employment? Effects of the 1988 Wage Increase", *Economic Development and Cultural Change*, 42, 2.

RBI (1981-82). "All India Debt and investment Survey 1982- Statistical tables relating to capital expenditures and Capital Formation of Households during the year ended 30th June 1982", Department of Statistical Analysis and Computer Services, Reserve Bank of India, Bombay.

———. (2003). *State Finances – A Study of Budgets of 2001-02 and 2002-02*, Reserve Bank of India, Bombay.

———. (Various Years). Annual Reports for various years.

Registrar General, India (2001b). *Population in Urban Agglomerations/Cities 2001*.

———. (2001c). "Tables on Houses, Household Amenities and Assets", *Census of India 2001*, Series-1, India, The Controller of Publications, New Delhi.

Report on Monopoly Cotton Procurement Scheme, (2001). (Chairman: R.G Sanstha), Unpublished report, Mumbai.

Revenue and Forest Department (2001-2002). Karyakram Andaj-Patrak – Mahasul va Van Vibhag (Marathi), Government of Maharashtra, Mumbai.

Rural Employment Generation Programme of Khadi and Village Industries Commission- Margin Money Scheme - Khadi and Village Industries Commission - Gramodaya, Irla

Road, Vile Parle (West), Mumbai-400056. Sadhu, A. (2002). Jagatikikaranachya Zanzavatat Tikun Rahilelee Purogami Yojana, *Lokarajya*, 54 (4), (Marathi).

Saleth, R.M. (1996). *Water Institutions In India: Economics, Law and Policy*, Commonwealth Publishers, New Delhi.

Sampath Kumar, Rama (2001). "Corruption in Transitional Russia", Paper presented at the Eighth International Police Executive

Symposium, Szczytno, Poland, May 27 printed in *Policing Corruption: Proceedings of the IPES Conference, Poland 2001*, Sarre, R., Das, D., Albrecht, H-J. (Eds), Lexington Books, 2003.

Sanyal, Bishwapriya (1994). "Cooperative Autonomy: The Dialectic of State - NGOs Relationship in Developing Countries", *Research Series 100*, International Institute for Labour Studies, Geneva.

Sarkar, Sravani (2000). "Nagpur Hospitals to Follow Waste Management Rules", *Express Healthcare Management*, July 6th, 2002, Indian Express Group, Mumbai.

Sarvekshana (1987). Vol. X. (3), 30.

Sathe, V. (2000). "Katkaryanchya Vikasasathi Chaar Kalami Karyakram", *Adivasai Sanvad*, Issue 6 (Marathi).

Sawant, S.D. and Sandhya Mhatre (2000). "Urban- Rural Levels of Living in India: Trends in Disparity and Policy Implications", *Indian Journal of Agricultural Economics*, Vol. 55 (2), April-June, pp. 99-115.

Sawant, S.D. *et al.* (1999). "Agricultural Development in Maharashtra: Problems and Prospects", *Occasional Paper No. 7*, NABARD.

Saxena, N.C. (2001). "Quality of Government Spending, India: Fiscal Policies to Accelerate Economic Growth", May 21- 22.

Seemanthini, Niranjane and Vinaya Saumya (2001). For DASTKAR Andhra Pradesh- "Report on Growth and Prospectus of the Handloom Industry", Study commissioned by the Planning Commission, 2001.

Sehgal, Bittu (2002). *India's Dismembered Network of Sanctuaries and National Parks*, Inter University Centre for Astronomy and Astrophysics, Pune.

Sen, Amartya (1984). "Food Battles: Conflicts in the Access to Food", *Food and Nutrition*, 10(1).

———. (1999). "Democracy as a Universal Value", Keynote Address, Building the World Movement for Democracy, New Delhi, India.

Sen, Somit (2003). "BMC's Garbage Contracts are a Load of Junk", *Times of India*, January 24th, Mumbai.

Sethi, Nitin (2003). "236,800 Hectares More", *Down to Earth*, Centre for Science and Environment, March 15th, New Delhi.

Shah, Deepak (1997). "Bovine Stock in Maharashtra: Changing Structure of Draught Power", *Productivity*, 37(4), pp. 685-697.

———. (2000). "Lessons from Management of Forest Resources in Maharashtra", *Artha Vijnana*, XLII (3), pp. 268-285.

Sharma, V.K. (1994). *Atmospheric Pollution by Aerosols*, Scientific Publishers, Jodhpur .

———. (1995). "Environmental Regulatory Measures and their Economic Impact on the Indian Leather Industry", *Natural Resources Forum*, 19(2), pp. 153-160.

Sharma, Vinod K. (1998a). Development of Climate Change Impact Model (Water Resources and Agriculture) for India, Report submitted to the National Institute for Environmental Studies, Japan Environment Agency, Onogawa, Tsukuba, Ibaraki, 305 Japan.

———. (1998b). "Gaps in Environmental Policy: A Focus on General and Air Pollution Problems", *Environmental Policy and Law*, 28(2), pp. 90-96.

———. (2002). "Water Facts in India: A Focus on Water Quantity, Quality and Regulatory Measures", *International Seminar on Water Management*, Organised by the Centre de Sciences Humaines and India International Centre, New Delhi, December 17.

———. (2004). *Handbook of Environment*, Bookwell, Delhi.

Sharma, Vinod K., Peiter Van Beukering and Barnali Nag (1997). "Environmental and Economic Policy Analysis of Waste Paper Trade and Recycling in India", *Resources, Conservation and Recycling*, 21(1), pp. 55-70.

Sharma, Vinod K., Y. Singh, S. Sinha and P.P.S. Gosain (2002). Environment Education and Capacity Building for Promoting Nature Conservation and Environmental Protection, India Canada Environment Facility and World Wide Fund for Nature, India, August.

Shome, P. (1997). *Fiscal Policy, Public Finance and Governance*, NIPFP.

———. (2002). *India's Fiscal Matters*, Oxford University Press.

Shrivastava K.C and S.J. Kunte (2003). Personal Communication with the Municipal Corporation of Greater Mumbai, Mumbai.

Shukla, Vibhuti (1988). *Urban Development and Regional Policy in India An Econometric Analysis*, Himalaya Publishing House, Bombay.

Shah, Shekhar (2002). "Unbundling Good Governance", Empowerment Retreat, The World Bank, May.

Sikidar, S. (1990). *Economic Development of Tribal India*, Ashish Publication House, New Delhi.

Singh, Harsha Vardhana, Anita Soni and R Kathuria (2003). "Telecom Policy Reform in India", *http://www1.worldbank.org/wbiep/trade/ services_files/ Singh.pdf*, 20th May.

Singh, K.S. (1994). *The Scheduled Tribes*, Oxford University Press, Mumbai.

Singh, Rajendra (2003). "Scope of Good Governance in Maharashtra", Presentation at the *Workshop on Governance: The Maharashtra Experience*, jointly by JBIMS and IIPA.

Singh, Vijay (2003). "Investigating the health of Mumbai's Lungs", The Indian Express, March 20th, Mumbai.

Sirsikar, V.M. (1995). *Politics of Modern Maharashtra*, Orient Longman, Bombay.

Sivakumar, N., A. Bheemappa and K.B. Umesh (1995). "A Study on the Adoption of Scientific Fish Culture by the Farmers of Tungabhadra Command Area in Raichur District, Karnataka", *Agricultural Situation in India*, 49(12), pp. 907-910.

Social Welfare Department (2002). National Seminar on Social Security, Rajasthan, Rajiv Gandhi Social Security Mission, Jaipur, Government of Rajasthan.

Sondhi, Sunil (2000). "Combating Corruption in India: The Role of Civil Society", *The XVIII World Congress of International Political Science Association*, Quebec City, Canada. August 1-5.

Soundarapandian, M. (2002). "Growth and Prospects of Handloom Sector in India", *Occasional Paper-22*, Mumbai, National Bank for Agriculture and Rural Development.

SRS Bulletin (2004). Vol. 38, No.1, April 2004 (Supplement) and Vol.36, No.2, October 2002.

State Folder (Maharashtra). Office of the Development Commissioner, Handicrafts.

State Minorities Commission (2002). First Report of the Maharashtra State Minorities Commission, April 2000 to March 2002, Mumbai, Government of Maharashtra.

Statement showing physical performance under normal, CBC and AEG Scheme during the year 2000-2001- Maharashtra State Khadi and Village Industries Board, Mumbai.

Steering Committee on Voluntary Sector the Xth Plan (2002). Promotion of Voluntary Action and Capacity Building of the Voluntary Sector, People's Action (CAPART), Vol. 22, pp. 1-12.

Stern, Nicholas (2001). "Reform, Investment Climate and Economic Growth", Keynote address at ICRIER, New Delhi, India.

Stuart, William (2002). "A Comparitive Analysis of the Practical Functioning Access to Information Legislation in South Africa and India", research paper, University of Cape Town.

Sundaram, K (2001). "Employment-Unemployment Situation in the Nineties", *Economic and Political Weekly*, March 17.

Sundaram, K. and Suresh Tendulkar (2003). "Poverty has Declined in the 1991s: A Resolution of Comparability Problems in NSS Consumer Expenditure Data", *Economic and Political weekly*, January 25, pp. 327-337.

Suresh, V. (2002). *India Vision 2020*, Asha, New Delhi.

Swaminathan, M.S. (2002). *Swaminathan, Report of the High Level Committee – To Prepare An Action Plan For Agriculture For Coming 25 Years*, Vol. 1, Commission of Agriculture, Pune.

Swamy, T.L.N. (1994). "Public and Private Sector Industries in India: A Comparative Analysis", *Productivity*, 35 (1), April- June, pp. 128-31.

Tata, R. (2002). "Partnership between Corporate and Voluntary Sectors", *People's Action*, (CAPART), Vol. 22, pp. 21-25.

Teltumbde, A. (2000). "Impact of New Economic Reforms on Dalits", in Joghud, P.G. (Ed.), *Economic Policy and Dalits*, Rawal Publication, Jaipur.

TERI (2002). *India Specific Impacts of Climate Change*, The Energy and Resources Institute (TERI), New Delhi.

Thakre, S.D. (2002). "Status of Rural Sanitation in Maharashtra", Paper presented at *Workshop on Strategy for Rural Sanitation in Maharashtra*, Organised by the Government of Maharashtra and Water and Sanitation Programme, South Asia, August .

Thakur, Manish K and Pattnaik, Binay K. (2002). "How Effective are 'Pani Panchayats'? A Field View from Maharashtra", *Sociological Bulletin*, 51(2), pp. 243-268.

Thamarajakshi, R. (1999). "Agriculture and Economic Reforms", *Economic and Political Weekly*, August 14, pp. 2293.

Thorat, V. (2002). "The Least of the Oppressed", *Combat Law The Human Rights Magazine*, 1(4).

Thorat, S.K (2000). "Human Rights of Ex-untouchables in India: Violations and Enforcement", *Indian Journal of Human Rights*, 4(1 and 2).

———. (2000a). "Programmes for Empowerment and Reducing Inequality: Long Way to Go for Untouchables", *Journal of Rural Development*, 19 (4).

———. (2003). "Economic Inequality and Deprivation: Unsolved Problem of Dalits and Adivasi in Maharashtra", in Mungekar, B.L. (ed.), *Economic of Maharashtra: Changing Structure and Imaging Issues*, Mumbai: Ambedkar Institute of Social and Economic Change, pp. 413-428.

Tilak, J.B. (2002). "Household Expenditure on Elementary Education In India: A Few Stylised Facts", *Indian Journal of Social Development*, 2 (2), TRTI, 1997, Bench Mark Survey, Pune, TRTI.

TMC (2001). *Environmental Status Report 2001*, Thane Municipal Corporation, Thane.

ToI (2003a). "Lack of Garbage Disposal Solutions Worries Experts", April 7th, Mumbai.

———. (2003b). "Mckinsey-Bombay First Study Recommendations", July 20th, p.1.

———. (2003c). "Indian Merhants Chamber (IMC), July 4th, Mumbai.

Trivedi, Pushpa and Shimane, Yoshie: "Growth and Productivity in Selected Manufacturing Industries in India: Regional Perspective", Project Report, The International Exchange Division, Institute of Developing Economies, Japan.

Tribal Research Bulletin (2000). Vol XXII, (1) p.1.

TRTI (2002). "Malnutrition Related Deaths of Tribal Children in Nandurbar District of Maharashtra: A Report", Tribal Research and Training Institute, Pune.

UNDP Human Development Report (2003). *Millennium Development Goals*, Oxford University Press, New York.

UNEP (2001). *State of India's Environment: India – 2000*, UNEP, Thailand.

United Nations (1995). *World Urbanisation Prospects, The 1994 Revision Estimates and Projections of Urban and Rural Populations and of Urban Agglomerations*, New York.

USAID (2001). *State Activities, Environment, 2001*.

Vaidya, Abhay (2000). "Solid Waste Power Plant Set up in City", *Times of India*, November 14.

Vaidyanathan, A. (1999). *Water Resources Management: Institutions and Irrigation Development in India*, Oxford University Press, New Delhi.

———. (1987). "Role of Bovine in Indian Agriculture: A Study of Size, Composition and Productivity", Centre for Development Studies, Trivendrum (*Mimeo*).

———. (2001). *Tanks in South India*, Center for Science and Environment, New Delhi.

Vaidyanathan, A. *et al.*, (1994). "Impact of Irrigation on Productivity of Land", *Journal of Indian School of Political Economy*, 6(4), pp. 601-645.

Vashisht, D.C. and T.R. Kundu (1990). "Productivity of Public and Private Enterprises" , *Productivity*, 31(2), July- September, pp. 197-204.

Velaskar, P. (2000). "The Politics of Untouchability and Social Change: A Study of the Scheduled Castes of Maharashtra", *Journal of Indian School of Political Economy*, XII(3 and 4).

Vermillion, Douglas, L (1997). *Impacts of Irrigation Management Transfer: A Review of the Evidence*, Research Report 11, International Irrigation Management Institute, Colombo, Sri Lanka.

Vigyan Ashram (1998). *Education Through Development and Development Through Education*, Pune:, CAPART - TRC project.

Vijapurkar, Mahesh (2001). "Maharashtra Remains Backward Despite Increased Fund Allocation", *The Hindu*, Chennai, July 12.

Visaria, P., N.A. Majumdar and T.R. Sundaram (1996). *Dilemmas of Growth–The Indian Experience*, Sage Publications, New Delhi.

Visaria, Pravin (1997). "Urbanisation in India: An Overview", in Jones, G. and Visaria, P. (Eds.) *Urbanisation in Large Developing Countries*, Clarendon Press, Oxford.

Vithal, C.P. and Y. Bhaskar Rao (1997). "Management of Panchayati Raj Finances in Maharashtra: An Analysis", *Journal of Rural Development*, 16(4), pp. 701-711.

Vittal N. (2001). "Corruption in Governance: The Role of the Central Vigilence Commission", talk delivered in JNU Academic Staff College, March 5, New Delhi.

Vyas, V.S. and Vidyasagar (1993). "Alleviation of Rural Poverty in the States: Lessons of the 1980's", in K. S. Parikh and R. Sudarshan, (Eds.), *Human Development and Structural Adjustment*, Macmillian India, Madras, pp. 89-115.

Vyasulu, Poornima and Vinod Vyasulu (1999). "Women in Panchayati Raj Grass Roots Democracy in Malgudi", *Economic and Political Weekly*, 34(52), pp. 3677- 3686.

Wadhwa, D.C. (2000). "Zoning for Sugar Cooperatives (A note of dissent)", *Economic and Political Weekly*, June 17, p. 2115.

Wake up India (2003). "An I Watch Publication....", The Times Foundation, Mumbai, March.

Wankhede, G.G. (1998). *The Post Matric Scholarship Scheme for SC/ST in Maharashtra and Go—An Evaluation*, Mumbai, TISS (unpublished report).

———. (2001). "Educational Inequalities among Scheduled Castes in Maharashtra", *Economic and Political Weekly*, 36(18), pp. 1153-1558.

———. (2002). "Dalits in India: A Critique of the Issues and Challenges", *Think India*, Oct.-Dec., 5(4).

Warade, G.N. (2003). Personal Communication with Shri G.N. Warade, Director, Department of Environment, Government of Maharashtra, Mumbai.

World Bank (1989). *India: Poverty, Employment and Social Services-A World Bank Country Study*, Washington D.C.

———. (1998). *Reducing Poverty in India- Options for More Effective Public Services*, Washington D.C..

———. (2000). Indoor Air Pollution Newsletter, Energy and Health for the Poor 2.

———. (2000a). *Overview of Rural Decentralisation in India*, Vol. II, Washington.

———. (2001). Indoor Air Pollution Newsletter, Energy and Health for the Poor, 4.

———. (2002). *INDIA, Maharashtra: Reorienting* Government *to Facilitate Growth and Reduce Poverty*, Vol. I and II, Report No. 25053-IN, Poverty Reduction and Economic Management Unit, South Asia Region, USA.

World Bank Country Study (1998). *Reducing Poverty in India- Options for More Effective Public Services - A World Bank Country Study*, Washington D.C: The World Bank.

World Bank Report (1994). "Governance the World Bank Experience", World Bank.

———. (2002). *Maharashtra: Reorienting Government to Facilitate Growth and Reduce Poverty*, World Bank, June.

World Commission on Dams (2000). *Dams and Development- A New Framework for Decision Making*, pp. 11-12.

WSP and DFID (2000). *Sustainable Community Management of a Multi-village Water Supply Scheme in Kolhapur, Maharashtra, India*, Water and Sanitation Programme, New Delhi.

WTTC (2002). *Executive Summary Impact of Travel and Tourism on Jobs and Economy*, World Travel and Tourism Council, 2002.

———. and Deloitte Touche Tahmatsu (2003). *Navigator 2003, The Indian Tourism Strategist*, an Express Travel and Tourism initiative.

WTO (1997). *What Tourism Managers Need to Know: A Practical Guide to the Development and Use of Indicators of Sustainable Tourism*, WTO.

Yadav, J.S.P. (1980). "Salt Affected Soil and Their Afforestation", *The Indian Forester*, 106(4), pp. 19-27, *www.agri.mah.nic.in*.

YUVA *et al.* (1996). YUVA and Regional Centre for Urban and Environmental Studies in the All India Institute of Local Self Government; "Partnerships for a Better Urban Future: A Question of Political Will" cited by Mani, Susan, 2003, "Govt. and Non-Govt. Organisations: Partnerships."